004.16.

D1433153

Items s
shown l
borrow
telepho
barcode
This car
Renew c
Fines cha
incurred
be charge

Leabhar

Baile Átha
Dublin City

D

IT Essentials:

PC Hardware and Software
Companion Guide

Fifth Edition

Cisco Networking Academy

Cisco Press

800 East 96th Street

Indianapolis, Indiana 46240 USA

IT Essentials: PC Hardware and Software Companion Guide, Fifth Edition

Copyright© 2014 Cisco Systems, Inc.

Published by:
Cisco Press
800 East 96th Street
Indianapolis, IN 46240 USA

All rights reserved. No part of this book may be reproduced or transmitted in any form or by any means, electronic or mechanical, including photocopying, recording, or by any information storage and retrieval system, without written permission from the publisher, except for the inclusion of brief quotations in a review.

Printed in the United States of America

First Printing July 2013

Library of Congress Control Number: 2013939397

ISBN-13: 978-1-58713-308-4

ISBN-10: 1-58713-308-3

Trademark Acknowledgments

All terms mentioned in this book that are known to be trademarks or service marks have been appropriately capitalized. Cisco Press or Cisco Systems, Inc., cannot attest to the accuracy of this information. Use of a term in this book should not be regarded as affecting the validity of any trademark or service mark.

Publisher
Paul Boger

Associate Publisher
Dave Dusthimer

Business Operation Manager, Cisco Press
Jan Cornelssen

Executive Editor
Mary Beth Ray

Managing Editor
Sandra Schroeder

Development Editor
Ellie C. Bru

Senior Project Editor
Tonya Simpson

Copy Editor
Keith Cline

Technical Editor
Jeff McDowell

Editorial Assistant
Vanessa Evans

Book Designer
Mark Shirar

Composition
Trina Wurst,
TnT Design, Inc.

Indexer
Brad Herriman

Proofreader
Megan Wade-Taxter

This book is part of the Cisco Networking Academy® series from Cisco Press. The products in this series support and complement the Cisco Networking Academy curriculum. If you are using this book outside the Networking Academy, then you are not preparing with a Cisco trained and authorized Networking Academy provider.

For more information on the Cisco Networking Academy or to locate a Networking Academy, Please visit www.cisco.com/edu.

CISCO

Warning and Disclaimer

This book is designed to provide information about the Cisco Networking Academy IT Essentials: PC Hardware and Software course. Every effort has been made to make this book as complete and as accurate as possible, but no warranty or fitness is implied.

The information is provided on an "as is" basis. The authors, Cisco Press, and Cisco Systems, Inc. shall have neither liability nor responsibility to any person or entity with respect to any loss or damages arising from the information contained in this book or from the use of the discs or programs that may accompany it.

The opinions expressed in this book belong to the author and are not necessarily those of Cisco Systems, Inc.

Corporate and Government Sales

The publisher offers excellent discounts on this book when ordered in quantity for bulk purchases or special sales, which may include electronic versions and/or custom covers and content particular to your business, training goals, marketing focus, and branding interests. For more information, please contact: **U.S. Corporate and Government Sales**   1-800-382-3419   corpsales@pearsontechgroup.com

For sales outside the United States, please contact: **International Sales**   international@pearsoned.com

Feedback Information

At Cisco Press, our goal is to create in-depth technical books of the highest quality and value. Each book is crafted with care and precision, undergoing rigorous development that involves the unique expertise of members from the professional technical community.

Readers' feedback is a natural continuation of this process. If you have any comments regarding how we could improve the quality of this book, or otherwise alter it to better suit your needs, you can contact us through email at feedback@ciscopress.com. Please make sure to include the book title and ISBN in your message.

We greatly appreciate your assistance.

Americas Headquarters	Asia Pacific Headquarters	Europe Headquarters
Cisco Systems, Inc.	Cisco Systems, Inc.	Cisco Systems International BV
170 West Tasman Drive	168 Robinson Road	Haarlerbergpark
San Jose, CA 95134-1706	#28-01 Capital Tower	Haarlerbergweg 13-19
USA	Singapore 068912	1101 CH Amsterdam
www.cisco.com	www.cisco.com	The Netherlands
Tel: 408 526-4000	Tel: +65 6317 7777	www-europe.cisco.com
800 553-NETS (6387)	Fax: +65 6317 7799	Tel: +31 0 800 020 0791
Fax: 408 527-0883		Fax: +31 0 20 357 1100

Cisco has more than 200 offices worldwide. Addresses, phone numbers, and fax numbers are listed on the Cisco Website at **www.cisco.com/go/offices.**

©2007 Cisco Systems, Inc. All rights reserved. CCVP, the Cisco logo, and the Cisco Square Bridge logo are trademarks of Cisco Systems, Inc.; Changing the Way We Work, Live, Play, and Learn is a service mark of Cisco Systems, Inc.; and Access Registrar, Aironet, BPX, Catalyst, CCDA, CCDP, CCIE, CCIP, CCNA, CCNP, CCSP, Cisco, the Cisco Certified Internetwork Expert logo, Cisco IOS, Cisco Press, Cisco Systems, Cisco Systems Capital, the Cisco Systems logo, Cisco Unity, Enterprise/Solver, EtherChannel, EtherFast, EtherSwitch, Fast Step, Follow Me Browsing, FormShare, GigaDrive, GigaStack, HomeLink, Internet Quotient, IOS, IP/TV, iQ Expertise, the iQ logo, iQ Net Readiness Scorecard, iQuick Study, LightStream, Linksys, MeetingPlace, MGX, Networking Academy, Network Registrar, Packet, PIX, ProConnect, RateMUX, ScriptShare, SlideCast, SMARTnet, StackWise, The Fastest Way to Increase Your Internet Quotient, and TransPath are registered trademarks of Cisco Systems, Inc. and/or its affiliates in the United States and certain other countries.

All other trademarks mentioned in this document or Website are the property of their respective owners. The use of the word partner does not imply a partnership relationship between Cisco and any other company. (0609R)

About the Contributing Authors

Kathleen Czurda-Page is the lead instructor for the Cisco Networking Academy at North Idaho College. She teaches IT Essentials and CCNA courses, along with introduction to computers in business courses and business leadership. Kathleen has a degree in Computer Applications in Business from North Idaho College. She earned her bachelor's degree in professional technical education, her master's degree in adult and organizational learning, and education specialist degree in adult/organizational learning and leadership at the University of Idaho. She also holds Cisco and CompTIA certifications. Kathleen lives with her lovely family in Coeur d'Alene, Idaho.

Laura Kier is the Cisco Networking Academy Lead at Spokane Community College in Spokane, Washington. She teaches CCNA Exploration, ITE, and CCNA Security, in addition to business software computer courses. Laura has a BS from Oregon State University and a certificate in Computer Forensics and Network Security from Spokane Falls Community College. She is a Certified Cisco Academy Instructor and has her CCNA, A+, and Net+ certificates. She and her husband live in Spokane, Washington.

Contents At a Glance

Contents

Introduction

IT Essentials: PC Hardware and Software Companion Guide, Fifth Edition, is a supplemental book to the Cisco Networking Academy IT Essentials: PC Hardware and Software Version 5 course. The course teaches you how to build a computer and troubleshoot problems that occur in everyday use. The course is designed to prepare you to take and pass the CompTIA A+ exams (based on the 2012 objectives). By reading and completing this book, you have the opportunity to review all key concepts that the CompTIA A+ exams cover. If you use this book along with its companion, *IT Essentials: PC Hardware and Software Lab Manual*, Fifth Edition (ISBN 1-58713-310-5), you can reinforce those concepts with hands-on exercises and test that knowledge with review questions and exercises.

The IT Essentials: PC Hardware and Software course aligns with the CompTIA A+ (220-801) exam and CompTIA A+ (220-802) exam. You must pass both exams to earn the CompTIA A+ certification.

Who Should Read This Book

This book is intended for students in the Cisco Networking Academy IT Essentials: PC Hardware and Software Version 5 course. This student is usually pursuing a career in information technology (IT) or wants to have the knowledge of how a computer works, how to assemble a computer, and how to troubleshoot hardware and software issues.

Book Features

The features in this book facilitate an understanding of computer systems and troubleshooting system problems. The highlights of each chapter are as follows:

- **Objectives:** Each chapter starts with a list of objectives that should be mastered by the end of the chapter. The objectives are framed as focus questions addressing the concepts covered in the chapter.

- **Key terms:** Each chapter includes a list of the key terms identified in the chapter, listed in the order in which they appear in the chapter. These terms serve as a study aid and are defined in the book's Glossary. The key terms reinforce the concepts introduced in the chapter and help you understand the chapter material before you move on to new concepts. You can find the key terms highlighted in blue throughout the chapter, in the context in which they are most important.

- **Explanatory text, lists, figures, and tables:** This book co. figures, proce-dures, and tables to accompany the thorough text explanat f the objective content and to help explain and visualize theories, concepts, nands, and setup sequences.

- **Chapter summaries:** At the end of each chapter is a summary o concepts covered in the chapter. The summary provides a synopsis of the c er and serves as a study aid.

- **Lab, worksheet, and class discussion references:** There are reference the labs, worksheets, and class discussion exercises that can be found in the com-panying *IT Essentials: PC Hardware and Software Lab Manual*, Fifth ion (ISBN 1-58713-310-5).

- **Virtual Desktop activity and Virtual Laptop activity references:** Designed and developed by the Cisco Networking Academy, these activities are virtual learning tools to help you develop critical thinking and complex problem-solving skills. How to access these activities is discussed in the following section, "Accessing Packet Tracer, Virtual Laptop, and Virtual Desktop Activities."

- **Packet Tracer activities:** Cisco Packet Tracer simulation-based learning activity files promote the exploration of networking and network security concepts and enable you to experiment with network behavior. How to access these activities is discussed in the following section, "Accessing Packet Tracer, Virtual Laptop, and Virtual Desktop Activities."

- **"Check Your Understanding" review questions:** Review questions are presented at the end of each chapter to serve as an assessment. In addition, the questions reinforce the concepts introduced in the chapter and help test your understand-ing before you move on to subsequent chapters. Answers to the questions are available in the Appendix.

Accessing Packet Tracer, Virtual Laptop, and Virtual Desktop Activities

All the Packet Tracer activities, Virtual Laptop, and Virtual Desktop activities are available within your IT Essentials Version 5 course in Netspace. However, you can also get easy access just to these activities if you register this Companion Guide on the Cisco Press website. Please visit http://ciscopress.com/register, create an account, and register your book. Once you have an account and have registered your book, follow the Access Bonus Content link to view the downloadable activities.

ote that you need to have the Packet Tracer software to use these Packet Tracer activity files. Packet Tracer is available only through the Cisco Networking Academy. Ask your instructor for a copy of this software. Also note that the most current files will always be found within the course on Netspace. Access to these files on the Cisco Press site is intended only for convenience of access for those of you using the Companion Guide textbook accompanying your course.

How This Book Is Organized

This book corresponds closely to the Cisco IT Essentials course and is divided into 12 chapters, one appendix, and a glossary of key terms:

- **Chapter 1, "Introduction to the Personal Computer"**: Information technology (IT) is the design, development, implementation, support, and management of computer hardware and software applications. A computer is an electronic machine that performs calculations based on a set of instructions. A computer system consists of hardware and software components. This chapter discusses hardware components found in a computer system, selecting replacement computer components, and configurations for specialized computer systems.

- **Chapter 2, "Lab Procedures and Tool Use"**: This chapter covers basic safety practices for the workplace, hardware and software tools, and the disposal of hazardous materials. Safety guidelines help protect individuals from accidents and injury and protect equipment from damage. Some of these guidelines are designed to protect the environment from contamination by discarded materials. You will also learn how to protect equipment and data and how to properly use hand and software tools.

- **Chapter 3, "Computer Assembly"**: Assembling computers is a large part of a technician's job. As a technician, you must work in a logical, methodical manner when working with computer components. At times, you might have to determine whether a component for a customer's computer needs to be upgraded or replaced. It is important that you develop advanced skills in installation procedures, troubleshooting techniques, and diagnostic methods. This chapter discusses the importance of component compatibility across hardware and software.

- **Chapter 4, "Overview of Preventive Maintenance"**: Troubleshooting is the systematic process used to locate the cause of a fault in a computer system and correct the relevant hardware and software issues. In this chapter, you will learn general guidelines for creating preventive maintenance programs and troubleshooting procedures. These guidelines are a starting point to help you develop your preventive maintenance and troubleshooting skills.

- **Chapter 5, "Operating Systems"**: The operating system (OS) controls almost all functions on a computer. In this chapter, you learn about the components, functions, and terminology related to the Windows 2000, Windows XP, Windows Vista, and Windows 7 operating systems.

- **Chapter 6, "Networks"**: This chapter provides an overview of network principles, standards, and purposes. The different types of network topologies, protocols, and logical models, in addition to the hardware needed to create a network, are also discussed in this chapter. Configuration, troubleshooting, and preventive maintenance are covered. You also learn about network software, communication methods, and hardware relationships.

- **Chapter 7, "Laptops"**: With the increase in demand for mobility, the popularity of mobile devices will continue to grow. During the course of your career, you will be expected to know how to configure, repair, and maintain these devices. The knowledge you acquire about desktop computers will help you service laptops and portable devices. However, there are important differences between the two technologies. This chapter examines these differences and how to techniques to use specific to laptops.

- **Chapter 8, "Mobile Devices"**: A mobile device is any device that is handheld, is light, and typically uses a touchscreen for input. Like a desktop or laptop computer, mobile devices use an operating system to run applications (apps) and games and play movies and music. It is important to become familiar with as many different mobile devices as possible. You may be required to know how to configure, maintain, and repair various mobile devices. Mastering the skills necessary to work on mobile devices is important to your career advancement. This chapter focuses on the many features of mobile devices and their capabilities, including configuration, synchronization, and data backup.

- **Chapter 9, "Printers"**: This chapter provides essential information about printers. You will learn how printers operate, what to consider when purchasing a printer, and how to connect printers to an individual computer or to a network.

- **Chapter 10, "Security"**: Technicians need to understand computer and network security. Failure to implement proper security procedures can have an impact on users, computers, and the general public. Private information, company secrets, financial data, computer equipment, and items of national security are placed at risk if proper security procedures are not followed. This chapter covers why security is important, security threats, security procedures, how to troubleshoot security issues, and how you can work with customers to ensure that the best possible protection is in place.

- **Chapter 11, "The IT Professional"**: As a computer technician, you not only fix computers, but also interact with people. In fact, troubleshooting is as much about communicating with the customer as it is about knowing how to fix a computer. In this chapter, you learn to use good communication skills as confidently as you use a screwdriver.

- **Chapter 12, "Advanced Troubleshooting"**: In your career as a technician, it is important that you develop advanced skills in troubleshooting techniques and diagnostic methods for computer components, operating systems, networks, laptops, printers, and security issues. Advanced troubleshooting can sometimes mean that the problem is unique or that the solution is difficult to perform. In this chapter, you will learn how to apply a troubleshooting process to solve computer problems.

- **Appendix A, "Answers to 'Check Your Understanding' Questions"**: This appendix lists the answers to the "Check Your Understanding" review questions that are included at the end of each chapter.

- **Glossary**: The Glossary provides you with definitions for all the key terms identified in each chapter.

About the CompTIA A+ Certification

As a CompTIA Authorized Quality Curriculum, IT Essentials: PC Hardware and Software v5 will help prepare you for the new CompTIA A+ Essentials and Practical Applications certification exams. To become A+ certified, you need to pass two exams to become certified in your chosen career area:

- CompTIA A+ (220-801)

- CompTIA A+ (220-802)

After becoming certified, you will be qualified to work as a computer support professional and technician in a variety of work environments and industries.

The CompTIA A+ exam is explained in detail, including a list of the objectives, at the following website:

http://www.comptia.org/certifications/listed/a.aspx

When you are ready to take the exam, you must purchase and schedule your two CompTIA A+ exams. You can find the necessary information to accomplish this at the following website:

http://certification.comptia.org/getCertified/certifications/a.aspx

Syntax Conventions

The conventions used to present command syntax in this book are the same conventions used in the IOS Command Reference. The Command Reference describes these conventions as follows:

- **Boldface** indicates commands and keywords that are entered literally as shown. In actual configuration examples and output (not general command syntax), boldface indicates commands that are manually input by the user (such as a show command).

- *Italic* indicates arguments for which you supply actual values.

- Vertical bars (|) separate alternative, mutually exclusive elements.

- Square brackets ([ ]) indicate an optional element.

- Braces ({ }) indicate a required choice.

- Braces within brackets ([{ }]) indicate a required choice within an optional element.

CHAPTER 1

Introduction to the Personal Computer

Objectives

Upon completion of this chapter, you will be able to answer the following questions:

- What is a computer system?
- How can I identify the names, purposes, and characteristics of cases and power supplies?
- What are the names, purposes, and characteristics of internal PC components?
- What are the names, purposes, and characteristics of ports and cables?
- How can I identify the names, purposes, and characteristics of input devices?
- How can I identify the names, purposes, and characteristics of output devices?

- What situations require replacement of computer components?
- How do I determine what purchases or upgrades are needed?
- How do I select replacement or upgrade components?
- What are some types of specialty computer systems?
- What are some of the hardware and software requirements for specialty computer systems?

Key Terms

This chapter uses the following key terms. You can find the definitions in the Glossary.

hardware   page 4

software   page 4

power supply   page 4

alternating current (AC)   page 4

direct current (DC)   page 4

form factor   page 5

uninterruptible power supply (UPS)   page 7

keyed connector   page 7

Ohm's law   page 9

field replaceable unit (FRU)   page 10

motherboard   page 11

chipset   page 13

Northbridge   page 13

Southbridge   page 13

central processing unit (CPU)   page 13

cache   page 15

Reduced Instruction Set Computer (RISC)   page 15

Complex Instruction Set Computer (CISC)   page 15

hyperthreading   page 15

hypertransport   page 15

front side bus (FSB)   page 15

Introduction (1.0.1)

A computer is an electronic machine that performs calculations based on a set of instructions. The first computers were huge room-sized machines that took teams of people to build, manage, and maintain. The computer systems of today are exponentially faster and only a fraction of the size of those original computers.

A computer system consists of hardware and software components. *Hardware* refers to the physical equipment. It includes the case, storage drives, keyboards, monitors, cables, speakers, and printers. *Software* includes the operating system and programs. The operating system instructs computer operations. These operations can include identifying, accessing, and processing information. Programs or applications perform different functions. Programs vary widely depending on the type of information that is accessed or generated. For example, instructions for balancing a checkbook differ from instructions for simulating a virtual reality world on the Internet.

This chapter discusses hardware components found in a computer system, selecting replacement computer components, and configurations for specialized computer systems.

Cases and Power Supplies (1.1.1)

The computer case is a vital component of the computer system; it provides both protection and cooling for the internal components. The size, location of the I/O ports, and number of internal drive bays are a few attributes to consider when buying a case. It needs to be compatible with the form factor of the motherboard in addition to the power supply.

Computer Cases (1.1.1.1)

The computer case contains the framework to support the internal components of a computer while providing an enclosure for added protection. Computer cases are usually made of plastic, steel, or aluminum and are available in a variety of styles.

In addition to providing protection and support, cases also provide an environment designed to keep the internal components cool. Case fans move air through the computer case. As the air passes warm components, it absorbs heat and then exits the case. This process keeps the computer components from overheating. Cases also help to prevent damage from static electricity. The computer's internal components are grounded via attachment to the case.

All computers need a *power supply* to convert *alternating current (AC)* power from the wall socket into *direct current (DC)* power. Every computer also needs a motherboard. The motherboard is the main circuit board in a computer. The size and shape of the computer case are usually determined by the motherboard, power supply, and other internal components.

The size and layout of a case is called the *form factor*. The basic form factors for computer cases include desktop and tower, as shown in Figure 1-1. Desktop cases can be slimline or full-sized. Tower cases can be mini or full-sized.

Figure 1-1   Types of Computer Cases

You can select a larger computer case to accommodate additional components that may be required in the future. Or you might select a smaller case that requires minimal space. In general, the computer case should be durable, be easy to service, and have enough room for expansion.

Computer cases are referred to in a number of ways:

- Computer chassis
- Cabinet
- Tower
- Box
- Housing

You need to consider several factors when choosing a case:

- Size of the motherboard
- Number of external or internal drive locations, called bays
- Available space

See Table 1-1 for a list of computer case features.

Leabharlanna Poibli Chathair Bhaile Átha Cliath
Dublin City Public Libraries

Table 1-1   Choosing a Computer Case

Factor	Rationale
Model type	There are two main case models. One type is for desktop PCs, and the other type is for tower computers. The type of motherboard you choose determines the type of case that can be used. The size and shape must match exactly.
Size	If a computer has many components, it will need more room for airflow to keep the system cool.
Available space	Desktop cases allow space conservation in tight areas because the monitor can be placed on top of the unit. The design of the desktop case may limit the number and size of the components that can be added.
Power supply	You must match the power rating and connection type of the power supply to the type of motherboard you have chosen.
Appearance	For some people, how the case looks does not matter at all. For others, it is critical. If you find it necessary to have an attractive case, you have many case designs to choose from.
Status display	What is going on inside the case can be very important. LED indicators that are mounted on the outside of the case can tell you if the system is receiving power, when the hard drive is being used, and when the computer is in sleep or hibernate mode.
Vents	All cases have a vent on the power supply, and some have another vent on the back to help draw air into or out of the system. Some cases are designed with more vents in the event that the system needs a way to dissipate an unusual amount of heat. This situation may occur when many devices are installed close together in the case.

Note

Select a case that matches the physical dimensions of the power supply and motherboard.

Power Supplies (1.1.1.2)

The power supply must provide enough power for the components that are currently installed and allow for other components that may be added at a later time. If you choose a power supply that powers only the current components, you might need to replace the power supply when other components are upgraded.

The power supply, shown in Figure 1-2, converts alternating current (AC) power coming from a wall outlet into direct current (DC) power, which is a lower voltage. DC power is required for all components inside the computer. There are three main form factors for power supplies, Advanced Technology (AT), AT Extended (ATX), and ATX12V. The ATX12V is the most common form factor used in computers today.

Figure 1-2   Power Supply

A computer can tolerate slight fluctuations in power, but a significant deviation can cause the power supply to fail. An *uninterruptible power supply (UPS)* can protect a computer from problems caused by changes in power. A UPS uses a power inverter. A power inverter provides AC power to the computer from a built-in battery by converting the DC current of the UPS battery into AC power. This built-in battery is continually charged via DC current that is converted from the AC supply.

Connectors

Most connectors today are keyed. A *keyed connector* is designed to be inserted in only one direction. Each power supply connector uses a different voltage, as described in Table 1-2. Different connectors are used to connect specific components to various ports on the motherboard:

- A Molex keyed connector connects to optical drives, hard drives, or other devices that use older technology.

- A Berg keyed connector connects to a floppy drive. A Berg connector is smaller than a Molex connector.

- A SATA keyed connector connects to an optical drive or a hard drive. The SATA connector is wider and thinner than a Molex connector.

- A 20-pin or 24-pin slotted connector connects to the motherboard. The 24-pin connector has two rows of 12 pins each, and the 20-pin connector has 2 rows of 10 pins each.

- A 4-pin to 8-pin auxiliary power connector has 2 rows of 2 to 4 pins and supplies power to all areas of the motherboard. The auxiliary power connector is the same shape as the main power connector but smaller. It can also power other devices within the computer.

- A 6/8-pin PCIe power connector has 2 rows of 3 to 4 pins and supplies power to other internal components.

Older standard power supplies used two connectors called P8 and P9 to connect to the motherboard. P8 and P9 were unkeyed connectors. They could be installed backward, potentially damaging the motherboard or power supply. The installation required that the connectors be lined up with the black wires together in the middle.

Note

If you have a difficult time inserting a connector, try repositioning it, or check to make sure that no bent pins or foreign objects are in the way. If it is difficult to plug in a cable or other part, something is wrong. Cables, connectors, and components are designed to fit together snugly. Never force a connector or component. If a connector is plugged in incorrectly, it can damage the plug and the connector. Take your time and make sure that you are handling the hardware correctly.

Table 1-2   Power Color Codes

Voltage	Wire Color	Use
+12V	Yellow	Disk drive motors, fans, cooling devices, and system bus slots
–12V	Blue	Some serial port circuits and early PROMs
+3.3V	Orange	Modern CPU, some memory, and AGP video cards
+5V	Red	Motherboard, early processors, many motherboard components
–5V	White	ISA bus cards and early PROMs
0V	Black	Ground (the return loop for circuits)

Electricity and Ohm's Law (1.1.1.3)

These are the four basic units of electricity:

- Voltage (V)
- Current (I)
- Power (P)
- Resistance (R)

Voltage, current, power, and resistance are electronic terms that a computer technician must know.

- **Voltage** is a measure of the force required to push electrons through a circuit. Voltage is measured in volts (V). A computer power supply usually produces several different voltages.

- **Current** is a measure of the amount of electrons going through a circuit. Current is measured in amperes, or amps (A). Computer power supplies deliver different amperages for each output voltage.

- **Power** is a measure of the pressure required to push electrons through a circuit (voltage), multiplied by the number of electrons going through that circuit (current). The measurement is called watts (W). Computer power supplies are rated in watts.

- **Resistance** is the opposition to the flow of current in a circuit, measured in ohms. Lower resistance allows more current, and therefore more power, to flow through a circuit. A good fuse has low resistance or almost 0 ohms.

A basic equation, known as *Ohm's law*, expresses how three of the terms relate to each other. It states that voltage is equal to the current multiplied by the resistance:

$V = IR$

In an electrical system, power is equal to the voltage multiplied by the current:

$P = VI$

In an electrical circuit, increasing the current or the voltage results in higher power.

Note

For example, imagine a simple circuit that has a 9V light bulb hooked up to a 9V battery. The power output of the light bulb is 100W. Using the P = VI equation, you can calculate how much current in amps is required to get 100W out of this 9V bulb.

To solve this equation, we know that P = 100W and V = 9V.

$I = P/V = 100W / 9V = 11.11A$

What happens if a 12V battery and a 12V light bulb are used to get 100W of power?

$I = P/V = 100W / 12V = 8.33A$

This system produces the same power but with less current.

You can use Ohm's triangle, shown in Figure 1-3, to calculate voltage, current, or resistance when two of the variables are known. To see the correct formula, cover up the variable that is not known and perform the resulting calculation. For example, if voltage and current are known, cover the R to reveal the formula V / I. Calculate V / I to find R. You can use the Ohm's law chart shown in Figure 1-3 to calculate any of the four basic units of electricity using any two known units.

Figure 1-3a   Ohm's Triangle   **Figure 1-3b**   Ohm's Law Chart

Computers normally use power supplies ranging from 250W to 800W output capacity. However, some computers need 1200W and higher-capacity power supplies. When building a computer, select a power supply with sufficient wattage to power all components. Each component inside the computer uses a certain amount of power. Obtain the wattage information from the manufacturer's documentation. When deciding on a power supply, choose one that has more than enough power for the current components. A power supply with a higher wattage rating has more capacity; therefore, it can handle more devices.

On the back of most power supplies is a small switch called the voltage selector switch. This switch sets the input voltage to the power supply to either 110V/115V or 220V/230V. A power supply with this switch is called a dual-voltage power supply. The correct voltage setting is determined by the country where the power supply is used. Setting the voltage switch to the incorrect input voltage could damage the power supply and other parts of your computer. If a power supply does not have this switch, it automatically detects and sets the correct voltage.

Caution

Do not open a power supply. Electronic capacitors located inside of a power supply, shown in Figure 1-4, can hold a charge for extended periods of time. The power supply is considered to be a *field replaceable unit (FRU)*, which means that if it no longer works, don't fix it, but instead replace it.

Figure 1-4   Power Supply Capacitors

Worksheet 1.1.1.4: Ohm's Law

In this worksheet, you answer questions based on electricity and Ohm's law. Refer to the worksheet in *IT Essentials: PC Hardware and Software Lab Manual*, Fifth Edition.

Internal PC Components (1.1.2)

This section discusses the names, purposes, and characteristics of the internal components of a computer.

Motherboards (1.1.2.1)

The *motherboard* is the main printed circuit board and contains the buses, or electrical pathways, found in a computer. These buses allow data to travel between the various components that comprise a computer. Figure 1-5 shows a variety of motherboards. A motherboard is also known as the system board or the main board.

Figure 1-5   Motherboards

The motherboard accommodates the central processing unit (CPU), random-access memory (RAM), expansion slots, heat sink and fan assembly, basic input/output system (BIOS) chip, chipset, and the circuitry that interconnects the motherboard components. Sockets, internal and external connectors, and various ports are also placed on the motherboard.

The form factor of motherboards pertains to the size and shape of the board. It also describes the physical layout of the different components and devices on the motherboard. The form factor determines how individual components attach to the motherboard and the shape of the computer case. Various form factors exist for motherboards, as shown in Table 1-3.

Table 1-3   Form Factors

AT	Advanced Technology
ATX	Advanced Technology Extended
Mini-ATX	Smaller footprint of Advanced Technology Extended
Micro-ATX	Smaller footprint of Advanced Technology Extended
LPX	Low-Profile Extended
BTX	Balanced Technology Extended
Mini-ITX	Smaller than the Micro-ATX format
Nano-ITX	Smaller footprint of the mini-ITX
Pico-ITX	Half the size of the Mini-ITX
Mobile-ITX	Smallest ITX motherboard

The most common form factor in desktop computers was the AT, based on the IBM AT motherboard. The AT motherboard can be up to approximately 1 foot (about 30 cm) wide. This cumbersome size led to the development of smaller form factors. The placement of heat sinks and fans often interferes with the use of expansion slots in smaller form factors.

A newer motherboard form factor, ATX, improved on the AT design. The ATX case accommodates the integrated I/O ports on the ATX motherboard. The ATX power supply connects to the motherboard via a single 20-pin connector, instead of the confusing P8 and P9 connectors used with some earlier form factors. Instead of using a physical toggle switch, the ATX power supply can be powered on and off with signaling from the motherboard.

A smaller form factor designed to be backward compatible with ATX is the Micro-ATX. Because the mounting points of a Micro-ATX motherboard are a subset of those used on an ATX board, and the I/O panel is identical, you can use the Micro-ATX motherboard in a full-size ATX case.

Because Micro-ATX boards often use the same chipsets (Northbridge and Southbridge) and power connectors as full-size ATX boards, they can use many of the same components. However, Micro-ATX cases are usually much smaller than ATX cases and have fewer expansion slots.

Some manufacturers have proprietary form factors based on the ATX design. This causes some motherboards, power supplies, and other components to be incompatible with standard ATX cases.

The ITX form factor has gained in popularity because of its very small size. There are many types of ITX motherboards. Mini-ITX is one of the most popular. The Mini-ITX form factor uses very little power, so fans are not needed to keep it cool. A Mini-ITX motherboard has only one PCI slot for expansion cards. A computer based on a Mini-ITX form factor can be used in places where it is inconvenient to have a large or noisy computer.

An important set of components on the motherboard is the chipset. The *chipset* is composed of various integrated circuits attached to the motherboard. They control how system hardware interacts with the CPU and motherboard. The CPU is installed into a slot or socket on the motherboard. The socket on the motherboard determines the type of CPU that can be installed.

The chipset allows the CPU to communicate and interact with the other components of the computer and to exchange data with system memory, or RAM, hard disk drives, video cards, and other output devices. The chipset establishes how much memory can be added to a motherboard. The chipset also determines the type of connectors on the motherboard.

Most chipsets are divided into two distinct components, Northbridge and Southbridge. What each component does varies from manufacturer to manufacturer. In general, the *Northbridge* controls access to the RAM, video card, and the speeds at which the CPU can communicate with them. The video card is sometimes integrated into the Northbridge. AMD and Intel have chips that integrate the memory controller onto the CPU die, which improves performance and power consumption. The *Southbridge*, in most cases, allows the CPU to communicate with the hard drive, sound card, USB ports, and other I/O ports.

CPUs (1.1.2.2)

The *central processing unit (CPU)* is considered the brain of the computer. It is sometimes referred to as the processor. Most calculations take place in the CPU. In terms of computing power, the CPU is the most important element of a computer system. CPUs come in different form factors, each style requiring a particular slot or socket on the motherboard. Common CPU manufacturers include Intel and AMD.

The CPU socket or slot is the connection between the motherboard and the processor. Most CPU sockets and processors in use today are built around the architectures of the pin grid array (PGA), shown in Figure 1-6, and land grid array (LGA), shown in Figure 1-7. In a PGA architecture, pins on the underside of the processor are inserted into the socket, usually with zero insertion force (ZIF). ZIF refers to the amount of force needed to install a CPU into the motherboard socket or slot. In an LGA architecture, the pins are in the socket instead of on the processor.

Figure 1-6   PGA CPU and Socket

Figure 1-7   LGA CPU and Socket

Slot-based processors, shown in Figure 1-8, are cartridge-shaped and fit into a slot that looks similar to an expansion slot, shown at the bottom left of Figure 1-9.

Figure 1-8   Slot CPU

Figure 1-9   Motherboard with CPU Slot

The CPU executes a program, which is a sequence of stored instructions. Each model of processor has an instruction set, which it executes. The CPU executes the program by processing each piece of data as directed by the program and the instruction set. While the CPU is executing one step of the program, the remaining instructions and the data are stored nearby in a special memory called *cache*. Two major CPU architectures are related to instruction sets:

- *Reduced Instruction Set Computer (RISC)*: Architectures use a relatively small set of instructions. RISC chips are designed to execute these instructions very rapidly.

- *Complex Instruction Set Computer (CISC)*: Architectures use a broad set of instructions, resulting in fewer steps per operation.

Some Intel CPUs incorporate hyperthreading to enhance the performance of the CPU. With *hyperthreading*, multiple pieces of code (threads) are executed simultaneously in the CPU. To an operating system, a single CPU with hyperthreading performs as though there are two CPUs when multiple threads are being processed.

Some AMD processors use hypertransport to enhance CPU performance. *Hypertransport* is a high-speed, low-latency connection between the CPU and the Northbridge chip.

The power of a CPU is measured by the speed and the amount of data that it can process. The speed of a CPU is rated in cycles per second, such as millions of cycles per second, called megahertz (MHz), or billions of cycles per second, called gigahertz (GHz). The amount of data that a CPU can process at one time depends on the size of the *front side bus (FSB)*. This is also called the CPU bus or the processor data bus. Higher performance can be achieved when the width of the FSB increases. The width of the FSB is measured in bits. A bit is the smallest unit of data in a computer and is the binary format in which data is processed. Current processors use a 32-bit or 64-bit FSB.

Overclocking is a technique used to make a processor work at a faster speed than its original specification. Overclocking is not a recommended way to improve computer performance and can result in damage to the CPU. The opposite of overclocking is CPU throttling. *CPU throttling* is a technique used when the processor runs at less than the rated speed to conserve power or produce less heat. Throttling is commonly used on laptops and other mobile devices.

The latest processor technology has resulted in CPU manufacturers finding ways to incorporate more than one CPU core onto a single chip. These CPUs can process multiple instructions concurrently:

- *Single-core CPU*: One core inside a single CPU that handles all the processing. A motherboard manufacturer might provide sockets for more than one single processor, providing the ability to build a powerful, multiprocessor computer.

- *Dual-core CPU*: Two cores inside a single CPU in which both cores can process information at the same time.

- **Triple-core CPU**: Three cores inside a single CPU that is actually a quad-core processor with one of the cores disabled.

- **Quad-core CPU**: Four cores inside a single CPU.

- **Hexa-core CPU**: Six cores inside a single CPU.

- **Octa-core CPU**: Eight cores inside a single CPU.

Cooling Systems (1.1.2.3)

The flow of current between the electronic components generates heat. Computer components perform better when kept cool. If the heat is not removed, the computer may run slower. If too much heat builds up, computer components can be damaged.

Increasing the airflow in the computer case allows more heat to be removed. A case fan installed in the computer case, as shown in Figure 1-10, makes the cooling process more efficient.

Figure 1-10   Case Fan

In addition to a case fan, a *heat sink* draws heat away from the CPU core. A fan on top of the heat sink, as shown in Figure 1-11, moves the heat away from the CPU.

Figure 1-11   CPU Fan

Other components are also susceptible to heat damage and are sometimes equipped with fans. Video adapter cards also produce a lot of heat. Fans are dedicated to cool the graphics processing unit (GPU), as shown in Figure 1-12.

Figure 1-12   Graphics Card Cooling System

Computers with extremely fast CPUs and GPUs might use a water-cooling system. A metal plate is placed over the processor, and water is pumped over the top to collect the heat that the processor generates. The water is pumped to a radiator to release the heat into the air and is then recirculated.

ROM and RAM

ROM and RAM provide memory for a vast amount of computer equipment. They come in different memory sizes and module sizes and have different features. ROM contains basic instructions for computers such as booting and loading the operating system. RAM chips are stored on memory modules that can easily be installed and removed to expedite upgrades. Some RAM uses parity to increase data integrity and reliability. Another kind of specialized memory is called cache. It stores frequently used data and commands. The following sections cover ROM, RAM, modules, parity, and cache in greater detail.

ROM (1.1.2.4)

Memory chips store data in the form of bytes. Bytes represent information such as letters, numbers, and symbols. A byte is a grouping of 8 bits. Each bit is stored as either 0 or 1 in the memory chip.

ROM chips are located on the motherboard and other circuit boards. ROM chips contain instructions that can be directly accessed by a CPU. Basic instructions for operation, such as booting the computer and loading the operating system, are stored in ROM. ROM chips retain their contents even when the computer is powered down. The contents cannot be erased or changed by normal means. ROM types include the following:

- *Read-only memory (ROM)*: Information is written to a ROM chip when it is manufactured. A ROM chip cannot be erased or rewritten. This type of ROM is obsolete.

- *Programmable read-only memory (PROM)*: Information is written to a PROM chip after it is manufactured. A PROM chip cannot be erased or rewritten.

- *Erasable programmable read-only memory (EPROM)*: Information is written to an EPROM chip after it is manufactured. An EPROM chip can be erased with exposure to UV light. Special equipment is required.

- *Electrically erasable programmable read-only memory (EEPROM)*: Information is written to an EEPROM chip after it is manufactured. EEPROM chips are also called flash ROMs. An EEPROM chip can be erased and rewritten without having to remove the chip from the computer.

Note

ROM is sometimes called firmware. This is misleading because firmware is actually the software that is stored in a ROM chip.

RAM (1.1.2.5)

Random-access memory (RAM) is the temporary storage for data and programs that are being accessed by the CPU. RAM is *volatile memory*, which means that the contents are erased when the computer is powered off. The more RAM in a computer, the more capacity the computer has to hold and process large programs and files. More RAM also enhances system performance. The maximum amount of RAM that can be installed is limited by the motherboard and the operating system. The different types of RAM are as follows:

- *Dynamic RAM (DRAM)* is a memory chip that is used as main memory. DRAM must be constantly refreshed with pulses of electricity to maintain the data stored within the chip.

- *Static RAM (SRAM)* is a memory chip that is used as cache memory. SRAM is much faster than DRAM and does not have to be refreshed as often. SRAM is much more expensive than DRAM.

- *Fast Page Mode (FPM)* DRAM is memory that supports paging. Paging enables faster access to the data than regular DRAM. FPM memory was used in Intel 486 and Pentium systems.

- *Extended Data Out (EDO)* RAM is memory that overlaps consecutive data accesses. This speeds up the access time to retrieve data from memory because the CPU does not have to wait for one data access cycle to end before another data access cycle begins.

- *Synchronous DRAM (SDRAM)* is DRAM that operates in synchronization with the memory bus. The memory bus is the data path between the CPU and the main memory. Control signals are used to coordinate the exchange of data between SDRAM and the CPU.

- *Double data rate SDRAM (DDR SDRAM)* is memory that transfers data twice as fast as SDRAM. DDR SDRAM increases performance by transferring data twice per clock cycle.

- *Double data rate 2 SDRAM (DDR2 SDRAM)* is a faster than DDR-SDRAM memory. DDR2 SDRAM improves performance over DDR SDRAM by decreasing noise and crosstalk between the signal wires.

- *Double data rate 3 SDRAM (DDR3 SDRAM)* expands memory bandwidth by doubling the clock rate of DDR2 SDRAM. DDR3 SDRAM consumes less power and generates less heat than DDR2 SDRAM.

- *Rambus DRAM (RDRAM)* is a memory chip that was developed to communicate at very high rates of speed. RDRAM chips are not commonly used.

Memory Modules (1.1.2.6)

Early computers had RAM installed on the motherboard as individual chips. The individual memory chips, called *dual in-line package (DIP)* chips, were difficult to install and often became loose. To solve this problem, designers soldered the memory chips on a special circuit board to create a *memory module*. Table 1-4 describes the different types of memory modules.

Note

Memory modules can be single sided or double sided. Single-sided memory modules contain RAM only on one side of the module. Double-sided memory modules contain RAM on both sides.

Table 1-4   Memory Modules

DIP	Dual in-line package is an individual memory chip. A DIP has dual rows of pins used to attach it to the motherboard.
SIMM	*Single in-line memory module* is a small circuit board that holds several memory chips. SIMMs have 30-pin or 72-pin configurations.
DIMM	*Dual in-line memory module* is a circuit board that holds SDRAM, DDR SDRAM, DDR2 SDRAM, and DDR3 SDRAM chips. There are 168-pin SDRAM DIMMs, 184-pin DDR DIMMs, and 240-pin DDR2 and DDR3 DIMMs.

RIMM	*Rambus in-line memory module* is a circuit board that holds RDRAM chips. A typical RIMM has a 184-pin configuration.
SODIMM	*Small outline DIMM* has a 72-pin and 100-pin configurations for support of 32-bit transfers or 144-pin, 200-pin, and 204-pin configurations for support of 64-bit transfers. This smaller, more condensed version of DIMM provides random-access data storage that is ideal for use in laptops, printers, and other devices where conserving space is desirable.

The speed of memory has a direct impact on how much data a processor can process because faster memory improves the performance of the processor. As processor speed increases, memory speed must also increase. For example, single-channel memory can transfer data at 64 bits per clock cycle. Dual-channel memory increases the speed by using a second channel of memory, creating a data transfer rate of 128 bits.

DDR technology doubles the maximum bandwidth of SDRAM. DDR2 offers faster performance and uses less energy. DDR3 operates at even higher speeds than DDR2. However, none of these DDR technologies are backward or forward compatible. Table 1-5 shows many common memory types and speeds.

Table 1-5   Common Memory Types and Characteristics

Memory Type	Industry Name	Peak Transfer Rate	Front Side Bus
PC100 SDRAM	PC-100	800 MB/s	100 MHz
PC133 SDRAM	PC-133	1060 MB/s	133 MHz
DDR-333	PC-2700	2700 MB/s	166 MHz
DDR-400	PC-3200	3200 MB/s	200 MHz
DDR2-667	PC2-5300	5333 MB/s	667 MHz
DDR2-800	PC2-6400	6400 MB/s	400 MHz
DDR3-1333	PC3-10600	10667 MB/s	1333 MHz
DDR3-1600	PC3-12800	12800 MB/s	1600 MHz
DDR3-1866	PC3-14900	14933 MB/s	1867 MHz
DDR3-2133	PC3-17000	17066 MB/s	2133 MHz

Cache Memory

Static RAM (SRAM) is used as *cache memory* to store the most recently used data and instructions. SRAM provides the processor with faster access to the data than retrieving it from the slower DRAM, or main memory. The three most common types of cache memory are as follows:

- L1 cache is internal cache and is integrated into the CPU.

- L2 cache is external cache and was originally mounted on the motherboard near the CPU. L2 cache is now integrated into the CPU.

- L3 cache is used on some high-end workstations and server CPUs.

Error Checking

Memory errors occur when the data is not stored correctly in the RAM chips. The computer uses different methods to detect and correct data errors in memory. Three different types of error checking are as follows:

- *Nonparity* memory does not check for errors in memory.

- *Parity* memory contains eight bits for data and one bit for error checking. The error-checking bit is called a parity bit.

- *Error-correcting code (ECC)* memory can detect multiple bit errors in memory and correct single bit errors in memory.

Adapter Cards and Expansion Slots (1.1.2.7)

Adapter cards increase the functionality of a computer by adding controllers for specific devices or by replacing malfunctioning ports. Figure 1-13 shows several types of adapter cards, many of which can be integrated into the motherboard.

Sound Adapter   NIC

RAID Adapter   Video Adapter

Figure 1-13 Adapter Cards

Some common adapter cards are used to expand and customize the capability of a computer:

- *Network interface card (NIC)*: Connects a computer to a network using a network cable

- **Wireless NIC:** Connects a computer to a network using radio frequencies

- **Sound adapter:** Provides audio capability

- **Video adapter:** Provides graphic capability

- **Capture card:** Sends a video signal to a computer so that the signal can be recorded to the computer hard drive with video-capture software

- **TV tuner card:** Provides the ability to watch and record television signals on a PC by connecting a cable television, satellite, or antenna to the installed tuner card

- **Modem adapter:** Connects a computer to the Internet using a phone line

- **Small Computer System Interface (SCSI) adapter:** Connects SCSI devices, such as hard drives or tape drives, to a computer

- *Redundant array of independent disks (RAID)* **adapter:** Connects multiple hard drives to a computer to provide redundancy and to improve performance

- **Universal Serial Bus (USB) port:** Connects a computer to peripheral devices

- *Parallel port*: Connects a computer to peripheral devices

- *Serial port*: Connects a computer to peripheral devices

Computers have *expansion slots* on the motherboard to install adapter cards. The type of adapter card connector must match the expansion slot. Table 1-6 shows the different types of expansion slots.

Table 1-6   Expansion Slots

Peripheral Component Interconnect (PCI) is a 32-bit or 64-bit expansion slot. PCI is the standard slot currently used in most computers.

Figure 1-14   PCI

Figure 1-15   AGP

Accelerated Graphics Port (AGP) is designed to be used by video adapters. Advancements in the specification for AGP allow for bandwidth increases. The bandwidth of the port can be multiplied 2X, 4X, or 8X.

Figure 1-16   PCIe

PCI Express is a serial bus expansion slot. PCIe has x1, x4, x8, and x16 slots. PCIe is replacing AGP as an expansion slot for video adapters and can be used for other types of adapters.

Figure 1-17   ISA

Industry Standard Architecture (ISA) is an 8-bit or 16-bit expansion slot. This is older technology and is seldom used.

Figure 1-18   EISA

Extended ISA is a 32-bit expansion slot. This is older technology and is seldom used.

Microchannel Architecture (MCA) is an IBM proprietary 32-bit expansion slot. This is older technology and is seldom used.

Figure 1-19   MCA

PCI-Extended (PCI-X) is a 32-bit bus with higher bandwidth than the PCI bus. PCI-X can run up to four times faster than PCI.

Figure 1-20   PCI-X

Mini-PCI is a 32-bit bus used by laptops. Mini-PCI has three different form factors: Type I, Type II, and Type III.

Figure 1-21   Mini PCI

Storage Devices and RAID (1.1.2.8)

Storage drives, as shown in Figure 1-22, read or write information to magnetic, optical, or semiconductor storage media. The drive can be used to store data permanently or to retrieve information from a media disk.

Figure 1-12   Storage Drives

Storage drives can be installed inside the computer case, such as a hard drive. For portability, some storage drives can connect to the computer using a USB port, a FireWire port, eSATA, or a SCSI port. These portable storage drives are sometimes referred to as removable drives and can be used on multiple computers. Here are some common types of storage drives:

- Floppy drive
- Hard drive
- Optical drive
- Flash drive

Floppy Drive

A *floppy drive*, or floppy disk drive, is a storage device that uses removable 3.5-inch floppy disks. These magnetic floppy disks can store 720 KB or 1.44 MB of data. In a computer, the floppy drive is usually configured as the A: drive. The floppy drive can be used to boot the computer if it contains a bootable floppy disk. A 5.25-inch floppy drive is older technology and is seldom used.

Hard Drive

A *hard drive*, or hard disk drive, is a magnetic device used to store data. In a Windows computer, the hard drive is usually configured as the C: drive and contains the operating system and applications. The storage capacity of a hard drive ranges from gigabytes (GB) to terabytes (TB). The speed of a hard drive is measured in revolutions per minute (RPM). This is how fast the spindle turns the platters that hold data. The faster the spindle speed, the faster a hard drive can retrieve data from the platters. Common hard drive spindle speeds include 5400, 7200, 10,000, and up to 15,000 RPM in high-end server hard drives. Multiple hard drives can be added to increase storage capacity.

Traditional hard drives use magnetic-based storage. Magnetic hard drives have drive motors that are designed to spin the magnetic platters and move the drive heads. In contrast, the newer *solid state drives (SSD)* do not have moving parts and use semiconductors to store data. Because an SSD has no drive motors and moving parts, it uses much less energy than a magnetic hard drive. Nonvolatile flash memory chips manage all storage on an SSD, which results in faster access to data, higher reliability, and reduced power usage. SSDs have the same form factor as magnetic hard drives and use ATA or SATA interfaces. You can replace a magnetic drive with an SSD.

Tape Drive

Magnetic tapes are most often used for backups or archiving data. The tape uses a magnetic read/write head. Although data retrieval using a tape drive can be fast, locating specific data is slow because the tape must be wound on a reel until the data is found. Common tape capacities vary between a few gigabytes to many terabytes.

Optical Drive

An *optical drive* uses lasers to read data on the optical media. There are three types of optical drives:

- Compact disc (CD)

- Digital versatile disc (DVD)

- Blu-ray disc (BD)

CD, DVD, and BD media can be prerecorded (read only), recordable (write once), or re-recordable (read and write multiple times). CDs have a data storage capacity of approximately 700 MB. DVDs have a data storage capacity of approximately 4.7 GB on a single-layer disc and approximately 8.5 GB on a dual-layer disc. BDs have a storage capacity of 25 GB on a single-layer disc and 50 GB on a dual-layer disc.

There are several types of optical media:

- **CD-ROM:** CD read-only memory media that is prerecorded

- **CD-R:** CD recordable media that can be recorded one time

- **CD-RW:** CD rewritable media that can be recorded, erased, and re-recorded

- **DVD-ROM:** DVD read-only memory media that is pre-recorded

- **DVD-RAM:** DVD RAM media that can be recorded, erased, and re-recorded

- **DVD+/-R:** DVD recordable media that can be recorded one time

- **DVD+/-RW:** DVD rewritable media that can be recorded, erased, and re-recorded

- **BD-ROM:** Blu-ray read-only media that is pre-recorded with movies, games, or software
- **BD-R:** Blu-ray recordable media that can record high-definition (HD) video and PC data storage one time
- **BD-RE:** Blu-ray rewritable format for HD video recording and PC data storage

External Flash Drive

An external *flash drive*, also known as a thumb drive, is a removable storage device that connects to a USB port. An external flash drive uses the same type of nonvolatile memory chips as SSDs and does not require power to maintain the data. These drives can be accessed by the operating system in the same way that other types of drives are accessed.

Types of Drive Interfaces

Hard drives and optical drives are manufactured with different interfaces that are used to connect the drive to the computer. To install a storage drive in a computer, the connection interface on the drive must be the same as the controller on the motherboard. Here are some common drive interfaces:

- *IDE: Integrated Drive Electronics*, also called *Advanced Technology Attachment (ATA)*, is an early drive controller interface that connects computers and hard disk drives. An IDE interface uses a 40-pin connector.

- *EIDE: Enhanced Integrated Drive Electronics*, also called *ATA-2*, is an updated version of the IDE drive controller interface. EIDE supports hard drives larger than 512 MB, enables direct memory access (DMA) for speed, and uses the AT Attachment Packet Interface (ATAPI) to accommodate optical drives and tape drives on the EIDE bus. An EIDE interface uses a 40-pin connector.

- *PATA: Parallel ATA* refers to the parallel version of the ATA drive controller interface.

- *SATA: Serial ATA* refers to the serial version of the ATA drive controller interface. A SATA interface uses a 7-pin data connector.

- *eSATA: External Serial ATA* provides a hot-swappable, external interface for SATA drives. Hot-swapping is the ability to connect and disconnect a device while a computer is powered on. The eSATA interface connects an external SATA drive using a 7-pin connector. The cable can be up to 6.56 ft (2 m) in length.

- *SCSI: Small Computer System Interface* is a drive controller interface that can connect up to 15 drives. SCSI can connect both internal and external drives. An SCSI interface uses a 25-pin, 50-pin, or 68-pin connector.

RAID provides a way to store data across multiple hard disks for redundancy. To the operating system, RAID appears as one logical disk. Table 1-7 shows a comparison of the different RAID levels. The following terms describe how RAID stores data on the various disks:

- **Parity:** Detects data errors

- **Striping:** Writes data across multiple drives

- **Mirroring:** Stores duplicate data on a second drive

Table 1-7   RAID Level Comparison

RAID	Minimum Number of Drives	Description	Advantages	Disadvantages
0	2	Data striping without redundancy	High performance.	No data protection and failure of one drive results in loss of all data.
1	2	Disk mirroring	High-performance and high data protection because all data is duplicated.	Highest cost of implementation because an additional drive of equal or larger capacity is required.
2	2	Error-correcting code	This level is no longer used.	Same performance can be achieved at a lower cost using RAID 3.
3	3	Byte-level data striping with dedicated parity	For large sequential data requests.	Does not support multiple, simultaneous read and write requests.
4	3	Block-level data striping with dedicated parity	Supports multiple read requests, and if a disk fails the dedicated parity is used to create a replacement disk.	Write requests are bottlenecked due to the dedicated parity.
5	3	Combination of data striping and parity	Supports multiple simultaneous reads and writes, data is written across all drives with parity, and data can be rebuilt from information found on the other drives.	Write performance is slower than RAID 0 and 1.

RAID	Minimum Number of Drives	Description	Advantages	Disadvantages
6	4	Independent data disks with double parity	Block-level data striping with parity data distributed across all disks can handle two simultaneous drive failures.	Lower performance than RAID 5, and not supported on all disk controllers.
0+1	4	Combination of data striping and mirroring	High performance, highest data protection.	High cost overhead because duplication of data requires twice the storage capacity.
10	4 (must be an even number)	Mirrored set in a striped set	Provides fault tolerance and improved performance.	High cost overhead because duplication of data requires twice the storage capacity.

Internal Cables (1.1.2.9)

Drives require both a power cable and a data cable. A power supply might have SATA power connectors for SATA drives, Molex power connectors for PATA drives, and Berg connectors for floppy drives. The buttons and the LED lights on the front of the case connect to the motherboard with the front panel cables. Figure 1-23 displays internal data cables.

Figure 1-23   Internal PC Cables

Data cables connect drives to the drive controller, which is located on an adapter card or on the motherboard. Here are some common types of data cables:

- **Floppy disk drive (FDD) data cable:** Has up to two 34-pin drive connectors and one 34-pin connector for the drive controller.

- **PATA (IDE/EIDE) 40-conductor data cable:** Originally, the IDE interface supported two devices on a single controller. With the introduction of Extended IDE, two controllers capable of supporting two devices each were introduced. The 40-conductor ribbon cable uses 40-pin connectors. The cable has two connectors for the drives and one connector for the controller.

- **PATA (EIDE) 80-conductor data cable:** As the data rates available over the EIDE interface increased, the chance of data corruption during transmission increased. An 80-conductor cable was introduced for devices transmitting at 33.3 MB/s and over, allowing for a more reliable balanced data transmission. The 80-conductor cable uses 40-pin connectors.

- **SATA data cable:** This cable has seven conductors, one keyed connector for the drive, and one keyed connector for the drive controller.

- **SCSI data cable:** There are three types of SCSI data cables. A narrow SCSI data cable has 50 conductors, up to seven 50-pin connectors for drives, and one 50-pin connector for the drive controller, also called the host adapter. A wide SCSI data cable has 68 conductors, up to 15 68-pin connectors for drives, and one 68-pin connector for the host adapter. An Alt-4 SCSI data cable has 80 conductors, up to 15 80-pin connectors for drives, and one 80-pin connector for the host adapter.

Note

A colored stripe on a floppy or PATA cable identifies Pin 1 on the cable. When installing a data cable, always ensure that Pin 1 on the cable aligns with Pin 1 on the drive or drive controller. Keyed cables can be connected only one way to the drive and drive controller.

External Ports and Cables (1.1.3)

Input/output (I/O) ports on a computer connect peripheral devices, such as displays, printers, scanners, portable drives, and audio devices. They also connect the computer to network resources, such as modems or external network drives. This section discusses a variety of the ports and cables available.

Video Ports and Cables (1.1.3.1)

A *video port* connects a monitor to a computer using a cable. Video ports and monitor cables transfer analog signals, digital signals, or both. Computers are digital devices that create digital signals. The digital signals are sent to the graphics card where they are transmitted through a cable to a digital display. Digital signals can also be converted to analog signals by the graphics card and transferred to an analog display. Converting a digital signal to an analog signal usually results in lower image quality. A display and a monitor cable that support digital signals should provide higher image quality than those supporting only analog signals.

There are several video ports and connector types, as shown in Table 1-8.

Table 1-8   Video Ports and Connectors

Digital Visual Interface (DVI) has 24 pins for digital signals and 4 pins for analog signals. DVI-I is used for both analog and digital signals. DVI-D handles digital signals only, while DVI-A handles only analog signals.

Figure 1-24   DVI

Displayport has 20 pins and can be used for audio, video, or both audio and video transmission.

Figure 1-25   Displayport

RCA connectors have a central plug with a ring around it and can be used to carry audio or video. It is common to find RCA connectors in groups of three, where a yellow connector carries video and a pair of red and white connectors carries left and right channel audio.

Figure 1-26   RCA

DB-15 has 3 rows and 15 pins and is commonly used for analog video.

Figure 1-27   DB-15

BNC connectors connect coaxial cable to devices using a quarter-turn connection scheme. BNC is used with digital or analog audio or video.

Figure 1-28   BNC

RJ-45 has 8 pins and can be used with digital or analog audio or video.

Figure 1-29   RJ-45

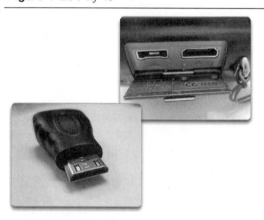

MiniHDMI, also called Type C, has 19 pins, is much smaller than an HDMI connector, and carries the same signals as an HDMI connector.

Figure 1-30   miniHDMI

Display cables transfer video signals from the computer to display devices. There are several display cable types, as shown in Figure 1-31:

- *High-Definition Multimedia Interface (HDMI):* Carries digital video and digital audio signals. Digital signals provide high-quality video and high resolutions.

- **DVI:** Carries analog, digital, or both analog and digital video signals.

- *Video Graphics Array (VGA):* Carries analog video signals. Analog video is low quality and can be interfered with by electrical and radio signals.

- **Component/RGB:** Carries analog video signals over three shielded cables (red, green, blue).

- **Composite:** Carries analog audio or video signals.

- *S-Video:* Carries analog video signals.

- **Coaxial:** Carries analog, digital, or both analog and digital video or audio signals.

- **Ethernet:** Carries analog, digital, or both analog and digital video or audio signals. Ethernet can also carry power.

Figure 1-31   Internal PC Cables

Other Ports and Cables (1.1.3.2)

Input/output (I/O) ports on a computer connect peripheral devices, such as printers, scanners, and portable drives. The following ports and cables are commonly used:

- Serial

- USB

- FireWire

- Parallel

- SCSI

- Network

- PS/2

- Audio

- Apple Thunderbolt

Serial Ports and Cables

A serial port can be either a DB-9, as shown in Figure 1-32, or a DB-25 male connector. Serial ports transmit one bit of data at a time. To connect a serial device, such as a modem or printer, you must use a serial cable. A serial cable has a maximum length of 50 ft. (15.2 m).

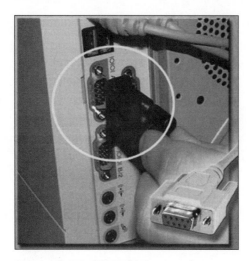

Figure 1-32   Serial Ports and Cables

Modem Ports and Cables

In addition to the serial cable used to connect an external modem to a computer, a telephone cable connects the modem to a telephone outlet. This cable uses an RJ-11 connector, as shown in Figure 1-33.

Figure 1-33   Telephone and Modem Cable and Connector

USB Ports and Cables

The *Universal Serial Bus (USB)* is a standard interface that connects peripheral devices to a computer. It was originally designed to replace serial and parallel connections. USB devices are hot-swappable, which means that users can connect and disconnect the devices while the computer is powered on. USB connections can be found on computers, cameras, printers, scanners, storage devices, and many other electronic devices. A USB hub connects multiple USB devices. A single USB port in a computer can support up to 127 separate devices with the use of multiple USB hubs.

Some devices can also be powered through the USB port, eliminating the need for an external power source. Figure 1-34 shows USB cables with connectors.

Figure 1-34 USB Cable and Connector

USB 1.1 allowed transmission rates of up to 12 Mb/s in full-speed mode and 1.5 Mb/s in low-speed mode. A USB 1.1 cable has a maximum length of 9.8 ft (3 m). USB 2.0 allows transmission speeds up to 480 Mb/s. A USB 2.0 cable has a maximum length of 16.4 ft (5 m). USB devices can only transfer data up to the maximum speed allowed by the specific port. USB 3.0 allows transmission speeds up to 5 Gb/s. USB 3.0 is backward compatible with previous versions of USB. A USB 3.0 cable does not have a maximum defined length, although a maximum length of 9.8 ft (3 m) is generally accepted.

FireWire Ports and Cables

FireWire is a high-speed, hot-swappable interface that connects peripheral devices to a computer. A single FireWire port in a computer can support up to 63 devices. Some devices can also be powered through the FireWire port, eliminating the need for an external power source. FireWire uses the Institute of Electrical and Electronics Engineers (IEEE) 1394 standard and is also known as i.Link. The IEEE creates publications and standards for technology. Figure 1-35 shows FireWire cables with connectors.

Figure 1-35 FireWire Cable and Connectors

The IEEE 1394a standard supports data rates up to 400 Mb/s for cable lengths of 15 ft. (4.5 m) or less. This standard uses a 4-pin or 6-pin connector. The IEEE 1394b and IEEE 1394c standards allow for a greater range of connections, including CAT5 UTP and optical fiber. Depending on the media used, data rates are supported up to 3.2 Gb/s for distances of 328 ft. (100 m) or less.

Parallel Ports and Cables

A parallel port on a computer is a standard Type A DB-25 female connector. The parallel connector on a printer is a standard Type B 36-pin Centronics connector. Some newer printers may use a Type C high-density 36-pin connector. Parallel ports can transmit 8 bits of data at one time and use the IEEE 1284 standard. To connect a parallel device, such as a printer, you must use a parallel cable. A parallel cable, as shown in Figure 1-36, has a maximum length of 15 ft. (4.5 m).

Figure 1-36   Parallel Cable and Connector

eSATA Data Cables

The eSATA cable connects SATA devices to the eSATA interface using a 7-pin data cable. This cable does not supply any power to the SATA external disk. A separate power cable provides power to the disk.

SCSI Ports and Cables

A SCSI port can transmit parallel data at rates in excess of 320 Mb/s and can support up to 15 devices. If a single SCSI device is connected to a SCSI port, the cable can be up to 80 ft. long (24.4 m). If multiple SCSI devices are connected to a SCSI port, the cable can be up to 40 ft. (12.2 m). A SCSI port on a computer can be a 25-pin, 50-pin, or 80-pin connector, as shown in Figure 1-37.

Figure 1-37   50-Pin SCSI Cable and SCSI Connectors

Note

A SCSI device must terminate at the endpoint of the SCSI chain. Check the device manual for termination procedures.

Caution

Some SCSI connectors resemble parallel connectors. Be careful not to connect the cable to the wrong port. The voltage used in the SCSI format may damage the parallel interface. SCSI connectors should be clearly labeled.

Network Ports and Cables

A network port, also known as an RJ-45 port, has 8 pins and connects a computer to a network. The connection speed depends on the type of network port. Standard Ethernet can transmit up to 10 Mb/s, Fast Ethernet can transmit up to 100 Mb/s, and Gigabit Ethernet can transmit up to 1000 Mb/s. The maximum length of network cable is 328 ft. (100 m). A network connector is shown in Figure 1-38.

Figure 1-38   Network Cable and Connector

PS/2 Ports

A *PS/2 port* connects a keyboard or a mouse to a computer. The PS/2 port is a
6-pin mini-DIN female connector. The connectors for the keyboard and mouse are
often colored differently, as shown in Figure 1-39. If the ports are not color-coded,
look for a small figure of a mouse or keyboard next to each port.

Figure 1-39   PS/2 Cable and Connector

Audio Ports

An audio port connects audio devices to the computer. Some of the following audio
ports are commonly used, as shown in Figure 1-40:

- **Line in:** Connects to an external source, such as a stereo system

- **Microphone:** Connects to a microphone

- **Line out:** Connects to speakers or headphones

- **Sony/Philips Digital Interface Format (S/PDIF):** Connects to coaxial cable
  using RCA connectors or fiber-optic cable using TosLink connectors to support
  digital audio

- **Gameport/MIDI:** Connects to a joystick or MIDI-interfaced device

Line In | Line Out | gameport/MIDI
Microphone In
Auxiliary In

Figure 1-40   Audio and Gameport Connectors

Input and Output Devices (1.1.4)

Input and output devices are used for communication between a computer and a user. This section discusses types of input and output devices.

Input Devices (1.1.4.1)

An *input device* enters data or instructions into a computer. Here are some examples of input devices:

- Mouse and keyboard
- Gamepad and joystick
- Digital camera and digital video camera
- Biometric authentication device
- Touchscreen
- Digitizer
- Scanner

Mice and Keyboards

The mouse and keyboard are the two most commonly used input devices. The mouse is used to navigate the graphical user interface (GUI). The keyboard is used to enter text commands that control the computer.

A *keyboard, video, mouse (KVM) switch* is a hardware device that can be used to control more than one computer while using a single keyboard, monitor, and mouse. For businesses, KVM switches provide cost-efficient access to multiple servers. Home users can save space using a KVM switch, as seen in Figure 1-41, to connect multiple computers to one keyboard, monitor, and mouse.

Figure 1-41   KVM Switch

Newer KVM switches have added the capability to share USB devices and speakers with multiple computers. Typically, by pressing a button on the KVM switch, the user can change the control from one connected computer to another connected computer. Some models of the switch transfer control from one computer to another using a specific key sequence on a keyboard, such as **Ctrl > Ctrl > A > Enter** to control the first computer connected to the switch, and then **Ctrl > Ctrl > B > Enter** to transfer control to the next computer.

Gamepads and Joysticks

Input devices for playing games include gamepads and joysticks. Gamepads allow the player to control movement and views with small sticks moved by the player's thumbs. Multiple buttons are pressed to achieve specific results within a game, such as jumping or shooting. Many gamepads even have triggers that register the amount of pressure the player puts on them. For example, applying more pressure exerted on the trigger accelerates the player faster in a driving game.

Joysticks are also used to play games and run simulations. Joysticks are best when simulating flight where actions such as pulling the joystick toward you allow the simulated plane to climb.

Digital Cameras and Digital Video Cameras

Digital cameras and digital video cameras create images that can be stored on magnetic media. The image is stored as a file that can be displayed, printed, or altered. Webcams can be built in to monitors or laptops, or stand alone to capture images in real time. Webcams are often used to create video for posting on the Internet or performing video chat sessions with others. They can also take still images that can be saved to the computer. A microphone allows the user to communicate audibly with others during a video chat session or record voice while creating a video.

Biometric Identification Devices

Biometric identification makes use of features that are unique to an individual user, such as fingerprints, voice recognition, or a retinal scan. When combined with ordinary usernames, biometrics guarantees that the authorized person is accessing the data. Figure 1-42 shows a laptop that has a built-in fingerprint scanner. By measuring the physical characteristics of the fingerprint of the user, the user is granted access if the fingerprint characteristics match the database and the correct login information is supplied.

Figure 1-42   Fingerprint Scanner

Touchscreens

A touchscreen has a pressure-sensitive transparent panel. The computer receives instructions specific to the place on the screen that the user touches.

Digitizers

A digitizer, shown in Figure 1-43, allows a designer or artist to create blueprints, images, or other artwork by using a pen-like tool called a stylus against a surface that senses where the stylus is located. Some digitizers have more than one surface or sensor and allow the user to create 3D models by performing actions with the stylus in mid-air.

Figure 1-43   Digitizer

Scanners

A scanner digitizes an image or document. The digitization of the image is stored as a file that can be displayed, printed, or altered. A bar code reader is a type of scanner that reads universal product code (UPC) bar codes. It is widely used for pricing and inventory information.

Output Devices (1.1.4.2)

An *output device* presents information to the user from a computer. Here are some examples of output devices:

- Monitors and projectors
- Printers, scanners, and fax machines
- Speakers and headphones

Monitors and Projectors

Monitors and projectors are primary output devices for a computer. There are different types of monitors, as shown in Figure 1-44. The most important difference between these monitor types is the technology used to create an image.

Figure 1-44   Types of Monitors

The following is an explanation of display technologies:

- **CRT:** The *cathode-ray tube (CRT)* has three electron beams. Each beam is directed at colored phosphor dots on the screen that glow red, blue, or green when struck by the beam. Areas not struck by an electron beam do not glow. The combination of glowing and non-glowing areas creates the image on the screen. Some televisions use this technology. CRTs usually have a degauss button on the front that the user can press to remove discoloration caused by magnetic interference.

- **LCD:** *Liquid crystal display (LCD)* is commonly used in flat-panel monitors, laptops, and some projectors. It consists of two polarizing filters with a liquid crystal solution between them. An electronic current aligns the crystals so that light can either pass through or not pass through. The effect of light passing through in certain areas and not in others is what creates the image. LCD comes in two forms, active matrix and passive matrix. Active matrix is sometimes called thin film transistor (TFT). TFT allows each pixel to be controlled, which creates very sharp color images. Passive matrix is less expensive than active matrix but does not provide the same level of image control. Passive matrix is not commonly used in laptops.

- **LED:** A *light-emitting diode (LED)* display is an LCD display that uses LED backlighting to light the display. LED has lower power consumption than standard LCD backlighting, allows the panel to be thinner, lighter, brighter, and display better contrast.

- **OLED:** An *organic LED (OLED)* display uses a layer of organic material that responds to electrical stimulus to emit light. This process allows each pixel to light individually, resulting in much deeper black levels than LED. OLED displays are also thinner and lighter than LED displays.

- **Plasma:** *Plasma* displays are another type of flat-panel monitor that can achieve high levels of brightness, deep black levels, and a very wide range of colors. Plasma displays can be created in sizes of up to 150 inches (381 cm) or more. Plasma displays get their name from the use of tiny cells of ionized gas that light up when stimulated by electricity. Plasma displays are often used in home theater applications because of their accurate representation of video.

- **DLP:** *Digital Light Processing (DLP)* is another technology used in projectors. DLP projectors use a spinning color wheel with a microprocessor-controlled array of mirrors called a digital micromirror device (DMD). Each mirror corresponds to a specific pixel. Each mirror reflects light toward or away from the projector optics. This creates a monochromatic image of up to 1024 shades of gray in between white and black. The color wheel then adds the color data to complete the projected color image.

All-in-One Printers

Printers are output devices that create hard copies of computer files. Some printers specialize in particular applications, such as printing color photographs. All-in-one printers are designed to provide multiple services, such as printing, scanning, faxing, and copying.

Speakers and Headphones

Speakers and headphones are output devices for audio signals. Most computers have audio support either integrated into the motherboard or on an adapter card. Audio support includes ports that allow input and output of audio signals. The audio card has an amplifier to power headphones and external speakers.

Monitor Characteristics (1.1.4.3)

Monitor resolution refers to the level of image detail that can be reproduced. Table 1-9 is a chart of common monitor resolutions.

Table 1-9   Display Resolutions

Display Standard	Linear Pixels (Height x Vertical)	Aspect Ration
CGA	320x200	16:10
EGA	640x350	11:6
VGA	640x480	4:3
WVGA	854x480	16:9
SVGA	800x600	4:3

Display Standard	Linear Pixels (Height x Vertical)	Aspect Ration
XGA	1024x768	4:3
WXGA	1280x800	16:10
SXGA	1280x1024	5:4
SXGA+	1400x1050	4:3
WSXGA	1600x1024	25:16
UXGA	16x1200	4:3
HDTV	1920x1080	16:9
WUXGA	1920x1200	16:10
QXGA	2048x1536	4:3
QSXGA	2560x2048	5:4
WQUXGA	3840x2400	16:10
HXGA	4096x3072	4:3
WHXGA	5120x3200	8:5
HSXGA	5120x4096	5:4
WHSXGA	6400x4096	25:16
HUXGA	6400x4800	4:3
WHUXGA	7680x4800	8:5

Higher-resolution settings produce better image quality. Several factors are involved in monitor resolution:

- *Pixel:* The term pixel is an abbreviation for picture element. Pixels are the tiny dots that comprise a screen. Each pixel consists of red, green, and blue.

- *Dot pitch:* Dot pitch is the distance between pixels on the screen. A lower dot pitch number produces a better image.

- *Contrast ratio:* The contrast ratio is a measurement of the difference in intensity of light between the brightest point (white) and the darkest point (black). A 10,000:1 contrast ratio shows dimmer whites and lighter blacks than a monitor with a contrast ratio of 1,000,000:1.

- *Refresh rate:* The refresh rate is how often per second the image is rebuilt. A higher refresh rate produces a better image and reduces the level of flicker.

- *Interlace/noninterlace:* Interlaced monitors create the image by scanning the screen two times. The first scan covers the odd lines, top to bottom, and the second scan covers the even lines. *Noninterlaced* monitors create the image by scanning the screen, one line at a time from top to bottom. Most CRT monitors today are noninterlaced.

- **Horizontal, vertical, and color resolution:** The number of pixels in a line is the horizontal resolution. The number of lines in a screen is the vertical resolution. The number of colors that can be reproduced is the color resolution.

- *Aspect ratio:* Aspect ratio is the horizontal to vertical measurement of the viewing area of a monitor. For example, a 4:3 aspect ratio applies to a viewing area that is 16 inches wide by 12 inches high. A 4:3 aspect radio also applies to a viewing area that is 24 inches wide by 18 inches high. A viewing area that is 22 inches wide by 12 inches high has an aspect ratio of 11:6.

- *Native resolution:* Native resolution is the number of pixels that a monitor has. A monitor with a resolution of 1280x1024 has 1280 horizontal pixels and 1024 vertical pixels. Native mode is when the image sent to the monitor matches the native resolution of the monitor.

Monitors have controls for adjusting the quality of the image. Here are some common monitor settings:

- **Brightness:** Intensity of the image

- **Contrast:** Ratio of light to dark

- **Position:** Vertical and horizontal location of the image on the screen

- **Reset:** Returns the monitor settings to factory settings

Adding additional monitors can increase work efficiency. The added monitors allow you to expand the size of the desktop so you can view more open windows. Many computers have built-in support for multiple monitors.

Connecting Multiple Monitors to a Single Computer

Note

To use multiple monitors, you need two or more video ports available.

How To

Step 1. Click **Start > Control Panel > Display**.

Step 2. Click **Change display settings.** (The Screen Resolution window should show two monitor icons. If multiple monitors are not displayed on the screen, the monitor may not be supported.)

Step 3. Click the monitor icon that represents your main display. If the monitor is not already the main display, check the box next to **Make this my main display**.

Step 4. Choose Extend these displays from the **Multiple displays** drop-down box.

Step 5. Click **Identify**. Windows 7 will display large numbers to identify the two monitors. Drag and drop the monitor icons to match the physical arrangement of the monitors.

Step 6. Choose the desired resolution and orientation from the drop-down boxes.

Step 7. Click OK.

Selecting PC Components (1.2.1)

Many circumstances require that you have knowledge and skills in selecting computer components. Situations such as building a new computer, upgrading an old computer or repair a malfunctioning computer are some the reasons to understand the selection of PC components.

Case and Power Supply (1.2.1.1)

Before making any purchases or performing upgrades, first determine the customer's needs. Ask the customer which devices will be connected to the computer both internally and externally. The computer case must be able to accommodate the size and shape of the power supply.

The computer case holds the power supply, motherboard, memory, and other components as show in Figure 1-45. If you are purchasing a computer case and power supply separately, ensure that all components fit into the new case and that the power supply is powerful enough to operate all the components. Many times a case comes with a power supply preinstalled. In this situation, you still need to verify that the power supply provides enough power to operate all the components that will be installed in the case.

Figure 1-45   Computer Case and Power Supply

Power supplies convert AC input to DC output voltages. Power supplies usually provide voltages of 3.3, 5, and 12, and are measured in wattage. It is recommended that the power supply has approximately 25 percent more wattage than all the attached components require. To determine the total wattage required, add the wattage for each component. If the wattage is not listed on a component, calculate it by multiplying its voltage and amperage. If the component requires different levels of wattage, use the higher requirement. After determining the necessary wattage, ensure that the power supply has the required connectors for all the components.

Selecting Motherboards (1.2.1.2)

New motherboards, as shown in Figure 1-46, often have new features or standards that may be incompatible with older components. When you select a replacement motherboard, make sure that it supports the CPU, RAM, video adapter, and other adapter cards. The socket and chipset on the motherboard must be compatible with the CPU. The motherboard must also accommodate the existing heat sink and fan assembly when reusing the CPU. Pay particular attention to the number and type of expansion slots. Make sure that they match the existing adapter cards and allow for new cards that will be used. The existing power supply must have connections that fit the new motherboard. Finally, the new motherboard must physically fit into the current computer case.

Figure 1-46   Motherboard

Different motherboards use different chipsets. A chipset consists of integrated circuits that control the communication between the CPU and the other components. The chipset establishes how much memory can be added to a motherboard and the type of connectors on the motherboard. When building a computer, choose a chipset that provides the capabilities that you need. For example, you can purchase a motherboard with a chipset that enables multiple USB ports, eSATA connections, surround sound, and video.

Motherboards have different types of CPU sockets and CPU slots. This socket or slot provides the connection point and the electrical interface for the CPU. The CPU package must match the motherboard socket type or CPU slot type. A CPU package contains the CPU, connection points, and materials that surround the CPU and dissipate heat.

Data travels from one part of a computer to another through a collection of wires known as the bus. The bus has two parts. The data portion of the bus, known as the *data bus*, carries data between the computer components. The address portion, known as the *address bus*, carries the memory addresses of the locations where data is read or written by the CPU.

The bus size determines how much data can be transmitted at one time. A 32-bit bus transmits 32 bits of data at one time from the processor to RAM or to other motherboard components, while a 64-bit bus transmits 64 bits of data at one time. The speed at which data travels through the bus is determined by the *clock speed*, measured in megahertz (MHz) or gigahertz (GHz).

PCI expansion slots connect to a parallel bus, which sends multiple bits over multiple wires simultaneously. PCI expansion slots are being replaced with PCIe expansion slots that connect to a serial bus, which sends one bit at a time at a faster rate. When building a computer, choose a motherboard that has slots to meet your current and future needs. For example, if you are building a computer for advanced gaming that needs dual graphics cards, you might choose a motherboard with dual PCIe x16 slots. Figure 1-46 shows a motherboard.

Selecting the CPU and Heat Sink and Fan Assembly (1.2.1.3)

Before you buy a CPU, make sure that it is compatible with the existing motherboard. Manufacturers' websites are a good resource to investigate the compatibility between CPUs and other devices. When upgrading the CPU, make sure the correct voltage is maintained. A Voltage Regulator Module (VRM) is integrated into the motherboard. You can configure the CPU voltage setting with jumpers, switches located on the motherboard, or settings in the BIOS.

Multicore processors have two or more processors on the same integrated circuit. Integrating the processors on the same chip creates a very fast connection between them. Multicore processors execute instructions more quickly than single-core processors and have increased data throughput. Instructions can be distributed to all the processors at the same time. RAM is shared between the processors because the cores reside on the same chip. A multicore processor is recommended for applications such as video editing, gaming, and photo manipulation.

High-power consumption creates more heat in the computer case. Multicore processors conserve power and produce less heat than multiple single-core processors, thus increasing performance and efficiency.

The speed of a modern processor is measured in GHz. A maximum speed rating refers to the maximum speed at which a processor can function without errors. Two primary factors can limit the speed of a processor:

- The processor chip is a collection of transistors interconnected by wires. Transmitting data through the transistors and wires creates delays.

- As the transistors change state from on to off or off to on, a small amount of heat is generated. The amount of heat generated increases as the speed of the processor increases. When the processor becomes too hot, it begins to produce errors.

The FSB is the path between the CPU and the Northbridge. It is used to connect various components, such as the chipset and expansion cards, and RAM. Data can travel in both directions across the FSB. The *frequency* of the bus is measured in megahertz (MHz). The frequency at which a CPU operates is determined by applying a clock multiplier to the FSB speed. For example, a processor running at 3200 MHz might be using a 400 MHz FSB. 3200 MHz divided by 400 MHz is 8, so the CPU is eight times faster than the FSB.

Processors are further classified as 32-bit and 64-bit. The primary difference is the number of instructions that can be handled by the processor at one time. A 64-bit processor processes more instructions per clock cycle than a 32-bit processor. A 64-bit processor can also support more memory. To utilize the 64-bit processor capabilities, ensure that the operating system and applications installed support a 64-bit processor.

One of the most expensive and sensitive components in the computer case is the CPU. The CPU can become very hot. Many CPUs require a heat sink, combined with a fan for cooling. A heat sink is a piece of copper or aluminum that sits between the processor and the CPU fan. The heat sink absorbs the heat from the processor and then the fan disperses the heat. When choosing a heat sink or fan, there are several factors to consider:

- **Socket type:** The heat sink or fan type must match the socket type of the motherboard.

- **Motherboard physical specifications:** The heat sink or fan must not interfere with any components attached to the motherboard.

- **Case size:** The heat sink or fan must fit within the case.

- **Physical environment:** The heat sink or fan must be able to disperse enough heat to keep the CPU cool in warm environments.

The CPU is not the only component in a computer case that can be adversely affected by heat. A computer has many internal components that generate heat while the computer is running. Case fans should be installed to move cooler air into the computer case while moving heat out of the case. When choosing case fans, there are several factors to consider:

- **Case size:** Larger cases often require larger fans because smaller fans cannot create enough airflow.

- **Fan speed:** Larger fans spin more slowly than smaller fans, which reduces fan noise.

- **Number of components in the case:** Multiple components in a computer create additional heat, which requires more fans, larger fans, or faster fans.

- **Physical environment:** The case fans must be able to disperse enough heat to keep the interior of the case cool.

- **Number of mounting places available:** Different cases have different numbers of mounting places for fans.

- **Location of mounting places available:** Different cases have different locations for mounting fans.

- **Electrical connections:** Some case fans are connected directly to the motherboard, while others are connected directly to the power supply.

Note

The direction of airflow created by all the fans in the case must work together to bring the cooler air in while moving the hotter air out. Installing a fan backward or using fans with the incorrect size or speed for the case can cause the airflows to work against each other.

Selecting RAM (1.2.1.4)

New RAM may be needed when an application locks up or the computer displays frequent error messages. To determine if the problem is the RAM, replace the old RAM module as shown in Figure 1-47. Restart the computer to see if the computer runs without error messages.

Figure 1-47   RAM Module

When selecting new RAM, you must ensure that it is compatible with the current motherboard. It must also be the same type of RAM that is currently installed in the computer. The speed of the new RAM must be supported by the chipset. It may help to take the original memory module with you when you shop for the replacement RAM.

Selecting Adapter Cards (1.2.1.5)

Adapter cards, also called expansion cards, are designed for a specific task and add extra functionality to a computer. Figure 1-48 shows types of the adapter cards available.

Sound Adapter   NIC

RAID Adapter   Video Adapter

Figure 1-48 Adapter Cards

Before you purchase an adapter card, answer the following questions:

- Is there an open expansion slot?
- Is the adapter card compatible with the open slot?
- What are the customer's current and future needs?
- What are the possible configuration options?
- What are the reasons for the best choice?

If the motherboard does not have a compatible expansion slot, an external device may be an option. Other factors that affect the selection process include cost, warranty, brand name, availability, and form factor.

Graphics Cards

The type of graphics card installed affects the overall performance of a computer. The programs and tasks that the graphics card may need to support could be RAM intensive, CPU intensive, or both. There are several factors to consider when purchasing a new graphics card:

- Slot type
- Port type
- Amount and speed of video RAM (VRAM)
- Graphics processing unit (GPU)
- Maximum resolution

A computer system must have the slots, RAM, and CPU to support the full functionality of an upgraded graphics card to receive all the benefits of the card. Choose the correct graphics card based on your customer's current and future needs. For example, if a customer wants to play 3D games, the graphics card must meet or exceed the minimum requirements for any game they want to play.

Some GPUs are integrated into the CPU. When the GPU is integrated into the CPU, there is no need to purchase a graphics card unless advanced video features such as 3D graphics or very high resolution are required. To use the built-in graphics capability of a CPU, purchase a motherboard that supports this feature.

Sound Cards

The type of sound card installed determines the sound quality of your computer. There are several factors to consider when purchasing a new sound card:

- Slot type
- Digital signal processor (DSP)
- Sample rate
- Port and connection types
- Hardware decoder
- Signal-to-noise ratio

A computer system must have quality speakers and a subwoofer to support the full functionality of an upgraded sound card. Choose the correct sound card based on your customer's current and future needs. For example, if a customer wants to hear a specific type of surround sound, the sound card must have the correct hardware decoder to reproduce it. In addition, the customer can get improved sound accuracy with a sound card that has a higher sample rate.

Storage Controllers

A storage controller is a chip that can be integrated into the motherboard or on an expansion card. Storage controllers allow for the expansion of internal and external drives for a computer system. Storage controllers, such as RAID controllers, can also provide fault tolerance or increased speed. There are several factors to consider when purchasing a new storage controller card:

- Slot type
- Drive type
- Connector quantity
- Connector location

- Card size

- Controller card RAM

- Controller card processor

- RAID type

The amount of data and the level of data protection needed for the customer influence the type of storage controller required. Choose the correct storage controller based on your customer's current and future needs. For example, if a customer wants to implement RAID 5, a RAID storage controller with at least three drives is needed.

I/O Cards

Installing an I/O card in a computer is a fast and easy way to add I/O ports. There are several factors to consider when purchasing an I/O card:

- Slot type

- I/O port type

- I/O port quantity

- Additional power requirements

FireWire, USB, parallel, and serial ports are some of the most common ports to install on a computer. Choose the correct I/O card based on your customer's current and future needs. For example, if a customer wants to add an internal card reader, and the motherboard has no internal USB connection, a USB I/O card with an internal USB connection is needed.

NICs

Customers upgrade a network interface card (NIC) to get faster speeds, more bandwidth, and better access. There are several factors to consider when purchasing a NIC:

- Slot type

- Speed

- Connector type

- Connection type

- Standards compatibility

Capture Cards

A capture card imports video into a computer and records it on a hard drive. The addition of a capture card with a television tuner allows you to view and record television programming. There are several factors to consider when purchasing a capture card:

- Slot type
- Resolution and frame rate
- I/O port
- Format standards

The computer system must have enough CPU power, adequate RAM, and a high-speed storage system to support the capture, recording, and editing demands of the customer. Choose the correct capture card based on your customer's current and future needs. For example, if a customer wants to record one program while watching another, either multiple capture cards or a capture card with dual TV tuners must be installed.

Selecting Hard Drives and Floppy Drives (1.2.1.6)

You might need to replace a storage device when it no longer meets your customer's needs or it fails. The signs that a storage device is failing might include the following:

- Unusual noises
- Unusual vibrations
- Error messages
- Corrupt data or applications

Floppy Disk Drive

While floppy disk drives (FDD) still have some limited uses, they have been largely superseded by USB flash drives, external hard drives, CDs, DVDs, and memory cards. If an existing FDD fails, replace it with one of the newer storage devices.

Hard Drives

A hard drive stores data on magnetic platters. There are several different types and sizes of hard drives. There are several factors to consider when purchasing a new hard drive:

- Adding or replacing
- Internal or external
- Case location
- System compatibility
- Heat generation
- Noise generation
- Power requirements
- Capacity
- Mechanical or solid state
- Cost (What is the price/GB?)
- Speed of rotation

Figure 1-49 shows types of hard drive connectors.

Figure 1-49   PATA, SATA, eSATA, and SCSI Connectors

PATA hard drives use a 40-pin/80-conductor cable or a 40-pin/40-conductor cable. Choose the PATA hard drive if your customer has a legacy motherboard or one that does not support SATA.

SATA and eSATA hard drives use a 7-pin/4-conductor cable. Although SATA and eSATA cables are similar, they are not interchangeable. SATA drives are internal. eSATA drives are external. Choose a SATA or eSATA hard drive if your customer needs a much higher data-transfer rate than PATA and the motherboard supports SATA or eSATA.

SCSI hard drives use a 50-pin, 68-pin, or 80-pin connector. Up to 15 SCSI drives can be connected to a SCSI drive controller. A typical use for SCSI drives is to run a server or to implement RAID. SCSI devices are usually connected in a series, forming a chain that is commonly called a daisy chain, as shown in Figure 1-50.

Figure 1-50   Daisy-Chained SCSI Devices

Each device in the SCSI chain must have a unique ID for the computer to communicate with the right device. This includes the SCSI adapter. The SCSI adapter is usually given the highest number. For narrow SCSI, the IDs 0–7 are available. For wide SCSI, the IDs 0–15 are available. The controller is 7 or 15, and the other devices in the chain use the remaining IDs. In early SCSI installations, jumpers were used to assign SCSI IDs to adapters and devices. Modern adapters most often assign IDs using a program installed on the adapter or in the operating system.

Some drives might be capable of hot-swapping. Hot-swappable drives can be connected and disconnected to the computer without turning the computer off. Normally, to install an eSATA hard disk, you shut down the computer, connect the drive, and turn the computer back on. A hot-swappable eSATA drive can be plugged into the computer at any time. External USB hard drives are also capable of hot-swapping. Check the documentation of your motherboard to determine if you can use hot-swappable drives.

See Table 1-10 for a list of SCSI types.

Table 1-10   SCSI Types

SCSI Type	Also Called	Connector	Maximum Throughput
SCSI-1		50-pin	5 MB/s
		Centronics 50-pin	
Fast SCSI	Plain SCSI	50-pin	10 MB/s
		Centronics 50-pin	
Fast Wide SCSI		50-pin	20 MB/s
		68-pin	
Ultra SCSI	Fast-20	50-pin	20 MB/s
Ultra Wide SCSI		68-pin	40 MB/s

SCSI Type	Also Called	Connector	Maximum Throughput
Ultra2 SCSI	Fast-40	50-pin	40 MB/s
Ultra2 Wide SCSI		68-pin	80 MB/s
		80-pin	
Ultra3 SCSI	Ultra-160	68-pin	160 MB/s
		80-pin	
Ultra320 SCSI		68-pin	320 MB/s
		80-pin	

Selecting Solid State Drives and Media Readers (1.2.1.7)

Solid State Drives

SSD can use different types of memory such as static RAM (SRAM) and dynamic RAM (DRAM) both of these are volatile memory and need batteries to maintain power to prevent data loss. These are called RAM-based SSD and are often used in industries that cannot tolerate high latency or downtime. Amazon, an e-commerce company, is an example of such an industry. NAND, another type of flash memory used in SSD, retains data without power; it is nonvolatile and is what is used in the SSD of the consumer market. They are less expensive and have all the other characteristics of an SSD; instead of magnetic platters to store data, as shown in Figures 1-51a and 1-51b. SSDs are considered to be highly reliable because they have no moving parts.

Figure 1-51a   Nonmechanical SSD

Figure 1-51b   Component and Mechanical HHD Components

Choose an SSD if your customer needs to do any of the following:

- Operate in extreme environments
- Use less power
- Produce less heat
- Reduce startup time

Media Readers

A *media reader* is a device that reads and writes to different types of media cards, for example, those found in a digital camera, smart phone, or MP3 player. When replacing a media reader, ensure that it supports the type of cards used and the storage capacity of the cards to be read. There are several factors to consider when purchasing a new media reader:

- Internal or external
- Type of connector used
- Type of media cards supported

Choose the correct media reader based on your customer's current and future needs. For example, if a customer needs to use multiple types of media cards, a multiple format media reader is needed. These are some common media cards:

- **Secure digital (SD):** SD cards were designed for use in portable devices such as cameras, MP3 players, and tablets. SD cards can hold as much as 4 GB. SD High Capacity (SDHC) cards can hold as much as 32 GB, while SD Extended Capacity (SDXC) cards can hold as much as 2 TB of data.
- **microSD:** A much smaller version of SD, commonly used in cellular phones.
- **CompactFlash:** CompactFlash is an older format, but still in wide use because of its high capacity (up to 128 GB is common) and high speed. CompactFlash is often used as storage for video cameras.
- **Memory Stick:** A proprietary flash memory created by Sony Corporation. Memory Stick is used in cameras, MP3 players, handheld video game systems, mobile phones, cameras, and other portable electronics.

Another type of media card is the Extreme Digital (xD or xD-Picture Card). xD cards were developed for use in many cameras and voice recorders but have since become obsolete with the broad use of SD cards. xD cards have a maximum capacity of 2 GB.

Selecting Optical Drives (1.2.1.8)

An optical drive uses a laser to read and write data to and from optical media. There are several factors to consider when purchasing an optical drive:

- Interface type
- Reading capability
- Writing capability
- Format

A CD-ROM drive can only read CDs. A CD-RW can read and write to CDs. Choose a CD-RW if your customer needs to read and write to CDs.

A DVD-ROM drive can only read DVDs and CDs. A DVD-RW can read and write to DVDs and CDs. DVDs hold significantly more data than CDs. Choose a DVD-RW if your customer needs to read and write to DVDs and CDs.

A Blu-ray reader (BD-R) can only read Blu-ray discs, DVDs, and CDs. A Blu-ray writer (BD-RE) can read and write to Blu-ray discs and DVDs. Blu-ray discs hold significantly more data than DVDs. Choose a BD-RE drive if your customer needs to read and write to Blu-ray discs.

Selecting External Storage (1.2.1.9)

External storage connects to an external port, such as a USB, IEEE 1394, SCSI, or eSATA. External flash drives, sometimes called thumb drives, that connect to a USB port are a type of removable storage. There are several factors to consider when purchasing external storage:

- Port type
- Storage capacity
- Speed
- Portability
- Power requirements

External storage offers portability and convenience when working with multiple computers. Choose the correct type of external storage for your customer's needs. For example, if your customer needs to transfer a small amount of data, such as a single presentation, an external flash drive is a good choice. If your customer needs to back up or transfer large amounts of data, choose an external hard drive.

Selecting Input and Output Devices (1.2.1.10)

To select input and output devices, first find out what the customer wants to do with the device. Next, research the Internet for possible solutions and discuss these with the customer, and examine the system to which the device will be added. After you determine which input or output device the customer needs, you must determine how to connect it to the computer. Figure 1-52 shows common input and output connectors.

Figure 1-52   Common Input/Output Connectors

Technicians should have a good understanding of several types of interfaces:

- **FireWire (IEEE 1394):** Transfers data at 100, 200, or 400 Mb/s and IEEE 1394b at 800 Mb/s.

- **Parallel (IEEE 1284):** Transfers data at a maximum speed of 3 MB/s.

- **Serial (RS-232):** Early versions were limited to 20 Kb/s, but newer versions can reach transfer rates of 1.5 Mb/s.

- **SCSI (Ultra-320 SCSI):** Connects as many as 15 devices with a transfer rate of 320 MB/s.

The USB interface is widespread and used with many different devices. Figure 1-53a and 1-53b shows plugs and connectors for USB 1.1, USB 2.0, and USB 3.0.

Figure 1-53a   USB 1.1 and USB 2.0   **Figure 1-53b**   USB 3.0

The SATA interface has become common in recent years. SATA is replacing IDE and EIDE as the standard interface for hard drives and SSDs. SATA cables are easier to connect because they only have two ends, drives do not need to be jumpered, and eSATA drives can be hot-plugged if the motherboard supports hot-plugging. See Table 1-11 for a comparison of PATA and SATA speeds.

Table 1-11   PATA and SATA Speeds

Interface	Speed
ATA-1 (IDE)	8.3 MB/s
ATA–2 (EIDE)	16.6 MB/s
ATA-3 (EIDE) Minor Revision	16.6 MB/s
ATA-4 (Ultra-ATA/33)	33.3 MB/s
ATA-5 (Ultra-ATA/66)	66.7 MB/s
ATA-6 (Ultra-ATA/100)	100 MB/s
ATA-7 (Ultra-ATA/133)	133 MB/s
SATA 1.0	1.5 Gb/s
SATA 2.0	3 Gb/s
SATA 3.0	6 Gb/s

Worksheet: 1.2.1.11 Research Computer Components

In this worksheet, you use the Internet, a newspaper, or a local store to gather information about the components you need to complete your customer's computer. Refer to the worksheet in *IT Essentials: PC Hardware and Software Lab Manual*, Fifth Edition.

Specialized Computer Systems (1.3.1)

When designing and building a computer system the technician must always ask the question "why?" to determine what components and type of computer the user or customer will need. What tasks will they be performing on their computer; will it be for everyday uses such as email or web surfing or will the use be more focused toward video editing, gaming, or some other tasks that will require a high performance system?

CAx Workstations (1.3.1.1)

You might need to design, build, and install computers for a customer that can accomplish a specific task. All computers can run programs, store data, and use I/O devices. A specialized computer must support hardware and software that allows a user to perform tasks that an off-the-shelf system cannot perform. One example of a specialized computer is a workstation used to run computer-aided design (CAD) or computer-aided manufacturing (CAM) software.

A CAD or CAM *(CAx)* workstation is used to design products and control the manufacturing process. CAx workstations are used to create blueprints, design homes, cars, airplanes, and many of the parts in the products that you use every day. CAx is even used to develop the computer parts used in CAx workstations. A computer used to run CAx software must support the needs of the software and the I/O devices that the user needs to design and manufacture products. CAx software is often complex and requires robust hardware. Consider the following hardware when you need to run CAx software:

- **Powerful processor:** CAx software must make enormous amounts of calculations very quickly. You must meet the needs of the software when choosing a CPU.

- **High-end video card:** Some CAx software is used to create 3D models. Realistic shading and texturing add to the complexity of the models, and a video card that can handle high resolutions and high detail is needed. Often, multiple monitors are desired or even required so that the user can work with code, 2D renderings, and 3D models all at the same time. Choose a video card that supports multiple monitors.

- **RAM:** Because of the high amount of data processed by a CAx workstation, RAM is very important. The more RAM that is installed, the more data the processor can calculate before needing to read from slower storage, such as hard drives. Install as much memory as is supported by the motherboard and the operating system. The quantity and speed of the memory should exceed the minimums recommended by the CAx application.

Audio and Video Editing Workstations (1.3.1.2)

An *audio and video editing workstation* is used during many stages of development when creating audio and video material. An audio editing workstation is used to record music and create music CDs and CD labels. A video editing workstation can be used to create television commercials, prime-time programming, and movies for the theater or home movies.

Specialized hardware and software are combined to build a computer to perform audio and video editing. Audio software on an audio editing workstation, shown in Figure 1-54, is used to record audio, manipulate how the audio sounds through mixing and special effects, and finalize recordings for publication. Video software is used to cut, copy, combine, and change video clips. Special effects are also added to video using video software. Consider the following hardware when you need to run audio and video-editing software:

- **Specialized audio card:** When recording music to a computer in a studio, multiple inputs from microphones and many outputs to effects equipment may be needed. An audio card capable of handling all these inputs and outputs is needed. Research different audio card manufacturers and understand the needs of your customer to install an audio card that will meet all the needs of a modern recording or mastering studio.

- **Specialized video card:** A video card that can handle high resolutions and multiple displays is necessary to combine and edit different video feeds and special effects in real time. You must understand the needs of the customer and research video cards to install a card that can handle the high amounts of information that comes from modern cameras and effects equipment.

- **Large, fast hard drive:** Modern video cameras record in high resolution at fast frame rates. This translates into a high amount of data. Small hard drives will fill up very quickly, and slow hard drives will not be able to keep up with demands, even dropping frames at times. A large, fast hard drive is necessary to record high-end video without errors or missed frames. RAID levels such as 0 or 5, where striping is used, can help to increase storage speed.

- **Dual monitors:** When working with audio and video, two, three, or even more monitors can be very helpful to keep track of everything that is going on with multiple tracks, scenes, equipment, and software. Find out how your customer likes to work to decide how many monitors is most beneficial. If multiple monitors are required, specialized video cards are necessary when building an audio or video workstation.

Figure 1-54   Audio-Editing Workstation

Virtualization Workstations (1.3.1.3)

You might need to build a computer for a client that uses virtualization technologies. Simultaneously running two or more operating systems on one computer is called *virtualization*. Often, an operating system is installed, and virtualization software is used to install and manage additional installations of other operating systems. Different operating systems from multiple software companies may be used.

There is also another type of virtualization. *Virtual Desktop Infrastructure (VDI)* allows users to log in to a server to access their own virtual computers. Input from the mouse and keyboard is sent to the server to manipulate the virtual computer. Output such as sound and video is sent back to the speakers and display of the computer accessing the virtual computer. Low-powered devices, such as old laptops, can perform difficult calculations quickly because they are being performed on a server that is much more powerful. Laptops, smart phones, and tablets can also access the VDI to use the virtual computers. These are some other functions of virtual computing:

- Test software or software upgrades in an environment that does not hurt your current operating system environment.

- Use other operating systems on one computer, such as Linux or Ubuntu.

- Browse the Internet without harmful software hurting your main installation.

- Run old applications that are not compatible with modern operating systems.

Virtual computing requires more powerful hardware configurations because each installation needs its own resources. One or two virtual environments can be run on a modern computer with modest hardware, but a complete VDI installation may require fast, expensive hardware to support multiple users in many different environments. This is some of the hardware required to run virtual computers:

- **Maximum RAM:** You need enough RAM to meet the requirements of each virtual environment and the host computer. A standard installation using only a few virtual machines might require as little as 64 MB of RAM to support a modern operating system such as Windows XP. With multiple users, supporting many virtual computers for each user, you might need to install as much as 64 GB of RAM or more.

- **CPU cores:** Although a single-core CPU can perform virtual computing, a CPU with additional cores increases speed and responsiveness when hosting multiple users and virtual machines. Some VDI installations use computers that have multiple CPUs that have multiple cores.

Gaming PCs (1.3.1.4)

Many people enjoy playing computer games. Each year, games become more advanced and require more powerful hardware, new hardware types, and additional resources to ensure a smooth and enjoyable gaming experience.

You may be required to build a computer for a customer designed specifically for playing games (see Figure 1-55). This is some of the hardware required when building a gaming computer:

- **Powerful processor:** Games require all the components in the computer to work together seamlessly. A powerful processor helps ensure that all the software and hardware data can be addressed in a timely fashion. Multiple-core processors can help increase the responsiveness of hardware and software.

Figure 1-55   Gaming PC

- **High-end video card:** Modern games use high resolutions and intricate detail. A video card that has a fast, specialized GPU and high amounts of fast video memory is necessary to ensure that the images displayed on the monitor are high quality, clear, and smooth. Some gaming machines use multiple video cards to produce high frame rates or use multiple monitors.

- **High-end sound card:** Video games use multiple channels of high-quality sound to immerse the player in games. A high-quality sound card increases the quality of sound above that of built-in sound on a computer. A dedicated sound card also helps improve overall performance by taking some of the demand off of the processor.

- **High-end cooling:** High-end components often produce more heat than standard components. More robust cooling hardware is often needed to make sure that the computer stays cool under heavy loads while playing advanced games. Oversized fans, heat sinks, and water cooling devices are often used to keep CPUs, GPUs, and RAM cool.

- **Large amounts of fast RAM:** Computer games require large amounts of memory to function. Video data, sound data, and all the information needed to play the game are constantly being accessed. The more RAM that the computer has, the less often the computer needs to read from slower storage, such as hard drives or SSDs. Faster RAM helps the processor keep all the data in sync because the data that it needs to calculate can be retrieved when it is needed.

- **Fast storage:** 7200 RPM and 10000 RPM drives can retrieve data at a much faster rate than 5400 RPM hard drives. SSD drives are more expensive, but they improve the performance of games dramatically.

- **Gaming-specific hardware:** Some games involve communicating with other players. A microphone is required to talk to them, and speakers or headphones are required to hear them. Find out what type of games your customer plays to determine if a microphone or headset is needed. Some games can be played in 3D. Special glasses and specific video cards may be required to use this feature. Also, some games might benefit from the use of more than one monitor. Flight simulators, for example, can be configured to display cockpit images across two, three, or even more monitors at the same time.

Home Theater PCs (1.3.1.5)

Building a *Home Theater Personal Computer (HTPC)* requires specialized hardware to deliver a high-quality viewing experience for the customer. Each piece of equipment must connect and properly provide the necessary services and resources to support the different demands required from an HTPC system.

A useful feature of an HTPC is the ability to record a video program to watch at a later time. HTPC systems can be designed to display live television, stream movies and Internet content, display family photos and videos, and even surf the Internet on a television. Consider the following hardware when building an HTPC:

- **Specialized cases and power supplies:** Smaller motherboards can be used when building an HTPC so that the components can fit into a more compact form factor case. This small form factor looks like a component usually found in a home theater. Usually an HTPC case contains large fans that move more slowly and create less noise than those found in an average workstation. Power supplies that do not have fans can be used (depending on power requirements) to further reduce the amount of noise created by the HTPC. Some HTPC designs contain high-efficient components and require no fans for cooling.

- **Surround-sound audio:** Surround sound helps to bring the viewer into the video program. An HTPC can use surround sound from the motherboard when the chipset supports it, or a dedicated sound card can be installed to output high-quality surround sound to speakers or an additional amplifier for even better sound.

- **HDMI output:** The HDMI standard allows for transmission of high-definition video, surround sound, and data to televisions, media receivers, and projectors.

- *TV tuners and cable cards*: A tuner must be used for the HTPC to display television signals. A TV tuner converts analog and digital television signals into audio and video signals that the computer can use and store. Cable cards can be used to receive television signals from a cable company. A cable card is required for access to premium cable channels. Some cable cards can receive as many as six channels simultaneously.

- **Specialized hard drive:** Hard drives that have low noise levels and that have reduced power consumption are commonly known as audio/video drives (A/V).

Worksheet: 1.3.1.6 Research Computer Components

In this worksheet, you use the Internet, a newspaper, or a local store to gather information about building a specialized computer system. Refer to the worksheet in *IT Essentials: PC Hardware and Software Lab Manual*, Fifth Edition.

Summary (1.4.1)

This chapter introduced the components that comprise a personal computer system and how to consider upgrade components. Much of the content in this chapter will help you throughout this course.

- Information technology encompasses the use of computers, network hardware, and software to process, store, transmit, and retrieve information.

- A personal computer system consists of hardware components and software applications.

- The computer case and power supply must be chosen carefully to support the hardware inside the case and allow for the addition of components.

- The internal components of a computer are selected for specific features and functions. All internal components must be compatible with the motherboard.

- Use the correct type of ports and cables when connecting devices.

- Typical input devices include the keyboard, mouse, touchscreen, and digital cameras.

- Typical output devices include monitors, printers, and speakers.

- Cases, power supplies, the CPU and cooling system, RAM, hard drives, and adapter cards, must be upgraded when devices fail or no longer meet customer needs.

- Specialized computers require hardware specific to their function. The type of hardware used in specialized computers is determined by how a customer works and what a customer wants to accomplish.

Summary of Exercises

This is a summary of the worksheets associated with this chapter. Refer to the worksheets in the *IT Essentials: PC Hardware and Software Lab Manual*, Fifth Edition.

Worksheets

The following worksheets cover material from this chapter. Refer to the worksheets in the *IT Essentials: PC Hardware and Software Lab Manual*, Fifth Edition.

Worksheet 1.1.1.4: Ohm's Law

Worksheet 1.2.1.11: Research Computer Components

Worksheet 1.3.1.6: Build a Specialized Computer System

Check Your Understanding

You can find the answers to these questions in Appendix A, "Answers to 'Check Your Understanding' Questions."

1. What is the purpose of the voltage selector switch?

   A. It sets the power supply voltage to accommodate the voltage needs of computer components.

   B. It sets the correct input voltage to the power supply, depending on the country where the power supply is used.

   C. It allows the user to increase the number of devices the power supply can support.

   D. It changes the voltage to match the type of motherboard used in the computer.

2. Which IEEE standard defines the FireWire technology?

   A. 1284

   B. 1394

   C. 1451

   D. 1539

3. What is the maximum data speed of high-speed USB 2.0?

   A. 1.5 Mb/s

   B. 12 Mb/s

   C. 380 Mb/s

   D. 480 Mb/s

   E. 480 Gb/s

   F. 840 Gb/s

4. A network administrator currently has three servers and needs to add a fourth but does not have enough room for an additional monitor and keyboard. Which device allows the administrator to connect all the servers to a single monitor and keyboard?

   A. Touchscreen monitor

   B. PS/2 hub

   C. USB switch

   D. KVM switch

   E. UPS

5. What danger is posed to a technician by opening a power supply even after it has been unplugged for an extended period of time?

    A. Shock from stored high voltage

    B. Burns from hot components

    C. Exposure to heavy metals

    D. Poisoning from toxic fumes

6. Which term refers to the technique of increasing the speed of a processor from the specified value of its manufacturer?

    A. Throttling

    B. Multitasking

    C. Overclocking

    D. Hyperthreading

7. Which technology would be best to use for drive redundancy and data protection?

    A. CD

    B. DVD

    C. PATA

    D. RAID

    E. SCSI

8. What is a characteristic of a hot-swappable eSATA drive?

    A. The computer must be shut down for the drive to be connected.

    B. A hot-swappable eSATA drive produces less heat.

    C. It can be connected and disconnected to the computer without turning off the computer.

    D. It has a lower spin rate (RPM).

9. Which is a possible use for virtual computing?

    A. To allow users to browse the Internet without the risk of malware infecting the host software installation

    B. To allow computer hardware to be tested

    C. To allow computer hardware upgrades to be tested

    D. To allow ROM firmware upgrades to be tested

10. When a computer is being built, which three components must have the same form factor? (Choose three.)

    A. Case

    B. Power supply

    C. Monitor

    D. Video card

    E. Motherboard

    F. Keyboard

11. What is the function of the power supply?

    A. To convert AC power into a lower-voltage DC power

    B. To convert AC power into a higher-voltage DC power

    C. To convert DC power into a lower-voltage AC power

    D. To convert DC power into a higher-voltage AC power

CHAPTER 2

Lab Procedures and Tool Use

Objectives

Upon completion of this chapter, you will be able to answer the following questions:

- What are safe working conditions and procedures?

- What procedures help protect equipment and data?

- What procedures help to properly dispose of hazardous computer components and related material?

- What tools and software are used with personal computer components, and what is their purpose?

- What is proper tool use?

Key Terms

This chapter uses the following key terms. You can find the definitions in the Glossary.

electrostatic discharge (ESD)   page 79

antistatic wrist strap   page 80

electromagnetic interference (EMI)   page 80

radio frequency interference (RFI)   page 80

current   page 80

power fluctuation   page 80

blackout   page 80

brownout   page 81

noise   page 81

spike   page 81

power surge   page 81

power protection device   page 81

surge suppressor   page 81

uninterruptible power supply   page 81

standby power supply (SPS)   page 81

Material Safety and Data Sheet (MSDS)   page 82

Occupational Safety and Health Administration (OSHA)   page 82

Registration, Evaluation, Authorization and restriction of Chemicals (REACH)   page 83

antistatic mat   page 85

hand tools   page 85

flat-head screwdriver   page 85

Phillips-head screwdriver   page 85

hex driver   page 86

Torx screwdriver   page 86

part retriever   page 86

wire stripper   page 86

crimper   page 86

punch-down tool   page 86

Introduction (2.0.1)

This chapter covers basic safety practices for the workplace, hardware and software tools, and the disposal of hazardous materials. Safety guidelines help protect individuals from accidents and injury. They also help to protect equipment from damage. Some of these guidelines are designed to protect the environment from contamination caused by improperly discarded materials. You will also learn how to protect equipment and data and how to properly use hand and software tools.

Safe Lab Procedures (2.1)

This section discusses safety in the lab. Safety guidelines help protect individuals from accidents and injury. They also help to protect equipment from damage. Some of these guidelines are designed to protect the environment from contamination caused by improperly discarded materials.

General Safety (2.1.1.1)

Safe working conditions help prevent injury to people and damage to computer equipment. A safe workspace is clean, organized, and properly lighted. Everyone must understand and follow safety procedures.

Follow the basic safety guidelines to prevent cuts, burns, electrical shock, and damage to eyesight. As a best practice, make sure that a fire extinguisher and first-aid kit are available in case of fire or injury. Poorly placed or unsecured cables can cause tripping hazards in a network installation. Cables should be installed in conduit or cable trays to prevent hazards.

This is a partial list of basic safety precautions to use when working on a computer:

- Remove your watch and jewelry and secure loose clothing.
- Turn off the power and unplug equipment before performing service.
- Cover sharp edges inside the computer case with tape.
- Never open a power supply or a CRT monitor.
- Do not touch areas in printers that are hot or that use high voltage.
- Know where the fire extinguisher is located and how to use it.
- Keep food and drinks out of your workspace.
- Keep your workspace clean and free of clutter.
- Bend your knees when lifting heavy objects to avoid injuring your back.

Electrical Safety (2.1.1.2)

Follow electrical safety guidelines to prevent electrical fires, injuries, and fatalities in the home and the workplace. Power supplies and CRT monitors contain high voltage.

Caution

Only experienced technicians should attempt to repair power supplies and CRT monitors. Do not wear the antistatic wrist strap when repairing power supplies or CRT monitors.

Some printer parts become hot during use, and other parts might contain high voltage. Check the printer manual for the location of high-voltage components. Some components retain a high voltage even after the printer is turned off. Make sure that the printer has had time to cool before making the repair.

Electrical devices have certain power requirements. For example, AC adapters are manufactured for specific laptops. Exchanging power cords with a different type of laptop or device may cause damage to both the AC adapter and the laptop.

Fire Safety (2.1.1.3)

Follow fire safety guidelines to protect lives, structures, and equipment. To avoid an electrical shock and to prevent damage to the computer, turn off and unplug the computer before beginning a repair.

Fire can spread rapidly and be very costly. Proper use of a fire extinguisher can prevent a small fire from getting out of control. When working with computer components, be aware of the possibility of an accidental fire and know how to react. Be alert for odors emitting from computers and electronic devices. When electronic components overheat or short out, they emit a burning odor. If there is a fire, follow these safety procedures:

- Never fight a fire that is out of control or not contained.
- Always have a planned fire escape route before beginning any work.
- Get out of the building quickly.
- Contact emergency services for help.
- Locate and read the instructions on the fire extinguishers in your workplace before you have to use them.

Be familiar with the types of fire extinguishers used in your country or region. Each type of fire extinguisher has specific chemicals to fight different types of fires:

- Paper, wood, plastics, cardboard
- Gasoline, kerosene, organic solvents

- Electrical equipment
- Combustible metals

It is important to know how to use a fire extinguisher. Use the memory aid P-A-S-S to remember the basic rules of fire extinguisher operation:

- **P:** Pull the pin.
- **A:** Aim at the base of the fire, not at the flames.
- **S:** Squeeze the lever.
- **S:** Sweep the nozzle from side to side.

Procedures to Protect Equipment and Data (2.1.2)

Replacing equipment and recovering data is expensive and time consuming. This section identifies potential threats to systems and describes procedures to help prevent loss and damage.

ESD and EMI (2.1.2.1)

Electrostatic discharge (ESD), harsh climates, and poor-quality sources of electricity can cause damage to computer equipment. Follow proper handling guidelines, be aware of environmental issues, and use equipment that stabilizes power to prevent equipment damage and data loss.

Static electricity is the buildup of an electric charge resting on a surface. *Electrostatic discharge (ESD)* occurs when this buildup jumps to a component and causes damage. ESD can be destructive to the electronics in a computer system.

At least 3000 volts of static electricity must build up before a person can feel ESD. For example, static electricity can build up on you as you walk across a carpeted floor. When you touch another person, you both receive a shock. If the discharge causes pain or makes a noise, the charge was probably above 10,000 volts. By comparison, less than 30 volts of static electricity can damage a computer component.

ESD can cause permanent damage to electrical components. Follow these recommendations to help prevent ESD damage:

- Keep all components in antistatic bags until you are ready to install them.
- Use grounded mats on workbenches.

- Use grounded floor mats in work areas.

- Use *antistatic wrist straps* when working on computers.

Electromagnetic interference (EMI) is the intrusion of outside electromagnetic signals in a transmission media, such as copper cabling. In a network environment, EMI distorts the signals so that the receiving devices have difficulty interpreting them.

EMI does not always come from expected sources, such as cellular phones. Other types of electric equipment can emit a silent, invisible electromagnetic field that can extend for more than a mile (1.6 km).

There are many sources of EMI:

- Any source designed to generate electromagnetic energy

- Manmade sources like power lines or motors

- Natural events such as electrical storms, or solar and interstellar radiations

Wireless networks are affected by *radio frequency interference (RFI)*. RFI is caused by radio transmitters and other devices transmitting in the same frequency. For example, a cordless telephone can cause problems with a wireless network when both devices use the same frequency. Microwaves can also cause interference when positioned in close proximity to wireless networking devices.

Climate

Climate affects computer equipment in a variety of ways:

- If the environment temperature is too high, equipment can overheat.

- If the humidity level is too low, the chance of ESD increases.

- If the humidity level is too high, equipment can suffer from moisture damage.

Power Fluctuation Types (2.1.2.2)

Voltage is the force that moves electrons through a circuit. The movement of electrons is called *current*. Computer circuits need voltage and current to operate electronic components. When the voltage in a computer is not accurate or steady, computer components might not operate correctly. Unsteady voltages are called *power fluctuations*.

The following types of AC power fluctuations can cause data loss or hardware failure:

- *Blackout*: Complete loss of AC power. A blown fuse, damaged transformer, or downed power line can cause a blackout.

- *Brownout*: Reduced voltage level of AC power that lasts for a period of time. Brownouts occur when the power line voltage drops below 80 percent of the normal voltage level. Overloading electrical circuits can cause a brownout.

- *Noise*: Interference from generators and lightning. Noise results in poor quality power, which can cause errors in a computer system.

- *Spike*: Sudden increase in voltage that lasts for a short period and exceeds 100 percent of the normal voltage on a line. Spikes can be caused by lightning strikes but can also occur when the electrical system comes back on after a blackout.

- *Power surge*: Dramatic increase in voltage above the normal flow of electrical current. A power surge lasts for a few nanoseconds, or one-billionth of a second.

Power Protection Devices (2.1.2.3)

To help shield against power fluctuation problems, use *power protection devices* to protect the data and computer equipment:

- *Surge suppressor*: Helps protect against damage from surges and spikes. A surge suppressor diverts extra electrical voltage that is on the line to the ground.

- *Uninterruptible power supply (UPS)*: Helps protect against potential electrical power problems by supplying a consistent level of electrical power to a computer or other device. The battery is constantly recharging while the UPS is in use. The UPS provides a consistent quality of power when brownouts and blackouts occur. Many UPS devices can communicate directly with the computer operating system. This communication allows the UPS to safely shut down the computer and save data prior to the UPS losing all electrical power.

- *Standby power supply (SPS)*: Helps protect against potential electrical power problems by providing a backup battery to supply power when the incoming voltage drops below the normal level. The battery is on standby during normal operation. When the voltage decreases, the battery provides DC power to a power inverter, which converts it to AC power for the computer. This device is not as reliable as a UPS because of the time it takes to switch over to the battery. If the switching device fails, the battery cannot supply power to the computer.

Caution

UPS manufacturers suggest never plugging in a laser printer to a UPS because the printer could overload the UPS.

Procedures to Protect the Environment (2.1.3)

Most computers and peripherals use and contain at least some materials that can be considered toxic to the environment. This section describes tools and procedures that help identify these materials and the steps for the proper handling and disposal of the materials.

Material Safety and Data Sheet (2.1.3.1)

Computers and peripherals contain materials that can be harmful to the environment. Hazardous materials are sometimes called toxic waste. These materials can contain high concentrations of heavy metals such as cadmium, lead, or mercury. The regulations for the disposal of hazardous materials vary by state or country. Contact the local recycling or waste removal authorities in your community for information about disposal procedures and services.

A *Material Safety and Data Sheet (MSDS)* is a fact sheet that summarizes information about material identification, including hazardous ingredients that can affect personal health, fire hazards, and first-aid requirements. The MSDS contains chemical reactivity and incompatibility information. It also includes protective measures for the safe handling and storage of materials and spill, leak, and disposal procedures.

To determine whether a material is classified as hazardous, consult the manufacturer's MSDS. In the United States, the *Occupational Safety and Health Administration (OSHA)* requires that all hazardous materials be accompanied by an MSDS when transferred to a new owner. The MSDS information included with products purchased for computer repairs or maintenance can be relevant to computer technicians. OSHA also requires that employees be informed about the materials that they are working with and be provided with material safety information. Figure 2-1 shows the OSHA website where you can find the MSDS form and more information.

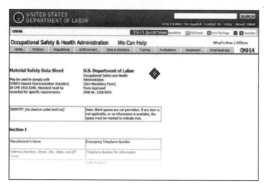

Figure 2-1   MSDS

Note

The MSDS is valuable in determining how to dispose of potentially hazardous materials in the safest manner. Always check local regulations concerning acceptable disposal methods before disposing of any electronic equipment.

The MSDS contains valuable information:

- Name of the material
- Physical properties of the material
- Hazardous ingredients contained in the material
- Reactivity data, such as fire and explosion data
- Procedures for spills and leaks
- Special precautions
- Health hazards
- Special protection requirements

In the European Union, the regulation *Registration, Evaluation, Authorization and restriction of Chemicals (REACH)* came into effect on June 1, 2007, replacing various directives and regulations with a single system.

Equipment Disposal (2.1.3.2)

The proper disposal or recycling of hazardous computer components is a global issue. Make sure to follow regulations that govern how to dispose of specific items. Organizations that violate these regulations can be fined or face expensive legal battles.

Batteries

Batteries often contain rare earth metals that can be harmful to the environment. Batteries from portable computer systems can contain lead, cadmium, lithium, alkaline manganese, and mercury. These metals do not decay and remain in the environment for many years. Mercury is commonly used in the manufacturing of batteries and is extremely toxic and harmful to humans.

Recycling batteries should be a standard practice for a technician. All batteries, including lithium-ion, nickel-cadmium, nickel-metal hydride, and lead-acid, are subject to disposal procedures that comply with local environmental regulations.

Monitors

Monitors contain glass, metal, plastics, lead, barium, and rare earth metals. According to the U.S. Environmental Protection Agency (EPA), monitors can contain approximately 4 pounds (1.8 kg) of lead. Monitors must be disposed of in compliance with environmental regulations.

Handle CRT monitors with care. Extremely high voltage can be stored in CRT monitors, even after being disconnected from a power source.

Toner Kits, Cartridges, and Developers

Used printer toner kits and printer cartridges must be disposed of properly or recycled. Some toner cartridge suppliers and manufacturers take empty cartridges for refilling. Some companies specialize in refilling empty cartridges. Kits to refill inkjet printer cartridges are available but are not recommended because the ink might leak into the printer, causing irreparable damage. Using refilled inkjet cartridges might also void the inkjet printer warranty.

Chemical Solvents and Aerosol Cans

Contact the local sanitation company to learn how and where to dispose of the chemicals and solvents used to clean computers. Never dump chemicals or solvents down a sink or dispose of them in a drain that connects to public sewers.

The cans or bottles that contain solvents and other cleaning supplies must be handled carefully. Make sure that they are identified and treated as special hazardous waste. For example, some aerosol cans explode when exposed to heat if the contents are not completely used.

Proper Use of Tools (2.2)

Using tools properly helps prevent accidents and damage to equipment and people. This section describes and covers the proper use of a variety of hardware, software, and organizational tools specific to working with computers and peripherals.

Hardware Tools (2.2.1)

For every job there is the right tool. Make sure that you are familiar with the correct use of each tool and that the correct tool is used for the current task. Skilled use of tools and software makes the job less difficult and ensures that tasks are performed properly and safely.

A toolkit should contain all the tools necessary to complete hardware repairs. As you gain experience, you learn which tools to have available for different types of jobs. Hardware tools are grouped into four categories:

- ESD tools
- Hand tools
- Cleaning tools
- Diagnostic tools

Figure 2-2 shows some common tools used in computer repair.

Figure 2-2   Computer Tools

ESD Tools (2.2.1.2)

There are two ESD tools: the antistatic wrist strap and the *antistatic mat*. The antistatic wrist strap protects computer equipment when grounded to a computer chassis. The antistatic mat protects computer equipment by preventing static electricity from accumulating on the hardware or on the technician.

Hand Tools (2.2.1.3)

Most tools used in the computer assembly process are small *hand tools*. They are available individually or as part of a computer repair toolkit. Toolkits range widely in size, quality, and price. Some common hand tools and their uses are

- *Flat-head screwdriver*: Used to tighten or loosen slotted screws.
- *Phillips-head screwdriver*: Used to tighten or loosen cross-headed screws.

- *Torx screwdriver*: Used to tighten or loosen screws that have a star-like depression on the top, a feature that is mainly found on laptops.

- *Hex driver*: Used to tighten or loosen nuts in the same way that a screwdriver tightens or loosens screws (sometimes called a nut driver).

- **Needle-nose pliers:** Used to hold small parts.

- **Wire cutters:** Used to strip and cut wires.

- **Tweezers:** Used to manipulate small parts.

- *Part retriever*: Used to retrieve parts from locations that are too small for your hand to fit.

- **Flashlight:** Used to light up areas that you cannot see well.

- *Wire stripper*: A wire stripper is used to remove the insulation from wire so that it can be twisted to other wires or crimped to connectors to make a cable.

- *Crimper*: Used to attach connectors to wires.

- *Punch-down tool*: Used to terminate wire into termination blocks. Some cable connectors must be connected to cables using a punch down tool.

Cleaning Tools (2.2.1.4)

Having the appropriate *cleaning tools* is essential when maintaining and repairing computers. Using the appropriate cleaning tools helps ensure that computer components are not damaged during cleaning. Cleaning tools include the following:

- **Soft cloth:** Used to clean different computer components without scratching or leaving debris

- **Compressed air:** Used to blow away dust and debris from different computer parts without touching the components

- **Cable ties:** Used to bundle cables neatly inside and outside of a computer

- **Parts organizer:** Used to hold screws, jumpers, fasteners, and other small parts and prevents them from getting mixed together

Diagnostic Tools (2.2.1.5)

Diagnostic tools are used to test and diagnose equipment. Diagnostic tools include the following:

- A *digital multimeter*, as shown in Figure 2-3, is a device that can take many types of measurements. It tests the integrity of circuits and the quality of electricity in computer components. A digital multimeter displays the information on an LCD or LED.

Figure 2-3 Multimeter

- A *loopback adapter*, also called a loopback plug, tests the basic functionality of computer ports. The adapter is specific to the port that you want to test.

- The *toner probe*, as shown in Figure 2-4, is a two-part tool. The toner part is connected to a cable at one end using specific adapters, such as an RJ-45, coaxial, or metal clips. The toner generates a tone that travels the length of the cable. The probe part traces the cable. When the probe is in near proximity to the cable to which the toner is attached, the tone can be heard through a speaker in the probe.

Figure 2-4 Toner Probe

Although an *external hard drive enclosure* is not a diagnostic tool, it is often used when diagnosing and repairing computers. The customer hard drive is placed into the external enclosure for inspection, diagnosis, and repair using a known-working computer. Backups can also be recorded to a drive in an external enclosure to prevent data corruption during a computer repair.

Software Tools (2.2.2)

Like hardware tools, there are a variety of software tools that can be used to help technicians pinpoint and troubleshoot problems. Many of these tools are free and several come with the Windows operating system.

Disk Management Tools (2.2.2.1)

Software tools help diagnose computer and network problems and determine which computer device is not functioning correctly. A technician must be able to use a range of software tools to diagnose problems, maintain hardware, and protect the data stored on a computer.

You must be able to identify which software to use in different situations. *Disk management tools* help detect and correct disk errors, prepare a disk for data storage, and remove unwanted files.

The following are some disk management tools:

- **FDISK:** A command-line tool that creates and deletes partitions on a hard drive. The FDISK tool is not available in Windows XP, Vista, or 7. It has been replaced with the Disk Management tool.

- **Disk Management Tool:** Initializes disks, creates partitions, and formats partitions.

- *Format*: Prepares a hard drive to store information.

- *ScanDisk or CHKDSK*: Checks the integrity of files and folders on a hard drive by scanning the file system. These tools might also check the disk surface for physical errors.

- *Defrag*: Optimizes space on a hard drive to allow faster access to programs and data.

- *Disk Cleanup*: Clears space on a hard drive by searching for files that can be safely deleted.

- *System File Checker (SFC)*: A command-line tool that scans the operating system critical files and replaces files that are corrupted.

Use the Windows 7 boot disk for troubleshooting and repairing corrupted files. The Windows 7 boot disk repairs Windows system files, restores damaged or lost files, and reinstalls the operating system.

Third-party software tools are also available to assist in troubleshooting problems.

Protection Software Tools (2.2.2.2)

Each year, viruses, spyware, and other types of malicious attacks infect millions of computers. These attacks can damage operating systems, applications, and data. Computers that have been infected may even have problems with hardware performance or component failure.

To protect data and the integrity of the operating system and hardware, use software designed to guard against attacks and to remove malicious programs.

Various types of software protect hardware and data:

- *Windows 7 Action Center*: Checks the status of essential security settings. The Action Center continuously checks to make sure that the software firewall and antivirus programs are running. It also ensures that automatic updates download and install automatically.

- **Antivirus program:** Protects against virus attacks.

- *Antispyware program*: Protects against software that sends information about web surfing habits to an attacker. Spyware can be installed without the knowledge or consent of the user.

- *Windows 7 Firewall*: Runs continuously to protect against unauthorized communications to and from your computer.

Worksheet 2.2.2.3: Diagnostic Software

In this worksheet, you use the Internet, a newspaper, or a local store to gather information about a hard drive diagnostic program. Be prepared to discuss the diagnostic software you researched. Refer to the worksheet in *IT Essentials: PC Hardware and Software Lab Manual*, Fifth Edition.

Organizational Tools (2.2.3)

Keeping accurate records and journals during a busy workday can be challenging. Many organizational tools, such as work-order systems, can help the technician document their work.

Reference Tools (2.2.3.1)

A technician must document all repairs and computer problems. The documentation can then be used as a reference for future problems or for other technicians who may not have encountered the problem before. The documents can be paper based, but electronic forms are preferred because they can be easily searched for specific problems.

It is important that a technician document all services and repairs. These documents need to be stored centrally and made available to all other technicians. The documentation can then be used as reference material for similar problems that are encountered in the future. Good customer service includes providing the customer with a detailed description of the problem and the solution.

Personal Reference Tools

Personal reference tools include troubleshooting guides, manufacturer manuals, quick reference guides, and repair journals. In addition to an invoice, a technician keeps a journal of upgrades and repairs. The documentation in the journal includes descriptions of the problem, possible solutions that have been attempted, and the steps taken to repair the problem. Note any configuration changes made to the equipment and any replacement parts used in the repair. This documentation is valuable when you encounter similar situations in the future.

■ **Notes:** Make notes as you go through the troubleshooting and repair process. Refer to these notes to avoid repeating previous steps and to determine what steps to take next.

■ **Journal:** Document the upgrades and repairs that you perform. Include descriptions of the problem, possible solutions that have been tried to correct the problem, and the steps taken to repair the problem. Note any configuration changes made to the equipment and any replacement parts used in the repair. Your journal, along with your notes, can be valuable when you encounter similar situations in the future.

■ **History of repairs:** Make a detailed list of problems and repairs, including the date, replacement parts, and customer information. The history allows a technician to determine what work has been performed on a specific computer in the past.

Internet Reference Tools

The Internet is an excellent source of information about specific hardware problems and possible solutions:

■ Internet search engines

■ News groups

■ Manufacturer FAQs

■ Online computer manuals

■ Online forums and chat

■ Technical websites

Miscellaneous Tools (2.2.3.2)

With experience, you will discover many additional items to add to the toolkit. Figure 2-5 shows how a roll of masking tape can be used to label parts that have been removed from a computer when a parts organizer is not available.

Figure 2-5 Parts Labels

A working computer is also a valuable resource to take with you on computer repairs in the field. A working computer can be used to research information, download tools or drivers, and communicate with other technicians.

Figure 2-6 shows the types of computer replacement parts to include in a toolkit. Make sure that the parts are in good working order before you use them. Using known good components to replace possible bad ones in computers helps you quickly determine which component is not working properly.

Figure 2-6 Replacement Computer Parts

Demonstrate Proper Tool Use (2.2.4)

This section describes the proper use of common tools used to protect, repair, and clean computers and peripherals.

Antistatic Wrist Strap (2.2.4.1)

Safety in the workplace is everyone's responsibility. You are much less likely to injure yourself or damage components when using the proper tool for the job.

Before cleaning or repairing equipment, make sure that your tools are in good condition. Clean, repair, or replace items that are not functioning adequately.

An example of ESD is the small shock that you receive when you walk across a carpeted room and touch a doorknob. Although the small shock is harmless to you, the same electrical charge passing from you to a computer can damage its components. Self-grounding or wearing an antistatic wrist strap can prevent ESD damage to computer components.

The purpose of self-grounding or wearing an antistatic wrist strap is to equalize the electrical charge between you and the equipment. Self-grounding is done by touching a bare metal part of a computer case. The antistatic wrist strap is a conductor that connects your body to the equipment that you are working on. When static electricity builds up in your body, the connection made by the wrist strap to the equipment, or ground, channels the electricity through the wire that connects the strap.

As shown in Figure 2-7, the wrist strap has two parts and is easy to wear. Following is the proper procedure for using an antistatic wrist strap:

Step 1.   Wrap the strap around your wrist and secure it using the snap or Velcro. The metal on the back of the wrist strap must remain in contact with your skin at all times.

Step 2.   Snap the connector on the end of the wire to the wrist strap, and connect the other end either to the equipment or to the same grounding point that the antistatic mat is connected to. The metal skeleton of the case is a good place to connect the wire. When connecting the wire to equipment that you are working on, choose an unpainted metal surface. A painted surface does not conduct electricity as well as unpainted metal.

Figure 2-7   Antistatic Wrist Strap

Note

Attach the wire on the same side of the equipment as the arm wearing the antistatic wrist strap. This helps keep the wire out of the way while you are working.

Although wearing a wrist strap helps prevent ESD, you can further reduce the risks by not wearing clothing made of silk, polyester, or wool. These fabrics are more likely to generate a static charge.

Note

Technicians should roll up their sleeves, remove scarves or ties, and tuck in shirts to prevent interference from clothing. Ensure that earrings, necklaces, and other loose jewelry are properly secured.

Caution

Never wear an antistatic wrist strap if you are repairing a CRT monitor or a power supply unit.

Antistatic Mat (2.2.4.2)

You might not always have the option to work on a computer in a properly equipped workspace. If you can control the environment, try to set up your workspace away from carpeted areas. Carpets can cause the buildup of electrostatic charges. If you cannot avoid the carpeting, ground yourself to the unpainted portion of the case of the computer on which you are working before touching any components.

An antistatic mat is slightly conductive. It works by drawing static electricity away from a component and transferring it safely from equipment to a grounding point, as shown in Figure 2-8. Following is the proper procedure for using an antistatic mat:

How To

Step 1.   Lay the mat on the workspace next to or under the computer case.

Step 2.   Clip the mat to the case to provide a grounded surface on which you can place parts as you remove them from the system.

Figure 2-8   Antistatic Mat

When you are working at a workbench, ground the workbench and the antistatic floor mat. By standing on the mat and wearing the wrist strap, your body has the same charge as the equipment and reduces the probability of ESD. Either connect the table-top mat and the floor mat to each other or connect both to the electrical earth ground.

Reducing the potential for ESD reduces the likelihood of damage to delicate circuits or components.

Note

Always handle components by the edges.

Hand Tools (2.2.4.3)

A technician needs to be able to properly use each tool in the toolkit. This topic covers many of the various hand tools used when repairing computers.

Screws

Match each screw with the proper screwdriver. Place the tip of the screwdriver on the head of the screw. Turn the screwdriver clockwise to tighten the screw and counterclockwise to loosen the screw.

Screws can become stripped if you over-tighten them with a screwdriver. A stripped screw, as shown in Figure 2-9, may get stuck in the screw hole, or it may not tighten firmly. Discard stripped screws.

Figure 2-9   Stripped Screw

Flat-Head Screwdriver

Use a flat-head screwdriver when you are working with a slotted screw. Do not use a flat-head screwdriver to remove a Phillips-head screw. Never use a screwdriver as a pry bar. If you cannot remove a component, check to see if there is a clip or latch that is securing the component in place.

> **Caution**
>
> If excessive force is needed to remove or add a component, something is probably wrong. Take a second look to make sure that you have not missed a screw or a locking clip that is holding the component in place. Refer to the device manual or diagram for additional information.

Phillips-Head Screwdriver

Use a Phillips-head screwdriver with crosshead screws. Do not use this type of screwdriver to puncture anything. This will damage the head of the screwdriver.

Hex Driver

Use a hex driver, shown in Figure 2-10, to loosen and tighten bolts that have a hexagonal (six-sided) head. Hex bolts should not be over-tightened because the threads of the bolts can be stripped. Do not use a hex driver that is too large for the bolt that you are using.

Figure 2-10   Hex Driver

Caution

Some tools are magnetized. When working around electronic devices, be sure that the tools you are using have not been magnetized. Magnetic fields can be harmful to data stored on magnetic media. Test your tool by touching the tool with a screw. If the screw is attracted to the tool, do not use the tool.

Component Retrieving Tools

Needle-nose pliers and tweezers can be used to place and retrieve parts that may be hard to reach with your fingers. There are also tools called part retrievers that are specifically designed for this task. Do not scratch or hit any components when using these tools.

Caution

Pencils should not be used inside the computer to change the setting of switches or to pry off jumpers. The pencil lead can act as a conductor and may damage the computer components.

A computer technician needs proper tools to work safely and prevent damage to the computer equipment. A technician uses many tools to diagnose and repair computer problems:

- Straight-head screwdriver, large and small
- Phillips-head screwdriver, large and small

- Tweezers or part retriever
- Needle-nosed pliers
- Wire cutters
- Chip extractor

- Hex wrench set
- Torx screwdriver
- Nut driver, large and small
- Three-claw component holder
- Wire stripper
- Crimper
- Punch-down tool
- Digital multimeter
- Wrap plugs

- Small mirror
- Small dust brush
- Soft, lint-free cloth
- Cable ties
- Scissors
- Small flashlight
- Electrical tape
- Pencil or pen
- Compressed air

Various specialty tools, such as Torx bits, *antistatic bags* and gloves, and integrated circuit pullers, can be used to repair and maintain computers. Always avoid magnetized tools, such as screwdrivers with magnetic heads, or tools that use extension magnets to retrieve small metal objects that are out of reach. Using magnetic tools can cause loss of data on hard drives and floppy disks. Magnetic tools can also induce current, which can damage internal computer components.

Additionally, there are specialized testing devices used to diagnose computer and cable problems:

- **Multimeter:** A device that measures AC/DC voltage, electric current, and other cable and electrical characteristics.

- *Power supply tester*: A device that checks whether the computer power supply is working properly. A simple power supply tester might just have indicator lights, while more advanced versions show the amount of voltage and amperage.

- *Cable tester*: A device that checks for wiring shorts or faults, such as wires connected to the wrong pin.

- *Loopback plug*: A device that connects to a computer, hub, switch, or router port to perform a diagnostic procedure called a loopback test. In a loopback test, a signal is transmitted through a circuit and then returned to the sending device to test the integrity of the data transmission.

Lab 2.2.4.4: Using a Multimeter and a Power Supply Tester

In this lab, you learn how to use and handle a multimeter and a power supply tester. Refer to Lab 2.2.4.4 in *IT Essentials: PC Hardware and Software Lab Manual*, Fifth Edition.

Lab 2.2.4.5: Testing UTP Cables Using a Loopback Plug and a Cable Meter

In this lab, you use a loopback plug and a cable meter to test an Ethernet cable. Refer to Lab 2.2.4.5 in *IT Essentials: PC Hardware and Software Lab Manual*, Fifth Edition.

Cleaning Materials (2.2.4.6)

Keeping computers clean inside and out is a vital part of a maintenance program. Dirt can cause problems with the physical operation of fans, buttons, and other mechanical components. On electrical components, an excessive buildup of dust acts like an insulator and traps the heat. This insulation impairs the ability of heat sinks and cooling fans to keep components cool, causing chips and circuits to overheat and fail.

Note

When using compressed air to clean inside the computer, blow the air around the components with a minimum distance of 4 in. (10 cm) from the nozzle. Clean the power supply and the fan from the back of the case.

Caution

Before cleaning any device, turn it off and unplug the device from the power source.

Computer Cases and Monitors

Clean computer cases and the outside of monitors with a mild cleaning solution on a damp, lint-free cloth. Mix one drop of dishwashing liquid with 4 oz. (118 ml) of water to create the cleaning solution. If water drips inside the case, allow enough time for the liquid to dry before powering on the computer.

LCD Screens

Do not use ammoniated glass cleaners or any other solution on an LCD screen, unless the cleaner is specifically designed for the purpose. Harsh chemicals damage the coating on the screen. There is no glass protecting these screens, so be gentle when cleaning them and do not press firmly on the screen.

CRT Screens

To clean the screens of CRT monitors, dampen a soft, clean, lint-free cloth with distilled water and wipe the screen from top to bottom. Then use a soft, dry cloth to wipe the screen and remove streaking.

Components

Clean dusty components with a can of compressed air. Compressed air does not cause electrostatic buildup on components. Make sure that you are in a well-ventilated area before blowing the dust out of the computer. A best practice is to wear a dust mask to make sure that you do not breathe in the dust particles.

Blow out the dust using short bursts from the can. Never tip the can or use the can upside down. Do not allow the fan blades to spin from the force of the compressed air. Hold the fan in place. Fan motors can be ruined from spinning when the motor is not turned on.

Component Contacts

Clean the contacts on components with isopropyl alcohol. Do not use rubbing alcohol. Rubbing alcohol contains impurities that can damage contacts. Make sure that the contacts do not collect lint from the cloth or cotton swab. Before reinstallation, use compressed air to blow lint off the contacts.

Keyboards

Clean a desktop keyboard with compressed air and then use a handheld vacuum cleaner with a brush attachment to remove the loose dust.

Caution

Never use a standard vacuum cleaner inside a computer case. The plastic parts of the vacuum cleaner can build up static electricity and discharge to the components. Use only vacuums that are approved for electronic components.

Mice

Use glass cleaner and a soft cloth to clean the outside of the mouse. Do not spray glass cleaner directly on the mouse. If cleaning a ball mouse, you can remove the ball and clean it with glass cleaner and a soft cloth. Wipe the rollers clean inside the mouse with the same cloth. Do not spray any liquids inside the mouse.

Table 2-1 shows the computer items that you should clean and the cleaning materials to use.

Table 2-1   Computer Cleaning Materials

Computer case and outside of monitor	Mild cleaning solution and lint-free cloth
LCD screen	LCD cleaning solution or distilled water and lint-free cloth
CRT screen	Distilled water and lint-free cloth

Heat sink	Compressed air
RAM	Isopropyl alcohol and lint-free swab
Keyboard	Handheld vacuum cleaner with a brush attachment
Mouse	Glass cleaner and a soft cloth

Lab 2.2.4.7: Computer Disassembly

In this lab, you disassemble a computer using safe lab procedures and the proper tools. Use extreme care and follow all safety procedures. Familiarize yourself with the tools you will be using in this lab. Refer to Lab 2.2.4.7 in *IT Essentials: PC Hardware and Software Lab Manual*, Fifth Edition.

Summary (2.3.1)

This chapter discussed safe lab procedures, correct tool usage, and the proper disposal of computer components and supplies. You have familiarized yourself in the lab with many of the tools used to build, service, and clean computer and electronic components. You have also learned the importance of organizational tools and how these tools help you work more efficiently.

Some of the important concepts to remember from this chapter:

- Work in a safe manner to protect users and equipment.
- Follow all safety guidelines to prevent injuries to yourself and others.
- Know how to protect equipment from ESD damage.
- Know about and be able to prevent power issues that can cause equipment damage or data loss.
- Know which products and supplies require special disposal procedures.
- Familiarize yourself with the MSDS for safety issues and disposal restrictions to help protect the environment.
- Be able to use the correct tools for the task.
- Know how to clean components safely.
- Use organizational tools during computer repairs.

Summary of Exercises

The following labs and worksheets cover material from this chapter. Refer to the labs and worksheets in *IT Essentials: PC Hardware and Software Lab Manual*, Fifth Edition.

Labs

The following labs cover material from this chapter. Refer to the labs in *IT Essentials: PC Hardware and Software Lab Manual*, Fifth Edition:

Lab 2.2.4.4: Using a Multimeter and a Power Supply Tester

Lab 2.2.4.5: Testing UTP Cables Using a Loopback Plug and a Cable Meter

Lab 2.2.4.7: Computer Disassembly

Worksheets

The following worksheets cover material from this chapter. Refer to the worksheets in *IT Essentials: PC Hardware and Software Lab Manual*, Fifth Edition:

Worksheet 2.2.2.3: Diagnostic Software

Check Your Understanding

You can find the answers to these questions in Appendix A, "Answers to 'Check Your Understanding' Questions."

1. How should a technician discharge static buildup while working on a computer system?

    A. Maintain contact with the painted part of the computer case.

    B. Maintain contact with an unpainted part of the computer case.

    C. Touch an antistatic wrist strap before touching any computer equipment.

    D. Touch an antistatic mat before touching any computer equipment.

2. Which of the following is a fact sheet that summarizes information about material identification, including hazardous ingredients that can affect personal health, fire hazards, and first aid requirements?

    A. ESD

    B. MSDS

    C. OSHA

    D. UPS

3. Which two statements are true of static electricity? (Choose two.)

    A. It can distort wireless signals.

    B. More than 10,000 volts can build up on a person.

    C. As few as 30 volts can damage computer components.

    E. It will not harm computer components as long as the computer is plugged in.

    F. Keeping the air cool and dry can decrease the buildup of static electricity.

    G. It is generated by devices such as motors, power lines, and radio transmitters.

4. Which recommendation should be followed first when a fire in the workplace is out of control?

   A. Try to use the elevators to get to the lowest floor faster.

   B. Get out of the room or building and contact emergency services for help.

   C. Use the company water system to stop the fire from extending to other areas.

   D. Try to control the fire with proper extinguishers.

5. Which device is designed specifically to protect computers and electrical devices from excess electrical voltage?

   A. Power strip

   B. Standby power supply

   C. Surge protector

   D. Uninterruptible power supply

6. Which piece of software is designed to protect against unauthorized communications to and from a computer?

   A. Security center

   B. Port scanner

   C. Antimalware

   D. Antivirus

   E. Firewall

7. What is an accepted method for cleaning computer components?

   A. Using ammonia to clean the LCD screen

   B. Using rubbing alcohol to clean component contacts

   C. Using a lint-free cloth to remove dust inside the computer case

   D. Using glass cleaner on a soft cloth to clean the outside of the mouse

8. Which tool would be used to scan Windows critical system files and replace any corrupted files?

   A. SFC

   B. CHKDSK

   C. Fdisk

   D. Defrag

9. Which condition refers to a sudden and dramatic increase in voltage, which is usually caused by lighting?

   A. Brownout

   B. Sag

   C. Spike

   D. Surge

10. Which tool can be used to take resistance and voltage measurements?

   A. Multimeter

   B. Power supply tester

   C. Cable tester

   D. Loopback plug

CHAPTER 3

Computer Assembly

Objectives

Upon completion of this chapter, you will be able to answer the following questions:

- How do I open the computer case?
- What is the process to install a power supply?
- How do I attach the components to the motherboard?
- How do I install a motherboard into a computer case?
- How do I handle and install a CPU with a fan and heat sink assembly?
- How do I install internal drives into a computer case?
- How do I install external devices?
- How do I install adapter cards?
- What is the process to connect all internal cables?
- How do I reassemble the computer case?
- What should I expect the first time I boot the computer?

Key Terms

This chapter uses the following key terms. You can find the definitions in the Glossary.

Introduction (3.0.1)

Assembling computers is a large part of a technician's job. As a technician, you must work in a logical, methodical manner when working with computer components. At times, you might have to determine whether a component for a customer's computer needs to be upgraded or replaced. It is important that you develop advanced skills in installation procedures, troubleshooting techniques, and diagnostic methods. This chapter discusses the importance of component compatibility across hardware and software. It also covers the need for adequate system resources to efficiently run the customer's hardware and software. Figure 3-1 shows the computer case and components used to assemble a computer system.

Figure 3-1   Case and Components

Open the Case and Install the Power Supply (3.1.1)

This section discusses gaining access to inside the computer case and the steps to install a power supply. To install the power supply, you must open the case, and the method to do this will vary by manufacturer. If you are upgrading a power supply, you need to disconnect cables before removing the old power supply; if you are doing a new installation, opening the case and situating the power supply properly is all that will be necessary.

Open the Case (3.1.1.1)

Computer cases are produced in a variety of form factors. Form factors refer to the size and shape of the case.

Prepare the workspace before opening the *computer case*. You want adequate lighting, good ventilation, and a comfortable room temperature. The workbench or table should be accessible from all sides. Avoid cluttering the surface of the work area with tools and computer components. Place an *antistatic mat* on the table to help prevent physical and *electrostatic discharge (ESD)* damage to equipment. It is helpful to use small containers to hold screws and other parts as you remove them.

There are different methods for opening cases. To learn how to open a particular computer case, consult the user manual or manufacturer's website. Most computer cases are opened in one of the following ways:

- The computer case cover is removed as one piece.

- The top and side panels of the case are removed.

- The top of the case is removed before the side panels can be removed.

- A latch is pulled to release the side panel, which can swing open.

Install the Power Supply (3.1.1.2)

A technician might be required to replace or install a power supply. Most power supplies can only fit one way in the computer case. Three or four screws usually attach the power supply to the case. Power supplies have fans that can vibrate and loosen screws that are not properly tightened. When installing a power supply, make sure that all the screws are used and tightened correctly.

To install a power supply, follow these steps:

Step 1.   Insert the power supply into the case.

Step 2.   Align the holes in the power supply with the holes in the case.

Step 3.   Secure the power supply to the case using the proper screws.

Virtual Desktop Activity: Power Supply

System requirements for the Virtual Desktop include a minimum of 512 MB RAM and Windows XP or Windows 7 operating systems. Complete the power supply installation in the Virtual Desktop power supply layer. To access the activities found in this book, please refer to the instructions found in the Introduction.

Figure 3-2 shows the power supply placement in a computer case.

Figure 3-2   Install the Power Supply

Lab 3.1.1.3: Install the Power Supply

In this lab, you install a power supply. Refer to Lab 3.1.1.3 in *IT Essentials: PC Hardware and Software Lab Manual*, Fifth Edition.

Install the Motherboard (3.1.2)

This section examines the installation of many of the components that are directly installed on a motherboard and the installation of the motherboard itself into a computer case. You also learn throughout this chapter that all components in your computer system are in some way attached to your motherboard.

Install the CPU, Heat Sink, and Fan Assembly (3.1.2.1)

The CPU, heat sink, and fan assembly might be installed on the motherboard before the motherboard is placed in the computer case. This allows for extra room to see and maneuver components during installation.

CPU

Figure 3-3a shows a close-up of the CPU and the motherboard. The CPU and motherboard are sensitive to electrostatic discharge. When handling a CPU and motherboard, make sure that you place them on a grounded antistatic mat. Wear an *antistatic wrist strap* while working with these components.

Figure 3-3a   CPU and Motherboard

Caution

When handling a CPU, do not touch the CPU contacts at any time.

The CPU is secured to the socket on the motherboard with a locking assembly. Before installing a CPU into the socket on the motherboard, make sure that the processor is compatible with the motherboard socket and you are familiar with the locking assembly.

Thermal compound helps to conduct heat away from the CPU. When you are installing a used CPU, clean the top of the CPU and the base of the heat sink with isopropyl alcohol and a lint-free cloth. A paper coffee filter works well as a lint-free cloth. This removes the old thermal compound. The surfaces are now ready for a new layer of thermal compound. Follow the manufacturer recommendations about applying the thermal compound.

Figure 3-3b shows thermal compound being applied to the CPU. In most cases, apply a very small amount of thermal compound to the CPU. It is important to remember more is not always better. Over-use can result in insulating the processor and the cooling effect is reduced which will impact its ability to conduct heat away from the CPU. The compound spreads out evenly under the weight and pressure of the *heat sink/fan assembly*.

Figure 3-3b   Thermal Paste Application

Heat Sink and Fan Assembly

Figure 3-3c shows the heat sink and fan assembly. It is a two-part cooling device. The heat sink draws heat away from the CPU. The fan moves the heat away from the heat sink. The assembly usually has a three-pin power connector. Some manufacturers include thermal compound pre-applied on the heat sink/fan assembly with the processors that are shipped with a heat sink and fan assembly included in a boxed purchase. This pre-applied thermal paste is convenient but can also have disadvantages such as not always being of the highest quality or having just a single use and if you need to reposition the CPU during installation the compound needs to be removed and new applied for effective heat dissipation.

Figure 3-3c   Heat Sink and Assembly Fan Installation

To install a CPU and heat sink and fan assembly, follow these steps:

Step 1.   Align the CPU so that the Connection 1 indicator is lined up with Pin 1 on the CPU socket. This ensures that the orientation notches on the CPU are aligned with the orientation keys on the CPU socket.

Step 2.   Place the CPU gently into the socket.

Step 3.   Close the CPU load plate. Secure it in place by closing the load lever and moving it under the load lever retention tab.

Step 4.   Apply a small amount of thermal compound to the CPU. Follow the application instructions provided by the manufacturer of the thermal compound.

Step 5.   Align the heat sink and fan assembly retainers with the holes on the motherboard.

Step 6.   Place the assembly onto the CPU socket, being careful not to pinch the CPU fan wires.

Step 7.   Tighten the assembly retainers to secure the assembly in place.

Step 8.   Connect the assembly power cable to the CPU fan connector on the motherboard.

Figure 3-3d shows the cable, the motherboard connector, and the locking assembly for the heat sink and fan.

Figure 3-3d   Heat Sink/Fan Cable, Motherboard Connector, and Locking Assembly

Install RAM (3.1.2.2)

RAM may be installed on the motherboard before the motherboard is secured in the computer case. Before installation, consult the motherboard documentation or website of the motherboard manufacturer to ensure that the RAM is compatible with the motherboard.

RAM provides fast, temporary data storage for the CPU while the computer is operating. RAM is volatile memory, which means that its contents are lost when the computer is powered off. More RAM usually enhances computer performance. Figure 3-4 shows the installation of a RAM module.

Figure 3-4   RAM Installation

To install RAM, follow these steps:

Step 1.   Align the notches on the RAM DIMM module to the keys in the slot and press down until the side tabs click into place.

Step 2.   Make sure that the side tabs have locked the RAM module.

Step 3.   Visually check for exposed contacts.

Step 4.   Repeat these steps for additional RAM modules.

Install the Motherboard (3.1.2.3)

The motherboard is now ready to be installed in the computer case. Plastic and metal *standoffs* are used to mount the motherboard and to prevent it from touching the metal portions of the case. Install only the standoffs that align with the holes on the case and in the motherboard. Installing additional standoffs might prevent the motherboard from being seated properly in the computer case.

Because the I/O connections on each motherboard vary, an *I/O connector plate*, is supplied with the motherboard. The I/O plate has cutouts on the back of the motherboard specifically for the connectors. The I/O connector plate is installed on the inside of the back of the computer case to allow the connectors to be used when the motherboard is installed in the case.

To install the motherboard, follow these steps:

Step 1.   Install the standoffs in the computer case aligned with the locations of the mounting holes in the motherboard.

Step 2.   Install the I/O plate on the inside of the back of the computer case.

Step 3.   Align the I/O connectors on the back of the motherboard with the openings in the I/O plate.

Step 4.   Align the screw holes of the motherboard with the standoffs.

Step 5.   Insert all the motherboard screws.

Step 6.   Tighten all the motherboard screws.

Virtual Desktop Activity: Motherboard

Complete the motherboard assembly in the Virtual Desktop motherboard layer.

System requirements for the Virtual Desktop include a minimum of 512 MB RAM and Windows XP or Windows 7 operating systems. Complete the motherboard assembly in the Virtual Desktop motherboard layer. To access the activities found in this book, please refer to the instructions found in the Introduction.

Lab 3.1.2.4: Install the Motherboard

In this lab, you install a CPU, a heat sink/fan assembly, and a RAM module on the motherboard. You then install the motherboard in the computer case. Refer to Lab 3.1.2.4 in *IT Essentials: PC Hardware and Software Lab Manual*, Fifth Edition.

Install the Drives (3.1.3)

In this section, you learn the steps to install a variety of disk drives in both internal and external bays.

Install the Internal Drive (3.1.3.1)

Drives that are installed in internal bays are called internal drives. A hard disk drive (HDD) is an example of an internal drive.

To install the HDD, follow these steps:

Step 1. Position the HDD so that it aligns with the 3.5-inch (8.9-cm) drive bay opening.

Step 2. Insert the HDD into the drive bay so that the screw holes in the drive line up with the screw holes in the case.

Step 3. Secure the HDD to the case using the proper screws.

Virtual Desktop Activity: Internal Drives

Complete the HDD drive installation in the Virtual Desktop internal drive layer. To access the activities found in this book, please refer to the instructions found in the Introduction.

System requirements for the Virtual Desktop include a minimum of 512 MB RAM and Windows XP or Windows 7 operating systems.

Install the Optical Drive (3.1.3.2)

Optical drives store data on removable media, such as CDs, DVDs, and Blu-rays. Optical drives are installed in drive bays that are accessed from the front of the case. The external bays allow access to the media without opening the case. Figure 3-5 shows an external bay installation.

Figure 3-5   Optical Drive Installation in an External Bay

A Molex or SATA power connector provides the optical drive with power from the power supply. A *PATA or SATA data cable* connects the optical drive to the motherboard.

To install an optical drive, follow these steps:

Step 1.   Position the optical drive so that it aligns with the 5.25-inch (13.34-cm) drive bay opening.

Step 2.   Insert the optical drive into the drive bay so that the optical drive screw holes align with the screw holes in the case.

Step 3.   Secure the optical drive to the case using the proper screws.

Caution

If you use screws that are too long, you may damage the drive you are mounting.

Install the Floppy Drive (3.1.3.3)

A floppy disk drive (FDD) is a storage device that reads and writes information to a floppy disk. A *Berg power connector* provides the FDD with power from the power supply. A floppy drive data cable connects the FDD to the motherboard.

A floppy disk drive fits into the 3.5-inch (8.9-cm) bay on the front of the computer case.

To install an FDD, follow these steps:

Step 1.   Position the FDD so that it aligns with the drive bay opening.

Step 2.   Insert the FDD into the drive bay so that the FDD screw holes align with the screw holes in the case.

Step 3.   Secure the FDD to the case using the proper screws.

Virtual Desktop Activity: External Drive Bays

Complete the optical and floppy drive installation in the Virtual Desktop external drive bays layer. To access the activities found in this book, please refer to the instructions found in the Introduction.

System requirements for the Virtual Desktop include a minimum of 512 MB RAM and Windows XP or Windows 7 operating systems.

Lab 3.1.3.4: Install the Drives

In this lab, you will install the hard disk drive, the optical drive, and the floppy drive. Refer to Lab 3.1.3.4 in *IT Essentials: PC Hardware and Software Lab Manual*, Fifth Edition.

Install the Adapter Cards (3.1.4)

In this section, you learn about different types of adapter cards and the expansion slots that they can be installed in on the motherboard. You will also go through the steps of installation.

Types of Adapter Cards (3.1.4.1)

Adapter cards add functionality to a computer. Adapter cards must be compatible with the expansion slots on the motherboard. You will install three types of adapter cards as shown in Table 3-1.

Table 3-1   Adapter Cards and Expansion Slots

	PCIe x1 NIC: PCI x1 is a short slot that has data throughput speeds faster than PCI slots, making it a good choice for high-speed NIC.

Figure 3-6a   PCIe x1 NIC

	PCI wireless NIC: PCI is a slot usually used for legacy adapter cards that do not require the faster throughput rates.

Figure 3-6b   PCI Wireless NIC

	PCIe x16: PCIe x16 supports fast data transfer rates, making that slot a good choice for video cards.

Figure 3-6c   PCIe x16 Video Adapter Card

Install a NIC (3.1.4.2)

A *NIC* enables a computer to connect to a network. NICs use PCI and PCIe expansion slots on the motherboard. Figure 3-7 shows the PCIe expansion slot and NIC connector.

Figure 3-7 PCIe NIC Installation

To install a NIC, follow these steps:

Step 1. Align the NIC to the appropriate expansion slot on the motherboard.

Step 2. Press down gently on the NIC until the card is fully seated.

Step 3. Secure the NIC mounting bracket to the case with the appropriate screw.

Install a Wireless NIC (3.1.4.3)

A *wireless NIC* enables a computer to connect to a wireless network. Wireless NICs use PCI and PCIe expansion slots on the motherboard. Some wireless NICs are installed externally with a USB connector.

To install a wireless NIC, follow these steps:

Step 1. Align the wireless NIC to the appropriate expansion slot on the motherboard.

Step 2. Press down gently on the wireless NIC until the card is fully seated.

Step 3. Secure the wireless NIC mounting bracket to the case with the appropriate screw.

As shown in Figure 3-8, a wireless NIC can be installed internally in a PCI slot.

Figure 3-8   PCI Wireless NIC

Install a Video Adapter Card (3.1.4.4)

A video adapter card, as shown in Figure 3-9, is the interface between a computer and a display monitor. An upgraded video adapter card can provide improved graphic capabilities for games and graphic programs. Video adapter cards use PCI, AGP, and PCIe expansion slots on the motherboard. If you install a video card on a motherboard with integrated graphics, you may need to disable the onboard video in the BIOS so that the new peripheral video card is recognized.

How To Q

To install a video adapter card, follow these steps:

Step 1.   Align the video adapter card to the appropriate expansion slot on the motherboard.

Step 2.   Press down gently on the video adapter card until the card is fully seated.

Step 3.   Secure the video adapter card mounting bracket to the case with the appropriate screw.

Figure 3-9   PCIe x16 Video Adapter Card Installation

Virtual Desktop Activity: Adapter Cards

Complete the NIC, wireless NIC, and video adapter card installation in the Virtual Desktop adapter card layer. To access the activities found in this book, please refer to the instructions found in the Introduction.

System requirements for the Virtual Desktop include a minimum of 512 MB RAM and Windows XP or Windows 7 operating systems.

Lab 3.1.4.5: Install Adapter Cards

In this lab, you install a NIC, a wireless NIC, and a video adapter card on the motherboard. Refer to Lab 3.1.4.5 in *IT Essentials: PC Hardware and Software Lab Manual*, Fifth Edition.

Install the Cables (3.1.5)

Computers use cables for different purposes. Cables can be used to transport data to input and output devices and storage devices, to connect to communication networks, and to connect to a monitor. Additional cables connect buttons and lights on the computer case. An AC power cable is an example of another type of computer cable. The power supply uses this AC power and converts it into DC power to give the motherboard the power it needs to operate. In this section, you learn about the many cables and connections that you need to attach to your motherboard to provide power to the components.

Install the Internal Power Cables (3.1.5.1)

Motherboard Power Connections

Motherboards require power to operate. The *Advanced Technology Extended (ATX)* main power connector has either 20 or 24 pins. The power supply can also have a 4-pin, 6-pin, or 8-pin Auxiliary (AUX) power connector that connects to the motherboard. A 20-pin connector works in a motherboard with a 24-pin socket.

To install a motherboard 20+4 pin ATX power connector, follow these steps:

Step 1.   Align the 20-pin ATX power connector to the socket on the motherboard (see Figure 3-10).

Step 2.   Gently press down on the connector until the clip clicks into place.

Step 3.   Align the 4-pin AUX power connector to the socket on the motherboard (see Figure 3-11).

Step 4.   Gently press down on the connector until the clip clicks into place.

Align the motherboard power connector to the motherboard socket as shown in Figure 3-10.

Figure 3-10   Motherboard 20-Pin Power Connection

Figure 3-11   Motherboard 4-Pin AUX Power Connection

SATA Power Connectors

SATA power connectors use a 15-pin connector. *SATA power connectors* are used to connect to hard disk drives, optical drives, or any devices that have a SATA power socket.

Molex Power Connectors

Hard disk drives and optical drives that do not have SATA power sockets use a *Molex power connector*.

Caution

Do not use a Molex connector and a SATA connector on the same drive at the same time. It will prevent the drive from operating properly.

Berg Power Connectors

The 4-pin Berg power connector supplies power to a floppy drive.

How To

To install a SATA, Molex, or Berg power connector, follow these steps:

Step 1.   Plug the SATA power connector into the HDD.

Step 2.   Plug the Molex power connector into the optical drive.

Step 3.   Plug the 4-pin Berg power connector into the FDD.

Step 4.   Connect the 3-pin fan power connector into the appropriate fan header on the motherboard according to the motherboard manual.

Step 5.   Plug the additional cables from the case into the appropriate connectors according to the motherboard manual.

Table 3-2 shows examples of various power supply connectors.

Table 3-2   SATA, Molex, and Berg Power Connectors

Figure 3-12   SATA Power Connector

Figure 3-14   Berg Power Connector

Figure 3-13   Molex Power Connector

Figure 3-15   Fan Power Connector

Install the Internal Data Cables (3.1.5.2)

Drives connect to the motherboard using data cables. The type of drive determines the type of data cable to use.

PATA Data Cables

The PATA cable is sometimes called a ribbon cable because it is wide and flat. The PATA cable can have either 40 or 80 conductors. A PATA cable usually has three

40-pin connectors. The end connector connects to the motherboard. The other two connectors connect to drives. If multiple hard drives are installed, the master drive connects to the end connector. The slave drive connects to the middle connector.

A stripe on the data cable indicates the location of Pin 1. Plug the PATA cable into the drive with the Pin 1 indicator on the cable aligned to the Pin 1 indicator on the drive connector. The Pin 1 indicator on the drive connector is usually closest to the power connector on the drive. Many older motherboards have two PATA drive controllers, providing support for a maximum of four PATA drives.

SATA Data Cables

The SATA data cable has a 7-pin connector as shown in Figure 3-16. One end of the cable is connected to the motherboard; Figure 3-17 shows the motherboard controller. The other end is connected to any drive that has a SATA data connector. Many motherboards have four or more SATA drive controllers.

Figure 3-16   SATA Data Connector to Disk Drive

Figure 3-17   SATA Data Connector to the Motherboard

Floppy Data Cables

The floppy data cable usually has three 34-pin connectors. A stripe on the cable indicates the location of Pin 1. The end connector connects to the motherboard. The other two connectors connect to drives. If multiple floppy drives are installed, the A: drive connects to the end connector. The B: drive connects to the middle connector. A twist in many floppy drive ribbon cables allows the drive connected to the end of the cable to be identified as the A: drive by the computer when two floppy drives are installed.

Plug the floppy data cable into the drive with the Pin 1 indicator on the cable aligned to the Pin 1 indicator on the drive connector. Motherboards have one floppy drive controller, providing support for a maximum of two floppy drives.

Note

If Pin 1 on the floppy data cable is not aligned with Pin 1 on the drive connector, the floppy drive does not function. This misalignment does not damage the drive, but the drive activity light displays continuously. To fix this problem, turn off the computer and reconnect the data cable so that Pin 1 on the cable and Pin 1 on the connector are aligned. Reboot the computer.

To install a PATA, SATA, or FDD data cable, follow these steps:

Step 1. Plug the motherboard end of the PATA cable into the motherboard socket.

Step 2. Plug the connector at the far end of the PATA cable into the optical drive.

Step 3. Plug one end of the SATA cable into the motherboard socket.

Step 4. Plug the other end of the SATA cable into the HDD.

Step 5. Plug the motherboard end of the FDD cable into the motherboard socket.

Step 6. Plug the connector at the far end of the FDD cable into the floppy drive.

Virtual Desktop Activity: Install Internal Cables

Complete the internal cable installation in the Virtual Desktop internal cable layer. To access the activities found in this book, please refer to the instructions found in the Introduction.

System requirements for the Virtual Desktop include a minimum of 512 MB RAM and Windows XP or Windows 7 operating systems.

Lab 3.1.5.3: Install Internal Cables

In this lab, you install the internal power and data cables in the computer. Refer to Lab 3.1.5.3 in *IT Essentials: PC Hardware and Software Lab Manual*, Fifth Edition.

Install the Front Panel Cables (3.1.5.4)

A computer case has buttons to control the power to the motherboard and lights to indicate motherboard activities. You must connect these buttons and lights to the motherboard with the cables from the front of the case. Writing on the motherboard near the system panel connector shows where each cable is connected.

System panel connectors are not keyed. The following guidelines for connecting cables to the system panel connectors are generic because no standards for labeling the case cables or the system panel connectors are defined. The markings on your front panel cables and system panel connectors may be different from what is shown. Always consult the manual of your motherboard for diagrams and additional information about connecting front panel cables.

Power and Reset Buttons

The power button turns the computer on or off. If the power button fails to turn off the computer, hold down the power button for 5 seconds. The reset button restarts the computer without turning it off. Some motherboards do not support a reset button. In this case, you might need to depress the power button for a short time to reboot the computer.

Figure 3-18 shows some of the front panel cables commonly found in a computer case with the Pin 1 indicated. Each front panel cable has a small arrow indicating Pin 1. To connect the power button, align Pin 1 of the front panel power button cable with the pin marked PWR. To connect the reset button, align Pin 1 of the front panel reset button cable with the pin marked RESET. Figure 3-19 shows a common system panel connector on a motherboard where the cables are connected with a plus sign indication Pin 1.

Figure 3-18   Front Panel Connectors with Pin 1 Indicator

Figure 3-19   System Panel Connectors with Pin 1 Indicator

Power and Drive Activity LEDs

The power LED remains lit when the computer is on and blinks when the computer is in sleep mode. The drive activity LED remains lit or blinks when the computer is reading or writing from the hard drive. Each pair of LED pins on the system panel connector has Pin 1 marked with a plus sign (+). To connect the power LED, align Pin 1 of the front panel power LED cable with the pin marked PLED+. To connect the IDE LED, align Pin 1 of the front panel drive activity LED cable with the pin marked IDE_LED+.

System Speaker

The motherboard uses the system speaker to indicate the computer's status. (The system speaker is not the same as the speakers that a computer uses to play music and other entertainment audio.) One beep indicates that the computer started without problems. If there is a hardware problem, a series of beeps is issued to indicate the type of problem. Diagnostic beeps are discussed later in this chapter.

The system speaker cable usually uses four pins on the system panel connector. To connect the speaker, align Pin 1 of the front panel system speaker cable with the pin marked + or +5V.

USB

USB ports are located on the outside of many computer cases. USB motherboard connectors often consist of 9 or 10 pins arranged in two rows. This arrangement allows for two USB connections, so USB connectors are often in pairs. Sometimes the two connectors are together in one piece and can be connected to the entire USB motherboard connector. USB connectors can also have four or five pins or individual groups of four or five pins.

Most USB devices only require the connection of four pins. The fifth pin is used to ground the shielding of some USB cables. To connect the USB port, align Pin 1 of the USB cable with the pin marked USB +5V or +5V.

Caution

Make sure that the motherboard connector is marked USB. FireWire connectors are similar. Connecting USB cables to FireWire connectors causes damage.

New cases and motherboards may have USB 3.0 capabilities. The USB 3.0 motherboard connector is similar in design to a USB connector but has additional pins.

Audio

Some cases have audio ports and jacks on the outside to connect microphones, external audio equipment such as signal processors, mixing boards, and instruments. Special audio panels can also be purchased and connected directly to the motherboard. These panels can either install into one or more external drive bays or be standalone. Due to the specialized function and variety of the hardware, consult the documentation of the motherboard, case, and audio panel for specific instructions for connecting the cables to the motherboard connectors.

How To

To install front panel cables, follow these steps:

Step 1. Plug the power cable into the system panel connector in the location marked POWER.

Step 2. Plug the reset cable into the system panel connector in the location marked RESET.

Step 3. Plug the power LED cable into the system panel connector in the location marked power LED.

Step 4. Plug the drive activity LED cable into the system panel connector in the location marked IDE LED.

Step 5. Plug the speaker cable into the system panel connector in the location marked SPEAKER.

Step 6. Plug the USB cable into the USB connector.

Step 7. Plug the audio cable into the audio connector.

Generally, if a button or LED does not function, the connector might be improperly oriented. To correct this, shut down the computer and unplug it, open the case, and turn the connector around for the button or LED that does not function.

Caution

When attaching cables, never force a connection.

Note

Plug in the power cable after you have connected all other cables.

Lab 3.1.5.5 Install Front Panel Cables

In this lab, install the front panel cables in the computer. Refer to Lab 3.1.5.5 in *IT Essentials: PC Hardware and Software Lab Manual*, Fifth Edition.

Install the Case Assembly (3.1.5.6)

Before reattaching the side panels to the computer case, make sure that all items are correctly aligned and seated properly. This list includes the CPU, RAM, adapter cards, data cables, front panel cables, and power cables.

When the cover is in place, make sure that it is secured at all screw locations. Some computer cases use screws that are inserted with a screwdriver. Other cases have knob-type screws that you can tighten by hand.

If you are unsure about how to remove or replace the computer case, refer to the manufacturer's documentation or website.

Caution

Handle case parts with care. Some computer case covers have sharp or jagged edges.

Install the External Cables (3.1.5.7)

After the case panels are reattached, connect the cables to the back of the computer. Here are some common external cable connections:

- Monitor
- Keyboard
- Mouse
- USB
- Ethernet
- Power

Note

Plug in the power cable after you have connected all other cables.

When attaching cables, ensure that they are connected to the correct locations on the computer. For example, older systems use the same type of PS/2 connector for the mouse and keyboard cables, but are color-coded to avoid being connected incorrectly. Often, an icon of the connected device, such as a keyboard, mouse, monitor, or USB symbol, is shown on the connector.

Caution

When attaching cables, never force a connection.

To install the various external cables, follow these steps:

Step 1. Attach the monitor cable to the video port. Secure the cable by tightening the screws on the connector.

Step 2. Plug the keyboard cable into the PS/2 keyboard port.

Step 3. Plug the mouse cable into the PS/2 mouse port.

Step 4. Plug the USB cable into a USB port.

Step 5. Plug the network cable into the network port.

Step 6. Connect the wireless antenna to the antenna connector.

Step 7. Plug the power cable into the power supply.

Note

Some motherboards do not have PS/2 ports for connecting the keyboard and mouse. Connect a USB keyboard and a USB mouse to this type of motherboard.

Figure 3-20 shows all of the external cables plugged into the back of the computer.

Figure 3-20   External Cables Attached

Virtual Desktop Activity: External Cables

Complete the external cable installation in the Virtual Desktop external cable layer. To access the activities found in this book, please refer to the instructions found in the Introduction.

System requirements for the Virtual Desktop include a minimum of 512 MB RAM and Windows XP or Windows 7 operating systems.

Lab 3.1.5.8: Complete the Computer Assembly

In this lab, you install the side panels and the external cables on the computer. Refer to Lab 3.1.5.8 in *IT Essentials: PC Hardware and Software Lab Manual*, Fifth Edition.

POST and BIOS (3.2.1)

The BIOS controls many computer functions; it provides instructions to the processing unit on a PC at startup of the system and takes control of the boot process. During the first part of the process, the BIOS runs a series of hardware diagnostic routines called POST, power-on-self-test. This sections looks at the BIOS setup and the POST.

BIOS Beep Codes and Setup (3.2.1.1)

When the computer is booted, the *basic input/output system (BIOS)* performs a basic hardware check. This check is called a *power-on self-test (POST)*. The POST, as shown in Figure 3-21, checks whether the computer hardware is operating correctly.

Figure 3-21   Power-On Self-Test (POST)

If a device is malfunctioning, an error or a beep code alerts the technician of the problem. A single beep usually means that the computer is functioning properly. If there is a hardware problem, a blank screen might appear at boot, and the computer emits a series of beeps. Each BIOS manufacturer uses different codes to indicate hardware problems. Table 3-3 shows a chart of *beep codes*. The beep codes for your computer might be different. Consult the motherboard documentation to get the beep codes for your computer.

Table 3-3   Common Beep Codes

Beep Code	Meaning	Cause
1 beep (no video)	Memory refresh failure	Bad memory
2 beeps	Memory parity error	Bad memory
3 beeps	Base 64 mem failure	Bad memory
4 beeps	Time not operational	Bad motherboard
5 beeps	Processor error	Bad processor

Beep Code	Meaning	Cause
6 beeps	8042 Gate A20 failure	Bad CPU or motherboard
7 beeps	Processor exception	Bad processor
8 beeps	Video memory error	Bad video or memory
9 beeps	ROM checksum error	Bad BIOS
10 beeps	CMOS checksum error	Bad motherboard
11 beeps	Cache memory bad	Bad CPU or motherboard

POST Card

When troubleshooting a computer problem when no video is available, you can use a POST card. A POST card is installed in a port on the motherboard, such as PCI or PCIe. When the computer is started, and errors are encountered, the computer issues a code that is displayed on the POST card in hexadecimal. This code is used to diagnose the cause of the problem through the motherboard, BIOS, or POST card manufacturer. Some motherboards have digital POST readouts on the motherboard itself.

BIOS Setup (3.2.1.2)

The BIOS contains a setup program to configure settings for the hardware devices. BIOS is a firmware chip that holds the instructions to control low-level hardware. The configuration data is saved to a memory chip called a *complementary metal-oxide semiconductor (CMOS)*, as shown in Figure 3-22. CMOS is maintained by the battery in the computer. If the battery dies, the BIOS setup configuration data is lost. If this occurs, replace the battery and reconfigure the BIOS settings that do not use the default settings.

Figure 3-22   CMOS Chip

Many modern motherboards use *nonvolatile memory* to store BIOS configuration settings. This type of memory does not need power to retain the settings. The battery in these systems is used only to keep the correct time and date in the clock. Configuration settings in the BIOS are not lost when the battery dies or is removed. Many modern motherboards also have the real-time clock and CMOS chip integrated into the chipset on the Southbridge.

To enter the BIOS setup program, you press the proper key or key sequence during POST. Many motherboards display graphics, called a splash screen, while the computer goes through the POST process. The computer might not display information about the key or key sequence required because of the splash screen. Most computers use the DEL key or a Function key to enter the BIOS setup program. Consult the motherboard documentation for the correct key or combination of keys for your computer.

Figure 3-23 shows the output when accessing one type of BIOS setup program. The interface of the setup programs and their features will vary by manufacturer. Even different versions of a BIOS from the same manufacturer may have different options and output.

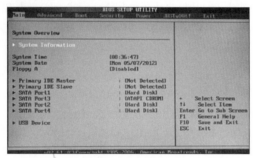

Figure 3-23   BIOS Setup Program

Here are examples of some common BIOS setup menu options:

- **Main:** Basic system configuration
- **Advanced:** Advanced system settings
- **Boot:** Boot device options and boot order
- **Security:** Security settings
- **Power:** Advanced power management configurations
- **JUSTw00t!:** Advanced voltage and clock settings
- **Exit:** BIOS exit options and loading default settings

BIOS Configuration (3.2.2)

In this section, you explore using the BIOS to learn about system hardware and various BIOS configuration options. These configuration options can vary a great deal depending on the BIOS manufacturer. The options mentioned in the previous section are some of the most common among manufacturers.

BIOS Component Information (3.2.2.1)

A technician can use the BIOS information to learn which components are installed in the computer and some of their attributes. This information can be useful when troubleshooting hardware that is not working properly and to determine upgrade options. These are some of the common component information items that are displayed in the BIOS:

- **CPU:** Displays the CPU manufacturer and speed. The number of installed processors is also displayed.

- **RAM:** Displays the RAM manufacturer and speed. The number of slots and which slots the RAM modules are installed in might also be displayed.

- **Hard drive:** Displays the manufacturer, size, and type of the hard drives. The type and number of hard disk controllers might also be displayed.

- **Optical drive:** Displays the manufacturer and type of optical drives.

BIOS Configurations (3.2.2.2)

Another function of the BIOS setup program is to customize specific aspects of the computer hardware to fit individual needs. The features that can be customized are determined by the BIOS manufacturer and version. Before making changes to the BIOS, it is important to have a clear understanding of how the changes can affect the computer. Incorrect settings can have an adverse effect.

Caution

Be careful when making changes to the BIOS. Some changes may cause your computer to malfunction or even prevent it from booting.

Time and Date

The main page of the BIOS has a System Time field and a System Date field to set the system clock. It is important to set these fields to the correct time and date because they are referenced by the operating system and other programs. If the date and time are not set properly, a maintenance program might think that it is out of date and constantly try to update files, or a calendar program will not display reminders on the correct date or time.

Disabling Devices

You can configure advanced BIOS settings to disable devices that are not needed or not used by the computer. For instance, a motherboard might have built-in video, sound, or network capabilities and installing a dedicated adapter card for one or more of these capabilities renders the built-in device redundant. Instead of wasting resources on the built-in device, you can disable the feature in the BIOS.

You can also disable extra hard drive controllers, serial ports, FireWire ports, or infrared hardware. If a device is not working, check the advanced BIOS settings to see if the device is disabled by default or has been disabled by someone. Enable the device in the BIOS so that it can be used by the computer.

Boot Order

When you turn on your computer the BIOS will check a predetermined list of devices that may contain an operating system. The order in which the devices are checked is configurable in BIOS. A computer can load an operating system from a hard drive, optical drive, USB device, or network. The ordered list that a computer is allowed to boot from is called the boot order or boot sequence. This list is usually located in the BIOS under the Boot tab. You can designate hard drives, optical drives, floppy drives, network boot, and flash media in the boot order. To allow USB booting, enable this option in the BIOS.

Shortly after completing POST, the computer attempts to load the operating system. The BIOS checks the first device in the boot order for a bootable partition. If the device has no bootable partition, the computer checks the next device in the list when a device with a bootable partition is found, the BIOS checks for an installed operating system.

The order in which devices are listed in the boot order depends on user needs. For example, when installing an operating system, an optical drive, network boot, or USB drive might need to be listed before a bootable hard drive. It is recommended to reorder the list after installing all operating systems to boot first from a bootable hard drive. The BIOS also allows you to disable or remove devices from the boot order list.

Clock Speed

Some BIOS setup programs allow you to change the CPU clock speed. Reducing the CPU clock speed makes the computer run slower and cooler. This might result in less noise from fans and can be useful if a quieter computer is desired, such as in a home theater or bedroom.

Increasing the CPU clock speed makes the computer run faster but also hotter, possibly causing the computer to be louder due to increased fan speeds. Increasing the CPU clock speed beyond the manufacturer recommendations is known as overclocking. Overclocking a CPU is risky and voids the warranty of the CPU. Overclocking can result in a shorter life span or cause damage to the CPU if the clock speed is increased too much. It is a common practice to install a cooling system capable of dissipating the extra heat created by overclocking so that the CPU is not damaged.

Virtualization

Virtualization technology allows a computer to run multiple operating systems in separate files or partitions. To accomplish this, a computer virtualization program emulates the characteristics of an entire computer system, including the hardware, BIOS, operating system, and programs. Enable the virtualization setting in the BIOS for a computer that will be using virtualization technology. Disable this setting if virtualization does not perform correctly or will not be used.

BIOS Security Configurations (3.2.2.3)

The BIOS might support many different security features to protect BIOS settings and data on the hard drive and to help recover the computer if it is stolen. The BIOS usually contains several common security features. BIOS passwords allow different levels of access to the BIOS settings. Two types of BIOS passwords are as follows:

- **Supervisor password:** This password can access all user-access passwords and all BIOS screens and settings.
- **User password:** This password becomes available after the supervisor password is enabled. Use this password to define the level of access to users.

Common levels of user access include the following:

- **Full access:** All screens and settings are available, except the supervisor password setting.
- **Limited:** Changes can be made to certain settings only (for example, the time and date).
- **View only:** All screens are available, but no settings can be changed.
- **No access:** No access is provided to the BIOS setup utility.

The BIOS includes additional security features, such as the following:

- *Drive encryption:* A hard drive can be encrypted to prevent data theft. Encrypting changes the data into code that cannot be understood. Without the correct password, the computer does not boot, and the computer cannot decrypt the data. Even if the hard drive is placed in another computer, the encrypted data remains encrypted.

- **Trusted Platform Module:** The TPM chip contains security items, such as encryption keys and passwords.

- **LoJack:** This two-part system from Absolute Software helps protect computers. The first part is a program called the Persistence Module that is installed in the BIOS by the manufacturer. The second part is a program called the Application Agent and is installed by the user. When the Application Agent is installed, the Persistence Module is activated. The Persistence Module installs the Application Agent if it is removed from the computer. The Persistence Module cannot be turned off after it is activated. The Application Agent calls the Absolute Monitoring Center over the Internet to report device information and location on a set schedule. If the computer is stolen, the owner can contact Absolute Software and perform the following functions:

  - Lock the computer remotely.

  - Display a message so that a lost computer can be returned to the owner.

  - Delete sensitive data on the computer.

  - Locate the computer using geotechnology.

BIOS Hardware Diagnostics and Monitoring (3.2.2.4)

The BIOS built-in hardware monitoring features are useful for collecting information and monitoring the activity of the hardware connected to the motherboard. The type and number of monitoring features varies by motherboard model. Use the hardware monitoring page to view temperatures, fan speeds, voltages, and other items. This area might also have information about intrusion detection devices.

Temperatures

Motherboards have heat sensors to monitor heat-sensitive hardware. A common heat sensor is under the CPU socket. This sensor monitors the temperature of the CPU and might increase the speed of the CPU fan to cool the CPU if it becomes too hot. Some BIOS setups also slow the speed of the CPU to reduce the CPU temperature. In some cases, the BIOS shuts down the computer to prevent damage to the CPU.

Other heat sensors monitor the temperature inside the case or power supply. Additionally, heat sensors monitor the temperatures of the RAM modules, chipsets, and other specialized hardware. The BIOS increases the speed of the fans or shuts down the computer to prevent overheating and damage.

Fan Speeds

Fan speeds are monitored by the BIOS. Some BIOS setups allow you to configure profiles to set the fan speeds to achieve a specific result. These are some common CPU fan speed profiles:

- **Standard:** The fan automatically adjusts depending on the temperature of the CPU, case, power supply, or other hardware.

- **Turbo:** Maximum fan speed.

- **Silent:** Minimizes the fan speed to decrease fan noise.

- **Manual:** The user can assign fan speed control settings.

Voltages

You can monitor the voltage of the CPU or the voltage regulators on the motherboard through the BIOS setup utility. If voltages are too high or too low, computer components can be damaged. If you find that voltages are not at or near the correct amount, make sure that the power supply is operating properly. If the power supply is delivering the correct voltages, the motherboard voltage regulators might be damaged. In this case, the motherboard might need to be repaired or replaced.

Clock and Bus Speeds

In some BIOS setups, you can monitor the speed of the CPU, as shown in Figure 3-24.

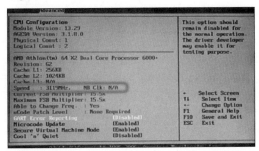

Figure 3-24   BIOS Clock and Bus Speed Settings

Some BIOS setups may also allow you to monitor one or more of the buses. You might need to look at these items to determine if the correct CPU settings have been detected by the BIOS or manually entered by a client or computer builder. Incorrect bus speeds can cause increased heat within the CPU and connected hardware or cause adapter cards and RAM to malfunction.

Intrusion Detection

Some computer cases have a switch that triggers when a computer case is opened. You can set the BIOS to record when the switch is triggered so that the owner can tell if the case has been tampered with. The switch is connected to the motherboard.

Built-In Diagnostics

If you notice a problem with a device connected to the system or a basic function, such as a fan or temperature and voltage control, you might be able to use built-in system diagnostics to determine where the problem is. Many times, the program provides a description of the problem or an error code for further troubleshooting. These are some common built-in diagnostics:

- **Start test:** Checks the main components to make sure that they are functioning properly. Use this test when the computer does not boot correctly.

- **Hard drive test:** Checks the hard drive for damaged areas. If a damaged area is found, it tries to retrieve the data and move it to a good area and mark the damaged area as bad so that the area is not used any more. Use this test if you suspect that the hard drive is not functioning properly, the computer does not boot, or the hard drive makes unusual noises.

- **Memory test:** Checks the memory modules to make sure that they are working properly. Use this test if the computer exhibits erratic behavior or fails to boot. Replace the memory immediately if this test reports errors.

- **Battery test:** Checks that the battery is functioning properly. Use this test if your battery is not functioning properly, does not hold a charge, or reports an incorrect charge level. Replace the battery if the battery fails this test.

Many built-in diagnostic programs retain a log that contains a record of the problems encountered. You can use this information to investigate issues and error codes. When a device is under warranty, you can use this information to convey the problem to product support.

Lab 3.2.2.5: Boot the Computer

In this lab, you boot the computer for the first time, explore the BIOS setup program, and change the boot order sequence. Refer to Lab 3.2.2.5 in *IT Essentials: PC Hardware and Software Lab Manual*, Fifth Edition.

Motherboard and Related Components (3.3.1)

All components in a computer system connect to the motherboard. As user requirements change, components may need to be upgraded to meet their needs. Reasons for upgrading or replacing computer components will vary from user to user and system to system. This section examines reasons why a user would upgrade and methods for upgrading a variety of components.

Motherboard Component Upgrades (3.3.1.1)

Computer systems need periodic upgrades for various reasons:

- User requirements change.

- Upgraded software packages require new hardware.

- New hardware offers enhanced performance.

Changes to the computer may cause you to upgrade or replace components and peripherals. Research the effectiveness and cost for both upgrading and replacing components.

If you upgrade or replace a motherboard, you might have to replace other components, such as the CPU, heat sink and fan assembly, and RAM. A new motherboard must fit into the old computer case. The power supply must also be compatible for the new motherboard and be able to support all new computer components.

Figure 3-25 shows the comparison of an older motherboard and a newer one that could be used to upgrade.

Figure 3-25 supports the earlier statement that upgrading the motherboard may lead to having to replace other components, too. These motherboards have different CPU sockets, RAM slots, and expansion buses.

Figure 3-25   Motherboard Upgrade

Begin the upgrade by moving the CPU and the heat sink and fan assembly to the new motherboard. These items are much easier to work with when they are outside of the case. Work on an antistatic mat, and wear a wrist strap to avoid damaging the CPU. If the new motherboard requires a different CPU and RAM, install them at this time. Clean the thermal compound from the CPU and heat sink you removed from the older system. Remember you will need to replace the old thermal compound with fresh compound. Always use a new application of thermal compound between the CPU and the heat sink.

CPU Installation

Different CPU architectures are installed in these common socket connection designs:

- Single-edge connector (SEC)
- Low-insertion force (LIF)
- Zero-insertion force (ZIF)
- Land grid array (LGA)
- Pin grid array (PGA)

SEC and LIF sockets are no longer commonly used. Compatibility between the processor type and the motherboard socket is essential. You can only use a processor with the same socket type as your existing motherboard. That means it must be from the same CPU manufacturer and product family. Consult the motherboard documentation on the type of processors it supports and on how to physically install the CPU.

Jumper Settings

Jumpers are upright gold pins on the motherboard. Each grouping of two or more pins is called a jumper block. A motherboard might use a dual in-line package (DIP) switch instead of jumpers. Both methods are used to complete electrical circuits that provide a variety of options supported by the motherboard. The motherboard documentation indicates which pins to connect to accommodate the various options:

- CPU voltage
- CPU speed
- Bus speed
- Cache size and type
- Flash BIOS enabled
- Clear CMOS
- Size of system memory

Newer motherboards rarely have jumpers. Advanced electronics allow these options to be configured from within the BIOS setup program.

CMOS Battery Installation

A CMOS battery might need to be replaced after several years. If the computer does not keep the correct time and date or loses configuration settings between shutdowns, the battery is most likely very weak or dead and needs to be replaced. Make sure that the new battery matches the model required by the motherboard.

How To

To install a CMOS battery, follow these steps:

Step 1.   Gently slide aside, or raise, the thin metal clips to remove the old battery.

Step 2.   Line up the positive and negative poles to the correct orientation.

Step 3.   Gently slide aside, or raise, the thin metal clips to insert the new battery.

Upgrade the Motherboard (3.3.1.2)

To remove and replace the old motherboard, remove the cables from the motherboard that attach to the case LEDs and buttons. Make notes in your journal to know where and how everything is connected before you start the upgrade. Documentation is a key aspect of a successful upgrade or computer building experience.

Document how the motherboard secures to the case. Some mounting screws provide support, and some may provide an important grounding connection between the motherboard and chassis. In particular, pay attention to screws and standoffs that are non-metallic because these may be insulators. Replacing insulating screws and supports with metal hardware that conducts electricity might damage electrical components.

Before installing the new motherboard into the computer case, examine the I/O shield located at the back of the computer case.

Figure 3-26 shows an example of an I/O shield.

Figure 3-26   Motherboard I/O Shield

Replace the old I/O shield if the new motherboard has different I/O ports or if the ports are in different locations.

Make sure that you use the correct screws. Do not swap threaded screws with self-tapping metal screws because they will damage the threaded screw holes and might not be secure. Make sure that the threaded screws are the correct length and have the same number of threads per inch. If the thread is correct, they fit easily. If you force a screw to fit, you can damage the threaded hole, and it will not hold the motherboard securely.

Caution

Using the wrong screws can also produce metal shavings that can cause short circuits.

Note

It does not matter whether you replace a flat-head screw with a Phillips-head screw as long as the threaded part of the screw is the same length and the threads are the same.

Next, connect the power supply cables. If the ATX power connectors are not the same size (some have more pins than others), you might need to use an adapter. Connect the cables for the case LEDs and buttons. Refer to the motherboard documentation for the layout of these connections. Often these connectors are not keyed and can be connected backwards. Pay careful attention to the orientation of the cable in the documentation.

After the new motherboard is in place and the cables are connected, install and secure the expansion cards.

It is now time to check your work. Make sure that there are no loose parts or leftover wires. Connect the keyboard, mouse, monitor, and power. If a problem is detected, shut off the power supply immediately.

BIOS Updates

The firmware encoded in the motherboard CMOS chip might need to be updated so that the motherboard can support newer hardware. Updating the firmware can be risky. Before updating motherboard firmware, record the manufacturer of the BIOS and the motherboard and the motherboard model. You need this information when you go to the motherboard manufacturer's site to get the correct installation software and BIOS firmware. Only update the firmware if there are problems with the system hardware or to add functionality to the system.

Upgrade CPU and Heat Sink and Fan Assembly (3.3.1.3)

One way to increase the power of a computer is to increase the processing speed. You can do this by upgrading the CPU. However, you must meet some requirements:

- The new CPU must fit into the existing CPU socket.

- The new CPU must be compatible with the motherboard chipset.

- The new CPU must operate with the existing motherboard and power supply.

- The new CPU must operate with the existing RAM. The RAM may need to be upgraded or expanded to take advantage of the faster CPU.

If the motherboard is older, you might not be able to find a compatible CPU. In that case, you must replace the motherboard.

Caution

Always work on an antistatic mat and wear a wrist strap when installing and removing CPUs. Place a CPU on the antistatic mat until you are ready to use it. Store CPUs in antistatic packaging.

To change the CPU, remove the existing CPU by releasing it from the socket using the *zero insertion force (ZIF) lever*. Different sockets have slightly different mechanisms, but all serve to lock the CPU in place after it is correctly oriented in the socket.

Insert the new CPU into place. Do not force the CPU into its socket or use excessive force to close the locking bars. Excessive force can damage the CPU or its socket. If you encounter resistance, make sure that you have aligned the CPU properly. Most have a pattern of pins that fit only one way:

- **SEC socket:** Align the notches on the CPU to the keys in the SEC socket.

- **PGA, LIF, or ZIF socket:** Align the CPU so that the Connection 1 indicator is lined up with Pin 1 on the CPU socket.

- **LGA socket:** Align the CPU so that the two notches on the CPU fit into the two socket extensions.

The new CPU might require a different heat sink and fan assembly. The assembly must physically fit the CPU and be compatible with the CPU socket. It must also be adequate to remove the heat of the faster CPU.

Caution

You must apply thermal compound between the new CPU and the heat sink and fan assembly.

View thermal settings in the BIOS to determine if there are any problems with the CPU and the heat sink and fan assembly. Third-party software applications can also report CPU temperature information in an easy-to-read format. Refer to the motherboard or CPU user documentation to determine if the chip is operating in the correct temperature range.

How To

To install additional fans in the case to help cool the motherboard and CPU, follow these steps:

Step 1. Align the fan so that it faces the correct direction to either draw air in or blow air out.

Step 2. Mount the fan using the predrilled holes in the case. To draw air into the case, mount the fan at the bottom of the case. To direct hot air out of the case, mount the fan at the top of the case.

Step 3. Connect the fan to the power supply or the motherboard, depending on the case fan plug type.

Figure 3-27 show an example of a heat sink and fan assembly.

Figure 3-27   CPU Heat Sink/Fan Assembly Upgrade

Upgrade the RAM (3.3.1.4)

Increasing the amount of system RAM almost always improves overall system performance. Before upgrading or replacing the RAM, answer the following questions:

- What type of RAM does the motherboard currently use?

- Can the RAM be installed one module at a time, or must it be grouped into matching banks?

- Are there available RAM slots?

- Does the new RAM chip match the speed, latency, type, and voltage of the existing RAM?

Caution

When working with system RAM, work on an antistatic mat and wear a wrist strap. Place the RAM on the mat until you are ready to install it. Store RAM in antistatic packaging.

Remove the existing RAM module by freeing the retaining clips that secure it. Pull it from the socket. Current DIMMs pull straight out and insert straight down. Earlier SIMMs were inserted at an angle to lock into place.

As shown in Figure 3-28, when inserting the new RAM module, make sure that the notches in the RAM and RAM slot on the motherboard align properly. Press down firmly, and lock the RAM into place with the retaining clips.

Figure 3-28   RAM Upgrade

Caution

Make sure to insert the memory module completely into the socket. RAM can cause serious damage to the motherboard if it is incorrectly aligned and shorts the main system bus.

The system discovers the newly installed RAM if it is compatible and installed correctly. If the BIOS does not indicate the presence of the correct amount of RAM, make sure that the RAM is compatible with the motherboard and is correctly installed.

Upgrade the BIOS (3.3.1.5)

Motherboard manufacturers periodically release updates for their BIOS. The release notes describe the upgrade to the product, compatibility improvements, and the known bugs that have been addressed. Searching your BIOS manufacturer and current BIOS version number will lead you to the release notes for your specific BIOS. Some newer devices operate properly only with an updated BIOS installed. To check the version of the BIOS installed in your computer, consult the BIOS Setup Utility; you can usually find this information on the main tab.

Early computer BIOS information was contained in ROM chips. To upgrade the BIOS information, the ROM chip had to be replaced, which was not always possible.

Modern BIOS chips are EEPROM, or flash memory, which can be upgraded by the user without opening the computer case. This process is called flashing the BIOS.

To download a new BIOS, consult the manufacturer's website and follow the recommended installation procedures. Installing BIOS software online may involve downloading a new BIOS file, copying or extracting files to removable media, and then booting from the removable media. An installation program prompts the user for information to complete the process.

Although it is still common to flash the BIOS through a command prompt, several motherboard manufacturers provide software on their websites that allow a user to flash the BIOS from within Windows. The procedure varies from manufacturer to manufacturer.

Caution

An improperly installed or aborted BIOS update can cause the computer to become unusable.

Lab 3.3.1.6: BIOS File Search

In this lab, you identify the current BIOS version, and then search for BIOS update files. Refer to Lab 3.3.1.6 in *IT Essentials: PC Hardware and Software Lab Manual*, Fifth Edition.

Storage Devices (3.3.2)

Storage devices are used for many purposes in a computer system. One critical use is the storage of user data. As users collect more data, they may need to increase their storage amounts or want to back up to protect it. This section discusses how to add more storage and methods for protecting data.

Upgrade Hard Drives and RAID (3.3.2.1)

Instead of purchasing a new computer to get increased access speed and storage space, you might consider adding another hard drive. There are several reasons for installing an additional drive:

- Install a second operating system.
- Provide additional storage space.
- Provide a faster hard drive.
- Hold the system swap file.

- Back up the original hard drive.

- Increase fault tolerance.

When two PATA hard drives are connected to the same data cable, one drive must be jumpered as the master drive, and the other drive must be jumpered as the slave drive. This allows the computer to communicate with both drives individually. As shown in Figure 3-29, jumper pins are located on the back of the hard drive and can configure a hard drive to be a standalone drive, a master drive, or a slave drive. Some drives can be jumpered to Cable Select (CS). The CS setting allows the BIOS to automatically configure the master and slave drives according to the order they are attached to the cable. Refer to the hard drive diagram or manual for the correct jumper settings.

Hard Drive Jumper Pins   Hard Drive Jumper Pin
                                      Diagram

Figure 3-29   Hard Drive Jumpers

Each SATA hard drive has its own data cable; therefore, there is no master-slave relationship between drives.

A redundant array of independent disks (RAID) installation can provide data protection or increased performance when connecting multiple hard drives, as shown in Table 3-4. RAID requires two or more hard drives. You can install RAID using hardware or software. Hardware installations are usually more dependable but more expensive. In a hardware implementation, a dedicated processor on a RAID adapter card or the motherboard makes the calculations needed to perform the special storage functions across multiple disks. Software installations are created and managed by some operating systems. It is important to understand the cost, performance, and reliability of each RAID array configuration.

After selecting the appropriate hard drive for the computer, follow these general guidelines during installation:

Step 1.   Place the hard drive in an empty drive bay and tighten the screws to secure the hard drive.

Step 2.   Configure a PATA hard drive as either master, slave, or cable select. If you have a SCSI hard drive, set the ID number and terminate the SCSI chain.

Step 3.   Attach the power cable and the data cable to the hard drive. Ensure that Pin 1 of the PATA data cable is properly aligned.

Table 3-4   RAID Level Comparison

RAID Level	Minimum Number of Drives	Description	Advantages	Disadvantages
0	2	Data striping without redundancy	Highest performance.	No data protection. Failure of one drive results in loss of all data.
1	2	Disk mirroring	High performance and high data protection because all data is duplicated.	High cost of implementation because an additional drive of equal or larger capacity is required.
2	2	Error-correcting coding	This level is no longer used.	Same performance using lower-cost RAID 3.
3	3	Byte-level data striping with dedicated parity	For large sequential data requests.	Does not support multiple simultaneous read and write requests.
4	3	Block-level data striping with dedicated parity	Supports multiple read requests. If a disk fails, the dedicated parity disk is used to create a replacement disk.	Write requests are bottlenecked due to the dedicated parity drive.
5	3	Combination of data striping and parity	Supports multiple simultaneous reads and writes, data is written across all drives with parity, and data can be rebuilt from information found on the other drives.	Write performance is slower than RAID 0 and 1.
6	4	Independent data disks with double parity	Block-level data striping with parity data distributed across all disks can handle two simultaneous drive failures.	Lower performance than RAID 5, and not supported on all disk controllers.
RAID 0+1	4	Combination of data striping and mirroring	High performance, highest data protection.	High cost overhead because of data duplication requires twice the storage capacity.

Input and Output Devices (3.3.3)

Users employ input devices to enter data into a computer and the resulting information is returned to the user through an output device. Sometimes it is necessary to change input and output devices if they fail or for personal preference like exchanging mouse to trackball for comfort. This section looks at reasons to and ways to upgrade input and output devices.

Upgrade Input and Output Devices (3.3.3.1)

If an input or output device stops operating, you may have to replace the device. Some customers want to upgrade their input or output devices to increase performance and productivity.

An ergonomic keyboard or mouse, shown in Figure 3-30, may be more comfortable to use. Sometimes a reconfiguration is necessary to enable a user to perform special tasks, such as typing in a second language with additional characters. Replacing or reconfiguring an input or output device might also make it easier to accommodate users with disabilities.

Figure 3-30   Ergonomic Input Devices

You can add privacy and antiglare filters to a monitor. A privacy filter is specially made to attach to the screen and prevent people to the side of a monitor from reading information on the screen. Only the user and people directly behind the user are able to read the screen. An antiglare filter attaches to the screen and helps prevent the glare of the sun and bright lights from reflecting off the screen. An antiglare filter makes it much easier to read the screen in the daylight or when a light is behind the user.

Some customers need to add additional monitors running multiple physical display devices at once. Often, a more advanced video adapter card is needed to support the additional connections, or a second video adapter card must be installed. Adding monitors to a system can increase productivity by allowing the user to display more information and move data between open programs more easily and quickly.

Sometimes it is not possible to perform an upgrade using the existing expansion slots or sockets. In this case, you may be able to accomplish the upgrade using a USB connection. If the computer does not have an extra USB connection, you must install a USB adapter card or purchase a USB hub, as shown in Figure 3-31.

Figure 3-31   USB Hub

After obtaining new hardware, you may have to install new drivers. You can usually do this by using the installation media. If you do not have the installation media, you can obtain updated drivers from the manufacturer's website.

Note

A signed driver is a driver that has passed the Windows hardware quality lab test and has been given a driver signature by Microsoft. Installing an unsigned driver can cause system instability, error messages, and boot problems. During hardware installation, if an unsigned driver is detected, you are asked whether you want to stop or continue the installation. Only install unsigned drivers if you trust the source of the drivers.

Worksheet 3.3.3.2: Upgrade Hardware

In this worksheet, you use the Internet, a newspaper, or a local store to gather information about hardware components. Your customer's computer currently has one module of 2 GB of RAM, a 500 GB hard disk drive, and a PCIe video adapter card with 256 MB of RAM. Your customer wants to be able to play advanced video games. Refer to Worksheet 3.3.3.2 in *IT Essentials: PC Hardware and Software Lab Manual*, Fifth Edition.

Summary (3.4.1.1)

This chapter detailed the steps used to assemble a computer and to boot the system for the first time. These are some important points to remember:

- Computer cases come in a variety of sizes and configurations. Many of the computer components must match the form factor of the case.

- The CPU is installed on the motherboard with a heat sink and fan assembly.

- RAM is installed in RAM slots on the motherboard.

- Adapter cards are installed in PCI and PCIe expansion slots on the motherboard.

- Hard disk drives are installed in 3.5-inch (8.9-cm) drive bays located inside the case.

- Optical drives are installed in 5.25-inch (13.34-cm) drive bays that can be accessed from outside the case.

- Floppy drives are installed in 3.5-inch (8.9-cm) drive bays that can be accessed from outside the case.

- Power supply cables are connected to all drives and the motherboard.

- Internal data cables transfer data to all drives.

- External cables connect peripheral devices to the computer.

- BIOS Beep codes signify when hardware malfunctions.

- The BIOS setup program displays information about the computer components and allows the user to change system settings.

- Computer components require periodic upgrades and replacement parts.

- Additional hard drives can provide fault tolerance and the ability to install additional operating systems.

Summary of Exercises

This is a summary of the labs, worksheets, and virtual desktop activities associated with this chapter. Refer to the labs, worksheets, and virtual desktop activities in the *IT Essentials: PC Hardware and Software Lab Manual*, Fifth Edition.

Virtual Desktop Activities

The following virtual desktop activities cover material from this chapter. To access the activities found in this book, please refer to the instructions found in the Introduction:

Virtual Desktop Activity: Power Supply

Virtual Desktop Activity: Motherboard

Virtual Desktop Activity: Internal Drives

Virtual Desktop Activity: Drives in External Bays

Virtual Desktop Activity: Adapter Cards

Virtual Desktop Activity: Internal Cables

Virtual Desktop Activity: External Cables

Labs

The following labs cover material from this chapter. Refer to the labs in the *IT Essentials: PC Hardware and Software Lab Manual*, Fifth Edition.

Lab 3.1.1.3: Install the Power Supply

Lab 3.1.2.4: Install the Motherboard

Lab 3.1.3.4: Install the Drives

Lab 3.1.5.3: Install Internal Cables

Lab 3.1.5.5: Install Front Panel Cables

Lab 3.2.2.5: Boot the Computer

Lab 3.3.1.6: BIOS File Search

Worksheets

The following worksheets cover material from this chapter. Refer to the worksheets in the *IT Essentials: PC Hardware and Software Lab Manual*, Fifth Edition.

Worksheet 3.3.3.2: Upgrade Hardware

Check Your Understanding

You can find the answers to these questions in Appendix A, "Answers to 'Check Your Understanding' Questions."

1. When mounting a motherboard in a computer case, what is used to prevent the motherboard from touching the bottom of the case?

    A. Standoffs

    B. Ground-fault isolators

    C. Silicon spray

    D. Grounding straps

2. Which two connectors are used to connect external peripherals? (Choose two.)

    A. EIDE

    B. Molex

    C. PATA

    D. PS/2

    E. USB

3. What should be used to clean the base of the CPU heat sink prior to reinstallation?

    A. Rubbing alcohol

    B. Water

    C. Isopropyl alcohol

    D. Thermal compound

4. What should be done prior to the installation of RAM onto the motherboard?

    A. Consult the motherboard documentation or website of the manufacturer to ensure that the RAM is compatible with the motherboard.

    B. Change the voltage selector to meet with the voltage specification of the RAM.

    C. Ensure the memory expansion slot tabs are in the locked position before inserting the RAM module.

    D. Populate the center memory slots first before inserting the new RAM.

5. A motherboard has a 24-pin socket for the main power connector. Which ATX power supply connector will work?

   A. 12-pin connector

   B. 16-pin connector

   C. 18-pin connector

   D. 20-pin connector

6. Which website should a technician consult to find instructions for updating the BIOS on a computer?

   A. CPU manufacturer

   B. Case manufacturer

   C. Motherboard manufacturer

   D. Operating system developer

7. What are two features of the LoJack system? (Choose two.)

   A. The LoJack system uses an Application Agent that is installed by the user.

   B. It uses geotechnology to locate a lost computer.

   C. It allows the user to deactivate the Persistence Module.

   D. It prevents data from being retrieved from a hard drive if the hard drive is removed and installed into a different computer.

   E. It emulates the characteristics of an entire computer system, including hardware, BIOS, operating system, and programs.

8. Which procedure is performed last when installing a new motherboard?

   A. Install the I/O shield.

   B. Secure the expansion cards.

   C. Connect the peripheral devices.

   D. Tighten the motherboard screws.

9. What type of disk drives need to be configured with either a master/slave or auto-detect setting to work correctly?

   A. PATA

   B. SATA

   C. SCSI

   D. FDD

10. Which definition describes the term *overclocking*?

    A. Changing the bus speed of the motherboard to increase the speed of attached adapters

    B. Increasing the speed of the CPU beyond the recommendations of the manufacturer

    C. Modifying the motherboard clocking crystal to increase the timing signals

    D. Replacing slower SDRAM with faster memory

11. A technician is installing a new power supply in a computer. Which type of power connector should be used to connect a CD- ROM drive?

    A. Berg

    B. Mini Molex

    C. Molex

    D. 20-pin ATX connector

12. A technician is installing additional memory in a computer. How can the technician guarantee that the memory is correctly aligned?

    A. The label on the memory module should always face the CPU.

    B. A notch in the memory module should be aligned with a notch in the slot on the motherboard.

    C. The arrows on the memory module should be aligned with the arrows on the motherboard slot.

    D. All memory and motherboard slots are color-coded, with one red end and one blue end.

CHAPTER 4

Overview of Preventive Maintenance

Objectives

Upon completion of this chapter, you will be able to answer the following questions:

- What are the benefits of preventive maintenance?

- What are the most common preventive maintenance tasks?

- What are the elements of the troubleshooting process?

- What are common problems and solutions when troubleshooting PCs?

Key Terms

This chapter uses the following key terms. You can find the definitions in the Glossary.

preventive maintenance   *page 156*

troubleshooting   *page 156*

data backup   *page 161*

open-ended questions   *page 163*

closed-ended questions   *page 163*

power-on self-test (POST)   *page 163*

Event Viewer   *page 164*

Device Manager   *page 164*

Task Manager   *page 165*

theory of probable cause   *page 166*

Introduction (4.0.1)

Preventive maintenance is the regular and systematic inspection, cleaning, and replacement of worn parts, materials, and systems. Effective preventive maintenance reduces part, material, and system faults and keeps hardware and software in good working condition.

Troubleshooting is the systematic process used to locate the cause of a fault in a computer system and correct the relevant hardware and software issues.

In this chapter, you learn general guidelines for creating preventive maintenance programs and troubleshooting procedures. These guidelines are a starting point to help you develop your preventive maintenance and troubleshooting skills.

Preventive Maintenance (4.1)

Preventive maintenance reduces the probability of hardware or software problems by systematically and periodically checking hardware and software to ensure proper operation. This section introduces some of the benefits of preventive maintenance and discusses how to plan and implement preventive maintenance practices.

Benefits of Preventive Maintenance (4.1.1.1)

Preventive maintenance is implemented via a plan. While there are several considerations for preventive maintenance needs, preventive maintenance plans are developed based on at least two factors:

- **Computer location or environment:** Computers that are exposed to dusty environments, such as those used on construction sites, require more attention than computers located in an office environment.

- **Computer use:** High-traffic networks, such as a school network, might require additional scanning and removal of malicious software and unwanted files.

To create a preventive maintenance plan, document the routine maintenance tasks that must be performed on the computer components and the frequency of each task. You can then use this list of tasks to create a maintenance program.

Be proactive in computer maintenance and data protection. By performing regular maintenance routines, you can reduce potential hardware and software problems. Regular maintenance routines reduce computer downtime and repair costs. Preventive maintenance also offers these benefits:

- Improves data protection
- Extends the life of the components

- Improves equipment stability

- Reduces the number of equipment failures

Preventive Maintenance Tasks (4.1.1.2)

Hardware

Check the condition of the cables, components, and peripherals. Clean components to reduce the likelihood of overheating. Repair or replace any component that shows signs of damage or excess wear.

Use these tasks as a guide to creating a hardware maintenance program:

- Remove dust from fan intakes.

- Remove dust from the power supply.

- Remove dust from the components inside the computer and peripheral equipment such as printers.

- Clean the mouse, keyboard, and display.

- Check for and secure any loose cables.

Software

Verify that installed software is current. Follow the policies of the organization when installing security updates, operating system updates, and program updates. Many organizations do not allow updates until extensive testing has been completed. This testing is done to confirm that the update will not cause problems with the operating system and software. Use these tasks as a guide to creating a software maintenance schedule that fits the needs of your computer:

- Review and install the appropriate security updates.

- Review and install the appropriate software updates.

- Review and install the appropriate driver updates.

- Update the virus definition files.

- Scan for viruses and spyware.

- Remove unwanted or unused programs.

- Scan hard drives for errors.

- Defragment non-SSD hard drives.

Clean the Case and Internal Components (4.1.1.3)

An important part of hardware preventive maintenance is to keep the computer case and internal components clean. The amount of dust and other airborne particles in the environment and the habits of the user determine how often to clean the computer components. Regularly cleaned or replaced air filters in the building in which the computer is used will significantly reduce the amount of dust in the air.

Dust or dirt on the outside of a computer can travel through cooling fans and loose computer case covers to the inside. When dust accumulates inside the computer, it prevents the flow of air and reduces the cooling of components. Hot computer components are more likely to break down than properly cooled components. Most cleaning is to prevent this accumulation of dust. When dust accumulates inside the computer, it prevents the flow of air and reduces the cooling of components. Several components are important to keep clean:

- Heat sink and fan assembly
- RAM
- Adapter cards
- Motherboard
- Fans
- Power supply
- Internal drives

To remove dust from the inside of a computer, use a combination of compressed air, a low-air-flow ESD vacuum cleaner, and a small lint-free cloth. The air pressure from some cleaning devices can generate static and damage or loosen components and jumpers.

You can use a low-air-flow ESD vacuum cleaner to remove collected dust and materials from inside the bottom of the case. You can also use the vacuum cleaner to pull in the dust blown around from the compressed air. If you use compressed air from a can, keep the can upright to prevent the fluid from leaking onto computer components. Always follow the instructions and warnings on the compressed air can to keep a safe distance from sensitive devices and components. Use the lint-free cloth to remove any dust left behind on the component.

Caution

When you clean a fan with compressed air, hold the fan blades in place. This prevents over-spinning the rotor or moving the fan in the wrong direction.

Regular cleaning also gives you a chance to inspect components for loose screws and connectors. Look for things that might cause a problem later and correct them, such as the following:

- Missing expansion slot covers that let dust, dirt, or living pests into the computer

- Loose or missing screws that secure adapter cards

- Missing cables

- Loose or tangled cables that can pull free from the case

Use a cloth or a duster to clean the outside of the computer case. If you use a cleaning product, do not spray it directly on the case. Instead, put a small amount onto a cleaning cloth or a duster and wipe the outside of the case.

Inspect Internal Components (4.1.1.4)

The best method of keeping a computer in good condition is to examine the computer on a regular schedule. This is a basic checklist of components to inspect:

- **CPU heat sink and fan assembly:** Examine the CPU heat sink and fan assembly for dust buildup. Make sure that the fan can spin freely. Check that the fan power cable is secure. Check the fan while the power is on to see the fan turn.

- **RAM connections:** The RAM chips should be seated securely in the RAM slots. Sometimes the retaining clips can loosen. Reseat them, if necessary. Use compressed air to remove dust.

- **Storage devices:** Inspect all storage devices. All cables should be firmly connected. Check for loose, missing, or incorrectly set jumpers. A drive should not produce rattling, knocking, or grinding sounds. Read the manufacturer's documentation to learn how to clean the optical drive and tape heads. You can buy laser lens cleaning kits for computer optical drives. Tape head cleaning kits are also available.

- **Adapter cards:** Adapter cards should be seated properly in their expansion slots. Loose cards can cause short circuits. Secure adapter cards with the retaining screw or clip to avoid having the cards come loose in their expansion slots. Use compressed air to remove dirt and dust on the adapter cards and the expansion slots.

- **Screws:** Loose screws can cause problems if they are not immediately fixed or removed. A loose screw in the case can cause a short circuit or roll into a position where the screw is hard to remove.

- **Cables:** Examine all cable connections. Look for broken and bent pins. Ensure that all connector retaining screws are finger-tight. Make sure cables are not crimped, pinched, or severely bent.

- **Power devices:** Inspect power strips, surge suppressors (surge protectors), and UPS devices. Make sure that there is proper and unobstructed ventilation. Replace the power device if it does not work properly.

- **Keyboard and mouse:** Use compressed air to clean the keyboard, mouse, and mouse sensor.

Environmental Concerns (4.1.1.5)

An optimal operating environment for a computer is clean, free of potential contaminants, and within the temperature and humidity range specified by the manufacturer. With most desktop computers, the operating environment can be controlled. However, due to the portable nature of laptops, it is not always possible to control the temperature, humidity, and working conditions. Computers are built to resist adverse environments, but technicians should always take precautions to protect the computer from damage and loss of data.

Follow these guidelines to help ensure optimal computer operating performance:

- Do not obstruct vents or airflow to the internal components. A computer can overheat if air circulation is obstructed.

- Keep the room temperature between 45 to 90 degrees Fahrenheit (7 to 32 degrees Celsius).

- Keep the humidity level between 10 to 80 percent.

Temperature and humidity recommendations vary by computer manufacturer. You should research these recommended values, especially if you plan to use the computer in extreme conditions.

Caution
To avoid damaging computer surfaces, use a soft, lint-free cloth with an approved cleaning solution. Apply the cleaning solution to the lint-free cloth, not directly to the computer.

Troubleshooting Process Steps (4.2.1)

This section introduces a process for troubleshooting that will be used throughout the rest of the course as a method for identifying and solving problems.

Introduction to Troubleshooting (4.2.1.1)

Troubleshooting requires an organized and logical approach to problems with computers and other components. Sometimes issues arise during preventive maintenance. At other times, a customer may contact you with a problem. A logical approach to troubleshooting allows you to eliminate variables and identify causes of problems in a systematic order. Asking the right questions, testing the right hardware, and examining the right data helps you understand the problem and form a proposed solution to try.

This section presents an approach to problem solving that you can apply to both hardware and software. You can also apply many of the steps to problem solving to other work-related areas.

Note

The term *customer*, as used in this course, is any user that requires technical computer assistance.

Troubleshooting is a skill that you refine over time. Each time you solve a problem, you increase your troubleshooting skills by gaining more experience. You learn how and when to combine steps or skip steps to reach a solution quickly. The troubleshooting process is a guideline that is modified to fit your needs.

Before you begin troubleshooting problems, always follow the necessary precautions to protect data on a computer. Some repairs, such as replacing a hard drive or reinstalling an operating system, might put the data on the computer at risk. Make sure you do everything possible to prevent data loss while attempting repairs.

Caution

Always perform a backup before beginning any troubleshooting. You must protect data before beginning any work on a customer's computer. If your work results in data loss for the customer, you or your company could be held liable.

Data Backup

A *data backup* is a copy of the data on a computer hard drive that is saved to another storage device or to cloud storage. Cloud storage is online storage that is accessed via the Internet. In an organization, backups may be performed on a daily, weekly, or monthly basis.

If you are unsure that a backup has been done, do not attempt any troubleshooting activities until you check with the customer. Here is a list of items to verify with the customer about data backups:

- Date of the last backup

- Contents of the backup

- Data integrity of the backup

- Availability of all backup media for a data restore

If the customer does not have a current backup and you are not able to create one, ask the customer to sign a liability release form. A liability release form contains at least the following information:

- Permission to work on the computer without a current backup available

- Release from liability if data is lost or corrupted

- Description of the work to be performed

Identify the Problem (4.2.1.2)

The first step in the troubleshooting process is to identify the problem. During this step, gather as much information as possible from the customer and then from the computer.

Conversation Etiquette

When you are talking to the customer, follow these guidelines:

- Ask direct questions to gather information.

- Do not use industry jargon.

- Do not talk down to the customer.

- Do not insult the customer.

- Do not accuse the customer of causing the problem.

By communicating effectively, you can elicit the most relevant information about the problem from the customer. The following is some of the important information to gather from the customer:

Step 1:   Identify the Problem

- Customer information

  - Company name

  - Contact name

  - Address

  - Phone number

- Computer configuration

    - Manufacturer and model

    - Operating system

    - Network environment

    - Connection type

- Problem description

    - Open-ended questions

    - Closed-ended questions

- Error messages

- Beep sequences

- LEDs

- POST

Open-Ended and Closed-Ended Questions

Open-ended questions allow customers to explain the details of the problem in their own words. Use open-ended questions to obtain general information.

Based on the information from the customer, you can proceed with *closed-ended questions*. Closed-ended questions generally require a yes or no answer. These questions are intended to get the most relevant information in the shortest time possible.

Documenting Responses

Document the information obtained from the customer in the work order and in the repair journal. Write down anything that you think might be important for you or another technician. The small details often lead to the solution of a difficult or complicated problem.

Beep Codes

Each BIOS manufacturer uses a unique beep sequence, a combination of long and short beeps, for hardware failures during the boot process. When troubleshooting, power on the computer and listen. As the system proceeds through the *power-on self-test (POST),* most computers emit one beep to indicate that the system is booting properly. If there is an error, you might hear multiple beeps. Document the beep code sequence, and research the code to determine the specific hardware failure.

BIOS Information

If the computer boots and stops after the POST, investigate the BIOS settings to determine where to find the problem. A device might not be detected or configured properly. Refer to the motherboard documentation to make sure that the BIOS settings are accurate.

Event Viewer

When system, user, or software errors occur on a computer, the *Event Viewer* is updated with information about the errors. The Event Viewer application shown in Figure 4-1 records the following information about the problem:

- What problem occurred

- Date and time of the problem

- Severity of the problem

- Source of the problem

- Event ID number

- Which user was logged in when the problem occurred

Although the Event Viewer lists details about the error, you might need to further research the solution.

Figure 4-1   Event Viewer

Device Manager

The *Device Manager* shown in Figure 4-2 displays all the devices that are configured on a computer. The operating system flags the devices that are not operating correctly with an error icon. A yellow circle with an exclamation point (!) indicates that the device is in a problem state. A red circle and an X means that the device is disabled. A yellow question mark (?) indicates that the system does not know which driver to install for the hardware.

Figure 4-2   Device Manager

Task Manager

The *Task Manager*, shown in Figure 4-3, displays the applications that are currently running. With the Task Manager, you can close applications that have stopped responding. You can also monitor the performance of the CPU and virtual memory, view all processes that are currently running, and view information about the network connections.

Figure 4-3   Task Manager

Diagnostic Tools

Conduct research to determine which software is available to help diagnose and solve problems. Many programs to help you troubleshoot hardware are available.

Manufacturers of system hardware usually provide diagnostic tools of their own. For instance, a hard drive manufacturer might provide a tool to boot the computer and diagnose why the hard drive does not boot Windows.

Establish a Theory of Probable Cause (4.2.1.3)

The second step in the troubleshooting process is to establish a *theory of probable cause*. First, create a list of the most common reasons why the error would occur. Even though the customer may think that there is a major problem, start with the obvious issues before moving to more complex diagnoses. List the easiest or most obvious causes at the top. List the more complex causes at the bottom. The following list is a sample of potential causes of a problem, listed from easiest to most complex.

Step 2:   Establish a Theory of Probable Cause

- Device is powered off.
- Power switch for an outlet is turned off.
- Surge protector is turned off.
- Loose external connections.
- Non-bootable disk in floppy drive.
- Incorrect boot order in BIOS setup.

The next steps of the troubleshooting process involve testing each possible cause.

Test the Theory to Determine Cause (4.2.1.4)

You determine an exact cause by testing your theories of probable causes one at a time, starting with the quickest and easiest. After identifying an exact cause of the problem, you then determine the steps to resolve the problem. As you become more experienced at troubleshooting computers, you will work through the steps in the process faster. For now, practice each step to better understand the troubleshooting process.

If you cannot determine the exact cause of the problem after testing all your theories, establish a new theory of probable cause and test it. If necessary, escalate the problem to a technician with more experience. Before you escalate, document each test that you tried and the results. The following list identifies some common steps to determine the cause of the problem.

Step 3: Test the Theory to Determine Cause

- Ensure the device is powered on.

- Ensure the power switch for an outlet is turned on.

- Ensure the surge protector is turned on.

- Ensure external cable connections are secure.

- Ensure that there are no disks in the floppy drive.

- Verify the boot order in BIOS setup.

Establish a Plan of Action to Resolve the Problem and Implement the Solution (4.2.1.5)

After you have determined the exact cause of the problem, establish a plan of action to resolve the problem and implement the solution. Sometimes quick procedures can correct the problem. If a quick procedure does correct the problem, verify full system functionality and, if applicable, implement preventive measures. If a quick procedure does not correct the problem, research the problem further and then return to Step 2 to establish a new theory of the probable cause.

After you have established a plan of action, you should research possible solutions. Following are possible research locations:

Step 4: Establish a Plan of Action to Resolve the Problem and Implement the Solution

- Help desk repair logs

- Other technicians

- Manufacturer FAQs

- News groups

- Computer manuals

- Device manuals

- Online forums

- Internet search

Divide larger problems into smaller problems that can be analyzed and solved individually. Prioritize solutions starting with the easiest and fastest to implement. Create a list of possible solutions and implement them one at a time. If you implement a possible solution and it does not correct the problem, reverse the action you just took and then try another solution. Continue this process until you have found the appropriate solution.

Verify Full System Functionality and, If Applicable, Implement Preventive Measures (4.2.1.6)

After the repairs to the computer have been completed, continue the troubleshooting process by verifying full system functionality and implementing the preventive measures needed. Verifying full system functionality confirms that you have solved the original problem and ensures that you have not created another problem while repairing the computer. Whenever possible, have the customer verify the solution and system functionality. The following list shows steps you can use to determine full system functionality:

Step 5:   Verify Full System Functionality and, If Applicable, Implement Preventive Measures

- Reboot the computer.

- Ensure multiple applications work properly.

- Verify network and Internet connections.

- Print a document from one application.

- Ensure all attached devices work properly.

- Ensure no error messages are received.

Document Findings, Actions, and Outcomes (4.2.1.7)

After the repairs to the computer have been completed, finish the troubleshooting process with the customer. Communicate the problem and the solution to the customer verbally and in writing. The following list shows the steps to be taken when you have finished a repair:

Step 6:   Document Findings, Actions, and Outcomes

- Discuss the solution implemented with the customer.

- Have the customer verify that the problem has been solved.

- Provide the customer with all paperwork.

- Document the steps taken to solve the problem in the work order and in the technician's journal.

- Document any components used in the repair.

- Document the amount of time spent to resolve the problem.

Verify the solution with the customer. If the customer is available, demonstrate how the solution has corrected the computer problem. Have the customer test the solution and try to reproduce the problem. When the customer can verify that the problem has been resolved, you can complete the documentation for the repair in the work order and in your journal. Include the following information in the documentation:

- Description of the problem
- Steps to resolve the problem
- Components used in the repair

PC Common Problems and Solutions (4.2.2.1)

Computer problems can be attributed to hardware, software, networks, or some combination of the three. You will resolve some types of problems more often than others. Common hardware problems include the following:

- **Storage device:** Storage device problems are often related to loose or incorrect cable connections, incorrect drive and media formats, and incorrect jumper and BIOS settings, as shown in Table 4-2.

- **Motherboard and internal component:** These problems are often caused by incorrect or loose cables, failed components, incorrect drivers, and corrupted updates, as shown in Table 4-3.

- **Power supply:** Power problems are often caused by a faulty power supply, loose connections, and inadequate wattage, as shown in Table 4-4.

- **CPU and memory:** Processor and memory problems are often caused by faulty installations, incorrect BIOS settings, inadequate cooling and ventilation, and compatibility issues, as shown in Table 4-5.

Table 4-2   Common Problems and Solutions for Storage Devices

Identify the Problem	Probable Causes	Possible Solutions
The computer does not recognize a storage device.	The power cable is loose.	Secure the power cable.
	The data cable is loose.	Secure the data cable.
	The jumpers are set incorrectly.	Reset the jumpers.
	The storage device has failed.	Replace the storage device.
	The storage device settings in BIOS are incorrect.	Reset the storage device settings in BIOS.

Identify the Problem	Probable Causes	Possible Solutions
The floppy disk drive will not read media or the drive light stays on constantly.	The power cable or the data cable connection is loose. Pin 1 on the data cable is not connected to Pin 1 on the drive. The FDD settings in BIOS are incorrect. The disc is bad or not formatted. The disc is inserted upside down.	Secure the power cable or the data cable to the drive and the motherboard. Correctly connect the data cable. Reset the FDD settings in BIOS. Try another disc or format the disc. Re-insert the disc correctly.
The computer fails to recognize an optical disc.	The optical drive is faulty. The disc is inserted upside down. There is more than one disc inserted in the drive. The disc is damaged. The disc is the wrong format.	Replace the optical drive. Insert the disc correctly. Ensure that there is only one disc inserted in the drive. Replace the disc. Use the correct type of disc.
The computer will not eject the optical disc.	The optical drive is jammed. The optical drive has been locked by software. The optical drive is faulty.	Insert a pin in the small hole next to the eject button on the drive to open the tray. Reboot the computer. Replace the optical drive.
The computer does not recognize a SCSI drive.	The SCSI drive has an incorrect SCSI ID. The SCSI termination is not set correctly. The external SCSI drive was not powered on prior to booting the computer.	Reconfigure the SCSI ID. Ensure that the SCSI chain is terminated at the correct end points. Turn on the drive before booting the computer.
The computer does not recognize a removable external drive.	The removable external drive is faulty. The removable external drive is not seated properly. The external ports are disabled in the BIOS settings.	Replace the removable external drive. Remove and re-insert the drive. Enable the ports in the BIOS settings.

Identify the Problem	Probable Causes	Possible Solutions
A media reader cannot read a memory card that works properly in the camera.	The media reader does not support the memory card type.	Use a different memory card type.
	The media reader is not connected correctly.	Ensure the media reader is connected correctly in the computer.
	The media reader is not configured properly in the BIOS settings.	Reconfigure the media reader in the BIOS settings.
	The media reader is faulty.	Install a known good media reader.

Table 4-3   Common Problems and Solutions for Motherboards and Internal Components

Identify the Problem	Probable Causes	Possible Solutions
The clock on the computer is no longer keeping the correct time or the BIOS settings are changing when the computer is rebooted.	The CMOS battery may be loose.	Secure the battery.
	The CMOS battery may be failing.	Replace the battery.
Retrieving or saving data from the USB flash drive is slow.	The motherboard does not support USB 3.0.	Update the motherboard or USB flash drive to support USB 3.0.
	The USB flash drive does not support USB 3.0.	Set the port speed in the BIOS setting to high speed.
	The port is set to full speed in the BIOS setting.	
After updating the BIOS firmware, the computer will not start.	The BIOS firmware update did not install correctly.	Contact the motherboard manufacturer to obtain a new BIOS chip. (If the mother board has two BIOS chips, the second BIOS chip can be used.
The computer displays the incorrect CPU information when the computer boots.	The motherboard has incorrect jumper settings.	Set the appropriate CPU jumper settings on the motherboard.
	The CPU settings are not correct in the advanced BIOS settings.	Set the advanced BIOS settings correctly for the CPU.
	BIOS does not properly recognize the CPU.	Update the BIOS.

Identify the Problem	Probable Causes	Possible Solutions
The hard drive LED on the front of the computer does not light.	The hard drive LED cable is not connected or is loose.	Reconnect hard drive LED cable to motherboard.
	The hard drive LED cable is incorrectly oriented to the front case panel connections	Correctly orient the hard drive LED cable to the front case panel connection and reconnect.
The built-in NIC has stopped working on a computer.	The NIC hardware has failed.	Add a new NIC to an open expansion slot.
The computer does not display any video after installing a new PCI-E video card.	BIOS settings are set to use the built-in video.	Disable the built-in video in the BIOS settings.
	The cable is still connected to the built-in video.	Connect the cable to the new video card.
	The new video card is faulty.	Install a known good video card.
The new sound card does not work.	The speakers are not connected to the correct jack.	Connect the speakers to the correct jack.
	The audio is muted.	Unmute the audio.
	The sound card is faulty.	Install a known good sound card.
	BIOS settings are set to use the onboard sound device.	Disable the onboard audio device in the BIOS settings.

Table 4-4   Common Problems and Solutions for Power Supplies

Identify the Problem	Probable Causes	Possible Solutions
The computer will not turn on.	The computer is not plugged in to the AC outlet.	Plug the computer into a known good AC outlet.
	The AC outlet is faulty.	Use a known good power cord.
	The power cord is faulty.	Turn on the power supply switch.
	The power supply switch is not turned on.	Set the power supply switch to the correct voltage setting.
	The power supply switch is set to the incorrect voltage.	Correctly orient the power button to the front case panel connector and reconnect.
	The power button is not connected correctly to the front panel connector.	Install a known good power supply.
	The power supply has failed.	

Identify the Problem	Probable Causes	Possible Solutions
The computer reboots and turns off unexpectedly or there is smoke or the smell of burning electronics.	The power supply is starting to fail.	Replace the power supply.

Table 4-5   Common Problems and Solutions for CPUs and Memory

Identify the Problem	Probable Causes	Possible Solutions
The computer will not boot or it locks up.	The CPU has overheated.	Reinstall the CPU.
	The CPU fan is failing.	Replace the CPU fan.
	The CPU has failed.	Add fan(s) to the case.
		Replace the CPU.
The CPU fan is making an unusual noise.	The CPU fan is failing.	Replace the CPU fan.
The computer reboots without warning, locks up, or displays error messages.	The front-side bus is set too high.	Reset to the factory default settings for the motherboard.
	The CPU multiplier is set too high.	Lower the front-side bus settings.
	The CPU voltage is set too high.	Lower the multiplier settings.
		Lower the CPU voltage settings.
After upgrading from a single core CPU to a dual core CPU, the computer runs more slowly and only shows one CPU graph in the Task Manager.	The BIOS does not recognize the dual core CPU.	Update the BIOS firmware to support the dual core CPU.
A CPU will not install onto the motherboard.	The CPU is the incorrect type.	Replace the CPU with a CPU that matches the motherboard socket type.
The computer does not recognize the RAM that was added.	The new RAM is faulty.	Replace the RAM.
	The incorrect type of RAM was installed.	Install the correct type of RAM.
	The new RAM is loose in the memory slot.	Secure the RAM in the memory slot.

Identify the Problem	Probable Causes	Possible Solutions
After upgrading Windows, the computer runs very slowly.	The computer does not have enough RAM. The video card does not have enough memory.	Install additional RAM. Install a video card that has more memory.
A computer with both DDR2 and DDR3 RAM installed only recognizes DDR3 RAM.	The motherboard does not support the installation of both DDR2 and DDR3 RAM.	Check the motherboard manual to see if the computer will support both types of RAM simultaneously.

Summary (4.3.1)

This chapter discussed the concepts of preventive maintenance and the trouble-shooting process, including the following important points:

- Regular preventive maintenance reduces hardware and software problems.

- Before beginning any repair, back up the data on a computer.

- The troubleshooting process is a guideline to help you solve computer problems in an efficient manner:

  1. Identify the problem.

  2. Establish a theory of probable cause.

  3. Test the theory to determine cause.

  4. Establish a plan of action to resolve the problem and implement the solution.

  5. Verify Full system functionality and, if applicable, implement preventive measures.

  6. Document findings, actions, and outcomes.

  7. Document everything that you try, even if it fails. The documentation that you create is a useful resource for you and other technicians.

Summary of Exercises

There are no labs or worksheets associated with this chapter.

Check Your Understanding

You can find the answers to these questions in Appendix A, "Answers to 'Check Your Understanding' Questions."

1. After a problem is identified, what is the next step for the troubleshooter?

   A. Establish a theory of probable cause.

   B. Determine the exact cause.

   C. Implement a solution.

   D. Document the findings.

   E. Verify the solution.

2. Which procedure is recommended when cleaning inside a computer?

   A. Remove the CPU before cleaning.

   B. Hold the CPU fan to prevent it from spinning and blow it with compressed air.

   C. Clean the hard drive heads with a cotton swab.

   D. Invert the can of compressed air while spraying.

3. What is a symptom of a failing power supply?

   A. The computer sometimes does not turn on.

   B. The display has only a blinking cursor.

   C. The computer displays a POST error code.

   D. The power cord will not attach properly to either the power supply or wall outlet or both.

4. What are two common problems that are encountered with PATA hard drives? (Choose two.)

   A. Loose cable connections

   B. Incorrect jumper settings

   C. Incorrect drivers

   D. Overheating

   E. Dirty read and write heads

5. An employee mentions that opening a large document file is taking longer than usual. The desktop support technician suspects that there might be a fault in the hard disk. What should the technician do next?

   A. Perform the disk cleanup procedure.

   B. Back up the user data from the workstation.

   C. Contact a data-recovery company for service.

   D. Replace the hard disk with a new one to pinpoint the exact problem.

6. An employee reports that the output of a workstation display is distorted. The technician checks the manufacturer website and downloads the latest version of the video driver. After the video driver is installed, what should the technician do next?

   A. Schedule the next system checkup with the employee.

   B. Log the previous and current version numbers of the video driver.

   C. Move the display card to another slot to see if the video performs better.

   D. Open a video-editing application to verify the video performance.

7. After a workstation is upgraded from a single core to a new dual core CPU, a user complains that the workstation seems to be performing slower. The workstation is running Windows XP Professional as its operating system. A support technician opens the Task Manager - Resource Monitor and notices that only one CPU core is displayed. What is the possible cause of the problem?

   A. The new CPU is the wrong type.

   B. The RAM installed is insufficient.

   C. The BIOS does not support a dual-core CPU.

   D. The operating system needs to be upgraded in order to support a dual-core CPU.

8. What is a primary benefit of preventive maintenance on a PC?

   A. It extends the life of the components.

   B. It enhances the troubleshooting processes.

   C. It simplifies PC use for the end user.

   D. It assists the user in software development.

9. What is the best way to determine if a CPU fan is spinning properly?

   A. Spin the blades of the fan quickly with a finger.

   B. Spray compressed air on the fan to make the blades spin.

   C. Visually inspect the fan when the power is on to ensure it is spinning.

   D. Listen for the sound of the fan spinning when the power is on.

10. A user has noticed that the hard drive LED on the front of the computer has stopped working. However, the computer seems to be functioning normally. What is the most likely cause of the problem?

    A. The hard drive data cable is malfunctioning.

    B. The motherboard BIOS needs to be updated.

    C. The hard drive LED cable has come loose from the motherboard.

    D. The power supply is not providing enough voltage to the motherboard.

CHAPTER 5

Operating Systems

Objectives

Upon completion of this chapter, you will be able to answer the following questions:

- What is the purpose of an operating system?

- How do different operating systems compare with one another based on purpose, limitations, and compatibilities?

- How do you determine the appropriate operating system based on customer needs?

- How do you install an operating system?

- How do I upgrade operating systems?

- How do you navigate within an operating system GUI?

- What are some common preventive maintenance techniques for operating systems, and how are they applied?

- What can be done to troubleshoot operating systems?

Key Terms

This chapter uses the following key terms. You can find the definitions in the Glossary.

operating system (OS)   page 181

multitasking   page 181

multiprocessing   page 181

multithreading   page 181

device driver   page 182

plug-and-play (PnP)   page 182

command-line interface (CLI)   page 182

graphical user interface (GUI)   page 182

application programming interface (API)   page 183

Open Graphics Library (OpenGL)   page 183

DirectX   page 183

Windows API   page 183

Java APIs   page 183

Registers   page 183

Microsoft Windows   page 185

Apple OS X   page 186

Linux   page 186

network operating system (NOS)   page 186

hardware compatibility list (HCL)   page 192

Upgrade Advisor   page 192

Windows User State Migration Tool (USMT)   page 195

Windows Easy Transfer   page 195

primary partition   page 197

active partition   page 197

extended partition   page 197

logical drive   page 197

Introduction 5.0.1.1

The *operating system (OS)* controls almost all functions on a computer. In this chapter, you learn about the components, functions, and terminology related to the Windows 7, Windows Vista, and Windows XP operating systems.

Modern Operating Systems (5.1)

Some basic terms and functions are common to computer operating systems. All computers rely on an OS to provide the interface for the interaction between users, applications, and hardware. The computer boots the OS and manages the file system. Operating systems can support more than one user, task, or CPU.

Terms (5.1.1.1)

To understand the capabilities of an operating system, it is important to first understand some basic terms. The following terms are often used when describing operating systems:

- **Multiuser:** Two or more users have individual accounts that allow them to work with programs and peripheral devices at the same time.

- *Multitasking*: The computer is capable of operating multiple applications at the same time.

- *Multiprocessing*: The operating system can support two or more CPUs.

- *Multithreading*: Programs can be broken into smaller parts that are loaded as needed by the operating system. Multithreading allows different parts of a program to be run at the same time.

Basic Functions of an Operating System (5.1.1.2)

Regardless of the size and complexity of the computer and the operating system, all operating systems perform the same four basic functions:

- Control hardware access

- Manage files and folders

- Provide a user interface

- Manage applications

Hardware Access

The OS manages the interaction between applications and the hardware. To access and communicate with each hardware component, the OS uses a program called a *device driver*. When a hardware device is installed, the OS locates and installs the device driver for that component. Assigning system resources and installing drivers are performed with a *plug-and-play (PnP)* process. The OS then configures the device and updates the Registry, which is a database that contains all the information about the computer.

If the OS cannot locate a device driver, a technician must install the driver manually either by using the media that came with the device or downloading it from the manufacturer's website.

File and Folder Management

The OS creates a file structure on the hard disk drive to store data. A file is a block of related data that is given a single name and treated as a single unit. Program and data files are grouped together in a directory. The files and directories are organized for easy retrieval and use. Directories can be kept inside other directories. These nested directories are referred to as subdirectories. Directories are called folders in Windows operating systems, and subdirectories are called subfolders.

User Interface

The OS enables the user to interact with the software and hardware. Operating systems include two types of user interfaces:

- *Command-line interface (CLI)*: The user types commands at a prompt, as shown in Figure 5-1.

- *Graphical user interface (GUI)*: The user interacts with menus and icons, as shown in Figure 5-2.

Figure 5-1 Command-Line Interface

Figure 5-2   Graphical User Interface

Application Management

The OS locates an application and loads it into the RAM of the computer. Applications are software programs, such as word processors, databases, spreadsheets, and games. The OS allocates available system resources to running applications.

To ensure that a new application is compatible with an OS, programmers follow a set of guidelines known as an *application programming interface (API)*. An API allows programs to access the resources managed by the operating system in a consistent and reliable manner. Here are some examples of APIs:

- *Open Graphics Library (OpenGL)*: Cross-platform standard specification for multimedia graphics

- *DirectX*: Collection of APIs related to multimedia tasks for Microsoft Windows

- *Windows API*: Allows applications from older versions of Windows to operate on newer versions

- *Java APIs*: Collection of APIs related to the development of Java programming

Processor Architecture (5.1.1.3)

The way that a CPU handles information can affect the performance of the OS. Two common architectures used to process data are as follows:

- **x86:** A 32-bit architecture that processes multiple instructions with a single request. An x86 processor uses fewer registers than an x64 processor. *Registers* are storage areas used by the CPU when performing calculations. An x86 processor can support a 32-bit operating system.

■ **x64:** This 64-bit architecture adds additional registers specifically for instructions that use a 64-bit address space. The additional registers allow the CPU to process instructions much faster than x86. The x64 processor is backward compatible with the x86 processor. An x64 processor can support 32-bit and 64-bit operating systems.

A 32-bit OS is capable of addressing only 4 GB of system memory, while a 64-bit OS can address more than 128 GB. Memory management differs between the two systems. A 64-bit system has better performance. A 64-bit OS also includes features that provide additional security. Table 5-1 summarizes the 32-bit and 64-bit Windows operating systems

Table 5-1   32-bit and 64-bit Compatibility in Windows

Windows Operating System	32-bit	64-bit
Windows 7 Starter	X	
Windows 7 Home Premium	X	X
Windows 7 Professional	X	X
Windows 7 Ultimate	X	X
Windows Vista Home Basic	X	X
Windows Vista Home Premium	X	X
Windows Vista Business	X	X
Windows Vista Ultimate	X	X
Windows XP Professional	X	X
Windows XP Home	X	
Windows XP Media Center	X	

Types of Operating Systems (5.1.2)

The choice of which operating system to install is a significant one. It is an important decision because the OS controls the major functions of the computer. One of the decision points in choosing the operating system to install is the intended use of the computer and its role in the network. In this section two types of operating systems are explained, the desktop operating system and the network operating system.

Desktop Operating Systems (5.1.2.1)

A technician might be asked to choose and install an OS for a customer. There are two distinct types of operating systems: desktop and network. A desktop operating system is intended for use in a small office, home office (SOHO) environment with a limited number of users. A network operating system (NOS) is designed for a corporate environment serving multiple users with a wide range of needs.

A desktop OS has the following characteristics:

- Supports a single user

- Runs single-user applications

- Shares files and folders on a small network with limited security

In the current software market, the most commonly used desktop operating systems fall into three groups: Microsoft Windows, Apple OS X, and Linux. This chapter focuses on Microsoft operating systems.

Microsoft Windows

Microsoft Windows is one of the most popular operating systems today. The following versions of Windows are available:

- **Windows 7 Starter:** Used on netbook computers to make networking easy

- **Windows 7 Home Premium:** Used on home computers to easily share media

- **Windows 7 Professional:** Used on small business computers to secure critical information and to make routine tasks easier to complete

- **Windows 7 Enterprise:** Used on large business computers to provide more enhanced productivity, security, and management features

- **Windows 7 Ultimate:** Used on computers to combine the ease of use of Windows 7 Home Premium with the business capabilities of Windows 7 Professional and provide added data security

- **Windows Vista Home Basic:** Used on home computers for basic computing

- **Windows Vista Home Premium:** Used on home computers to expand personal productivity and digital entertainment beyond the basics

- **Windows Vista Business:** Used on small business computers for enhanced security and enhanced mobility technology

- **Windows Vista Enterprise:** Used on large business computers to provide more enhanced productivity, security, and management features

- **Windows Vista Ultimate:** Used on computers to combine all the needs of both home and business users

- **Windows XP Professional:** Used on most computers that connect to a Windows Server on a network

- **Windows XP Home:** Used on home computers and has limited security

- **Windows XP Media Center:** Used on entertainment computers for viewing movies and listening to music

- **Windows XP 64-bit Professional:** Used for computers with 64-bit processors

Apple OS X

Apple computers are proprietary and use an operating system called OS X. OS X is designed to be a user-friendly GUI operating system. Current versions of OS X are based on a customized version of UNIX.

Linux

Linux is based on UNIX, which was introduced in the late 1960s and is one of the oldest operating systems. Linus Torvalds designed Linux in 1991 as an open-source OS. Open-source programs allow the source code to be distributed and changed by anyone as a free download or by developers at a much lower cost than other operating systems.

Note

In this course, all command paths refer to Microsoft Windows, unless otherwise noted.

Network Operating Systems (5.1.2.2)

A *network operating system (NOS)* contains additional features to increase functionality and manageability in a networked environment. A NOS has the following characteristics:

- Supports multiple users

- Runs multiuser applications

- Provides increased security compared to desktop operating systems

A NOS provides network resources to computers, including the following:

- Server applications, such as shared databases

- Centralized data storage

- Centralized repository of user accounts and resources on the network

- Network print queue

- Redundant storage systems, such as RAID and backups

The following are examples of network operating systems:

- Windows Server

- Red Hat Linux

- Mac OS X Server

Worksheet 5.1.2.3: Search NOS Certifications and Jobs

In this worksheet, you use the Internet, a newspaper, or magazines to gather information about network operating system certifications and jobs that require these certifications. Refer to the worksheet in *IT Essentials: PC Hardware and Software Lab Manual*, Fifth Edition.

Customer Requirements for an Operating System (5.1.3)

Many factors need to be assessed when choosing an operating system. Conducting the proper research to make a sound decision is crucial. This section provides guidelines for how to conduct the research and considerations to be studied when making the choice to upgrade.

OS-Compatible Applications and Environments (5.1.3.1)

Understanding how a computer will be used is important when recommending an OS to a customer. The OS must be compatible with the existing hardware and the required applications. Before recommending an OS to a customer, investigate the types of applications that the customer will be using and whether new computers will be purchased.

To make an OS recommendation, a technician must review budget constraints, learn how the computer will be used, and determine which types of applications will be installed. These are some guidelines to help determine the best OS for a customer:

- Does the customer use off-the-shelf applications for this computer? Off-the-shelf applications specify a list of compatible operating systems on the application package.

- Does the customer use customized applications that were programmed specifically for the customer? If the customer is using a customized application, the programmer of that application specifies which OS to use.

Minimum Hardware Requirements and Compatibility with the OS Platform (5.1.3.2)

Operating systems have minimum hardware requirements that must be met for the OS to install and function correctly.

Identify the equipment that your customer has in place. If hardware upgrades are necessary to meet the minimum requirements for an OS, conduct a cost analysis to determine the best course of action. In some cases, it might be less expensive for the customer to purchase a new computer than to upgrade the current system. In other cases, it might be cost effective to upgrade one or more of the following components:

- RAM
- Hard disk drive
- CPU
- Video adapter card
- Motherboard

Note

If the application requirements exceed the hardware requirements of the OS, you must meet the additional requirements for the application to function properly.

After you have determined the minimum hardware requirements, ensure that all hardware in the computer is compatible with the OS that you have selected for the customer.

Microsoft Compatibility Center

Windows 7 and Windows Vista have an online Compatibility Center that allows technicians to check the compatibility of both software and hardware, as shown in Figure 5-3. The tool provides a detailed inventory of hardware that has been tested and proven to work with Windows 7 and Windows Vista. If any of the customer's existing hardware is not on the list, those components might need to be upgraded.

The Microsoft Compatibility Center does not support Windows XP. Windows XP has a hardware compatibility list (HCL) that can be found on the manufacturer's website.

Note

An HCL specified for an OS might not be continuously maintained and therefore may not contain all compatible hardware.

Figure 5-3   Windows Compatibility Center

Comparing OS Requirements (5.1.3.3)

When selecting an operating system to install, just knowing that an operating system is compatible with the hardware in a computer is not enough. It is also necessary to be aware of the hardware requirements of the operating system. Table 5-2 outlines requirements of various Windows OSes.

Table 5-2   Installation Requirements for Windows Operating Systems

	CPU	RAM	HHD	Video Adapter Card
Windows 7 Starter	1 GHz or faster 32-bit (x86) or 64-bit (x64) processor	1 GB RAM	16 GB of available space (32-bit)	DirectX 9 graphics device with WDDM 1.0 or later driver
Windows 7 Home Premium	1 GHz or faster 32-bit (x86) or 64-bit (x64) processor	1 GB RAM (32-bit) or 2 GB RAM (64-bit)	16 GB of available space (32-bit) or 20 GB (64-bit)	
Windows 7 Professional	1 GHz or faster 32-bit (x86) or 64-bit (x64) processor	1 GB RAM (32-bit) or 2 GB RAM (64-bit)	16 GB of available space (32-bit) or 20 GB (64-bit)	DirectX 9 graphics device with WDDM 1.0 or later driver
Windows 7 Ultimate	GHz 32-bit (x86) or 64-bit (x64) processor	1 GB RAM (32-bit) or 2 GB RAM (64-bit)	16 GB of available space (32-bit) or 20 GB (64-bit)	DirectX 9 graphics device with WDDM 1.0 or later driver
Windows 7 Enterprise	GHz 32-bit (x86) or 64-bit (x64) processor	1 GB RAM (32-bit) or 2 GB RAM (64-bit)	16 GB of available space (32-bit) or 20 GB (64-bit)	DirectX 9 graphics device with WDDM 1.0 or later driver

	CPU	RAM	HHD	Video Adapter Card
Windows Vista Home Basic	1 GHz 32-bit (x86) or 64-bit (x64) processor	512 MB of RAM	20 GB hard drive with at least 15 GB available space	DirectX 9 graphics and 32 MB of graphics memory
Windows Vista Home Premium	1 GHZ or 32-bit (x86) or 64-bit (x64) processor	1 GB RAM	40 GB hard drive with at least 15 GB available space	Supports graphics device with: WDDM driver 128 MB of graphics memory (minimum) Pixel Shader 2.0 in hardware 32 bits per pixel
Windows Vista Business	1 GHz 32-bit (x86) or 64-bit (x64) processor	1 GB RAM	40 GB hard drive with at least 15 GB available space	Supports graphics device with: WDDM driver 128 MB of graphics memory (minimum) Pixel Shader 2.0 in hardware 32 bits per pixel
Windows Vista Ultimate	1 GHz 32-bit (x86) or 64-bit (x64) processor	1 GB RAM	40 GB hard drive with at least 15 GB available space	Supports graphics device with: WDDM driver 128 MB of graphics memory (minimum) Pixel Shader 2.0 in hardware 32 bits per pixel
Windows Vista Enterprise	1 GHz 32-bit (x86) or 64-bit (x64) processor	1 GB RAM	40 GB hard drive with at least 15 GB available space	Supports graphics device with: WDDM driver 128 MB of graphics memory (minimum) Pixel Shader 2.0 in hardware 32 bits per pixel

	CPU	RAM	HHD	Video Adapter Card
Windows XP Professional	233 MHZ minimum required 300 MHZ or higher recommended Intel Pentium/ Celeron Family64 MB minimum required 128 MB or higher recommended AMD K6/Athlon/ Duran family or compatible	64 MB minimum required 128 MB or higher recommended	1.5 GB available hard disk space minimum required (More is recommended if installing over a network.)	Super VGA (800 x 600) minimum required higher resolution recommended
Windows XP Home	233 MHZ minimum required 300 MHZ or higher recommended Intel Pentium/ Celeron Family64 MB minimum required 128 MB or higher recommended AMD K6/Athlon/ Duran family or compatible	64 MB minimum required 128 MB or higher recommended	1.5 GB available hard disk space minimum required (More is recommended if installing over a network.)	Super VGA (800 x 600) minimum required higher resolution recommended
Windows XP Media Center	1.6 GHZ or higher	256 MB	1.5 GB available hard disk space minimum required (More is recommended if installing over a network.)	Support for Direct X graphics

Operating System Upgrades (5.1.4)

While there are many reasons to upgrade an operating system, the decision to do so should be a well thought-out and carefully evaluated plan. This section discusses reasons for upgrading, steps to choose the best upgrade path, and methods for upgrading.

Checking OS Compatibility (5.1.4.1)

An OS must be upgraded periodically to remain compatible with the latest hardware and software. It is also necessary to upgrade an OS when a manufacturer stops supporting it. Upgrading an OS can increase performance. New hardware products often require that the latest OS version be installed to operate correctly. While upgrading an OS may be expensive, you can gain enhanced functionality through new features and support for newer hardware.

Before upgrading the operating system, check the minimum hardware requirements of the new OS to ensure that it can be installed successfully on the computer. Also check the Windows Compatibility Center for Windows 7 and Vista or the Windows XP *hardware compatibility list (HCL)* to ensure that the hardware is compatible with the new OS.

Note

When newer versions of an OS are released, support for older versions is eventually withdrawn.

Upgrade Advisor

Microsoft provides a free utility called the *Upgrade Advisor*, which scans the system for hardware and software incompatibility issues in hardware before upgrading to newer editions of the Windows OS. The Upgrade Advisor creates a report of any problems and then guides you through the steps to resolve them. You can download the Upgrade Advisor from the Microsoft Windows website.

How To

To use the Windows 7 Upgrade Advisor, follow these steps:

Step 1.   Download and run the Windows 7 Upgrade Advisor from the Microsoft website.

Step 2.   Click **Start Check**. The program scans your computer hardware, devices, and installed software. A compatibility report is presented.

Step 3.   Click **Save Report** if you want to keep it or print it later.

Step 4.   Examine the report. Record any recommended fixes for the issues found.

Step 5.   Click **Close**.

After making the changes to hardware, devices, or software, Microsoft recommends running the Upgrade Advisor again before installing the new OS. Figure 5-4 shows the Windows 7 Upgrade Advisor.

Figure 5-4   Windows 7 Upgrade Advisor

Windows OS Upgrades (5.1.4.2)

The process of upgrading a computer's OS can be quicker than performing a new installation. The upgrade process varies depending on the version. For example, the Windows 7 setup utility replaces existing Windows Vista files with Windows 7 files. However, the existing applications and settings are saved.

The version of an OS determines available upgrade options. For example, a 32-bit OS cannot be upgraded to a 64-bit OS. Another example is that Windows XP cannot be upgraded to Windows 7. Before attempting an upgrade, check the OS developer's website for a list of possible upgrade paths. Table 5-3 shows the upgrade paths for Windows operating system upgrades.

Table 5-3   Operating Systems Upgrades

OS can upgrade to	Windows 2000	Windows XP	Windows Vista	Windows 7
Windows 98	Supported	Supported	Supported	Unsupported
Windows 2000	N/A	Supported	Supported	Unsupported
Windows XP	N/A	N/A	Supported	Unsupported
Windows Vista	N/A	N/A	N/A	Supported

Note

Before performing an upgrade, back up all data in case a problem occurs with the installation.

How To

To upgrade the Windows Vista OS to Windows 7, follow these steps:

Step 1.   Insert the Windows 7 installation disc into the optical drive. The Set Up window appears.

Step 2.   Select the **Install now** option.

Step 3.   You are prompted to download any important updates for installation.

Step 4.   Agree to the End User License Agreement (EULA), and click **Next**.

Step 5.   Click **Upgrade**. The system begins copying the installation files.

Step 6.   Follow the prompts to complete the upgrade. When the install is complete, the computer restarts.

Note

Before you can upgrade from Windows XP to Windows Vista, you must install Windows XP Service Pack 2 or 3.

How To

To upgrade the OS to Windows Vista, follow these steps:

Step 1.   Insert the Windows Vista installation disc into the optical drive. The Set Up window appears.

Step 2.   Select **Install Windows Vista**.

Step 3.   You are prompted to download any important updates.

Step 4.   Enter your product key, and then agree to the End User License Agreement (EULA). Click Next.

Step 5.   Click **Upgrade**. The system begins copying the installation files.

Step 6.   Follow the prompts to complete the upgrade. When the install is complete, the computer restarts.

How To

To upgrade the OS to Windows XP, follow these steps:

Step 1.   Insert the Windows XP installation disc into the optical drive.

Step 2.   Select **Start > Run**. (The Setup Wizard might automatically start when the disc is inserted in the optical drive.)

Step 3.   In the Run box, where D is the drive for the optical drive, type **D:\i386\winnt32** and press **Enter**. The Welcome to the Windows XP Setup Wizard displays.

Step 4.   Choose **Upgrade to Windows XP** and click **Next**. The License Agreement page displays.

Step 5.   Read the license agreement and click the button to accept this agreement.

Step 6.   Click **Next**. The Upgrading to the Windows XP NTFS File System page displays.

Step 7.   Follow the prompts to complete the upgrade. When the install is complete, the computer restarts.

Data Migration (5.1.4.3)

When a new installation is required, user data must be migrated from the old OS to the new one. There are three tools available to transfer data and settings. The tool you select depends on your level of experience and your requirements.

User State Migration Tool

The *Windows User State Migration Tool (USMT)* migrates all user files and settings to the new OS, as shown in Figure 5-5. Download and install USMT from Microsoft. Use the software to create a store of user files and settings that are saved in a different location from the OS. After the new OS is installed, download and install USMT again to the new installation to load the user files and settings on the new OS.

Figure 5-5   User State Migration Tool

Windows Easy Transfer

If a user is switching from an old computer to a new one, you can use *Windows Easy Transfer* to migrate personal files and settings. You can perform the file transfer using a USB cable, a CD or DVD, a USB flash drive, an external drive, or a network connection.

After running Windows Easy Transfer, you can view a log of the files transferred. To access Windows Easy Transfer in Windows 7 or Windows Vista, use the following path:

Start > All Programs > Accessories > System Tools > Windows Easy Transfer

On Windows XP, you must first download the Windows Easy Transfer program. After it has been downloaded, access it using the following path:

Start > All Programs > Windows Easy Transfer

Windows Easy Transfer replaced the Windows XP File and Settings Transfer Wizard.

File and Settings Transfer Wizard for Windows XP

The File and Settings Transfer Wizard for Windows XP transfers files and settings from an old computer to a new computer. It allows the user to select which files and settings to transfer. You can transfer files using storage media, a cabled connection, or a network connection. To access the Files and Settings Transfer Wizard, use the following path:

Start > All Programs > Accessories > System Tools > Files and Settings Transfer Wizard

Lab 5.1.4.4: Data Migration in Windows 7

In this lab, you use Windows Easy Transfer to transfer files. Refer to Lab 5.1.4.4 in *IT Essentials: PC Hardware and Software Lab Manual*, Fifth Edition.

Lab 5.1.4.5: Data Migration in Windows Vista

In this lab, you use Windows Easy Transfer to transfer files. Refer to Lab 5.1.4.5 in *IT Essentials: PC Hardware and Software Lab Manual*, Fifth Edition.

Lab 5.1.4.6: Data Migration in Windows XP

In this lab, you use Files and Settings Transfer Wizard to transfer files. Refer to Lab 5.1.4.6 in *IT Essentials: PC Hardware and Software Lab Manual*, Fifth Edition.

Operating System Installation (5.2)

This section discusses preparation and options for installing a Windows operating system. Installing an operating system involves an understanding of both the software and hardware that is compatible with the operating system as well as the process for readying components for installation.

Hard Drive Partitioning (5.2.1.1)

As a technician, you might have to perform a clean installation of an OS. Perform a clean install in the following situations:

- When a computer is passed from one employee to another
- When the OS is corrupt
- When the primary hard drive is replaced in a computer

The installation and initial booting of the OS is called the operating system setup. Although it is possible to install an OS over a network from a server or from a local hard drive, the most common installation method for a home or small business is with CDs or DVDs. To install an OS from a CD or DVD, first configure the BIOS setup to boot the system from the CD or DVD.

Important

If the hardware is not supported by the OS, you may need to install third-party drivers when performing a clean installation.

Partitioning

A hard drive is divided into specific areas called partitions. Each partition is a logical storage unit that can be formatted to store information, such as data files and applications. During the installation process, most operating systems automatically partition and format available hard drive space.

A technician should understand the process and terms relating to hard drive setup:

- *Primary partition*: This primary partition containing the operating system files is usually the first partition. There can be up to four primary partitions per hard drive. A primary partition cannot be subdivided into smaller sections.

- *Active partition*: The OS uses the active partition to boot the computer. Only one primary partition per disk can be marked active. In most cases, the C: drive is the active partition and contains the boot and system files. Some users create additional partitions to organize files or to be able to dual-boot the computer.

- *Extended partition*: The extended partition normally uses the remaining free space on a hard drive or takes the place of a primary partition. There can be only one extended partition per hard drive, but it can be subdivided into smaller sections called logical drives.

- *Logical drive*: A logical drive is a section of an extended partition. It can be used to separate information for administrative purposes.

- *Basic disk*: A basic disk (the default) contains primary and extended partitions, as well as logical drives. A basic disk is limited to four partitions.

- **Dynamic disk:** A dynamic disk has the ability to create volumes that span across more than one disk. The size of the partitions can be changed after they have been set. Free space can be added from the same disk or a different disk, allowing a user to efficiently store large files. After a partition has been extended, it cannot be shrunk without deleting the entire partition.

- *Formatting*: This process prepares a file system in a partition for files to be stored.

- *Sector*: A sector contains 512 bytes.

- *Cluster*: A cluster is also called a file allocation unit. It is the smallest unit of space used for storing data. It is made up of one or more sectors.

- *Track*: A track is one complete circle that can contain data on one side of a hard drive platter. A track is broken into groups of sectors.

- *Cylinder*: A cylinder is a stack of tracks lined up one on top of another to form a cylinder shape.

Figure 5-6 illustrates both the physical and logical structure of a hard drive. It shows how different parts of the hard drive relate.

Figure 5-6   Structure of a Hard Drive

Hard Drive Formatting (5.2.1.2)

A clean installation of an OS proceeds as if the disk were brand new. No information that is currently on the hard drive is preserved. The first phase of the installation process partitions and formats the hard drive. This process prepares the disk to accept the new file system. The file system provides the directory structure that organizes the user's operating system, application, configuration, and data files.

Windows operating systems use one of these file systems:

- *New Technology File System (NTFS)*: Supports partition sizes up to 16 exabytes, in theory. NTFS incorporates more file system security features and extended attributes than the FAT file system.

- *File Allocation Table, 32-bit (FAT32)*: Supports partition sizes up to 2 TB or 2048 GB. The FAT32 file system is used by Windows XP and earlier OS versions.

The preferred file system type for a clean installation of Windows is NTFS. Security is one of the most important differences between FAT32 and NTFS. NTFS can support more and larger files than FAT32 and also provides more flexible security features for files and folders. Table 5-4 is a comparison of the Windows file systems.

Table 5-4 Operating System Upgrades

	FAT32	NTFS	exFAT (FAT64)
Security	Low security	File and folder level permissions and encryption	exFAT can support access control lists that define permissions for user access.
Compatibility	Compatible with Windows 95 OEM Service Release 2 (OSR2) and newer operating systems	Compatible with Windows NT 3.1, Windows 2000 and newer operating systems	Compatible with Windows XP with SP2 or SP3, Windows 7, Windows Server 2003 SP2, Windows server 2008, and Linux.
File Size	Limit of 4 GB files. Limit of 32 GB of volumes	Limit of 16 TB files. Limit of 256 TB of volumes	Limit of 64 zetabytes (ZB) files. Limit of 512 TB of volumes.
Files per Volume	4.17 million	4.29 billion	Max 16 exabytes (EBs).

To use the extra security advantages of NTFS, you can convert partitions from FAT32 to NTFS using the convert.exe utility. To make an NTFS partition a FAT32 partition, back up the data, reformat the partition, and restore the data from a backup.

Caution

Before converting a file system, remember to back up the data.

Windows 7 and Windows Vista automatically create a partition using the entire hard drive. If a user does not create custom partitions using the New option the system formats the partition and begins installing Windows. If users create a partition, they will be able to determine the size of the partition. Windows 7 and Windows Vista have no option to select a file system. All partitions are formatted with NTFS.

Before users can install Windows XP, they must create a new partition. When users create a new partition, they are prompted to choose the size of the partition. After a partition has been created, Windows XP provides users with a choice of formatting it with the NTFS or FAT file systems. A technician should also be familiar with the following multimedia file systems:

- **exFAT (FAT 64):** Created to address some of the limitations of FAT, FAT32, and NTFS when formatting USB flash drives, such as file size and directory size

- **Compact Disc File System (CDFS):** Created specifically for optical disk media

Quick Format Versus Full Format

When installing Windows XP, you can format a partition using a quick format or full format, as shown in Figure 5-7. The quick format removes files from the partition but does not scan the disk for bad sectors. Scanning a disk for bad sectors can prevent data loss in the future. For this reason, do not use the quick format for disks that have been previously formatted. The quick format option is not available when installing Windows 7 or Windows Vista.

The full format removes files from the partition while scanning the disk for bad sectors. It is required for all new hard drives. The full format option takes more time to complete.

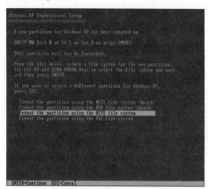

Figure 5-7   Quick Format Versus Full Format

Worksheet 5.2.1.3: Answer NTFS and FAT32 Questions

In this worksheet, you answer questions about the NTFS and FAT32 file systems. Refer to the worksheet in *IT Essentials: PC Hardware and Software Lab Manual*, Fifth Edition.

OS Installation with Default Settings (5.2.1.4)

When a computer boots with the Windows 7 installation disc (or USB flash drive), the installation wizard presents three options:

- **Install now:** Sets up and installs the Windows 7 OS.

- **What to know before installing Windows:** Opens a Help and Support window describing the Upgrade and Custom options for installing Windows 7. The window also describes how to prepare for and install Windows 7.

- **Repair your computer:** Opens the System Recovery Options utility to repair an installation. Select the Windows 7 installation that needs repair and click **Next**. You can then select from a number of recovery tools, such as Startup Repair.

Startup Repair locates and repairs problems with the OS files. If Startup Repair does not solve the problem, additional options, such as System Restore or System Image Recovery, are available.

Note

Before performing a repair installation, back up important files to a different physical location, such as a second hard drive, optical disc, or USB storage device.

For this section, select the **Install now** option. Three options are available:

- **Upgrade:** Upgrades Windows but keeps your current files, settings, and programs. You can use this option to repair an installation.

- **Custom (advanced):** Installs a clean copy of Windows in your choice of location and allows you to change disks and partitions. It is also known as a clean installation. Selecting a custom installation increases the likelihood of a successful installation.

- **Quit:** Exits Setup.

If existing Windows installations are not found, the Upgrade option is disabled.

Note

Unless you perform a clean installation of Windows 7, the previous Windows folder is kept, along with the Documents and Settings and Program Files folders. During the Windows 7 installation, these folders are moved to a folder named Windows.old. You can copy files from the previous installation to the new installation if you need them.

During an installation, you must provide the following information:

- Language to install
- Standards and formats that define currency and numerals
- Keyboard or input method
- Physical location of the installation
- Username and computer name
- Password for the administrative account
- Product key
- Time and date settings
- Network settings

Network Settings

When configuring initial network settings during installation, you are prompted to select one of the following current locations:

- Home network
- Work network
- Public network

Depending on the current location of the computer and version of the OS, you are prompted to select a method for organizing computers and sharing resources on a network. The options are HomeGroup, Workgroup, and Domain.

If **Home network** is selected, you are prompted to enter the name of a workgroup, with the option of configuring a homegroup. A workgroup provides a network structure that permits file and printer sharing. All computers in a workgroup must have the same workgroup name. A homegroup allows computers on the same network to automatically share files, such as music and pictures, as well as printers.

If **Work network** is selected, you can choose to enter the name of a domain or a workgroup. A computer on a domain is governed by a central administrator and must follow the rules and procedures set by the administrator. A domain, like a workgroup, provides users with the ability to share files and devices.

Lab 5.2.1.5: Install Windows 7

In this lab, you install the Windows 7 operating system. Refer to Lab 5.2.1.5 in *IT Essentials: PC Hardware and Software Lab Manual*, Fifth Edition.

Lab 5.2.1.6: Install Windows Vista

In this lab, you install the Windows Vista operating system. Refer to Lab 5.2.1.6 in *IT Essentials: PC Hardware and Software Lab Manual*, Fifth Edition.

Lab 5.2.1.7: Install Windows XP

In this lab, you install the Windows XP operating system. Refer to Lab 5.2.1.7 in *IT Essentials: PC Hardware and Software Lab Manual*, Fifth Edition.

Account Creation (5.2.1.8)

When users attempt to log in to a device or to access system resources, Windows uses the process of authentication to verify that the users are who they say they are. Authentication occurs when users enter a username and password to access a user account. Windows OSes use Single-Sign On (SSO) authentication, which allows users to log in once to access all system features versus requiring them to log in each time they need to access an individual resource.

User accounts allow multiple users to share a single computer, with each user having his or her own files and settings. Windows 7 and Windows Vista have three types of user accounts: Administrator, Standard, and Guest. Each account type provides a user with a different level of control over system resources.

An account with administrator privileges must be created when Windows 7 is installed, as shown in Figure 5-8.

Figure 5-8   Creating a User Account

During setup, you create your first user as shown in Figure 5-8.

A user with administrator privileges can make changes that impact all users of the computer, such as altering security settings or installing software for all users. Accounts with administrator privileges should be used only to manage a computer and not for regular use because drastic changes that affect everyone can be made when using the administrator account. Attackers also seek out an administrator account because it is so powerful. For this reason, it is recommended that a standard user account is created for regular use.

Standard user accounts can be created at any time. A standard user account has fewer permissions than an administrator account. For example, users might have the right to only read, but not modify, a file.

Individuals without a standard user account on the computer can use a guest account. A Guest account has limited permissions and must be turned on by an administrator.

To create or remove a user account in Windows 7 and Windows Vista, use the following path:

Start > Control Panel > User Accounts > Add or remove user accounts

Windows XP features a fourth group of users called Power Users. Power Users have privileges that are extended beyond those of Standard users, providing them with some of the capabilities given to administrator accounts. Power Users are not able to fully administrate system resources. The group has not been included in Windows 7 or Windows Vista.

To create or remove a user account in Windows XP, use the following path:

Start > Control Panel > User Accounts > select the **Users** tab, and then click **Add**.

Lab 5.2.1.9: Check for Updates in Windows 7

In this lab, you configure the operating system so that you can select which updates are installed and then change the settings so that updates are downloaded and installed automatically. Refer to Lab 5.2.1.9 in *IT Essentials: PC Hardware and Software Lab Manual*, Fifth Edition.

Lab 5.2.1.10: Check for Updates in Windows Vista

In this lab, you configure the operating system so that you can select which updates are installed and then change the settings so that updates are downloaded and installed automatically. Refer to Lab 5.2.1.10 in *IT Essentials: PC Hardware and Software Lab Manual*, Fifth Edition.

Lab 5.2.1.11: Check for Updates in Windows XP

In this lab, you configure the operating system so that you can select which updates are installed and then change the settings so that updates are downloaded and installed automatically. Refer to Lab 5.2.1.11 in *IT Essentials: PC Hardware and Software Lab Manual*, Fifth Edition.

Complete the Installation (5.2.1.12)

After the Windows installation copies all the necessary OS files to the hard drive, the computer reboots and prompts you to create a user account.

Windows 7 must be activated. Doing so enables you to download individual updates called patches. A service pack is just several patches grouped together. Windows 7 uses the term *activated* to authenticate that the operating system is a legal copy.

It is not necessary to enter the owner's name and other information as a normal "registration" process usually requests. Microsoft states that Windows 7 can be used for 30 days without activation.

As shown in Figure 5-9, you must also complete the activation that ensures that you are using a legal copy.

Figure 5-9   Windows 7 Verification

Windows Update

Depending on the age of the media at the time of your installation, there might be updates to install. To install patches and service packs in Windows 7 or Windows Vista, use the following path:

Start > All Programs > Windows Update

To install patches and service packs in Windows XP, use the following path:

Start > All Programs > Accessories > System Tools > Windows Update

As shown in Figure 5-10, Microsoft Update Manager can be used to check for important and optional updates.

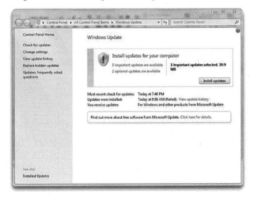

Figure 5-10   Windows Update

Device Manager

After installation, verify that all hardware is installed correctly. In Windows 7 and Windows Vista, use the following path:

Start > Control Panel > Device Manager

In Windows XP, use the following path:

Start > Control Panel > System > Hardware > Device Manager

As shown in Figure 5-11, you can use Device Manager to locate problems and to install the correct or updated drivers.

Figure 5-11   Device Manager

In Device Manager for Windows 7 and Windows Vista, a yellow triangle with an exclamation point indicates a problem with a device. To view a description of the problem, right-click the device and select **Properties**. A gray circle with a downward-pointing arrow means that a device is disabled. To enable the device, right-click the device and select **Enable**. To expand a device category, click the right-pointing triangle next to the category.

Note

In Windows XP, a red circle with a white X indicates a disabled device.

Note

When Windows detects a system error, a dialog box is displayed. If you choose to send the report, Microsoft Windows Error Reporting (WER) collects information about the application involved in the error and sends the information to Microsoft.

Custom Installation Options (5.2.2)

Installing an OS on a single computer takes time. Imagine the time it would take to install operating systems on multiple computers, one at a time. To simplify this activity, you can use the *Microsoft System Preparation (sysprep)* tool to install and configure the same OS on multiple computers. Sysprep prepares the OS with different hardware configurations. The sysprep tool is shown in Figure 5-12.

Figure 5-12   Sysprep

With sysprep and a disk-cloning application, technicians can quickly install the OS, complete the last configuration steps, and install applications.

Disk Cloning (5.2.2.1)

Disk cloning creates an image of a hard drive in a computer. For disk cloning, follow these steps:

Step 1.   Create a master installation on one computer. This master installation includes the OS, software applications, and common configuration settings that will be used by the other computers in the organization.

Step 2.   Run sysprep.

Step 3.   Create a disk image of the configured computer using a third-party disk-cloning program.

Copy the disk image onto a server. When the destination computer is booted, a shortened version of the Windows setup program runs. The setup installs the drivers for the hardware components, creates user accounts, and configures network settings to finish the installation.

Other Installation Methods (5.2.2.2)

A standard installation of Windows 7 is sufficient for most computers used in a home or small office environment. A custom installation of Windows 7 can save time and provide a consistent configuration across computers on a large network. When deploying Windows to multiple computers, technicians may elect to use a pre-installation environment such as Windows PE. Preinstallation environments are basic operating systems that enable a user to partition and format drives or to start an installation from a network.

Windows 7 has several different types of custom installations:

- *Network Installation*: Requires all setup files to be copied to a network server.

- *Preboot Execution Environment (PXE) Installation*: Uses a PXE boot program and a client's network card to access the setup files.

- *Unattended Installation*: Uses a network distribution point that uses an answer file.

- *Image-Based Installation*: Uses Sysprep and a disk-imaging program, such as ImageX, that copies an image of the OS directly to the hard drive with no user intervention.

- *Remote Installation*: Downloads the installation across the network. The installation can be requested by the user or forced on to a computer by an administrator.

Note

To simplify OS deployment across an organization, consider using an OS Deployment Feature Pack using Microsoft System Center Configuration Manager (SCCM).

Network Installation

To install Windows 7 or Windows Vista over a network, follow these steps:

Step 1. Prepare the computer by creating an NTFS partition of at least 5 GB. You must make the partition bootable and include a network client. You can also use a boot disk that contains a network client so that the computer can connect to a file server over the network.

Step 2. Copy the installation media to the network server. Make sure to share the directory so that clients can connect and use the files.

Step 3. Boot the computer and connect to the shared directory.

Step 4. From the shared directory, run the setup program, setup.exe, located in the directory called Sources. The setup program copies the installation files to your hard drive. After the installation files have been copied, the installation continues.

How To Q

To install Windows XP over a network, follow these steps:

Step 1. Prepare the computer by creating a FAT or FAT32 partition of at least 1.5 GB. You must make the partition bootable and include a network client. You can also use a boot disk that contains a network client so that the computer can connect to a file server over the network.

Step 2. Copy the Windows XP installation files (the I386 folder from the installation disc) to the network server. Make sure to share the directory so that clients can connect and use the files.

Step 3. Boot the computer and connect to the shared directory.

Step 4. From the shared directory, run the setup program, winnt.exe. The setup program copies the installation files from the network onto your hard drive. After the installation files have been copied, the installation continues.

PXE Installation

A PXE installation uses a method similar to a network installation. The only difference is that a PXE installation uses a PXE boot file instead of a boot disk. The PXE boot file allows the network interface card (NIC) to communicate with the server and obtain setup files. After a client has access to the setup files, it boots to a command window, where the user is prompted for the network username and password.

Unattended Installation in Windows 7 and Vista

An unattended installation using an unattend.txt answer file or an autounattend.xml file is the easiest alternative installation method to perform on a network. To customize a standard Windows 7 or Windows Vista installation, the System Image Manager (SIM) is used to create the setup answer file. You can also add packages, such as applications or drivers, to an unattended answer file and an autounattend.xml file.

After all questions have been answered, the file is copied to the distribution shared folder on a server. At this point, you can do one of two things:

- Run the unattended.bat file on the client machine to prepare the hard drive and install the OS from the server over the network.

- Create a boot disk that boots the computer and connects to the distribution share on the server. You then run the batch file to install the OS over the network.

Figure 5-13 shows an example of an answer file.

```
[Data]
    AutoPartition=0
    MsDosInitiated="0"
    UnattendedInstall="Yes"
    UseBIOSToBoot=1
[Unattended]
    UnattendMode=FullUnattended
    OemSkipEula=Yes
    OemPreinstall=No
    ExtendOemPartition=0
    TargetPath=*
    Repartition=No
[GuiUnattended]
    AdminPassword=*
    AutoLogon=Yes
    OEMSkipWelcome=1
    TimeZone=20
[UserData]
    ComputerName=OEMComputerName
    FullName="Windows Storage Server 2003"
    OrgName="OEM Name"
    ProductID="XXXXX-XXXXX-XXXXX-XXXXX-XXXXX"
```

Figure 5-13   Unattended.txt File Example

Note

Windows SIM is part of the Windows Automated Installation Kit (AIK). You can download it from the Microsoft website.

Note

In Windows XP, you can create an answer file with the application setupmgr.exe, located in the deploy.cab file on the Windows XP media.

Image-Based Installation

To perform image-based installations, begin by completely configuring one computer to an operational state. Then run Sysprep to prepare the system for imaging. A third-party drive-imaging application prepares an image of the completed computer, which can be burned onto a DVD. You can then copy the image onto computers with compatible Hardware Abstraction Layers (HAL) to complete the installation of multiple computers. After the image is copied, boot up the computer, but you might have to configure some settings, such as the computer name and domain membership.

Remote Installation

With Remote Installation Services (RIS), the process is similar to an image-based installation except that you do not use a drive-imaging utility. You use an RIS network shared folder as the source of the Windows OS files. You can install operating systems on remote boot-enabled client computers. You can also start user computers that are connected to the network with a remote boot disk or network adapter capable of booting the computer. The user then logs in with valid user account credentials.

Lab 5.2.2.3: Advanced Installation of Windows 7

In this lab, you install a Windows 7 operating system by using an answer file for automation. You customize partition settings and create an administrator account and user accounts. Refer to Lab 5.2.2.3 in *IT Essentials: PC Hardware and Software Lab Manual*, Fifth Edition.

Lab 5.2.2.4: Advanced Installation of Windows Vista

In this lab, you install a Windows 7 operating system by using an answer file for automation. You customize partition settings and create an administrator account and user accounts. Refer to Lab 5.2.2.4 in *IT Essentials: PC Hardware and Software Lab Manual*, Fifth Edition.

Lab 5.2.2.5: Advanced Installation of Windows XP

In this lab, you install a Windows XP operating system by using an answer file for automation. You customize partition settings and create an administrator account and user accounts. Refer to Lab 5.2.2.5 in *IT Essentials: PC Hardware and Software Lab Manual*, Fifth Edition.

System Recovery Options (5.2.2.6)

When a system failure occurs users can employ the following recovery tools:

- System Recovery Options
- Automated System Recovery (Windows XP Professional only)
- Factory recovery partition

System Recovery Options

The System Recovery Options are a set of tools that allow users to recover or restore an operating system when it has failed. The System Recovery Options are a part of the *Windows Recovery Environment (WinRE)*. WinRE is a recovery platform based on the *Windows Preinstallation Environment (PE)*. Windows PE is a basic operating system created to prepare a computer for Windows installation and help users troubleshoot operating system failures when no OS is available.

WinRE can be accessed by pressing and holding the **F8** key when starting a computer. Once the Advanced Boot Options screen appears, highlight **Repair your computer** and press **Enter** to access the System Recovery Options. You can then use system recovery tools to repair errors that prevent system startup. The following tools are available in the System Recovery Options menu:

- **Startup Repair:** Scans the hard drive for problems and automatically fixes missing or corrupt system files that prevent Windows from starting

- **System Restore:** Uses *restore points* to restore Windows system files to an earlier point in time

- **System Image Recovery:** Creates a system image that replicates the system drive that Windows requires to operate

- **Windows Memory Diagnostic:** Examines computer memory to detect malfunctions and diagnose problems

- **Command Prompt:** Opens a command prompt window where the bootrec.exe tool can be used to repair and troubleshoot startup issues for Windows. The bootrec.exe utility can be used with the **fixmbr** command to repair the Master Boot Record or the **fixboot** command to write a new boot sector that is compatible with the OS. This command prompt replaces the Recovery Console from Windows XP.

If Repair your computer does not appear as an option, users can access the System Recovery Options in WinRE by booting the computer from installation media or a system repair disc. A system repair disc allows users to access the System Recovery Options in the same way that installation media would. Before a system repair disc can be used to boot a computer, it must be created. Figure 5-14 shows a screenshot of the Create a system repair disk utility.

Figure 5-14   System Repair Disk Utility

To create a Windows 7 system repair disc, follow these steps:

Step 1.   Select **Start > Control Panel > Backup and Restore > Create a system repair disc.**

Step 2.   Insert a blank disc in the optical disc drive and click **Create Disc.**

Step 3.   Test the disc by using it to boot the computer.

Step 4.   After the System Recovery Options window is displayed, highlight the OS that needs to be restored and click **Next.** The following tools should be available:

- Startup Repair

- System Restore

- System Image Recovery

- Windows Memory Diagnostic

- Command Prompt

Note

When using a recovery disc, make sure that it uses the same architecture as the OS being recovered. For example, if the computer is running a 64-bit version of Windows 7, the recovery disc must use a 64-bit architecture.

System Image Recovery

The *System Image Recovery utility*, shown in Figure 5-15, is a new recovery option that is included in all versions of Windows 7. It allows users to back up the contents of their hard drive, including personal files and settings, if an operating system needs to be restored.

Figure 5-15   System Image Recovery Tool

To create a system image in Windows 7, follow these steps:

Step 1.   Select **Start > Control Panel > Backup and Restore > Create a system image**.

Step 2.   Select a location for the system image:

- **On a hard disk:** Stores the system image on an external hard drive

- **On one or more DVDs:** Burns the system image to a DVD

- **On a network location:** Stores the system image in a shared folder on a network

Step 3.   Click **Next** and confirm the selections. A system image is created and stored in the selected location.

Automated System Recovery in Windows XP Professional

You must create an *Automated System Recovery (ASR)* set to use for the recovery. The ASR Wizard creates a backup of the system state, services, and OS components. It also creates a file containing information about your disks, the backup, and how to restore the backup.

Use the following path:

Start > All Programs > Accessories > System Tools > Backup > click the **Advanced Mode** link **> Automated System Recovery Wizard**

To restore your system, press **F2** after booting the Windows XP installation disc. ASR reads the set and restores the disc needed to start the computer. After the basic disk information has been restored, ASR installs a basic version of Windows and begins restoring the backup created by the ASR Wizard.

Factory Recovery Partition

Some computers that have Windows 7 preinstalled from the factory contain a section of the disk that is inaccessible to the user. This partition, called a *factory recovery partition,* contains an image of the bootable partition created when the computer was built. You can use this partition to restore the computer to its original configuration.

Occasionally, the option to reach this partition is hidden, and you must use a special key or key combination when the computer is starting to access the hidden partition. Sometimes, the option to restore from the factory recovery partition is located in the BIOS. Contact the computer manufacturer to find out how to access the partition and restore the original configuration of the computer.

Boot Sequence and Registry Files (5.2.3)

The boot sequence is the initial processes a computer goes through as it boots or "starts up." Basic instructions in the BIOS tell the computer how to boot and where to locate the operating system to load. Windows operating systems store configuration information in the Registry database.

Windows Boot Process (5.2.3.1)

Understanding the boot process in Windows can help a technician troubleshoot boot problems. Table 5-5 displays the boot sequence for Windows 7.

Table 5-5   Boot Sequence for Windows 7

Power-On Self-Test (POST).
POST for each adapter card that has a BIOS.
BIOS reads the MBR.
MBR takes over control of the boot process and starts BOOTMGR.
BOOTMGR reads the Boot Configuration Data file to know which OS to load and where to find the OS on the boot partition.
BOOTMGR invokes WINLOAD.EXE in order to load the NTOSKRNL.EXE file and HAL.DLL.
BOOTMGR reads the Registry files and loads *device drivers*.
NTOSKRNL>EXE starts the WINLOGON.EXE program and displays the Windows login screen.

Windows Boot Process

To begin the boot process, turn on the computer. This is called a cold boot. When the computer is powered on, it performs a Power-On Self-Test (POST). Because the video adapter has not yet been initialized, errors that occur at this point in the boot process are reported by a series of audible tones, called beep codes.

After POST, the BIOS locates and reads the configuration settings that are stored in the CMOS memory. The boot device priority, as shown in Figure 5-16, is the order in which devices are checked to locate the operating system. The boot device priority is set in the BIOS and can be arranged in any order. The BIOS boots the computer using the first drive that contains an operating system.

Hard drives, network drives, USB drives, and even removable magnetic media, such as CompactFlash or Secure Digital (SD) cards, can be used in the boot order, depending on the capabilities of the motherboard. Some BIOS also have a boot device priority menu that is accessed with a special key combination while the computer is starting but before the boot sequence begins. You can use this menu to select the device to boot, which is useful if multiple drives can boot the computer.

Figure 5-16   Boot Device Priority

Windows Boot Loader and Windows Boot Manager in Windows 7 and Windows Vista

When the drive storing the OS is located, the BIOS finds the Master Boot Record (MBR). At this point, *Windows Boot Manager (BOOTMGR)* controls several installation steps. For instance, if more than one OS is present on the disk, BOOTMGR gives the user a chance to select which one to use. If there are no other operating systems, or if the user does not make a selection before the timer expires, the following process occurs:

1. WinLoad uses the path specified in BOOTMGR to find the boot partition.

2. WinLoad loads two files that make up the core of Windows 7: NTOSKRNL.EXE and HAL.DLL.

3. WinLoad reads the Registry files, chooses a hardware profile, and loads the device drivers.

Note

If another OS version is on the disk that is Windows Vista or later, BOOTMGR repeats the process. If another OS version is on the disk that is Windows XP or earlier, BOOTMGR invokes the Windows XP boot loader (NTLDR).

NTLDR and the Windows Boot Menu in Windows XP

When the drive with the OS is located on a computer running Windows XP, the BIOS locates the MBR. The MBR locates the OS boot loader *NTLDR*. At this point, NTLDR controls several installation steps. For instance, if more than one OS is present on the disk, BOOT.INI gives the user a chance to select which one to use. If there are no other operating systems, or if the user does not make a selection before the timer expires, the following process occurs:

1. NTLDR runs NTDETECT.COM to get information about the installed hardware.

2. NTLDR uses the path specified in the BOOT.INI to find the boot partition.

3. NTLDR loads two files that make up the core of XP: NTOSKRNL.EXE and HAL.DLL.

4. NTLDR reads the Registry files, chooses a hardware profile, and loads the device drivers.

NT Kernel

At this point, the NT kernel takes over. The NT kernel is the heart of all Windows operating systems. The name of this file is NTOSKRNL.EXE. It starts the login file called WINLOGON.EXE and displays the Windows Welcome screen.

Startup Modes (5.2.3.2)

Windows can boot in one of many different modes. Pressing the F8 key during the boot process opens the Windows Advanced Startup Options menu, as shown in Figure 5-17. This allows users to select how to boot Windows. The following startup options are commonly used:

- **Safe Mode:** Starts Windows but only loads drivers for basic components, such as the keyboard and display.

- **Safe Mode with Networking:** Starts Windows as for safe mode but also loads the drivers for network components.

- **Safe Mode with Command Prompt:** Starts Windows and loads the command prompt instead of the GUI.

- **Last Known Good Configuration:** Loads the configuration settings that were used the last time that Windows started successfully. It does this by accessing a copy of the Registry that is created for this purpose.

Note

Last Known Good Configuration is not useful unless it is applied immediately after a failure occurs. If the machine is restarted and manages to open Windows, the Registry is updated with the faulty information.

Figure 5-17   Advanced Startup Options

Windows Registry (5.2.3.3)

The *Windows Registry* files are an important part of the Windows boot process. These files are recognized by their distinctive names, which begin with HKEY_, followed by the name of the portion of the OS under their control. Every setting in Windows, from the background of the desktop and the color of the screen buttons, to the licensing of applications, is stored in the Registry. When a user makes changes to the Control Panel settings, file associations, system policies, or installed software, the changes are stored in the Registry. Table 5-6 shows the Windows Registry keys and their descriptions.

Table 5-6 Registry Keys

HKEY	Description
HKEY_CLASSES_ROOT	Information about which file extensions map to a particular application
HKEY_CURRENT_USER	Information, such as desktop settings and history, related to the current user of a PC
HKEY_USERS	Information about all users who have logged on to a system
HKEY_LOCAL_MACHINE	Information relating to the hardware and software
HKEY_CURRENT_CONFIG	Information relating to all active devices on a system

Each user account has a unique section of the Registry. The Windows login process pulls system settings from the Registry to reconfigure the system for each individual user account.

The Registry is also responsible for recording the location of *dynamic link library (DLL)* files. A DLL file consists of program code that can be used by different programs to perform common functions. As a result, DLL files are very important to the functionality of an operating system and any application users may install.

To ensure that a DLL can be located by the operating system or a program, it must be registered. It is usually registered automatically during the installation process. A user may need to manually register a DLL file when a problem is encountered. Registering a DLL maps the path to the file, making it easier for programs to locate necessary files. To register a DLL file in Windows using the command-line tool, use the following path:

Start > type **cmd** in the **Search Programs and Files** bar **>** type **regsvr32** *filename.***dll**

Lab 5.2.3.4: Registry Backup and Recovery in Windows XP

In this lab, you back up a computer Registry. You also perform a recovery of a computer Registry. The Registry is also called system state data. Refer to Lab 5.2.3.4 in *IT Essentials: PC Hardware and Software Lab Manual*, Fifth Edition.

Multiboot (5.2.4)

Sometimes it is necessary or just desired to have more than one operating system running on a single computer; this is known as multiboot or dual boot. Testing an OS, testing compatibility of applications, and customer support are some reasons for a multiboot setup.

Multiboot Procedures (5.2.4.1)

You can have multiple operating systems on a single computer. Some software applications may require the most recent version of an OS, while other applications require an older version. There is a dual-boot process for multiple operating systems on a computer. During the boot process, if the Windows Boot Manager (BOOTMGR) determines that more than one OS is present, you are prompted to choose the OS that you want to load, as shown in Figure 5-18.

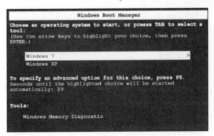

Figure 5-18   Windows Boot Manager

To create a dual-boot system in Microsoft Windows, the hard drive must contain more than one partition.

The oldest OS should be installed on the primary partition or the hard drive marked as the active partition first. Install the second OS on the second partition or hard drive. The boot files are automatically installed in the active partition.

BOOTMGR File

During the installation, the BOOTMGR file is created on the active partition to allow selecting the OS to boot on startup. You can edit the BOOTMGR file to change the order of the operating systems. You can also change the length of time allowed during the boot phase to select the OS. Typically, the default time is 30 seconds. This time period delays the boot time of the computer by the specified time, unless the user intervenes to select a particular OS. If the disk has only one OS, change the time to 5 or 10 seconds to boot the computer faster.

Note

In Windows XP, the BOOT.INI file fills the role of the BOOTMGR file.

To change the time to display the operating systems, use the following path:

Select **Start > Control Panel > System and Security > System > Advanced System Settings > Advanced tab >** in the Startup and Recovery area, select **Settings**.

To edit general boot configuration data in Windows 7 and Vista, use the bcdedit.exe command-line tool, as shown in Figure 5-19. To access the bcdedit.exe tool, use the following path:

Select **Start > All Programs > Accessories >** right-click **Command Prompt > Run as administrator > Continue >** type **bcdedit.exe.**

To edit the boot.ini file in Windows XP, use the following path:

Select **Start >** right-click **My Computer > Properties > Advanced tab >** in the Startup and Recovery area, select **Settings >** click **Edit.**

Figure 5-19   bcdedit.exe Tool

Disk Management Utility (5.2.4.2)

A multiboot setup requires multiple hard drives or a hard drive that has multiple partitions. To create a new partition, access the Disk Management utility, as shown in Figure 5-20. You can also use the Disk Management utility to complete the following tasks:

- View drive status
- Extend partitions
- Split partitions
- Assign drive letters
- Add drives
- Add arrays

Figure 5-20   Disk Management Utility

To access the Disk Management utility in Windows 7 and Windows Vista, use the following path:

Start > right-click **Computer > Manage >** select **Disk Management**

To access the Disk Management utility in Windows XP, use the following path:

Start > right-click **My Computer > Manage >** select **Disk** Management

Drive Status

The Disk Management utility displays the status of each disk. The drives in the computer display one of the following conditions:

- **Foreign:** A dynamic disk that has been moved to a computer from another computer running Windows XP

- **Healthy:** A volume that is functioning properly

- **Initializing:** A basic disk that is being converted into a dynamic disk

- **Missing:** A dynamic disk that is corrupted, turned off, or disconnected

- **Not Initialized:** A disk that does not contain a valid signature

- **Online:** A basic or dynamic disk that is accessible and shows no problems

- **Online (Errors):** I/O errors detected on a dynamic disk

- **Offline:** A dynamic disk that is corrupted or unavailable

- **Unreadable:** A basic or dynamic disk that has experienced hardware failure, corruption, or I/O errors

Other drive status indicators might be displayed when using drives other than hard drives, such as an audio CD that is in the optical drive or a removable drive that is empty.

Extending Partitions

In Disk Manager, you can extend primary partitions and logical drives if there is unallocated space on the hard disk. To extend a basic disk, it must be formatted with the NTFS file format. Extending a hard disk increases the amount of space available on a primary partition or logical drive. Logical drives and system volumes must be extended into contiguous space, and the disk type must be converted to dynamic. Other partitions can be extended into noncontiguous space, and the disk type must be converted to dynamic.

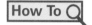

To extend a partition in the Disk Manager, follow these steps:

Step 1. Right-click the desired partition.

Step 2. Click **Extend Volume**.

Step 3. Follow the instructions on the screen.

Splitting Partitions

If a hard drive is partitioned automatically in Windows 7 and Windows Vista, there is only one partition. If you want to split the partition, you can use the Shrink Volume feature. This feature reduces the size of the original partition, which creates unallocated disk space that is used to create a new partition. You must format the unallocated space and assign it a drive letter.

To shrink a partition in Windows 7 and Windows Vista from the Disk Management utility, right-click the drive and select **Shrink Volume**.

Assigning Drive Letters

You can change, add, and remove drive letters and paths. By default, Windows assigns a letter to a partition or drive after it is created or added. You can change the drive designation to any letter as long as that letter is not already in use.

To change a drive letter in Windows 7 from the Disk Management utility, right-click the drive and select **Change Drive Letter and Paths**.

Adding Drives

To increase the amount of storage space available on a computer, or implement a RAID setup, you can add drives to the computer. If the additional hard drive has been installed correctly, the BIOS should automatically recognize it. After the drive is installed, you can check if it is recognized using the Disk Management utility. If the disk is available, it probably requires formatting before it can be used. If it does not appear, troubleshoot the problem.

Adding Arrays

To set up a RAID, two or more drives must be installed in a computer. You can add an array with the Disk Management utility. You have the following options:

- **New Spanned Volume:** Creates a disk partition that consists of disk space from more than one physical disk. The data on a spanned volume is not fault tolerant.

- **New Striped Volume:** A dynamic partition that stores data in stripes on more than one physical disk. The data on a striped volume is not fault tolerant.

- **New Mirrored Volume:** Duplicates data from one disk to one or more additional physical disks. The data on a mirrored volume is fault tolerant.

- **New RAID-5 Volume:** A dynamic partition that stores data in stripes on more than one physical disk, while also providing parity for each stripe. The data on a RAID-5 volume is fault tolerant.

Note

The options available for adding an array are based on system limitations. Not all options may be available.

To add an array in the Disk Management utility, right-click the desired disk and select an option.

Lab 5.2.4.3: Create a Partition in Windows 7

In this lab, you create a FAT32 formatted partition on a disk. You convert the partition to NTFS. You identify the differences between the FAT32 format and the NTFS format. Refer to Lab 5.2.4.3 in *IT Essentials: PC Hardware and Software Lab Manual*, Fifth Edition.

Lab 5.2.4.4: Create a Partition in Windows Vista

In this lab, you create a FAT32 formatted partition on a disk. You convert the partition to NTFS. You identify the differences between the FAT32 format and the NTFS format. Refer to Lab 5.2.4.4 in *IT Essentials: PC Hardware and Software Lab Manual*, Fifth Edition.

Lab 5.2.4.5: Create a Partition in Windows XP

In this lab, you create a FAT32 formatted partition on a disk. You will convert the partition to NTFS. You identify the differences between the FAT32 format and the NTFS format. Refer to Lab 5.2.4.5 in *IT Essentials: PC Hardware and Software Lab Manual*, Fifth Edition.

Directory Structure and File Attributes (5.2)

The Windows directory structure is the organization of folders and files within the operating system. It is a hierarchical structure that starts at the root and has folders and subfolders within the root that contain software files and user's files. It is a way for the OS to catalog files.

Directory Structures (5.2.5.1)

In Windows, files are organized in a directory structure. A directory structure is designed to store system files, user files, and program files. A path is a description of where a file is located in a directory structure. The root level of the Windows directory structure, the partition, is usually labeled drive C. Drive C contains a set of standardized directories, called folders, for the operating system, applications, configuration information, and data files. Directories may contain subdirectories. Subdirectories are commonly called subfolders.

Following the initial installation, you can install most applications and data in whichever directory you choose. The Windows setup program creates directories that have specific purposes, such as storing photos or music files. When files of the same type are saved to a certain location, it is easier to find things.

> **Note**
>
> It is a best practice to store files in folders and subfolders rather than at the root level of a drive.

Drive Mapping

In Windows, letters are used to name physical or logical drives. This process is called drive mapping. A Windows computer can have up to 26 physical and logical drives because there are 26 letters in the English alphabet. Drives A and B have traditionally been reserved for floppy disk drives, and drive C is reserved for the primary, active partition. In Windows Vista and Windows 7, you can assign drives A and B to volumes if you do not have floppy drives. An optical drive is traditionally labeled as drive D. The maximum number of additional drives is dependent on the hardware of a specific computer.

Mounting a Volume

With the NTFS file system, you can map a drive to an empty folder on a volume. This is referred to as a mounted drive. Mounted drives are assigned drive paths instead of letters and are displayed as a drive icon in Windows Explorer. Windows Explorer is a tool that allows users to view all the drives, folders, and files on a computer in an organized manner. Use a mounted drive to configure more than 26 drives on your computer or when you need additional storage space on a volume.

To mount a volume in Windows, follow these steps:

Step 1. Select **Start > Control Panel > Administrative Tools > Computer Management.**

Step 2. Click **Disk Management** in the left pane.

Step 3. Right-click the partition or volume to mount.

Step 4. Click **Change Drive Letter and Paths.**

Step 5. Click **Add.**

Step 6. Click **Mount in the following empty NTFS folder.**

Step 7. Browse to an empty folder on an NTFS volume or create one, and click **OK.**

Step 8. Close Computer Management.

User and System File Locations (5.2.5.2)

During installation, the Windows operating system's essential folders are created. They contain operating system files and other system files necessary for the function of the OS as well as a default folder location for user-created files.

User File Locations

By default, Windows 7 and Windows Vista stores most of the files created by users in the folder C:\Users*User_name*\. Windows XP uses the folder C:\Documents and Settings*User_name*\.

Each user's folder contains folders for music, videos, websites, and pictures, among others. Many programs also store specific user data here. If a single computer has many users, each user has their own folder containing their favorites, desktop items, and cookies. Cookies are files that contain information from web pages that the user has visited.

System Folder

When the Windows OS is installed, all files that are used to run the computer are located in the folder C:\Windows\system32.

Fonts

In Windows XP, the folder C:\Windows\Fonts contains the fonts installed on the computer. Fonts come in several formats, including TrueType, OpenType,

Composite, and PostScript. Some examples of font typefaces are Arial, Times New Roman, and Courier. You can access the Fonts folder through the Control Panel. You can install fonts using the **File > Install New Font** menu.

In Windows 7, fonts are installed from the Font Help menu.

If you want to install additional fonts, you must first download them. You can download fonts from a software program, the Internet, or your organization's network.

Note

Before you download a font, make sure you trust the source.

To install a font, right-click the font you want to install and click **Install**.

Temporary Files

The Temporary Files folder contains files created by the OS and programs that are needed for a short period of time. For example, temporary files might be created while an application is being installed to make more RAM available for other applications.

Almost every program uses temporary files, which are usually automatically deleted when the application or the OS is finished using them. However, some temporary files must be deleted manually. Because temporary files take up hard drive space that could be used for other files, it is a good idea to delete them as necessary every 2 or 3 months.

In Windows Vista and Windows 7, temporary files are usually located in the following folders:

- C:\Windows\Temp
- C:\Users\User_Name\AppData\Local\Temp
- %USERPROFILE%\AppData\Local\Temp

In Windows XP, temporary files are usually located in the following folders:

- C:\Temp
- C:\Tmp
- C:\Windows\Temp
- C:\Windows\Tmp
- C:\Documents and Settings\%USERPROFILE%\Local Settings\Temp

Note

%USERPROFILE% is an environment variable set by the OS with the username that is currently logged on to the computer. Environment variables are used by the operating system, applications, and software installation programs.

To see the environment variables that are configured on Windows 7, use the following path:

Start > Control Panel > System > Advanced System Settings > Advanced tab > Environment Variables

To see the environment variables that are configured on Windows Vista, use the following path:

Start > Control Panel > System > Advance System Settings > Advanced tab > Environmental Variables

To see the environment variables that are configured on Windows XP, use the following path:

Start > Control Panel > System > Advanced > Environment Variables

Program Files

The Program Files folder is used by most application installation programs to install software. In 32-bit systems, programs are usually installed in the folder C:\Program Files. In 64-bit systems, 64-bit programs are usually installed in the folder C:\ Program Files, while 32-bit programs are usually installed in the folder C:\Program Files (x86).

File Extensions and Attributes (5.2.5.3)

Files in the directory structure adhere to a Windows naming convention:

- A maximum of 255 characters is allowed.

- Characters such as a slash or a backslash (/ \) are not allowed.

- An extension of three or four letters is added to the filename to identify the file type.

- Filenames are not case sensitive.

By default, file extensions are hidden. To display the file extensions, you must disable the **Hide extensions for known file types** setting in the Folder Options control panel utility, as shown in Figure 5-21.

Figure 5-21   Show Known File Types

To display file extensions, use the following path:

Start > Control Panel > Folder Options > View > uncheck **Hide extensions for known file types**

The following filename extensions are commonly used:

- **.docx:** Microsoft Word
- **.txt:** ASCII text only
- **.jpg:** Graphics format
- **.pptx:** Microsoft PowerPoint
- **.zip:** Compression format

The directory structure maintains a set of attributes for each file that controls how the file can be viewed or altered. These are the most common file attributes:

- **R:** The file is read-only.
- **A:** The file will be archived the next time that the disk is backed up.
- **S:** The file is marked as a system file, and a warning is given if an attempt is made to delete or modify the file.
- **H:** The file is hidden in the directory display.

Application, File, and Folder Properties (5.2.5.4)

To view or change the properties of an application, file, or folder, right-click the icon and select **Properties**.

Application and File Properties

The Properties view, as shown in Figure 5-22, for an application or file may contain the following tabs:

- **General:** Displays basic information, including location and the attributes.

- **Security:** Provides the option to change file access permissions for user accounts and the system.

- **Details:** Displays basic information for the file, including attributes.

- **Compatibility:** Provides options for configuring file compatibility mode and operational settings. In Windows 7, compatibility mode allows a user to run a program created for earlier versions of the Windows OS. For Windows Vista and Windows XP, the number of options available in compatibility mode is limited.

Figure 5-22   Application Properties

Folder Properties

The Properties view for an individual folder may contain the following tabs:

- **General:** Displays basic information, such as location and size. Provides options to change attributes, such as making a folder read-only or hidden.

- **Sharing:** Displays options for folder sharing. Users can share folders with computers on the same network. Password protection settings can also be configured.

- **Security:** Displays options for basic and advanced security settings.

- **Previous Versions:** Displays options for restoring a folder from a previous version.

- **Customize:** Displays options for customizing the appearance of the folder and optimizing it for specific file types, such as music or photo files.

Shadow Copy

Shadow Copy is a feature of Windows operating systems that automatically creates backup copies of files and data on a hard drive. It can be found under the Previous Versions tab and is often referred to as the previous versions feature. Shadow Copy requires the hard disk to be formatted as NTFS and works in conjunction with System Restore and Windows Backups. Before Shadow Copy can be used, it must be enabled. To enable Shadow Copy, use the following path:

Start > Control Panel > System Protection link **>** check the check boxes next to the desired drives **>** click **OK**

After Shadow Copy has been enabled, users can view, copy, or restore previous versions of the file. Selecting the view option will open the file as read-only, while the copy option will save an older version of the file in another folder. Restore will overwrite the file in its current state.

The Windows GUI and Control Panel (5.3)

This section examines the graphical user interface (GUI) that allows users to interact with the computer. It also explores the Windows Control Panel. This is where Windows centralizes the settings for many features that control the behavior and appearance of the computer. These settings are categorized in *Control Panel applets*, or small programs, found in the Control Panel.

Windows Desktop (5.3.1.1)

After the OS has been installed, you can customize the computer desktop to suit individual needs. A computer desktop is a graphical representation of the workspace and is commonly called a GUI. The desktop has icons, toolbars, and menus to manipulate files. You can add or change images, sounds, and colors to provide a more personalized look and feel. Together, these customizable items make up a theme. Windows 7 and Windows Vista have a default theme called Aero. Aero has translucent window borders, numerous animations, and icons that are thumbnail images of the contents of a file. Because of the advanced graphics required to support the theme, Aero is available only on computers that meet the following hardware requirements:

- 1 GHz 32-bit or 64-bit processor
- 1 GB of RAM
- 128 MB graphics card
- DirectX 9 class graphics processor that supports a Windows Display Driver Model driver, Pixel Shader 2.0 in hardware, and 32 bits per pixel

Note

Windows 7 Starter and Windows Vista Home Basic do not include the Aero theme.

Windows 7 includes the following new Aero features:

- **Shake:** Minimize all windows that are not being used by clicking the title bar of one window and shaking the mouse. To maximize the windows again, click the title bar of the visible window and shake the mouse.

- **Peek:** View the icons and gadgets on the desktop by pointing the mouse at the right edge of the taskbar to make all windows transparent.

- **Snap:** Resize a window by dragging it to one of the edges of the screen. Dragging the window to the left edge of the desktop fits the window to the left half of the screen. Dragging the window to the right edge of the desktop fits the window to the right half of the screen. Dragging the window to the top edge of the desktop maximizes the window to fill the entire screen.

Gadgets

In Windows 7 and Windows Vista, users can place gadgets on the desktop. Gadgets are small applications such as games, sticky notes, or a clock. Thousands of gadgets are available for accessing different types of data. Figure 5-23 displays weather, calendar, and clock gadgets on a Windows 7 desktop. You can snap or position gadgets to the sides and corners of the desktop, in addition to aligning them to other gadgets.

Note

Microsoft no longer hosts the Gadget Gallery for downloading new gadgets.
http://windows.microsoft.com/en-ca/windows/downloads/personalize/gadgets

See: Microsoft Security Advisory (2719662), "Vulnerabilities in Gadgets Could Allow Remote Code Execution": http://technet.microsoft.com/en-us/security/advisory/2719662

Note

Windows XP does not feature gadgets.

Figure 5-23   Gadgets

To add gadgets to the desktop, follow these steps:

Step 1.   Right-click anywhere on the desktop and choose **Gadgets**.

Step 2.   Do any of the following:

- Drag and drop the gadget from the menu to the desktop.

- Double-click the gadget to add it to the desktop.

- Right-click the gadget and choose **Add**.

Step 3.   To snap a gadget, drag it to the desired desktop location. The gadget aligns itself with the screen edges and other gadgets.

In Windows Vista, you can also personalize a feature called Sidebar. Sidebar is a graphical pane on the desktop that keeps gadgets organized. Sidebar is not available in Windows 7.

Desktop Properties (5.3.1.2)

To customize the desktop in Windows 7 and Windows Vista, right-click anywhere on the desktop and choose **Personalize**. In Windows 7, the Personalization window, as shown in Figure 5-24, has three links on the left to change desktop icons, mouse pointers, and your account picture. Themes are chosen from the right panel. You can modify a theme's background, color, sound, and screensaver using the four items under the window.

The Personalization window in Windows Vista has seven links that allow users to adjust window color and appearance, change the desktop background, configure the display settings, and more. Each link customizes the desktop in a particular way.

To customize the desktop in Windows XP, right-click anywhere on the desktop and choose **Properties**. The Display Properties window, as shown in Figure 5-25, uses tabs.

Figure 5-24   Windows 7 Personalization Window

Figure 5-25   Windows XP Display Properties Window

Each tab customizes the display settings in a particular way.

Start Menu and Taskbar (5.3.1.3)

The Start menu and taskbar allow users to manage programs, search the computer, and manipulate running applications. To customize the Start menu or the taskbar, right-click it and choose **Properties**.

Start Menu

On the desktop, the Start menu is accessed by clicking the Windows icon in the bottom left of the desktop. The Start menu displays all the applications installed in the computer, a list of recently opened documents, and a list of other elements, such as the search feature, help center, and system settings. You can customize different aspects of the Start menu, as shown in Figure 5-26.

Figure 5-26   Customize the Start Menu

To customize Start menu settings, use the following path:

Right-click an empty section of the taskbar and choose **Properties > Start menu > Customize.**

In Windows XP, you can change the style of the Start menu: XP or Classic. In Windows 7, the option for Start menu styles has been removed.

Taskbar

In Windows 7, the following new features have been added to the taskbar to make navigating, organizing, and accessing windows and notifications easier:

- **Jump list:** To display a list of tasks that are unique to the application, right-click the application's icon in the taskbar.

- **Pinned applications:** To add an application to the taskbar for easy access, right-click the icon of an application and select **Pin to taskbar.**

- **Thumbnail previews:** To view a thumbnail image of a running program, hover the mouse over the program icon on the taskbar.

Task Manager (5.3.1.4)

The *Task Manager* allows you to view all applications that are running and to close any applications that have stopped responding.

The Task Manager has the following tabs:

- **Applications:** This tab shows all running applications. From this tab, you can create, switch to, or close any applications that have stopped responding using the buttons at the bottom.

- **Processes:** This tab shows all running processes. A process is a set of instructions started by the user, a program, or the OS. From this tab, you can end processes or set process priorities.

- **Services:** This tab shows the available services, including their operational status (not included in Windows XP).

- **Performance:** This tab shows the CPU and page file usage.

- **Networking:** This tab shows the usage of all network adapters.

- **Users:** This tab shows all users who are logged in to the computer. From this tab, you can disconnect remote users or log out local users.

To view information in the Task Manager for Windows 7 and Windows Vista, use the following path:

Ctrl+Alt+Del and select **Start Task Manager**

Alternatively, you can access the Task Manager by right-clicking the taskbar and selecting **Start Task Manager.**

In Windows XP, use the following path:

Ctrl+Alt+Del and select **Task Manager**

Alternatively, you can access the Task Manager by right-clicking the taskbar and selecting **Task Manager.**

Be careful when ending a process or changing the priority of processes. Ending a process causes the program to end immediately without saving any information. Ending a process might prevent the system from running correctly. Changing the priority of a process might adversely affect the performance of the computer.

Lab 5.3.1.5: Task Manager (Managing Processes) Windows 7

In this lab, you explore Task Manager and manage processes from within Task Manager. Refer to Lab 5.3.1.5 in *IT Essentials: PC Hardware and Software Lab Manual*, Fifth Edition.

Lab 5.3.1.6: Task Manager (Managing Processes) Windows Vista

In this lab, you explore Task Manager and manage processes from within Task Manager. Refer to Lab 5.3.1.6 in *IT Essentials: PC Hardware and Software Lab Manual*, Fifth Edition.

Lab 5.3.1.7: Task Manager (Managing Processes) Windows XP

In this lab, you explore Task Manager and manage processes from within Task Manager. Refer to Lab 5.3.1.7 in *IT Essentials: PC Hardware and Software Lab Manual*, Fifth Edition.

Computer and Windows Explorer (5.3.1.8)

Computer

The Computer feature allows you to access the various drives installed in the computer. With Windows 7 or Windows Vista, click **Start** and select **Computer**. With Windows XP, this feature is called My Computer, and you can access it by double-clicking the **My Computer** icon on the desktop.

Windows Explorer

Windows Explorer allows you to navigate the file system. The navigation pane in Windows 7 includes the path of the currently accessed folder or file at the top, a search bar on the top right, a toolbar directly under the path listing and search bar, a navigation panel on the left, and a viewing pane to the right of the navigation panel. You can use the search bar to find a specific application, file, or folder. The toolbar allows you to organize files, add new folders, change the layout of files in Windows Explorer, display a preview pane for files and folders, and open the help feature for Windows. The navigation panel includes a default list of folders, including Favorites, Libraries, Computer, and Network. You can use the viewing pane to access or manipulate applications, files, and folders.

Windows 7 adds the following features to Windows Explorer:

- **Search box:** Access previous searches. You can also filter search results.

- **New folder button:** Create new folders with one click.

- **Arrange by:** Organize items easily according to different criteria.

- **Preview pane button:** Turn the preview pane on or off as needed.

Launching Applications and Opening Files

You can launch an application in several ways:

- Click an application icon on the Start menu or the taskbar.

- Double-click the application executable or shortcut icon on the desktop or in Windows Explorer.

- Launch the application from the Run window or command line.

You can open files in the same manner as applications. When you open a file, Windows determines which application is associated with the file. Windows compares the file extension with the installed applications that are capable of opening the file. For example, if you open a .docx file, Windows launches Microsoft Word and opens the file.

Windows 7 Libraries (5.3.1.9)

Libraries is a new Windows 7 feature that allows you to easily organize content from various storage devices on your local computer and network, including removable media, without actually moving the files. A library is a virtual folder that presents content from different locations within the same view. You can search a library, and you can filter the content using criteria such as filename, file type, or date modified.

When Windows 7 is installed, each user has four default libraries: Documents, Music, Pictures, and Videos, as shown in Figure 5-27. To access a library, open Windows Explorer and click **Libraries** in the left column. To add a file or folder to a library, right-click it, select **Include in library**, and then choose to which library to add the item. The file or folder is available when you open that library.

Figure 5-27   Windows 7 Libraries

To create a new library, open a folder and select **Libraries > New library**.

To customize a library, right-click the library and click **Properties**. The Properties window allows you to add folders to the library by clicking **Include a folder**. You can also change the icon for the library and customize how items are arranged.

Install and Uninstall Applications (5.3.1.10)

As a technician, you will be responsible for adding and removing software from your customers' computers. Most applications use an automatic installation process when the application installation disc is inserted in the optical drive. The installation process updates the Add or Remove Programs utility. The user is required to click through the installation wizard and provide information when requested.

Adding an Application

In Windows 7 and Windows Vista, insert the CD or DVD or open the downloaded program file. The program installer should start. If it does not start, run the setup or install file on the disc to begin installation or download the program again.

After the application is installed, you can start the application from the Start menu or the shortcut icon that the application installs on the desktop. Check the application to ensure that it is functioning properly. If there are problems, repair or uninstall the application using the Uninstall or Change a Program utility. Some applications, such as Microsoft Office, provide a repair option in the install process. You can use this function to try to correct a program that is not working properly.

Note

In Windows XP, if a program or application is not automatically installed when the disc is inserted, you can use the Add or Remove Programs utility to install the application. Click the **Add New Programs** button and select the location where the application is located.

Uninstalling or Changing a Program

If an application is not uninstalled properly, you might be leaving files on the hard drive and unnecessary settings in the Registry, which depletes the hard drive space and system resources. Unnecessary files might also reduce the speed at which the Registry is read. Microsoft recommends that you always use the Programs and Features utility, as shown in Figure 5-28, when removing, changing, or repairing applications. The utility guides you through the software removal process and removes every file that was installed.

In some instances, you can install or uninstall optional features of an application using the Programs and Features utility. Not all programs offer this option.

Figure 5-28 Programs and Features Utility

To open the Programs and Features utility in Windows 7 and Windows Vista, use the following path:

Start > Control Panel > Programs and Features

In Windows XP, use the following path:

Start > Control Panel > Add or Remove Programs

Lab 5.3.1.11: Install Third-Party Software in Windows 7

In this lab, you install and remove a third-party software application supplied by your instructor. You install the Packet Tracer Windows application. Refer to Lab 5.3.1.11 in *IT Essentials: PC Hardware and Software Lab Manual*, Fifth Edition.

Lab 5.3.1.12 Install Third-Party Software in Windows Vista

In this lab, you install and remove a third-party software application supplied by your instructor. You install the Packet Tracer Windows application. Refer to Lab 5.3.1.12 in *IT Essentials: PC Hardware and Software Lab Manual*, Fifth Edition.

Lab 5.3.1.13: Install Third-Party Software in Windows XP

In this lab, you install and remove a third-party software application supplied by your instructor. You install the Packet Tracer Windows application. Refer to Lab 5.3.1.13 in *IT Essentials: PC Hardware and Software Lab Manual*, Fifth Edition.

Control Panel Utilities (5.3.2)

Microsoft Windows Control Panel is the focal point for programs that can be used to make configuration changes in many areas of the Windows operating system. This section evaluates various Control Panel utilities.

Introduction to Control Panel Utilities (5.3.2.1)

Windows centralizes the settings for many features that control the behavior and appearance of the computer. These settings are categorized in utilities, or small programs, found in the Control Panel. Adding or removing programs, changing network settings, and changing the security settings are some of the configuration options available in the Control Panel.

The names of various categories in the Control Panel differ slightly depending on the version of Windows installed. By default, icons are grouped into the following eight categories in Windows 7:

- **System and Security:** To configure system and security settings
- **Network and Internet:** To configure network connection types
- **Hardware and Sound:** To configure devices connected to the computer and settings for sound

- **Programs:** To remove, change, and repair applications

- **User Accounts and Family Safety:** To create and remove user accounts and set up parental controls

- **Appearance and Personalization:** To control the look and feel of the Windows GUI

- **Clock, Language, and Region:** To specify location and language

- **Ease of Access:** To configure Windows for vision, hearing, and mobility needs

In Windows you can change how the Control Panel is displayed. The view that you select determines which utilities are immediately accessible in the Control Panel. In Windows 7, the view options include the following:

- **Category:** Groups the Control Panel utilities into easy-to-navigate groups

- **Large icons:** Displays the utilities in alphabetical order using large icons

- **Small icons:** Displays the utilities in alphabetical order using small icons

---

Note

This book uses the large icon view, shown in Figure 5-29.

Figure 5-29   Control Panel in Large Icon View

In Windows Vista, there are two view options:

- **Control Panel Home:** Groups the Control Panel utilities into easy-to-navigate groups

- **Classic View:** Displays all of the Control Panel utilities individually

In Windows XP, there are two view options:

- **Category:** Groups the Control Panel utilities into easy-to-navigate groups

- **Classic View:** Displays all of the Control Panel utilities individually

User Accounts (5.3.2.2)

An administrative account is created when the Windows OS is installed. To create additional user accounts, open the User Accounts utility, as shown in Figure 5-30, by selecting **Start > Control Panel > User Accounts**.

Figure 5-30 User Accounts

The User Accounts utility provides options to help you manage your password, change your picture, change your account name and type, manage another account, and change *User Account Control (UAC) settings*.

Note

Some features of the User Accounts utility require administrative privileges and might not be accessible with a standard user account.

User Account Control Settings

The UAC monitors programs on a computer and warns users when an action might present a threat to the system. In Windows 7, you can adjust the level of monitoring that the UAC performs. When Windows 7 is installed, the UAC for the primary account is set to Default - Notify me only when programs try to make changes to my computer.

To adjust the level of UAC monitoring, use the following path:

Start > Control Panel > User Accounts > Change User Account Control settings

Lab 5.3.2.3: Create User Accounts in Windows 7

In this lab, you create user accounts. Refer to Lab 5.3.2.3 in *IT Essentials: PC Hardware and Software Lab Manual*, Fifth Edition.

Lab 5.3.2.4: Create User Accounts in Windows Vista

In this lab, you create user accounts. Refer to Lab 5.3.2.4 in *IT Essentials: PC Hardware and Software Lab Manual*, Fifth Edition.

Lab 5.3.2.5: Create User Accounts in Windows XP

In this lab, you create user accounts. Refer to Lab 5.3.2.5 in *IT Essentials: PC Hardware and Software Lab Manual*, Fifth Edition.

Internet Options (5.3.2.6)

To access the Internet Options, use the following path:

Start > Control Panel > Internet Options

As shown in Figure 5-31, Internet Options has the following tabs:

- **General:** Configure basic Internet settings, such as selecting the Internet Explorer (IE) home page, viewing and deleting browsing history, adjusting search settings, and customizing browser appearance.

- **Security:** Adjust the security settings for the Internet, local intranet, trusted sites, and restricted sites. Security levels for each zone can range from low (minimal security) to high (maximum security).

- **Privacy:** Configure privacy settings for the Internet zone, manage location services, and enable Pop-Up Blocker.

- **Content:** Access Parental Controls, control content viewed on the computer, adjust AutoComplete settings, and configure the feeds and web slices that can be viewed in IE.

- **Connections:** Set up an Internet connection and adjust network settings.

- **Programs:** Choose the default web browser, enable browser add-ons, select the HTML editor for IE, and select programs used for Internet services.

- **Advanced:** Adjust advanced settings, and reset Internet Explorer's settings to the default state.

Figure 5-31   Internet Options Properties

Lab 5.3.2.7: Configure Browser Settings in Windows 7

In this lab, you configure browser settings. Refer to Lab 5.3.2.7 in *IT Essentials: PC Hardware and Software Lab Manual*, Fifth Edition.

Lab 5.3.2.8: Configure Browser Settings in Windows Vista

In this lab, you configure browser settings. Refer to Lab 5.3.2.8 in *IT Essentials: PC Hardware and Software Lab Manual*, Fifth Edition.

Lab 5.3.2.9: Configure Browser Settings in Windows XP

In this lab, you configure browser settings. Refer to Lab 5.3.2.9 in *IT Essentials: PC Hardware and Software Lab Manual*, Fifth Edition.

Display Settings (5.3.2.10)

When using an LCD screen, set the resolution to native mode or native resolution. Native mode has the same number of pixels that the monitor has. If you do not use native mode, the monitor does not produce the best picture.

You can change the display settings with the Display Settings utility. You can change the appearance of the desktop by modifying the resolution and color quality, as shown in Figure 5-32. If the screen resolution is not set properly, you might get unexpected display results from different video cards and monitors. You can also change more advanced display settings, such as the wallpaper, screensaver, power settings, and other options.

With Windows 7, use the following path:

Start > Control Panel > Display > Change display settings

With Windows Vista, use the following path:

Start > Control Panel > Personalization > Display Settings

With Windows XP, use the following path:

Start > Control Panel > Display > Settings

Figure 5-32 Display Settings

You can adjust the following features in Windows 7:

- **Screen resolution:** Specifies the number of pixels. A higher number of pixels provides better resolution and picture.

- **Orientation:** Determines whether the display appears in Landscape, Portrait, flipped Landscape, or flipped Portrait orientations.

- **Refresh rate:** Sets how often the image in the screen is redrawn. The refresh rate is in hertz (Hz). The higher the refresh rate, the more steady the screen image.

- **Display colors:** Specifies the number of colors visible on the screen at once. The more bits, the greater the number of colors. The 8-bit color palette contains 256 colors. The 16-bit color (High Color) palette contains 65,536 colors. The 24-bit color (True Color) palette contains 16 million colors. The 32-bit color palette contains 24-bit color and 8 bits for other data such as transparency.

Note

You can also access the display settings in Windows 7 and Windows Vista in the Display link of the Personalization Control Panel utility.

Folder Options (5.3.2.11)

Ensuring proper access to files requires managing the directory and folder settings. To configure settings for folders in Windows, use the Folder Options utility.

To access the Folder Options utility in Windows 7, use the following path:

Start > Control Panel > Folder Options

Folder Options has three tabs: General, View, and Search.

General Tab

Use the General tab to adjust basic display and access settings:

- **Browse folders:** Configures how a folder is displayed when it is opened
- **Click items as follows:** Specifies the number of clicks required to open a file
- **Navigation pane:** Determines whether all folders are displayed and whether a folder is automatically expanded when it is selected in the navigation pane

View Tab

Use the View tab to adjust view settings and attributes for folders, including the ability to see hidden folders:

- **Folder views:** Applies the view settings for a folder being viewed to all folders of the same type
- **Advanced settings:** Customizes the viewing experiences

Search Tab

Use the Search tab to customize folder search settings:

- **What to search:** Configures search settings based on indexed and non-indexed locations to make files and folders easier to find
- **How to search:** Determines which options to take into account during a search
- **When searching non-indexed locations:** Determines whether system directories and compressed files are included when searching non-indexed locations

Action Center (5.3.2.12)

Security settings are an important aspect of maintaining an operating system because they protect your computer from security threats. The Action Center in Windows 7 and Windows Vista allows you to configure security settings. In Windows XP, the Action Center is called the Security Center.

To access the Action Center in Windows 7 and Windows Vista, use the following path:

Start > Control Panel > Action Center

To access the Security Center in Windows XP, use the following path:

Start > Control Panel > Security Center

The Action Center has a number of utilities:

- **Virus Protection:** Turn virus protection programs on or off.

- **Setup Backup:** Users with administrative privileges can set up a Windows backup.

- **Change Action Center settings:** Turn messaging for security and maintenance programs on or off.

- **Change User Account Control settings:** Users with administrative privileges can adjust settings for the UAC.

- **View archived messages:** View archived messages about past computer problems.

- **View performance information:** View and rate the performance of system components.

Windows Firewall (5.3.2.13)

In addition to the security settings available in the Action Center, you can prevent malicious attacks on your system with the Windows Firewall utility. A firewall implements a security policy by selectively permitting and denying data traffic to a computer. A firewall gets its name from a brick and mortar firewall designed to prevent fire from spreading from one part of a building to another.

You can configure firewall settings for home networks, work networks, and public networks. Further changes can be made by using the following options:

- **Allow a program or feature through Windows Firewall:** Determine which programs can communicate through the Windows Firewall.

- **Change notification settings:** Users with administrative privileges can manage notifications from the Windows Firewall.

- **Turn Windows Firewall on or off:** Users with administrative privileges can turn the Windows Firewall on or off.

- **Restore defaults:** Users with administrative privileges can restore the Windows Firewall to the default settings.

- **Advanced settings:** Users with administrative privileges can adjust advanced security settings.

To access the Windows Firewall utility in Windows 7, use the following path:

Start > Control Panel > Windows Firewall

Power Options (5.3.2.14)

The Power Options utility in Windows allows you to reduce the power consumption of certain devices or of the entire system. Use Power Options to maximize performance or conserve energy by configuring a system's power plan. Power plans are a collection of hardware and system settings that manage the power usage of the computer, as shown in Figure 5-33. In Windows XP, power plans are called power schemes.

Figure 5-33   Power Options

Windows 7 and Windows Vista have preset power plans, while Windows XP has preset power schemes. These are the default settings and were created when the OS was installed. You can use the default settings or the customized plans that are based on specific work requirements.

Note

Power Options automatically detects some devices that are connected to the computer. Therefore, the Power Options windows will vary based on the hardware that is detected.

To access the Power Options utility, use the following path:

Start > Control Panel > Power Options

You can choose from the following options:

- Require a password on wakeup
- Choose what the power buttons do
- Choose what closing the lid does (for laptops only)

- Create a power plan
- Choose when to turn off the display
- Change when the computer sleeps

Selecting Choose what the power buttons do or Choose what closing the lid does configures how a computer acts when power or sleep buttons are pressed or when the lid on a laptop is closed. If users do not want to completely shut down a computer, the following options are available:

- **Do nothing:** The computer continues to run at full power.
- **Sleep:** Documents and applications are saved in RAM, allowing the computer to power on quickly. In Windows XP, this option is called Standby.
- **Hibernate:** Documents and applications are saved to a temporary file on the hard drive. With this option, the computer takes a little longer than Sleep to power on.

System Utility (5.3.2.15)

The System utility in the Windows Control Panel allows all users to view basic system information, access tools, and configure advanced system settings.

To access the System utility, use the following path:

Start > Control Panel > System

You access the various settings by clicking the links in the Control Panel Home pane.

When a user clicks the link for the Device Manager, the Device Manager utility opens. When one of the other links is clicked, the System Properties utility appears with the following tabs:

- **Computer Name:** View or modify the name and workgroup settings for a computer, as well as change the domain or workgroup.
- **Hardware:** Access the Device Manager or adjust the device installation settings.
- **Advanced:** Configure settings for performance, user profiles, startup, and recovery.
- **System Protection:** Access System Restore and configure protection settings.
- **Remote:** Adjust settings for Remote Assistance and Remote Desktop.

Performance Settings

To enhance the performance of the OS, you can change some of the settings that your computer uses, such as virtual memory configuration settings, as shown in

Figure 5-34. The OS uses virtual memory when a computer does not have enough RAM available to run a program. If enough RAM is not available, virtual memory moves data from the RAM and places it in a paging file on the hard drive. A paging file is a place where data is stored until enough RAM is available to process the data. This process is much slower than accessing the RAM directly. If a computer has a small amount of RAM, consider purchasing additional RAM to reduce paging.

To view the virtual memory setting in Windows 7, use the following path:

Start > Control Panel > System > Advanced system settings > Performance > Settings button > Advanced > Change

In Windows Vista, use the following path:

Start > Control Panel > System > Advanced system settings > Continue > Advanced tab > Performance area > Settings button > Advanced > Change

In Windows XP, use the following path:

Start > Control Panel > System > Advanced > Performance area > Settings button > Advanced tab > Change

Figure 5-34   Performance Options

Windows ReadyBoost

If users are unable to install more RAM, they can use an external flash device and Windows ReadyBoost to enhance performance in Windows 7 and Windows Vista. Windows ReadyBoost enables the OS to treat an external flash device, such as a USB thumb drive, as hard drive cache when there is not enough RAM available. To activate Windows ReadyBoost, a user must insert a flash device and use the following path:

Start > Computer > right-click the desired external flash device **>** select **Properties > click the ReadyBoost tab**

Leabharlanna Poiblí Chathair Bhaile Átha Cliath

Dublin City Public Libraries

Once ReadyBoost has been activated for the desired device, a user must determine how much space on the device will be reserved as cache. A minimum of 256 MB must be selected, with a maximum of 4GB for FAT32 file systems and 32GB on NTFS file systems.

Lab 5.3.2.16: Managing Virtual Memory Windows 7

In this lab, you customize virtual memory settings. Refer to Lab 5.3.2.16 in *IT Essentials: PC Hardware and Software Lab Manual*, Fifth Edition.

Lab 5.3.2.17: Managing Virtual Memory Windows Vista

In this lab, you customize virtual memory settings. Refer to Lab 5.3.2.17 in *IT Essentials: PC Hardware and Software Lab Manual*, Fifth Edition.

Lab 5.3.2.18: Managing Virtual Memory Windows XP

In this lab, you customize virtual memory settings. Refer to Lab 5.3.2.18 in *IT Essentials: PC Hardware and Software Lab Manual*, Fifth Edition.

Device Manager (5.3.2.19)

Device Manager, as shown in Figure 5-35, displays the hardware in a computer. Device Manager allows you to diagnose and resolve device conflicts. You can view details about the installed hardware and drivers such as the currently installed version to compare with the manufacturer's website to see if a driver needs to be updated as well as perform the following functions:

- **Update a driver:** Change the currently installed driver.
- **Roll back a driver:** Change the currently installed driver to the previously installed driver.
- **Uninstall a driver:** Remove a driver.
- **Disable a device:** Disable a device.

To access the Device Manager in Windows 7 and Windows Vista, use the following path:

Start > Control Panel > System > Device Manager

In Windows XP, use the following path:

Start > Control Panel > System > Hardware > Device Manager

You can view the properties of any properly installed device in the system by double-clicking the device name.

Figure 5-35   Device Manager

The Device Manager utility uses icons to indicate a problem with a device, as shown in Figure 5-36.

Device Manager Icon	Explanation
⚠️	An exclamation point in a yellow triangle the device has an error. A problem code is displayed to explain the problem.
❎	Red X appears when the device is disabled. The device is installed in the computer, but no driver is loaded for it.
ⓘ	A blue I appears if the device was manually selected . The Use Automatic Setting options is not selected for the device.
?	A green question mark appears a device specific driver is not available. A compatible driver has been installed.

Figure 5-36   Device Manager Icons

Lab 5.3.2.20: Managing Device Drivers with Device Manager in Windows 7

In this lab, you use Windows Device Manager to gather information about different drivers and learn how Device Manager manages drivers. Refer to Lab 5.3.2.20 in *IT Essentials: PC Hardware and Software Lab Manual*, Fifth Edition.

Lab 5.3.2.21: Managing Device Drivers with Device Manager in Windows Vista

In this lab, you use Windows Device Manager to gather information about different drivers and learn how Device Manager manages drivers. Refer to Lab 5.3.2.21 in *IT Essentials: PC Hardware and Software Lab Manual*, Fifth Edition.

Lab 5.3.2.22: Managing Device Drivers with Device Manager in Windows XP

In this lab, you use Windows Device Manager to gather information about different drivers and learn how Device Manager manages drivers. Refer to Lab 5.3.2.22 in *IT Essentials: PC Hardware and Software Lab Manual*, Fifth Edition.

Regional and Language Options (5.3.2.23)

You can change the formats for numbers, currencies, dates, and time by using the Regional and Language Options settings. You can also change the primary language or install an additional language.

To access the Regional and Language Options settings, as shown in the figure, use the following path:

Start > Control Panel > Regional and Language Options

Lab 5.3.2.24: Regional and Language Options in Windows 7

In this lab, you examine regional and language settings. Refer to Lab 5.3.2.24 in *IT Essentials: PC Hardware and Software Lab Manual*, Fifth Edition.

Lab 5.3.2.25: Regional and Language Options in Windows Vista

In this lab, you examine regional and language settings. Refer to Lab 5.3.2.25 in *IT Essentials: PC Hardware and Software Lab Manual*, Fifth Edition.

Lab 5.3.2.26: Regional and Language Options in Windows XP

In this lab, you examine regional and language settings. Refer to Lab 5.3.2.26 in *IT Essentials: PC Hardware and Software Lab Manual*, Fifth Edition.

Administrative Tools (5.3.3)

Administrative Tools is a collection of very powerful tools that fundamentally change the OS. Unlike customizing the color of the desktop, these utilities create partitions, install drivers, enable services, and perform other significant modifications.

Computer Management (5.3.3.1)

Windows contains many utilities to manage permissions and users or configure computer components and services. The Computer Management console allows you to manage many aspects of your computer and remote computers.

The Computer Management console provides access to a number of utilities, including the following:

- Task Scheduler
- Event Viewer
- Shared Folders
- Local Users and Groups
- Performance
- Device Manager
- Disk Management

To open the Computer Management console, use the following path:

Start > Control Panel > Administrative Tools > Computer Management

How To

To view the Computer Management console for a remote computer, follow these steps:

Step 1.   In the console tree, right-click **Computer Management (Local)** and select **Connect to another computer.**

Step 2.   In the Another computer box, type the name of the computer or browse to find the computer you want to manage.

Event Viewer, Component Services, and Data Sources (5.3.3.2)

The Event Viewer, as shown in the Figure 5-37, logs the history of events regarding applications, security, and the system. These log files are a valuable troubleshooting tool because they provide information necessary to identify a problem.

To access the Event Viewer, use the following path:

Start > Control Panel > Administrative Tools > Event Viewer

Figure 5-37   Event Viewer

Component Services is an administrative tool used by administrators and developers to deploy, configure, and administer Component Object Model (COM) components. COM is a way to allow the use of components in environments other than the environment in which they were created.

To access Component Services, use the following path:

Start > Control Panel > Administrative Tools > Component Services

Data Sources is an administrative tool used by administrators to manage, add, or remove data sources using Open Database Connectivity (ODBC). ODBC is a technology that programs use to access a wide range of databases or data sources.

To access Data Sources (ODBC), use the following path:

Start > Control Panel > Administrative Tools > Data Sources (ODBC)

Services (5.3.3.3)

The Services console allows you to manage all the services on your computer and remote computers. A service is a type of application that runs in the background to achieve a specific goal or wait for a request; they require little or no user input. To reduce security risks, only start necessary services. You need to have administrative privileges to have full access to the Service Console. You can use the following settings, or states, to control a service:

- **Automatic:** The service starts when the computer is started. This prioritizes the most important services to start up immediately when an OS starts up.

- **Automatic (delayed):** The service starts after services that are set to Automatic have started. The Automatic (delayed) setting is available only in Windows 7 and Windows Vista.

- **Manual:** The service must be started manually.

- **Disabled:** The service cannot be started until it is enabled.

- **Stopped:** The service is not running.

To open the Services console, use the following path:

Start > Control Panel > Administrative Tools > Services

To view the Services console for a remote computer, follow these steps:

Step 1. In the console tree, right-click **Services (Local)** and select **Connect to another computer.**

Step 2. In the Another computer box, type the name of the computer or browse to find the computer you want to manage.

Performance and Windows Memory Diagnostic (5.3.3.4)

The *Performance Monitor* console has two distinct parts: the System Monitor and Performance Logs and Alerts. You must have administrative privileges to access the Performance Monitor console.

The System Monitor displays real-time information about the processors, disks, memory, and network usage. Use the System Monitor to display detailed data about the resources that you are using when performing specific tasks or multiple tasks. The data displayed can help you understand how the computer workload affects system resources, such as the CPU, memory, and network. You can easily summarize usage data with histograms, graphs, and reports. The data can also help determine when an upgrade might be necessary.

Performance Logs and Alerts allows you to record the performance data and configure alerts. Alerts notify you when a specified usage falls below or rises above a threshold. You can set alerts to create entries in the event log, send a network message, begin a performance log, run a specific program, or any combination of these.

To open the Performance Monitor console in Windows 7, use the following path:

Start > Control Panel > Administrative Tools > Performance Monitor

In Windows Vista, use the following path:

Start > Control Panel > Administrative Tools > Reliability and Performance Monitor > Continue

In Windows XP, use the following path:

Start > Control Panel > Administrative Tools > Performance

Windows Memory Diagnostic is an administrative tool that checks the physical memory that is installed on a computer for errors.

To access Windows Memory Diagnostic in Windows 7, use the following path:

Start> Control Panel > Administrative Tools> Windows Memory Diagnostic

To access Windows Memory Diagnostic in Windows Vista, use the following path:

Start> Control Panel > Administrative Tools> Memory Diagnostic Tool

The Windows Memory Diagnostic is not included in Windows XP.

Lab 5.3.3.5: Monitor and Manage System Resources in Windows 7

In this lab, you use administrative tools to monitor and manage system resources. Refer to Lab 5.3.3.5 in *IT Essentials: PC Hardware and Software Lab Manual*, Fifth Edition.

Lab 5.3.3.6: Monitor and Manage System Resources in Windows Vista

In this lab, you use administrative tools to monitor and manage system resources. Refer to Lab 5.3.3.6 in *IT Essentials: PC Hardware and Software Lab Manual*, Fifth Edition.

Lab 5.3.3.7: Monitor and Manage System Resources in Windows XP

In this lab, you use administrative tools to monitor and manage system resources. Refer to Lab 5.3.3.7 in *IT Essentials: PC Hardware and Software Lab Manual*, Fifth Edition.

System Tools (5.3.4)

Several tools are available to optimize the performance of an operating system. The concepts may be the same across operating systems, but the optimization methods and procedures are different. For example, while virtual memory performs the same function on a Windows 7 OS and a Windows XP OS, the path to find and set virtual memory settings is different.

Disk Defragmenter and Disk Error-Checking Tool (5.3.4.1)

To maintain and optimize an operating system, you can access various tools within Windows. Some of these tools include hard drive defragmentation, which consolidates files for faster access, and disk error checking, which scans the hard drive for file structure errors.

Several utilities included with Windows help maintain system integrity. Two utilities that are useful tools for preventive maintenance are Disk Defragmenter and the Disk Error-Checking tool, or *chkdsk*.

Disk Defragmenter

As files increase in size, some data is written to the next available cluster on the disk. In time, data becomes fragmented and spread over nonadjacent clusters on the hard drive. As a result, it takes longer to locate and retrieve each section of the data. A disk defragmenter gathers the noncontiguous data into one place, making the OS run faster. In Windows 7, the Disk Defragmenter tool is automatically scheduled to run on Wednesday morning or the next time the computer is powered on.

> **Note**
>
> It is not recommended to perform Windows disk defragmentation on solid state drives (SSD). SSDs are optimized by the controller and firmware they use. Determine if a hard drive is an SSD by viewing available disk drives in Device Manager.

To access the Disk Defragmenter in Windows 7, use the following path:

Start > All Programs > Accessories > System Tools > Disk Defragmenter

In Windows Vista, use the following path:

Start > Computer > right-click **Drive** *x* **> Properties > Tools**

In Windows XP, use the following path:

Start > All Programs > Accessories > System Tools > Disk Defragmenter

Disk Error-Checking Tool

The Disk Error-Checking tool checks the integrity of files and folders by scanning the hard disk surface for physical errors. If errors are detected, the tool repairs them. You can access chkdsk through the Disk Defragmenter or by entering **chkdsk** on the command line.

Alternatively, you can check a drive for errors using the following steps:

Step 1.   Click **Start** and select **Computer.**

Step 2.   Right-click the drive to check and select **Properties.**

Step 3.   Click the **Tools** tab.

Step 4.   Under Error-checking, click **Check Now.**

Step 5.   Under Check disk options, select **Scan for and attempt recovery of bad sectors.**

The tool fixes file system errors and checks the disk for bad sectors. It also attempts to recover data from bad sectors.

> **Note**
>
> Use the Disk Error-Checking tool at least once a month and whenever a sudden loss of power causes the system to shut down.

Lab 5.3.4.2: Hard Drive Maintenance in Windows 7

In this lab, you examine the results after using Disk Check and Disk Defragmenter on a hard drive. Refer to Lab 5.3.4.2 in *IT Essentials: PC Hardware and Software Lab Manual*, Fifth Edition.

Lab 5.3.4.3: Hard Drive Maintenance in Windows Vista

In this lab, you examine the results after using Disk Check and Disk Defragmenter on a hard drive. Refer to Lab 5.3.4.3 in *IT Essentials: PC Hardware and Software Lab Manual*, Fifth Edition.

Lab 5.3.4.4: Hard Drive Maintenance in Windows XP

In this lab, you examine the results after using Disk Check and Disk Defragmenter on a hard drive. Refer to Lab 5.3.4.4 in *IT Essentials: PC Hardware and Software Lab Manual*, Fifth Edition.

System Information (5.3.4.5)

Administrators can use the *System Information tool* to collect and display information about local and remote computers. The System Information tool quickly finds information about software, drivers, hardware configurations, and computer components. Support personnel can use this information to diagnose and troubleshoot a computer.

To access the System Information tool, use the following path:

Start > All Programs > Accessories > System Tools > System Information

You can also create a file containing all the information about the computer to send to another technician or help desk. To export a System Information file, select **File > Export**, type the filename, choose a location, and click **Save**.

The System Information tool in Windows XP provides access to many other tools:

- **Net Diagnostics:** Runs a variety of network tests to troubleshoot network-related problems

- **System Restore:** Creates or loads a restore point for restoring the computer's system files and settings

- **File Signature Verification Utility:** Checks for system files that are not digitally signed

- **DirectX Diagnostic Tool:** Reports detailed information about the DirectX components that are installed on your computer

- **Dr Watson:** Debugs Windows to help diagnose program errors

Lab 5.3.4.6: Managing System Files with Built-In Utilities in Windows 7

In this lab, you use Windows built-in utilities to gather information about the system and to troubleshoot system resources. Refer to Lab 5.3.4.6 in *IT Essentials: PC Hardware and Software Lab Manual*, Fifth Edition.

Lab 5.3.4.7: Managing System Files with Built-In Utilities in Windows Vista

In this lab, you use Windows built-in utilities to gather information about the system and to troubleshoot system resources. Refer to Lab 5.3.4.7 in *IT Essentials: PC Hardware and Software Lab Manual*, Fifth Edition.

Lab 5.3.4.8: Managing System Files with Built-In Utilities in Windows XP

In this lab, you use Windows built-in utilities to gather information about the system and to troubleshoot system resources. Refer to Lab 5.3.4.8 in *IT Essentials: PC Hardware and Software Lab Manual*, Fifth Edition.

Accessories (5.3.5)

Windows includes in its operating systems accessories that are preinstalled programs or tools to help users to increase productivity and manage their computers without having to purchase additional third-party applications. Types of programs included are calculator, text editor, and remote-access tools.

Remote Desktop (5.3.5.1)

Technicians can use Remote Desktop and Remote Assistance to repair and upgrade computers. *Remote Desktop* allows technicians to view and control a computer from a remote location. *Remote Assistance* allows technicians to assist customers with problems from a remote location. Remote Assistance also allows the customer to view what is being repaired or upgraded on the computer.

To access Remote Desktop in Windows 7 or Windows Vista, use the following path:

Start > All Programs > Accessories > Remote Desktop Connection

For Windows XP, Remote Desktop is available only on Windows XP Professional. To access Remote Desktop in Windows XP Professional, use the following path:

Start > All Programs > Accessories > Communications > Remote Desktop Connection

Before Remote Assistance can be used in Windows, it must be enabled. To enable and access Remote Assistance, follow these steps:

Step 1.   Click **Start > right-click Computer > Properties**.

Step 2.   Click the **Remote Settings** link in the System window.

Step 3.   Check the **Allow Remote Assistance Connections to This Computer** box.

Step 4.   Click **Apply > OK**.

To access Remote Assistance in Windows 7 or Windows Vista, use the following path:

Start > All Programs > Maintenance > Windows Remote Assistance

To access Remote Assistance in Windows XP, use the following path:

Start > All Programs > Remote Assistance

Lab 5.3.5.2: Remote Desktop and Remote Assistance in Windows 7

In this lab, you remotely connect to a computer, examine device drivers, and provide remote assistance. Refer to Lab 5.3.5.2 in *IT Essentials: PC Hardware and Software Lab Manual*, Fifth Edition.

Lab 5.3.5.3: Remote Desktop and Remote Assistance in Windows Vista

In this lab, you remotely connect to a computer, examine device drivers, and provide remote assistance. Refer to Lab 5.3.5.3 in *IT Essentials: PC Hardware and Software Lab Manual*, Fifth Edition.

Lab 5.3.5.4: Remote Desktop and Remote Assistance in Windows XP

In this lab, you remotely connect to a computer, examine device drivers, and provide remote assistance. Refer to Lab 5.3.5.4 in *IT Essentials: PC Hardware and Software Lab Manual*, Fifth Edition.

Control Panel Utilities Unique to Specific Windows Versions (5.3.6)

Control Panel is the central location for the Windows operating system configuration utilities. When you make changes in the Control Panel, you are making changes to the Registry. The utilities available vary slightly depending on the version of the Windows operating system you are running.

Windows 7 Unique Utilities (5.3.6.1)

A number of Control Panel utilities are unique to Windows 7, including the following:

- HomeGroup
- Action Center
- Windows Defender
- RemoteApp and Desktop Connections
- Troubleshooting

HomeGroup

A homegroup is a network setting that allows users to share files and folders easily on a home network. The *HomeGroup* utility, shown in Figure 5-38, is not available on a work network or a public network.

Figure 5-38   HomeGroup Utility

Action Center

Action Center replaces the Security Center that is found in XP and Vista. The Action Center is described in more detail on the page titled Action Center, found elsewhere in this course.

Windows Defender

Windows Defender is an antispyware program that scans the operating system for unwanted software that might pose a security threat. Windows Defender protects computers from harmful software, such as spyware, that is created to perform malicious attacks. If Windows Defender detects any unwanted software, users can delete or quarantine the harmful files. To access Windows Defender, use the following path:

Start > Control Panel > Windows Defender

Windows Defender is available on Windows 7 and Windows Vista by default and can be downloaded for Windows XP.

RemoteApp and Desktop Connections

The RemoteApp and Desktop Connections utility provides access to remote computers and programs from a single folder in Windows Explorer. To access the RemoteApp and Desktop Connections utility, use the following path:

Start > Control Panel > RemoteApp and Desktop Connections

Troubleshooting

The Troubleshooting utility allows you to troubleshoot problems within the following categories:

- **Programs:** Solve compatibility issues with programs made for prior versions of Windows.

- **Hardware and Sound:** Diagnose and solve device configuration problems and audio issues.

- **Network and Internet:** Solve problems with Internet connections, as well as shared files and folders.

- **Appearance and Personalization:** Solve problems associated with desktop appearance.

- **System and Security:** Perform maintenance tasks, check for performance issues, and improve power usage.

To access the Troubleshooting utility, use the following path:

Start > Control Panel > Troubleshooting

Windows Vista Unique Utilities (5.3.6.2)

A number of Control Panel utilities are unique to Windows Vista, including the following:

- **Tablet PC settings:** The Tablet PC Settings utility allows you to customize the functionality of your tablet PC.

  To access the Tablet PC Settings utility, use the following path: **Start > Control Panel > Tablet PC Settings**

- **Pen and Input Devices:** Allows you to configure settings for digital pens and other input devices.

To access the Pen and Input Devices utility, use the following path:

Start > Control Panel > Pen and Input Devices

- **Offline Files:** Allows you to select shared files and folders from a network to be stored on a computer. These files are available after the computer is disconnected from the network. When you reconnect to the network, the changes made offline are applied to the original files on the network.

  To set up a computer to use offline files and folders, use the following path:
  Start > Control Panel > Offline Files > click the **General tab > Enable Offline Files**

  To view a list of all offline files, use the following path:

  Start > Control Panel > Offline Files > click the **General tab > View your offline files**

- **Problem Reports and Solutions:** The Problem Reports and Solutions utility maintains a log of problems that have occurred in the system and solutions that have been provided by Microsoft. This utility has been moved into the Action Center in Windows 7.

  To access the Problem Reports and Solutions utility, use the following path:
  Start > Control Panel > Problem Reports and Solutions

- **Printers:** The Printers utility allows you to add, remove, and configure printers.

  To access the Printers utility, use the following path:

  Start > Control Panel > Printers

Windows XP Unique Utilities (5.3.6.3)

A number of Control Panel utilities are unique to Windows XP, including the following:

- **Add/Remove Programs:** The Add/Remove Programs utility provides the same functionality in Windows XP as the Programs and Features utility in Windows 7 and Windows Vista.

  To access the Add/Remove Programs utility in Windows XP, use the following path:

  Start > Control Panel > Add/Remove Programs

- **Printers and Faxes:** Allows you to add printers and set up faxing. Similar functionality is provided by the Devices and Printers utility in Windows 7 and Windows Vista.

To access the Printers and Faxes utility, use the following path:

Start > Control Panel > Printers and Faxes

- **Automatic Updates:** The Automatic Updates utility ensures that the OS and applications are constantly being updated for security purposes and added functionality. The Automatic Updates utility scans the system for needed updates and then recommends what should be downloaded and installed. It can download and install updates as soon as they are available, or it can download updates as required and install them when the computer is next rebooted.

  To access the Automatic Updates utility, use the following path:

  Start > Control Panel > System > Automatic Updates

- **Network Connections:** The Network Connections utility allows you to enable and disable network connections. It was replaced in Windows 7 and Windows Vista by the Network and Sharing Center.

  To access the Network Connections utility, use the following path:

  Start > Control Panel > Network Connections

- **Network Setup Wizard:** The Network Setup Wizard guides you through the setup of a small office or home office network. The setup allows users on the network to share files, folders, and devices, such as printers.

  To access the Network Setup Wizard, use the following path:

  Start > Control Panel > Network Connections > Common Tasks > Network Setup Wizard

Command-Line Tools (5.3.7)

A command-line interface (CLI) is text based. You must type commands to manipulate files and execute programs; there are no icons available in the CLI.

Windows CLI Commands (5.3.7.1)

When troubleshooting problems with the OS, you may need to use CLI commands and options to perform tasks. To access the CLI, in Windows Vista and Windows 7 use the following path:

Start > type **cmd** in the search box **>** press **Enter**

To access the CLI in Windows XP, use the following path:

Start > Run > type **cmd** or **command** in the Run box > press **Enter**

After the command window opens, you can enter commands to execute specific functions. Table 5-7 describes some common commands and what they do.

If you are denied the use of one of these commands, you may need to access the CLI as an administrator. To access the CLI as an administrator, use the following path:

Start > type **cmd** in the search box **>** right-click **cmd.exe >** click **Run as administrator >** Yes

Table 5-7   Common CLI Commands

Command	Function
Help [command-name]	Provides specific information for any CLI command Alternatively, you can use [command-name]/?
Taskkill	Stops a running application
Bootrec	Repairs the MBR
Shutdown	Shuts down a local or remote computer
COPY	Copies file from one location to another
XCOPY	Copies files and subdirectories
MD	Creates a new directory
CD	Changes to a different directory
RD	Removes a directory
FORMAT	Formats a drive, mount point, or volume with a file system

Lab 5.3.7.2: Working with CLI Commands in Windows

In this lab, you use Windows CLI commands to manage folders, files, and programs in Windows 7/Vista/XP. Refer to Lab 5.3.7.2 in *IT Essentials: PC Hardware and Software Lab Manual*, Fifth Edition.

Run Line Utility (5.3.7.3)

The Run Line utility, shown in Figure 5-39, allows you to enter commands to configure settings in Windows. Many of these commands are used for system diagnostics and modifications.

To access the Run Line utility in Windows 7, use the following path:

Start > type **run** in the search box **>** press **Enter**

To access the Run Line utility in Windows Vista, use the following path:

Start > Start Search > type **run >** press **Enter**

To access the Run Line utility in Windows XP, use the following path:

Start > run

Figure 5-39   Run Line Utility

This is a list of common commands:

- **CMD:** Used to execute command-line programs and utilities.

- *DXDIAG*: Displays details for all DirectX components and drivers that are installed in a computer. Use this utility to ensure that DirectX is installed properly and configured correctly, as shown in Figure 5-40.

- **EXPLORER:** Opens Windows Explorer.

- **MMC:** Opens the Microsoft Management Console (MMC), which allows you to organize management tools, called snap-ins, in one location for easy administration. You can also add web page links, tasks, ActiveX controls, and folders. You can create as many customized MMCs as needed, each with a different name. This is useful when multiple administrators manage different aspects of the same computer. Each administrator can have an individualized MMC for monitoring and configuring computer settings. You must have administrative privileges to access the MMC.

- *MSCONFIG*: Opens the System Configuration utility, which performs diagnostic procedures on the Windows startup files. You must be logged in with administrator permissions to complete the troubleshooting procedure. Use **MSCONFIG** when the computer boots but does not load Windows correctly.

- *MSINFO32*: Displays a complete system summary of the computer, including hardware components and software information.

- **MSTSC:** Opens Remote Desktop Connection.

- **NOTEPAD:** Opens the Notepad utility, which is a basic text editor.

- *REGEDIT*: Opens the Registry Editor utility, which allows a user to edit the Registry. Using the Registry Editor utility incorrectly could cause hardware, application, or OS problems, including problems that require you to reinstall the operating system.

- **SERVICES.MSC:** Opens the Services utility.

Figure 5-40   DXDiag

MSCONFIG

MSCONFIG, as shown in Figure 5-41, is officially called System Configuration in Windows 7 and Windows Vista and is called Microsoft System Configuration Utility in Windows XP. System Configuration can be used to disable or reenable device drives, Windows services, and software programs. It can also change boot parameters.

The following five tabs are used to manage the different features:

- **General:** Used to select Normal, Diagnostic, and Selective startup methods

- **Boot:** Provides boot options that can be turned on and off

- **Services:** Used to disable and enable running services

- **Startup:** Used to disable and enable items that are loaded automatically when the computer is turned on

- **Tools:** Used to launch Windows features that are usually found in the Control Panel

Figure 5-41   MSCONFIG

Lab 5.3.7.4: Run Line Utilities in Windows 7

In this lab, you use Windows Run Line utilities to access and use tools to configure settings in Windows 7. Refer to Lab 5.3.7.4 in *IT Essentials: PC Hardware and Software Lab Manual*, Fifth Edition.

Lab 5.3.7.5: Run Line Utilities in Windows Vista

In this lab, you use Windows Run Line utilities to access and use tools to configure settings in Windows Vista. Refer to Lab 5.3.7.5 in *IT Essentials: PC Hardware and Software Lab Manual*, Fifth Edition.

Lab 5.3.7.6: Run Line Utilities in Windows XP

In this lab, you use Windows Run Line utilities to access and use tools to configure settings in Windows XP. Refer to Lab 5.3.7.6 in *IT Essentials: PC Hardware and Software Lab Manual*, Fifth Edition.

Client-Side Virtualization (5.4)

Client-side virtualization provides flexibility to businesses in application deployment and operating system usage. It can also help to lower costs when it comes to purchasing PC hardware and OS licenses. This section addresses the purpose of virtualization and various implementation types.

Purpose of Virtual Machines (5.4.1.1)

In a business environment, companies must manage technological resources in a way that allows them to stay competitive by cutting costs and allocating resources wisely. As a result, client-side virtualization has become a popular method of providing staff with critical resources, such as applications, file-sharing services, and other productivity tools. Virtualization also has advantages for SOHO users because it can provide access to programs that are not available on a specific OS.

PC virtualization occurs when a host machine uses its system resources to host a virtual machine. A virtual machine is sometimes called a guest. A host machine must be a physical machine that is powered on and controlled by a user. A virtual machine uses the system resources on the host machine to boot and run an OS. The OS of the virtual machine is independent of the OS installed on the host machine.

Hosting a virtual machine allows users to access the functionality and resources provided by an OS that is completely isolated from the OS of the host computer.

This virtual machine can run software specific to Windows XP. The Windows XP installation does not interfere with the Windows 7 installation on the host machine. If needed, users can further increase the functionality of their system resources by running multiple virtual machines. For example, a host machine running Windows 7 can host a virtual machine that has Windows XP installed, as shown in Figure 5-42.

Figure 5-42   Windows Virtual PC Console

Hypervisor: Virtual Machine Manager (5.4.1.2)

The software that creates and manages a virtual machine on a host machine is called the *hypervisor*, or Virtual Machine Manager (VMM) . A hypervisor can run multiple virtual machines on a single host computer. Each virtual machine runs its own operating system. The number of virtual machines that can be made available depends on the host machine's hardware resources. The hypervisor allocates the physical system resources, such as CPU, RAM, and hard drive, to each virtual machine as needed. This ensures that the operation of one virtual machine does not interfere with another.

There are two types of hypervisors: Type 1 (native) and Type 2 (hosted). A Type 1 hypervisor runs directly on the hardware of a host and manages the allocation of system resources to guest operating systems. A Type 2 hypervisor is hosted by an OS. The Windows Virtual PC is an example of a Type 2 hypervisor.

Windows Virtual PC

Windows Virtual PC is the virtualization platform for Windows 7. Virtual PC allows you to partition system resources for a Windows OS among virtual machines running a licensed copy of Windows 7, Windows Vista, or Windows XP. You can download Virtual PC from the Microsoft Windows website. Virtual PC is required to run the Windows XP Mode program in Windows 7.

Windows XP Mode

Windows XP Mode is a program available for Windows 7 Professional, Enterprise, and Ultimate. *Windows XP Mode* uses virtualization technology to allow users to run Windows XP programs in Windows 7. It opens a virtual machine on the Windows 7 desktop that provides a fully functional version of Windows XP, including access to all system resources. After installing a program in Windows XP Mode, you can run the program in XP Mode and access it from the Windows 7 Start menu.

Note

Before using Windows XP Mode, download and install Windows Virtual PC.

To access XP Mode in Windows 7, follow these steps:

Step 1.   Select **Start > All Programs.**

Step 2.   Select **Windows Virtual PC > Windows XP Mode.**

Virtual Machine Requirements (5.4.1.3)

All virtual machines require that basic system requirements are met, such as a minimum amount of hard disk space or RAM. Table 5-8 displays the minimum hardware requirements for running Virtual PC. Like physical computers, virtual machines are susceptible to threats and malicious attacks. Users should install security software, run the Windows Firewall, and update patches and drivers.

Table 5-8   Virtual PC Requirements

Processor	1 GHz
	32-bit/64-bit processor
Hard disk space	15 GB per virtual OS
Memory	2 GB
Supported host operating systems	Windows 7 Home Basic
	Windows 7 Home Premium
	Windows 7 Enterprise
	Windows 7 Professional
	Windows 7 Ultimate
Supported guest operating systems	Windows XP
	Windows Vista
	Windows 7

To connect to the Internet, a virtual machine uses a virtual network adapter. The virtual network adapter acts like a real adapter in a physical computer, except that it connects through the physical adapter on the host to establish a connection to the Internet.

Lab 5.4.1.4: Install Virtual PC

In this lab, you install and configure Windows XP Mode in Windows 7. You will then run a Windows XP-based application in Windows XP Mode. Refer to Lab 5.4.1.4 in *IT Essentials: PC Hardware and Software Lab Manual*, Fifth Edition.

Common Preventive Maintenance Techniques for Operating Systems (5.5)

The goal of an operating system preventive maintenance plan is to avoid problems in the future. *Preventive maintenance* for an operating system includes organizing the system, defragmenting the hard drive, keeping applications current, removing unused applications, and checking the system for errors.

Preventive Maintenance Plan Contents (5.5.1.1)

To ensure that an OS remains fully functional, you must implement a preventive maintenance plan. A preventive maintenance plan provides the following benefits to users and organizations:

- Decreased downtime

- Improved performance

- Improved reliability

- Decreased repair costs

Preventive Maintenance Planning

Preventive maintenance plans should include detailed information about the maintenance of all computers and network equipment. The plan should prioritize equipment that would affect the organization the most if it goes down. Preventive maintenance for an OS includes automating tasks to perform scheduled updates. Preventive maintenance also includes installing service packs that help keep the system up to date and compatible with new software and hardware. Preventive maintenance includes the following important tasks:

- Hard drive backup

- Hard drive defragmentation

- Updates to the OS and applications

- Updates to antivirus and other protective software

- Hard drive error checking

Perform preventive maintenance regularly, and record all actions taken and observations made. A repair log helps you determine which equipment is the most or least reliable. It also provides a history of when a computer was last fixed, how it was fixed, and what the problem was.

Some preventive maintenance should take place when it causes the least amount of disruption to the people who use the computers. This often means scheduling tasks at night, early in the morning, or over the weekend. There are also tools and techniques that can automate many preventive maintenance tasks.

Security

Security is an important aspect of your preventive maintenance program. Install virus and malware protection software, and perform regular scans on computers to help ensure that they remain free of malicious software. Use the Windows Malicious Software Removal Tool to check a computer for specific, prevalent malicious software. If an infection is found, the tool removes it. Each time a new version of the tool is available from Microsoft, download it and scan your computer for new threats. This should be a standard item in your preventive maintenance program, along with regular updates to your antivirus and spyware removal tools.

Startup Programs

Some programs, such as antivirus scanners and spyware-removal tools, do not automatically start when the computer boots. To ensure that these programs run each time the computer boots, add the program to the Startup folder of the Start menu. Many programs have switches to allow the program to perform a specific action, start up without being displayed, or go to the Windows Tray. Check the documentation to determine if your programs allow the use of special switches.

Lab 5.5.1.2: Managing the Startup Folder in Windows 7

In this lab, you customize the Startup folder and the RunOnce key in the Registry. Refer to Lab 5.5.1.2 in *IT Essentials: PC Hardware and Software Lab Manual*, Fifth Edition.

Lab 5.5.1.3: Managing the Startup Folder in Windows Vista

In this lab, you customize the Startup folder and the RunOnce key in the Registry. Refer to Lab 5.5.1.3 in *IT Essentials: PC Hardware and Software Lab Manual*, Fifth Edition.

Lab 5.5.1.4: Managing the Startup Folder in Windows XP

In this lab, you customize the Startup folder and the RunOnce key in the Registry. Refer to Lab 5.5.1.4 in *IT Essentials: PC Hardware and Software Lab Manual*, Fifth Edition.

Updates (5.5.1.5)

Operating systems are complex programs and can be released for usage with undetected imperfections. These undetected imperfections can cause operational issues and security incidents. As these imperfections are exposed, vendors release patches to fix them. Updating your operating system and other system software adds all the latest patches and necessary fixes to your computer.

Device Driver Updates

Updating device drivers regularly should be part of your preventive maintenance program to ensure that your drivers are always current. Manufacturers occasionally release new drivers to address issues with the current drivers. Check for updated drivers when your hardware does not work properly or to prevent future problems. It is also important to update drivers that patch or correct security problems. If a driver update does not work properly, use the Roll Back Driver feature to revert back to the previously installed driver.

Operating System Updates

Microsoft releases updates to address security issues and other functionality problems. You can install individual updates manually from the Microsoft website or automatically using the *Windows Automatic Updates* utility. Downloads that contain multiple updates are called service packs. A service pack usually contains all the updates for an OS. Installing a service pack is a good way to bring your OS up-to-date quickly. Set a restore point and back up critical data prior to installing a service pack. Add OS updates to your preventive maintenance program to ensure that your OS has the latest functionality and security fixes.

Firmware Updates

Firmware updates are less common than driver updates. Manufacturers release new firmware updates to address issues that might not be fixed with driver updates. Firmware updates can increase the speed of certain types of hardware, enable new features, or increase the stability of a product. Follow the manufacturer's instructions carefully when performing a firmware update to avoid making the hardware unusable. Research the update completely because it might not be possible to revert to the original firmware. Checking for firmware updates should be part of your preventive maintenance program.

Scheduling Tasks (5.5.1.6)

You can schedule preventive maintenance applications to run at an assigned time. You can schedule tasks using the GUI-based Windows Task Scheduler or the CLI **at** command. Both these tools allow you to run a command once at a specific time or on an ongoing basis on selected days or times. For recurring tasks and deleting tasks already scheduled, the Windows Task Scheduler, shown in Figure 5-43, is easier to learn and use than the **at** command.

Figure 5-43   Task Scheduler

Windows Task Scheduler

You can automate tasks using the Task Scheduler. The Task Scheduler monitors selected user-defined criteria and then executes the tasks when the criteria have been met. Some common tasks that are automated using Task Scheduler include the following:

- Disk cleanup
- Backup
- Disk defragmenter
- Restore point
- Starting other applications

To access the Windows Task Scheduler in Windows 7 and Windows Vista, use the following path:

Start > All Programs > Accessories > System Tools > Task Scheduler

In Windows XP, use the following path:

Start > All Programs > Accessories > System Tools > Scheduled Tasks

at Command

You can use the **at** command to schedule a command, script file, or application to run at a specific date and time. To use the **at** command, you must be logged in as an administrator.

To access more information about the **at** command in Windows 7 and Windows Vista, use the following path:

Start > Start Search > type **cmd >** press **Enter**

Then type **at /?** in the command line and press **Enter**.

To access information about the **at** command in Windows XP, use the following path:

Start > Run > type **cmd >** press **Enter**

Then type **at /?** in the command line and press **Enter**.

Lab 5.5.1.7: Schedule a Task Using the GUI and the at Command in Windows 7

In this lab, you schedule a task using the Windows 7 GUI and schedule a task in a command window using the **at** command. Refer to Lab 5.5.1.7 in *IT Essentials: PC Hardware and Software Lab Manual*, Fifth Edition.

Lab 5.5.1.8 Schedule a Task Using the GUI and the at Command in Windows Vista

In this lab, you schedule a task using the Windows Vista GUI and schedule a task in a command window using the **at** command. Refer to Lab 5.5.1.8 in *IT Essentials: PC Hardware and Software Lab Manual*, Fifth Edition.

Lab 5.5.1.9: Schedule a Task Using the GUI and the at Command in Windows XP

In this lab, you schedule a task using the Windows XP GUI and schedule a task in a command window using the **at** command. Refer to Lab 5.5.1.9 in *IT Essentials: PC Hardware and Software Lab Manual*, Fifth Edition.

Restore Points (5.5.1.10)

Sometimes installing an application or hardware driver can cause instability or create unexpected problems. Uninstalling the application or hardware driver usually corrects the problem. If uninstalling does not solve the problem, restore the computer to an earlier time when the system worked properly with the System Restore utility, as shown in Figure 5-44.

Figure 5-44 System Restore Tool

Restore points contain information about the system and Registry settings. If a computer crashes or an update causes problems, the computer can be rolled back to a previous configuration using a restore point. System restore does not back up personal data files nor recover personal files that have been corrupted or deleted. Always use a dedicated backup system, such as a tape drive, optical disc, or USB storage device.

A technician should always create a restore point before making changes to a system in the following situations:

- When updating the OS
- When installing or upgrading hardware
- When installing an application
- When installing a driver

Note

A restore point backs up drivers, system files, and Registry settings but not application data.

To open the System Restore utility and create a restore point, use the following path:

Start > All Programs > Accessories > System Tools > System Restore

Lab 5.5.1.11: Use the System Restore Tool in Windows 7

In this lab, you create a restore point and return your computer back to that point in time. Refer to Lab 5.5.1.11 in *IT Essentials: PC Hardware and Software Lab Manual*, Fifth Edition.

Lab 5.5.1.12: Use the System Restore Tool in Windows Vista

In this lab, you create a restore point and return your computer back to that point in time. Refer to Lab 5.5.1.12 in *IT Essentials: PC Hardware and Software Lab Manual*, Fifth Edition.

Lab 5.5.1.13: Use the System Restore Tool in Windows XP

In this lab, you create a restore point and return your computer back to that point in time. Refer to Lab 5.5.1.13 in *IT Essentials: PC Hardware and Software Lab Manual*, Fifth Edition.

Hard Drive Backup (5.5.1.14)

It is important to establish a backup strategy that includes data recovery, including personal files. You can use the Microsoft *Backup Utility*, shown in Figure 5-45, to perform backups as required. How the computer system is used, in addition to organizational requirements, determines how often the data must be backed up and the type of backup to perform.

You can choose from several different types of backups depending on your requirements.

Figure 5-45   Backup Utility

Normal Backup

A normal backup is also called a *full backup*. During a *normal backup*, all selected files on the disk are archived to the backup medium. These files are marked as having been archived by clearing the archive bit.

Copy Backup

A *copy backup* copies all selected files. It does not mark the files as archived.

Incremental Backup

An *incremental backup* backs up all the files and folders that have been created or modified since either the last normal or incremental backup. It marks the files as archived by clearing the archive bit. This has the effect of advancing the starting point of differential backups without having to re-archive the entire contents of the drive. To recover an incremental backup, the last full backup must be recovered, followed by all incremental backups in order.

Differential Backup

A *differential backup* backs up all the files and folders that have been created or modified since either the last normal backup or the last incremental backup. A differential backup does not mark the files as archived. Copies are made from the same starting point until the next incremental or full backup is performed. Making differential backups is important because only the last full and differential backups are needed to restore all the data.

Daily Backup

Daily backups only back up the files that are modified on the day of the backup. Daily backups do not modify the archive bit.

It can take a long time to run a backup. If the backup strategy is followed carefully, it is not necessary to back up all files every time. Instead, only the files that have changed since the last backup need to be backed up.

To access the backup utility in Windows 7, use the following path:

Start > Control Panel > Backup and Restore

To access the backup utility in Windows Vista, use the following path:

Start > All Programs > Accessories > System Tools > Backup Status and Configuration

To access the backup utility in Windows XP Professional, use the following path:

Start > All Programs > Accessories > System Tools > Backup

Basic Troubleshooting Process for Operating Systems (5.6)

The troubleshooting process helps resolve problems with the operating system. OS problems can result from a combination of hardware, software, and network issues. These problems range from simple, such as a driver that does not operate properly, to complex, such as a system that locks up. Computer technicians must be able to analyze a problem and determine the cause to be able to come up with solutions. This process is called troubleshooting. This section explores the troubleshooting steps to guide a technician in how to accurately identify, repair, and document problems.

Identify the Problem (5.6.1.1)

OS problems can result from a combination of hardware, software, and network issues. Computer technicians must be able to analyze a problem and determine the cause to be able to repair the computer. The first step in the troubleshooting process is to identify the problem. Table 5-9 is a list of open-ended and closed-ended questions to ask the customer.

Table 5-9   Step 1: Identify the Problem

Open-ended questions	What problems are you having?
	What operating system is installed on the computer?
	What updates have you performed lately?
	What programs have you recently installed?
	What were you doing when the problem was discovered?
Closed-ended questions	Can you boot the operating system?
	Can you boot in safe mode?
	Have you changed your password lately?
	Have you seen any error messages on the computer?
	Has anyone else used the computer recently?
	Has any hardware been added recently?
Problem description	Open-ended questions.
	Closed ended questions.

Establish a Theory of Probable Cause (5.6.1.2)

After you have talked to the customer, you can establish a theory of probable causes. Table 5-10 lists some common probable causes for OS problems.

Table 5-10   Step 2: Establish a Theory of Probable Cause

Common causes of operating system problems	Incorrect settings in BIOS.
	Caps lock key is set to on.
	Nonbootable media in the floppy drive during computer boot.
	Password has changed.
	Incorrect monitor setting in Control Panel.
	Operating system update failure.
	Driver update failure.
	Malware infection.
	Hard drive failure.
	Corrupt operating system files.

Test the Theory to Determine Cause (5.6.1.3)

After you have developed some theories about what is wrong, test your theories to determine the cause of the problem. Table 5-11 shows a list of quick procedures that can help determine the exact cause of the problem or even correct the problem. If a quick procedure does correct the problem, you can jump to verifying the full system functionality. If a quick procedure does not correct the problem, you need to research the problem further to establish the exact cause.

Table 5-11   Step 3: Test the Theory to Determine Cause

Common steps to determine cause	Log in as a different user.
	Use third-party diagnostic software.
	Determine whether new software or software updates have just been installed.
	Uninstall recently installed applications.
	Boot into safe mode to determine if the problem is driver related.
	Roll back newly updated drivers.
	Examine Device Manager for device conflicts.
	Examine event logs for warnings or errors.
	Check the hard drive for errors and fix file system issues.
	Use the System File Checker to recover corrupt system files.
	Use System Restore if a system update or service pack has been installed.

Establish a Plan of Action to Resolve the Problem and Implement the Solution (5.6.1.4)

After you have determined the exact cause of the problem, establish a plan of action to resolve the problem and implement the solution. Table 5-12 shows some sources you can use to gather additional information to resolve an issue.

Table 5-12   Step 4: Establish a Plan of Action to Resolve the Problem and Implement the Solution

If no solution is achieved in the previous step, further research is needed to implement the solution.	Help desk repair logs
	Other technicians
	Manufacturer FAQs
	Technical websites
	News groups
	Manuals
	Online forums
	Internet research

Verify Full System Functionality and Implement Preventive Measures (5.6.1.5)

After you have corrected the problem, verify full system functionality and, if applicable, implement preventive measures. Table 5-13 lists the steps to verify full system functionality.

Table 5-13   Step 5: Verify Full System Functionality and, If Applicable, Implement Preventive Measures

Verify full functionality.	Shut down and restart computer.
	Check event logs to make sure there are no warnings or errors.
	Check Device Manager to see that there are no warnings or errors.
	Run DXDiag to make sure DirectX is running correctly.
	Make sure network shares are accessible.
	Make sure the Internet can be accessed.
	Rerun System File Checker to ensure all files are correct.
	Check Task Manager to ensure that the status of all programs is running.
	Rerun any diagnostic tools.

Document Findings, Actions, and Outcomes (5.6.1.6)

In the final step of the troubleshooting process, you must document your findings, actions, and outcomes. Table 5-14 lists the tasks required to document the problem and the solution.

Table 5-14   Step 6: Document Your Findings, Actions, and Outcomes

Document your findings, actions, and outcomes.	Discuss the solution implemented with the customer.
	Have the customer verify that the problem has been solved.
	Provide the customer with all paperwork.
	Document the steps taken to solve the problem in the work order and technician's journal.
	Document any components used in the repair.
	Document the time spent to resolve the problem.

Common Problems and Solutions (5.6.2.1)

OS problems can be attributed to hardware, application, or configuration issues, or to some combination of the three. You will resolve some types of OS problems more often than others. Table 5-15 is a chart of some of common operating system problems and solutions.

Table 5-15   Common Problems and Solutions

Identify the Problem	Probable Causes	Possible Solutions
OS locks up.	Computer is overheating. Some of the operating system files may be corrupted. The power supply, RAM, HDD, or motherboard may be defective. The BIOS settings may be incorrect. An incorrect driver has been installed.	Clean internal components. Check the fan connections. Run System File Checker to replace corrupt OS files. Test hardware components and replace if necessary. Address any events in the event logs. Examine and adjust the BIOS settings. Install or roll back drivers as necessary.
The keyboard or mouse does not respond.	Communication between the device and computer has failed. Computer has an incompatible or outdated driver. Cable is damaged. Device is defective. KVM switch is being used, and the active computer is not displayed.	Reboot the system. Install or roll back drivers. Replace the defective power supply, RAM, HDD, or motherboard with a known good component. Change input on the KVM switch.

Identify the Problem	Probable Causes	Possible Solutions
The operating system will not start.	A hardware device has failed. No bootable disk is available. OS file corrupt. MBR is corrupt. The power supply, RAM, HDD, or motherboard may be defective. Hardware drivers did not install properly. Windows updates have corrupted the OS.	Reboot the computer. Remove all nonbootable media from the drives. Restore Windows using the System Restore tool. Recover the system disk using System Image Recovery tool. Perform a repair installation on the operating system. Use the Recovery Console to fix the Master Boot Record. Replace the defective power supply, RAM, HDD, or motherboard with a known good component. Disconnect any newly connected devices and use the Last Known Good Configuration option to start the operating system. Boot the computer into safe mode and address all the events in the event logs.
The computer displays an "Invalid Boot Disk Error" after the POST.	Media that does not have an operating system is in the drive. The boot order is not set correctly in the BIOS. The hard drive is not detected, or the jumpers are not set correctly. Hard drive does not have an operating system installed. MBR is corrupted. Hard drive is failing. Computer has a boot sector virus.	Remove all media from the drives. Change the boot order in the BIOS. Reconnect the hard drive or reset the jumpers. Install an OS. Run **fdisk /mbr** in Windows XP only. Run virus-removal software. Replace the hard drive.

Identify the Problem	Probable Causes	Possible Solutions
The computer displays an "Invalid Boot Disk Error" after the POST.	A recently installed device driver is incompatible with the boot controller. BOOTMGR is corrupted in Windows 7 or Windows Vista. NTLDR is corrupted in Windows XP.	Use the Last Known Good Configuration to boot the computer. Boot the computer in safe mode and load a restore point from before the installation of new hardware. Restore the BOOTMGR file from Windows 7 or Windows Vista installation media. Restore NTLDR for Windows XP installation media.
The computer displays a "BOOTMGR" error after POST in Windows 7 and Windows Vista.	BOOTMGR is missing or damaged. Boot configuration data is missing or damaged. The boot order is not set correctly in BIOS. MBR is corrupt. Hard drive is failing. Hard drive jumpers are not set correctly.	Restore BOOTMGR from installation media. Restore boot configuration data from installation media. Set the correct boot order in BIOS. Run **chkdsk /F/R** from Recovery Console. Change hard drive jumper to correct setting.
The computer displays a "BOOTMGR Is Missing" error after POST in Windows Vista and Windows 7.	BOOTMGR is missing or damaged. Boot configuration data is missing or damaged. The boot order is set incorrectly in BIOS. The MBR is corrupted. The hard drive is failing. The hard drive jumpers are set incorrectly.	Restore BOOTMGR from installation media. Restore boot configuration data from installation media. Change the boot order in BIOS to correct boot drive. Run **chkdsk /F/R** from Recovery Console. Change hard drive jumper to correct setting.
A service failed to start when the computer booted.	The service is not enabled. The service is set to Manual. The failed service requires another service to be enabled.	Enable the service. Set the service to Automatic. Reenable or reinstall the required service.

Identify the Problem	Probable Causes	Possible Solutions
A device did not start when the computer booted.	The external power is not on. The data cable or power cable is not connected to the device. The device has been disabled in the BIOS. The device has failed. The device has a conflict with a newly installed device. The driver is corrupted.	Power on external device. Secure the data and power cables to the device. Enable the device in the BIOS. Replace the device. Remove the newly installed device. Reinstall or roll back the driver.
The program listed in the Registry is not found.	One of more program files has been deleted. The uninstall program did not work correctly. The installation directory has been removed. The hard drive has become corrupt. The computer has a virus.	Reinstall the program. Reinstall the program and run the uninstall program again. Run **chkdsk /F/R** to fix the hard drive file entries. Scan for and remove the virus.
The computer continually restarts without displaying the desktop.	The computer is set to restart when there is a failure. A startup file has become corrupted.	Press **F8** to open the Advanced Options menu and choose **Disable automatic restart on system failure**. Run **chkdsk /F/R** from the Recovery Console.
The CPU locks without an error message.	The CPU or FSB settings are incorrect on the motherboard or in the BIOS. The computer is overheating. RAM is failing. Hard drive is failing. Power supply is failing.	Check and reset the CPU and FSB settings as necessary. Check and replace any cooling devices as necessary. Replace any failing devices with known good replacement components.

Identify the Problem	Probable Causes	Possible Solutions
An application does not install.	The downloaded application installer contains a virus and was prevented from installing by the virus-protection software. The installation disk of file is corrupted. The installation application is not compatible with the operating system. There are too many programs running and not enough system memory remaining to install the application. The minimum hardware requirements of the application are not met.	Replace the installation disk or downloaded file with one that is virus free or not corrupt. Run the installation application in compatibility mode. Close other applications before attempting the installation. Install hardware to meet the minimum hardware requirements of the application.
A computer with Windows 7 installed does not run Aero.	The computer does not meet the minimum hardware requirements for running Aero.	Upgrade the processor, RAM, and video card to meet the minimum Microsoft requirements for Aero.
The search feature takes a long time to find results.	The index service is not running. The index service is not indexing the correct locations.	Start the index service using services.msc. Change the settings of the index service in the Advanced Options panel.
The UAC no longer prompts the user for permissions.	The UAC has been turned off.	Turn on the UAC in the User Account applet in the Control Panel.
No gadgets appear on the desktop.	The gadgets have never been installed or have been uninstalled. The XML necessary to render the gadget is broken, corrupt, or not installed.	Right-click the desktop > choose **Gadgets** > right-click a gadget > click **Add**. Register the file msxml3.dll by entering **regsvr32 msxml3.dll>** at the command prompt.

Identify the Problem	Probable Causes	Possible Solutions
The computer is running slowly and has a delayed response.	A process is using most of the CPU resources.	Restart the process with services.msc. If the process is not needed, end it with Task Manager. Restart the computer.
The computer does not recognize an external drive.	The OS does not have the correct drivers for the external drive.	Download the correct drivers.
A new sound card does not work.	The volume has been muted.	Unmute the volume in the Sound Control Panel applet.
Some external devices from a 32-bit OS computer do not work in the 64-bit OS computer.	Incorrect devices drivers.	Update to the 64-bit device drivers.
After upgrade to Windows 7, the computer runs very slowly.	Aero is causing the slowdown.	Turn off Aero in Window 7.

Summary (5.7.1.1)

This chapter introduced computer operating systems. As a technician, you should be skilled at installing, configuring, and troubleshooting an OS. The following concepts from this chapter are important to remember:

- Several different operating systems are available, and you must consider the customer's needs and environment when choosing an OS.

- The main steps in setting up a customer's computer include preparing the hard drive, installing the OS, creating user accounts, and configuring installation options.

- A GUI shows icons of all files, folders, and applications on the computer. A pointing device, such as a mouse, is used to navigate in a GUI desktop.

- A CLI uses commands to complete tasks and navigate the file system.

- You should establish a backup strategy that allows for the recovery of data.

- Normal, copy, differential, incremental, and daily backups are all optional backup tools available in Windows operating systems.

- With a virtual machine manager, system resources on a host computer can be allocated to run virtual machines. Virtual machines run operating systems, and using them can provide users with greater system functionality.

- Preventive maintenance techniques help to ensure optimal performance of the OS.

- Some of the tools available for troubleshooting an OS problem include administrative tools, system tools, and CLI commands.

Summary of Exercises

This is a summary of the labs and worksheets associated with this chapter. Refer to the worksheets in the *IT Essentials: PC Hardware and Software Lab Manual*, Fifth Edition.

Labs

The following labs cover material from this chapter. Refer to the labs in the *IT Essentials: PC Hardware and Software Lab Manual*, Fifth Edition.

Lab 5.1.4.4: Data Migration in Windows 7

Lab 5.1.4.5: Data Migration in Windows Vista

Lab 5.3.2.20: Managing Device Drivers with Device Manager in Windows 7

Lab 5.3.2.21: Managing Device Drivers with Device Manager in Windows Vista

Lab 5.3.2.22: Managing Device Drivers with Device Manager in Windows XP

Lab 5.3.2.24: Regional and Language Options in Windows 7

Lab 5.3.2.25: Regional and Language Options in Windows Vista

Lab 5.3.2.26: Regional and Language Options in Windows XP

Lab 5.3.3.5: Monitor and Manage System Resources in Windows 7

Lab 5.3.3.6: Monitor and Manage System Resources in Windows Vista

Lab 5.3.3.7: Monitor and Manage System Resources in Windows XP

Lab 5.3.4.2: Hard Drive Maintenance in Windows 7

Lab 5.3.4.3: Hard Drive Maintenance in Windows Vista

Lab 5.3.4.4: Hard Drive Maintenance in Windows XP

Lab 5.3.4.6: Managing System Files with Built-in Utilities in Windows 7

Lab 5.3.4.7: Managing System Files with Built-in Utilities in Windows Vista

Lab 5.3.4.8: Managing System Files with Built-in Utilities in Windows XP

Lab 5.3.5.2: Remote Desktop and Remote Assistance in Windows 7

Lab 5.3.5.3: Remote Desktop and Remote Assistance in Windows Vista

Lab 5.3.5.4: Remote Desktop and Remote Assistance in Windows XP

Lab 5.3.7.2: Working with CLI Commands in Windows

Lab 5.3.7.4: Run Line Utilities in Windows 7

Lab 5.3.7.5: Run Line Utilities in Windows Vista

Lab 5.3.7.6: Run Line Utilities in Windows XP

Lab 5.4.1.4: Install Virtual PC

Lab 5.5.1.2: Managing the Startup Folder in Windows 7

Lab 5.5.1.3: Managing the Startup Folder in Windows Vista

Lab 5.5.1.4: Managing the Startup Folder in Windows XP

Lab 5.5.1.7: Schedule a Task Using the GUI and the at Command in Windows 7

Lab 5.5.1.8: Schedule a Task Using the GUI and the at Command in Windows Vista

Lab 5.5.1.9: Schedule a Task Using the GUI and the at Command in Windows XP

Lab 5.5.1.11: Use the System Restore Tool in Windows 7

Lab 5.5.1.12: Use the System Restore Tool in Windows Vista

Lab 5.5.1.13: Use the System Restore Tool in Windows XP

Worksheets

The following worksheets cover material from this chapter. Refer to the worksheets in the *IT Essentials: PC Hardware and Software Lab Manual*, Fifth Edition.

Worksheet 3.3.3.2: Upgrade Hardware

Check Your Understanding

You can find the answers to these questions in Appendix A, "Answers to 'Check Your Understanding' Questions."

1. What is the purpose of the Microsoft System Preparation (Sysprep) tool?

    A. To install updated drivers for hardware

    B. To create a disk image of the configured computer

    C. To enable Windows updates to be pushed out over a network to multiple computers

    D. To enable the same operating system to be installed and configured on multiple computers

2. A computer is suffering from poor performance after an upgrade from Windows XP to Windows Vista. Which action could improve the performance?

    A. Turn off Aero.

    B. Restore NTLDR from installation media.

    C. Update the device drivers to 64-bit drivers.

    D. Create a new NTFS partition.

3. Which term best describes the process of breaking a program into smaller parts that can be loaded as needed by the operating system?

    A. Multithreading

    B. Multiprocessing

    C. Multiuser

    D. Multitasking

4. A user reports to a technician that his computer freezes without any error messages. What are two probable causes?

    A. An update has corrupted the operating system.

    B. NTLDR is missing or damaged.

    C. The power supply is failing.

    D. The MBR is corrupted.

    E. The boot order is not set correctly in BIOS.

5. Which of these programs is an example of a Type 2 hypervisor?

    A. Virtual PC

    B. Windows XP Mode

    C. OpenGL

    D. DirectX

6. A technician is troubleshooting a PC. The display shows an "Invalid Boot Disk" error after the POST. What is a probable cause?

    A. The MBR is corrupted.

    B. A process is using most of the CPU resources.

    C. The date and time have been changed in the BIOS and do not reflect the correct time and date.

    D. The PC does not have a floppy drive or the floppy drive is broken.

    E. The PC has a BIOS password.

7. What command would allow a technician to receive help with the command-line options that are used to schedule a program to run at a specific time?

    A. **help at**

    B. **ask at**

    C. **cmd ?**

    D. **at /?**

    E. **help**

8. An application update causes the computer to function improperly. Which Windows function could be used to roll the operating system back to a previous state?

   A. Automatic Updates

   B. NTBackup

   C. Restore point

   D. Scanreg

   E. Driver rollback

9. Which question is an open-ended question that could be used when helping a customer troubleshoot a Windows problem?

   A. Can you boot the operating system?

   B. Have you changed your password recently?

   C. Do you get a login prompt when the computer boots?

   D. What programs have you installed recently?

10. A technician is having difficulty resolving what appears to be a Windows 7 problem. Previously documented known solutions did not work, and neither Device Manager nor Event Viewer provided useful information. Which two actions should the technician try next?

    A. Reinstall the operating system.

    B. Check any manuals that relate to the hardware and software.

    C. Check the Internet for possible solutions.

    D. Ask the customer for any idea about what may be wrong.

    E. Use the recovery CD to restore the operating system.

11. Which file attribute indicates that a file has been flagged for backup?

    A. r

    B. a

    C. s

    D. h

12. A technician is attempting to create multiple partitions on a hard disk. What is the maximum number of primary partitions allowed per hard drive?

    A. 1

    B. 2

    C. 4

    D. 16

    E. 32

13. Which partition is used by the Windows operating system to boot the computer?

    A. Active

    B. RAID

    C. Extended

    D. Logical

14. What would be a reason for a computer user to use the Task Manager Performance tab?

    A. To increase the performance of the CPU

    B. To check the CPU usage of the PC

    C. To view the services that are currently running on the PC

    D. To view the processes that are running and end a process if needed

CHAPTER 6

Networks

Objectives

Upon completion of this chapter, you will be able to answer the following questions:

- What are the principles of networking?

- What are the different types of networks?

- What are the basic networking concepts and technologies?

- What makes up the physical components of a network?

- What are the LAN topologies and architectures?

- What are some of the standards organizations?

- What are the Ethernet standards?

- What are the OSI and TCP/IP data models?

- How do I configure a NIC and a modem?

- What are the names, purposes, and characteristics of other technologies used to establish connectivity?

- How do I design a network based on the customer's needs?

- What are the potential safety hazards, and how do I implement proper safety procedures related to networks?

- How do I identify and apply common preventive maintenance techniques used with networks?

- How do I troubleshoot a network?

Key Terms

This chapter uses the following key terms. You can find the definitions in the Glossary.

Introduction (6.0.1)

This chapter provides an overview of network principles, standards, and purposes.

Different types of network topologies, protocols, logical models, and the hardware needed to create a network are discussed in this chapter. In addition, network component upgrades, and configuration, troubleshooting, and preventive maintenance are covered. You also learn about network software, communication methods, and hardware relationships.

To meet the expectations and needs of your customers and network users, you must be familiar with networking technologies. You will learn the basics of network design and how some components affect the flow of data on a network. This knowledge will help you successfully troubleshoot network problems.

Principles of Networking (6.1)

This section discusses how to define computer networks, the features and benefits of networking, and some of the advantages and disadvantages of networking.

Define Computer Networks (6.1.1.1)

Networks are systems that are formed by links. For example, roads that connect groups of people together create a physical network. Connections with your friends create your personal network. Websites that allow individuals to link to each other's pages are called social networking sites.

People use the following networks every day:

- Mail delivery system
- Telephone system
- Public transportation system
- Corporate computer network
- The Internet

Networks share information and use various methods to direct the manner in which information flows. The information on the network goes from one place to another, sometimes via different paths, to arrive at the appropriate destination. For example, the public transportation system is a network similar to a computer network. The cars, trucks, and other vehicles are like the messages that travel within the network. Each driver defines a starting point (source computer) and an ending point (destination computer). Within this system, there are rules such as stop signs and traffic lights that control the flow from the source to the destination. A computer network also uses rules to control the flow of data between hosts on a network. In the next section, you will learn about computer networks and the benefits of networking.

A *host* is any device that sends and receives information on the network. Some devices can serve either as hosts or peripherals. For example, a printer connected to your laptop that is on a network is acting as a peripheral. If the printer is connected directly to a network, it is acting as a host.

Many different types of devices can connect to a network:

- Desktop computers
- Laptop computers
- Tablet computers
- Smartphones
- Printers
- File and print servers
- Game consoles
- Home appliances

Computer networks are used globally in businesses, homes, schools, and government agencies. Many of the networks are connected to each other through the Internet. A network can share many different types of resources and data:

- Services, such as printing or scanning
- Storage space on removable devices, such as hard drives or optical drives
- Applications
- Databases
- Information, stored on other computers
- Documents
- Calendars, synchronizing between a computer and a smartphone

Network devices link together using a variety of connections:

- **Copper cabling:** Uses electrical signals to transmit data between devices
- **Fiber-optic cabling:** Uses glass or plastic fiber to carry information as pulses of light
- **Wireless connection:** Uses radio signals, infrared technology, or satellite transmissions

Features and Benefits (6.1.1.2)

The benefits of networking computers and other devices include lowered costs and increased productivity. In a network, resources can be shared to reduce data duplication and data corruption.

Require Fewer Peripherals

Figure 6.1 shows that many devices can be connected on a network. Each computer on the network does not need to have its own printer or backup device. Multiple printers can be set up in a central location and shared among the network users. All network users send print jobs to a central print server that manages the print requests. The print server can distribute print jobs over multiple printers or queue jobs that require a specific printer.

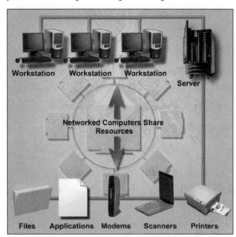

Figure 6-1 Shared Resources

Increase Communication Capabilities

Networks provide several different collaboration tools that can be used to communicate between network users. Online collaboration tools include email, forums and chats, voice and video, and instant messaging. With these tools, users can communicate with friends, family, and colleagues.

Avoid File Duplication and Corruption

A server manages network resources. Servers store data and share it with users on a network. Confidential or sensitive data can be protected and shared with the users who have permission to access that data. Document tracking software can be used to prevent users from overwriting files or changing files that others are accessing at the same time.

Lower the Cost of Licensing

Application licensing can be expensive for individual computers. Many software vendors offer site licenses for networks, which can dramatically reduce the cost of software. The site license allows a group of people or an entire organization to use the application for a single fee.

Centralize Administration

Centralized administration reduces the number of people needed to manage the devices and data on the network, reducing time and cost to the company. Individual network users do not need to manage their own data and devices. One administrator can control the data, devices, and permissions of users on the network. Backing up data is easier because the data is stored in a central location.

Conserve Resources

Data processing can be distributed across many computers to prevent one computer from becoming overloaded with processing tasks.

Identifying Networks (6.2)

There are many types of computer networks. This section describes and explains different types of computer networks and their basic characteristics.

LANs (6.2.1.1)

Data networks continue to evolve in complexity, use, and design. A computer network is identified by the following specific characteristics:

- The area it serves
- How data is stored
- How resources are managed
- How the network is organized
- Type of networking devices used
- Type of media used to connect the devices

Different types of networks are given different descriptive names. An individual network usually spans a single geographical area, providing services and applications to people within a common organizational structure. This type of network is called a *local-area network (LAN)*. A LAN can be made up of multiple local networks or a single network, as shown in Figure 6-2.

Figure 6-2   Local-Area Network

All of the local networks within a LAN are under one administrative control group. This group enforces the security and access control policies of the network. In this context, the word *local* refers to local consistent control rather than being physically close to each other. Devices in a LAN might be physically close, but this is not a requirement.

A LAN can be as small as a single local network installed in a home or small office. Over time, the definition of a LAN has evolved to include interconnected local networks consisting of many hundreds of devices that are installed in multiple buildings and locations.

WLANs (6.2.1.2)

A *wireless LAN (WLAN)* is a LAN that uses radio waves to transmit data between wireless devices. In a traditional LAN, devices are connected together using copper cabling. In some environments, installing copper cabling might not be practical, desirable, or even possible. In these situations, wireless devices are used to transmit and receive data using radio waves. As with LANs, on a WLAN you can share resources, such as files and printers, and access the Internet.

In a WLAN, wireless devices connect to access points within a specified area. Access points are typically connected to the network using copper cabling. Instead of providing copper cabling to every network host, only the wireless access point is connected to the network with copper cabling. The range (radius of coverage) for typical WLAN systems varies from under 98.4 feet (30 m) indoors to much greater distances outdoors, depending on the technology used.

PANs (6.2.1.3)

A *personal-area network (PAN)* is a network that connects devices, such as mice, keyboards, printers, smartphone, and tablets within the range of an individual person. All of these devices are dedicated to a single host and are most often connected with Bluetooth technology.

Bluetooth is a wireless technology that enables devices to communicate over short distances. A Bluetooth device can connect up to seven other Bluetooth devices. This technical specification is described by the IEEE 802.15.1 standard. Bluetooth devices are capable of handling voice and data. Bluetooth devices operate in the 2.4–2.485 GHz radio frequency range, which is in the Industrial, Scientific, and Medical (ISM) band. The Bluetooth standard incorporates Adaptive Frequency Hopping (AFH). AFH allows signals to "hop" around using different frequencies within the Bluetooth range, thereby reducing the chance of interference when multiple Bluetooth devices are present.

MANs (6.2.1.4)

A *metropolitan-area network (MAN)* is a network that spans across a large campus or a city. The network consists of various buildings interconnected through wireless or fiber-optic backbones, as shown in Figure 6-3. The communications links and equipment are generally owned by either a consortium of users or by a network service provider who sells the service to the users. A MAN can act as a high-speed network to allow sharing of regional resources.

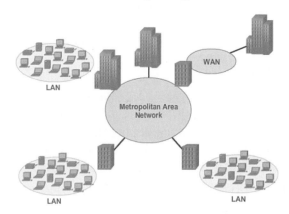

Figure 6-3   Metropolitan-Area Network

WANs (6.2.1.5)

A *wide-area network (WAN)* connects multiple smaller networks such as LANs that are in geographically separated locations, as shown in Figure 6-4. The most common example of a WAN is the Internet. The Internet is a large WAN that is composed of millions of interconnected LANs. WAN technology is also used to connect corporate or research networks. Telecommunications service providers are used to interconnect these LANs at different locations.

Figure 6-4   Wide-Area Network

Peer-to-Peer Networks (6.2.1.6)

In a *peer-to-peer network*, there is no hierarchy among the computers, nor are there any dedicated servers. Each device, also called a client, has equivalent capabilities and responsibilities. Individual users are responsible for their own resources and can decide which data and devices to share or install. Because individual users are responsible for the resources on their own computers, the network has no central point of control or administration.

Peer-to-peer networks work best in environments with ten or fewer computers. Peer-to-peer networks can also exist inside larger networks. Even on a large client network, users can still share resources directly with other users without using a network server. In your home, if you have more than one computer, you can set up a peer-to-peer network, as shown in Figure 6-5. You can share files with other computers, send messages between computers, and print documents to a shared printer.

Figure 6-5   Peer-to-Peer Network

Peer-to-peer networks have several disadvantages:

- There is no centralized network administration, which makes it difficult to determine who controls resources on the network.

- There is no centralized security. Each computer must use separate security measures for data protection.

- The network becomes more complex and difficult to manage as the number of computers on the network increases.

- There might not be any centralized data storage. Separate data backups must be maintained. This responsibility falls on the individual users.

Client/Server Networks (6.2.1.7)

Servers have software installed that enables them to provide services, such as email or web pages, to clients. Each service requires separate server software. For example, a server requires web server software to provide web services to the network.

In a *client/server network*, the client requests information or services from the server. The server provides the requested information or service to the client. Servers on a client/server network commonly perform some of the processing work for client machines, for example, sorting through a database before delivering only the records requested by the client. This provides for centralized network administration, which makes it easy to determine who controls resources on the network. Resources are controlled by a centralized network administration.

A computer with server software can provide services simultaneously to one or many clients, as shown in Figure 6-6.

Figure 6-6   Client/Server Network

Additionally, a single computer can run multiple types of server software. In a home or small business, it may be necessary for one computer to act as a file server, a web server, and an email server. In a corporate environment, employees may access a single computer that acts as an email server in the company. This email server is used only to send, receive, and store email. The email client on an employee computer issues a request to the email server for any unread email. The server responds by sending the requested email to the client.

A single computer can also run multiple types of client software. There must be client software for every service required. With multiple client software installed, a client can connect to multiple servers at the same time. For example, a user can check email and view a web page while instant messaging and listening to Internet radio.

A client/server model makes it easy to determine who controls resources on the network by providing central network administration. The network administrator implements data backups and security measures. The network administrator also controls user access to the network resources. All of the data on the network is stored on a centralized file server. A centralized print server manages shared printers on the network. Each user must provide an authorized username and password to gain access to network resources that each person is permitted to use.

Basic Networking Concepts and Technologies (6.3)

In this section, you are introduced to the basic concepts and technologies that allow data to travel through networks. You will learn about data transmission technologies, how IP addressing is implemented, and how ports and protocols are used by network software to perform functions and provide services over the network.

Bandwidth (6.3.1.1)

When data is sent over a computer network, it is broken up into small chunks called *packets*. Each packet contains source and destination address information. The packet, along with the address information, is called a *frame*. It also contains information that describes how to put all the packets back together again at the destination. The *bandwidth* determines the number of packets that can be transmitted within a fixed period of time.

Bandwidth is measured in bits per second and is usually denoted by any of the following units of measure:

- **bit/s:** Bits per second
- **Kb/s:** Kilobits per second
- **Mb/s:** Megabits per second
- **Gb/s:** Gigabits per second

Note

1 byte is equal to 8 bits, and is abbreviated with a capital letter B. 1 MB/s is approximately 8 Mb/s.

Figure 6-7 shows how bandwidth on a network can be compared to a highway.

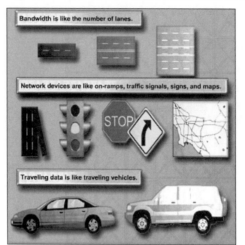

Figure 6-7   Highway Analogy

In the highway example, the cars and trucks represent the data. The number of lanes on the highway represents the amount of cars that could travel on the highway at the same time. An eight-lane highway can handle four times the number of cars that a two-lane highway can hold.

The amount of time it takes data to travel from source to destination is called *latency*. Like a car traveling across town that encounters stop lights or detours, data is delayed by network devices and cable length. Network devices add latency when processing and forwarding data. When surfing the Web or downloading a file, latency does not normally cause problems. Time-critical applications, such as Internet telephone calls, video, and gaming, can be significantly affected by latency.

Data Transmission (6.3.1.2)

The data that is transmitted over the network can flow using one of three modes: simplex, half-duplex, or full-duplex.

Simplex

Simplex, also called unidirectional, is a single, one-way transmission. An example of simplex transmission is the signal that is sent from a TV station to your home TV.

Half-Duplex

When data flows in one direction at a time it is known as *half-duplex*. With half-duplex, the channel of communications allows alternating transmission in two directions, but not in both directions simultaneously. Two-way radios, such as police or emergency communications mobile radios, work with half-duplex transmissions. When you press the button on the microphone to transmit, you cannot hear the person on the other end. If people at both ends try to talk at the same time, neither transmission gets through.

Full-Duplex

When data flows in both directions at the same time it is known as *full-duplex*. Although the data flows in both directions, the bandwidth is measured in only one direction. A network cable with 100 Mb/s in full-duplex mode has a bandwidth of 100 Mb/s.

A telephone conversation is an example of full-duplex communication. Both people can talk and be heard at the same time.

Full-duplex networking technology increases network performance because data can be sent and received at the same time. Broadband technologies, such as digital subscriber line (DSL) and cable, operate in full-duplex mode. Broadband technology allows multiple signals to travel on the same wire simultaneously. With a DSL connection, for example, users can download data to the computer and talk on the telephone at the same time.

IP Addressing (6.3.2.1)

Transmission Control Protocol/Internet Protocol (TCP/IP) defines the rules computers must follow to communicate with each other over the Internet. TCP is the primary Internet protocol for the reliable delivery of data. IP provides an addressing structure that is responsible for delivering data from the source computer to the destination computer.

As shown in Figure 6-8, an *IP address* is a number that is used to identify a device on the network. Each device on a network must have a unique IP address to communicate with other network devices. As noted earlier, a host is a device that sends or receives information on the network. Network devices are devices that move data across the network.

Figure 6-8   IP Address

A person's fingerprints usually do not change. They provide a way to physically identify people. The mailing address of a person can change, as it relates to where the person lives or picks up mail. This address can change. On a host, the *Media Access Control (MAC) address* is assigned to the host NIC and is known as the physical address. The physical address remains the same regardless of where the host is placed on the network, in the same way that fingerprints remain with the person regardless of where the person goes. MAC addresses consist of six groupings of two hexadecimal values separated by either a dash (-) or a colon (:), for example, 00-26-6C-FC-D5-AE. *Hexadecimal* values are defined as a range of the numbers from 0 to 9 and the letters *a* to *f*.

The IP address is similar to the mailing address of a person. It is known as a logical address because it is logically assigned based on the host location. The IP address, or network address, is based on the local network and is assigned to each host by a network administrator. This process is similar to the local government assigning a street address based on the logical description of the city or village and neighborhood.

IPv4 and IPv6

In the early 1990s, there was a concern about running out of IPv4 network addresses, which led the Internet Engineering Task Force to begin looking for a replacement. This led to the development of what is now known as IPv6. Currently IPv6 is operating alongside and is beginning to replace IPv4.

An IPv4 address consists of 32 bits with a potential address space of $2 \wedge 32$. In decimal notation that is approximately a 4 followed by 9 zeroes, an IPv6 address consists of 128 bits with a potential address space of $2 \wedge 128$. In decimal notation, that is approximately a 3 followed by 38 zeroes. With IPv6, the number of addresses available per person is approximately $10 \wedge 30$. If the IPv4 address space is represented by a marble, the IPv6 address space is represented by a sphere that is almost the size of the planet Saturn.

IPv4 (6.3.2.2)

An *IPv4 address* consists of a series of 32 binary bits (1s and 0s). It is difficult for humans to read a binary IPv4 address. For this reason, the 32 bits are grouped into four segments of 8 bits called octets. An IPv4 address, even in this grouped format, is hard for humans to read, write, and remember. Therefore, each octet is presented as its decimal value, separated by a decimal point or period. This format is referred to as dotted-decimal notation.

When a host is configured with an IPv4 address, it is entered as a dotted-decimal number, such as 192.168.1.5. Imagine if you had to enter the 32-bit binary equivalent of this: 11000000101010000000000100000101. If just 1 bit were mistyped, the address would be different, and the host might not be able to communicate on the network.

The logical 32-bit IPv4 address is hierarchical and is composed of two parts. The first part identifies the network, and the second part identifies a host on that network. Both parts are required. For example, if a host has the IPv4 address 192.168.18.57, the first three octets, 192.168.18, identify the network portion of the address, and the last octet, 57 identifies the host. This is known as *hierarchical addressing* because routers only need to communicate with networks and not individual hosts. A *router* is a networking device that forwards data packets across networks toward their destinations.

IPv4 addresses are divided into the following *classes*:

- **Class A:** Large networks implemented by large companies
- **Class B:** Medium-sized networks implemented by universities and other similar sized organizations
- **Class C:** Small networks implemented by small organizations or Internet service providers (ISP) for customer subscriptions
- **Class D:** Special use for multicasting
- **Class E:** Used for experimental testing

In addition to creating separate classes, the IETF reserved some Internet address space for private networks. Private networks have no connection to public networks. Private network addresses are not routed across the Internet. This allows networks in different locations to use the same private addressing scheme without creating addressing conflicts. An example of when these private addresses are useful is in a classroom lab where you want to prevent access outside of your network.

Each of these classes has a range of private IP addresses:

- **Class A:** 10.0.0.0 to 10.255.255.255
- **Class B:** 172.16.0.0 to 172.31.255.255
- **Class C:** 192.168.0.0 to 192.168.255.255

IPv4 Subnet Mask

The *subnet mask* indicates the network portion of an IPv4 address. Like the IPv4 address, the subnet mask is a dotted-decimal number. Usually all hosts within a LAN use the same subnet mask. Table 6-1 shows the default subnet masks for usable IPv4 addresses that are mapped to the first three classes of IPv4 addresses:

- **255.0.0.0**: Class A, which indicates that the first octet of the IPv4 address is the network portion

- **255.255.0.0**: Class B, which indicates that the first two octets of the IPv4 address is the network portion

- **255.255.255.0**: Class C, which indicates that the first three octets of the IPv4 address is the network portion

Table 6-1   IPV4

Class A	Network	Host		
Octet	1	2	3	4
Default subnet mask	255	0	0	0
IP address range	1.0.0.0 to 126.255.255.255			
Hosts per network	$2 \wedge 24 - 2 = 16,777,214$			

Class B	Network	Host		
Octet	1	2	3	4
Default subnet mask	255	255	0	0
IP address range	128.0.0.0 to 191.255.255.255			
Hosts per network	$2 \wedge 16 - 2 = 65,534$			

Class C	Network	Host		
Octet	1	2	3	4
Default subnet mask	255	255	255	0
IP address range	192.0.0.0 to 223.255.255.255			
Hosts per network	$2 \wedge 8 - 2 = 254$			

Class D addresses are used for multicast groups, such as webcasts or streaming video to a select group. Class E addresses are reserved for research use only.

If an organization owns one Class B network but needs to provide IPv4 addresses for four LANs, the organization must subdivide the Class B address into four smaller parts. *Subnetting* is a logical division of a network. It provides a way to divide a network, and the subnet mask specifies how it is subdivided. An experienced network administrator typically performs subnetting. After the subnetting scheme has been created, the proper IPv4 addresses and subnet masks can be configured on the hosts in the four LANs. These skills are taught in the Cisco Networking Academy courses related to Cisco Certified Network Associate (CCNA) level networking skills.

IPv6 (6.3.2.3)

Working with 128-bit numbers is difficult, so the *IPv6* address notation represents the 128 bits as 32 hexadecimal values. The 32 hexadecimal values are further subdivided into eight fields of four hexadecimal values, using colons as delimiters. Each field of four hexadecimal values is called a block.

The IPv6 address has a three-part hierarchy, as shown in Figure 6-9. The global prefix, also called a site prefix, is the first three blocks of the address and is assigned to an organization by an Internet names registry. The subnet ID includes the fourth block of the address, and the interface ID includes the last four blocks of the address. The network administrator controls both the subnet and interface ID.

Figure 6-9   Abbreviating IPV6 Addresses

As an example, if a host has an IPv6 address 3ffe:6a88:85a3:08d3:1319:8a2e: 0370:7344, the global prefix address is fe80:6a88:85a3, the subnet ID address is 08d3, and the interface ID address is 1319:8a2e:0370:7344.

An IPv6 address can be abbreviated with the following rules:

- Omit leading 0s in a 16-bit value.

- Replace one group of consecutive 0s by a double colon.

Table 6-2 is an example of how these rules are applied.

Table 6-2   Rules for Abbreviating IPV6 Addresses

Address	2001	:	0db8	:	0000	:	0000	:	0000	:	0000	:	1428:	:	57ab
After Rule 1	2001	:	db8	:	0	:	0	:	0	:	0	:	1428:	:	57ab
After Rule 2	2001	:	db8									:	1428	:	57ab

Here are the text representations of these addresses:

Address	2001:0db8:0000:0000:0000:0000:1428:57ab
After Rule 1	2001:db8:0:0:0:0:1428:57ab
After Rule 2	2001:db8::1428:57ab

Static Addressing (6.3.2.4)

In a network with a small number of hosts, it is easy to manually configure each device with the proper IP address. A network administrator who understands IP addressing should assign the addresses and should know how to choose a valid address for a particular network. The IP address that is assigned is unique for each host within the same network or subnet. This is known as *static IP addressing*.

To configure a static IP address on a host, go to the TCP/IPv4 Properties window of the NIC, as shown in Figure 6-10. The NIC enables a computer to connect to a network using a MAC address. Whereas the IP address is a logical address that is defined by the network administrator, a MAC address, or physical address, as shown in Figure 6-11, is permanently programmed (or burned in) into the NIC when it is manufactured. The IP address of a NIC can be changed, but the MAC address never changes.

Figure 6-10   Configure Static IP Address

Figure 6-11   MAC (Physical) Address

You can assign the following IP address configuration information to a host:

- **IP address:** Identifies the computer on the network

- **Subnet mask:** Is used to identify the network on which the computer is connected

- *Default gateway*: Identifies the device that the computer uses to access the Internet or another network

- **Optional values:** Such as the preferred Domain Name System (DNS) server address and the alternate DNS server address

In Windows 7, use the following path to configure a static IPv4 address:

Start > Control Panel > Network and Sharing Center > Change adapter setting > right-click **Local Area Connection >** click **Properties > TCP/IPv4 > Properties >** Use the following IP address > Use the following DNS server addresses > OK > OK

In Windows Vista, use the following path:

Start > Control Panel > Network and Sharing Center > Manage network connections > right-click **Local Area Connection >** click **Properties > TCP/IPv4 > Properties >** Use the following IP address > Use the following DNS server addresses > OK > OK

In Windows XP, use the following path:

Start > Control Panel > Network Connections > right-click **Local Area Connection >** click **Properties > TCP/IP > Properties >** Use the following IP address > Use the following DNS server addresses > OK > OK

DHCP Addressing (6.3.2.5)

If more than a few computers are a part of the LAN, manually configuring IP addresses for every host on the network can be time consuming and prone to errors. A *Dynamic Host Configuration Protocol (DHCP)* server automatically assigns IP addresses, which simplifies the addressing process. Automatically configuring TCP/IP also reduces the possibility of assigning duplicate or invalid IP addresses.

The DHCP server maintains a list of IP addresses to assign and manages the process so that every device on the network receives a unique IP address. When the DHCP server receives a request from a host, the server selects IP address information from a set of predefined addresses that are stored in a database. When the IP address information is selected, the DHCP server offers these values to the requesting host on the network. If the host accepts the offer, the DHCP server assigns the IP address for a specific period of time. This is called leasing. When the lease expires, the DHCP server can use this address for another computer that joins the network. A device, however, can renew its lease to retain the IP address.

Before a computer on the network can take advantage of the DHCP services, the computer must be able to identify the server on the local network. A computer can be configured to accept an IP address from a DHCP server by selecting the **Obtain an IP address automatically** option in the NIC configuration window, as shown in Figure 6-12. When a computer is set to obtain an IP address automatically, all other IP addressing configuration boxes are not available. The DHCP settings are configured the same for a wired or wireless NIC.

Figure 6-12   DNS Configurations While Using DHCP

A computer continually requests an IP address at 5-minute intervals from a DHCP server. If your computer cannot communicate with the DHCP server to obtain an IP address, the Windows OS automatically assigns a *link-local IP*. If your computer is assigned a link-local IP address, which is in the range of 169.254.0.0 to 169.254.255.255, your computer can only communicate with computers connected to the same network within this IP address range.

A DHCP server automatically assigns the following IP address configuration information to a host:

- IP address
- Subnet mask
- Default gateway
- Optional values, such as a DNS server address

In Windows 7, use the following path to configure a DHCP automatically assigned IPv4 address:

Start > Control Panel > Network and Sharing Center > Change adapter setting > right-click Local Area Connection > click Properties > TCP/IPv4 > Properties > select radio button Obtain an IP address automatically > click OK > OK

In Windows Vista, use the following path:

Start > Control Panel > Network and Sharing Center > Manage network connections > right-click Local Area Connection > click Properties > TCP/IPv4 > Properties > select radio button Obtain an IP address automatically > click OK > OK

In Windows XP, use the following path:

Start > Control Panel > Network Connections > right-click Local Area Connection > click Properties > TCP/IP > Properties > select radio button Obtain an IP address automatically > click OK > OK

Configuring Alternate IP Settings

Setting up an alternate IP configuration in Windows simplifies moving between a network that requires using DHCP and a network that uses static IP settings. If a computer cannot communicate with the DHCP server on the network, Windows uses the alternate IP configuration assigned to the NIC. The alternate IP configuration also replaces the Automatic IP Addressing (APIPA) address that is assigned by Windows when a DHCP server cannot be contacted.

To create the alternate IP configuration click the **Alternate Configuration** tab located in the NIC Properties window.

DNS

To access a *DNS* server, a computer uses the IP address configured in the DNS settings of the NIC in the computer. DNS resolves or maps hostnames and URLs to IP addresses.

All Windows computers contain a DNS cache that stores hostnames that have recently been resolved. The cache is the first place that the DNS client looks for host-name resolution. Because it is a location in memory, the cache retrieves resolved IP addresses more quickly than using a DNS server and does not create network traffic.

ICMP (6.3.2.6)

Internet Control Message Protocol (ICMP) is used by devices on a network to send control and error messages to computers and servers. There are several different uses for ICMP, such as announcing network errors, announcing network congestion, and troubleshooting.

Ping is commonly used to test connections between computers. Ping is a simple but highly useful command-line utility used to determine whether a specific IP address is accessible. To see a list of options that you can use with the **ping** command in Windows 7 and Windows Vista, select **Start** and type **cmd** in the search line. For Windows XP, select **Start > Run > cmd**. At the command prompt, enter **ping /?**.

The *ipconfig* command is another useful command-line utility used to verify that a NIC has a valid IP address. To display full configuration information of all network adapters in Windows 7 and Windows Vista, select **Start** and type **cmd** in the search line. For Windows XP, select **Start > Run > cmd**. At the command prompt, enter **ipconfig /all**. You can ping the IP address obtained from the **ipconfig /all** command to test IP connectivity.

Ping works by sending an ICMP echo request to a destination computer or other network device. The receiving device then sends back an ICMP echo reply message to confirm connectivity. Echo requests and echo replies are test messages that determine if devices can send packets to each other. Four ICMP echo requests (pings) are sent to the destination computer. If it is reachable, the destination computer responds with four ICMP echo replies. The percentage of successful replies can help you to determine the reliability and accessibility of the destination computer. Other ICMP messages report undelivered packets and whether a device is too busy to handle the packet.

You can also use ping to find the IP address of a host when that host's name is known. If you ping the name of a website (for example, cisco.com), as shown in Example 6-1, the IP address of the server displays.

Example 6-1   Using the ping Command to Find an IP Address

```
C:\> ping cisco.com
Pinging cisco.com [198.133.219.25] with 32 bytes of data:


Request timed out.
Request timed out.
Request timed out.
Request timed out.


Ping statistics for 198.133.219.25:
    Packets: Sent  = 4, Received = 0, Lost = 4 (100% loss),
```

Lab 6.3.2.7: Configure a NIC to Use DHCP in Windows 7

In this lab, you configure an Ethernet NIC to use DHCP to obtain an IP address and test connectivity between two computers.

Refer to Lab 6.3.2.7 in *IT Essentials: PC Hardware and Software Lab Manual*, Fifth Edition.

Lab 6.3.2.8: Configure a NIC to Use DHCP in Windows Vista

In this lab, you configure an Ethernet NIC to use DHCP to obtain an IP address and test connectivity between two computers.

Refer to Lab 6.3.2.8 in *IT Essentials: PC Hardware and Software Lab Manual*, Fifth Edition.

Lab 6.3.2.9: Configure a NIC to Use DHCP in Windows XP

In this lab, you configure an Ethernet NIC to use DHCP to obtain an IP address and test connectivity between two computers.

Refer to Lab 6.3.2.9 in *IT Essentials: PC Hardware and Software Lab Manual*, Fifth Edition.

Packet Tracer
☐ Activity

PT 6.3.2.10: Adding Computers to an Existing Network

In this Packet Tracer activity, you configure computers to use DHCP, configure static addressing, use ipconfig to retrieve host IP information, and use ping to verify connectivity. Refer to the website for this book to find the activity. To access the activities found in this book, please refer to the instructions found in the Introduction.

Common Ports and Protocols (6.3.3)

Ports and protocols are used in networking to allow communication between devices, applications, and networks. Protocols define how this communication occurs, and ports are used to track the various communication. This section explains common protocols and ports and how they are used in networking.

TCP and UDP (6.3.3.1)

A *protocol* is a set of rules. Internet protocols are sets of rules governing communication within and between computers on a network. Protocol specifications define the format of the messages that are exchanged. A letter sent through the postal system also uses protocols. Part of the protocol specifies where the delivery address on the envelope needs to be written. If the delivery address is written in the wrong place, the letter cannot be delivered.

Timing is crucial for the reliable delivery of packets. Protocols require messages to arrive within certain time intervals so that computers do not wait indefinitely for messages that might have been lost. Systems maintain one or more timers during the transmission of data. Protocols also initiate alternative actions if the network does not meet the timing rules.

These are the main functions of protocols:

- Identifying and handling errors
- Compressing the data
- Deciding how data is to be divided and packaged
- Addressing data packets
- Deciding how to announce the sending and receiving of data packets

Devices and computers connected to the Internet use a protocol suite called TCP/IP to communicate with each other. The information is transmitted most often via two protocols, TCP and UDP, as shown in Table 6-3.

Table 6-3   TCP and UDP

TCP	UDP
Advantages:	Advantages:
Error detection: TCP retransmits lost packets, drops duplicate packets, and guarantees that data is transmitted in the proper order. Reliable transport protocol: TCP tracks data to guarantee it is delivered to the destination.	Lower overhead: Uses less bandwidth than TCP. Connectionless: There is no requirement that the recipient is available and ready to receive data, and there is no requirement of acknowledgment of receipt.
Applications: Email Web browser	Applications: Simple file transfer: Sends data without security and does not require acknowledgment of receipt. Network file system: A system for accessing files over a network that is similar to the way files are accessed locally.

In the design of a network, you must determine the protocols that are going to be used. Some protocols are proprietary and only work on specific equipment, whereas other protocols are open standard and work on a variety of equipment.

TCP and UDP Protocols and Ports (6.3.3.3)

When the TCP/IP protocol stack is enabled, other protocols can communicate on specific ports. For example, HTTP uses port 80 by default. A *port* is a numeric identifier used to keep track of specific conversations. Every message that a host sends contains both a source and destination port.

Network software applications use these protocols and ports to perform functions over the Internet or over a network. Some network software applications include services to host a web page, send email, and transfer files. These services may be provided by a single server or by several servers. Clients use *well-known ports* for each service so that the client requests can be identified by using a specific destination port.

To understand how networks and the Internet work, you must be familiar with commonly used protocols and associated ports. Some uses of these protocols are to connect to a remote network device, convert a website URL to an IP address, and transfer data files. You will encounter other protocols as your experience in IT grows, but they are not used as often as the common protocols described here.

Table 6-4 summarizes some of the more common network and Internet protocols and the port number used by these protocols. The more you understand about each of these protocols, the more you will understand how networks and the Internet work.

Table 6-4   Common Network Protocols and Ports

Protocol	Port	Description
TCP/IP	NA	A suite of protocols used to transport data on the Internet
NetBEUI/NetBIOS	137, 139, 150	A small, fast protocol designed for a workgroup network that requires no connection to the Internet
HTTP	80	A communication protocol that establishes a request/response connection on the Internet
HTTP	443	Uses authentication and encryption to secure data as it travels between the client and web server
FTP	20/21	Provides services for file transfer and manipulation
SSH	22	Securely connects to a remote network device
Telnet	23	Connects to a remote network device
POP3	110	Downloads email messages from an email server
IMAP	143	Downloads email messages from an email server
SMTP	25	Sends email in a TCP/IP network
LDAP	389	Accesses information directories
SNMP	161	Manages and monitors devices on a network
SMB	445	Provides shared access to files, printers, and communication between points on a network
SFTP	115	Provides a secure file transfer service
DNS	53	Resolves hostnames to IP addresses
RDP	3389	Used to provide access to a remote computer

Worksheet 6.3.3.4: Protocol Definitions and Default Ports

In this worksheet, you write the name of the protocol and the default ports for each protocol definition in the table. Be prepared to discuss your answers. Refer to Worksheet 6.3.3.4 in *IT Essentials: PC Hardware and Software Lab Manual*, Fifth Edition.

Physical Components of a Network (6.4)

Network devices, hardware, cables, and connectors make up the physical components of networking. This section describes and explains common devices, cabling, and cabling standards.

Modems (6.4.1.1)

To support the immediate delivery of the millions of messages being exchanged between people all over the world, we rely on a web of interconnected networks. The standardization of the various elements of the network enables equipment and devices created by different companies to work together. It is important that IT technicians understand the purpose and function of different network equipment used to support personal and business operations.

A *modem* is an electronic device that connects to the Internet via an ISP. The modem converts digital data to analog signals for transmission over a phone line. Because the analog signals change gradually and continuously, they can be drawn as waves. In this system, the digital signals are represented as binary bits. The digital signals must be converted to a waveform to travel across telephone lines. They are converted back to bits by the receiving modem so that the receiving computer can process the data. Figure 6-13 shows two types of modems and a modem adapter.

Figure 6-13   Modems

The modem at the receiving end reconverts the analog signals back to digital data to be interpreted by the computer. The process of converting analog signals to digital and back again is called *modulation/demodulation*. The accuracy of modem-based transmission has increased with the development of error detection and correction protocols, which has reduced or eliminated noise and interference on telephone lines.

An internal modem plugs into an expansion slot on the motherboard. External modems connect to a computer through the serial and USB ports. Software drivers must be installed and connection ports configured for the modem to work properly.

When computers use the public telephone system to communicate, it is called *dialup networking (DUN)*. Modems communicate with each other using audio tone signals. This means that modems are able to duplicate the dialing characteristics of a telephone. DUN creates a *Point-to-Point Protocol (PPP)*. A PPP is simply a connection between two computers over a phone line.

Hubs, Bridges, and Switches (6.4.1.2)

To make data transmission more extensible and efficient than a simple peer-to-peer network, network designers use specialized network devices, such as hubs, bridges and switches, routers, and wireless access points, to send data between devices.

Hubs

Hubs, shown in Figure 6-14, extend the range of a network by receiving data on one port and then regenerating the data and sending it out to all other ports. A hub can also function as a repeater. A repeater extends the reach of a network because it rebuilds the signal, which overcomes the effects of data degradation over distance. The hub can also connect to another networking device, like a switch or router that connects to other sections of the network.

Figure 6-14   Hubs

Hubs are used less often today because of the effectiveness and low cost of switches. Hubs do not segment network traffic, so they decrease the amount of available bandwidth for all devices connected to them. In addition, because hubs cannot filter data, a lot of unnecessary network traffic constantly moves between all the devices connected to it.

Bridges and Switches

Files are broken up into small pieces of data, called packets, before they are transmitted over a network. This process allows for error checking and easier retransmission if the packet is lost or corrupted. Address information is added to the beginning and end of packets before they are transmitted. The packet, along with the address information, is called a frame.

LANs are often divided into sections called *segments*, similar to the way a company is divided into departments or a school is divided into classes. The boundaries of segments can be defined using a bridge. A *bridge* filters network traffic between LAN segments. Bridges keep a record of all the devices on each segment to which the bridge is connected. When the bridge receives a frame, the bridge examines the destination address to determine if the frame is to be sent to a different segment or dropped. The bridge also helps to improve the flow of data by keeping frames confined to only the segment to which the frame belongs.

Switches, shown in Figure 6-15, are sometimes called multiport bridges. A typical bridge has two ports, linking two segments of the same network. A switch has several ports, depending on how many network segments are to be linked. A switch is a more sophisticated device than a bridge.

Switch

Figure 6-15 Switch

In modern networks, switches have replaced hubs as the central point of connectivity. Like a hub, the speed of the switch determines the maximum speed of the network. However, switches filter and segment network traffic by sending data only to the device to which it is sent. This provides higher dedicated bandwidth to each device on the network.

Switches maintain a switching table. The switching table contains a list of all MAC addresses on the network and a list of which switch port can be used to reach a device with a given MAC address. The switching table records MAC addresses by inspecting the source MAC address of every incoming frame, as well as the port on which the frame arrives. The switch then creates a *switching table* that maps MAC addresses to outgoing ports. When a frame arrives that is destined for a particular

MAC address, the switch uses the switching table to determine which port to use to reach the MAC address. The frame is forwarded from the port to the destination. By sending frames out of only one port to the destination, other ports are not affected.

Power over Ethernet

A *Power over Ethernet (PoE) switch* transfers small amounts of DC current over Ethernet cable, along with data, to power PoE devices. Low-voltage devices that support PoE, such as Wi-Fi access points, surveillance video devices, and NICs, can be powered from remote locations. Devices that support PoE can receive power over an Ethernet connection at distances up to 330 feet (100 m) away.

Routers and Wireless Access Points (6.4.1.3)

When subscribing to an ISP, determine what type of equipment is available to select the most appropriate device. An *ISP* is a company that provides Internet services to individuals and businesses. An ISP usually provides a connection to the Internet, email accounts, and web pages for a monthly service fee. Some ISPs rent equipment on a month-to-month basis. This could be more attractive than purchasing the equipment because the ISP supports the equipment if there is a failure, change, or upgrade to the technology. Equipment that can be used to connect to an ISP is shown in Figure 6-16.

Figure 6-16   Devices Used to Connect to an ISP

Wireless Access Points

Wireless access points, shown in Figure 6-17, provide network access to wireless devices, such as laptops and tablets. The wireless access point uses radio waves to communicate with the wireless NIC in the devices and other wireless access points. An access point has a limited range of coverage. Large networks require several access points to provide adequate wireless coverage. A wireless access point provides connectivity only to the network, while a wireless router provides additional features, such as assigning IP addresses.

Figure 6-17 Wireless Access Point

Routers

Routers connect networks to each other. Switches use MAC addresses to forward a frame within a single network. Routers use IP addresses to forward packets to other networks. A router can be a computer with special network software installed or a device built by network equipment manufacturers.

On a corporate network, one router port connects to the WAN connection and the other ports connect to the corporate LANs. The router becomes the gateway, or path to the outside, for the LAN.

Multipurpose Devices

Multipurpose devices, shown in Figure 6-18, are network devices that perform more than one function. It is more convenient to purchase and configure one device that serves all your needs than to purchase a separate device for each function. This is especially true for the home user. In a home network, the router connects the computers and network devices in the home to the Internet. The router serves as a home gateway and a switch. The wireless router serves as a home gateway, wireless access point, and a switch. Multipurpose devices may also include a modem.

Figure 6-18   Multipurpose Device

NAS (6.4.1.4)

Network-attached storage (NAS) is a device consisting of one or more hard drives, an Ethernet connection, and an embedded operating system rather than a full-featured network operating system. The NAS device connects to the network, allowing users on the network to access and share files, stream media, and back up data to a central location. NAS devices that support multiple hard drives can provide RAID-level data protection.

NAS is a client/server design. A single hardware device, often called the NAS head, acts as the interface between the NAS and the network clients. Clients always connect to the NAS head, not the individual storage devices. A NAS device requires no monitor, keyboard, or mouse.

NAS systems provide easy administration. They often include built-in features, such as disk space quotas, secure authentication, and automatic sending of email alerts if an error is detected in the equipment.

VoIP Phones (6.4.1.5)

Voice over IP (VoIP) is a method to carry telephone calls over the data networks and Internet. VoIP converts the analog signals of voices into digital information that is transported in IP packets. VoIP can also use an existing IP network to provide access to the *public switched telephone network (PSTN)*.

VoIP phones look like normal phones, but instead of using the standard RJ-11 phone connector, they use an RJ-45 Ethernet connector. VoIP phones connect directly to a network and have all the hardware and software necessary to handle the IP communications.

When using VoIP to connect to the PSTN, you might be dependent on an Internet connection. This can be a disadvantage if the Internet connection experiences an interruption in service. When a service interruption occurs, the user cannot make phone calls.

You can use VoIP in several ways:

- *IP phone*: A device that connects to an IP network using an RJ-45 Ethernet connector or a wireless connection.

- *Analog telephone adapter (ATA)*: A device that connects standard analog devices, such as telephones, facsimile machines, or answering machines, to an IP network.

- *IP phone software*: This application connects by using a microphone, speakers, and a sound card to emulate the IP phone functionality.

Hardware Firewalls (6.4.1.6)

Hardware firewalls, such as integrated routers, protect data and equipment on a network from unauthorized access. A *hardware firewall* is a free-standing unit that resides between two or more networks, as shown in Figure 6-19. It does not use the resources of the computers it is protecting, so there is no impact on processing performance.

Figure 6-19 Hardware Firewall

A firewall should be used in addition to security software. A firewall resides between two or more networks and controls the traffic between them as well as helps prevent unauthorized access. Firewalls use various techniques for determining what is permitted or denied access to a network segment.

Considerations when selecting a hardware firewall include the following:

- **Space:** Free standing and uses dedicated hardware.

- **Cost:** Initial cost of hardware and software updates can be costly.

- **Number of computers:** Multiple computers can be protected.

- **Performance requirements:** Little impact on computer performance.

Note

On a secure network, if computer performance is not an issue, enable the internal operating system firewall for additional security. Some applications might not operate properly unless the firewall is configured correctly for them.

Internet Appliances (6.4.1.7)

An *Internet appliance* is also called a Net appliance, a smart appliance, or an information appliance. Examples of Internet appliance devices include televisions, game consoles, Blu-ray players, and streaming media players. The device is designed for the specific function and has built-in hardware for Internet connectivity. The Internet connection is either wired or wireless. Internet appliances include a CPU and RAM that support email, web surfing, gaming, as well as video streaming and social networking.

Purchasing Authentic Networking Devices (6.4.1.8)

Computer and network problems can be related to *counterfeit components*. The cosmetic differences between an authentic product and a counterfeit one can be subtle. There are also performance differentiators between authentic products and counterfeits. Many manufacturers have teams that are staffed with engineers well-versed in these differentiators.

Counterfeit products pose network as well as personal health and safety risks. The trafficking of counterfeit computer and networking equipment is a crime that carries serious penalties. In 2008, a former owner of a computer company was sentenced to 30 months in prison and ordered to pay a large sum in restitution as a result of his conviction for trafficking in counterfeit computer components. This type of case serves as an important reminder to customers about the risk of purchasing outside the manufacturer's authorized sales and distribution channels.

To help ensure that you are getting authentic products, consider these points when placing orders or requesting quotes:

- Always purchase your equipment directly from authorized channels.

- Confirm that the equipment is a new, authentic product and not previously owned.

- Be suspicious when prices seem too good to be true.

- Be suspicious if the product is offered at a much higher discount than authentic products. These discounts could be as high as 70 percent to 90 percent off.

- Check that the equipment comes with a valid software license.

- Check that the equipment has a full warranty enclosed.

- Ask whether the equipment includes service support.

- Be suspicious if the product appears to have proper labeling, logos, and trademarks, but the performance or appearance is substandard as compared to authentic products.

- Be suspicious of packaging that appears to be substandard, not original, tampered with, or previously used.

Do not do business with any supplier who insists that you

- Order immediately to beat a price increase.

- Take advantage of a special offer that is about to expire.

- Reserve the last few remaining products in stock.

- Purchase OEM specials.

- Take advantage of Internet, email, or telemarketing offers that send representatives to pick up your payment in person or demand cash on delivery.

Cables and Connectors (6.4.2)

There are many different types of network cables and connectors that can be used with network devices. It is important to understand the types of cables needed and how they are used.

Considerations for Cabling a Network (6.4.2.1)

A wide variety of networking cables is available, as shown in Figure 6-20. Coaxial and twisted-pair cables use copper to transmit data. Fiber-optic cables use glass or plastic to transmit data. These cables differ in bandwidth, size, and cost. You need to know what type of cable to use in different situations to install the correct cables for the job. You also need to be able to troubleshoot and repair problems that you encounter. Select the cable type that is the most beneficial and cost-effective for the users and services that will connect to the network.

Figure 6-20   Network Cables

Cost

When designing a network, cost is a consideration. Installing cables is expensive, but after a one-time expense, a wired network is normally inexpensive to maintain.

Security

A wired network is usually more secure than a wireless network. The cables in a wired network are usually installed in walls and ceilings and are therefore not easily accessible. It is easier to gain unauthorized access to the signals on a wireless network than a wired network. Radio signals are available to anyone who has a receiver. To make a wireless network as secure as a wired network requires using authentication and encryption.

Design for the Future

Many organizations install the highest grade of cable that is available. This ensures that the networks are prepared for additional bandwidth requirements in the future. To avoid expensive cable installations later, you and your customer must decide if the cost of installing a higher-grade cable is necessary.

Wireless

A wireless solution might be needed in places where cables cannot be installed, such as an older, historic building where local building codes do not permit structural modifications.

Coaxial Cables (6.4.2.2)

Coaxial cable is usually constructed of either copper or aluminum. It is used by cable television companies to provide service and for connecting the various components that make up satellite communication systems.

Coaxial cable (or coax) carries data in the form of electrical signals. It provides improved shielding compared to unshielded twisted-pair (UTP), so it has a higher signal-to-noise ratio and can therefore carry more data. However, twisted-pair cabling has replaced coax in LANs because, when compared to UTP, coax is physically harder to install, more expensive, and harder to troubleshoot.

Coaxial cable is enclosed in a sheath or jacket. There are several types of coaxial cable:

- *Thicknet or 10BASE5*: Used in networks and operated at 10 Mb/s with a maximum length of 1640.4 feet (500 m)
- *Thinnet 10BASE2*: Used in networks and operated at 10 Mb/s with a maximum length of 607 feet (185 m)
- **RG-59:** Most commonly used for cable television in the United States
- **RG-6:** Higher-quality cable than RG-59, with more bandwidth and less susceptibility to interference

Cable service provider wiring inside a customer's premises is coax. Several connecting methods are used to connect coaxial cable together. Two common connection types are as follows:

- **F series:** Primarily used in television cable and antenna applications up to 1 GHz
- **BNC:** Designed for military use and also used in video and RF applications to 2 GHz

The *F series connector* has a standard thread pattern, but push-on designs are also available. The *BNC* uses a push, twist, and lock connector. Coaxial cable has no specific maximum bandwidth, and the type of signaling technology used determines the speed and limiting factors.

Twisted-Pair Cables (6.4.2.3)

Twisted pair is a type of copper cabling used for telephone communications and most Ethernet networks. A pair of wires forms a circuit that can transmit data. The pair is twisted to provide protection against *crosstalk*, which is the noise generated by adjacent pairs of wires in the cable. Pairs of copper wires are encased in color-coded plastic insulation and twisted together. An outer jacket protects the bundles of twisted pairs.

When electricity flows through a copper wire, a magnetic field is created around the wire. A circuit has two wires. The two wires in that circuit have oppositely charged magnetic fields. When the two wires of the circuit are next to each other, the magnetic fields cancel each other out. This is called the *cancellation effect*. Without the cancellation effect, network communications become slow due to the interference caused by the magnetic fields.

There are two basic types of twisted-pair cables:

- *Unshielded twisted-pair (UTP)*: Cable that has two or four pairs of wires. This type of cable relies solely on the cancellation effect produced by the twisted-wire pairs that limits signal degradation caused by electromagnetic interference (EMI) and radio frequency interference (RFI). UTP is the most commonly used cabling in networks. UTP cable segments have a length up to 330 feet (100 m).

- *Shielded twisted-pair (STP)*: Each pair of wires is wrapped in metallic foil to better shield the wires from noise. Four pairs of wires are then wrapped in an overall metallic braid or foil. STP reduces electrical noise from within the cable. It also reduces EMI and RFI from outside the cable.

Although STP prevents interference better than UTP, STP is more expensive because of extra shielding and more difficult to install because of the thickness. In addition, the metallic shielding must be grounded at both ends. If improperly grounded, the shield acts like an antenna picking up unwanted signals. STP is primarily used outside of North America.

Category Rating

Twisted-pair cables come in several categories (Cat). These categories are based on the number of wires in the cable and the number of twists in those wires.

The size of the network determines the type of network cable that will be used. Most networks today are wired using twisted-pair copper cable. The characteristics of twisted-pair cable are shown in Table 6-5.

Table 6-5   Twisted-Pair Cable Features

	Speed	Features
Cat 3 UTP	10 MB/s at 16 MHz	Suitable for Ethernet LAN. Most often used for phone lines.
Cat 5 UTP	100 Mb/s at 100 MHz	Manufactured with higher standard than Cat 3 to allow for higher data transfer rates.

	Speed	Features
Cat 5e UTP	1000 Mb/s at 100 MHz	Manufactured with higher standard than Cat 5 to allow for higher data transfer rates.
		More twists per foot than Cat 5 to better prevent EMI and RFI from outside sources.
Cat 6 UTP	1000 Mb/s at 250 MHz	Manufactured with higher standard than Cat 5e.
		More twists per foot than Cat 5e to better prevent EMI and RFI from outside sources.
Cat 6a UTP	1000 Mb/s at 500 MHz	Cat 6a has better insulation and performance than Cat 6.
Cat 7 ScTP	10 Gb/s at 600 MHz	May have a plastic divider to separate pairs of wires inside the cable to better prevent EMI and RFI.
		Good choice for customers using applications that require large amounts of bandwidth, such as videoconferencing or gaming.
		ScTP (screened twisted-pair) is very expensive and not as flexible as UTP.

New or renovated office buildings often have some type of UTP cabling that connects every office to a central point called the *main distribution facility (MDF)*. The distance limitation of UTP cabling used for data is 330 feet (100 m). Cable runs in excess of this distance limitation need a switch, repeater, or hub to extend the connection to the MDF.

Cables that are installed inside the walls and ceilings of buildings must be plenum rated. A *plenum cable* is one that is safe for installation between a dropped ceiling and the structural ceiling of a building where air circulation takes place. Plenum-rated cables are made from a special plastic that retards fire and produces less smoke than other cable types.

Note

Cat 3 cables use a 6-pin RJ-11 connector, whereas all other twisted-pair cables use an 8-pin RJ-45 connector.

Wire Schemes

There are two different patterns, or wiring schemes, called *T568A* and *T568B*. Each wiring scheme defines the *pinout*, or order of wire connections, on the end of the cable. The two schemes are similar except that two of the four pairs are reversed in the termination order.

On a network installation, one of the two wiring schemes (T568A or T568B) should be chosen and followed. It is important that the same wiring scheme is used for every termination in that project. If working on an existing network, use the wiring scheme that already exists.

Using the T568A and T568B wiring schemes, two types of cables can be created: a straight-through cable and a crossover cable. These two types of cable are found in data installations.

Straight-Through Cables

A *straight-through cable* is the most common cable type. It maps a wire to the same pins on both ends of the cable. In other words, if T568A is on one end of the cable, T568A is also on the other. If T568B is on one end of the cable, T568B is on the other. This means that the order of connections (the pinout) for each color is the exact same on both ends.

Two devices directly connected and using different pins for transmit and receive are known as *unlike devices*. They require a straight-through cable to exchange data. There are two unlike devices that require a straight-through cable, a switch port to router port and a hub port to PC.

Crossover Cable

A *crossover cable* uses both wiring schemes. T568A on one end of the cable and T568B on the other end of the same cable. This means that the order of connection on one end of the cable does not match the order of connections on the other.

Devices that are directly connected and use the same pins for transmit and receive are known as *like devices*. They require the use of a crossover cable to exchange data. Like devices that require a crossover cable include the following:

- Switch port to switch port
- Switch port to hub port
- Hub port to hub port
- Router port to router port
- PC to router port
- PC to PC

If the incorrect cable type is used, the connection between network devices will not function.

Some devices can automatically sense which pins are used for transmit and receive and will adjust their internal connections accordingly.

Lab 6.4.2.4- Building Straight-Through and Crossover UTP Cables

In this lab, you build and test straight-through and crossover unshielded twisted-pair (UTP) Ethernet network cables. Refer to Lab 6.4.2.4 in *IT Essentials: PC Hardware and Software Lab Manual*, Fifth Edition.

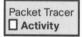

PT 6.4.2.5: Cabling a Simple Network

In this Packet Tracer activity, you create a simple network using two hosts. To access the activities found in this book, please refer to the instructions found in the Introduction.

Fiber-Optic Cables (6.4.2.6)

An *optical fiber* is a glass or plastic medium that transmits information using light. *Fiber-optic cable* has one or more optical fibers enclosed in a sheath or jacket, as shown in Figure 6-21. Because it uses light to transmit signals, fiber-optic cable is not affected by EMI or RFI. All signals are converted to light pulses as they enter the cable and converted back into electrical signals when they leave it. This means that fiber-optic cable can deliver signals that are clearer, can go farther, and have greater bandwidth than cable made of copper or other metals.

Figure 6-21   Fiber Media Cable Design

Fiber-optic cables can reach distances of several miles or kilometers before the signal needs to be regenerated. Either lasers or light-emitting diodes (LED) generate the light pulses that are used to represent the transmitted data as bits on the media. Bandwidth reaches speeds of 100 Gb/s and increases as standards are developed and adopted.

The speed of data transmitted over fiber-optic cable is limited by the devices connected to the cable, as well as impurities within the fiber cable. Electronic semiconductor devices called photodiodes detect the light pulses and convert them to voltages that can then be reconstructed into data frames.

Fiber-optic cable is usually more expensive to use than copper cable, and the connectors are more costly and harder to assemble. Common connectors for fiber-optic networks include the following:

- *SC*: 2.5-mm ferrule that uses a snap-in connector that latches with a simple push-pull motion
- *ST*: 2.5-mm ferrule that uses a bayonet mount connector that is spring loaded
- *LC*: 1.25-mm ferrule that uses a snap-in connector that latches with a simple push-pull motion

These three types of fiber-optic connectors are simplex, which allows data to flow in only one direction. Therefore, two cables are needed to provide data flow in both directions.

These are the two types of glass fiber-optic cable:

- *Multimode*: Cable that has a thicker core than single-mode cable. It is easier to make, can use simpler light sources (LED), and works well over distances up to 6560 feet (2 km). It often uses LEDs as the light source within LANs or distances of 200 meters within a campus network.
- *Single mode*: Cable that has a very thin core. It is harder to make, uses lasers as a light source, and can transmit signals up to 62.14 miles (100 km). It often uses lasers as the light source within campus backbones for distances of several thousand meters.

Network Topologies (6.5)

Network topologies describe the physical and logical layout of a network. It is important to clearly understand both types and to be able to read and create network topologies as you work with networks. The following section describes the elements of each topology, provides an explanation of common physical topologies, and explains how to determine a network topology by understanding a customer's network needs.

Logical and Physical Topologies (6.5.1.1)

A *logical topology* describes how the hosts access the medium and communicate on the network. The two most common types of logical topologies are broadcast and token passing. In a *broadcast topology*, a host broadcasts a message to all hosts on the same network segment. There is no order that hosts must follow to transmit data. Messages are sent on a first in, first out (FIFO) basis.

Token passing controls network access by passing an electronic token sequentially to each host. If a host wants to transmit data, the host adds the data and a destination address to the token, which is a specially formatted frame. The token then travels to another host with the destination address. The destination host takes the data out of the frame. If a host has no data to send, the token is passed to another host.

A *physical topology* defines the way in which computers, printers, and other devices are connected to a network. Figure 6-22 shows four physical topologies.

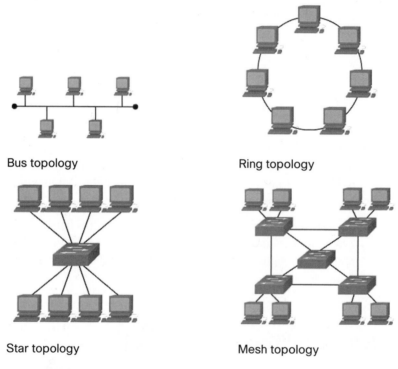

Bus topology

Ring topology

Star topology

Mesh topology

Figure 6-22   Physical Topologies

Bus

In a *bus topology*, each computer connects to a common cable. The cable connects one computer to the next, like a bus line going through a city. The cable has a small cap installed at the end called a terminator. The terminator prevents signals from bouncing back and causing network errors.

Ring

In a *ring topology*, hosts are connected in a physical ring or circle. Because the ring topology has no beginning or end, the cable is not terminated. A token travels around the ring stopping at each host. If a host wants to transmit data, the host adds the data and the destination address to the token. The token continues around the ring until it stops at the host with the destination address. The destination host takes the data out of the token.

Star

The *star topology* has a central connection point, which is normally a device such as a hub, switch, or router. Each host on a network has a cable segment that attaches the host directly to the central connection point. The advantage of a star topology is that it is easy to troubleshoot. Each host is connected to the central device with its own wire. If there is a problem with that cable, only that host is affected. The rest of the network remains operational.

Hierarchical

A *hierarchical or extended star topology* is a star network with an additional networking device connected to the main networking device. Typically, a network cable connects to one switch, and then several other switches connect to the first switch. Larger networks, such as those of corporations or universities, use the hierarchical star topology.

Mesh

The *mesh topology* connects all devices to each other. When every device is connected to every other device, a failure of any cable or device along a connection does not affect the network. The mesh topology is used in WANs that interconnect LANs.

Hybrid

A *hybrid topology* is a combination of two or more basic network topologies, such as a star-bus or star-ring topology. The advantage of a hybrid topology is that it can be implemented for a number of different network environments.

The type of topology determines the capabilities of the network, such as ease of setup, speed, and cable lengths. *LAN architecture* describes both the physical and logical topologies used in a network.

Packet Tracer
☐ Activity

PT 6.5.1.2: Physical Topologies

This Packet Tracer activity will familiarize you with star, extended star, and mesh physical topologies. To access the activities found in this book, please refer to the instructions found in the Introduction.

Determining the Network Topology (6.5.1.3)

Understanding the needs of the customer and determining the general layout of the new network are required to properly determine the network topology. These network decisions need to be discussed with the customer:

- Cable and wireless standards
- Expandability
- Number and location of users

The number of users and the estimated amount of future growth determine the initial physical and logical topology of the network. An inspection, called a site survey, should be done early in the project. A *site survey* is a physical inspection of the building that helps determine a basic physical topology. Create a checklist to record the needs of your customer to determine the physical topology:

- Location of users' computers
- Position of network equipment, such as switches and routers
- Position of the servers

A floor plan or blueprint is helpful to determine the physical layout of equipment and cables. The physical layout is often based on available space, power, security, and air conditioning. Figure 6-23 shows a typical network topology.

Figure 6-23   Network Topology

If a floor plan or blueprint is not available, make a drawing of where the network devices will be located, including the location of the server room, printers, end stations, and cable runs. This drawing can be used for discussions when the customer makes the final layout decisions.

Ethernet Standards (6.6)

Standards are needed to ensure consistency and interoperability between devices and network technology. This section discusses the organizations that set and maintain common technology standards and also provides descriptions of the most common standards for network communication.

Standards Organizations (6.6.1.1)

Several international standards organizations are responsible for setting networking standards. Standards are used by manufacturers as a basis for developing technology, especially communications and networking technologies. Standards ensure that the devices from one manufacturer will be compatible with devices made by another manufacturer using the same technology. The standards groups create, examine, and update standards. These standards are applied to the development of technology to meet the demands for higher bandwidth, efficient communication, and reliable service.

Table 6-6 provides information about several standards organizations.

Table 6-6   Standards Organizations

ITU-T	The International Telecommunication Unions Telecommunication Standardization Sector: The United Nations specialized agency for information and communication technologies (ICT)
IEEE	Institute of Electrical and Electronics Engineering: Develops standard for computer and electronic industry; for example, the IEEE 802 standard for local-area networks.
ISO	International Organization for Standardization: Defines computer standards (for example, the Open System Interconnection [OSI] model)
IAB	Internet Architecture Board: A committee that oversees the technical and engineering development of the Internet
IEC	International Electrotechnical Commission: Is the global organization that prepares and publishes international standards for all electrical, electronic, and related technologies
ANSI	American National Standards Institute: Facilitates the development of standards by establishing consensus processes among qualified groups
TIA/ EIA	Telecommunications Industry Association and Electronic Industries Alliance: Develop and publish standards covering structured voice and data wiring for LANs

IEEE 802.3 (6.6.1.2)

Ethernet protocols describe the rules that control how communication occurs on an Ethernet network. To ensure that all Ethernet devices are compatible with each other, the IEEE developed standards for manufacturers and programmers to follow when developing Ethernet devices.

The Ethernet architecture is based on the IEEE 802.3 standard. The *IEEE 802.3* standard specifies that a network implement the *carrier sense multiple access with collision detection (CSMA/CD)* access control method.

In CSMA/CD, all end stations listen to the network wire for clearance to send data. This process is similar to waiting to hear a dial tone on a phone before dialing a number. When the end station detects that no other host is transmitting, the end station attempts to send data. If no other station sends any data at the same time, this transmission arrives at the destination computer with no problems. If another end station observed the same clear signal and transmitted at the same time, a *collision* occurs on the network media.

The first station that detects the collision, or the doubling of voltage, sends out a jam signal that tells all stations to stop transmitting and to run a backoff algorithm. A *backoff algorithm* calculates random times in which the end station tries transmitting again. This random time is typically in 1 or 2 milliseconds (ms). This sequence occurs every time there is a collision on the network and can reduce Ethernet transmission by up to 40 percent.

Ethernet Technologies (6.6.1.3)

The IEEE 802.3 standard defines several physical implementations that support Ethernet. Table 6-7 summarizes the standards of different Ethernet cable types.

Table 6-7   Ethernet Standards

Ethernet Standards	Media	Transfer Rates
10BASE-T	Category 3	Transfers data at a rate of 10Mb/s.
100BASE-T	Category 5	At 100 Mb/s, transfer rates of 100BASE-TX are 10 times that of 10BASE-T.
1000BASE-T	Category 5e	The 1000BASE-T architecture supports data transfer rates of 1 Gb/s.
10GBASE-T	Category 6a, 7	The 10GBASE-T architecture supports data transfer rates of 10 Gb/s.

10BASE-T is an Ethernet technology that uses a star topology. 10BASE-T is a popular Ethernet architecture whose features are indicated in its name:

- The 10 represents a speed of 10 Mb/s.

- BASE represents baseband transmission. In baseband transmission, the entire bandwidth of a cable is used for one type of signal.

- The T represents twisted-pair copper cabling.

IEEE 802.11 (6.6.1.4)

IEEE 802.11 is the standard that specifies connectivity for wireless networks. IEEE 802.11, or Wi-Fi, refers to a collective group of standards, as shown in Table 6-8. These protocols specify the frequencies, speeds, and other capabilities of the different Wi-Fi standards.

Table 6-8   Wireless Ethernet Standards

Standard	Bandwidth	Frequency	Maximum Range	Interoperability
IEEE 802.11a	Up to 54 Mb/s	5 GHz	45.7 m (150 ft.)	Not interoperable with 802.11b
IEEE 802.11b	Up to 11 Mb/s	2.4-GHz band	91 m (300 ft.)	Interoperable with 802.11g
IEEE 802.11g	Up to 54 Mb/s	2.4-GHz band	91 m (300 ft.)	Interoperable with 802.11b
IEEE 802.11n	Up to 600 Mb/s	2.4-GHz or 5-GHz band	250 m (984 ft.)	Interoperable with 802.11a, 802.11b, and 802.11g

OSI and TCP/IP Data Models (6.7)

The TCP/IP and OSI models are used by those working with networks to provide a common ground for communicating about devices, processes, protocols, and services. They are also used for troubleshooting. These models describe the protocols and process in "layers" as data is moved through the network.

TCP/IP (6.7.1.1)

An *architectural model* is a common frame of reference for explaining Internet communications and developing communication protocols. It separates the functions of protocols into manageable layers. Each layer performs a specific function in the process of communicating over a network.

The *TCP/IP model* was created by researchers in the U.S. Department of Defense (DoD). The TCP/IP suite of protocols is the dominant standard for transporting data across networks and the Internet. It consists of layers that perform functions necessary to prepare data for transmission over a network. Table 6-9 shows the four layers of the TCP/IP model.

Table 6-9   TCP/IP Layer

TCP/IP Layer	Description
Application	Where high-level protocols such as SMTP and FTP operate
Transport	Specifies which application requested or is receiving data through specific ports
Internet	Where IP addressing and routing take place
Network access	Where MAC addressing and physical network components exist

A message begins at the top application layer and moves down the TCP/IP layers to the bottom network access layer. Header information is added to the message as it moves down through each layer and is then transmitted. After reaching the destination, the message travels back up through each layer. The header information that was added to the message is stripped away as the message moves up through the layers toward its destination.

Application Layer Protocols

Application layer protocols provide network services to user applications, such as web browsers and email programs. Common protocols that operate at the application layer include HTTP, Telnet, FTP, SMTP, DNS, and HTML.

Transport Layer Protocols

Transport layer protocols provide end-to-end management of the data. One of the functions of these protocols is to divide the data into manageable segments for easier transport across the network. Common protocols that operate at the transport layer include TCP and UDP.

Internet Layer Protocols

Internet layer protocols provide connectivity between hosts in the network. Common protocols that operate at the Internet layer include IP and ICMP.

Network Access Layer Protocols

Network access layer protocols describe the standards that hosts use to access the physical media. The IEEE 802.3 Ethernet standards and technologies, such as CSMA/CD and 10BASE-T, are defined in this layer.

OSI (6.7.1.2)

In the early 1980s, the International Standards Organization (ISO) developed the *Open Systems Interconnection (OSI)* reference model to standardize the way devices communicate on a network. This model was a major step toward ensuring interoperability between network devices.

The OSI model divides network communications into seven distinct layers. Although other models exist, most network vendors today build their products using this framework.

A system that implements protocol behavior consisting of a series of these layers is known as a protocol stack. Protocol stacks can be implemented either in hardware or software, or a combination of both. Typically, only the lower layers are implemented in hardware, and the higher layers are implemented in software. Each layer is responsible for part of the processing to prepare data for transmission on the network. Table 6-10 shows what each layer of the OSI model does.

Table 6-10   OSI Model

OSI Model	Layer	Description
Application	7	Responsible for network services to applications
Presentation	6	Transforms data formats to provide a standard interface for the application layer
Session	5	Establishes, manages, and terminates the connections between the local and remote applications
Transport	4	Provides reliable transport and flow control across a network
Network	3	Responsible for logical addressing and the domain of routing
Data link	2	Provides physical addressing and media access procedures
Physical	1	Defines all the electrical and physical specifications for devices

In the OSI model, when data is transferred, it is said to virtually travel down the OSI model layers of the sending computer and up the OSI model layers of the receiving computer.

When a user sends data, such as an email, the *encapsulation* process starts at the application layer. The application layer provides network access to applications. Information flows through the top three layers and is considered to be data when it gets down to the transport layer.

At the transport layer, the data is broken down into more manageable segments, called *protocol data units (PDU),* for orderly transport across the network. A PDU describes data as it moves from one layer of the OSI model to another. The transport layer PDU also contains information used for reliable data transport, such as port numbers, sequence numbers, and acknowledgement numbers.

At the network layer, each segment from the transport layer becomes a packet. The packet contains logical addressing and other Layer 3 control information.

At the data link layer, each packet from the network layer becomes a frame. The frame contains physical address and error correction information.

At the physical layer, the frame becomes bits. These bits are transmitted one at a time across the network medium.

At the receiving computer, the *de-encapsulation* process reverses the process of encapsulation. The bits arrive at the physical layer of the OSI model of the receiving computer. The process of traveling up the OSI model of the receiving computer brings the data to the application layer, where an email program displays the email.

Note

Mnemonics can help you remember the seven layers of the OSI. Some examples include "All People Seem To Need Data Processing" and "Please Do Not Throw Sausage Pizza Away."

Comparing the OSI and TCP/IP Models (6.7.1.3)

The OSI model and the TCP/IP model are both reference models used to describe the data communication process. The TCP/IP model is used specifically for the TCP/IP suite of protocols, and the OSI model is used for the development of standard communication for equipment and applications from different vendors.

The TCP/IP model performs the same process as the OSI model but uses four layers instead of seven. Figure 6-24 shows how the layers of the two models compare.

Figure 6-24 OSI Model and TCP/IP Model Compared

Computer-to-Network Connection (6.8)

Installing a network requires a solid understanding of the hardware and installation steps required for each project. This section introduces procedures for each segment of a network installation.

Network Installation Completion List (6.8.1.1)

Having a clear understanding of all the steps required to physically build a network improves the success of a project. You may need to install network cards and wireless and wired network devices and configure network equipment.

When installing a wireless network, you can use a wireless access point or a multipurpose device. The Linksys E2500 is a multipurpose device that provides both router and access point capabilities. You have to decide where you want to install access points to provide the maximum range of connectivity.

After you have determined the location of all the network devices, you are ready to install the network cables. If you are installing the cable yourself, make sure that all the necessary materials are available at the site, in addition to a blueprint of the network's physical topology.

To physically create a network, follow these steps:

How To Q

Step 1. Make sure all Ethernet wall port locations are properly marked and meet the current and future requirements for the customer. To install the cable in ceilings and behind walls, you perform a cable pull: One person pulls the cable, and another feeds the cable through the walls. Make sure to label the ends of every cable. Follow a labeling scheme that is already in place, or follow the guidelines outlined in TIA/EIA 606-A.

Step 2. After the cables are terminated at both ends, use a cable tester to make sure that there are no shorts or interference.

Step 3. Use a floor plan to find the locations for access points that allow maximum coverage. The best place for a wireless access point is at the center of the area you are covering, with line of sight between the wireless devices and the access point.

Step 4. Connect the access point to the existing network.

Step 5. Make sure that the network interfaces are properly installed in the desktops, laptops, and network printers. After the network interfaces are installed, configure the client software and the IP address information on all the devices.

Step 6. Make sure to install switches and routers in a secured, centralized location. All LAN connections terminate in this area. In a home network, you might need to install these devices in separate locations, or you might have only one device.

Step 7. Install an Ethernet patch cable from the wall connection to each network device. Check whether you have a link light on all network interfaces and on each network device port that connects to a device.

Step 8. When all devices are connected and all link lights are functioning, test the network for connectivity. Use the **ipconfig /all** command to view the IP configuration on each workstation. Use the **ping** command to test basic connectivity. You should be able to ping other computers on the network, including the default gateway and remote computers. After confirming basic connectivity, configure and test the network applications, such as email and the web browser.

Selecting a NIC (6.8.2.1)

A NIC is required to connect to the network. The NIC may come preinstalled on a computer, or you might have to purchase one on your own. You must be able to upgrade, install, and configure components when a customer asks for increased speed or new functionality to be added to a network. If your customer is adding additional computers or wireless functionality, you should be able to recommend equipment based on their needs, such as wireless access points and wireless network cards. The equipment that you suggest must work with the existing equipment and cabling, or the existing infrastructure must be upgraded. In rare cases, you might need to update the driver. You can use the driver disc that comes with the motherboard or adapter card, or you can supply a driver that you downloaded from the manufacturer.

There are many types of network interfaces:

- Most network interfaces for desktop computers are either integrated into the motherboard or are an expansion card that fits into an expansion slot.

- Most laptop network interfaces are either integrated into the motherboard or fit into a PC Card or ExpressBus expansion slot.

- USB network adapters plug into a USB port and can be used with both desktops and laptops.

Before purchasing a NIC, research the card's speed, form factor, and capabilities. Also check the speed and capabilities of the hub or switch connected to the computer.

Ethernet NICs will *auto-negotiate* the fastest speed that is common between the NIC and the other device. For instance, if you have a 10/100 Mb/s NIC and a hub that is only 10 Mb/s, the NIC operates at 10 Mb/s. If you have a 10/100/1000 Mb/s NIC and a switch that is only operating at 100 Mb/s, the NIC operates at 100 Mb/s.

If you have a gigabit switch, you most likely need to purchase a gigabit NIC to match speeds. If there are plans to upgrade the network in the future to Gigabit Ethernet, make sure to purchase NICs that can support the speed. Costs can vary greatly, so select NICs that match the needs of your customer.

To connect to a wireless network, the computer must have a wireless adapter. A wireless adapter communicates with other wireless devices, such as computers, printers, or wireless access points. Before purchasing a wireless adapter, make sure that it is compatible with the other wireless equipment that is already installed on the network. Verify that the wireless adapter is the correct form factor for the customer's computer. You can use a wireless USB adapter with any desktop or laptop computer that has a USB port.

Wireless NICs are available in different formats and capabilities. Select a wireless NIC based on the type of wireless network that is installed:

- 802.11b NICs can be used on 802.11g networks.

- 802.11a can be used only on a network that supports 802.11a.

- 802.11a dual-band, 802.11b, and 802.11g NICs can be used on 802.11n networks.

Worksheet 6.8.2.2: Internet Search for NIC Drivers

In this worksheet, you search the Internet for the latest NIC drivers for a network card. Refer to Worksheet 6.8.2.2 in *IT Essentials: PC Hardware and Software Lab Manual*, Fifth Edition.

Installing and Updating a NIC (6.8.2.3)

To install a NIC in a desktop computer, you must remove the case cover. Then remove the cover of the available PCI slot or PCI Express slot. After the NIC is securely installed, replace the case cover. A wireless NIC has an antenna connected to the back of the card or attached with a cable so that it can be positioned for the best signal reception. You must connect and position the antenna.

Sometimes a manufacturer publishes new driver software for a NIC. A new driver might enhance the functionality of the NIC, or it might be needed for operating system compatibility.

When installing a new driver, disable virus protection software to ensure that the driver installs correctly. Some virus scanners detect a driver update as a possible virus attack. Install only one driver at a time; otherwise, some updating processes might conflict. A best practice is to close all applications that are running so that they are not using any files associated with the driver update. Before updating a driver, visit the website of the manufacturer. In many cases, you can download a self-extracting executable driver file that automatically installs or updates the driver.

After the NIC and the driver are installed and configured, you might need to configure other OS settings. You might also need to install a modem to connect to the Internet. If not, you can simply connect the computer to the existing network.

You can also manually update a NIC driver. In Windows 7 and Windows Vista, use the following path:

Start > Control Panel > Device Manager

In Windows XP, use the following path:

Start > Control Panel > System > Hardware tab **> Device Manager**

In Windows 7, to view the network adapters installed, click the arrow next to the category. In Windows Vista and Windows XP, click the **+** next to the Network adapter category. To view and change the properties of the adapter, double-click the adapter. In the Adapter Properties window, select the **Driver** tab.

Note

Sometimes the driver installation process prompts you to reboot the computer.

If a new NIC driver does not perform as expected after it has been installed, you can uninstall the driver or roll back to the previous driver. Double-click the adapter in the Device Manager. In the Adapter Properties window, select the **Driver** tab and click **Roll Back Driver**. If no driver was installed before the update, this option is not available. In that case, you must find a driver for the device and install it manually if the operating system could not find a suitable driver for the NIC.

Lab 6.8.2.4: Install a Wireless NIC in Windows 7

In this lab, you install and configure a wireless NIC. Refer to Lab 6.8.2.4 *in IT Essentials: PC Hardware and Software Lab Manual*, Fifth Edition.

Lab 6.8.2.5: Install a Wireless NIC in Vista Windows

In this lab, you install and configure a wireless NIC. Refer to Lab 6.8.2.5 in *IT Essentials: PC Hardware and Software Lab Manual*, Fifth Edition.

Lab 6.8.2.6: Install a Wireless NIC in Windows XP

In this lab, you install and configure a wireless NIC. Refer to Lab 6.8.2.6 in *IT Essentials: PC Hardware and Software Lab Manual*, Fifth Edition.

Configuring a NIC (6.8.2.7)

After the NIC driver is installed, configure the IP address settings. If the NIC is configured with a static IP address, you might need to change the IP address if your computer joins a different network. Therefore, it might be more practical to enable DHCP on your computer to receive IP address information from the DHCP server.

Every NIC must be configured with the following information:

- **Protocols:** The same protocols must be implemented between any two computers that communicate on the same network.

- **IP address:** This address is configurable and must be unique to each device. The IP address can be manually configured or automatically assigned by DHCP.

- **MAC address:** Each device has a unique MAC address. The MAC address is assigned by the manufacturer and cannot be changed.

To configure a NIC in Windows 7, use the following path:

Start > Control Panel > Network and Sharing Center > Change adapter setting > right-click Local Area Connection > Properties > TCP/IPv4 > Properties > configure IP settings **> OK > OK**

In Windows Vista, use the following path:

Start > Control Panel > Network and Sharing Center > Manage network connections > right-click Local Area Connection > Properties > TCP/IPv4 > Properties > configure IP settings **> OK > OK**

In Windows XP, use the following path:

Start > Control Panel > Network Connections > right-click **Local Area Connection > Properties > TCP/IP > Properties >** configure IP settings **> OK > OK**

Configure Alternate IP Settings

Setting up an alternate IP configuration in Windows simplifies moving between a network that requires using DHCP and a network that uses static IP settings. If a computer cannot communicate with the DHCP server on the network, Windows uses the alternate IP configuration assigned to the NIC. The alternate IP configuration also replaces the APIPA address assigned when the DHCP server cannot be contacted.

To create an alternate IP configuration, click the **Alternate Configuration** tab in the Properties window for the NIC.

Advanced NIC Settings (6.8.2.8)

In most network environments, the only NIC setting that you must configure is the IP address information. You can leave the advanced NIC settings at their default values. However, when a computer connects to a network that does not support some or all the default settings, you must make the necessary changes to the advanced settings. These changes may be required so that the computer can connect to the network, enable features required by the network, or achieve a better network connection.

Improperly setting the advanced features can lead to connection failure or performance degradation. Advanced features are located in the Advanced tab in the NIC configuration window. The Advanced tab contains all the parameters that the NIC manufacturer has available.

Note

The Advanced features available and tab layout of features depend on the OS and the specific NIC adapter and driver installed.

Duplex and Speed

Duplex and speed settings for a NIC can slow down data transfer rates on a computer if they are not matched with the device to which they are connected. A duplex mismatch is when a NIC with a specific link speed or duplex is connected to a NIC set with different values. The default is auto, but you may have to change either the duplex or speed, or both.

Wake on LAN

Wake on LAN (WoL) settings are used to wake up a networked computer from a very low power mode state. Very low power mode means that the computer is turned off but is still connected to a power source. To support WoL, the computer must have an ATX-compatible power supply and a WoL-compatible NIC. A wake-up message, called a magic packet, is sent to the NIC of the computer. The magic packet contains the MAC address of the NIC connected to the computer. When the NIC receives the magic packet, the computer wakes up.

You configure WoL in either the motherboard BIOS or the NIC driver firmware.

Quality of Service

Quality of service (QoS), also called 802.1q QoS, is a variety of techniques that control the flow of network traffic, improve transmission speeds, and improve real-time communications traffic. Both the networked computer and the network device must have QoS enabled for the service to function. When QoS is installed and enabled on a computer, Windows can limit available bandwidth to accommodate high-priority traffic. When QoS is disabled, all traffic is treated equally. QoS is configured by installing the Network Service called QoS Packet Scheduler.

Packet Tracer
☐ Activity

PT 6.8.2.9: Install a Wireless NIC

In this Packet Tracer activity, you install a wireless NIC and configure a PC to join a wireless network. To access the activities found in this book, please refer to the instructions found in the Introduction.

Wireless and Wired Router Configurations (6.8.3)

Wireless and wired router connections require different planning and connection techniques. This section describes the basic setup and options and the steps required to connect a device to both kinds of router and test connectivity.

Connecting to the Router (6.8.3.1)

After the NIC drivers are installed, the network router can be connected for the first time. Plug a network cable, also called an Ethernet patch or straight-through cable, into the network port on the computer. Plug the other end into the network device or wall jack.

After connecting the network cable, look at the LEDs, or *link lights*, next to the Ethernet port on the NIC to see if there is any activity. If there is no activity, this might indicate a faulty cable, a faulty switch port, or even a faulty NIC. You might have to replace one or more of these devices to correct the problem.

After confirming that the computer is connected to the network and the link lights on the NIC indicate a working connection, the computer needs an IP address. Most networks are set up so that the computer receives an IP address automatically from a local DHCP server. If the computer does not have an IP address, enter a unique IP address in the TCP/IP properties of the NIC.

How To

To connect to an E2500 router for the first time, follow these steps:

Step 1. The back of the Linksys E2500 router has five Ethernet ports. Connect a DSL or cable modem to the port labeled Internet. The switching logic of the device forwards all the packets through this port when there is communication to and from the Internet and other connected computers. Connect one computer to any remaining port to access the configuration web pages.

Step 2. Turn on the broadband modem and plug in the power cord to the router. When the modem finishes establishing a connection to the ISP, the router automatically communicates with the modem to receive the network information from the ISP that is necessary to gain access to the Internet: IP address, subnet mask, and DNS server addresses. The Internet LED lights up to indicate communication with the modem.

Step 3. When the router has established communication with the modem, you must configure the router to communicate with the devices on the network. Turn on the computer that is connected to the router. The NIC LED on the computer lights up to indicate communication with the router.

Setting the Network Location (6.8.3.2)

The first time Windows 7 or Windows Vista connects to a network, a *network location profile* must be selected. Each network location profile has different default settings. Depending on the profile selected, file and printer sharing or network discovery can be turned off or on and different firewall settings can be applied.

Windows 7 and Windows Vista have three network locations profiles called Public network, Work network, and Home network. Computers that belong to and share resources on a Public, Work, or Home network must be members of the same workgroup. Computers on a Home network can also belong to a homegroup. A homegroup is a feature of Windows 7 that provides a simple method for file and printer sharing. Windows Vista does not support the homegroup feature.

There is a fourth network location profile called Domain network and is typically used for enterprise workplaces. This profile is controlled by the network administrator and cannot be selected or changed by users connected to the enterprise.

Windows XP does not support selecting a network location profile and is not a required step when connecting to a network.

When connecting to a network for the first time, use the following information to make the appropriate choice:

- **Home network:** Choose this network location for home networks or when you trust the people and devices on the network. *Network discovery* is turned on, which allows you to see other computers and devices on the network and other network users to see your computer.

- **Work network:** Choose this network location for a small office or other workplace network. Network discovery is turned on. A homegroup cannot be created or joined.

- **Public network:** Choose this network location for airports, coffee shops, and other public places. Network discovery is turned off. This network location provides the most protection. Also choose this network location if you connect directly to the Internet without using a router or if you have a mobile broadband connection. Homegroup is not available.

Note

If there is only one computer on a network and file or printer sharing is not needed, the most secure choice is Public.

If the Set Network Location window does not display when connecting to a network for the first time, you might need to release and renew the IP address for the computer. After opening the command prompt on the computer, type **ipconfig /release** and then type **ipconfig /renew** to receive an IP address from the router.

You can change the default settings for all network location profiles. Changes to the default profile are applied to every network that uses the same network location profile.

To change network location profile settings in Windows 7, use the following path:

Start > Control Panel > Network and Sharing Center > click the current network location profile > select a network location > view or change settings in Network and Sharing Center > choose homegroup and sharing option > change advanced sharing settings

To change network location profile settings in Windows Vista, use the following path:

Start > Control Panel > Network and Sharing Center > Customize > select a location type > click **Next** > view or change network and sharing settings in Network and Sharing Center

Logging In to the Router (6.8.3.3)

When the router has established communication with the modem, configure the router to communicate with the devices on the network. Open a web browser. In the Address field, enter 192.168.1.1. This is the default private IP address for the Linksys E2500 router configuration and management interface.

The first time you connect to the Linksys E2500, you are asked to either install the Cisco Connect software or manually connect to the router using the browser-based utility. When manually connecting to an E2500 router, a security window prompts for authentication to access the router configuration screens. The Username field must be left blank. Enter **admin** as the default password.

Basic Network Setup (6.8.3.4)

After you log in, the setup screen opens, as shown in Figure 6-25. The setup screen has tabs that help you configure the router. You must click **Save Settings** at the bottom of each screen after making any changes.

Figure 6-25   E2400 Router Setup Page

All routers that are designed for a home or a small business are preconfigured with basic settings. These settings can be located under different tabs depending on the make and model of the router. It is good practice to make changes to the following default settings:

- **Router name:** Provide a name that can be easily recognized. This name is displayed when viewing networked devices from an operating system.

- **Network device access permissions:** Many network devices built by a specific manufacturer have the same default username and password for accessing the device configuration screen. If left unchanged, unauthorized users can easily log in to the device and modify the settings. When first connecting to the network device, change the default username and password. On some devices, you can only reset the password.

- **Basic QoS:** The E2500 router supports QoS for applications, online gaming, VoIP, and video streaming.

While some default settings should be changed, others are best left alone. Most home or small business networks share a single Internet connection provided by the ISP. Routers in this type of network receive public addresses from the ISP, which allows the router to send and receive packets to and from the Internet. The router provides private addresses to local network hosts. Because private addresses cannot be used on the Internet, a process is used for translating private addresses into unique public addresses. This allows local hosts to communicate over the Internet.

Network Address Translation (NAT) is the process used to convert private addresses to Internet-routable addresses. With NAT, a private (local) source IP address is translated to a public (global) address. The process is reversed for incoming packets. The router is able to translate many internal IP addresses into public addresses, by using NAT.

Only packets destined for other networks need to be translated. These packets must pass through the gateway, where the router replaces the private IP addresses of the source hosts with the public IP addresses of the router.

Although each host on the internal network has a unique private IP address, the hosts share Internet routable addresses that have been assigned to the router by the ISP.

When using the configuration screens of the E2500 router, click the **Help** tab to see additional information about a tab. For information beyond what is shown on the help screen, consult the documentation.

Lab 6.8.3.5: Connect to a Router for the First Time

In this lab, you configure basic settings on the Linksys E2500. Refer to Lab 6.8.3.5 in *IT Essentials: PC Hardware and Software Lab Manual*, Fifth Edition.

PT 6.8.3.6: Connect to Wireless Router and Configure Basic Settings

In this Packet Tracer activity, you configure a PC to join a wireless network and test the wireless connection. To access the activities found in this book, please refer to the instructions found in the Introduction.

Basic Wireless Settings (6.8.3.7)

After establishing the connection to a router, it is good practice to configure some basic settings to help secure and increase the speed of the wireless network. All following wireless settings are under the Wireless tab, as shown in Figure 6-26:

- Network mode
- Service set identifier (SSID)
- Channel
- Wireless security modes

Figure 6-26   E2500 Wireless Setup Screen

Network Mode

The 802.11 protocol can provide increased throughput based on the wireless network environment. If all wireless devices connect with the same 802.11 standard, maximum speeds can be obtained for that standard. If the access point is configured to accept only one 802.11 standard, devices that do not use that standard cannot connect to the access point.

A mixed mode wireless network environment can include 802.11a, 802.11b, 802.11g, and 802.11n. This environment provides easy access for legacy devices that need a wireless connection.

SSID

The *service set identifier (SSID)* is the name of the wireless network. The SSID broadcast allows other devices to automatically discover the name of the wireless network. When the SSID broadcast is disabled, you must manually enter the SSID on wireless devices.

Disabling SSID broadcasting can make it more difficult for legitimate clients to find the wireless network. Simply turning off the SSID broadcast is not sufficient to prevent unauthorized clients from connecting to the wireless network. Instead of turning off the SSID broadcast, use stronger encryption, such as WPA or WPA2.

Channel

Wireless devices that transmit over the same frequency range create interference. Home electronic devices, such as cordless phones, other wireless networks, and baby monitors, may use this same frequency range. These devices can slow down the Wi-Fi performance and potentially break network connections.

802.11b and 802.11g standards transmit in a narrow radio frequency range of 2.4 GHz. The 2.4-GHz Wi-Fi signal range is divided into a number of smaller bands, also called channels. Setting this Wi-Fi channel number is a way to avoid wireless interference.

Channel 1 uses the lowest frequency band, and each subsequent channel slightly increases the frequency. The further apart two channel numbers are, the less the degree of overlap and likelihood of interference. Channels 1 and 11 do not overlap with the default channel 6. It is good practice to use one of these three channels for best results. For example, if you experience interference with a neighbor's WLAN, change to a distant channel.

Wireless Security

Most wireless access points support several different security modes. The most common ones include the following:

- *Wired Equivalent Privacy (WEP)*: Encrypts the broadcast data between the wireless access point and the client using a 64-bit or 128-bit encryption key.

- *Temporal Key Integrity Protocol (TKIP)*: This WEP patch automatically negotiates a new key every few minutes. TKIP helps to prevent attackers from gaining enough data to break the encryption key.

- *Advanced Encryption Standard (AES)*: A more secure encryption system than TKIP. AES also requires more computing power to run the stronger encryption.

- *Wi-Fi Protected Access (WPA)*: An improved version of WEP created as a temporary solution until 802.11i became ratified. Now that 802.11i has been ratified, WPA2 has been released. It covers the entire 802.11i standard. WPA uses much stronger encryption than WEP encryption.

- *Wi-Fi Protected Access 2 (WPA2)*: An improved version of WPA that supports robust encryption, which provides government-grade security. WPA2 can be enabled with password authentication (personal) or server authentication (enterprise).

Lab 6.8.3.8: Configure Wireless Router in Windows 7

In this lab, you configure and test the wireless settings on the Linksys E2500. Refer to Lab 6.8.3.8 in *IT Essentials: PC Hardware and Software Lab Manual*, Fifth Edition.

Lab 6.8.3.9: Configure Wireless Router in Windows Vista

In this lab, you configure and test the wireless settings on the Linksys E2500. Refer to Lab 6.8.3.9 in *IT Essentials: PC Hardware and Software Lab Manual*, Fifth Edition.

Lab 6.8.3.10: Configure Wireless Router in Windows XP

In this lab, you configure and test the wireless settings on the Linksys E2500. Refer to Lab 6.8.3.10 in *IT Essentials: PC Hardware and Software Lab Manual*, Fifth Edition.

PT 6.8.3.11: Connecting Wireless PCs to a Linksys WRT300N

In this Packet Tracer activity, you configure basic wireless settings on a PC, configure basic security on the Linksys-WRT300N, and verify full connectivity. To access the activities found in this book, please refer to the instructions found in the Introduction.

Testing Connectivity with the Windows GUI (6.8.3.12)

When all devices are connected and all link lights are functioning, test the network for connectivity. This test can determine if you are connected to a wireless access point, a home gateway, or the Internet. The easiest way to test for an Internet connection is to open a web browser and see if the Internet is available. To troubleshoot a wireless connection, you can use the Windows GUI or CLI.

To verify a wireless connection in Windows 7, use the following path:

Start > Control Panel > Network and Sharing Center > Change adapter settings

Then double-click **Wireless Network Connection** to display the status screen.

To verify a wireless connection in Windows Vista, use the following path:

Start > Control Panel > Network and Sharing Center > Manage Network Connections

Then double-click **Wireless Network Connection** to display the status screen.

To verify a wireless connection in Windows XP, use the following path:

Start > Control Panel > Network Connections

Then double-click **Wireless Network Connection** to display the status screen.

The Wireless Network Connection Status window, as shown in Figure 6-27, displays whether the computer is connected to the Internet, along with the duration of the connection. It also shows the number of sent and received bytes.

Figure 6-27   Wireless Network Connection Status Window

For Windows 7 or Windows Vista, click the **Details** button. The Connection Status information includes either a static address or a dynamic address. The subnet mask, default gateway, MAC address, and other information about the IP address are also listed. If the connection is not functioning correctly, click **Diagnose** to reset the connection information and attempt to establish a new connection.

For Windows XP, to display the address type, click the **Support** tab. The Connection Status information includes either a static address, which is assigned manually, or a dynamic address, which is assigned by a DHCP server. The subnet mask and default gateway are also listed. To access the MAC address and other information about the IP address, click **Details.** If the connection is not functioning correctly, click **Repair** to reset the connection information and attempt to establish a new connection.

To view more information about local wireless networks before connecting, you may need to use a *wireless locator*. Wireless locators are software utilities that allow a user to see SSID broadcasts, encryptions, channels, and locations of wireless networks in the immediate area.

Testing Connectivity with the Windows CLI (6.8.3.13)

You can use several CLI commands to test network connectivity. As a technician, it is essential that you become familiar with a basic set of these commands.

ipconfig Command Options

The **ipconfig** command displays basic configuration information of all network adapters. To perform specific tasks, you can add options to the **ipconfig** command, as shown in Table 6-11.

Table 6-11   ipconfig Command Options

ipconfig Command Options	Purpose
/all	Displays the full configuration of all network adapters
/release	Releases the IP address of a network adapter
/renew	Renews the IP address of a network adapter
/flushdns	Empties the cache that stores DNS information
/registerdns	Refreshes DHCP leases and reregisters the adapter with DNS
/displaydns	Shows DNS information in the cache

ping Command Options

ping tests basic connectivity between devices. You can test your own connection by pinging your computer. To test your computer, ping your NIC. In Windows 7 and Windows Vista, select **Start** and type **cmd**. For Windows XP, select **Start > Run > cmd**. At the command prompt, enter **ping localhost**.

Try to ping other computers on the network, including the default gateway and remote computers. You can find the address for the default gateway by using the **ipconfig** command.

Ping a public IP address outside of your network to check if your WAN connection is working properly. You can also test the Internet connection and DNS when you ping a popular website. At the command prompt, enter **ping** *destination_name*.

The response of the **ping** command displays the IP address resolution of the domain. The response shows replies from the ping or that the request timed out because there is a problem.

To perform other specific tasks, you can add options to the **ping** command, as shown in Table 6-12.

Table 6-12   ping Command Options

ping Command Options	Purpose
-t	Ping the specified host until stopped
-a	Resolve the address to a hostname

ping Command Options	Purpose
-n count	Number of echo requests to send
-l size	Send the buffer size
-f	Set the Don't Fragment flag in the packet
-I TTL	Time To Live
-v TOS	Type Of Services
-r count	Record the route for count hops
-s count	Time stamp for count hops
-j host-list	Loose source route along host list
K host-list	Strict source route along host list
-w timeout	Timeout in milliseconds to wait for each reply

net Commands

Use the *net* command to manage network computers, servers, and resources like drives and printers. **net** commands use the NetBIOS protocol in Windows. These commands start, stop, and configure networking services, as shown in Table 6-13.

Table 6-13   net Commands

net Commands	Purpose
net/? or net help	Displays the net commands
Nbtstat	Displays protocol statistics and current TCP/IP connections using NetBIOS over TCP/IP (NBT)
Netstat	Displays active TCP connections
net accounts	Updates the user accounts database and modifies password and login requirements
net computer	Adds or deletes computers
net config [workstation | server]	Displays configuration information
net continue	Continues a service that has been suspended by net pause
net file	Displays the names of all open shared files on a server
net group	Adds, displays, or modifies global groups
net help [command]	Displays information about specific net commands

net Commands	Purpose
net helpmsg	Provides error and problem-solving information
net localgroup	Adds, displays, or modifies local groups
net *name*	Adds or deletes a messaging name
net pause	Pauses services that are currently running
net print	Displays print queue or print job information, or controls a specified print job
net send	Sends messages
net session	Displays or disconnects sessions between computers
net share	Displays or manages shared printers or directories
net start	Displays started services
net statistics [**workstation** | **server**]	Displays workstation and server statistics
net stop [*service*]	Stops specified network service
net time	Displays or synchronizes network time
net use	Displays or manages remote connections
net user	Creates, modifies, or lists user accounts
net view	Displays network resources or computers

tracert Command

tracert traces the route that packets take from your computer to a destination host. At the command prompt, enter **tracert** *hostname*.

The first listing in the results is your default gateway. Each listing after that is the router that packets are traveling through to reach the destination. **tracert** shows you where packets are stopping, indicating where the problem is occurring. If listings show problems after the default gateway, it may mean that the problems are with the ISP, the Internet, or the destination server.

nslookup Command

nslookup tests and troubleshoots DNS servers. It queries the DNS server to discover IP addresses or hostnames. At the command prompt, enter **nslookup** *hostname*. **nslookup** returns the IP address for the hostname entered. A reverse **nslookup** command, **nslookup** *IP_address*, returns the corresponding hostname for the IP address entered.

Lab 6.8.3.14: Test the Wireless NIC in Windows 7

In this lab, you check the status of your wireless connection, investigate the availability of wireless networks, and test connectivity. Refer to Lab 6.8.3.14 in *IT Essentials: PC Hardware and Software Lab Manual*, Fifth Edition.

Lab 6.8.3.15: Test the Wireless NIC in Windows Vista

In this lab, you check the status of your wireless connection, investigate the availability of wireless networks, and test connectivity. Refer to Lab 6.8.3.15 in *IT Essentials: PC Hardware and Software Lab Manual*, Fifth Edition.

Lab 6.8.3.16: Test the Wireless NIC in Windows XP

In this lab, you check the status of your wireless connection, investigate the availability of wireless networks, and test connectivity. Refer to Lab 6.8.3.16 in *IT Essentials: PC Hardware and Software Lab Manual*, Fifth Edition.

PT 6.8.3.17: Test a Wireless Connection

In this Packet Tracer activity, you configure a PC to join a wireless network and test the wireless connection. To access the activities found in this book, please refer to the instructions found in the Introduction.

OS Configurations (6.8.4)

This section defines domains and workgroups and describes the steps for connecting to a workgroup or domain, sharing resources, and setting up and connecting with a virtual private network (VPN) connection.

Domain and Workgroup (6.8.4.1)

Domain and workgroup are methods for organizing and managing computers on a network. All computers on a network must be part of either a domain or a workgroup. When Windows is first installed on a computer, it is automatically assigned to a workgroup.

Domain

A *domain* is a group of computers and electronic devices with a common set of rules and procedures administered as a unit. A domain does not refer to a single location or specific type of network configuration. Computers in a domain are a logical grouping of connected computers that can be located in different locations in the world. A specialized server called a *domain controller* manages all security-related aspects of users and network resources, centralizing security and administration.

For data protection, an administrator performs a routine backup of all files on the servers. If a computer crashes, or data is lost, the administrator can easily recover the data from a recent backup.

Workgroup

A *workgroup* is a collection of workstations and servers on a LAN that are designed to communicate and exchange data with one another. Each individual workstation controls its user accounts, security information, and access to data and resources.

Connecting to a Workgroup or a Domain (6.8.4.2)

Before computers can share resources, they must share the same domain name or workgroup name. Older operating systems have more restrictions for naming a workgroup. If a workgroup is made up of newer and older operating systems, use the workgroup name from the computer with the oldest operating system.

Note

Before changing a computer from a domain to a workgroup, you need the username and the password for an account in the local administrator group.

To change the workgroup name for Windows 7 and Windows Vista, use the following path:

Start > right-click **Computer >** click **Properties > Change setting > Change**

To change the workgroup name for Windows XP, use the following path:

Start > right-click **My Computer >** click **Properties > Computer Name** tab **> Change**

Windows also has a wizard that guides you through the process for joining a domain or workgroup. After changing the domain name or workgroup name, you must restart the computer for the changes to take place.

Windows 7 Homegroup (6.8.4.3)

All Windows 7 computers that belong to the same workgroup can also belong to a *homegroup*. There can only be one homegroup per workgroup on a network. Computers can only be a member of one homegroup at a time. The homegroup option is not available in Windows Vista or Windows XP.

Only one user in the workgroup creates the homegroup. The other users can join the homegroup, provided they know the homegroup password. Homegroup availability depends on your network location profile:

- **Home network:** Allowed to create or join a homegroup

- **Work network:** Not allowed to create or join a homegroup, but you can see and share resources with other computers

- **Public network:** Homegroup not available

Note

Computers with Windows 7 Starter or Windows 7 Home Basic installed can join a homegroup but not create a homegroup.

How To

To change the network location profile of the computer to the Home Network, follow these steps:

Step 1.   Click **Start > Control Panel > Network and Sharing Center.**

Step 2.   Click the network location profile listed in the View your active networks section of the window, as shown in Figure 6-28.

Figure 6-28   Current Network Location Profile

Step 3.   Click **Home network.**

Step 4.   Select what you want to share (for example, Pictures, Music, Videos, Documents, and Printers), and then click **Next.**

Step 5.   Join or create a homegroup.

How To

To create a homegroup, follow these steps:

Step 1.   Click **Start > Control Panel > HomeGroup.**

Step 2.   Click **Create a homegroup.**

Step 3.   Select files to share, and then click **Next.**

Step 4.   Record the homegroup password.

Step 5.   Click **Finish**.

When a computer joins a homegroup, all user accounts on the computer, except the Guest account, become members of the homegroup. Being part of a homegroup makes it easy to share pictures, music, videos, documents, libraries, and printers with other people in the same homegroup. Users control access to their own resources. Users can also create or join a homegroup with a virtual machine in Windows Virtual PC.

How To

To join a computer to a homegroup, follow these steps:

Step 1.   Click **Start > Control Panel > HomeGroup**.

Step 2.   Click **Join now**.

Step 3.   Select files to share then click **Next**.

Step 4.   Type in the homegroup password; then click **Next**.

Step 5.   Click **Finish**.

To change the files shared on a computer, select **Start > Control Panel > HomeGroup**. After you make your changes, click **Save change**.

Note

If a computer belongs to a domain, you can join a homegroup and access files and resources on other homegroup computers. You are not allowed to create a new homegroup or share your own files and resources with a homegroup.

Sharing Resources in Windows Vista (6.8.4.4)

Windows Vista controls which resources are shared and how they are shared by turning specific sharing features on and off. Sharing and Discovery, located in the Network and Sharing Center, manages the settings for a home network. The following items can be controlled:

- Network discovery
- File sharing
- Public folder sharing
- Printer sharing
- Password-protected sharing
- Media sharing

To access Sharing and Discovery, use the following path:

Start > Control Panel > Network and Sharing Center

To enable sharing resources between computers connected to the same workgroup, Network Discovery and File Sharing must be turned on.

Sharing Resources in Windows XP (6.8.4.5)

The Windows XP Network Setup Wizard configures the computer settings for setting up a home network and sharing resources. The wizard sets up the following items:

- A connection to the Internet for the computer through a direct dialup or broadband connection or through another computer on the home network

- Internet Connection Sharing on a Windows XP-based computer for sharing a connection to the Internet with other computers on the home network

- Computer name, computer description, and workgroup name

- File and printer sharing

To access the Network Setup Wizard, use the following path:

Start > Control Panel > Network Setup Wizard

The Network Setup Wizard is portable. You can create a Network Setup Wizard disk to automatically configure other Windows XP computers to have the same settings.

Network Shares and Mapping Drives (6.8.4.6)

Network file sharing and mapping network drives is a secure and convenient way to provide easy access to network resources. This is especially true when different versions of Windows require access to network resources. Mapping a local drive is a useful way to access a single file, specific folders, or an entire drive between different operating systems over a network. Mapping a drive, which is done by assigning a letter (A–Z) to the resource on a remote drive, allows you to use the remote drive as if it were a local drive.

Network File Sharing

First determine which resources will be shared over the network and the type of permissions users will have to the resources. Permissions define the type of access a user has to a file or folder:

- **Read:** The user can view the file and subfolder names, navigate to subfolders, view data in files, and run program files.

- **Change:** In addition to Read permissions, the user can add files and subfolders, change the data in files, and delete subfolders and files.

- **Full Control:** In addition to Change and Read permissions, the user can change the permission of files and folders in an NTFS partition and take ownership of files and folders.

Copy or move the resources to a share folder.

To share resources in Windows 7 and Windows Vista, use the following path:

Right-click the folder > click **Properties > Advanced Sharing >** select **Share this folder > Permissions.** Identify who has access to the folder and which permissions by viewing the permissions window of a shared folder.

To share resources in Windows XP, use the following path:

Right-click the folder **>** select **Sharing and Security > Share this folder.** Identify who has access to the folder and which permissions.

Network Drive Mapping

To map a network drive to a shared folder, use the following path:

Start > right-click **Computer >** click **Map network drive.** Locate the shared folder over the network and assign a drive letter.

Windows 7 is limited to a maximum of 20 simultaneous file-sharing connections. Windows Vista Business and Windows XP Professional are limited to a maximum of 10 simultaneous file-sharing connections.

Lab 6.8.4.7: Share a Folder Create a Homegroup and Map a Network Drive in Windows 7

In this lab, you create and share a folder, set permissions for the shares, create a homegroup to share resources, and map a network drive. Refer to Lab 6.8.4.7 in *IT Essentials: PC Hardware and Software Lab Manual*, Fifth Edition.

Lab 6.8.4.8: Share a Folder and Map a Network Drive in Windows Vista

In this lab, you create and share a folder, set permissions for the shares and map a network drive. Refer to Lab 6.8.4.8 in *IT Essentials: PC Hardware and Software Lab Manual*, Fifth Edition.

Lab 6.8.4.9: Share a Folder and Map a Network Drive in Windows XP

In this lab, you create and share a folder, set permissions for the shares and map a network drive. Refer to Lab 6.8.4.9 in *IT Essentials: PC Hardware and Software Lab Manual*, Fifth Edition.

VPN (6.8.4.10)

A *virtual private network (VPN)* is a private network that connects remote sites or users together over a public network, like the Internet. The most common type of VPN is used to access a corporate private network. The VPN uses dedicated secure connections, routed through the Internet, from the corporate private network to the remote user. When connected to the corporate private network, users become part of that network and have access to all services and resources as if they were physically connected to the corporate LAN.

Remote-access users must install the VPN client on their computers to form a secure connection with the corporate private network. The VPN client software encrypts data before sending it over the Internet to the VPN gateway at the corporate private network. VPN gateways establish, manage, and control VPN connections, also known as VPN tunnels. Basic VPN connection software is shown in Figure 6-29.

Figure 6-29   VPN Software Connection

 To set up and configure Windows 7 and Windows Vista to use a VPN connection, follow these steps:

Step 1.   Select **Start > Network and Sharing Center.**

Step 2.   Select **Set up a new connection or network.**

Step 3.   After the New Connection Wizard window opens, select **Connect to a workplace** and click **Next**.

Step 4.   Select **Use my Internet connection (VPN)** and type the Internet address and the destination name.

Step 5.   Select **Don't connect now; just set it up so I can connect later** and click **Next**.

Step 6.   Type the username and password and click **Create**.

Step 7.   In the login window, enter the username and password and click **Connect**.

To set up and configure Windows XP to use a VPN connection, follow these steps:

Step 1.   Select **Start > Control Panel > Network Connections**.

Step 2.   Select **Create a new connection**.

Step 3.   After the New Connection Wizard window opens, click **Next**.

Step 4.   Select **Connect to the network at my workplace** and click **Next**.

Step 5.   Select **Virtual Private Network connection** and click **Next**.

Step 6.   Type the name for the connection and click **Next**.

Step 7.   Type in the name or IP address of the VPN server and click **Next** and **Finish**.

Step 8.   In the login window, enter the username and password and click **Connect**.

Select an ISP Connection Type (6.9)

It is very important to determine a customer's needs when choosing an Internet service provider and type of service. There are many considerations that should affect the decision. This section describes the common Internet connection types and choices and discusses advantages and disadvantages.

Brief History of Connection Technologies (6.9.1.1)

In the 1990s, the Internet was typically used for data transfer. Transmission speeds were slow compared to the high-speed connections that are available today. The additional bandwidth allows for transmission of voice and video as well as data. Today there are many ways to connect to the Internet. Phone, cable, satellite, and private telecommunications companies offer broadband Internet connections for businesses and home use.

Analog Telephone

Analog telephone, also called *plain old telephone service (POTS)*, transmits over standard voice telephone lines. This type of service uses an analog modem to place a telephone call to another modem at a remote site, such as an Internet service provider. The modem uses the telephone line to transmit and receive data. This method of connection is known as dialup.

Integrated Services Digital Network

Integrated Services Digital Network (ISDN) uses multiple channels and can carry different types of services; therefore, it is considered a type of broadband. ISDN is a standard for sending voice, video, and data over normal telephone wires. ISDN technology uses the telephone wires as an analog telephone service.

Broadband

Broadband is a technology that is used to transmit and receive multiple signals using different frequencies over one cable. For example, the cable used to bring cable television to your home can carry computer network transmissions at the same time. Because the two transmission types use different frequencies, they do not interfere with each other.

Broadband uses a wide range of frequencies that can be further divided into channels. In networking, the term broadband describes communication methods that transmit two or more signals at the same time. Sending two or more signals simultaneously increases the rate of transmission. Some common broadband network connections include cable, DSL, ISDN, and satellite.

DSL and ADSL (6.9.1.2)

Digital subscriber line (DSL) is an always-on service, which means that there is no need to dial up each time you want to connect to the Internet. DSL uses the existing copper telephone lines to provide high-speed digital data communication between end users and telephone companies. Unlike ISDN, where the digital data communications replaces the analog voice communications, DSL shares the telephone wire with analog signals.

With DSL, the voice and data signals are carried on different frequencies on the copper telephone wires. A filter prevents DSL signals from interfering with phone signals. A DSL filter is connected between each telephone and phone jack.

The DSL modem does not require a filter. The DSL modem is not affected by the frequencies of the telephone. A DSL modem can connect directly to your computer, or it can be connected to a networking device to share the Internet connection with multiple computers.

Asymmetric digital subscriber line (ADSL) has different bandwidth capabilities in each direction. *Downloading* is the receiving of data from the server to the end user. *Uploading* is the sending of data from the end user to the server. ADSL has a fast download rate which is beneficial to users who are downloading large amounts of data. The upload rate of ADSL is slower than the download rate. ADSL does not perform well when hosting a web server or FTP server, both of which involve upload-intensive Internet activities.

Line-of-Sight Wireless Internet Service (6.9.1.3)

Line-of-sight wireless Internet is an always-on service that uses radio signals for transmitting Internet access. Radio signals are sent from a tower to the receiver that the customer connects to a computer or network device. A clear path between the transmission tower and customer is required. The tower may connect to other towers or directly to an Internet backbone connection. The distance the radio signal can travel and still be strong enough to provide a clear signal depends on the frequency of the signal. A lower frequency of 900 MHz can travel up to 40 miles (65 km), whereas a higher frequency of 5.7 GHz can only travel 2 miles (3 km). Extreme weather condition, trees, and tall buildings can affect signal strength and performance.

WiMAX (6.9.1.4)

Worldwide Interoperability for Microwave Access (WiMAX) is an IP-based wireless 4G broadband technology that offers high-speed mobile Internet access for mobile devices. WiMAX is a standard called IEEE 802.16e. It supports a MAN network and has download speeds up to 70 Mb/s and distances up to 30 miles (50 km). Security and QoS for WiMAX are equivalent to cellular networks.

WiMAX uses a low wavelength transmission, usually between 2 GHz and 11 GHz. These frequencies are not as easily disrupted by physical obstructions because they can better bend around obstacles than higher frequencies. *Multiple-input and multiple-output (MIMO)* technology is supported, which means additional antennas can be added to increase the potential throughput.

There are two methods of transmitting a WiMAX signal:

- **Fixed WiMAX:** A point-to-point or point-to-multipoint service with speeds up to 72 Mb/s and a range of 30 miles (50 km)

- **Mobile WiMAX:** A mobile service, like Wi-Fi, but with higher speeds and a longer transmission range

Other Broadband Technologies (6.9.1.5)

Broadband technology provides several different options for connecting people and devices for the purpose of communicating and sharing information. Each offers different features or is designed to support specific needs. It is important to have a clear understanding of the several broadband technologies and how they can best support a customer.

Cellular

Cellular technology enables the transfer of voice, video, and data. With a cellular WAN adapter installed, a user can access the Internet over the cellular network. There are different cellular WAN characteristics:

- **1G:** Analog voice only

- **2G:** Digital voice, conference calls, and caller ID; data speeds less than 9.6 Kb/s

- **2.5G:** Data speeds between 30 Kb/s and 90 Kb/s; supports web browsing, short audio and video clips, games, and application and ring tone downloads

- **3G:** Data speeds between 144 Kb/s and 2 Mb/s; supports full-motion video, streaming music, 3D gaming, and faster web browsing

- **3.5G:** Data speeds between 384 Kb/s and 14.4 Mb/s; supports high-quality streaming video, high-quality videoconferencing, and VoIP

- **4G:** Data speeds between 5.8 Mb/s and 672 Mb/s when mobile, and up to 1 Gb/s when stationary; supports IP-based voice, gaming services, high-quality streamed multimedia, and IPv6

Cellular networks use one or more of the following technologies:

- **Global System for Mobile Communications (GSM):** Standard used by the worldwide cellular network

- **General Packet Radio Service (GPRS):** Data service for users of GSM

- **Quad-band:** Allows a cellular phone to operate on all four GSM frequencies: 850 MHz, 900 MHz, 1800 MHz, and 1900 MHz

- **Short Message Service (SMS):** Data service used to send and receive text messages

- **Multimedia Messaging Service (MMS):** Data service used to send and receive text messages and can include multimedia content

- **Enhanced Data Rates for GSM Evolution (EDGE):** Increased data rates and improved data reliability

- **Evolution-Data Optimized (EV-DO):** Improved upload speeds and QoS

- **High-Speed Downlink Packet Access (HSDPA):** Enhanced 3G access speed

Cable

A *cable* Internet connection does not use telephone lines. Cable uses coaxial cable lines originally designed to carry cable television. A cable modem connects your computer to the cable company. You can plug your computer directly into the cable modem, or you can connect a router, switch, hub, or multipurpose network device so that multiple computers can share the connection to the Internet. Like DSL, cable offers high speeds and an always-on service, which means that even when the connection is not in use, the connection to the Internet is still available.

Satellite

Broadband *satellite* is an alternative for customers who cannot get cable or DSL connections. A satellite connection does not require a phone line or cable, but uses a satellite dish for two-way communication. The satellite dish transmits and receives signals to and from a satellite that relays these signals back to a service provider. Download speeds are up to 1 Gb/s; uploads are closer to 10 Mb/s. It takes time for the signal from the satellite dish to relay to your ISP through the satellite orbiting the Earth. Due to this latency, it is difficult to use time-sensitive applications, such as videogaming, VoIP, and videoconferencing.

Fiber Broadband

Fiber broadband provides faster connection speeds and bandwidth than cable modems, DSL, and ISDN. Fiber broadband can deliver a multitude of digital services, such as telephone, video, data, and videoconferencing simultaneously.

 Worksheet 6.9.1.6: Answer Broadband Questions

In this worksheet, you answer questions about broadband technology and connections. Refer to Worksheet 6.9.1.6 in *IT Essentials: PC Hardware and Software Lab Manual*, Fifth Edition.

Selecting an ISP for the Customer (6.9.1.7)

Several WAN solutions are available for connecting between sites or to the Internet. WAN connection services provide different speeds and levels of service. You should understand how users connect to the Internet and the advantages and disadvantages of different connection types. The ISP that you choose can have a noticeable effect on network service. Some private resellers that connect to a phone company may sell more connections than allowed, which slows the overall speed of the service to customers.

There are four main considerations for an Internet connection:

- Cost

- Speed

- Reliability

- Availability

Research the connection types that the ISPs offer before selecting an ISP. Check the services available in your area. Compare connection speeds, reliability, and cost before committing to a service agreement. Table 6-14 describes ISP connection details.

Table 6-14   ISP Connection Details

Type	Advantages	Disadvantages	Speed
POTS	Widely available	Very slow speeds Cannot receive phone calls while connected	Maximum of 56 Kb/s
ISDN	Higher speeds than POTS	Still much slower than other broadband technologies	BRI: up to 128 Kb/s PRI: up to 2.048 Mb/s
DSL	Low cost	Distance from central office impacts speed	24 Mb/s to 100 Mb/s
Cable	Very high download speed	Slow upload speeds	27 Kb/s to 160 Mb/s
Satellite	Available where DSL and cable are not	More expensive than other broadband technologies Susceptible to weather conditions	9 Kb/s to 24 Mb/s
Cellular	Available to mobile users	Not accessible everywhere	20 Kb/s and up depending on the technology used

POTS

A POTS connection is extremely slow, but it is available wherever there is a telephone. There are two major disadvantages of using the phone line with an analog modem. The first is that the telephone line cannot be used for voice calls while the modem is in use. The second is the limited bandwidth provided by analog phone service. The maximum bandwidth using an analog modem is 56 Kb/s, but in reality, it is usually much lower than that. An analog modem is not a good solution for the demands of busy networks.

ISDN

ISDN is very reliable because it uses POTS lines. ISDN is available in most places where the telephone company supports digital signaling to carry the data. Because it uses digital technology, ISDN offers faster connection times, faster speeds, and higher-quality voice than traditional analog telephone service. It also allows multiple devices to share a single telephone line.

DSL

DSL allows multiple devices to share a single telephone line. DSL speeds are generally higher than ISDN. DSL allows the use of high-bandwidth applications or multiple users to share the same connection to the Internet. In most cases, the copper wires already in your home or business are capable of carrying the signals needed for DSL communication.

There are limitations to DSL technology:

- DSL service is not available everywhere, and it works better and faster the closer the installation is to the telephone provider's central office (CO).

- In some cases, installed telephone lines will not qualify to carry all DSL signals.

- The voice information and data carried by DSL must be separated at the customer site. A device called a filter prevents data signals from interfering with voice signals.

Cable

Most homes that have cable television have the option to install high-speed Internet service using that same cable. Many cable companies offer telephone service as well.

Satellite

People who live in rural areas often use satellite broadband because they need a faster connection than dialup and no other broadband connection is available. The cost of installation and the monthly service fees are generally much higher than those of DSL and cable. Heavy storm conditions can degrade the quality of the connection, slowing down or even disconnecting the connection.

Cellular

Many types of wireless Internet services are available. The same companies that offer cellular service may offer Internet service. PC Card/ExpressBus, USB, or PCI and PCIe cards are used to connect a computer to the Internet. Service providers may offer wireless Internet service using microwave technology in limited areas.

Worksheet 6.9.1.8: ISP Connection Types

In this worksheet, you determine the best ISP type for your customer. Refer to Worksheet 6.9.1.8 in *IT Essentials: PC Hardware and Software Lab Manual*, Fifth Edition.

Common Preventive Maintenance Techniques Used for Networks (6.10)

Preventive maintenance is vital for keeping network availability high and costs and downtime at a minimum. Having a preventive maintenance plan in place and routinely performing maintenance tasks is an important part of maintaining a network.

Preventive Maintenance Procedures (6.10.1.1)

There are common preventive maintenance techniques that should continually be performed for a network to operate properly. In an organization, if one computer is malfunctioning, generally only that user is affected. But if the network is malfunctioning, many or all users are unable to work.

Preventive maintenance is just as important for the network as it is for the computers on a network. You must check the condition of cables, network devices, servers, and computers to make sure that they are kept clean and are in good working order. One of the biggest problems with network devices, especially in the server room, is heat. Network devices do not perform well when overheated. When dust gathers in and on network devices, it impedes the proper flow of cool air and sometimes even clogs the fans. It is important to keep network rooms clean and change air filters often. It is also a good idea to have replacement filters available for prompt maintenance. You should develop a plan to perform scheduled maintenance and cleaning at regular intervals. A maintenance program helps prevent network downtime and equipment failures.

As part of a regularly scheduled maintenance program, inspect all cabling. Make sure that cables are labeled correctly and labels are not coming off. Replace worn or unreadable labels. Always follow the company's cable labeling guidelines. Check that cable supports are properly installed and no attachment points are coming loose. Cabling can become damaged and worn. Keep the cabling in good repair to maintain good network performance. Refer to wiring diagrams if needed.

Check cables at workstations and printers. Cables are often moved or kicked when they are underneath desks. These conditions can result in loss of bandwidth or connectivity.

As a technician, you may notice that equipment is failing, damaged, or making unusual sounds. Inform the network administrator if you notice any of these issues to prevent unnecessary network downtime. You should also be proactive in the education of network users. Demonstrate to network users how to properly connect and disconnect cables, as well as how to move them, if necessary.

Basic Troubleshooting Process for Networks (6.11)

Troubleshooting network problems requires a systematic approach that results in a minimum of downtime for the network users. This section applies the troubleshooting process to networks.

Identify the Problem (6.11.1.1)

Network problems can be simple or complex and can result from a combination of hardware, software, and connectivity issues. Computer technicians must be able to analyze the problem and determine the cause of the error to repair the network issue. This process is called troubleshooting.

To assess the problem, determine how many computers on the network are experiencing the problem. If there is a problem with one computer on the network, start the troubleshooting process at that computer. If there is a problem with all computers on the network, start the troubleshooting process in the network room where all computers are connected. As a technician, you should develop a logical and consistent method for diagnosing network problems by eliminating one problem at a time.

Follow the steps outlined in this section to accurately identify, repair, and document the problem. The first step in the troubleshooting process is to identify the problem. Table 6-15 shows a list of open-ended and closed-ended questions to ask the customer.

Table 6-15   Step 1: Identify the Problem

Open-ended questions	What problems are you experiencing with your computer or network device?
	What software has been installed on your computer recently?
	What were you doing when the problem was identified?
	What error message have you received?
	What type of network connection is the computer using?
Closed-ended questions	Has anyone else used your computer recently?
	Can you see any shared files or printers?
	Have you changed your password recently?
	Can you access the Internet?
	Are you currently logged in to the network?

Establish a Theory of Probable Cause (6.11.1.2)

After you have talked to the customer, you can establish a theory of probable causes. Table 6-16 shows a list of some common probable causes for network problems.

Table 6-16   Step 2: Establish a Theory of Probable Cause

Common causes of network problems	Loose cable connections
	Improperly installed NIC
	ISP down
	Low wireless signal strength
	Invalid IP address

Test the Theory to Determine Cause (6.11.1.3)

After you have developed some theories about what is wrong, test your theories to determine the cause of the problem. Table 6-17 shows a list of quick procedures that can determine the exact cause of the problem or even correct the problem. If a quick procedure does correct the problem, you can then verify full system functionality. If a quick procedure does not correct the problem, you might need to research the problem further to establish the exact cause.

Table 6-17   Step 3: Test the Theory to Determine Cause

Common steps to determine cause	Check that all cables are connected to the proper locations.
	Unseat and then reconnect cables and connectors.
	Reboot the computer or network device.
	Log in as a different user.
	Repair or reenable the network connection.
	Contact the network administrator.
	Ping your default gateway.
	Access a remote web page such as http://www.cisco.com.

Establish a Plan of Action to Resolve the Problem and Implement the Solution (6.11.1.4)

After you have determined the exact cause of the problem, establish a plan of action to resolve the problem and implement the solution. Table 6-18 shows some sources you can use to gather additional information to resolve an issue.

Table 6-18   Step 4: Establish a Plan of Action to Resolve the Problem and Implement the Solution

If no solution is achieved in the previous step, further research is needed to implement the solution.	Help desk repair logs
	Other technicians
	Manufacturer FAQ websites
	Technical websites
	Newsgroups
	Computer manuals
	Device manuals
	Online forums
	Internet search

Verify Full System Functionality and Implement Preventive Measures (6.11.1.5)

After you have corrected the problem, verify full functionality and, if applicable, implement preventive measures. Table 6-19 shows a list of the steps to verify the solution.

Table 6-19   Step 5: Verify Full System Functionality and, If Applicable, Implement Preventive Measures

Verify full functionality	Use **ipconfig /all** command to display IP address information for all network adapters.
	Use **ping** to check network connectivity. It will send a packet to the specified address and displays response information.
	Use **nslookup** to query an Internet domain name server. It will return a list of hosts in a domain or the information for one host.
	Use **tracert** to determine the route taken by the packets when they travel across the network. It will show where communications between your computer and another computer are having difficulty.
	Use **net view** to display a list of computers in a workgroup. It will show the available shared resources on a network.

Document Findings, Actions, and Outcomes (6.11.1.6)

In the final step of the troubleshooting process, document your findings, actions, and outcomes. Table 6-20 shows a list of the tasks required to document the problem and the solution.

Table 6-20 Step 6: Document Findings, Actions, and Outcomes

Document your findings, actions, and outcomes.	Discuss the solution implemented with the customer.
	Have the customer verify whether the problem has been solved.
	Provide the customer with all paperwork.
	Document the steps taken to solve the problem in the work order and technician's journal.
	Document any components used in the repair.
	Document the time spent to solve the problem.

Common Problems and Solutions for Networks (6.11.2)

This section provides solutions that can be applied to many common network problems.

Identify Common Problems and Solutions (6.11.2.1)

Network problems can be attributed to hardware, software, or configuration issues, or to some combination of the three. You will resolve some types of network problems more often than others. Table 6-21 is a chart of common network problems and solutions.

Table 6-21 Common Problems and Solutions for Networks

Identify the Problem	Probable Causes	Possible Solutions
NIC LED lights are not lit.	The network cable is unplugged, bad, or damaged.	Reconnect or replace the network connection to the computer.
User cannot telnet into a remote device.	The remote device is not configured for Telnet access.	Configure the remote device for Telnet access.
	Telnet is not allowed from the user or a particular network.	Allow Telnet access from the user or the network.
Older laptop cannot detect the wireless router.	The wireless router/access point is configured with a different 802.11 protocol.	Configure the wireless router with a compatible protocol for the laptop.
	The SSID is not being broadcast.	Configure the wireless router to broadcast the SSID.
	The wireless NIC in the laptop is disabled.	Enable the wireless NIC in the laptop

Identify the Problem	Probable Causes	Possible Solutions
Computer has an IP address of 169.254.x.x.	The network cable is unplugged. The router is powered off or the connection is bad. The NIC is bad.	Reconnect the network cable. Ensure the router is powered on and is properly connected to the network. Replace the NIC. Release and renew the IP address on the computer.
Remote device does not respond to a ping request.	Windows firewall disables ping by default. The remote device is configured to not respond to ping requests.	Set the firewall to enable the ping protocol. Configure the remote device to respond to the ping request.
One user can log in to the local network but cannot access the Internet.	The gateway address is incorrect.	Ensure the correct gateway address is assigned to the NIC.
The network is fully functional and the wireless laptop connection is enabled, but the laptop cannot connect to the network.	The laptop wireless capability is turned off. The external wireless antenna is misaligned. The laptop is out of wireless range. Interference from other wireless devices using the same frequency range.	Enable laptop wireless capability using the wireless NIC property or the Fn key along with the multipurpose key. Realign the external wireless antenna to pick up the wireless signal. Move closer to the wireless router/access point. Change wireless router to a different channel.
A Windows 7 computer, just connected to a network with only Windows 7 computers, cannot view shared resources.	Incorrect workgroup. Incorrect network location. Has not joined the homegroup. Network Discovery and File Sharing is turned off.	Change workgroup name. Change network location to Home Network. Join the homegroup. Turn on Network Discovery and File Sharing.
A user cannot map a drive over the network.	Incorrect workgroup. Network Discovery and File Sharing is turned off.	Change workgroup name. Turn on Network Discovery and File Sharing.

Summary (6.12.1)

This chapter introduced you to the fundamentals of networking; the benefits of having a network; the ways to connect computers to a network; and the planning, implementation, and upgrading of networks and network components. The different aspects of troubleshooting a network were discussed with examples of how to analyze and implement simple solutions. The following concepts from this chapter are important to remember:

- A computer network is composed of two or more computers that share data and resources.

- There are several different network types, including LAN, WLAN, PAN, MAN, and WAN.

- In a peer-to-peer network, devices are connected directly to each other. A peer-to-peer network is easy to install, and no additional equipment or dedicated administrator is required. Users control their own resources, and a network works best with a small number of computers. A client/server network uses a dedicated system that functions as the server. The server responds to requests made by users or clients connected to the network.

- The network topology defines the way in which computers, printers, and other devices are connected. Physical topology describes the layout of the wire and devices, as well as the paths used by data transmissions. Logical topology is the path that signals travel from one point to another. Topologies include bus, star, ring, mesh, and hybrid.

- Networking devices are used to connect computers and peripheral devices so that they can communicate. These include hubs, bridges, switches, routers, and multipurpose devices. The type of device implemented depends on the type of network.

- *Networking media* can be defined as the means by which signals, or data, are sent from one computer to another. Signals can be transmitted either by cable or wireless means. The media types discussed were coaxial, twisted pair, fiber-optic cabling, and radio frequencies.

- Ethernet architecture is now the most popular type of LAN architecture. Architecture refers to the overall structure of a computer or communications system. It determines the capabilities and limitations of the system. The Ethernet architecture is based on the IEEE 802.3 standard. The IEEE 802.3 standard specifies that a network implement the CSMA/CD access control method.

- The OSI reference model is an industry-standard framework that divides the functions of networking into seven distinct layers: application, presentation, session, transport, network, data link, and physical. It is important to understand the purpose of each layer.

- The TCP/IP suite of protocols has become the dominant standard for the Internet. TCP/IP represents a set of public standards that specify how packets of information are exchanged between computers over one or more networks.

- A NIC is a device that plugs into a motherboard and provides ports for the network cable connections. It is the computer interface with the LAN.

- Resources are shared over a network when computers belong to the same workgroup and homegroup.

- Testing network connectivity can be accomplished with CLI tools like ping, ipconfig, net, tracert, and nslookup.

- The three transmission methods for sending signals over data channels are simplex, half-duplex, and full-duplex. Full-duplex networking technology increases performance because data can be sent and received at the same time. DSL, cable, and other broadband technologies operate in full-duplex mode.

- Network devices and media, such as computer components, must be maintained. It is important to clean equipment regularly and use a proactive approach to prevent problems. Repair or replace broken equipment to prevent downtime.

- Many safety hazards are associated with network environments, devices, and media.

- Make network design decisions that will meet the needs and the goals of your customers.

- Select network components that offer the services and capabilities necessary to implement a network based on the needs of the customer.

- Plan network installations based on the needed services and equipment.

- Upgrading a network may involve additional equipment or cabling.

- Prevent network problems by developing and implementing a comprehensive preventive maintenance policy.

- When troubleshooting network problems, listen to what your customer tells you so that you can formulate open-ended and closed-ended questions that will help you determine where to begin fixing the problem. Verify obvious issues, and try quick solutions before escalating the troubleshooting process.

Summary of Exercises

Labs

The following labs, worksheets, and Packet Tracer activities cover material from this chapter. Refer to the labs and worksheets in *IT Essentials: PC Hardware and Software Lab Manual*, Fifth Edition.

Lab 6.3.2.7: Configure a NIC to Use DHCP in Windows 7

Lab 6.3.2.8: Configure a NIC to Use DHCP in Windows Vista

Lab 6.3.2.9: Configure a NIC to Use DHCP in Windows XP

Lab 6.4.2.4: Building Straight-Through and Crossover UTP Cables

Lab 6.8.2.4: Install a Wireless NIC in Windows 7

Lab 6.8.2.5: Install a Wireless NIC in Windows Vista

Lab 6.8.2.6: Install a Wireless NIC in Windows XP

Lab 6.8.3.5: Connect to a Router for the First Time

Lab 6.8.3.8: Configure Wireless Router in Windows 7

Lab 6.8.3.9: Configure Wireless Router in Windows Vista

Lab 6.8.3.10: Configure Wireless Router in Windows XP

Lab 6.8.3.14: Test the Wireless NIC in Windows 7

Lab 6.8.3.15: Test the Wireless NIC in Windows Vista

Lab 6.8.3.16: Test the Wireless NIC in Windows XP

Lab 6.8.4.7: Share a Folder, Create a Homegroup, and Map a Network Drive in Windows 7

Lab 6.8.4.8: Share a Folder and Map a Network Drive in Windows Vista

Lab 6.8.4.9: Share a Folder and Map a Network Drive in Windows XP

Worksheets

The following worksheets cover material from this chapter. Refer to the labs in *IT Essentials: PC Hardware and Software Lab Manual*, Fifth Edition.

Worksheet 6.3.3.4: Protocol Definitions and Default Ports

Worksheet 6.8.2.2: Internet Search for NIC Drivers

Worksheet 6.9.1.6: Answer Broadband Questions

Worksheet 6.9.1.8: ISP Connection Types

<table>
<tr><td>Packet Tracer
□ Activity</td></tr>
</table>

Packet Tracer Activities

The following Packet Tracer activities cover material from this chapter. To access the activities found in this book, please refer to the instructions found in the Introduction.

PT 6.3.2.10: Adding Computers to an Existing Network

PT 6.4.2.5: Cabling a Simple Network

PT 6.5.1.2: Physical Topologies

PT 6.8.2.9: Install a Wireless NIC

PT 6.8.3.6: Connect to Wireless Router and Configure Basic Settings.

PT 6.8.3.11: Connecting Wireless PCs to a Linksys WRT300N

PT 6.8.3.17: Test a Wireless Connection

Check Your Understanding

You can find the answers to these questions in Appendix A, "Answers to 'Check Your Understanding' Questions."

1. Which network device regenerates the data signal without segmenting the network?

    A. Hub

    B. Modem

    C. Switch

    D. Router

2. When planning the network in a new building, the technician notes that the company requires cabling that can extend up to 295 feet (90 m) with enhanced bandwidth support at an affordable price. Which cable type will the technician pick if the preference is for the most common type of cabling that is used on networks?

    A. Category 3

    B. Category 7

    C. Category 5e

    D. Category 6a

3. Which term is used to describe any device on a network that can send and receive information?

   A. Host

   B. Workstation

   C. Server

   D. Console

   E. Peripheral

4. Which standards organization publishes current Ethernet standards?

   A. EIA/TIA

   B. IEEE

   C. ANSI

   D. CCITT

5. Which technology requires customers to be within a particular range of the service provider facility in order to be provided the maximum bandwidth for Internet access?

   A. Cable

   B. DSL

   C. ISDN

   D. Satellite

6. A company has four sites: headquarters and three branch offices. The four sites are interconnected through WAN connections. For redundancy, a full-mesh topology is desirable for this WAN. How many individual WAN links are needed to create a full-mesh topology?

   A. 4

   B. 6

   C. 8

   D. 12

7. Which statement describes the physical topology for a LAN?

   A. It depicts the addressing scheme that is employed in the LAN.

   B. It describes whether the LAN is a broadcast or token-passing network.

   C. It defines how hosts and network devices connect to the LAN.

   D. It shows the order in which hosts access the network.

8. A technician is troubleshooting a computer that has lost connectivity to the network. After data is gathered from the customer, which two tasks should the technician complete next?

   A. Verify that the computer has a valid IP address.

   B. Verify that the computer has the most up-to-date version of the OS.

   C. Try to log in as a different user.

   D. Repair the network cable.

   E. Check that the NIC link light is lit.

9. Which type of network spans a single building or campus and provides services and applications to people within a common organizational structure?

   A. PAN

   B. WAN

   C. LAN

   D. MAN

10. Which protocol operates at the application layer of the TCP/IP model?

    A. IP

    B. TCP

    C. HTTP

    D. ICMP

11. A company purchases several inexpensive wireless NICs. After installing the NICs, the company finds that users cannot connect to the 2.4-GHz wireless network. What is a possible cause of the problem?

    A. The NICs are designed for the 802.11a standard.

    B. The NICs are designed for the 802.11b standard.

    C. The NICs are designed for the 802.11g standard.

    D. The NICs are dual standard 802.11b/g.

12. A technician wishes to update the NIC driver for a computer. What is the best location for finding new drivers for the NIC?

    A. The installation media that came with the NIC

    B. Windows Update

    C. The website for the manufacturer of the NIC

    D. The website for Microsoft

13. A student is helping a friend with a home computer that can no longer access the Internet. Upon investigation, the student discovers that the computer has been assigned the IP address 169.254.100.88. What could cause a computer to get such an IP address?

   A. Static IP addressing with incomplete information
   B. Interference from surrounding devices
   C. Reduced computer power supply output
   D. Unreachable DHCP server

CHAPTER 7

Laptops

Objectives

Upon completion of this chapter, you will be able to answer the following questions:

- What are laptops and their common uses?

- What are the components of laptops?

- What are the best ways to select laptop components?

- What are different ways to configure a laptop?

- How can I repair a laptop?

- What wireless communication methods are used with laptops?

- Some common preventive maintenance techniques used for laptops are?

- What are some ways to troubleshoot laptops?

- What are common problems and solutions when troubleshooting PCs?

Key Terms

This chapter uses the following key terms. You can find the definitions in the Glossary.

Introduction (7.0.1.1)

The first laptops were used primarily by businesspeople who needed to access and enter data when they were away from the office. The use of laptops was limited due to expense, weight, and limited capabilities compared to less-expensive desktops.

The most significant feature of a *laptop* is its compact size. The design of the laptop places the keyboard, screen, and internal components into a small, portable case. As a result, laptops can be used to take notes in school, present information in a business meeting, or access the Internet in a coffee shop. A rechargeable battery allows the laptop to function when it is disconnected from an external power source. The compact design, convenience, and evolving technology of laptops have made them popular.

Common uses for laptops include the following:

- Taking notes in school
- Researching papers
- Presenting information in business meetings
- Accessing data away from home or the office
- Playing games while traveling
- Watching movies while traveling
- Accessing the Internet in a public place
- Sending and receiving email in a public place

Laptop Components (7.1)

The following section looks closely at both internal and external laptop components. Components can be located in different places on different laptop models. It is important to know each component to make informed decisions on the selection of components for purchases and upgrades. Understanding laptop components is necessary for troubleshooting when they malfunction or fail.

External Features Unique to Laptops (7.1.1.1)

Laptop and desktop computers use the same types of ports so that peripherals can be interchangeable. These ports are specifically designed for connecting peripherals.

The placement of ports, connections, and drives is unique because of the compact design of a laptop. Ports, connections, and drives are located on the exterior of the laptop, in the front, back, and side panels. Some laptops contain PC Card or ExpressCard slots to add functionality, such as removable memory cards, a modem, or a network connection.

Laptops require a port for external power. Laptops can operate using either a *battery* or an *AC power adapter*. You can use this port to power the computer or to charge the battery.

LEDs or status indicators, ports, slots, connectors, bays, jacks, vents, and a keyhole are on the exterior of the laptop.

> **Note**
>
> LED displays vary among laptops. Consult the laptop manual for a list of specific status displays.

Figure 7-1 shows three components on the back of the laptop.

Figure 7-1   Laptop: Rear View

A laptop operates using either a battery or an AC power adapter. Laptop batteries are manufactured in various shapes and sizes. They use different types of chemicals and metals to store power. Table 7-1 compares rechargeable batteries.

Table 7-1   Laptop Battery Comparison

Type of Battery	Characteristics	Common Use
Nickel-cadmium "Ni-Cad" (NiCd)	Heavy for the power it holds, long life (many charging cycles), may exhibit memory effect.	Toys, cordless phones, emergency lighting, power tools, camera flash
Nickel-metal hydride (NiMH)	Moderate weight for power; moderate lifespan; may experience "polarity reversal" at end of cycle, shut down, or recharge at once. May need several charge/discharge cycles to reach full capability.	Cell phones, digital cameras, GPS units, flashlights, and other consumer electronics
Lithium-ion (Li-Ion)	Lightweight battery for power, no memory effect, can easily overheat. Keep cool, charge often, seek freshest batteries (most recently manufactured).	Cell phones, laptops

Type of Battery	Characteristics	Common Use
Lithium-polymer (Li-Poly or LiPo)	Costly, small, lightweight battery for power, moderate capacity, fast recharge, moderate life span, does not short circuit, is not flammable.	PDAs, laptops, portable MP3 players, portable gaming devices, radio-controlled airplanes

The left side of the laptop has the following 10 components.

- *Security keyhole*: A small slot designed to receive a specially shaped lock to reduce the risk of physical theft. A security keyhole enables a user to connect a laptop to a stationary location, such as a desk, by using a combination or keyed lock.

- *USB port*: Connects the laptop to most peripheral devices.

- *S-Video connector*: Connects the laptop to an external monitor or projector.

- *Modem port*: Communicates on analog phone networks.

- *Ethernet port*: Communicates on Ethernet networks.

- *Network LEDs*: Indicate network traffic activity.

- *Stereo headphone jack*: Allows the laptop to port audio to external speakers or headphones.

- *Microphone jack*: Allows a microphone to input sound.

- *Ventilation*: Removes heat from the case.

- *PC combo expansion slot*: Receives expansion cards like PCMCIA and PC Card/ExpressCard.

The left side components are shown in Figure 7-2.

Figure 7-2   Laptop: Left-Side View

The front of the laptop has the following components:

- **Ventilation:** Removes heat from the case

- *Infrared port*: Allows the laptop to communicate with other infrared-enabled devices

- **Speakers:** Provide sound output
- *Laptop latch*: Keeps the lid closed

The front of the laptop components are shown in Figure 7-3.

Figure 7-3   Laptop: Front View

The right side of the laptop contains four components:

- **Optical drive:** Reads CDs, DVDs, and Blu-ray discs
- **Optical drive status indicator:** Displays activity on the optical drive
- **Drive bay status indicator:** Displays activity on that drive bay
- **Video Graphics Array (VGA) port:** Allows for external monitor or projector

The right side of the laptop components are shown in Figure 7-4.

Figure 7-4   Laptop: Right-Side View

The bottom of the laptop has the following components:

- *Hard drive access panel*: Provides access to the hard drive
- *Battery latches* (**two areas**): Release the battery from the battery bay
- *Docking station connector*: Connects the laptop to a docking station or port replicator
- *RAM access panel*: Provides access to the RAM

The bottom of the laptop components are shown in Figure 7-5.

Docking Station Connector
Battery Latch | Battery Latch

RAM Access Panel

Hard Drive
Access Panel

Figure 7-5   Laptop: Bottom View

Virtual Laptop Activity: Explore Laptop

Explore the different views of the Virtual Laptop.

To access the activities found in this book, please refer to the instructions found in the Introduction.

Common Input Devices and LEDs in Laptops (7.1.1.2)

Laptops are designed to be compact and portable, while maintaining much of the functionality provided by desktop systems. As a result, essential input devices are built in to laptops. When a laptop is open, the following input devices may be present:

- Touchpad
- Pointing stick
- Keyboard
- Fingerprint readers
- Microphone
- Web camera

Some input devices are built in to the laptop. Typically, the laptop is closed when not in use. By opening the lid of the laptop, you can access a variety of input devices, LEDs, and a display screen. Several input devices are available when the laptop lid is open, as shown in Figure 7-6.

Figure 7-6   Open Laptop

Note

Input devices that are built in to laptops can be configured or optimized for speed, sensitivity, scrolling, or the number of taps needed in the same manner as input devices for desktops.

Laptops may feature LEDs that show the status of specific devices or components. LEDs are commonly found below the display screen or directly above the keyboard. Types of common status LEDs found on a laptop include the following:

- Wireless

- Bluetooth

- Num Lock

- Caps Lock

- Hard drive activity

- Power on

- Battery status

- Hibernate/standby

Note

LEDs vary by laptop model.

Virtual Laptop Activity: Keyboard

Explore the Virtual Laptop keyboard.

Refer to Virtual Laptop software on the CD that accompanies this book.

Internal Components (7.1.1.3)

The compact nature of laptops requires a number of internal components to fit in a small amount of space. The size restrictions result in a variety of form factors for a number of laptop components, such as the system board, RAM, and CPU. Some laptop components, such as the CPU, may be designed to use less power to ensure that the system can operate for a longer period of time when using a battery source.

Motherboards

Desktop motherboards have standard *form factors*. The standard size and shape allow motherboards from different manufacturers to be interchangeable. In comparison, laptop motherboards vary by manufacturer and are proprietary. When you repair a laptop, it is recommended that you obtain a replacement system board from the laptop manufacturer. Figure 7-7 shows a comparison between a desktop motherboard and a laptop motherboard.

Figure 7-7   Motherboard Comparison

Laptop system boards and desktop motherboards are designed differently. Components designed for a laptop generally cannot be used in a desktop. Laptop and desktop designs are compared in Table 7-2.

Table 7-2   Laptop and Desktop Comparison

Component	Laptop	Desktop
Motherboard form factor	Proprietary	AT, LPX, NLX, ATX, BTX
Expansion slot	Mini-PCI	PCI, PCIe, ISA, AGP
RAM slot type	SODIMM	SIMM, DIMM, RIMM

RAM

Due to space restrictions laptops use *small outline dual in-line memory modules (SODIMM),* shown in Figure 7-8.

Figure 7-8   SODIMM

CPUs

Laptop processors are designed to use less power and create less heat than desktop processors. As a result, laptop processors do not require cooling devices that are as large as those found in desktops. Laptop processors also use *CPU throttling* to modify the clock speed as needed to reduce power consumption and heat. This results in a slight decrease in performance, but it increases the lifespan of some components. These specially designed processors allow laptops to operate for a longer period of time when using a battery power source.

Note

Refer to the laptop manual for compatible processors and for replacement instructions.

Special Function Keys (7.1.1.4)

The purpose of the *Function (Fn) key* is to activate a second function on a dual-purpose key. The feature that is accessed by pressing the Fn key in combination with another key is printed on the key in a smaller font or different color. Several functions can be accessed:

- Display settings
- Display brightness
- Keyboard backlight brightness
- Volume setting
- Sleep states
- Wireless functionality
- Bluetooth functionality
- Battery status

Note

Some laptops may have dedicated function keys that perform functions without requiring users to press the Fn key.

A laptop monitor is a *built-in LCD*. It is similar to a desktop LCD monitor, except that you can adjust the resolution, brightness, and contrast settings using software or button controls. You cannot adjust the laptop monitor for height and distance because it is integrated into the lid of the case. You can connect a desktop monitor to a laptop. Pressing the Fn key with the appropriate Function key on the laptop keyboard toggles between the laptop display and the desktop monitor.

Do not confuse the Fn key with Function keys F1 through F12. These keys are typically located in a row across the top of the keyboard. Their function depends on the operating system (OS) and application that is running when they are pressed. Each key can perform up to seven different operations by pressing it with one or more combinations of the Shift, Control, and Alt keys.

Docking Station Versus Port Replicator (7.1.1.5)

A *base station* attaches to AC power and to desktop peripherals. When you plug the laptop into the base station, you have access to power and the attached peripherals as well as an increased number of ports.

There are two types of base stations that are used for the same purpose: *docking stations* and *port replicators.* A port replicator may contain a SCSI port, a networking port, PS/2 ports, USB ports, and a game port. A docking station has the same ports as a port replicator, but adds the ability to connect to PCI cards, additional hard drives, optical drives, and floppy drives. A laptop connected to a docking station has the same functionalities as a desktop computer.

Docking stations and port replicators use a variety of connection types:

- Manufacturer and model specific
- USB and FireWire
- PC Card or ExpressCard

Some docking stations connect to a laptop using a port that is located on the top of the docking station. Other docking stations are designed to plug directly into a USB port of the laptop. Most laptops can be docked when in use or while shut off. Adding devices when docking can be handled with plug-and-play technology or by having a separate hardware profile for the docked and undocked state. Figure 7-9 shows an example of a docking station with the connection port on top.

Eject Button
Power Button
Laptop Connector

Figure 7-9   Docking Station: Top View

Note

Many base stations are proprietary and work only with particular laptops. Before buying a base station, check the laptop documentation or the website of the manufacturer to determine the appropriate make and model for the laptop.

The back of the docking station contains ports and connectors used to attach to desktop peripherals such as a mouse, a monitor, or a printer. A vent is also necessary to expel hot air from the docking station.

The following components are typically located on the back of the docking station:

- *Exhaust vent*: Lets hot air out of the laptop
- *AC power connector*: Provides power to charge the battery
- *PC Card/ExpressCard slot*: Connects laptops to expansion cards
- *VGA port*: Allows for external monitor or projector
- *Digital Visual Interface (DVI) port*: Allows for external monitor or projector
- *Line In connector*: Allows audio input from pre-amplified sources like iPods
- *Headphone connector*: Allows audio output for headphones
- USB port: Connects the laptop to most peripheral devices
- *Mouse port*: Connects older mice to the laptop
- *Keyboard port*: Connects older keyboards to the laptop
- *External diskette drive connector*: Connects laptop to an external diskette drive
- *Parallel port*: Connects legacy devices such as printers and scanners that do not support USB
- *Serial port*: A legacy port that connects devices like mice, keyboards, and modems before widespread use of USB
- *RJ-11 (modem port)*: Communicates on analog phone networks
- Ethernet port: Communicates on Ethernet networks

Figure 7-10 shows components that are typically located on the back of the docking station.

Figure 7-10   Docking Station: Rear View

Docking stations can also have a key lock to secure the laptop to the docking station, as shown in Figure 7-11.

Figure 7-11   Docking Station: Right-Side View

Worksheet 7.1.1.6: Research Docking Stations

In this activity, you use the Internet, a newspaper, or a local store to gather information and then enter the specifications for a laptop docking station onto this worksheet. Be prepared to discuss your decisions regarding the docking station you select. Refer to the 7.1.1.6 worksheet in *IT Essentials: PC Hardware and Software Lab Manual*, Fifth Edition.

Virtual Laptop Activity: Docking Station

Explore the different views of the docking station in the Virtual Laptop. To access the activities found in this book, please refer to the instructions found in the Introduction.

Laptop Display Components (7.2)

Laptop display is the output device that shows all the onscreen content and one of the most expensive components of the laptop. There are four different display types, and they come in various sizes and resolutions. Understanding the screen display types and the internal display components of a laptop is important when purchasing or repairing a system. This section describes the different types of displays and the internal components for each type.

LCD, LED, OLED, and Plasma Monitors (7.2.1.1)

Laptop monitors are built-in displays. They are similar to desktop monitors, except that you can adjust the resolution, brightness, and contrast using software or button controls. You cannot adjust the laptop monitor for height and distance because it is integrated into the lid of the case. You can connect a desktop monitor to a laptop, providing the user with multiple screens and increased functionality.

There are four types of laptop displays:

- LCD
- LED
- OLED
- Plasma

LED monitors use less power and have a longer lifespan than LCD monitors. *Organic LED (OLED)* technology is commonly used for mobile devices and digital cameras but can also be found in laptop concept designs. OLED monitors will become more popular as the technology improves. *Plasma displays* are rarely found in laptops because they consume a large amount of power.

On many laptops, a small pin on the laptop cover contacts a switch when the case is closed, called an *LCD cutoff switch*. The LCD cutoff switch helps conserve power by extinguishing the backlight and turning off the LCD. If this switch breaks or is dirty, the LCD remains dark while the laptop is open. Carefully clean this switch to restore normal operation.

Internal Components (7.2.2)

An inverter and backlight are two important display components. The *inverter* is essentially the power supply for the backlight, and the *backlight* supplies the main source of light to the screen without it the image on the screen would not be visible.

Backlights and Inverters (7.2.2.1)

The inverter converts DC power to the higher voltage AC power that is required by the backlight. The backlight shines through the screen and illuminates the display. Two common types of backlights are cold cathode fluorescent lamp (CCFL) and LED. LED monitors use LED-based backlights that do not have fluorescent tubes or inverters.

LCD monitors use CCFL technology for the backlight. The fluorescent tube is connected to an inverter. In most laptops, the inverter, as shown in Figure 7-12, is behind the screen panel and close to the LCD.

Figure 7-12   Inverter

The backlight, as shown in Figure 7-13, is behind the LCD screen. To replace the backlight, you must completely disassemble the display unit.

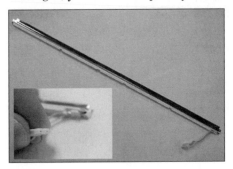

Figure 7-13   Backlight

Wi-Fi Antenna Connectors (7.2.2.2)

Wi-Fi antennas transmit and receive data carried out over wireless signals. Wi-Fi antennas in laptops are typically located above the screen. The Wi-Fi antenna is connected to a wireless card by an antenna wire and antenna leads, as shown in Figure 7-14.

Figure 7-14   Wi-Fi Antenna Leads

The wires are fastened to the display unit by wire guides located on the sides of the screen.

Laptop Power (7.3)

Power conservation and management are important aspects to consider for laptops because they are intended for portable use. Laptops use batteries as a power source when disconnected from an external power source. Software can be used to extend the life of the laptop battery and maximize battery usage. This section introduces methods of power management and settings for optimizing power management through software and the BIOS on a laptop.

Power Management (7.3.1.1)

Advances in power management and battery technology are increasing the time that a laptop can be disconnected from AC power. Current batteries can last up to 10 hours or more without recharging. Configuring laptop power settings to better manage power usage is important to ensure that the battery is used efficiently.

Power management controls the flow of electricity to the components of a computer. There are two methods of power management:

- *Advanced Power Management (APM)*

- *Advanced Configuration and Power Interface (ACPI)*

APM is an earlier version of power management. The BIOS controls the power management setting with APM. ACPI has replaced APM. ACPI standards create a bridge between the hardware and OS and allow technicians to create power management schemes to get the best performance from a laptop. The ACPI standards are applicable to most computers, but they are particularly important when managing power in laptops. Table 7-3 shows the ACPI standards

Table 7-3   ACPI Standards

Standard	Description
S0	The computer is on and the CPU is running.
S1	The CPU and RAM are stilling receiving power, but unused devices are powered down.
S2	The CPU is off, but RAM is refreshed. The system is in a lower mode than S1.
S3	The CPU is off, and the RAM is set to a slow refresh rate. This mode is often called "save to RAM." In Windows XP, this state is known as suspend mode.
S4	The CPU and RAM are off. The contents of RAM have been saved to a temporary file on the hard disk. This mode is also called "save to disk." In Windows 7, Windows Vista, and Windows XP, this state is known as hibernate mode.
S5	The computer is off.

Managing ACPI Settings in the BIOS (7.3.1.2)

Technicians are often required to configure power settings by changing the settings in the BIOS setup. Figure 7-15 shows an example of power settings in the BIOS setup.

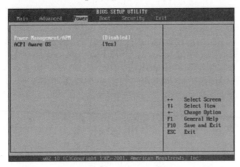

Figure 7-15   BIOS: Power Settings

Configuring the power settings in BIOS setup affects the following:

- System states
- Battery and AC modes
- Thermal management
- CPU PCI bus power management
- Wake on LAN (WOL)

Note

WOL might require a cable connection inside the computer from the network adapter to the motherboard.

In Windows, the ACPI power management mode must be enabled in the BIOS setup to allow the OS to configure the power management states.

To enable ACPI mode in the BIOS setup, follow these steps:

Step 1.   Enter BIOS setup.

Step 2.   Locate and enter the Power Management settings menu item.

Step 3.   Use the appropriate keys to enable ACPI mode.

Step 4.   Save and exit BIOS setup.

Note

These steps are common to most laptops, but be sure to check the laptop documentation for specific configuration settings. There is no standard name for each power management state. Manufacturers might use different names for the same state.

Worksheet 7.3.1.3: Match ACPI Standards

In this activity, you enter the ACPI standard next to the matching power management state description. Refer to Worksheet 7.3.1.3 in *IT Essentials: PC Hardware and Software Lab Manual*, Fifth Edition.

Managing Laptop Power Options (7.3.1.4)

The Power Options utility in Windows allows you to reduce the power consumption of specific devices or the entire system. You can manage power usage for the following:

- Laptop
- Hard drive
- Display
- Sleep timers
- Low-battery warnings

To configure power settings in Windows 7 and Windows Vista, use the following path:

Start > Control Panel > Power Options

To configure power settings in Windows XP, use the following path:

Start > Control Panel > Power Options

Laptop Power Options

If you do not want to completely shut down the laptop when you press the power button, you can adjust settings to reduce power usage.

To access the Define power buttons and turn on the password protection menu in Windows 7 and Windows Vista, click the **Choose what the power buttons do** link on the left side of the Power Options utility. In Windows XP, the Power buttons settings can be accessed by selecting the **Advanced** tab in the Power Options utility.

In Windows 7 and Windows Vista, the options are as follows:

- **Do nothing:** The computer continues to run at full power.
- **Sleep:** Documents and applications are saved in RAM, allowing the computer to power on quickly.
- *Hibernate*: Documents and applications are saved to a temporary file on the hard drive. The laptop takes a little longer than Sleep to power on.

In Windows XP, the options are

- *Standby*: Documents and applications are saved in RAM, allowing the computer to power on quickly.

- **Hibernate:** Documents and applications are saved to a temporary file on the hard drive. The laptop takes a little longer than Standby to power on.

Figure 7-16 shows Hibernate enabled in the Power Options utility of Windows 7.

Figure 7-16   Hibernate Enabled in Windows 7 Power Options Utility

Hard Drive and Display Power Management

Two of the biggest power consumers on a laptop are the hard drive and display. As shown in Figure 7-17, you can select when to turn the hard drive or display off when the laptop is running on a battery or AC adapter.

Figure 7-17   XP Power Options Advanced Settings

To adjust the power settings for a hard drive, display, or other computer component in Windows 7 and Windows Vista, follow these steps:

Step 1.   Click **Start > Control Panel > Power Options**.

Step 2.   Locate the power plan.

Step 3.   Click **Change plan settings.**

Step 4.   Click **Change advanced power settings.**

To access the Advanced Power Settings in Windows XP, use the following path:

Start > Control Panel > Power Options > Advanced tab

Sleep Timers

Customized sleep timers for Windows 7 and Windows Vista Power Plans settings
are shown in Figure 7-18. The Windows XP Power Schemes settings are shown in
Figure 7-19.

Figure 7-18   Windows 7 Power
Plans settings

Figure 7-19   Edit Power Scheme
Settings in Windows XP

To configure sleep timers in Windows 7 and Windows Vista, follow these steps:

Step 1.   Click **Start > Control Panel > Power Options.**

Step 2.   Click **Change when the computer sleeps** and select the desired time.

To configure sleep timers in Windows XP, use the following path:

Start > Control Panel > Power Options and select the desired time

Battery Warnings

In Windows, you can set the levels for battery warnings. The default for a *low-
battery warning* is 10 percent remaining capacity. The default for *critical battery*
level is 5 percent. You can also set the type of notification and the action to take,
such as whether to sleep, hibernate, or shut down the laptop when the battery
capacity reaches the specified level.

Laptop Wireless Communication Technologies (7.4)

A major advantage of a laptop is that it is portable and adding the use of wireless technologies increases the functionality of the laptop in any location. Laptop users can connect to the Internet, wireless peripheral devices, or other laptops through the use of wireless technologies. Most laptops have built -in wireless devices, adding to their flexibility and portability compared to desktop computers. This section takes a look at various wireless technologies available.

Bluetooth (7.4.1.1)

The *Bluetooth* technical specification is described by the Institute of Electrical and Electronics Engineers (IEEE) 802.15.1 standard. Bluetooth devices are capable of handling voice, music, videos, and data.

Table 7-4 shows common Bluetooth characteristics.

Table 7-4 Bluetooth Characteristics

A short-range wireless technology designed to eliminate the need for cables between portable or fixed-configuration devices.
Operates at 2.4 to 2.48 GHz in the unlicensed Industrial, Scientific, and Medical band.
Low power, low cost, and small size.
Uses adaptive frequency hopping.
Version 1.2 operates at up to 1.2 Mbps.
Version 2.0 + Enhanced Data Rate (EDR) operates at up to 3 Mbps.
Version 3.0 + High Speed (HS) operates at up to 24 Mbps.

The distance of a Bluetooth PAN is limited by the amount of power used by the devices in the PAN. Bluetooth devices are broken into three classifications, as shown in Table 7-5. The most common Bluetooth network is Class 2, which has a range of approximately 33 feet (10 m).

Table 7-5 Bluetooth Classifications

Class	Maximum Permitted Power (mW)	Approximate Distance
Class 1	100 mW	~330 feet (100 m)
Class2	2.5 mW	~33 feet (10 m)
Class3	1 mW	~3 feet (1 m)

Four specifications of Bluetooth technology define the standards for data transfer rates. Each subsequent version offers enhanced capabilities. For instance, Version 1 is older technology with limited capabilities, and Version 4 features more advanced capabilities.

Table 7-6 shows the four Bluetooth technology specifications that define the standards for data transfer rates.

Table 7-6   Bluetooth Specifications

Specification	Version	Data Transfer Rate
1.0	v1.2	1 Mb/s
2.0	v2.0 + EDR	3 Mb/s
3.0	v3.0 +HS	24 Mb/s
4.0	v4.0 +LE	24 Mb/s

Security measures are included in the Bluetooth standard. The first time that a Bluetooth device connects, the device is authenticated using a PIN. Bluetooth supports both 128-bit encryption and PIN authentication.

Bluetooth Installation and Configuration

Windows activates connections to Bluetooth devices by default. If the connection is not active, look for a switch on the front face or on the side of the laptop to enable the connection. If a laptop does not feature Bluetooth technology, you can purchase USB Bluetooth adapters that plug into a USB port.

Before installing and configuring a device, make sure that Bluetooth is enabled in the BIOS.

Turn on the device and make it discoverable to Windows. Check the device documentation to learn how to make the device discoverable. Use the Bluetooth Wizard to search and discover Bluetooth devices that are in Discoverable mode.

How To

To discover a Bluetooth device in Windows 7, follow these steps:

Step 1.   Click **Start > Control Panel > Devices and Printers > Add a device.**

Step 2.   Select the discovered device and click **Next.**

Step 3.   Enter the pairing code provided by Windows 7 into the Bluetooth device.

Step 4.   When the device has been successfully added, click **Close.**

In Windows Vista, follow these steps:

Step 1.   Click **Start > Control Panel > Network and Internet > Set up a Bluetooth enabled device > Device > Add.**

Step 2.   If prompted, click **Continue.** The Add Bluetooth Device Wizard starts.

Step 3.   **Click My device is set up and ready to be found > Next.**

Step 4.   Select the discovered device and click **Next.**

Step 5.   If prompted, enter a passkey and click **Finish.**

In Windows XP, follow these steps:

Step 1.   Click **Start > Control Panel > Bluetooth Devices > Device > Add.**

Step 2.   The Add Bluetooth Device Wizard starts.

Step 3.   Click **My device is set up and ready to be found > Next.**

Step 4.   Select the discovered device and click **Next.**

Step 5.   If prompted, enter a passkey and click **Next.**

Step 6.   Click **Finish.**

Infrared (7.4.1.2)

Infrared (IR) wireless technology is a low-power, short-range wireless technology. IR transmits data using LEDs and receives data using photodiodes. IR wireless networks are globally unregulated. However, the Infrared Data Association (IrDA) defines the specifications for IR wireless communication. Common IR characteristics include the following:

- It is low-power, short-range, wireless technology that uses LEDs.

- Infrared light signals operate in the lowest light frequency, and transmission distances are limited to a few feet or meters.

- Infrared light cannot penetrate ceilings or walls.

Three common types of IR networks:

- *Line of sight*: The signal is transmitted only if there is a clear, unobstructed view between devices.

- *Scatter*: The signal is bounced off ceilings and walls.

- *Reflective*: The signal is sent to an optical transceiver and is redirected to the receiving device.

Setting up and configuring IR devices is simple. Many IR devices connect to the USB port on a laptop or desktop computer. When the computer detects the new device, Windows 7 installs the appropriate drivers. The installation is similar to setting up a LAN connection.

IR is a practical, short-range connection solution, but it has some limitations:

- IR light cannot penetrate ceilings or walls.

- IR signals are susceptible to interference and dilution by strong light sources, such as fluorescent lighting.

- Scatter IR devices can connect without the line of sight, but data transfer rates are lower and distances are shorter.

- IR distances should be 3 feet (1 m) or less when used for computer communications.

How To

Before installing and configuring a device, make sure that IR is enabled in the BIOS by following these steps:

Step 1. Turn on the device to make it discoverable to Windows.

Step 2. Align the devices.

Step 3. When the devices are correctly aligned, an icon appears on the taskbar with a pop-up message.

Step 4. Click the pop-up message to display the Infrared dialog box.

Laptops without an internal IR device can connect a serial IR transceiver to a serial port or USB port. Figure 7-20 shows an internal IR port transceiver.

Internal IR Port Transceiver

Figure 7-20   Internal IR Port Transceiver

You can also access the Infrared dialog box in the Control Panel. You can configure the following settings:

- **Infrared:** Controls how you are notified about an IR connection and controls how files are transferred

- **Image Transfer:** Controls how images are transferred from a digital camera

- **Hardware:** Lists IR devices that are installed on the computer

Cellular WAN (7.4.1.3)

To connect a laptop to a cellular WAN, you install an adapter that is designed to work with cellular networks. *Cellular WAN cards*, as shown in Figure 7-21, are plug-and-play (PnP). The card plugs in to the PC Card slot or is built in to the laptop.

Figure 7-21   Cellular WAN Card

You can also access a cellular WAN with a USB adapter or by using a mobile hotspot. The mobile hotspot can be connected to the laptop using Wi-Fi technology. Some cell phones offer mobile hotspot functionality.

Laptops with integrated cellular WAN capabilities require no software installation and no additional antenna or accessories. When you turn on the laptop, the integrated WAN capabilities are ready to use. If the connection is not active, look for a switch on the front face or on the side of the laptop.

To enable the connection, follow these steps:

Step 1.   Before installing and configuring the device, make sure that cellular WAN is enabled in the BIOS.

Step 2.   Install the manufacturer's broadband card utility software.

Step 3.   Use the utility software to manage the network connection.

The cellular WAN utility software is usually located in the taskbar or in **Start > Programs**.

Wi-Fi (7.4.1.4)

Laptops access the Internet by using wireless adapters. *Wireless adapters* can be built in to the laptop or attached to the laptop through a laptop expansion port. Three major types of wireless adapters used in laptops are as follows:

- *Mini-PCI*: Commonly used by older laptops. Mini-PCI cards have 124 pins and are capable of 802.11a, 802.11b, and 802.11g wireless LAN connection standards.

- *Mini-PCIe*: Most common type of wireless card in laptops. Mini-PCIe cards have 54 pins and support all wireless LAN standards.

- *PCI Express Micro*: Commonly found in newer and smaller laptops, such as Ultrabooks, because they are half the size of Mini-PCIe cards. PCI Express Micro cards have 54 pins and support all wireless LAN standards.

Figure 7-22 shows the three major types of wireless adapters used in laptops.

Figure 7-22   Wireless Adapter Types

Wireless expansion cards are not commonly used in newer laptops, because most of them have built-in wireless adapter cards. It is more common to use a USB adapter to add or upgrade wireless capabilities for a laptop.

 To configure wireless Ethernet settings on a laptop running Windows 7 and Windows Vista, follow these steps:

Step 1.   Make sure that the modem and router software is installed and that both devices are turned on.

Step 2.   Select **Start > Control Panel > Network and Sharing Center > Set up a new connection or network.**

Step 3.   If a connection or network has already been established, click **Connect** and select the network.

Step 4.   Use the Set Up a New Connection or Network Wizard to establish the new connection or configure the new network.

 To configure wireless Ethernet settings on a laptop running Windows XP, follow these steps:

Step 1.   Make sure that the modem and router software is installed and that both devices are turned on.

Step 2.   Select **Start > Control Panel > Network and Internet Connections > Network Connections.**

Step 3.   If a connection or network has already been established, click **Connect** and select the network.

Step 4.   If a connection or network has not been established, click the **Create a new connection** link.

Step 5.   Use the Set Up a New Connection or Network Wizard to establish the new connection or configure the new network.

Laptop Hardware and Component Installation and Configuration (7.5)

Compactness and portability are two major reasons laptops are so popular. These two factors also cause the limitations in some areas of technology that users want to have available. This section discusses enhancing the functionality of a laptop through the installation and configuration of expansion devices.

Expansion Cards (7.5.1.1)

One of the disadvantages of laptops in comparison to desktops is that their compact design might limit the availability of some functions. To address this problem, many laptops contain PC Card or ExpressCard slots to add functionality, such as more memory, a modem, or a network connection.

Cards follow the PCMCIA standard. They come in three types: Type I, Type II, and Type III. Each type is different in size and can attach to different devices.

The PC Card slot uses an open standard interface to connect to peripheral devices using the CardBus standard. The ExpressCard is the newer model of expansion card and is the most commonly used.

Table 7-7 shows a comparison of PC Cards.

Table 7-7   PC Card Specifications

PC Bus	Size (mm)	Thickness (mm)	Interface	Examples
Type I	85.6 mm x 54 mm	3.3 mm	Memory, I/O, CardBus	SRAM flash
Type II	85.6 mm x 54 mm	5.5 mm	Memory, I/O, CardBus	Modem, LAN, and wireless
Type III	85.6 mm x 54 mm	10.5 mm	Memory, I/O, CardBus	Hard drive

Table 7-8 shows a comparison of PC ExpressCards.

Table 7-8   PCExpress Card Specifications

PC Bus	Size (mm)	Thickness (mm)	Interface	Examples
ExpressCard/34	75 mm x 34 mm	5 mm	PCI Express or USB 2.0 or USB 3.0	FireWire, TV tuner, wireless NIC
ExpressCard/54	75 mm x 54 mm	5 mm	PCI Express or USB 2.0 or USB 3.0	Smart card reader, CompactFlash reader, 1.8-inch disk drive

The PC ExpressCard comes in two models: ExpressCard/34 and ExpressCard/54. The models are 34 mm and 54 mm in width, respectively. Figure 7-23 shows an example of a PC Card and PC ExpressCard.

Figure 7-23   Laptop Expansion Cards

Here are some examples of functionality that can be added when using PC Cards and ExpressCards:

- Wi-Fi connectivity
- Ethernet access
- USB and FireWire ports
- External hard drive access
- Additional memory

All PC expansion cards are inserted and removed using similar steps. To install a card, insert the card into the slot. To remove the card, press the eject button to release it.

If a PC Card is hot-swappable, safely remove it by following these steps:

Step 1.   Left-click the **Safely Remove Hardware** icon in the Windows System Tray to ensure that the device is not in use.

Step 2.   Left-click the device that you want to remove. A message pops up to tell you that it is safe to remove the device.

Step 3.   Remove the hot-swappable device from the laptop.

Caution

PC Cards and USB devices are commonly hot-swappable. In some instances, the optical drive and battery can also be hot-swappable. However, the internal hard drive and RAM are never hot-swappable. Removing a device that is not hot-swappable while the computer is powered on can cause damage to data and devices.

Flash Memory (7.5.1.2)

External Flash Drive

An external *flash drive*, also known as a thumb drive, is a removable storage device that connects to a USB port. An external flash drive uses the same type of nonvolatile memory chips as a solid state drive (SSD). As a result, flash drives provide fast access to data, high reliability, and reduced power usage. An external flash drive is shown in Figure 7-24.

Figure 7-24   Flash Drive

External flash drives expand the amount of storage space on a laptop and can connect to USB ports. These drives are accessed by the operating system in the same way that other types of drives are accessed.

Flash Cards and Flash Card Readers

A *flash card* is a data storage device that uses flash memory to store information. Flash cards are small, are portable, and require no power to maintain data. They are commonly used in laptops, mobile devices, and digital cameras. A large variety of flash card models are available, and each varies in size and shape. Most modern laptops feature a *flash card reader* for Secure Digital (SD) and Secure Digital High Capacity (SDHC) flash cards, as shown in Figure 7-25.

Figure 7-25   Digital Flash Card

A flash card reader on a standard laptop is shown in Figure 7-26.

Figure 7-26   Flash Card Reader

Note

Flash memory cards are hot-swappable and should be removed by following the standard procedure for hot-swappable device removal.

SODIMM Memory (7.5.1.3)

Additional RAM improves laptop performance by decreasing the number of times the operating system reads and writes data to the hard drive in the form of virtual memory. Additional RAM also helps the operating system to run multiple applications more efficiently.

The make and model of the laptop determine the type of RAM chip needed. It is important to select the memory type that is physically compatible with the laptop. Most desktop computers use memory that fits into a DIMM slot. Most laptops use a smaller profile memory chip that is called a small outline dual in-line memory module (SODIMM). SODIMM has 72-pin and 100-pin configurations for support of 32-bit transfers and 144-pin, 200-pin, and 204-pin configurations for support of 64-bit transfers.

Note

SODIMMs can be further classified as DDR, DDR2, and DDR3. Different laptop models require different types of SODIMMs.

Before purchasing and installing additional RAM, consult the laptop documentation or the website of the manufacturer for form-factor specifications. Use the documentation to find where to install RAM on the laptop. On most laptops, RAM is inserted into slots behind a cover on the underside of the case. On some laptops, the keyboard must be removed to access the RAM slots.

As shown in Figure 7-27, SODIMM is installed into the underside of the case.

Figure 7-27   SODIMM Installed in a Laptop

Consult the manufacturer of the laptop to confirm the maximum amount of RAM each slot can support. You can view the currently installed amount of RAM in the POST screen, BIOS, or System Properties window.

Figure 7-28 shows where the amount of RAM is displayed in the System utility.

Figure 7-28   RAM Information in the System Utility

The System utility allows you to view basic information about your system such as the amount of RAM.

In Windows 7 and Windows Vista, use the following path:

Start > Control Panel > System

In Windows XP, use the following path:

Start > Control Panel > System > General tab

To replace or add memory, determine if the laptop has available slots and that it supports the quantity and type of memory to be added. In some instances, there are no available slots for the new SODIMM.

To remove the existing SODIMM, follow these steps:

Step 1.   Remove the AC adapter and battery from the laptop, along with any other components designated by the manufacturer.

Step 2.   Remove the screws on the cover above the memory socket to expose the SODIMM.

Step 3.   Press outward on the clips that hold the sides of the SODIMM.

Step 4.   Lift up to loosen the SODIMM from the slot and remove the SODIMM.

To install a SODIMM, follow these steps:

Step 1.   Align the notch of the SODIMM memory module at a 45-degree angle, and gently press it into the socket.

Step 2.   Gently press the memory module into the socket until the clips lock.

Step 3.   Replace the cover and install the screws.

Step 4.   Insert the battery and connect the AC adapter. Turn the computer on and access the System utility to ensure that the RAM has been installed successfully.

Worksheet 7.5.1.4: Laptop RAM

In this activity, you use the Internet, a newspaper, or a local store to gather information about expansion memory for a laptop. Refer to Worksheet 7.5.1.4 in *IT Essentials: PC Hardware and Software Lab Manual*, Fifth Edition.

Replacing Hardware Devices (7.5.2)

Some components of a laptop might need to be replaced. Always remember to make sure that you have the correct replacement component and tools as recommended by the manufacturer.

Overview of Hardware Replacement (7.5.2.1)

Some parts of a laptop, typically called *customer-replaceable units (CRU)*, can be replaced by the customer. CRUs include such components as the laptop battery and RAM. Parts that should not be replaced by the customer are called *field-replaceable units (FRU)*.

FRUs include components such as the motherboard and LCD display, as shown in Figure 7-29.

Figure 7-29   Laptop Display Screen

Another component considered a FRU is the keyboard, as shown in Figure 7-30.

Figure 7-30   Removing the Laptop Keyboard

Replacing FRUs usually requires a considerable amount of technical skill. In many cases, the device may need to be returned to the place of purchase, a certified service center, or the manufacturer.

A repair center might provide service on laptops made by different manufacturers or just specialize in a specific brand and be considered an authorized dealer for warranty work and repair. The following are common repairs performed at local repair centers:

- Hardware and software diagnostics
- Data transfer and recovery
- Hard drive installation and upgrades
- RAM installation and upgrades
- Keyboard and fan replacement
- Internal laptop cleaning
- LCD screen repair
- LCD inverter and backlight repair

Most repairs to LCD displays must be performed in a repair center. The repairs include replacing the screen, the backlight that shines through the screen to illuminate the display, and the inverter that produces the high voltage required by the backlight.

If no local services are available, you might need to send the laptop to a regional repair center or to the manufacturer. If the laptop damage is severe or requires specialized software and tools, the manufacturer can decide to replace the laptop instead of attempting a repair.

Caution

Before attempting to repair a laptop or portable device, check the warranty to see if repairs during the warranty period must be done at an authorized service center to avoid invalidating the warranty. If you repair a laptop yourself, always back up the data and disconnect the device from the power source. This chapter provides general instructions for replacing and repairing laptop components. Always consult the service manual before beginning a laptop repair.

Power (7.5.2.2)

These are some signs that the battery may need to be replaced:

- The laptop shuts off immediately when AC power is removed.
- The battery is leaking.
- The battery overheats.
- The battery does not hold a charge.

If you experience problems that you suspect are battery related, exchange the battery with a known good battery that is compatible with the laptop. If a replacement battery cannot be located, take the battery to an authorized repair center for testing.

A replacement battery must meet or exceed the specifications of the laptop manufacturer. New batteries must use the same form factor as the original battery. Voltages, power ratings, and AC adapters must also meet manufacturer specifications.

Note

Always follow the instructions provided by the manufacturer when charging a new battery. The laptop can be used during an initial charge, but do not unplug the AC adapter. Ni-Cad and NiMH rechargeable batteries should occasionally be discharged completely to remove the memory effect. When the battery is completely discharged, it should then be charged to maximum capacity.

Caution

Handle batteries with care. Batteries can explode if they are shorted, mishandled, or improperly charged. Be sure that the battery charger is designed for the chemistry, size, and voltage of your battery. Batteries are considered toxic waste and must be disposed of according to local laws.

Replacing a Battery

To remove and install a battery, follow these steps:

Step 1. Power off the laptop and disconnect the AC adapter.

Step 2. Remove the cover for the battery, if needed.

Step 3. Move the battery lock to the unlocked position.

Step 4. Hold the release lever in the unlock position and remove the battery.

Step 5. Ensure that the battery contacts inside of the laptop and on the battery are clear of dirt and corrosion.

Step 6. Insert the new battery.

Step 7. Make sure that both battery levers are locked.

Step 8. Replace the cover for the battery, if needed.

Step 9. Connect the AC adapter to the laptop and power on the computer.

Replacing a DC Jack

A *DC jack* receives power from a laptop's AC/DC power converter and supplies the power to the system board.

If your DC jack is replaceable, follow these steps:

Step 1. Power off the laptop and disconnect the AC adapter.

Step 2. Remove the battery and any other components as described by the manufacturer.

Step 3. Unfasten the DC jack from the case.

Step 4. Unfasten the power cable that is attached to the DC jack.

Step 5. Disconnect the power cable connector from the motherboard, and remove the DC jack from the case.

Step 6. Connect the power cable connector to the motherboard.

Step 7. Secure the power cables that are attached to the new DC jack to the case.

Step 8.   Secure the new DC jack to the case.

Step 9.   Insert the battery and reinstall any other components that were removed.

Step 10.   Connect the AC adapter to the laptop and power on the computer.

A laptop DC jack is shown in Figure 7-31.

Figure 7-31   DC Jack

> **Note**
>
> If the DC jack is soldered onto the motherboard, the motherboard should be replaced according to the manufacturer of the laptop.

Worksheet 7.5.2.3: Laptop Batteries

In this activity, you use the Internet, a newspaper, or a local store to gather information and then enter the specifications for a laptop battery onto this worksheet.

Refer to the 7.5.2.3 worksheet in *IT Essentials: PC Hardware and Software Lab Manual*, Fifth Edition.

Keyboard, Touchpad, and Screen (7.5.2.4)

The keyboard and *touchpad* are input devices considered to be FRUs. Replacing a keyboard or touchpad typically requires removing the plastic casing that covers the inside of a laptop, as shown in Figure 7-32.

Figure 7-32   Plastic Casing Surrounding a Laptop Keyboard

Replacing a Keyboard

To remove and replace a keyboard, follow these steps:

Step 1.   Power off the laptop, disconnect the AC adapter, and remove the battery.

Step 2.   Open the laptop.

Step 3.   Remove any screws holding the keyboard in place.

Step 4.   Remove any plastics holding the keyboard in place.

Step 5.   Lift up the keyboard and detach the keyboard cable from the motherboard.

Step 6.   Remove the keyboard.

Step 7.   Plug the new keyboard cable into the motherboard.

Step 8.   Insert the keyboard and attach any plastics that hold the keyboard in place.

Step 9.   Replace all necessary screws to secure the keyboard.

Step 10.   Close the screen and turn the laptop over.

Step 11.   Connect the AC adapter to the laptop, and power on the computer.

Replacing a Touchpad

To remove and replace a touchpad as shown in Figure 7-33, follow these steps:

Step 1.   If the touchpad is attached to the laptop casing, remove the casing. If it is a separate component, remove all devices that block access to the touchpad.

Step 2.   Close the screen and turn the computer over.

Step 3.   Remove the bottom casing of the laptop.

Step 4.   Disconnect the cables that connect the touchpad to the motherboard.

Step 5.   Remove the screws holding the touchpad in place.

Step 6.   Remove the touchpad.

Step 7.   Insert the new touchpad and fasten it to the laptop casing.

Step 8.   Replace the screws to hold the touchpad in place.

Step 9.   Connect the cables from the touchpad to the motherboard.

Step 10.   Replace the bottom casing of the laptop.

Step 11.   Turn over the laptop and open the screen.

Step 12.   Turn on the laptop and ensure that the touchpad is working correctly.

Figure 7-33 shows disconnecting the cables that connect the touchpad to the motherboard.

Figure 7-33   Touchpad Attached to Plastic Casing

Replacing a Screen

A laptop's display screen is often the most expensive component to replace. Unfortunately, it is also one of the most susceptible to damage as a result of pressure or a collision.

To replace a screen, follow these steps:

Step 1.   Remove the AC adapter and battery from the laptop, along with any other components designated by the manufacturer.

Step 2.   Remove the top part of the laptop case and the keyboard.

Step 3.   Disconnect the display cable from the motherboard.

Step 4.   Remove any screws securing the display to the laptop frame.

Step 5.   Detach the display assembly from the laptop frame.

Step 6.   Insert the new display assembly into the laptop frame.

Step 7.   Secure the new display assembly by replacing the screws.

Step 8.   Connect the display cable to the motherboard.

Step 9.   Reattach the keyboard and the top part of the laptop case.

Step 10.   Insert the battery and connect the AC adapter. Turn the computer on to check that the new display unit is working.

Worksheet 7.5.2.5: Laptop Screens

In this activity, you use the Internet, a newspaper, or a local store to gather information and then enter the specifications for a laptop display onto this worksheet. Refer to the 7.5.2.5 worksheet in *IT Essentials: PC Hardware and Software Lab Manual*, Fifth Edition.

Hard Drive and Optical Drive (7.5.2.6)

The form factor of an internal hard drive storage device is smaller for a laptop than for a desktop computer. Laptop hard drives are 1.8 inches (4.57 cm) or 2.5 inches (6.35 cm) in width, while desktop hard drives are 3.5 inches (8.9 cm). Storage devices are CRUs, unless a warranty requires technical assistance.

An external USB hard drive connects to a laptop using the USB port. Another type of external drive is the IEEE 1394 external hard drive that connects to the FireWire port. A laptop automatically detects when an external hard drive is plugged in to a USB or FireWire port.

Before purchasing a new internal or external storage device, check the laptop documentation or the website of the manufacturer for compatibility requirements. Documentation often contains FAQs that may be helpful. It is also important to research known laptop component issues on the Internet.

On most laptops, the internal hard drive and the internal optical drive are connected behind a cover on the underside of the case. On some laptops, the keyboard must be removed to access these drives. Blu-ray, DVD, and CD drives might not be interchangeable in the laptop. Some laptops may not include optical drives.

To view the currently installed storage device, check the POST screen or BIOS. If installing a second hard drive or an optical drive, confirm that there are no error icons next to the device in the Device Manager.

Replacing a Hard Drive

To remove and replace a hard drive, follow these steps:

Step 1.   Power off the laptop and disconnect the AC adapter.

Step 2.   On the bottom of the laptop, remove the screw that holds the hard drive in place.

Step 3.   Slide the assembly outward. Remove the hard drive assembly.

Step 4.   Remove the hard drive faceplate from the hard drive.

Step 5.   Attach the new hard drive faceplate to the hard drive.

Step 6.   Slide the hard drive into the hard drive bay.

Step 7.   On the bottom of the laptop, install the screw that holds the hard drive in place.

Step 8.   Connect the AC adapter to the laptop, and power on the computer.

Replacing an Optical Drive

To remove and replace an optical drive, follow these steps:

Step 1.   Power off the laptop and disconnect the AC adapter.

Step 2.   Press the button to open the drive and remove any media in the drive. Close the tray.

Step 3.   On the bottom of the laptop, remove the screw that holds the optical drive in place.

Step 4.   Slide the latch to release the lever that secures the drive.

Step 5.   Pull on the lever to expose the drive. Remove the drive.

Step 6.   Insert the new drive securely.

Step 7.   Push the lever inward.

Step 8.   Replace the screw that holds the hard drive in place.

Step 9.   Connect the AC adapter to the laptop, and power on the computer.

Worksheet 7.5.2.7: Laptop Hard Drives

In this activity, you use the Internet, a newspaper, or a local store to gather information about laptop hard drives. Refer to the 7.5.2.7 worksheet in *IT Essentials: PC Hardware and Software Lab Manual*, Fifth Edition.

Virtual Laptop Activity: Components and Devices

Replace components and devices in the Virtual Laptop. Refer to Virtual Laptop software on the CD that accompanies this book.

Wireless Card (7.5.2.8)

Before replacing a wireless card, determine which form factor is required by the laptop by checking the label on the wireless card or the laptop documentation.

To remove and install a wireless card, follow these steps:

How To

Step 1. Power off the laptop and disconnect the AC adapter.

Step 2. Locate the wireless card compartment on the bottom of the computer.

Step 3. Remove the cover if needed.

Step 4. Disconnect all wires and remove any screws holding the wireless card in place.

Step 5. Slide the wireless card out of the compartment and remove it.

Step 6. Slide the new wireless card into its compartment.

Step 7. Connect all wires and replace any screws holding the wireless card in place.

Step 8. Replace the cover if needed, including any screws holding it into place.

Step 9. Connect the AC adapter to the laptop, and power on the computer.

Speakers (7.5.2.9)

Before replacing laptop speakers, check that the volume is not muted by increasing volume or unmuting the sound.

To remove and replace the speaker unit, follow these steps:

How To

Step 1. Power off the computer and then disconnect the AC adapter.

Step 2. Remove the battery and any other components recommended by the manufacturer, including the keyboard or top casing.

Step 3. Disconnect any cables connecting the laptop to the motherboard.

Step 4. Remove any screws securing the speakers to the laptop frame.

Step 5. Remove the speakers.

Step 6. Insert the new speakers.

Step 7. Tighten all screws to secure the speakers to the laptop frame.

Step 8. Connect any cables connecting the laptop to the motherboard.

Step 9. Insert the battery, along with all other components that were removed.

Step 10. Connect the AC adapter and power on the computer to check for functionality.

CPU (7.5.2.10)

Before a CPU can be replaced, a technician must remove the fan or heatsink. Fans and heatsinks might be joined together as a single module or installed as separate units. If the fan and heatsink are separate, remove both components individually.

To replace a CPU with a separate fan and heatsink, follow these steps:

How To

Step 1. Power off the computer and disconnect the AC adapter.

Step 2. Remove the battery and any other components recommended by the manufacturer.

Step 3. Turn the laptop over, if necessary, and remove any plastics covering the fan.

Step 4. Locate the fan and remove any screws holding the fan in place.

Step 5. Disconnect the power cable connecting the fan to the motherboard.

Step 6. Remove the fan from the laptop.

Step 7. Remove the heatsink from the CPU by removing any screws holding it in place.

Step 8. Remove the screw that locks the latch holding the CPU in the socket.

Step 9. Open the latch and remove the CPU from the socket.

Step 10. Remove any thermal paste from the CPU, and store the CPU in an antistatic bag.

Step 11. Gently place the new CPU into the socket.

Step 12. Fasten the latch that holds the CPU in place and tighten the screws holding it down.

Step 13. Apply thermal paste to the CPU before replacing the heatsink.

Step 14. Insert the heatsink and replace all necessary screws.

Step 15. Insert the fan and connect the power cable to the motherboard.

Step 16. Fasten the fan to the motherboard by replacing all necessary screws.

Step 17. Replace the base cover of the laptop.

Step 18. Insert the battery and replace all necessary components.

If the fan and heatsink are joined together, use the following procedure.

How To 🔍   To remove and replace a CPU and heatsink assembly, follow these steps:

Step 1.   Power off the computer and disconnect the AC adapter.

Step 2.   Remove the battery and any other components recommended by the manufacturer.

Step 3.   Turn the laptop over, if necessary, and remove any plastics covering the heatsink.

Step 4.   Locate the heatsink assembly and remove any screws holding it in place.

Step 5.   Disconnect the fan power cable from the motherboard.

Step 6.   Remove the heatsink assembly.

Step 7.   Remove the screw that locks the latch holding the CPU in the socket.

Step 8.   Open the latch and remove the CPU from the socket.

Step 9.   Remove any thermal paste from the CPU, and store the CPU in an antistatic bag.

Step 10.   Gently place the new CPU into the socket.

Step 11.   Fasten the latch that holds the CPU in place and tighten the screws holding it down.

Step 12.   Apply thermal paste to the CPU before replacing the heatsink assembly.

Step 13.   Insert the heatsink assembly and connect the power cable to the motherboard.

Step 14.   Fasten heatsink assembly to the system frame by replacing all necessary screws.

Step 15.   Replace the base cover of the laptop.

Step 16.   Insert the battery and replace all necessary components.

Note

A CPU is one of the most fragile components in a laptop. It should be handled with great care.

Note

It is important to note how the CPU is positioned. The replacement must be installed the same way.

System Board (7.5.2.11)

Replacing the system board in a laptop normally requires a technician to remove all other components from a laptop. Before replacing a laptop motherboard, make sure that the replacement meets the design specifications of the laptop model.

How To

To remove and replace the system board, follow these steps:

Step 1.   Power off the computer and disconnect the AC adapter.

Step 2.   Remove the battery and any other components recommended by the manufacturer.

Step 3.   Detach the DC jack from the laptop casing. Unclip the power cable from the case and disconnect it from the system board.

Step 4.   Remove any remaining screws connecting the system board to the case.

Step 5.   Remove the system board.

Step 6.   Attach the new system board to the laptop casing. Tighten any necessary screws.

Step 7.   Attach the DC jack to the laptop casing, clip the power cable to the case, and connect it to the system board.

Step 8.   Replace any removed components.

Step 9.   Insert the battery, connect the AC adapter, and power on the computer to ensure that the system is functioning.

Plastics (7.5.2.12)

The exterior of a laptop is typically comprised of multiple plastic parts. This includes the plastic parts that are responsible for covering the memory, wireless card, and hard drive, in addition to the casing that surrounds the touchpad and keyboard.

How To

To remove and replace the plastics, follow these steps:

Step 1.   Disconnect the AC adapter and remove the battery.

Step 2.   Adjust the positioning of the laptop so that the desired plastic component is facing upward.

Step 3.   Unscrew the desired plastic component, or pry it off gently using the technique suggested by the manufacturer.

Step 4.   Attach the new plastic component and replace all necessary screws, or insert and fasten the component.

Step 5.   Insert the battery and connect the AC adapter.

Worksheet 7.5.2.13: Build a Specialized Laptop

In this worksheet, you use the Internet, a newspaper, or a local store to gather information about building a specialized laptop that supports hardware and software that allows a user to perform tasks that an off-the-shelf system cannot perform. Be prepared to discuss your selections. Refer to the 7.5.2.13 worksheet in *IT Essentials: PC Hardware and Software Lab Manual*, Fifth Edition.

Preventive Maintenance Techniques for Laptops (7.6)

Preventive maintenance should be scheduled at regular intervals to keep laptops running properly. It is important to keep a laptop clean and to ensure that it is being used in the most optimal environment. The following section covers preventive maintenance techniques for the laptop.

Scheduling Maintenance (7.6.1.1)

Because laptops are portable, they are used in different types of environments. As a result, they are more likely than desktop computers to be exposed to these harmful materials and situations:

- Dirt and contamination
- Spills
- Wear and tear
- Drops
- Excessive heat or cold
- Excessive moisture

Many components are placed in a very small area directly beneath the keyboard. Spilling liquid or dropping debris onto the keyboard can result in severe internal damage.

It is important to keep a laptop clean and to ensure that it is being used in the most optimal environment possible. Proper care and maintenance can help laptop components run more efficiently and extend the life of the equipment.

Preventive Maintenance Program

A preventive maintenance program is important in addressing such issues and must include a routine schedule for maintenance. Most organizations have a preventive maintenance schedule in place. If a schedule does not exist, work with the manager to create one. The most effective preventive maintenance programs require a set of routines to be conducted monthly but still allow for maintenance to be performed when usage demands it.

The preventive maintenance schedule for a laptop may include practices that are unique to a particular organization but should also include these standard procedures:

- Cleaning
- Hard drive maintenance
- Software updates

To keep a laptop clean, be proactive, not reactive. Keep fluids and food away from the laptop. Close the laptop when it is not in use. When cleaning a laptop, never use harsh cleaners or solutions that contain ammonia. Nonabrasive materials for cleaning a laptop include the following:

- Compressed air
- Mild cleaning solution
- Cotton swabs
- Soft, lint-free cleaning cloth

Caution

Before you clean a laptop, disconnect it from all power sources and remove the battery.

Routine maintenance includes the monthly cleaning of these laptop components:

- Exterior case
- Cooling vents
- I/O ports
- Display
- Keyboard

Note

If it is obvious that the laptop needs to be cleaned, clean it. Do not wait for the next scheduled maintenance.

Cleaning Procedures (7.6.1.2)

Proper routine cleaning is the easiest, least expensive way to protect and to extend the life of a laptop. It is important to use the right product and procedures when cleaning a laptop. Always read the warning labels on the cleaning products. The components are sensitive and should be handled with care. Consult the laptop manual for additional information and cleaning suggestion.

Figure 7-34 shows proper cleaning products and tools.

Figure 7-34   Cleaning Supplies

The following common cleaning procedures help maintain and extend the life of a laptop.

Caution

Use a soft, lint-free cloth with an approved cleaning solution to avoid damaging laptop surfaces. Apply the cleaning solution to the lint-free cloth, not directly to the laptop.

How To

Before cleaning laptop components, follow these steps:

Step 1.   Turn off the laptop.

Step 2.   Disconnect all attached devices.

Step 3.   Disconnect the laptop from the electrical outlet.

Step 4.   Remove the batteries.

Keyboard

Wipe the laptop and the keyboard with a soft, lint-free cloth that is lightly moistened with water or mild cleaning solution.

Vents

Use compressed air or a non-electrostatic vacuum to clean out the dust from the vents and from the fan behind the vent. Use tweezers to remove any debris.

LCD Display

Wipe the display with a soft, lint-free cloth that is lightly moistened with a computer-screen cleaner.

Caution

Do not spray cleaning solution directly onto the LCD display. Use products specifically designed for cleaning LCD displays.

Touchpad

Wipe the surface of the touchpad gently with a soft, lint-free cloth that is moistened with an approved cleaner. Never use a wet cloth.

Optical Drive

Dirt, dust, and other contaminants can collect in the optical drives. Contaminated drives can cause malfunctions, missing data, error messages, and lost productivity.

How To

To clean an optical drive, follow these steps:

Step 1.   Use a commercially available CD or DVD drive cleaning disc.

Step 2.   Remove all media from the optical drive.

Step 3.   Insert the cleaning disc and let it spin for the suggested amount of time to clean all contact areas.

CD and DVD Discs

Inspect the disc for scratches on both sides. Replace discs that contain deep scratches because they can create data errors. If you notice problems, such as skipping or degraded playback quality, clean the discs. Commercial products that clean discs and provide protection from dust, fingerprints, and scratches are available. Cleaning products for CDs are safe to use on DVDs.

How To

To clean CDs or DVDs, follow these steps:

Step 1.   Hold the disc by the outer edge or by the inside edge.

Step 2.   Gently wipe the disc with a lint-free cotton cloth. Never use paper or any material that can scratch the disc or leave streaks.

Step 3.   Wipe from the center of the disc outward. Never use a circular motion.

Step 4.   Apply a CD or DVD cleaning solution to the lint-free cotton cloth, and wipe again if any contaminates remain on the disc.

Step 5.   Allow the disc to dry before inserting it into the drive.

Basic Troubleshooting Process for Laptops (7.7)

Troubleshooting is a skill that is developed with experience. Technicians can better develop their troubleshooting skills through gaining experience and using an organized approach to problem solving. This section outlines a systematic approach that can be employed to properly troubleshoot and gives specifics on how to address issues that are particular to laptop systems.

Identify the Problem (7.7.1.1)

Laptop problems can result from a combination of hardware, software, and network issues. Computer technicians must be able to analyze the problem and determine the cause of the error to repair the laptop. This process is called troubleshooting.

The first step in the troubleshooting process is to identify the problem. Table 7-9 shows a list of open-ended and closed-ended questions to ask the customer.

Table 7-9 Identify the Problem

Open-ended questions	What problems are you experiencing with your laptop?
	What software has recently been installed?
	What were you doing when the problem was identified?
	What error messages have you received?
Close-ended questions	Is the laptop under warranty?
	Is the laptop currently using the battery?
	Can the laptop operate using the AC adapter?
	Can the laptop boot and show the desktop OS?

Establish a Theory of Probable Cause (7.7.1.2)

After you have talked to the customer, you can establish a theory of probable causes. Table 7-10 shows a list of some common probable causes for laptop problems.

Table 7-10 Establish a Theory of Probable Cause

Common causes of laptop problems	Battery does not have a charge.
	Battery will not charge.
	Loose cable connections.
	Keyboard does not lock.
	Num Lock key is on.
	Loose RAM.

Test the Theory to Determine Cause (7.7.1.3)

After you have developed some theories about what is wrong, test your theories to determine the cause of the problem. If a quick procedure does not correct the problem, research the problem further to establish the exact cause. Table 7-11 shows a list of quick procedures that can determine the exact cause of the problem or even correct the problem.

Table 7-11   Test the Theory to Determine Cause

Common steps to determine cause	Use an AC adapter with the laptop.
	Replace the battery.
	Reboot the laptop.
	Check BIOS settings.
	Disconnect and reconnect the cables.
	Disconnect the peripherals.
	Toggle Num Lock key.
	Remove and reinstall RAM.
	Check whether the Caps Lock key is on.
	Check for nonbootable media in a boot device.

Establish a Plan of Action to Resolve the Problem and Implement the Solution (7.7.1.4)

After you have determined the exact cause of the problem, establish a plan of action to resolve the problem and implement the solution. Table 7-12 shows some sources you can use to gather additional information to resolve an issue.

Table 7-12   Establish a Plan of Action to Resolve the Problem and Implement the Solution

If no solution is achieved in the previous step, further research is needed to implement the solution.	Help desk repair logs
	Other technicians
	Manufacturer FAQs
	Technical websites
	Newsgroups
	Manuals
	Online forums
	Internet research

Verify Full System Functionality and Implement Preventive Measures (7.7.1.5)

After you have corrected the problem, verify full functionality and, if applicable, implement preventive measures. Table 7-13 shows a list of steps to verify the solution.

Table 7-13   Verify Full System Functionality and, If Applicable, Implement Preventive Measures

Verify full functionality	Reboot the laptop.
	Attach all peripherals.
	Operate laptop using only battery.
	Print a document from an application.
	Type a sample document to test the keyboard.
	Check Event Viewer for warnings or errors.

Document Findings, Actions, and Outcomes (7.7.1.6)

In the final step of the troubleshooting process, document your findings, actions, and outcomes. Table 7-14 shows a list of the tasks required to document the problem and the solution.

Table 7-14   Document Your Findings, Actions, and Outcomes

Document your findings, actions, and outcomes.	Discuss the solution implemented with the customer.
	Have the customer verify that the problem has been solved.
	Provide the customer with all paperwork.
	Document the steps taken to solve the problem in the work order and technician's journal.
	Document any components used in the repair.
	Document the time spent to resolve the problem.

Identify Common Problems and Solutions (7.7.2.1)

Laptop problems can be attributed to hardware, software, networks, or some combination of the three. You will resolve some types of laptop problems more often than others. Table 7-15 shows common laptop problems and solutions.

Table 7-15 Common Problems and Solutions

Identify the Problem	Probable Causes	Possible Solutions
Laptop does not power on.	Laptop is not plugged in. Battery is not charged. Battery will not hold a charge.	Plug the laptop into AC power. Remove and reinstall the battery. Replace battery if will not charge.
Laptop battery supports the system for a reduced period of time.	Proper battery charging and discharging practices have not been followed. Extra peripherals are draining the battery. Power plan isn't correct. Battery is not holding a charge for very long.	Follow the battery charging procedures described in the manual. Remove unneeded peripherals and disable wireless NIC if possible. Modify power plan to decrease battery usage. Replace the battery.
External display has power but no image on the screen.	A video cable is loose or damaged. The laptop is not sending a video signal to the external display.	Reconnect or replace video cable. Use the Fn key along with the multipurpose key to toggle to the external display.
Laptop is powered on, but nothing is displayed on the LCD screen when the laptop lid is reopened.	LCD cutoff switch is dirty or damaged. The laptop has gone into sleep mode.	Check the laptop repair manual for instructions about cleaning or replacing the LCD cutoff switch. Press a key on the keyboard to bring the computer out of sleep mode.
The image on a laptop display is pixilated.	LCD display properties are incorrect.	Set the LCD screen to native resolution.
The laptop display is flickering.	Images on the screen are not refreshing fast enough. The display inverter is damaged or malfunctioning.	Adjust the screen refresh rate. Disassemble the display unit and replace the inverter.
A user is experiencing a ghost cursor that moves on its own.	The track pad is dirty. A track pad and mouse are being used at the same time. A part of the hand has touched the track pad while typing.	Clean the track pad. Disconnect the mouse. Try not to touch the track pad while typing.
Pixels on the screen are dead or not generating color.	Power to the pixels has been cut off.	Contact the manufacturer.

Identify the Problem	Probable Causes	Possible Solutions
The image on the screen appears to flash lines or patterns of different color and size (artifacts).	The display is not properly connected. The GPU is overheating. The GPU is faulty or malfunctioning.	Disassemble the laptop to check display connections. Disassemble and clean the computer, checking for dust and debris. Replace the GPU.
Color patterns on a screen are incorrect.	The display is not properly connected. The GPU is overheating. The GPU is faulty or malfunctioning.	Disassemble the laptop to check display connections. Disassemble and clean the computer, checking for dust and debris. Replace the GPU.
Images on a display screen are distorted.	Display settings have been changed. The display is not properly connected. The GPU is overheating. The GPU is faulty or malfunctioning.	Restore display settings to the original factory settings. Disassemble the laptop to check display connections. Disassemble and clean the computer, checking for dust and debris. Replace the GPU.
The network is fully functional and the wireless laptop connection is enabled, but the laptop cannot connect to the network.	Laptop wireless capability is turned off. External wireless antenna is misaligned. Out of wireless range.	Turn laptop wireless on using the wireless NIC properties or the Fn key along with the appropriate multipurpose key. Realign external wireless antenna to pick up wireless signal. Move closer to the wireless access point.
Input devices connected with Bluetooth are not functioning properly.	Bluetooth capability is turned off. Batteries in the input device are not providing enough power. The input device is out of range.	Turn laptop Bluetooth on by using the Bluetooth setting applet or the Fn key along with the appropriate multipurpose key. Replace the batteries. Move the input device closer to the laptop's Bluetooth receiver. Verify that the Bluetooth device is turned on.
Keyboard is inserting numbers instead of text, and Num Lock indicator light is on.	Num Lock is enabled.	Turn off Num Lock using the Num Lock key or the Fn key along with the appropriate multipurpose key.

Worksheet 7.7.2.2: Research Laptop Problems

Laptops often use proprietary parts. In this activity, you use the Internet to find information about the replacement parts; you may have to research the website of the laptop manufacturer. Refer to the 7.7.2.2 worksheet in *IT Essentials: PC Hardware and Software Lab Manual*, Fifth Edition.

Worksheet 7.7.2.3: Gather Information from the Customer

In this worksheet, you act as a call center technician and come up with closed-ended and open-ended questions to ask a customer about a laptop problem. Refer to the 7.7.2.3 worksheet in *IT Essentials: PC Hardware and Software Lab Manual*, Fifth Edition.

Worksheet 7.7.2.4: Investigating Support Websites and Repair Companies

For this worksheet, you investigate the services provided by a local laptop repair company or a laptop manufacturer support website. Use the Internet or a local phone directory to locate a local laptop repair company or laptop manufacturer support website. Refer to the 7.7.2.4 worksheet in *IT Essentials: PC Hardware and Software Lab Manual*, Fifth Edition.

Summary (7.8.1)

This chapter discussed the features and functionality of laptops, in addition to how to remove and install internal and external components. The following concepts from this chapter are important to remember:

- Laptops are unique because of their compact size and their ability to operate on battery power.

- Laptops use the same types of ports as desktop computers so that peripheral devices can be interchangeable.

- Essential input devices, such as a keyboard and track pad, are built in to laptops to provide similar functionality as desktop computers.

- Internal components of laptops are usually smaller than desktop components because they are designed to fit into compact spaces and conserve energy.

- Laptops feature function keys that can be pressed in combination with the Fn key. The functions performed by these keys are specific to the laptop model.

- Docking stations and port replicators can increase the functionality of laptops by providing the same types of ports that are featured on desktop computers.

- Laptops most commonly feature LCD and LED monitors.

- Backlights and inverters illuminate laptop displays.

- Power settings of laptop batteries can be configured to ensure that power is used efficiently.

- Laptops can feature a number of wireless technologies, including Bluetooth, infrared, Wi-Fi, and the ability to access cellular WANs.

- Laptops provide a number of expansion possibilities. Users can add memory to increase performance, make use of flash memory to increase storage capacity, or increase functionality by using expansion cards.

- Laptop components consist of CRUs and FRUs.

- Laptop components should be cleaned regularly in order to extend the life of the laptop.

Summary of Exercises

This is a summary of the worksheets and Virtual Laptop activities associated with this chapter. Refer to the worksheets in the *IT Essentials: PC Hardware and Software Lab Manual*, Fifth Edition.

Worksheets

The following worksheets cover material from this chapter. Refer to the worksheets in the *IT Essentials: PC Hardware and Software Lab Manual*, Fifth Edition.

Worksheet 7.1.1.6: Research Docking Stations

Worksheet 7.3.1.3: Match ACPI Standards

Worksheet 7.5.1.4: Laptop RAM

Worksheet 7.5.2.3: Laptop Batteries

Worksheet 7.5.2.5: Laptop Screens

Worksheet 7.5.2.7: Laptop Hard Drives

Worksheet 7.5.2.13: Build a Specialized Laptop

Worksheet 7.7.2.2: Research Laptop Problems

Worksheet 7.7.2.3: Gather Information from the Customer

Worksheet 7.7.2.4: Investigating Support Websites and Repair Companies

Virtual Laptop Activities

The following Virtual Laptop activities cover material from this chapter. To access the activities found in this book, please refer to the instructions found in the Introduction.

Virtual Laptop Activity: Explore Laptop

Virtual Laptop Activity: Keyboard

Virtual Laptop Activity: Docking Station

Virtual Laptop Activity: Components and Devices

Check Your Understanding

You can find the answers to these questions in the Appendix A, "Answers to 'Check Your Understanding' Questions."

1. Which type of RAM modules are designed for the space limitations of laptops?

   A. SODIMMs

   B. SRAM

   C. SIMMs

   D. DIMMs

2. What is a design consideration for mobile CPUs used in laptops compared with desktop CPUs?

   A. They are interchangeable with desktop CPUs.

   B. They require smaller cooling mechanisms than desktops do.

   C. They operate at higher clock speeds than desktops do.

   D. They consume more power than desktops do.

3. What is the maximum range of a Class 2 Bluetooth network?

   A. 2 meters

   B. 5 meters

   C. 10 meters

   D. 50 meters

4. What is an example of an expansion slot on a laptop?

   A. Internal USB

   B. External PCI

   C. ExpressCard

   D. AGP

   E. ISA

   F. EISA

5. What is a proactive way to keep a laptop clean?

   A. Keep fluids away from the laptop computer.

   B. Clean the keyboard using cotton swabs.

   C. Use mild soap to clean the screen.

   D. Use compressed air to blow the dust off the optical drive.

6. A technician is about to perform a routine cleaning on a laptop and notices that some dust has accumulated in the cooling vents. What should a technician use to remove the dust?

   A. Damp cloth

   B. Compressed air

   C. Cleaning disc

   D. Mild detergent

7. What is a closed-ended question that a technician may ask when troubleshooting a possible laptop battery failure?

   A. Can the laptop operate using the AC adapter?

   B. What problems are you experiencing with your laptop?

   C. What software has been installed recently?

   D. Have you recently upgraded your display driver?

8. A technician troubleshooting a laptop notices that some keyboard keys are not working properly. What should the technician check first?

   A. If the AC adapter is charging correctly

   B. If the touchpad is working

   C. If the WordPad program is not corrupted

   D. If the Num Lock key and Scroll Lock key are on

9. Which statement describes the S4 ACPI power state?

   A. The CPU and RAM are still receiving power, but unused devices are powered down.

   B. The laptop is on and the CPU is running.

   C. The CPU and RAM are off. The contents of the RAM have been saved to a temporary file on the hard disk.

   D. The laptop is off and nothing has been saved.

10. A technician is trying to configure an integrated cellular WAN adapter on a laptop. What is the first step the technician should take to configure the adapter?

    A. Uninstall the device driver in Device Manager.

    B. Run Windows Update.

    C. Download software from the cellular service provider.

    D. Ensure that the device is enabled in the BIOS settings.

CHAPTER 8

Mobile Devices

Objectives

Upon completion of this chapter, you will be able to answer the following questions:

- What kind of hardware is used in mobile devices?

- What are the characteristics of touchscreens on mobile devices?

- What are the main characteristics of the two most commonly used mobile operating systems

- What is the difference between closed source and open source operating systems?

- How are applications downloaded and installed on mobile devices?

- How do users interact with applications on mobile devices?

- How do users manage apps, widgets, and folders on an Android device?

- How do users manage apps and folders on an iOS device?

- What are common features of mobile devices?

- How do users connect to networks and use email on mobile devices?

- What security options are there for mobile devices?

- What are the troubleshooting processes for mobile devices?

- What are common problems and solutions for mobile devices?

Key Terms

This chapter uses the following key terms. You can find the definitions in the Glossary.

Introduction (8.0.1)

With the increase in demand for mobility, the popularity of mobile devices continues to grow. A *mobile device* is any device that is handheld, is light, and typically uses a touchscreen for input. Like a desktop or laptop computer, mobile devices use an operating system to run applications (apps) and games and play movies and music. Some examples of mobile devices include Android devices, such as the Samsung Galaxy tablet and Galaxy Nexus smartphone and the Apple iPad and iPhone.

To facilitate mobility, mobile devices use many different wireless technologies. Many mobile device components, operating systems, and software are proprietary. It is important to become familiar with as many different mobile devices as possible.

You may be required to know how to configure, maintain, and repair various mobile devices. Some of the knowledge you acquire about desktop and laptop computers will help you; however, there are important differences between these technologies.

Mastering the skills necessary to work on mobile devices is important to your career advancement. This chapter focuses on the many features of mobile devices and their capabilities, including configuration, synchronization, and data backup.

Mobile Device Hardware Overview (8.1)

While mobile devices have similar hardware to desktops and laptops, there are many important differences. Hardware in a mobile device usually is not repaired by a field technician, but some parts may be replaceable. This section discusses the types of hardware found in mobile devices.

Non-Field-Serviceable Parts (8.1.1.1)

Unlike laptops, mobile devices do not have *field-serviceable parts*. Mobile devices consist of several compact components integrated into a single unit. When a mobile device malfunctions, it is usually sent to the manufacturer for repair or replacement. If the device is still under warranty, it can often be returned to the place of purchase for an exchange.

Broken mobile devices must often be returned to the manufacturer for repair or replacement. There are parts and instructions available from many websites to repair mobile devices, including touchscreens, front or back glass, and batteries. Installing parts from sources other than the manufacturer voids the manufacturer's warranty and might harm the device. For example, a battery for an iPhone should not be replaced with a battery that does not come from Apple. If a replacement battery is installed that does not meet the exact electrical specifications for the phone, the phone could short out or overload, becoming unusable.

There are no field-serviceable parts for mobile devices, but a few mobile device parts are field replaceable:

- **Battery:** Some mobile device batteries can be replaced.

- *Memory card*: Many mobile devices use memory cards to add storage.

- *Subscriber Identity Module (SIM) card*: This small card contains information used to authenticate a device to mobile telephone and data services, as shown in Figure 8-1. SIM cards can also hold user data such as contacts and text messages.

Figure 8-1   SIM Card

Non-Upgradeable Hardware (8.1.1.2)

Mobile device hardware is usually not upgradeable. The design and dimensions of the internal hardware do not allow for replacement with upgraded hardware. Many of the components in a mobile device are connected directly to circuit boards, which cannot be replaced with upgraded components, as shown in Figure 8-2. Batteries and memory cards, however, can often be replaced with items that have larger capacities. This might not increase the speed or capability of the mobile device, but it does allow for longer runtimes between charges or increased storage capacity for data.

Figure 8-2   iPhone Circuit Board

Some functionality can be added to mobile devices through the use of built-in ports and docking stations. These connections offer expandability, such as video or audio output, a connection to a docking station, or docking to a clock radio. Some smartphones can even be docked to a device with a keyboard, track pad, and LCD monitor to create a version of a laptop. There are also tablet cases that have a keyboard on the inside.

When a mobile device no longer possesses the capabilities or operates at the speeds required by the user, it must be replaced. Often, old mobile devices can be traded in for credit when purchasing a new one. The items are refurbished and resold or donated. Basic mobile devices can be donated to be reused when they cannot be traded in. Check for local donation programs in your area to find where these devices can be taken.

Touchscreens (8.1.1.3)

Most mobile devices do not have a keyboard or a pointing device. They use *touchscreens* to allow users to physically interact with what is shown on the screen and type on a virtual keyboard. Fingers or a stylus are used in place of a mouse pointer. Icons, like those found on desktops and laptops, are clicked with a touch rather than a mouse button. Mobile device manufacturers use the word *tap* or *touch* when describing operations and steps when using a mobile device. You will see both of these terms in instruction manuals, and they mean the same thing. This course uses the term *touch*.

There are two types of touchscreens:

- *Capacitive*: Consists of a glass screen coated with a conductor. Because the human body is also a conductor, touching the screen interrupts the electrical field of the screen. This change is measured by the touch processor to determine the vertical and horizontal location of the touch on the screen.

- *Resistive*: Consists of transparent layers of material capable of conducting electricity. These layers have a small air gap between them. One layer conducts electricity from top to bottom, while the other conducts electricity from left to right. When pressure is exerted on the screen, the two layers touch. When the layers touch, the vertical and horizontal locations are calculated by the touch processor from where the electricity is interrupted.

In addition to a single touch, mobile devices have the ability to recognize when two or more points of contact are made on the screen. This is called *multi-touch*. These are some common *gestures* used to perform functions:

- *Slide or swipe*: Move between screens horizontally or vertically. Touch the screen, slide your finger quickly in the direction you want to move the screen, and let go.

- *Double touch*: Zoom items such as photographs, maps, and text. Touch the screen twice quickly to zoom in. Touch the screen twice quickly again to zoom out.

- *Long touch*: Select items, such as text, icons, or photos. Touch and hold the screen until options become available for the item you are touching.

- *Scroll*: Scroll items that are too large for the screen, such as photos or web pages. Touch and hold the screen, moving your finger in the direction you want to move the item. Lift your finger when you reach the area of the screen you want to see.

- *Pinch*: Zoom out from objects, such as photographs, maps, and text. Touch the screen with two fingers and pinch them together to zoom out from the object.

- *Spread*: Zoom in on objects, such as photographs, maps, and text. Touch the screen with two fingers and spread them apart to zoom in on the object.

These gestures may be different between devices. Many other gestures can also be used, depending on the device and operating system version. Check the device documentation for additional information.

Some smartphones have a ***proximity sensor*** that turns off the touchscreen when the phone is up to your ear and turns it on when you pull the device away from your ear. This prevents icons or numbers from being activated by contact with your face or ear and also saves power.

Solid State Drives (8.1.1.4)

Mobile devices use the same components found in solid state drives (SSD) to store data. To reduce the size requirements, there is no case surrounding the components, as shown in Figure 8-3. The circuit board, *flash memory chips*, and *memory controller* in SSDs are installed directly inside the mobile device.

Figure 8-3   SSD Board

These are some of the advantages of using flash memory storage in mobile devices:

- **Power efficiency:** Flash memory requires very little power to store and retrieve data. This reduces the frequency with which mobile devices need to be recharged.

- **Reliability:** Flash memory can withstand high levels of shock and vibration without failing. Flash memory is also highly resistant to heat and cold.

- **Lightweight:** The weight of mobile devices is not significantly affected by the amount of memory installed.

- **Compact:** Because flash memory is compact, mobile devices can remain small regardless of the amount of memory installed.

- **Performance:** Flash memory does not have any moving parts, so there is no spin-up time for platters like a conventional hard drive. There is also no drive head to move, reducing the seek time to locate data.

- **Noise:** Flash memory makes no noise.

Mobile Operating Systems (8.2)

Operating systems on mobile devices manage apps and services, and determine the ways users interact with the device. This section focuses on an introduction to mobile device operating systems and key features of each of the two main mobile operating systems, as well as the differences between them.

Open Source Versus Closed Source (8.2.1.1)

Mobile devices use an OS to run software similar to the way desktops and laptops do. This chapter focuses on the two most commonly used mobile operating systems: Android and iOS. Android is developed by Google, and iOS is developed by Apple.

Released in 2008 on the HTC Dream, the Android OS is open source. *Open source* means that the developer's programming code, known as *source code*, is published when it is released. The public can change, copy, or redistribute the code without paying royalty fees to the software developer.

Open source software allows anyone to contribute to the development and evolution of the software. Android has been customized for use on a wide range of electronic devices. Because Android is open and customizable, programmers can use it to operate devices like laptops, smart TVs, and e-book readers. There have even been Android installations in devices like cameras, navigation systems, and portable media players.

Released in 2007 on the first iPhone, iOS is *closed source*, which means that the source code is not released to the public. To copy or redistribute iOS with or without changes requires the permission of Apple. Apple would most likely charge royalty fees for any money made from using their OS.

Application and Content Sources (8.2.1.2)

Applications (apps) are the programs that are executed on mobile devices. Mobile devices come with a number of different apps preinstalled to provide basic functionality. There are apps to make phone calls, send and receive email, listen to music, take pictures, and play video or videogames. Many other types of apps enable information retrieval, device customization, and productivity.

Apps are used on mobile devices the same way that programs are used on PCs. Instead of being installed from an optical disk, apps are downloaded from a *content source*. Some apps can be downloaded for free, and others must be purchased. Often, free apps are loaded with advertisements to help pay for development costs. Several content sources are available for Android mobile devices:

- Google Play
- Amazon App Store
- AndroidZoom
- AppsAPK
- 1Mobile

There are many other websites where Android apps can be found. These sites usually offer safe content, but sometimes they offer unsafe content. It is important to install apps only from trusted sources. If a questionable site contains a desirable app, check Google Play or the Amazon App Store to see if it can be downloaded from there instead. This will ensure that it is a safe download. The Google Play app only allows installation of apps on devices that are compatible with them.

Sometimes a website contains a *Quick Response (QR) code*, as shown in Figure 8-4. QR codes are similar to a bar code but can contain much more information. To use a QR code, a special app accesses the camera on a mobile device to scan the code. The code contains a web link that allows the direct download of an app. Be careful when using QR codes, and only allow downloads and installations from trusted sources.

Figure 8-4   QR Code

The Apple App Store is the only content source that iOS users are allowed to use to get apps and content. This ensures that Apple has cleared the content to be free of harmful code and meet strict performance guidelines and that it does not infringe on copyrights.

Other types of content are also available for download. Like apps, some content is free, whereas other content must be purchased. Content that you currently own can also be loaded onto mobile devices through a data cable connection or over Wi-Fi. Types of available content include the following:

- Music
- Television programs
- Movies
- Magazines
- Books

Push Versus Pull

There are two main methods for installing content on mobile devices: *push and pull*. Both Google Play and the Apple App Store support push and pull. When a user runs the Google Play app or the Apple App Store app from a mobile device, apps and content that are downloaded are pulled from a server to the device.

With Android devices, a user can browse Google Play using any desktop or laptop computer and purchase content. The content is pushed to the Android device from the server. iOS users are able to purchase content from iTunes on a desktop or laptop computer that is then pushed to an iOS device.

When an Android app is being installed, a list of all the required permissions is displayed. A game may need to access the Internet, manage sound settings, or enable vibration, for example. The game does not, however, need to access the list of contacts stored in a smartphone. You must agree to grant the listed permissions to the app so that it can be installed. Always read the list of permissions carefully and do not install apps that request permission to access items and features that it should not need.

Sideloading

There is another way to install apps on mobile devices. Apps can be downloaded from different sources on the Internet and transferred to a mobile device through Wi-Fi, Bluetooth, data cable, or other methods. This is called *sideloading*. After the app is transferred to the mobile device, it can be installed by touching it using a file explorer app. However, sideloading apps is not recommended because many sources for apps cannot be trusted. Only install apps from trusted sources and developers.

Android Touch Interface (8.2.2)

The Android touch interface allows users to interact with the system and apps through icons and menus on the touchscreen. Some devices have an onscreen keyboard that can be used like the keyboard on your laptop or PC by touching the keys on the screen.

Home Screen Items (8.2.2.1)

Much like a desktop or laptop computer, mobile devices organize icons and widgets on multiple screens for easy access. These are called the *home screens*. One screen is designated as the main home screen, as shown in Figure 8-5. Additional home screens are accessed by sliding the main home screen to the left or right. Each home screen contains *navigation icons*, the main area where icons and widgets are accessed, and notification and system icons. The home screen indicator displays which home screen is currently being used.

Figure 8-5   Android Main Home Screen

Navigation Icons

The Android OS uses the system bar to navigate apps and screens. The system bar is always displayed at the bottom of every screen.

The system bar contains the following buttons:

- **Back:** Returns focus to the previous screen that was being used. If the onscreen keyboard is displayed, this button closes it. Continuing to press the Back button navigates to through each previous screen until the main home screen is displayed.

- **Home:** Returns focus to the last home screen used. If you are viewing a left or right home screen, the Home button opens the main home screen.

- **Recent Apps:** Opens thumbnail images of recently used apps. To open an app, touch its thumbnail. Swipe a thumbnail to remove it from the list.

- **Menu:** Shows additional options for the current screen if available.

Google Search

Android devices often come with a default Google search app preinstalled. Touch and then type text into the box to search the device and the Internet for anything. Touch the microphone icon to enter the search using speech.

Special Enhancements

Some manufacturers add functionality to the Android OS. For example, some Samsung Android tablets have a feature called the Mini App Tray, which contains shortcuts to apps that can be used at any time. The Mini App Tray is opened by touching the arrow at the bottom of the screen. This feature is useful because the user does not have to navigate away from what they are doing to run a specific app.

Notification and System Icons

Each Android device has an area that contains system icons, such as the clock, battery status, and radio signal status for Wi-Fi and provider networks. Apps such as email, text messaging, and Facebook often display status icons to indicate communication activity.

To open the notification area on Android phones, touch and hold the top of the screen and swipe your finger down the screen. On Android tablets, touch the notification and system icons at the bottom of the screen, as shown in Figure 8-6.

Figure 8-6   Notification Area

You can do the following when notifications are open:

- Respond to a notification by touching it.
- Dismiss a notification by swiping it off the screen to either side.
- Dismiss all notifications with the icon.
- Toggle often-used settings.
- Adjust the brightness of the screen.
- Open the Settings menu with the quick settings icon.

TouchFLO

Instead of using the standard Android interface on its phones, HTC designed the TouchFLO interface over Android. With TouchFLO, use a special menu accessed by dragging your finger up the screen and then selecting common tasks by moving your finger left or right. TouchFLO was replaced by TouchFLO 3D. TouchFLO 3D had a collection of tabs along the bottom of the screen to easily access tasks. TouchFLO 3D has been replaced by HTC Sense. HTC Sense uses desktop apps and widgets but has many interface modifications exclusive to HTC devices, such as locking screen apps and widgets and 3D home screen effects.

Managing Apps, Widgets, and Folders (8.2.2.2)

Managing programs and folders on mobile devices can be very different from managing them on desktops and PCs. The following paragraphs explain how to add, remove, and move apps, widgets, and folders. Figure 8-7 shows an example of these items on an Android device.

Figure 8-7   Apps, Widgets, and Folders

Apps

How To 🔍

Each home screen is set up with a grid where apps can be placed. To move an app, follow these steps:

Step 1.   Touch and hold the app.

Step 2.   Drag it to an empty area of any home screen.

Step 3.   Release the app.

How To 🔍

To remove an app from a home screen, follow these steps:

Step 1.   Touch and hold the app.

Step 2.   Drag it to the trashcan or X icon on the screen.

Step 3.   Release the app.

To execute an app, touch it. After the app is running, there are often options that can be configured by touching the menu button.

There are usually three different ways to close an app:

- Touch the **Back** button continually to reach the home screen. It is common for the program to prompt to exit the app.

- Touch the **Home** button.

- Touch the **Exit** option in the menu for the app.

Widgets

Widgets are programs (or pieces of programs) that display information. For example, a weather widget can be placed on the Home screen to display weather conditions. Often, a widget can be touched to launch an associated app. In the case of a weather widget, touching the widget would open a weather app on the full screen with more information and details about the weather. Widgets are helpful because they give you quick access to often-used information or functions. Examples of popular widgets include the following:

- **Clock:** Displays a large version of a customizable clock

- **Weather:** Displays current conditions for one or more locations

- **Wi-Fi On/Off:** Allows the user to turn Wi-Fi on or off quickly without navigating to the settings menu

- **Power Control:** Displays multiple widgets like Wi-Fi On/Off, Bluetooth, and vibrate in a group that is always visible

- **Notes:** Allows the user to create notes that are shown on a home screen

- **Facebook:** Provides access to Facebook postings and allows the user to post to Facebook quickly

- **Last Call:** Displays the last incoming or outgoing call that was received or placed

There are many other types of widgets that can be used to customize Android screens. Refer to the documentation of programs or Google Play to determine which apps have widgets.

Folders

On some mobile devices, multiple apps can be grouped into folders to help organize them. If folders are not available, an app can be installed to provide this feature. Apps can be grouped in any way you want.

To create a folder on an Android smartphone, follow these steps:

Step 1.   Touch and hold an app on a home screen.

Step 2.   Drag the app onto another app that you want in the same folder.

Step 3.   Release the app.

To create a folder on an Android tablet, follow these steps:

Step 1.   Touch and hold an app on a home screen.

Step 2.   Drag the app onto the folder icon at the top of the screen.

Step 3.   Release the app.

Touch any folder to open it. Touch any app in the folder to open it. To rename a folder, touch the folder, touch the folder name, and type a new name for the folder. To close a folder, touch outside the folder or touch the **Back** or **Home** button. Move folders around on home screens the same way apps are moved.

To remove an app from a folder, follow these steps:

Step 1.   Open the folder.

Step 2.   Touch and hold the app to remove.

Step 3.   Drag the app to an empty area of a home screen.

Step 4.   Release the app.

On Android smartphones, if a folder has two apps and one is removed, the folder is removed but the remaining app replaces the folder on the home screen. On Android tablets, if all apps are removed from a folder, the folder remains. Remove a folder from a home screen the same way apps are removed.

All Apps Icon

The All Apps icon opens the All Apps screen that displays all of the apps that are installed on the device. These are some common tasks that can be performed from the All Apps screen:

- **Launch an app:** Touch any app to launch it.

- **Place apps on a home screen:** Touch and hold an app. The home screen is displayed. Release the app on any open area of any home screen.

- **Uninstall apps:** Touch and hold an app. Drag the app to either the trashcan icon or the X icon.

- **Access the Play Store:** Touch the **menu** icon and touch **Google Play.**

- **Access Widgets:** Touch the **Widgets** tab to see all the widgets installed. Place widgets on home screens using the same method for placing apps on the home screens.

Lab 8.2.2.3: Working with Android

In this lab, you place apps and widgets on the home screen and move them between different home screens. You also create folders to which apps will be added and removed. Finally, you uninstall apps from the Android device. Refer to Lab 8.2.2.3 in *IT Essentials: PC Hardware and Software Lab Manual*, Fifth Edition.

iOS Touch Interface (8.2.3)

Like the Android interface, the iOS touch interface uses a touchscreen that allows users to access apps and device features. This section describes the ways users can interact with an iOS device and points out important differences between the two operating systems.

Home Screen Items (8.2.3.1)

The iOS interface works in much the same way as the Android interface. It is similar to the Android touchscreen, but there are some very important differences.

iOS Home screens are used to organize apps, and apps are launched with a touch. Some of the differences from the Android OS are as follows:

- **No navigation icons:** A physical button is pressed instead of touching navigation icons.

- **No widgets:** Only apps and other content can be installed on iOS devices.

- **No app shortcuts:** Each app on a home screen is the actual app, not a shortcut.

Home Button

Unlike Android, iOS devices do not use navigation icons to perform functions. A single button called the *Home button* performs many of the same functions as the Android navigation buttons. The Home button is at the bottom of the device, with the image of a square on it, as shown in Figure 8-8.

Figure 8-8   iOS Home Button

The Home button performs the following functions:

- **Wake the device:** When the device's screen is off, press the **Home** button once to turn it on.

- **Return to the home screen:** Press the **Home** button while using an app to bring up the last home screen that was used.

- **Return to the main home screen:** Press the **Home** button while on any other home screen or the search screen to go to the main home screen.

- **Open the multitasking bar:** Double-press the **Home** button to open the multitasking bar. The multitasking bar shows the most recent apps that have been used.

- **Start Siri or voice control:** Hold down the **Home** button to start Siri or *voice control*. *Siri* is special software that understands advanced voice controls. On devices without Siri, basic voice controls can be used.

- **Open audio controls:** Double-press the **Home** button when the screen is locked to open the audio controls.

- **Open the search screen:** Press the **Home** button while on the main home screen to go to the search screen.

Notification Center

iOS devices have a *notification center* that displays all of the alerts from apps in one location, as shown in Figure 8-9. To open the notification area on iOS devices, touch and hold the top of the screen and swipe a finger down the screen.

Figure 8-9   Notification Center

The following actions can be taken when notifications are open:

- Respond to an alert by touching it.

- Remove an alert by touching the **X** icon and touching clear.

To change the options for notifications, use the following path:

Settings > Notifications

Search

Swipe the main home screen from left to right or double-click the **Home** button to open the search feature called *Spotlight*. Enter the search item. All results are listed in accordance with the app that contains the results. To search the Internet instead, touch **Search web** at the bottom of the list after the search results appear.

Managing Apps and Folders (8.2.3.2)

Like the Android OS, iOS has specific steps for managing programs and folders on mobile devices. The following paragraphs explain how to add, remove, and move apps and folders in iOS.

Apps

iOS apps and folders work similarly to the Android OS. Instead of an All Apps button, all the apps that are installed on the device are located on the home screens. Apps can be uninstalled from the device but can be reinstalled on the device using *iTunes*.

How To Q

Each home screen has a grid in which apps can be placed. To move an app, follow these steps:

Step 1.   Touch and hold the app until it jiggles.

Step 2.   Drag it to an empty area of any home screen.

Step 3.   Release the app.

Step 4.   Move any additional apps.

Step 5.   Press the **Home** button to save the changes.

How To Q

To remove an app from an iOS device, follow these steps:

Step 1.   Touch and hold the app until it jiggles.

Step 2.   Touch the X icon on the app.

Step 3.   Delete any additional apps.

Step 4.   Press the **Home** button to save the changes.

Multitasking Bar

iOS allows multiple apps to run at the same time. While you are working in one app, others may run in the background. The *multitasking bar* is used to quickly switch between the apps that have been used recently, close apps that are running, and access commonly used settings. To open the multitasking bar, double-click the **Home** button. The following actions can be performed in the multitasking bar:

- Touch any app to open it.
- Swipe the multitasking bar left to see more apps.
- Swipe the multitasking bar right to access commonly used settings.
- Touch and hold an app until it jiggles, and touch the small red circle with the white dash to force the app to close.

Folders

How To Q

Folders can also be created on iOS devices to help organize them. To create a folder, follow these steps:

Step 1.   Touch and hold an app on a home screen until it jiggles.

Step 2.   Drag the app onto another app that you want in the same folder.

Step 3.   Release the app.

Step 4.   Add any additional apps to the folder.

Step 5.   Touch the **Home** button to save changes

Touch any folder to open it. Touch any app in the folder to open it. To rename a folder, touch the folder, touch the folder name, and type a new name for the folder. To close a folder, touch outside the folder or touch the **Home** button. Move folders around on home screens the same way apps are moved.

How To

To remove an app from a folder, follow these steps:

Step 1.   Open the folder.

Step 2.   Touch and hold the app you want to remove.

Step 3.   Drag the app to an empty area of a home screen.

Step 4.   Release the app.

To remove a folder, remove all apps from the folder.

Many of the apps on iOS devices are able to show an *alert badge*. An alert badge is displayed as a small icon over an app. This icon is a number that indicates the amount of alerts from the app that need attending. This might be how many missed calls you have, how many text messages that you have, or how many updates are available. If an alert badge displays an exclamation mark, there is a problem with the app. Alert badges for apps inside a folder are displayed on the folder. Touch the app to attend to the alerts.

Lab 8.2.3.3: Working with iOS

In this lab, you place apps on the home screen and move them between different home screens. You also create folders to which apps will be added and removed. Finally, you uninstall apps from the iOS device. Refer to Lab 8.2.3.3 in *IT Essentials: PC Hardware and Software Lab Manual*, Fifth Edition.

Common Mobile Device Features (8.2.4)

The following paragraphs describe common features of mobile devices.

Screen Orientation and Calibration (8.2.4.1)

Screen Orientation

Most mobile device screens are rectangular in shape. This shape allows content to be viewed in two different ways: portrait and landscape. Some content fits better in a specific view. For example, video fills the screen in landscape mode but may not fill the screen in portrait mode. Also, a book or magazine viewed in portrait mode seems very natural because it is similar in shape to the real thing. Users can usually choose the viewing mode that is the most comfortable for them for each type of content.

Many mobile devices contain sensors, such as an *accelerometer*, that can determine how they are being held. Content is automatically rotated to the position of the device, either landscape or portrait. This feature is useful, for example, when taking a photograph. When the device is turned to landscape mode, the camera app also turns to landscape mode. Also, when a user is creating a text, turning the device to landscape mode automatically turns the app to landscape mode, making the keyboard larger and wider, which is easier to use.

When using an Android device to enable automatic rotation, use the following path:

Settings > Display > check **Auto-rotate screen**

When using an iOS device, to enable *automatic rotation* use the following path:

Double-click the **Home** button > swipe the multitasking bar from left to right > touch the **lock** icon on the left.

Screen Calibration

When using a mobile device, you may need to adjust the brightness of the screen. Increase the *screen brightness* level when using a mobile device outdoors because bright sunlight makes the screen very difficult to read. In contrast, a very low brightness is helpful when reading a book on a mobile device at night. Some mobile devices can be configured to auto-adjust the brightness depending on the amount of surrounding light. The device must have a light sensor to use auto-brightness.

The LCD screen for most mobile devices uses the most battery power. Lowering the brightness or using auto-brightness helps conserve battery power. Set the brightness to the lowest setting to get the most battery life from the device.

When using an Android device, to configure screen brightness use the following path:

Settings > Display > Brightness > slide the brightness to the desired level or check **Automatic brightness > OK**

When using an iPad, to configure screen brightness, use the following path:

Double-click the **Home** button > swipe the multitasking bar from left to right > slide the brightness to the desired level > click the **Home** button

To configure brightness in the Settings menu, use the following path:

Settings > Brightness & Wallpaper > slide the brightness to the desired level or touch **Auto-Brightness >** click the **Home** button

GPS (8.2.4.2)

Another common feature of mobile devices is the *Global Positioning System (GPS)*. GPS is a navigation system that determines the time and location on Earth using messages from satellites in space and a receiver on Earth. A GPS radio receiver uses at least four satellites to calculate its position based on the messages. GPS is very accurate and can be used under most weather conditions. However, dense foliage, tunnels, and tall buildings can interrupt satellite signals.

There are GPS devices for cars, boats, and handheld devices used by hikers and backpackers. In mobile devices, GPS receivers have many different uses:

- *Navigation*: A mapping app that provides turn-by-turn directions to a place, an address, or coordinates.

- *Geocaching*: A mapping app that shows the location of geocaches (hidden containers around the world). Users find them and often sign a log book to show that they found it.

- *Geotagging*: Embeds location information into a digital object, like a photograph or a video, to record where it was taken.

- **Specialized search results:** For example, displays results based on proximity, such as restaurants that are close by when searching for the keyword restaurants.

- **Device tracking:** Locates the device on a map if it is lost or stolen.

To enable GPS on Android devices, use the following path:

Settings > Location services > Use GPS satellites

To enable GPS on iOS devices, use the following path:

Settings > Location services > turn location services on

> **Note**
>
> Some Android and iOS devices do not have GPS receivers. These devices use information from Wi-Fi networks and cellular networks, if available, to provide location services.

 Lab 8.2.4.3: Mobile Device Features - Android and iOS

In this lab, you set the autorotation and brightness and turn GPS on and off. Refer to Lab 8.2.4.3 in *IT Essentials: PC Hardware and Software Lab Manual*, Fifth Edition.

Worksheet 8.2.4.4: Mobile Device Information

In this activity, you use the Internet, a newspaper, or a local store to gather information and then enter the specifications for an Android and iOS device onto this worksheet. For both devices, you identify common operating system features. Be prepared to discuss your decisions regarding the devices you select. Refer to Worksheet 8.2.4.4 in *IT Essentials: PC Hardware and Software Lab Manual*, Fifth Edition.

Network Connectivity and Email (8.3)

One of the biggest benefits of mobile devices is the ability to connect to the Internet and send and receive email from any location that has a connection to a network. This section describes connection types and how devices connect to networks and the Internet and explains how to set up and manage connections that are secure and efficient.

Wireless Data Network (8.3.1.1)

Mobile devices give people the freedom to work, learn, play, and communicate wherever they want. People using mobile devices do not need to be tied to a physical location to send and receive voice, video, email, and data communications. In addition, wireless facilities, such as Internet cafes, are available in many countries. College campuses use wireless networks to allow students to sign up for classes, watch lectures, and submit assignments in areas where physical connections to the network are unavailable. With mobile devices becoming more powerful, many tasks that needed to be performed on large computers connected to physical networks can now be completed using mobile devices on wireless networks.

Almost all mobile devices are capable of connecting to *Wi-Fi networks*. It is advisable to connect to Wi-Fi networks when possible because data used over Wi-Fi does not count against the cellular data plan. Also, because Wi-Fi radios use less power than cellular radios, connecting to Wi-Fi networks conserves battery power. Like other Wi-Fi–enabled devices, it is important to use security when connecting to Wi-Fi networks. These precautions should be taken to protect Wi-Fi communications on mobile devices:

- Never send login or password information using clear, unencrypted text.

- Use a VPN connection when possible.

- Enable security on home networks.

- Use WPA2 security.

To turn Wi-Fi on or off, use the following path for Android and iOS:

Settings > turn **Wi-Fi** on or off

To connect an Android device when it is within the coverage range of a Wi-Fi network, turn on Wi-Fi, and the device then searches for all available Wi-Fi networks and displays them in a list. Touch a Wi-Fi network in the list to connect. Enter a password if needed.

When a mobile device roams out of the range of the Wi-Fi network, it attempts to connect to another Wi-Fi network in range. If no Wi-Fi networks are in range, the mobile device connects to the *cellular data network*. When Wi-Fi is on, it automatically connects to any Wi-Fi network that it has connected to previously. If the network is new, the mobile device either displays a list of available networks that can be used or asks if it should connect to it.

If a mobile device does not prompt to connect to a Wi-Fi network, the network SSID broadcast may be turned off or the device may not be set to connect automatically. Manually configure the Wi-Fi settings on the mobile device.

To connect to a Wi-Fi network manually on an Android device, follow these steps:

Step 1. Select **Settings > Add network**.

Step 2. Enter the network SSID.

Step 3. Touch **Security** and select a security type.

Step 4. Touch **Password** and enter the password.

Step 5. Touch **Save**.

To connect to a Wi-Fi network manually on an iOS device, follow these steps:

Step 1. Select **Settings > Wi-Fi > Other**.

Step 2. Enter the network SSID.

Step 3. Touch **Security** and select a security type.

Step 4. Touch **Other Network**.

Step 5. Touch **Password** and enter the password.

Step 6. Touch **Join**.

Lab 8.3.1.2: Mobile Wi-Fi - Android and iOS

In this lab, you turn the Wi-Fi radio on and off, forget a found Wi-Fi network, and find and connect to a Wi-Fi network.

Cellular Communications (8.3.1.3)

When people began to use cell phones, there were few industry-wide standards for cell phone technology. Without standards, it was difficult and expensive to make calls to people who were on another network. Today, cell phone providers use industry standards, making it easier to use cell phones to make calls.

Cellular standards have not been adopted uniformly around the world. Some cell phones are capable of using multiple standards, whereas others can use only one standard. As a result, some cell phones can operate in many countries, and other cell phones can only be used locally.

The *first generation (1G)* of cell phones began service in the 1980s. First-generation phones primarily used analog standards. With analog, interference and noise cannot easily be separated from the voice in the signal. This factor limits the usefulness of analog systems. Few 1G devices are in use today.

In the 1990s, the *second generation (2G)* of mobile devices was marked by a switch from analog to digital standards. Digital standards provide higher call quality. These are some common 2G standards:

- *Global System for Mobile (GSM)*
- *Integrated Digital Enhanced Network (iDEN)*
- *Code Division Multiple Access (CDMA)*
- *Personal Digital Cellular (PDC)*

As 3G cell phone standards were being developed, extensions to the existing 2G standards were added. These transitional standards are known as *2.5G* standards. These are some common 2.5G standards extensions:

- *General Packet Radio Service (GPRS)*
- *Enhanced Data Rates for GSM Evolution (EDGE)*
- *CDMA2000*

Third-generation (3G) standards enable mobile devices to go beyond simple voice and data communications. It is now common for mobile devices to send and receive text, photos, audio, and video. 3G even provides enough bandwidth for video conferencing. 3G mobile devices are also able to access the Internet to browse, play games, listen to music, and watch video. These are some common 3G standards:

- *Universal Mobile Telecommunications System (UMTS)*
- CDMA2000
- *Evolution-Data Optimized (EV-DO)*

- *Freedom of Mobile Multimedia Access (FOMA)*

- *Time Division Synchronous Code Division Multiple Access (TD-SCDMA)*

Fourth-generation (4G) standards provide ultra-broadband Internet access. Higher data rates allow users to download files much faster, perform videoconferencing, or watch high-definition television. These are some common 4G standards:

- *Mobile WiMAX*

- *Long Term Evolution (LTE)*

The specification for 4G devices requires a maximum of 100 Mb/s communication for highly mobile devices like those in a car. The specification also requires a maximum of 1 Gb/s for devices being used by people moving slowly or standing still.

WiMAX and LTE

Even though Mobile WiMAX and LTE fall short of the data rate to be compliant with 4G (128 Mb/s and 100 Mb/s, respectively), they are still considered 4G standards because they offer so much improvement over the performance of 3G. WiMAX and LTE are also forerunners to versions that will be compliant with the full specification of 4G.

Technologies that add multimedia and networking functionality can be bundled with cellular standards. The two most common are *Short Message Service (SMS),* used for text messaging, and *Multimedia Message Service (MMS),* used for sending and receiving photos and videos. Most cellular providers charge extra for adding these features.

To turn on or off cellular data on an Android device use the following path:

Settings > touch **More** under **Wireless and Networks >** touch **Mobile Networks >** touch **Data enabled**

To turn on or off cellular data on an iOS device, use the following path:

Settings > General > Cellular Data > turn cellular data on or off

As a mobile device moves from an area of 4G coverage to 3G coverage, the 4G radio shuts off and turns on the 3G radio. Connections are not lost during this transition.

Airplane Mode

Most mobile devices also have a setting called *Airplane Mode* that turns off all cellular, Wi-Fi, and Bluetooth radios. Airplane Mode is useful when traveling on an airplane or when located where accessing data is prohibited or expensive. Most mobile device functions are still usable, but communication is not possible.

To turn Airplane Mode on or off on an Android device, use the following path:

Settings > More > Airplane mode > OK

To turn Airplane Mode on or off on an iOS device, use the following path:

Settings > turn **Airplane mode** on or off

Bluetooth for Mobile Devices (8.3.2.1)

Mobile devices connect using many different methods. Cellular and Wi-Fi can be difficult to configure and require extra equipment such as towers and access points. Cable connections are not always practical when connecting headsets or speakers. *Bluetooth technology* provides a simple way for mobile devices to connect to each other and to wireless accessories. Bluetooth is wireless and automatic and uses very little power, which helps conserve battery life. Up to eight Bluetooth devices can be connected together at any one time.

These are some examples of how mobile devices use Bluetooth:

- **Handsfree headset:** A small earpiece with a microphone used for making and receiving calls.

- **Keyboard or mouse:** A keyboard or mouse can be connected to a mobile device to make input easier.

- **Stereo control:** A mobile device can connect to a home or car stereo to play music.

- **Car speakerphone:** A device that contains a speaker and a microphone used for making and receiving calls.

- *Tethering*: A mobile device can connect to another mobile device or computer to share a network connection. Tethering can also be performed with a Wi-Fi connection or a cable connection such as USB.

- **Mobile speaker:** Portable speakers can connect to mobile devices to provide high-quality audio without a stereo system.

Bluetooth is a networking standard that has two levels, physical and protocol. At the physical level, Bluetooth is a radio frequency standard. At the protocol level, devices agree on when bits are sent, how they are sent, and that what is received is the same as what was sent.

Bluetooth Pairing (8.3.2.2)

Bluetooth pairing is when two Bluetooth devices establish a connection to share resources. For the devices to pair, the Bluetooth radios are turned on, and one device begins searching for other devices. Other devices must be set to discoverable mode, also called visible, so that they can be detected. When a Bluetooth device is in discoverable mode, it transmits the following information when another Bluetooth device requests it:

- Name

- Bluetooth class

- Services that the device can use

- Technical information, such as the features or the Bluetooth specification that it supports

During the pairing process, a PIN may be requested to authenticate the pairing process. The PIN is often a number but can also be a numeric code or passkey. The PIN is stored using pairing services, so it does not have to be entered the next time the device tries to connect. This is convenient when using a headset with a smartphone because they are paired automatically when the headset is turned on and within range.

How To

To pair a Bluetooth device with an Android device, follow these steps:

Step 1. Follow the instructions for your device to place it in discoverable mode.

Step 2. Check the instructions for your device to find the connection PIN.

Step 3. Select **Settings > Wireless and networks.**

Step 4. Touch **Bluetooth** to turn it on.

Step 5. Touch the **Bluetooth** tab.

Step 6. Touch **Scan for devices.**

Step 7. Touch the discovered device to select it.

Step 8. Type the PIN.

Step 9. Touch the device name again to connect to it.

How To

To pair a Bluetooth device with an iOS device, follow these steps:

Step 1. Follow the instructions for your device to place it in discoverable mode.

Step 2. Check the instructions for your device to find the connection PIN.

Step 3. Select **Settings > General > Bluetooth.**

Step 4. Touch **Bluetooth** to turn it on.

Step 5. Touch the discovered device to select it.

Step 6. Type the PIN.

Introduction to Email (8.3.3.1)

Email software can be installed as part of a web browser or as a standalone application. Any email program can be used with Windows 7. Windows Live Mail is an email program that is recommended by Microsoft. It manages multiple email accounts, calendars, and contacts. To install Windows Live Mail, download and install Windows Essentials from Microsoft. Windows Live Mail is included in Windows Essentials.

You should have the following information available when setting up an email account:

- **Display name:** This can be your real name, nickname, or any other name that you want people to see.

- **Email address:** This is the address people need to send email to you. An email address is a username followed by the @ symbol and the domain of the email server (user@example.net).

- *Protocol*: Used by the incoming mail server. Different protocols provide different email services.

- **Incoming and outgoing mail server names:** These names are provided by the network administrator or ISP.

- **Username:** This is used to log in to the mail servers.

- **Account password:** The password should be strong because mail accounts are often available from websites.

The protocols used in email include the following:

- *Post Office Protocol Version 3 (POP3)*

- *Internet Message Access Protocol (IMAP)*

- *Simple Mail Transfer Protocol (SMTP)*

- *Multipurpose Internet Mail Extensions (MIME)*

- *Secure Sockets Layer (SSL)*

You need to know how to configure a device to accept the correct incoming mail format. You can configure the email client software manually or by using a wizard.

POP3

POP3 retrieves emails from a remote server over TCP/IP. POP3 does not leave a copy of the email on the server; however, some implementations allow users to specify that mail be saved for some period of time. POP3 supports end users that have intermittent connections, such as dialup. A POP3 user can connect, download email from the server, and then disconnect. POP3 usually uses port 110.

IMAP

IMAP allows local email clients to retrieve email from a server. Like POP3, IMAP allows you to download email from an email server using an email client. The difference is that IMAP allows the user to organize email on the network email server and download copies of email. The original email remains on the network email server. Unlike POP3, IMAP typically leaves the original email on the server until you move the email to a personal folder in your email application. IMAP synchronizes email folders between the server and client. IMAP is faster than POP3, but IMAP requires more disk space on the server and more CPU resources. The most recent version of IMAP is IMAP4. IMAP4 is often used in large networks, such as a university campus. IMAP usually uses port 143.

SMTP

SMTP is a simple text-based protocol that transmits emails across a TCP/IP network and is the email format for text that uses only ASCII encoding. SMTP must be implemented to send email. SMTP sends email from an email client to an email server or from one email server to another. A message is sent after recipients are identified and verified. SMTP usually uses port 25.

MIME

MIME extends the email format to include text in ASCII standard as well as other formats, such as pictures and word processor documents. MIME is normally used in conjunction with SMTP.

SSL

SSL was developed to transmit files securely. All data exchanged between the email client and the email server is encrypted. When configuring an email client to use SSL, make sure to use the correct port number for the email server.

Exchange

Exchange is a mail server, contact manager, and calendaring software created by Microsoft. Exchange uses a proprietary messaging architecture called *Messaging Application Programming Interface (MAPI)*. MAPI is used by Microsoft Office Outlook to connect to Exchange servers, to provide email, calendar, and contact management. Check your understanding of email protocols by completing activity 8.3.3.2, Matching Email Protocols, in your online curriculum.

Android Email Configuration (8.3.3.3)

Android devices are capable of using advanced communication applications and data services. Many of these applications and features require the use of web services provided by Google. When you configure an Android mobile device for the first time, you are prompted to sign in to your Google account with your Gmail email address and password.

By signing in to your Gmail account, the Google Play store, data and settings backup, and other Google services become accessible. The device synchronizes contacts, email messages, apps, downloaded content, and other information from the Google services that you use with your device. If you do not have a Gmail account, you can use the Google account sign-in page to create a new account.

Note

If you want to restore Android settings to a tablet that you have previously backed up, you must sign in to the account when setting up the tablet for the first time. You cannot restore your Android settings if you sign in after the initial setup.

After initial setup, access your mailbox by touching the Gmail app icon. Android devices also have an email app for connecting to other email accounts.

How To

To add an email account, perform the following steps:

Step 1.   Touch the **Email** app icon.

Step 2.   Touch the **Menu** button.

Step 3.   Touch **Account** settings.

Step 4.   Touch **Add account**.

Step 5.   Enter your email address and password.

Step 6.   Touch **Next**, or touch **Manual setup** to enter special account settings.

Step 7.   Touch **Done**.

Step 8.   Type a name for the email account.

Step 9.   Touch **Done**.

iOS Email Configuration (8.3.3.4)

An Apple ID is required to set up an iOS device. An Apple ID is used to access the Apple App Store, the iTunes Store, and iCloud. *iCloud* provides email and the ability to store content on remote servers. The iCloud email is free and comes with remote storage for backups, mail, and documents.

All of the iOS devices, apps, and content are linked to your Apple ID. When an iOS device is turned on for the first time, the Setup Assistant guides you through the process of connecting the device and signing in with or creating an Apple ID. The Setup Assistant also allows you to create an iCloud email account. You can restore settings, content, and apps from a different iOS device from an iCloud backup during the setup process.

If iCloud is not configured during the setup process, use the following path to set it up:

Settings > iCloud

How To

To set up additional email accounts, follow these steps:

Step 1.   Select **Settings > Mail, Contacts, Calendars > Add Account.**

Step 2.   Touch the account type.

Step 3.   If the account type is not listed, touch **Other.**

Step 4.   Enter the account information.

Step 5.   Touch **Save.**

Mobile Device Synchronization (8.3.4)

Using several mobile devices can cause information to be stored in different places. This can result in errors in calendars, contacts, and other types of stored data when one saved version is different than another on a different device. To avoid these problems, most devices allow data synchronization, which is explained in the sections below

Types of Data to Synchronize (8.3.4.1)

Many people use a combination of desktop, laptop, tablet, and smartphone devices to access and store information. It is helpful when specific information is the same across multiple devices. For example, when scheduling appointments using a calendar program, each new appointment would need to be entered in each device to ensure that each device is up to date. Data synchronization eliminates the need to constantly make changes to every device.

Data synchronization is the exchange of data between two or more devices, while maintaining consistent data on those devices. Some of the types of data that can be synchronized are as follows:

- Contacts
- Email
- Calendar entries

- Pictures

- Music

- Apps

- Video

- Browser links and settings

Application Installation Software Requirements (8.3.4.2)

To synchronize data on an iOS device, iTunes software must be installed. iTunes is a media player application that downloads, plays, and organizes content for use with iOS devices and computers. iTunes also manages iOS devices by activating them with Apple and restoring them when there is a malfunction. iTunes is also used to upgrade the iOS. These are the application installation software requirements for Windows:

- PC with a 1-GHz Intel or AMD processor.

- 512 MB of RAM.

- Windows XP Service Pack 2 or later, 32-bit editions of Windows Vista, or 32-bit editions of Windows 7.

- 64-bit editions of Windows Vista or Windows 7 require the iTunes 64-bit installer.

Requirements change with different versions, and there are additional requirements for special audio and video capabilities. For more information, refer to the Apple website.

No application is necessary to synchronize content for Android devices. Automatic synchronization for various types of data and content with Google is accessed by selecting **Settings > Personal > Accounts & sync.**

Use *Motocast USB* to synchronize data and content when using a Motorola device with the Android OS. These are the application installation software requirements for Windows:

- PC with a 3.0-GHz Intel Pentium IV or AMD Athlon XP 2600+ or faster single-core processor or a PC with a 1.8-GHz Core Duo, Pentium dual-core or multi-core Athlon/Phenom or faster processor

- 1 GB of RAM

- Windows XP Service Pack 3 or later, Windows Vista, or Windows 7

Additional hardware specifications for special audio and video capabilities may be required. For more information, refer to the Motorola website.

Synchronization Connection Types (8.3.4.3)

To synchronize data between devices, the devices must use a common communication medium. USB and Wi-Fi connections are the most common connection types used to synchronize data between devices.

Because most Android devices do not have a desktop program for performing data synchronization, most users sync with Google's different web services, even when synchronizing with a desktop or laptop computer. One benefit of synchronizing data using this method is that the data is accessible from any computer or mobile device at any time by signing in to a Google account. The disadvantage to this arrangement is that it can be difficult to synchronize data with programs that are installed locally on a computer, such as Outlook for email, calendar, and contacts, or iTunes for music and video.

Before iOS 5, synchronization was limited to using a USB connection cable to connect the device to a computer. You can now use *Wi-Fi Sync* to synchronize with iTunes wirelessly. To use Wi-Fi Sync, you must first synchronize the iOS device with iTunes using a USB cable. You must also turn on Sync over Wi-Fi Connection in the Summary pane of iTunes. After that, you can use Wi-Fi Sync or a USB cable. When the iOS device is on the same wireless network as the computer running iTunes and it is plugged into a power source, it automatically synchronizes with iTunes.

Cross-Platform Data Synchronization

Often, a user has devices that run different operating systems. Synchronization of data between different operating systems is called *cross-platform data synchronization*. Third-party applications that handle Android synchronization between Outlook or iTunes must be installed for synchronization to work. iTunes can be installed on either a Windows or Apple computer, and an Android or iOS device can synchronize data with either one.

Apps can also be used to perform synchronization between different computing platforms. Dropbox is an example of an application that can be installed on different platforms and synchronize different types of data. One particularly useful feature is the ability to set photographs from a mobile device to automatically sync. When a picture is taken, it is automatically sent to a remote server. When another device, such as a tablet or desktop computer, is running the software, the photograph is automatically downloaded.

Methods for Securing Mobile Devices (8.4)

Like laptops and PCs, mobile devices must be protected from security threats. This section discusses some types of security measures to help protect data and devices from loss and theft.

Overview of Passcode Locks (8.4.1.1)

Smartphones, tablets, and other mobile devices contain sensitive data. If a mobile device is lost, anyone who finds the device has access to contacts, text messages, and web accounts. One method to help prevent theft of private information from mobile devices is to use a *passcode lock*. A passcode lock locks a device and puts it in a power-saving state. The lock can also be delayed to engage after a specified amount of time passes after the device goes into the power-saving state. One common method for placing a mobile device into a sleep state is by quickly pressing the main power button. The device can also be set to enter a sleep state after a certain amount of time.

Many different types of passcode locks are available. Some types of passcode locks are more difficult to guess than others. The passcode must be entered each time the device is turned on or resumes from a power-saving state. These are some common types of passcode locks:

- **None:** Removes any other type of passcode lock if there is one set.
- **Slide:** The user slides an icon, such as a lock or arrow, to unlock the device. This option is the least secure.
- **Face Unlock:** Uses the camera to recognize faces. After a stored face is recognized, the device unlocks.
- **Pattern:** Locks the device when the user slides a finger over the screen in a certain pattern. To unlock the device, the exact pattern must be repeated on the screen.
- **PIN:** Uses a private pin to secure the device. When the pin is entered correctly, the device unlocks.
- **Password:** Uses a password to secure the device. This option is the least convenient, especially if the word is complicated or long, but can be the most secure.
- **Simple Passcode:** iOS devices only. When this option is set to On, the passcode must be a four-digit number. When set to Off, more complex passwords using characters, numbers, and symbols can be used.

After a passcode is set, it must be entered each time the device is turned on or resumes from a power saving state.

To set a passcode on an Android device, use the following path:

Settings > Location & Security > Screen Lock

Then choose the type of passcode to use from the list and set the remaining Screen Security settings.

To set a passcode on an iOS device, use the following path:

Settings > General > Passcode lock > turn Passcode on

Then, enter a four-digit number. Enter the same number a second time for verification.

If the passcode for an iOS device is forgotten, you must connect it to the computer to which it was last synchronized and a restore must be performed in iTunes.

You must also perform a restore for an Android device. This is accomplished by holding down the volume buttons while turning the power on, after which a restore option is presented. Check with the manufacturer of your Android device for specific instructions.

Lab 8.4.1.2: Passcode Locks - Android and iOS

In this lab, you set a passcode lock, change a passcode lock, and fail passcode authentication. You also remove a passcode lock. Refer to Lab 8.4.1.2 in *IT Essentials: PC Hardware and Software Lab Manual*, Fifth Edition.

Restrictions on Failed Login Attempts (8.4.1.3)

To unlock a mobile device when a passcode has been properly implemented requires entering the correct PIN, password, pattern, or other passcode. In theory, a passcode such as a PIN could be guessed given enough time and perseverance. To prevent someone from trying to guess a passcode over and over, mobile devices can be set to perform defined actions after a certain number of incorrect attempts have been made.

For iOS devices, the device is disabled after five failed attempts. On the sixth failed attempt, the device remains disabled for 1 minute. Each failed attempt after six results in additional waiting time. Table 8-1 shows the results of failing to enter the correct passcode.

Table 8-1   iOS Failed Passcode Attempts

Failed Attempts	Additional Time Device Is Disabled	Total Time Device Is Disabled
1 to 5	0	0
6	1 minute	1 minute
7	5 minutes	6 minutes

Failed Attempts	Additional Time Device Is Disabled	Total Time Device Is Disabled
8	15 minutes	21 minutes
9	60 minutes	81 minutes
10	60 minutes	141 minutes
11	Device data deleted	

For extra security, turn on the **Erase all data on this device after 10 failed passcode attempts** option. If the passcode fails 11 times, the screen goes black, and all data on the device is deleted. To restore the iOS device and data, you must connect it to the computer to which it was last synchronized and use the Restore option in iTunes.

With Android devices, the number of failed attempts before lockout depends on the device and version of the Android OS. It is common that an Android device will lock when a passcode has failed from 4 to 12 times. After a device is locked, you can unlock it by entering the Gmail account information used to set up the device.

Cloud-Enabled Services for Smart Devices (8.4.2)

Cloud-enabled services such as backup storage, locator services and security services can be accessed by most mobile devices. These services help users protect data and devices.

Remote Backup (8.4.2.1)

Like desktops and laptops, mobile device data can be lost due to device failures or loss of a device. It is necessary to back up data periodically to ensure that lost data can be recovered. With mobile devices, storage is often limited, and often it is not removable. To overcome these limitations, remote backups can be performed.

A *remote backup* is when a device copies its data to a website using a *backup app*. If data needs to be restored to a device, run the backup app, connect with the website where the data is stored, and retrieve it.

iOS users are given 5 GB of storage for free. Additional storage can be purchased for a yearly fee. These are the items that iCloud can back up:

- Calendar
- Mail
- Contacts

- Content that you have purchased from the Apple App Store (This content does not count against the 5 GB total.)

- Photos that you have taken with your device

- Settings that you have configured

- App data that has accumulated from running apps

- Screen icons and locations

- Text and media messages

- Ringtones

The following items are automatically remotely backed up for Android device users:

- Calendar

- Mail

- Contacts

Google also keeps track of all apps and content that you have purchased, so they can be downloaded again. Many apps are also available to remotely back up other items. Research the apps in the Google Play Store to find backup apps that meet your needs.

Locator Applications (8.4.2.2)

If a mobile device is misplaced or stolen, it is possible to find it using a *locator app*. A locator app is usually installed and configured on each mobile device before it is lost or taken. There is also an app that can be downloaded after an Android phone is missing to send an email or text message with the location of the missing phone.

Both Android and iOS have many different apps for remotely locating a device, but most iOS users use the Find My iPhone app. The first step is to install the app, start it, and follow the instructions to configure the software. The Find My iPhone app can be installed on a different iOS device to locate the lost device. If a second iOS device is not available, the device can also be found by logging in to the iCloud website and using the Find My iPhone feature.

On Android devices, the method for locating the device is specific to the app that was installed. Log in to the website indicated by the app to find the missing Android device. Often an account needs to be created when the app is first installed. Log in to the website using this account.

After initiating the location option from a website or second iOS device, the locator app uses radios to determine the device's location. Locator apps use location data from cellular towers, Wi-Fi hotspots, and GPS:

- **Cellular towers:** The app calculates the location of the device by analyzing the signal strength from the towers to which it can connect. Because the towers are at known locations, the location of the device can be determined. This is known as *triangulation*.

- **Wi-Fi hotspots:** The app looks up the approximate location of Wi-Fi hotspots that the missing device can detect. A file containing many known hotspots and their locations is stored on the device.

- **GPS:** The app uses data from the GPS receiver to determine the location of the device.

Note

If the app is unable to locate the lost device, the device might be either turned off or disconnected. The device must be connected to either a cellular or wireless network to receive commands from the app or to send location information to the user.

After the device is located, you might be able to perform additional functions, such as sending a message or playing a sound. These options are useful if you have misplaced your device. If the device is close by, playing a sound indicates exactly where it is. If the device is at another location, sending a message to display on the screen allows someone to contact you if it has been found.

Remote Lock and Remote Wipe (8.4.2.3)

If attempts to locate a mobile device have failed, there are still security measures that can be used to prevent data on the device from being compromised. These measures can be completed using Find My iPhone from an iOS device or by using apps created to perform them. Usually the same apps that perform remote location have security measures. Two of the most common remote security measures are as follows:

- *Remote lock*: The remote lock feature allows you to lock a device with a passcode.

- *Remote wipe*: The remote wipe feature deletes all data from the device and returns it to a factory state. To restore data to the device, Android users must set up the device using a Gmail account, and iOS users must synchronize their device to iTunes.

Note

For these remote security measures to function, the device must be powered on and connected to a cellular or Wi-Fi network.

Software Security (8.4.3)

Mobile devices are subject to the same types of threats as a desktop computer and must be protected. Many applications are available to help secure software on a mobile device.

Antivirus (8.4.3.1)

Computers are vulnerable to malicious software. Smartphones and other mobile devices are computers, and therefore, also vulnerable. Antivirus apps are available for both Android and iOS. Depending on the permissions granted to antivirus apps when they are installed on an Android device, the app might not be able to scan files automatically or run scheduled scans. File scans must be initiated manually.

iOS never allows automatic or scheduled scans. This is a safety feature to prevent malicious programs from using unauthorized resources or contaminating other apps or the OS. Some antivirus apps also provide locator services, remote lock, or remote wipe.

Mobile device apps run in a sandbox. A *sandbox* is a location of the OS that keeps code isolated from other resources or code. It is difficult for malicious programs to infect a mobile device because apps are run inside the sandbox. An Android app asks for permission to access certain resources upon installation. A malicious app has access to any resources that were allowed permission during installation. It is important to download apps only from trusted sources.

Due to the nature of the sandbox, it is far more likely that a mobile device could transfer a malicious program to another device such as a laptop or desktop. For example, if a malicious program is downloaded from email, the Internet, or another device, the program could be placed on a laptop the next time it is connected.

Rooting and Jailbreaking

Mobile devices contain a *bootloader*. A bootloader is code that is run before the OS starts. This is similar to the code found in the BIOS of PCs and laptops. The bootloader provides instructions for the hardware to start the OS. Bootloaders are locked to prevent modification and access to sensitive areas of the file system. Manufacturers lock bootloaders for many reasons:

- Altering system software may damage a device.

- Untested software may be detrimental to a cellular carrier network.

- A modified OS may provide capabilities beyond what is included in a service contract.

- Access to the root directory is prevented.

The process of *rooting* Android devices and *jailbreaking* iOS devices involves unlocking the bootloader. After the bootloader is unlocked, a custom OS can be installed. Thousands of custom operating systems are available for mobile devices. These are some of the benefits of rooting or jailbreaking a mobile device:

- The user interface (UI) can be heavily customized.
- Tweaks can be made to the OS to improve the speed and responsiveness of the device.
- The CPU and graphics processing unit (GPU) can be overclocked to increase performance of the device.
- Features such as tethering that are disabled by a carrier can be enabled.
- Apps that cannot be removed from within the default OS, known as bloatware, can be removed.

Rooting and jailbreaking devices is very risky and voids the manufacturer warranty. Loading a custom OS can open up the device to malicious attacks. The custom OS may contain malicious programs, or it may not provide the same security found in the default OS. A rooted or jailbroken device greatly increases the risk of infection by a virus because it might not properly create or maintain sandboxing features. A custom OS also provides access for the user to the root directory, which means that malicious programs might also be granted access to this sensitive area of the file system.

Patching and Updating Operating Systems (8.4.3.2)

Like the OS on a desktop or laptop, you can update or patch the OS on mobile devices. Updates add functionality or increase performance. Patches can fix security problems or issues with hardware and software that do not work properly.

Because there are so many different Android mobile devices, updates and patches are not released as one package for all devices. Sometimes a new version of Android cannot install on older devices where the hardware does not meet the minimum specifications. These devices might receive patches to fix known issues, but not receive OS upgrades.

Android updates and patches use an automated process for delivery. When a carrier or manufacturer has an update for a device, it shows up as a notification on the device that an update is ready. Touch the update to begin the download and installation process.

iOS updates also use an automated process for delivery, and devices that do not meet the hardware requirements are also excluded. To check for updates to iOS, connect the device to iTunes. A notice to download opens if updates are available. To manually check for updates, click the **Check for Update** button in the iTunes Summary pane.

Applying the Troubleshooting Process to Mobile Devices (8.5.1)

This section describes how to apply the six-step troubleshooting process to mobile devices and provides some common problems and solutions for troubleshooting mobile devices.

Identify the Problem (8.5.1.1)

When troubleshooting problems with mobile devices, check to make sure the device is under warranty. If so, it can often be returned to the place of purchase for an exchange. If the device in no longer under warranty, determine if a repair is cost-effective. To determine the best course of action, compare the cost of the repair with the replacement cost of the mobile device. Because many mobile devices change rapidly in design and functionality, they are often more expensive to repair than to replace. For this reason, mobile devices are usually replaced.

Follow the steps outlined in this section to accurately identify, repair, and document the problem.

Mobile device problems can result from a combination of hardware, software, and network issues. Mobile technicians must be able to analyze the problem and determine the cause of the error to repair the mobile device. This process is called *troubleshooting*.

The first step in the troubleshooting process is to identify the problem. Table 8-2 shows a list of open-ended and closed-ended questions to ask the customer.

Table 8-2   Step 1. Identify the Problem

Open-ended questions	What is the problem you are experiencing?
	What is the make and model of your mobile device?
	What service provider do you have?
	What apps have you installed recently?
Closed-ended questions	Has this problem happened before?
	Has anyone else used the mobile device?
	Is your mobile device under warranty?
	Have you modified the operating system of the mobile device?
	Have you installed any apps from an unapproved source?
	Does the mobile device connect to the Internet?

Establish a Theory of Probable Cause (8.5.1.2)

After you have talked to the customer, you can establish a theory of probable causes. Table 8-3 shows a list of some common probable causes for mobile device problems.

Table 8-3   Step 2. Establish a Theory of Probably Cause

Common causes of mobile device problems	The power button is broken.
	The battery can no longer hold a charge.
	The mobile device cannot send or receive email.
	There is excessive dirt in the speaker, microphone, or charging port.
	The mobile device has been dropped.
	The mobile device has been submerged.
	An app has stopped working.
	A malicious app has been sideloaded.
	The mobile device has frozen.
	Mobile device software or apps are not up to date.
	A user has forgotten his or her passcode.

Test the Theory to Determine Cause (8.5.1.3)

After you have developed some theories about what is wrong, test your theories to determine the cause of the problem. Table 8-4 shows a list of quick procedures that can determine the exact cause of the problem or even correct the problem. If a quick procedure does correct the problem, you can then verify full system functionality. If a quick procedure does not correct the problem, you may need to research the problem further to establish the exact cause.

Table 8-4   Step 3. Test the Theory to Determine Cause

Common steps to determine cause	Force a running app to close.
	Reconfigure email account settings.
	Restart the mobile device.
	Plug the mobile device into an AC outlet.
	Replace the mobile device battery.
	Reset the mobile device to factory defaults.
	Restore the mobile device from a backup.
	Remove any removable battery and reinstall it.
	Connect an iOS device to iTunes.
	Clean the speaker, microphone, charging port, or other connection ports.
	Update the mobile device software and apps.

Establish a Plan of Action to Resolve the Problem and Implement the Solution (8.5.1.4)

After you have determined the exact cause of the problem, establish a plan of action to resolve the problem and implement the solution. Table 8-5 shows some sources you can use to gather additional information to resolve an issue.

Table 8-5   Step 4. Establish a Plan of Action to Resolve the Problem and Implement the Solution

If no solution is achieved in the previous step, further research is needed to implement the solution.	Help desk repair logs
	Other technicians
	Manufacturer FAQs
	Technical websites
	Device manual
	Online forums
	Internet Search

Verify Full System Functionality and Implement Preventive Measures (8.5.1.5)

After you have corrected the problem, verify full functionality and, if applicable, implement preventive measures. Table 8-6 shows a list of the steps to verify the solution.

Table 8-6   Step 5. Verify Full System Functionality and, If Applicable, Implement Preventive Measures

Verify full system functionality and, if applicable, implement preventive measures.	Reboot the mobile device.
	Browse the Internet using Wi-Fi.
	Browse the Internet using 4G, 3G, or another carrier network type.
	Make a phone call.
	Send a text message.
	Open different types of apps.
	Operate the mobile device using only the battery.

Document Findings, Actions, and Outcomes (8.5.1.6)

In the final step of the troubleshooting process, you must document your findings, actions, and outcomes. Table 8-7 shows a list of the tasks required to document the problem and the solution.

Table 8-7   Step 6. Document Findings, Actions, and Outcomes

Document your findings, actions, and outcomes	Discuss the solution implemented with the customer.
	Have the customer verify the problem has been solved.
	Provide the customer with all paperwork.
	Document the steps taken to solve the problem in the work order and technician's journal.
	Document any components used in the repair.
	Document the time spent to solve the problem.

Identify Common Problems and Solutions (8.5.2.1)

Mobile device problems can be attributed to hardware, software, networks, or some combination of the three. You will resolve some types of mobile device problems more often than others. Table 8-8 shows common mobile device problems and solutions.

Table 8-8   Common Problems and Solutions

Identify the Problem	Probable Causes	Possible Solutions
The mobile device will not connect to the Internet.	Wi-Fi is not available. Wi-Fi is turned off. Wi-Fi settings are incorrect. There is no carrier data network in range.	Move to within the boundaries of a Wi-Fi network. Turn on Wi-Fi. Reconfigure the Wi-Fi settings. Move to within the boundaries of a carrier data network.
The mobile device will not turn on.	The battery is drained. The power button is broken. The device has failed.	Charge the mobile device or replace the battery with a charged battery. Contact customer support to determine the next course of action.
An app fails to respond.	The app does not work correctly. The app failed to close correctly.	Force the app to close. Restart the mobile device. Reset the mobile device. Remove and reinsert the mobile device battery.
The mobile device cannot send or receive email.	The mobile device is not connected to the Internet. The email account settings are incorrect.	Connect the device to a Wi-Fi or cellular data network. Reconfigure the email account settings.

Identify the Problem	Probable Causes	Possible Solutions
A tablet fails to charge or charges very slowly when connected to AC power.	The tablet is in use when charging. The AC adapter does not have enough amperage.	Turn off the tablet when charging. Use the AC adapter that came with the tablet. Use an AC adapter that has the correct amount of amperage.
A smartphone cannot connect to the carrier's network.	The SIM card is not installed.	Install the SIM card.
The mobile device cannot install additional apps or save photos.	The mobile device is out of memory.	Insert a memory card or replace the memory card with a larger one. Remove unnecessary files. Uninstall unnecessary apps.
A mobile device cannot sync with a Bluetooth device.	The Bluetooth device is out of range of the mobile device. The PIN code is incorrect. The Bluetooth device is not compatible with the mobile device.	Move the Bluetooth device to within range of the mobile device. Enter the correct PIN code. Update the Bluetooth device or replace it with a compatible one.

Many mobile device problems can be solved by simply turning off the device and turning it back on. When a mobile device does not respond to a reboot, a reset may need to be performed.

These are some of the ways that Android devices can be reset, check the documentation for your mobile device to determine how to reset your device:

- Hold down the **power** button until the mobile device turns off. Turn the device on again.

- Hold down the **power** button and the **volume down** button until the mobile device turns off. Turn the device on again.

This is how iOS devices can be reset:

- Press and hold both the **Sleep/Wake** button and the **Home** button for 10 seconds, until the Apple logo appears.

In some cases, when a standard reset does not correct the problem, a factory reset may need to be performed. To perform a factory reset on an Android device, use the following path:

Settings > Backup and reset > Factory data reset > Reset device

To perform a factory reset on an iOS device, use the following path:

Settings > General > Reset > Erase All Content and Settings

Caution
A factory reset restores the device to the state it was in when it left the factory. All settings and user data are deleted from the device when a factory reset is performed. Be sure to back up any data and record any settings before performing a factory reset because all data and settings will be lost when you perform a factory reset.

Lab 8.5.2.2: Troubleshooting Mobile Devices

In this lab, you analyze scenarios involving common problems for mobile devices and identify the solutions. You have been provided with a list of solutions for common problems. Each solution may be used more than once.

After the solutions have been identified, you research and list the steps for implementing them. Refer to Lab 8.5.2.2 in *IT Essentials: PC Hardware and Software Lab Manual*, Fifth Edition.

Summary (8.6.1)

This chapter introduced you to mobile devices; the operating systems used on mobile devices; how to secure mobile devices; the uses of cloud-enabled services for mobile devices; and the way that mobile devices connect to networks, devices, and peripherals. The basics of troubleshooting mobile devices were discussed with examples of simple solutions for common problems. The following concepts from this chapter are important to remember:

- Mobile device hardware has few field-repairable units.

- Mobile devices are often replaced instead of repaired due to the high cost of repairs.

- Mobile devices often contain proprietary parts that cannot be interchanged.

- Touchscreens are used instead of other input devices, such as mice and keyboards.

- SSDs are used in mobile devices because of their size, energy efficiency, and lack of noise.

- Open source software can be modified by anyone with little or no cost.

- Use only trusted content sources to avoid malware and unreliable content.

- Both Android and iOS have similar GUIs for using apps and other content.

- Mobile devices use sensors, such as GPS and accelerometers, to enhance their functionality.

- Network connections for mobile devices are made with cellular, Wi-Fi, and Bluetooth connections.

- Email accounts are closely tied to mobile devices and provide many different data synchronization services.

- Android devices use apps to synchronize data not automatically synchronized by Google.

- iOS devices use iTunes to synchronize data and other content.

- Passcode locks secure mobile devices.

- Remote backups can be performed to back up mobile device data to the cloud.

- Remote lock and remote wipe are features to secure a mobile device that has been lost or stolen.

- Antivirus software is often used on mobile devices to prevent the transfer of malicious programs to other devices or computers.

Summary of Exercises

Labs

The following labs and worksheets cover material from this chapter. Refer to the labs and worksheets in *IT Essentials: PC Hardware and Software Lab Manual*, Fifth Edition.

Lab 8.2.2.3: Working with Android

Lab 8.2.3.3: Working with iOS

Lab 8.2.4.3: Mobile Device Features - Android and iOS

Lab 8.3.1.2: Mobile Wi-Fi - Android and iOS

Lab 8.5.2.2: Troubleshooting Mobile Devices

Worksheets

The following worksheet covers material from this chapter. Refer to the labs in *IT Essentials: PC Hardware and Software Lab Manual*, Fifth Edition.

Worksheet 8.2.4.4: Mobile Device Information

Check Your Understanding

You can find the answers to these questions in Appendix A, "Answers to 'Check Your Understanding' Questions."

1. Refer to the exhibit. Which expression best describes the pattern that is shown?

   A. A Quick Response code, which may represent a link to a download or website

   B. A 3D pattern that helps visually impaired users

   C. A standard bar code that indicates the price of an app

   D. The camera calibration pattern of a mobile device

2. What two sources of information are used to enable geocaching, geotagging, and device tracking on Android and iOS devices? (Choose two.)

   A. GPS signals

   B. Cellular or Wi-Fi network

   C. The user profile

   D. Images of the environment from the integrated camera

   E. The relative position to other mobile devices

3. Which feature of an Android or iOS mobile device helps prevent malicious programs from infecting the device?

   A. The phone carrier prevents the mobile device app from accessing some smartphone features and programs.

   B. The passcode restricts the mobile device app from access to other programs.

   C. Mobile device apps are run in a sandbox that isolates them from other resources.

   D. The remote lock feature prevents malicious programs from infecting the device.

4. Which two terms describe unlocking the bootloader of Android and iOS mobile devices to allow a new operating system to be installed? (Choose two.)

   A. Patching

   B. Rooting

   C. Remote wipe

   D. Sandboxing

   E. Jailbreaking

5. While troubleshooting a mobile device, a technician determines that the battery is not holding a charge. What is the next step in the troubleshooting process?

   A. Implement a solution.

   B. Document the findings.

   C. Determine the exact cause.

   D. Verify the solution and full system functionality.

6. A customer brings in a mobile device for repair. After asking a few questions, the service technician determines that the device is unable to connect to any Wi-Fi network. Which step of the troubleshooting process has just taken place?

   A. Identify the problem.

   B. Determine the exact cause.

   C. Implement a solution.

   D. Document findings.

   E. Establish a theory of probable causes.

7. Which statement describes a mobile device feature?

   A. When a mobile device is not operating at the speed required by the user, the user must perform a memory upgrade.

   B. Docking stations can add some functionality to mobile devices such as video output.

   C. There are no field-replaceable parts for mobile devices, but there are some that are field serviceable.

   D. Like laptops and desktops, most mobile device hardware is upgradeable.

8. Which cellular standard is an example of a 2.5G transitional standard?

   A. CDMA

   B. LTE

   C. GPRS

   D. GSM

9. Which term is used to describe the process of establishing a connection between any two Bluetooth devices?

   A. Pairing

   B. Syncing

   C. Joining

   D. Matching

10. Which statement describes the Airplane Mode feature found on most mobile devices?

   A. It automatically lowers the volume of the audio output from the device.

   B. It turns off cellular, Wi-Fi, and Bluetooth radios on the device.

   C. It allows the device to roam from one cellular network to another.

   D. It locks the device so that it cannot be used by someone else if it is lost or stolen.

Objectives

Upon completion of this chapter, you will be able to answer the following questions:

- What types of printers are currently available?
- What is the process of installation and configuration for local printers?
- How do I install and configure a local printer and scanner?
- How do I share a printer on a network?
- What does it take to upgrade printers?
- How can I identify and apply common preventive maintenance techniques to printers?
- How can I troubleshoot printers?

Key Terms

This chapter uses the following key terms. You can find the definitions in the Glossary.

pages per minute (ppm)   page 505

dots per inch (dpi)   page 505

mean time between failures (MTBF)   page 505

total cost of ownership (TCO)   page 506

serial data transfer   page 506

parallel data transfer   507

IEEE 1284   page 507

Small Computer System Interface (SCSI)   page 507

FireWire (i.LINK or IEEE 1394)   page 507

inkjet printer   page 508

thermal   page 508

piezoelectric   page 508

laser printer   page 509

processing   page 510

charging   page 510

primary corona   page 510

exposing   page 510

developing   page 510

transferring   page 510

fusing   page 510

cleaning   page 510

thermal printer   page 511

impact printer   page 511

Ethernet connection   page 513

page description language (PDL)   page 514

Printer Command Language (PCL)   page 514

PostScript (PS)   page 514

printer drivers   page 514

all-in-one device   page 518

print server   page 526

High Efficiency Particulate Air (HEPA) filtration   page 531

Introduction (9.0.1)

This chapter provides essential information about printers. You will learn how printers operate, what to consider when purchasing a printer, and how to connect printers to an individual computer or to a network.

Printers produce paper copies of electronic files. Many government regulations require physical records; therefore, hard copies of computer documents are often as important today as they were when the paperless revolution began several years ago.

You must understand the operation of various types of printers to be able to install and maintain them and to troubleshoot any problems that arise.

Common Printer Features (9.1)

The printers available today are usually either laser printers using imaging drums or inkjet printers using electrostatic spray technology. Dot-matrix printers using impact technology are used in applications that require carbon copies. Figure 9-1 shows three types of printers.

Figure 9-1   Printer Types

Characteristics and Capabilities of Printers (9.1.1.1)

As a computer technician, you might be required to purchase, repair, or maintain a printer. The customer might request that you perform the following tasks:

- Select a printer.
- Install and configure a printer.
- Troubleshoot a printer.

Capabilities and Speed

Printer capabilities and speed are factors to consider when selecting a printer. The speed of a printer is measured in *pages per minute (ppm)*. Printer speed varies between makes and models. Speed is also affected by the complexity of the image and the quality desired by the user. For example, a draft-quality page of text prints faster than a high-quality page of text. A draft-quality image of a color digital photograph prints faster than a photo-quality print. Inkjet printers are usually slower, but they are often sufficient for a home or small office.

Color or Black and White

A computer monitor produces colors through the additive mixing of dots that are displayed on the screen. The dots produce the color range using red, green, and blue (RGB) dots. In contrast, a printer produces colors using subtractive mixing. The CMYK color model is a subtractive color model used in color printing. CMYK is the acronym for a color system composed of four colors (cyan, magenta, yellow, and black, with black represented by Key, as a base color).

The choice between a black-and-white printer and a color printer depends on the needs of the customer. If the customer is primarily printing letters and does not need color capability, a black-and-white printer is sufficient and can be less expensive. An elementary school teacher might need a color printer to add excitement to lessons.

Quality

The quality of printing is measured in *dots per inch (dpi)*. The larger the dpi number, the better the image resolution. When the resolution is higher, text and images are clearer. To produce the best high-resolution images, use high-quality ink or toner and high-quality paper.

Reliability

A printer should be reliable. Because so many types of printers are on the market, research the specifications of several printers before selecting one. Here are some manufacturer options to consider:

- **Warranty:** Identify what is covered within the warranty.
- **Scheduled servicing:** Servicing is based on expected usage. Usage information is in the documentation or on the manufacturer's website.
- *Mean time between failures (MTBF)*: The printer should work without failing for an average length of time. This information is in the documentation or on the manufacturer's website.

Total Cost of Ownership

When buying a printer, there is more than just the initial cost of the printer to consider. The *total cost of ownership (TCO)* includes a number of factors:

- Initial purchase price
- Cost of supplies, such as paper and ink
- Pages per month
- Price per page
- Maintenance costs
- Warranty costs

When calculating the TCO, consider the amount of printing required and the expected lifetime of the printer.

Wired Printer Connection Types (9.1.1.2)

A printer must have a compatible interface with the computer to print. Printers usually connect to home computers using a parallel, USB, or wireless interface. Figure 9-2 shows examples of the various connection types. Printers may connect to a network using a network cable or a wireless interface.

Figure 9-2   Printer Connection Types

Serial

Serial data transfer is the movement of single bits of information in a single cycle. A serial connection can be used for dot-matrix printers because the printers do not require high-speed data transfer.

Parallel

Parallel data transfer is faster than serial data transfer. Parallel data transfer moves multiple bits of information in a single cycle. The data transfer path is wider than the serial data transfer path, allowing data to move more quickly to or from the printer.

IEEE 1284 is the standard for parallel printer ports. Enhanced Parallel Port (EPP) and Enhanced Capabilities Port (ECP) are two modes of operation within the IEEE 1284 standard that allow bidirectional communication.

SCSI

Small Computer System Interface (SCSI) uses parallel communication technology to achieve high data-transfer rates.

USB

USB is a common interface for printers and other devices. When a USB device is added to a computer system that supports plug and play, the device is automatically detected and starts the driver installation process.

FireWire

FireWire, also known as i.LINK or IEEE 1394, is a high-speed communication bus that is platform independent. FireWire connects digital devices such as digital printers, scanners, digital cameras, and hard drives.

FireWire allows a peripheral device, such as a printer, to plug directly into a computer. It also allows the device to be hot-swappable. FireWire provides a single plug-and-socket connection that can attach up to 63 devices. FireWire has a data transfer rate of up to 400 Mb/s.

Ethernet

Connecting a printer to the network requires cabling that is compatible with both the network and the network port installed in the printer. Most network printers use an RJ-45 interface to connect to a network or wireless interface.

Types of Printers (9.2)

This section describes the characteristics of many types of printers. Knowing the features and characteristics of different printer types is necessary to make the best choice for the printer use.

Inkjet Printers (9.2.1.1)

Inkjet printers produce high-quality prints. Inkjet printers are easy to use and somewhat less expensive when compared with laser printers. The print quality of an inkjet printer is measured in dots per inch (dpi). Higher dpi numbers provide better image details. Some all-in-one devices contain inkjet printers. Figure 9-3 shows inkjet printer components.

Figure 9-3   Printer Types

Inkjet printers use ink cartridges that spray ink onto a page through tiny holes. The tiny holes are called nozzles and are located in the print head. The print head and ink cartridges are located on the carriage, which is attached to a belt and motor. As rollers pull paper in from the feeder, the belt moves the carriage back and forth along the paper as the ink is sprayed in a pattern on the page.

There are two types of inkjet nozzles:

- *Thermal*: A pulse of electrical current is applied to heating chambers around the nozzles. The heat creates a bubble of steam in the chamber. The steam forces ink out through the nozzle and onto the paper.

- *Piezoelectric*: Piezoelectric crystals are located in the ink reservoir at the back of each nozzle. A charge is applied to the crystal, causing it to vibrate. This vibration of the crystal controls the flow of ink onto the paper.

Inkjet printers use plain paper to make economical prints. Special-purpose paper can be used to create high-quality prints of photographs. An inkjet printer with a duplex assembly can print on both sides of a sheet of paper. When the paper leaves the printer, the ink is often wet. You should avoid touching printouts for 10 to 15 seconds to prevent smearing. If inkjet printer quality degrades, check the printer calibration by using the printer software.

Table 9-1 lists some advantages and disadvantages of an inkjet printer:

Table 9-1   Inkjet Printer Pros and Cons

Advantages	Disadvantages
Initial low cost	Nozzles are prone to clogging.
High resolution	Ink cartridges are expensive.
Quick to warm up	Ink is wet after printing.

Laser Printers (9.2.1.2)

A *laser printer* is a high-quality, fast printer that uses a laser beam to create an image. Figure 9-4 is an example of a laser printer.

Figure 9-4   Laser Printer

The central part of the laser printer is its imaging drum. The drum is a metal cylinder that is coated with a light-sensitive insulating material. When a beam of laser light strikes the drum, it becomes a conductor at the point where the light hits it.

As the drum rotates, the laser beam draws an electrostatic image upon the drum. The undeveloped or latent image is passed by a supply of dry ink or toner that is attracted to it. While the image is being exposed on the drum, an individual sheet of paper has been pressed between a separation pad and pickup roller and is fed toward the drum.

The drum turns and brings the exposed image in contact with the paper, which attracts the ink from the drum. The paper is then passed through a fuser assembly that is made up of hot rollers, which melts the toner into the paper.

Printing Process

The laser printer process involves seven steps to print information onto a single sheet of paper.

1. *Processing*: The data from the source must be converted into a printable form. The printer converts data from common languages, such as Adobe PostScript (PS) or HP Printer Command Language (PCL), to a bitmap image stored in the printer's memory. Some laser printers have built-in Graphical Device Interface (GDI) support. GDI is used by Windows applications to display printed images on a monitor so there is no need to convert the output to another format such as PostScript or PCL.

2. *Charging*: The previous latent image on the drum is removed and the drum is conditioned for the new latent image. A wire, grid, or roller receives a charge of approximately –600V DC uniformly across the surface of the drum. The charged wire or grid is called the *primary corona*. The roller is called a conditioning roller.

3. *Exposing*: To write the image, the photosensitive drum is exposed with the laser beam. Every portion of the drum that is scanned with the light has the surface charge reduced to about –100V DC. This electrical charge has a lower negative charge than the remainder of the drum. As the drum turns, an invisible latent image is created on the drum.

4. *Developing*: The toner is applied to the latent image on the drum. The toner is a negatively charged combination of plastic and metal particles. A control blade holds the toner at a microscopic distance from the drum. The toner then moves from the control blade to the more positively charged latent image on the drum.

5. *Transferring*: The toner attached to the latent image is transferred to the paper. A corona wire places a positive charge on the paper. Because the drum was charged negatively, the toner on the drum is attracted to the paper. The image is now on the paper and is held in place by the positive charge. Because color printers have three cartridges of ink, a colored image must go through multiple transfers to be complete. To ensure precise images, some color printers write multiple times onto a transfer belt that transfers the complete image to paper.

6. *Fusing*: The toner is permanently fused to the paper. The printing paper is rolled between a heated roller and a pressure roller. As the paper moves through the rollers, the loose toner is melted and fused with the fibers in the paper. The paper is then moved to the output tray as a printed page. Laser printers with duplex assemblies can print on both sides of a sheet of paper.

7. *Cleaning:* When an image has been deposited on the paper and the drum has separated from the paper, the remaining toner must be removed from the drum. A printer might have a blade that scrapes the excess toner. Some printers use an AC voltage on a wire that removes the charge from the drum surface and allows the excess toner to fall away from the drum. The excess toner is stored in a used toner container that is either emptied or discarded.

Table 9-2 lists some advantages and disadvantages of a laser printer:

Table 9-2   Laser Printer Pros and Cons

Advantages	Disadvantages
Low cost per page	High cost of startup
High ppm	Toner cartridges are expensive
High capacity	Requires a high level of maintenance
Prints are dry	

Thermal Printers (9.2.1.3)

Some retail cash registers or older fax machines might contain *thermal printers*. Thermal paper is chemically treated and has a waxy quality. Thermal paper becomes black when heated. After a roll of thermal paper is loaded, the feed assembly moves the paper through the printer. Electrical current is sent to the heating element in the print head to generate heat. The heated areas of the print head make the pattern on the paper.

Table 9-3 lists some advantages and disadvantages of a thermal printer:

Table 9-3   Thermal Printer Pros and Cons

Advantages	Disadvantages
Longer life because there are few moving parts	Paper is expensive.
Quiet operation	Paper has a short shelf life.
No cost for ink or toner	Images are poor quality.
	Paper must be stored at room temperature.
	Color printing is not available.

Impact Printers (9.2.1.4)

Impact printers have print heads that strike an inked ribbon, causing characters to be imprinted on the paper. Dot matrix and daisy wheel are examples of impact printers. Figure 9-5 is an example of an impact printer.

Figure 9-5   Impact Printer

Table 9-4 lists some advantages and disadvantages of an impact printer.

Table 9-4   Impact Printer Pros and Cons

Advantages	Disadvantages
Uses less-expensive ink than inkjet or laser printers	Noisy
	Low-resolution graphics
Uses continuous feed paper	Limited color capability
Has carbon-copy printing ability	

Types of Impact Printers

A daisy wheel printer uses a wheel that contains letters, numbers, and special characters. The wheel rotates until the required character is in place, and then an electromechanical hammer pushes the character into the ink ribbon. The character then strikes the paper, imprinting the character on the paper.

A dot-matrix printer is similar to a daisy wheel printer, except that it has a print head containing pins that are surrounded by electromagnets instead of a wheel. When energized, the pins push forward onto the ink ribbon, creating a character on the paper. The number of pins on a print head, 9 or 24, indicates the quality of the print. The highest quality of print that is produced by the dot-matrix printer is referred to as near letter quality (NLQ).

Most dot-matrix printers use continuous-feed paper, also known as tractor feed. The paper has perforations between each sheet, and perforated strips on the side are used to feed the paper and to prevent skewing or shifting. Sheet feeders that print one page at a time are available for some higher quality printers. A large roller, called the platen, applies pressure to keep the paper from slipping. If a multiple-copy paper is used, you can adjust the platen gap to the thickness of the paper.

Installing and Configuring Printers (9.3)

A printer has become a commonly added peripheral device for computer users. Once the type of printer needed has been decided and the printer purchased then next step is installing and configuring the device. This section provides information about both the installation and configuration of a printer.

Installing a Printer (9.3.1.1)

When you purchase a printer, the installation and configuration information is usually supplied by the manufacturer. An installation CD that includes the drivers, manuals, and diagnostic software is included with the printer. If there is no CD, you can download the tools from the manufacturer's website.

Although all types of printers are somewhat different to connect and configure, there are procedures that should be applied to all printers. Before you install a printer, remove all packing material. Remove anything that prevents moving parts from shifting during shipping. To return the printer to the manufacturer for warranty services, it should be returned in the original packing materials.

Note

Before connecting the printer to the PC, read the installation instructions. In some cases, the printer driver needs to be installed first before the printer is connected to the PC.

You can connect and use a printer as a local or network printer. Some printers can be connected as both local and network. A local printer is connected directly to a computer port, such as a USB, parallel, or serial port. The local computer manages and sends the print jobs to the printer. Local printers can be shared over the network with other users. A network printer is connected to a network using a wireless or *Ethernet connection*. The network printer allows multiple users to send documents to the printer over the network.

If the printer has a USB, FireWire, or parallel port, connect the corresponding cable to the printer port. Connect the other end of the data cable to the corresponding port on the back of the computer. If you are installing a network printer, connect the network cable to the network port.

After the data cable has been properly connected, attach the power cable to the printer. Connect the other end of the power cable to an available electrical outlet. When you turn on the power to the device, the computer tries to determine the correct device driver to install.

Caution

Never plug a printer into a UPS. The power surge that occurs when the printer is turned on damages the UPS unit.

Printers can be shared over a network. Connecting a printer to a network requires cabling that is compatible with both the existing network and the network port installed in the printer. Most network printers use an RJ-45 interface to connect to a network.

Note

Always check the packaging for cables when you buy a printer. Many manufacturers keep production costs down by not including a cable with the printer. If you have to buy a cable, be sure that you buy the correct type.

Lab 9.3.1.2: Install a Printer in Windows 7

In this lab, you install a printer. You will find, download, and update the driver and the software for the printer. Refer to Lab 9.3.1.2 in *IT Essentials: PC Hardware and Software Lab Manual*, Fifth Edition.

Lab 9.3.1.3: Install a Printer in Windows Vista

In this lab, you install a printer. You will find, download, and update the driver and the software for the printer. Refer to Lab 9.3.1.3 in *IT Essentials: PC Hardware and Software Lab Manual*, Fifth Edition.

Lab 9.3.1.4: Install a Printer in Windows XP

In this lab, you install a printer. You will find, download, and update the driver and the software for the printer. Refer to Lab 9.3.1.4 in *IT Essentials: PC Hardware and Software Lab Manual*, Fifth Edition.

Types of Print Drivers (9.3.1.5)

Printer drivers are software programs that make it possible for computers and printers to communicate with each other. Configuration software provides an interface that enables users to set and change printer options. Every printer model has its own type of driver and configuration software.

Page Description Language (PDL) is a type of code that describes the appearance of a document in a language that a printer can understand. The PDL for a page includes the text, graphics, and formatting information. A software application uses a PDL to send What You See Is What You Get (WYSIWYG) images to the printer. The printer translates the PDL file so that whatever is on the computer screen is what is printed. PDLs speed up the printing process by sending large amounts of data at one time. They also manage the computer fonts.

Adobe Systems developed *PostScript* to allow fonts and text types to share the same characteristics on the screen as on paper. Hewlett-Packard developed *Printer Command Language (PCL)* for communication with early inkjet printers. PCL is now an industry standard for nearly all printer types.

Table 9-5 is a PostScript and PCL comparison.

Table 9-5   PostScript and PCL Comparison

PostScript	PCL
Page is rendered by the printer.	Page is rendered on local workstation.
Better quality output.	Faster print job.
Handles more complex print jobs.	Requires less printer memory.
Output is identical on different printers.	Output varies slightly on different printers.

Updating and Installing Print Drivers (9.3.1.6)

After you have connected the power and data cables to the printer, the operating system discovers the printer and installs the driver.

A printer driver is a software program that enables the computer and the printer to communicate with each other. The driver also provides an interface for the user to configure printer options. Each printer model has a unique driver. Printer manufacturers often update drivers to increase the performance of the printer, to add options, or to fix problems. You can download updated printer drivers from the manufacturer's website.

How To

To install a printer driver, follow these steps:

Step 1.   **Determine whether a newer driver is available.** Most manufacturers' websites have a link to a page that offers drivers and support. Make sure that the driver is compatible with the computer and operating system that you are updating.

Step 2.   **Download the printer driver files to your computer.** Most driver files are compressed or "zipped." Download the file to a folder and uncompress the contents. Save instructions or documentation to a separate folder on your computer.

Step 3.   **Install the downloaded driver.** Install the downloaded driver automatically or manually. Most printer drivers have a setup file that automatically searches the system for older drivers and replaces them with the new one. If no setup file is available, follow the directions supplied by the manufacturer.

Step 4.   **Test the new printer driver.** Run multiple tests to make sure that the printer works properly. Use a variety of applications to print different types of documents. Change and test each printer option.

The printed test page should contain text that is readable. If the text is unreadable, the problem could be a bad driver program or the wrong PDL is being used.

Printer Test Page (9.3.1.7)

After installing a printer, print a test page to verify that the printer is operating properly. The test page confirms that the driver software is installed and working correctly and that the printer and computer are communicating.

Print Test Page

To manually print a test page in Windows 7, use the following path:

Step 1.   Choose **Start > Devices and Printers.**

Step 2.   The Devices and Printers control panel appears. Right-click the desired printer.

Step 3.   Follow this path: **Printer Properties > General** tab **> Print Test Page.**

To manually print a test page in Windows Vista, use the following path:

Step 1.   Choose **Start > Control Panel > Printers** to display the Printers and Faxes menu.

Step 2.   In the Printers and Faxes menu, right-click the desired printer.

Step 3.   Follow this path: **Properties > General** tab **> Print Test Page.**

A dialog box asks if the page printed correctly. If the page did not print, built-in help files assist you in troubleshooting the problem.

To manually print a test page in Windows XP, use the following path:

Step 1.   Choose **Start > Printers and Faxes** to display the Printers and Faxes menu.

Step 2.   In the Printers and Faxes menu, right-click the printer and select **Properties > General** tab > **Print Test Page**.

Print from an Application

You can test the printer by printing a test page from an application, such as Notepad or WordPad. To access Notepad in Windows 7, Windows Vista, and Windows XP, use the following path:

Start > All Programs > Accessories > Notepad

In the blank document that opens, type some text. Print the document using the following path:

File > Print

Test the Printer

You can print from the command line to test the printer. Printing from the command line is limited to ASCII files only, such as .txt and .bat files.

To send a file to the printer from the command line in Windows 7, complete the following steps:

Step 1.   Click the **Start** button. In the Search programs and files field, type **cmd** and then click **OK**.

Step 2.   At the command line prompt, enter the command **Print** *filename*.**txt.**

To send a file to the printer from the command line in Windows Vista, complete the following steps:

Step 1.   **Start > Start Search**. In the Run box, type **cmd** and then click **OK**.

Step 2.   At the command-line prompt, enter the command **Print** *filename*.txt.

To send a file to the printer from the command line in Windows XP, complete the following steps:

Step 1.   Select **Start > Run**. In the Run box, type **cmd**, and then click **OK**.

Step 2.   At the command-line prompt, enter the command **Print** *filename*.txt.

Test the Printer from the Printer Panel

Most printers have a front panel with controls to allow you to generate test pages. This method of printing enables you to verify the printer operation separately from the network or computer. Consult the printer manufacturer's website or documentation to learn how to print a test page from the front panel of the printer.

The installation of any device is not complete until you have successfully tested all its functions. Printer functions might include the following:

- Print double-sided documents.
- Use different paper trays for different paper sizes.
- Change the settings of a color printer so that it prints in black and white or grayscale.
- Print in draft mode.
- Use an optical character recognition (OCR) application.

For an *all-in-one device*, all the functions:

- Fax to another known working fax.
- Create a copy of a document.
- Scan a document.
- Print a document.

Note

For information on clearing paper jams, installing ink cartridges, and loading the paper trays, check the manufacturer's documentation or website.

Configuring Options and Default Settings (9.3.2)

For some installations using the default settings on the printer will be just fine, but others will require customization to the printer settings. This section identifies the common configurable settings and methods to configure them.

Common Configuration Settings (9.3.2.1)

Each printer may have different configurations and default options. Check the printer documentation for specific information about its configuration and default settings. Figure 9-6 shows an example of printer configuration settings.

Figure 9-6   Printer Configuration Settings

Here are some common configuration options available for printers:

- **Paper type:** Standard, draft, gloss, or photo

- **Print quality:** Draft, normal, or photo

- **Color printing:** Multiple colors are used

- **Black-and-white printing:** Only black ink is used

- **Grayscale printing:** Images printed using only black ink in different shades

- **Paper size:** Standard paper sizes or envelopes and business cards

- **Paper orientation:** Landscape or portrait

- **Print layout:** Normal, banner, booklet, or poster

- **Duplex:** Two-sided printing

Common printer options that the user can configure include media control and printer output.

The following media control options set the way a printer manages media:

- Input paper tray selection

- Output path selection

- Media size and orientation

- Paper weight selection

The following printer output options manage how the ink or toner goes on the media:

- Color management

- Print speed

Global and Individual Document Options (9.3.2.2)

Some printers have control panels with buttons to select options. Other printers use the printer driver options. You can set options globally or per document.

Global Method

The global method refers to printer options that are set to affect all documents. Each time a document is printed, the global options are used, unless they are overridden by per document selections.

To change the global configuration of a printer in Windows 7, use the following path:

Start > Control Panel > Devices and Printers > right-click the printer

To designate a default printer, right-click the printer and select **Set as default printer**, as shown in the figure.

To change the orientation of the page to landscape in Windows 7, right-click the printer and select **Printing Preferences**. In the Layout tab, select **Landscape** in the **Orientation** drop-down menu. Click **OK**.

To change the global configuration of a printer in Windows Vista and Windows XP, use the following path:

Start > Control Panel > Printers and Faxes > right-click the printer

To designate a default printer, right-click the printer and select **Set as default printer**.

> **Note**
>
> Depending on the driver installed, the Set as default printer option might not be available. In this case, double-click the printer to open the Document Status window, and then choose **Printer > Set as default printer**.

Per Document Method

Letters, spreadsheets, and digital images are some of the document types that may require special printer settings. You can change the settings for an individual document by changing the document print settings.

Optimizing Printer Performance (9.3.3)

This section discusses enhancing printer performance. Printer uses and installations vary; it is always a good practice to download the vendor drivers to have access to all the available printer features if they are needed. Many printers also have upgradable hardware components that can improve performance. Information on upgradable components can be found in the manufacturer's documentation.

Software Optimization (9.3.3.1)

With printers, most optimization is completed through the software supplied with the drivers.

The following tools optimize performance:

- **Print spool settings:** Cancel or pause current print jobs in the printer queue.
- **Color calibration:** Adjust settings to match the colors on the screen to the colors on the printed sheet.
- **Paper orientation:** Select landscape or portrait image layout.

Printers are calibrated using the print driver software. Calibration makes sure that the print heads are aligned and that they can print on different kinds of media, such as cardstock, photographic paper, and optical discs. Some inkjet print heads are fitted to the ink cartridge, so you might have to recalibrate the printer each time you change a cartridge.

Hardware Optimization (9.3.3.2)

Some printers can be upgraded to print faster and to accommodate more print jobs by adding hardware. The hardware may include additional paper trays, sheet feeders, network cards, and expansion memory.

Firmware

Firmware is a set of instructions stored on the printer. The firmware controls how the printer operates. The procedure to upgrade firmware is similar to installing printer drivers. Because firmware updates do not take place automatically, visit the home page of the printer manufacturer to check the availability of new firmware.

Printer Memory

Upgrading the printer memory increases the printing speed and enhances complex print job performance. All printers have RAM. The more memory a printer has, the more efficiently it works. The added memory helps with tasks such as job buffering, page creation, improved photo printing, and graphics.

Print job buffering is when a print job is captured in the internal printer memory. Buffering allows the computer to continue with other work instead of waiting for the printer to finish. Buffering is a common feature in laser printers and plotters, as well as in advanced inkjet and dot-matrix printers.

Printers usually arrive from the factory with enough memory to handle jobs that involve text. However, print jobs involving graphics, and especially photographs, run more efficiently if the printer memory is adequate to store the entire job before it starts. If you receive low memory errors, this can indicate that the printer is out of memory or has a memory overload. In this instance, you may need more memory.

Installing Printer Memory

Before installing additional printer memory, read the printer documentation to determine the following:

- **Memory type:** Physical type of memory, its speed, and capacity. Some memory types are standard, and some printers require special or proprietary memory.

- **Memory population and availability:** Number of memory upgrade slots in use and how many are available. You might have to open a compartment to check the RAM.

Printer manufacturers have set procedures for upgrading memory, including the following tasks:

- Removing covers to access the memory area

- Installing or removing memory

- Initializing the printer to recognize the new memory

- Installing updated drivers if needed

Additional Printer Upgrades

Some printers allow additional printer upgrades:

- Duplex printing to enable dual-sided printing

- Extra trays to hold more paper

- Specialized tray types for different media

- Network cards to access a wired or wireless network

- Firmware upgrades to add functionality or to fix bugs

Follow the instructions included with the printer when you install or upgrade components. Contact the manufacturer or an authorized service technician for additional information if you have any problems when installing upgrades. Follow all safety procedures outlined by the manufacturer.

Sharing Printers (9.4)

Printer sharing is an effective way to give users access to the printer while saving on hardware purchases. This section outlines the processes to share a printer in Windows operating systems.

Configuring Printer Sharing (9.4.1.1)

To connect to the printer from another computer on the network in Windows 7, follow these steps:

Step 1.   Choose **Start > Devices and Printers > Add a Printer.**

Step 2.   The Add Printer wizard appears.

Step 3.   Select **Add a network, wireless or Bluetooth printer.**

Step 4.   A list of shared printers will appear. If the printer is not listed, select **The printer that I wanted is not listed.**

Step 5.   After selecting the printer, click **Next.**

Step 6.   A virtual printer port is created and displayed in the Add a Printer window. The required print drivers are downloaded from the print server and installed on the computer. The wizard then finishes the installation.

To connect to the printer from another computer on the network in Windows Vista, follow these steps:

Step 1.   Choose **Start > Control Panel > Printers > Add a Printer.**

Step 2.   The Add Printer wizard appears.

Step 3.   Select **Add a network, wireless or Bluetooth printer.**

Step 4.   A list of shared printers will appear. If the printer is not listed, select **The printer that I wanted is not listed.**

Step 5.   After selecting the printer, click **Next.**

Step 6.   A virtual printer port is created and displayed in the Add a Printer window. The required print drivers are downloaded from the print server and installed on the computer. The wizard then finishes the installation.

To connect to the printer from another computer on the network in Windows XP, follow these steps:

Step 1.   Choose **Start > Devices and Printers > Add a Printer.**

Step 2.   The Add Printer wizard appears.

Step 3.   Select **Add a network, wireless or Bluetooth printer.**

Step 4.   A list of shared printers will appear. If the printer is not listed, select **The printer that I wanted is not listed.**

Step 5.   After selecting the printer, click **Next.**

Step 6.   A virtual printer port is created and displayed in the Add a Printer window. The required print drivers are downloaded from the print server and installed on the computer. The wizard then finishes the installation.

Windows allows computer users to share their printers with other users on the network.

In Windows 7, to configure the computer with the printer attached to accept print jobs from other network users, as shown in Figure 9-7, follow these steps:

Step 1.   Select **Start > Control Panel > Network and Sharing Center > Change advanced sharing settings.**

Step 2.   Expand the network listing to view the network profile.

Step 3.   If printer sharing is off, under File and printer sharing, select **Turn on file and printer sharing**, and then click **Save changes.**

Figure 9-7   Sharing a Printer

In Windows Vista, to configure the computer with the printer attached to accept print jobs from other network users, follow these steps:

Step 1.   Select **Start > Control Panel > Hardware and Sound > Printers.**

Step 2.   Right-click the printer to share and choose **Sharing.** The Printer Properties dialog box opens.

Step 3.   Select **Share this printer** and enter the desired shared printer name. This name is displayed to other users.

Step 4.   Verify that sharing has been successful. In the Printers window, check whether the printer has a share icon under it, indicating that it is a shared resource.

In Windows XP, to configure the computer with the printer attached to accept print jobs from other network users, as shown in Figure 9-8, follow these steps:

Step 1.   Select **Start > Control Panel > Printers and Other Hardware > Printers and Faxes.**

Step 2.   Select the printer to share. The **Printer Tasks** box appears on the left.

Step 3.   Select **Share this printer.** The Printer Properties dialog box opens.

Step 4.   In the Sharing tab, select **Share this printer** and enter the printer name. This name is displayed to other users.

Step 5.   Verify that sharing has been successful. In the Printers and Faxes folder, check whether the printer icon has a hand under it, indicating that it is a shared resource.

Figure 9-8   XP Share a Printer Wizard

Users who can now connect to the shared printer might not have the required drivers installed. They might also be using different operating systems than the computer that is hosting the shared printer. Windows can automatically download the correct drivers to these users. Click the **Additional Drivers** button to select operating systems that the other users are using. When you close that dialog box by clicking **OK,** Windows will ask to obtain those additional drivers. If the other users are also using the same Windows OS, you do not need to click the **Additional Drivers** button.

Wireless Printer Connections (9.4.1.2)

Wireless printers allow hosts to connect and print wirelessly using Bluetooth, 802.11x, or infrared (IR). For wireless printers to use Bluetooth, both the printer and the host device must have Bluetooth capabilities and be paired. If necessary, you can add a Bluetooth adapter to the computer, usually in a USB port. Wireless Bluetooth printers allow for easy printing from mobile devices.

Wireless printers designed for 802.11 standards are equipped with installed wireless NICs and connect directly to a wireless router or access point. Setup is completed by connecting the printer to the computer with the supplied software or using the printer display panel to connect to the wireless router

IR printing, the earliest form of wireless printing, requires transmitters and receivers on both devices. Both devices must have a clear line of sight between the transmitter and receiver, with a maximum distance of 12 feet (3.7 m).

Print Servers (9.4.2)

Print servers can be wireless, internal, external, or embedded devices. The *print server* is the device that interfaces between a computer and a printer. This section discusses the purpose and function of print servers.

Purposes of Print Servers (9.4.2.1)

Many printers usually require a separate print server to allow network connectivity because these printers do not have built-in network interfaces. A hardware print server is a device that is not a computer; it is a device with a network card and memory. It connects to the network and printers to enable printers to be shared over the network.

A computer can also be used as a print server. Most personal computer operating systems have built-in printer sharing capability.

Print servers enable multiple computer users to access a single printer. A print server has three functions:

- Provide client access to print resources
- Administrate print jobs by storing them in a queue until the print device is ready for them and then feeding or spooling the print information to the printer
- Provide feedback to users

Network, Dedicated, and Computer Shared Print Servers (9.4.2.2)

Hardware Print Servers

Hardware print servers allow many users on a network to access a single printer. A hardware print server can manage network printing through either wired or wireless connections. An advantage of using a hardware print server is that the server accepts incoming print jobs from computers, thereby freeing the computers for other tasks. A hardware print server is always available to users, unlike a printer shared from a user's computer.

Dedicated PC Print Servers

A dedicated PC print server handles client print jobs in the most efficient manner and can manage more than one printer at a time. A print server must have the following resources to meet the requests of print clients:

- **Powerful processor:** Because the PC print server uses its processor to manage and route printing information, it must be fast enough to handle all incoming requests.

- **Adequate hard disk space:** A PC print server captures print jobs from clients, places them in a print queue, and sends them to the printer in a timely way. This process requires the computer to have enough storage space to hold these jobs until completed.

- **Adequate memory:** The server processor and RAM handle sending print jobs to a printer. If server memory is not large enough to handle an entire print job, the hard drive must send the job, which is much slower.

Computer-Shared Printers

A computer that has a printer attached can share that printer with other users on the network. For example, in a home network, users can print documents from wherever they are in the house by using a wireless laptop. In a small office network, sharing a printer means one printer can serve many users.

Sharing a printer from a computer also has disadvantages. The computer sharing the printer uses its own resources to manage the print jobs coming to the printer. If the computer user on the desktop is working at the same time as a user on the network is printing, the desktop computer user might notice a performance slowdown. In addition, the printer is not available to others if the user reboots or powers off the computer with a shared printer.

 Lab 9.4.2.3: Share a Printer in Windows 7

In this lab, you share a printer, configure the printer on a networked computer, and print a test page from the remote computer. Refer to Lab 9.4.2.3 in *IT Essentials: PC Hardware and Software Lab Manual*, Fifth Edition.

Lab 9.4.2.4: Share a Printer in Windows Vista

In this lab, you install a printer. You will find, download, and update the driver and the software for the printer. Refer to Lab 9.4.2.4 in *IT Essentials: PC Hardware and Software Lab Manual*, Fifth Edition.

Lab 9.4.2.5: Share a Printer in Windows XP

In this lab, you install a printer. You will find, download, and update the driver and the software for the printer. Refer to Lab 9.4.2.5 in *IT Essentials: PC Hardware and Software Lab Manual*, Fifth Edition.

Preventive Maintenance Techniques for Printers (9.5)

Preventive maintenance is a proactive way to decrease printer problems and increase the life span of the hardware. Using manufacturer's guidelines, a preventive maintenance plan should be established and implemented. This section examines preventive maintenance guidelines and best practices.

Vendor Guidelines (9.5.1.1)

Preventive maintenance decreases downtime and increases the service life of the components. It is important to maintain printers to keep them working properly. A good maintenance program guarantees good quality prints and uninterrupted operation. The printer documentation contains information on how to maintain and clean the equipment.

Read the information manuals that come with every new piece of equipment. Follow the recommended maintenance instructions. Use the supplies listed by the manufacturer. Less expensive supplies can save money, but may produce poor results, damage the equipment, or void the warranty.

Caution

Be sure to unplug the printer from the electrical source before beginning any type of maintenance.

When maintenance is completed, reset the counters to allow the next maintenance to be completed at the correct time. On many types of printers, the page count is viewed through the LCD display or a counter located inside the main cover.

Most manufacturers sell maintenance kits for their printers. For laser printers, the kit might contain replacement parts that often break or wear out:

- Fuser assembly
- Transfer rollers
- Separation pads
- Pickup rollers

Figure 9-9 shows a maintenance kit that includes replacements for parts that often break or wear out.

Figure 9-9   Maintenance Kit

When you install new parts or replace toners and cartridges, visually inspect all internal components and perform the following tasks:

- Remove bits of paper and dust.
- Clean spilled ink or toner.
- Look for worn gears, cracked plastic, or broken parts.

If you do not know how to maintain printing equipment, call a manufacturer-certified technician.

Replacing Consumables (9.5.1.2)

The type and quality of paper and ink used can affect the life of the printer. Many types of printer paper are available, including inkjet and laser. The printer manufacturer might recommend which type of paper to use for best results. Some papers, especially photo paper, transparencies, and multilayered carbon paper, have a right and wrong side. Load the paper according to the manufacturer's instructions.

The manufacturer recommends the brand and type of ink to use. If the wrong type of ink is installed, the printer might not work or the print quality might deteriorate. Avoid refilling ink cartridges because the ink can leak.

When an inkjet printer produces blank pages, the ink cartridges might be empty. Some inkjet printers may refuse to print any pages if one of the ink cartridges is empty. Laser printers do not produce blank pages. Instead, they begin to print poor quality prints. Most inkjet printers have a utility that shows ink levels in each cartridge, as shown in Figure 9-10. Some printers have LCD message screens or LED lights that warn users when ink supplies are low.

Figure 9-10   Estimated Ink Levels

A method for checking ink levels is to look at the page counter inside the printer or the printer software to determine how many pages have been printed. Then look at the cartridge label information. The label should show how many pages the cartridge can print. You can then easily estimate how many more pages you can print. To help keep track of usage, each time you replace the cartridge, reset the counter. In addition, some printouts use more ink than others do. For example, a letter uses less ink than a photograph.

You can set the printer software to toner save or draft quality to reduce the amount of ink or toner that the printer uses. These settings also reduce the print quality of laser and inkjet products, as well as the time it takes to print a document on an inkjet printer.

An impact printer is similar to a typewriter because the print head strikes an inked ribbon to transfer ink to the printout. When the impact printer produces faded or light characters, the ribbon is worn out and needs to be replaced. If a consistent flaw is produced in all characters, the print head is stuck or broken and needs to be replaced.

Cleaning Methods (9.5.1.3)

Always follow the manufacturer's guidelines when cleaning printers. Information on the manufacturer's website or documentation explains the proper cleaning methods.

Caution

Unplug printers before cleaning to prevent danger from high voltage.

Printer Maintenance

Make sure that you turn off and unplug any printer before performing maintenance. Use a damp cloth to wipe off dirt, paper dust, and spilled ink on the exterior of the device.

On some printers, print heads in an inkjet printer are replaced when the cartridges are replaced. However, sometimes print heads become clogged and require cleaning. Use the utility supplied by the manufacturer to clean the print heads. After you clean them, test them. Repeat this process until the test shows a clean and uniform print.

Printers have many moving parts. Over time, the parts collect dust, dirt, and other debris. If not cleaned regularly, the printer may not work well or could stop working completely. When working with dot-matrix printers, clean the roller surfaces with a damp cloth. On inkjet printers, clean the paper-handling machinery with a damp cloth. Some printer parts must be lubricated with special grease. Check the documentation to determine if your printer needs this grease and the locations to use it.

Caution

Do not touch the drum of a laser printer while cleaning because you can damage the drum surface.

Laser printers do not usually require much maintenance unless they are in a dusty area or are very old. When cleaning a laser printer, use a specially designed vacuum cleaner to pick up toner particles. A standard vacuum cleaner cannot hold the tiny particles of toner and may scatter them about. Use only a vacuum cleaner with *High Efficiency Particulate Air (HEPA) filtration.* HEPA filtration catches microscopic particles within the filters.

Figure 9-11 displays a specially designed vacuum cleaner with HEPA filtration built to catch microscopic particles like toner from laser printers.

Figure 9-11 Printer Vacuum

Thermal printers use heat to create an image on special paper. To extend the life of the printer, clean the heating element of the thermal printer regularly with isopropyl alcohol.

Choosing the correct paper type for a printer helps the printer last longer and print more efficiently. Several types of paper are available. Each type of paper is labeled with the type of printer for which it is intended. The manufacturer of the printer may also recommend the best type of paper.

Operational Environment (9.5.1.4)

Printers, like all other electrical devices, are affected by temperature, humidity, and electrical interference. Laser printers produce heat and should be operated in well-ventilated areas to prevent overheating.

Keep paper and toner cartridges in their original wrappers. These supplies should also be stored a cool, dry, dust-free environment. High humidity causes paper to absorb moisture from the air. This can cause the paper to wave, which causes pieces of paper to stick together or jam during the printing process. High humidity can also make it difficult for the toner to attach to the paper correctly. If the paper and printer are dusty, you can use compressed air to blow away the dust. The following lists common operating environment guidelines:

- Keep paper dry.
- Keep printer in a cool, dust-free environment.
- Store toner in a clean, dry environment.
- Clean glass on scanners.

Worksheet 9.5.1.5: Search for Certified Printer Technician Jobs

In this activity, you use the Internet to gather information about becoming a certified printer technician. Refer to the worksheet in *IT Essentials: PC Hardware and Software Lab Manual*, Fifth Edition.

Basic Troubleshooting Process for Printers (9.6)

Troubleshooting is a valuable skill. Using an organized approach to problem solving will help technicians develop their troubleshooting skills. This section outlines a systematic troubleshooting approach and offers specifics on how to address issues that are particular to printers.

Identify the Problem (9.6.1.1)

Printer problems can result from a combination of hardware, software, and connectivity issues. This section studies a six-step troubleshooting model. Troubleshooting is an important skill for technicians. A technician must be able to determine whether the problem exists with the device, a cable connection, or the computer to which the printer is connected. Computer technicians must be able to analyze the problem and determine the cause of the error to repair the printer issues.

The first step in the troubleshooting process is to identify the problem. The following shows a list of open-ended and closed-ended questions to ask the customer:

Identify the Problem

Open-ended questions:

- What problems are you experiencing with your printer or scanner?
- What software or hardware has been changed recently on your computer?
- What error messages have you received?
- What were you doing when the problem was discovered?

Closed-ended questions:

- Is the printer under warranty?
- Can you print a test page?
- Is this a new printer?
- Is the printer powered on?

Establish a Theory of Probable Cause (9.6.1.2)

After you have talked to the customer, you can establish a theory of probable cause. The following shows a list of some common probable causes for printer problems:

Establish a Theory of Probable Cause

Common causes of printer problems:

- Loose cable connections
- Paper jams
- Equipment power
- Low ink warning
- Out of paper

- Error on equipment display
- Errors on computer screen

Test the Theory to Determine Cause (9.6.1.3)

After you have developed some theories about what is wrong, test them to determine the cause of the problem. The following shows a list of quick procedures that can determine the exact cause of the problem or even correct the problem. If a quick procedure does correct the problem, you can verify full system functionality. If a quick procedure does not correct the problem, you may need to research the problem further to establish the exact cause.

Test the Theory to Determine Cause

Common steps to determine cause:

- Restart the printer.
- Disconnect and reconnect the cables.
- Restart computer.
- Check for paper jams.
- Reseat paper in tray.
- Open and close printer tray.
- Ensure printer doors are closed.
- Install a new ink or toner cartridge.

Establish a Plan of Action to Resolve the Problem and Implement the Solution (9.6.1.4)

After you have determined the exact cause of the problem, establish a plan of action to resolve the problem and implement the solution. The following shows some sources you can use to gather additional information to resolve an issue:

Establish a Plan of Action to Resolve the Problem and Implement the Solution

If no solution is achieved in the previous step, further research is needed to implement the solution:

- Help desk repair logs
- Other technicians
- Manufacturer FAQs
- Technical websites

- Newsgroups

- Manuals

- Online forums

- Internet research

Verify Full System Functionality and Implement Preventive Measures (9.6.1.5)

After you have corrected the problem, verify full functionality and, if applicable, implement preventive measures. The following shows a list of the steps to verify the solution:

Verify Full System Functionality and, if Applicable, Implement Preventive Measures

Verify full functionality:

- Reboot the computer.

- Reboot the printer.

- Print a test page from the printer control panel.

- Print a document from an application.

- Reprint the customer's problem print job.

Document Findings, Actions, and Outcomes (9.6.1.6)

In the final step of the troubleshooting process, document your findings, actions, and outcomes. The following shows a list of the tasks required to document the problem and the solution:

Document Your Findings, Actions, and Outcomes

Document your findings, actions, and outcomes:

- Discuss the solution implemented with the customer.

- Have the customer verify that the problem has been solved.

- Provide the customer with all paperwork.

- Document the steps taken to solve the problem in the work order and technician's journal.

- Document any components used in the repair.

- Document the time spent to resolve the problem.

Common Problems and Solutions for Printers (9.6.2)

Printer problems can stem from many sources; the printer hardware, printer drivers, the print server, or in the case of a network printer the issues can be network related. Recognizing the source of a problem and identifying a solution are the topics of this section.

Identify Common Problems and Solutions (9.6.2.1)

Printer problems can be attributed to hardware, software, networks, or some combination of the three. You will resolve some types of problems more often than others.

Table 9-6 shows a chart of common problems and solutions.

Table 9-6   Common Problems and Solutions

Identify the Problem	Probable Causes	Possible Solutions
An application document does not print.	There is a document error in the print queue.	Manage the print jobs by deleting the document from the print queue and print again.
Printer cannot be added, or there is a spooler error.	The printer service is stopped or not working properly.	Start the print spooler and if necessary reboot.
User receives a "Document failed to print" message.	A cable is loose or disconnected. A printer is no longer shared.	Check and reconnect cables. Configure printer sharing.
Printer is printing incorrect colors.	Print cartridge is empty. Print cartridge is defective. Incorrect cartridge type installed. Print heads need to be cleaned and calibrated.	Replace cartridge with correct cartridge. Clean and calibrate print heads.

Summary (9.7.1.1)

In this chapter, various types of printers were discussed. You learned that there are many different types and sizes of printers, each with different capabilities, speeds, and uses. You also learned that printers can be connected directly to computers or shared across a network. The chapter introduced the different types of cables and interfaces available to connect a printer.

The following concepts from this chapter are important to remember:

- Some printers have low output and are adequate for home use, whereas other printers have high output and are designed for commercial use.

- Printers can have different speeds and quality of print.

- Older printers use parallel cables and ports. Newer printers usually use USB or FireWire cables and connectors.

- With newer operating systems, it is common for the computer to automatically recognize the printer and install the necessary drivers.

- If the device drivers are not automatically installed by the computer, download them from the manufacturer's website or use the supplied CD.

- Most optimization is done through software drivers and utilities.

- After you have set up the printer, you can share the device with other users on the network. This arrangement is cost-efficient because every user does not need to have a printer.

- A good preventive maintenance program extends the life of the printer and keeps it performing well.

- Always follow safety procedures when working with printers. Many parts inside printers contain high voltage or become very hot with use.

- Use a sequence of steps to fix a problem. Start with simple tasks before you decide on a course of action. Call a certified printer technician when a problem is too difficult for you to fix.

Summary of Exercises

This is a summary of the labs, worksheets, and virtual desktop activities associated with this chapter. Refer to the worksheets in the *IT Essentials: PC Hardware and Software Lab Manual*, Fifth Edition.

Labs

The following labs cover material from this chapter. Refer to the labs in the *IT Essentials: PC Hardware and Software Lab Manual*, Fifth Edition.

Lab 9.3.1.2: Install a Printer in Windows 7

Lab 9.3.1.3: Install a Printer in Windows Vista

Lab 9.3.1.4: Install a Printer in Windows XP

Lab 9.4.2.3: Share a Printer in Windows 7

Lab 9.4.2.4: Share a Printer in Windows Vista

Lab 9.4.2.5: Share a Printer in Windows XP

Worksheets

The following worksheets cover material from this chapter. Refer to the worksheets in the *IT Essentials: PC Hardware and Software Lab Manual*, Fifth Edition.

Worksheet 9.5.1.5: Search for Certified Printer Technician Jobs

Check Your Understanding

You can find the answers to these questions in Appendix A, "Answers to 'Check Your Understanding' Questions."

1. In most cases, which type of document takes longer to be printed?

   A. A draft photo-quality printout

   B. A digital color photograph

   C. A draft text

   D. A high-quality page of text

2. Dots per inch is used as a measure for which characteristic of a printer?

   A. Cost of ownership

   B. Speed

   C. Reliability

   D. Quality of printing

3. How could a user share a locally connected printer with other users on the same network?

   A. Install shared PCL drivers.

   B. Enable print sharing.

   C. Install a USB hub.

   D. Remove the PS drivers.

4. A technician wants to share a printer on the network but according to the company policy, no PC should have a directly connected printer. Which device would the technician need?

   A. A docking station

   B. A USB hub

   C. A hardware print server

   D. LAN switch

5. A technician has determined that uninstalling the current printer driver on a computer and then installing an updated driver could be a possible solution to a printer problem. Which printer problem could this solution resolve?

   A. The paper is jamming in the printer.

   B. The printer power LED does not come on.

   C. The printer does not print a test page.

   D. The printer does not print a document for one application but prints for all other applications.

6. While troubleshooting a printer problem, a technician discovers that the printer has been connected to the wrong computer port. Which printer problem would this mistake have caused?

   A. The print queue is functioning, but print jobs are not printed.

   B. Blank pages are printed by the printer.

   C. When a document is printed, there are unknown characters on the page.

   D. The print spooler displays an error.

7. What are two disadvantages of sharing a directly connected printer from a computer? (Choose two.)

   A. Only one computer at a time can use the printer.

   B. The computer sharing the printer uses its own resources to manage all the print jobs coming to the printer.

   C. Other computers do not need to be cabled directly to the printer.

   D. All the computers using the printer need to use the same operating system.

   E. The computer directly connected to the printer always needs to be powered on, even if not in use.

8. What is the first action that should be taken when performing preventive maintenance on a printer?

   A. Disconnect the printer from the power source.

   B. Disconnect the printer from the network.

   C. Remove the paper from the printer paper tray.

   D. Clean the print heads using the printer software utility.

9. What are two potential disadvantages of replacing printer consumables with parts or components that are not recommended by the manufacturer? (Choose two.)

   A. Print quality may be poor.

   B. The manufacturer warranty may be voided.

   C. Nonrecommended parts may be less expensive.

   D. The printer may need cleaning more often.

   E. Nonrecommended parts may be more readily available.

10. Which method is recommended for cleaning the print heads in an inkjet printer?

   A. Wipe the print heads with isopropyl alcohol.

   B. Wipe the print heads with a damp cloth.

   C. Use compressed air.

   D. Use the printer software utility.

CHAPTER 10

Security

Objectives

Upon completion of this chapter, you will be able to answer the following questions:

- What are some types of security threats that involve malicious software?

- What are some types of security threats that involve Internet security?

- What are some types of security threats that involve access to data and equipment?

- What are some types of security procedures?

- What are the elements of a strong security policy?

- What are some ways to secure data and account information?

- What are some ways to protect physical equipment?

- What are some preventive maintenance techniques for security?

- What can be done to troubleshoot security?

- What is the process to troubleshoot security?

Key Terms

This chapter uses the following key terms. You can find the definitions in the Glossary.

Introduction (10.0.1)

Computer and network security helps to ensure that only authorized personnel have access to networks and devices. It also helps to keep data and equipment functioning properly. Threats to security can be internal, coming from the inside, or external, coming from the outside of an organization, and the level of potential damage can vary greatly:

- *Internal threats*: Users and employees who have access to data, equipment, and the network

- *External threats*: Users outside of an organization who do not have authorized access to the network or resources

Theft, loss, network intrusion, and physical damage are some of the ways a network or computer can be harmed. Damage or loss of equipment can mean a loss of productivity. Repairing and replacing equipment can cost the company time and money. Unauthorized use of a network can expose confidential information, violate the integrity of data, and reduce network resources.

An attack that intentionally degrades the performance of a computer or network can also harm the production of an organization. Poorly implemented security measures on wireless network devices demonstrate that physical connectivity is not necessary for unauthorized access by intruders.

The primary responsibilities of a technician include data and network security. A customer or an organization might depend on you to ensure that their data and computer equipment are secure. You might perform tasks that are more sensitive than those assigned to the average employee. You might repair, adjust, and install equipment. You need to know how to configure settings to keep the network secure but still keep it available to those who need to access it. You must ensure that software patches and updates are applied, antivirus software is installed, and antispyware software is used. You can also be asked to instruct users how to maintain good security practices with computer equipment.

This chapter reviews the types of attacks that threaten the security of computers and the data contained on them. A technician is responsible for the security of data and computer equipment in an organization. This chapter describes how you can work with customers to ensure that the best possible protection is in place.

To successfully protect computers and the network, a technician must understand both types of threats to computer security:

- *Physical*: Events or attacks that steal, damage, or destroy equipment, such as servers, switches, and wiring

- *Data*: Events or attacks that remove, corrupt, deny access to authorized users, allow access to unauthorized users, or steal information

Security Threats (10.1)

There are many types of security threats to computers and networks. This section defines and explains several types of threats, including threats from malicious software, computer and network attacks, and threats from unauthorized access to data and equipment.

Adware, Spyware, and Phishing (10.1.1.1)

Malware is any software created to perform malicious acts. Malware includes adware, spyware, grayware, phishing, viruses, worms, Trojan horses, and rootkits. Malware is usually installed on a computer without the knowledge of the user. These programs open extra windows on the computer or change the computer configuration. Malware is capable of modifying web browsers to open to specific web pages that are not the desired web page. This is known as browser redirection. Malware can also collect information stored on the computer without the user's consent.

Adware

Adware is a software program that displays advertising on your computer. Adware is usually distributed with downloaded software. Most often, adware is displayed in a pop-up window. Adware pop-up windows are sometimes difficult to control and open new windows faster than users can close them.

Spyware

Spyware is similar to adware. It is distributed without user intervention or knowledge. After spyware is installed and run, it monitors activity on the computer. The spyware then sends this information to the individual or organization responsible for launching the spyware.

Grayware

Grayware is similar to adware. Grayware may be malicious and is sometimes installed with the user's consent. For example, a free software program may require the installation of a toolbar that displays advertising or tracks a user's website history.

Phishing

Phishing is where the attacker pretends to represent a legitimate outside organization, such as a bank. A potential victim is contacted via email, telephone, or text message. The attacker might ask for verification of information, such as a password or username, to possibly prevent some terrible consequence from occurring.

Many malware attacks are phishing attacks that try to persuade the user to unknowingly provide attackers with access to personal information. As you fill out an online form, the data is sent to the attacker. Malware can be removed using virus, spyware, or adware removal tools.

> **Note**
>
> There is rarely a need to provide sensitive personal or financial information online. Legitimate businesses will not ask for sensitive information through email. Be suspicious. When in doubt, make contact by mail or phone to ensure the validity of the request.

Viruses, Worms, Trojans, and Rootkits (10.1.1.2)

Viruses

A *virus* is a program written with malicious intent and sent by attackers. The virus is transferred to another computer through email, file transfers, and instant messaging. The virus hides by attaching itself to computer code, software, or documents on the computer. When the file is accessed, the virus executes and infects the computer. A virus has the potential to corrupt or even delete files on your computer, use your email to spread itself to other computers, prevent the computer from booting, cause applications to not load or operate correctly, or even erase your entire hard drive. If the virus is spread to other computers, those computers could continue to spread the virus.

Some viruses can be exceptionally dangerous. One of the most damaging types of virus is used to record keystrokes. Attackers can use these viruses to harvest sensitive information, such as passwords and credit card numbers. The virus sends the data that it collects back to the attacker. Viruses can also alter or destroy information on a computer. Stealth viruses can infect a computer and lay dormant until summoned by the attacker.

Worms

A *worm* is a self-replicating program that is harmful to networks. A worm uses the network to duplicate its code to the hosts on a network, often without user intervention. A worm is different from a virus because it does not need to attach to a program to infect a host. Worms typically spread by automatically exploiting known vulnerabilities in legitimate software.

Trojans

A *Trojan horse* is malicious software that is disguised as a legitimate program. A Trojan threat is hidden in software that appears to do one thing, but behind the scenes it does another. The Trojan program can reproduce like a virus and spread to other computers. Computer data damage, exposed login information, and production loss could be significant. A technician might be needed to perform repairs, and employees might lose or have to replace data. An infected computer could be sending critical data to competitors, while at the same time infecting other computers on the network.

Virus Protection Software

Virus protection software, also known as antivirus software, is designed to detect, disable, and remove viruses, worms, and Trojans before they infect a computer. However, antivirus software becomes outdated quickly, and it is the responsibility of the technician to apply the most recent updates, patches, and virus definitions as part of a regular maintenance schedule. Many organizations establish a written security policy stating that employees are not permitted to install any software that is not provided by the company. Organizations also make employees aware of the dangers of opening email attachments that may contain a virus or a worm.

Rootkits

A *rootkit* is a malicious program that gains full access to a computer system. Often, a direct attack on a system using a known vulnerability or password is used to gain Administrator-account level access. Because the rootkit has this privileged access, the program is able to hide the files, Registry edits, and folders that it uses from detection by typical virus or spyware programs. It is very difficult to detect the presence of a rootkit because it has the rights to control and modify security programs that may otherwise be able to detect a malicious software installation. Special rootkit removal software can be used to remove some rootkits, but sometimes a reinstallation of the operating system is necessary to ensure that the rootkit is completely removed.

> **Note**
>
> Do not assume that email attachments are safe, even when they are sent from a trusted contact. The sender's computer may be infected by a virus that is trying to spread itself. Always scan email attachments before opening them.

Web Security (10.1.1.3)

Tools that are used to make web pages more powerful and versatile can also make computers more vulnerable to attacks. These are some examples of *web tools*:

- **ActiveX:** Technology created by Microsoft to control interactivity on web pages. If ActiveX is enabled on a web page, an applet or a small program must be downloaded to gain access to the full functionality.

- **Java:** Programming language that allows applets to run within a web browser. Examples of Java applets include a calculator or a page-hit counter.

- **JavaScript:** Programming language developed to interact with HTML source code to allow websites to be interactive. Examples include a rotating banner or a pop-up window.

- **Adobe Flash:** Multimedia tool used to create interactive media for the web. Flash is used for creating animation, video, and games on web pages.

- **Microsoft Silverlight:** Tool used to create rich, interactive media for the web. Silverlight is similar to Flash with many of the same features.

Attackers might use any of these tools to install a program on a computer. To prevent against these attacks, most browsers have settings that force the computer user to authorize the downloading or use of these tools.

ActiveX Filtering

When browsing the web, some pages may not work properly unless you install an *ActiveX control*. Some ActiveX controls are written by third parties and may be malicious. *ActiveX filtering* allows web browsing without running ActiveX controls.

After an ActiveX control has been installed for a website, the control runs on other websites as well. This may degrade performance or introduce security risks. When ActiveX filtering is enabled, you can choose which websites are allowed to run ActiveX controls. Sites that are not approved cannot run these controls, and the browser does not show notifications for you to install or enable them.

To enable ActiveX Filtering in Internet Explorer 9, use the following path.

Tools > ActiveX Filtering

To view a website that contains ActiveX content when ActiveX filtering is enabled, click the blue **ActiveX Filtering** icon in the address bar, and click **Turn off ActiveX Filtering**.

After viewing the content, you can turn ActiveX filtering for the website back on by following the same steps.

Pop-Up Blocker

A *pop-up* is a web browser window that opens on top of another web browser window. Some pop-ups are initiated while browsing, such as a link on a page that opens a pop-up to deliver additional information or a close-up of a picture. Other pop-ups are initiated by a website or advertiser and are often unwanted or annoying, especially when multiple pop-ups are opened at the same time on a web page.

A *pop-up blocker* is a tool that is built in to a web browser or operates as a standalone program. It enables a user to limit or block most of the pop-ups that occur while browsing the web. The pop-up blocker built in to Internet Explorer is turned on by default when the browser is installed. When a web page is encountered that contains pop-ups, a message is displayed that a pop-up has been blocked. A button in the message can be used to allow the pop-up once or change the pop-up blocking options for the web page.

To turn off the pop-up blocker in Internet Explorer, use the following path:

Tools > Pop-up Blocker > Turn off Pop-up Blocker

To change the settings of the pop-up blocker in Internet Explorer, use the following path:

Tools > Pop-up Blocker > Pop-up Blocker settings

The following Pop-up Blocker settings can be configured, as shown in Figure 10-1:

- Add a website to allow pop-ups from it.

- Change notifications when blocking pop-ups.

- Change the level of blocking. High blocks all pop-ups, Medium blocks most automatic pop-ups, and Low allows pop-ups from secure sites.

Figure 10-1 Pop-Up Blocker Settings

SmartScreen Filter

In Internet Explorer, the *SmartScreen Filter*, shown in Figure 10-2, detects phishing websites, analyzes websites for suspicious items, and checks websites against a list of websites and files that are known to be malicious. SmartScreen Filter is turned on by default when Internet Explorer is installed. To turn off SmartScreen Filter, use the following path:

Tools > SmartScreen Filter > Turn off SmartScreen Filter

To analyze the current web page, use the following path:

Tools > SmartScreen Filter > Check this website

To report a suspicious web page, use the following path:

Tools > SmartScreen Filter > Report unsafe website

Figure 10-2   SmartScreen Filter

InPrivate Browsing (10.1.1.4)

Web browsers retain information about the web pages that you visit, the searches that you perform, usernames, passwords, and other identifiable information. This is a convenient feature when using a computer at home that is secured with a password. When using a laptop away from home, or a computer at a public location such as a library or Internet cafe, retained information from a web browser can be compromised. Anyone who uses that computer after you could use your information to steal your identity, steal your money, or change your passwords on important accounts.

It is possible to browse the web without the browser retaining personal information about you or your browsing habits. This is called *InPrivate browsing*. InPrivate browsing prevents the web browser from storing the following information:

- Usernames
- Passwords
- Cookies
- Browsing history

- Temporary Internet files

- Form data

To start InPrivate Browsing in Windows 7, use the following path:

Right-click **Internet Explorer > ** click **Start InPrivate Browsing.**

If Internet Explorer is already started, use the following path:

Tools > InPrivate Browsing

Alternatively, press **Ctrl+Shift+P.**

While you are browsing, the browser stores some information, such as temporary files and cookies, but after the InPrivate session is ended, the information is deleted.

Starting InPrivate browsing opens a new browser window. Only this window provides privacy, but any new tabs opened within the window have the same protection. Other browser windows are not protected by InPrivate browsing. Closing the browser window ends the InPrivate browsing session.

Spam (10.1.1.5)

Spam, also known as junk mail, is unsolicited email. In most cases, spam is used as a method of advertising. However, spam can be used to send harmful links, malicious programs, or deceptive content to try to obtain sensitive information such as a social security number or bank account information.

When used as an attack method, spam can include links to an infected website or an attachment that could infect a computer. These links or attachments can result in lots of pop-ups designed to capture your attention and lead you to advertising sites. Excessive pop-up windows can quickly cover a user's screen, taking up resources and slowing down a computer. In extreme cases, pop-ups can cause a computer to lock up or display a *Blue Screen of Death (BSOD).*

Many antivirus and email software programs automatically detect and remove spam from an email inbox. The ISP often filters most spam before it reaches the user's inbox. Some spam still might get through. Watch for some of the more common indicators of spam:

- An email has no subject line.

- An email is requesting an update to an account.

- The email is filled with misspelled words or strange punctuation.

- Links within the email are long/cryptic.

- An email is disguised as correspondence from a legitimate business.

- The email requests that you open an attachment.

Most spam is sent out by multiple computers on networks that have been infected by a virus or worm. These compromised computers send out as much bulk email as possible.

TCP/IP Attacks (10.1.1.6)

TCP/IP is the protocol suite that controls communications on the Internet. Unfortunately, some features of TCP/IP can be manipulated, resulting in network vulnerabilities.

Denial of Service

Denial of service (DoS) is a form of attack that prevents users from accessing normal services, such as email or a web server, because the system is busy responding to abnormally large amounts of requests. DoS works by sending so many requests for a system resource that the requested service is overloaded and ceases to operate.

Distributed DoS

A *distributed DoS (DDoS)* attack uses many infected computers, called *zombies* or *botnets*, to launch an attack. The intent is to obstruct or overwhelm access to the targeted server. Zombie computers located at different geographical locations make it difficult to trace the origin of the attack.

SYN Flood

A SYN (synchronize) request is the initial communication sent to establish a TCP connection. A *SYN flood* attack randomly opens TCP ports at the source of the attack and ties up the network equipment or computer with a large amount of false SYN requests. This causes sessions to be denied to others, as shown in Figure 10-3. A SYN flood attack is a type of DoS attack.

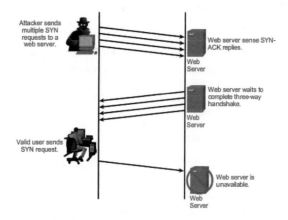

Figure 10-3 SYN Flood Attack

Spoofing

In a *spoofing* attack, a computer pretends to be a trusted computer to gain access to resources. The computer uses a forged IP or MAC address to impersonate a computer that is trusted on the network.

Man-in-the-Middle

An attacker performs a *man-in-the-middle attack* by intercepting communications between computers to steal information transiting through the network. A man-in-the-middle attack could also be used to manipulate messages and relay false information between hosts, as shown in Figure 10-4, because the hosts are unaware that the messages have been modified.

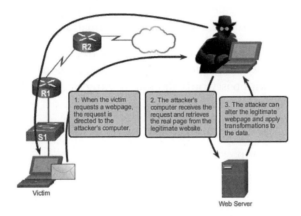

Figure 10-4   Man-in-the-Middle Attack

Replay

To perform a *replay attack*, data transmissions are intercepted and recorded by an attacker. These transmissions are then replayed to the destination computer. The destination computer handles these replayed transmissions as authentic and sent by the original source. This is how the attacker gains unauthorized entry into a system or network.

DNS Poisoning

With *DNS poisoning*, DNS records on a system are changed to point to imposter servers. The user attempts to access a legitimate site, but traffic is diverted to an imposter site. The imposter site is used to capture confidential information, such as usernames and passwords. An attacker can then retrieve the data from that location.

Worksheet 10.1.1.7: Security Attacks

In this activity, you use the Internet, a newspaper, or magazines to gather information to help you become familiar with computer crime and security attacks in your area. Be prepared to discuss your research with the class. Refer to Worksheet 10.1.1.7 in *IT Essentials: PC Hardware and Software Lab Manual*, Fifth Edition.

Social Engineering (10.1.2.1)

Social engineering occurs when an attacker tries to gain access to equipment or a network by tricking people into providing the necessary access information. Often, the social engineer gains the confidence of an employee and convinces the employee to divulge username and password information.

A social engineer might pose as a technician to try to gain entry into a facility. When inside, the social engineer might look over shoulders to gather information, seek out papers on desks with passwords and phone extensions, or obtain a company directory with email addresses.

Here are some basic precautions to help protect against social engineering:

- Never give out your password.
- Always ask for the ID of unknown persons.
- Restrict access to visitors.
- Escort all visitors.
- Never post your password in your work area.
- Lock your computer when you leave your desk.
- Do not let anyone follow you through a door that requires an access card.

Data Wiping, Hard Drive Destruction, and Recycling (10.1.2.2)

Deleting files from a hard drive does not remove them completely from the computer. The operating system removes the reference to the file in the file allocation table, but the data remains. This data is not completely removed until the hard drive stores other data in the same location, overwriting the previous data. Hard drives should be fully erased (data wiped) to prevent the possibility of recovery using specialized software. After the data on the hard drive has been completely erased, the hard drive can be destroyed or recycled.

Data Wiping

Data wiping, also known as secure erase, is a procedure performed to permanently delete data from a hard drive. Data wiping is often performed on hard drives containing sensitive data such as financial information. It is not enough to delete files or even format the drive. Software tools can still be used to recover folders, files, and even entire partitions if they are not erased properly. Use software specifically designed to overwrite data multiple times, rendering the data unusable. It is important to remember that data wiping is irreversible, and the data can never be recovered.

Secure erase software takes a long time to erase a disk. Many programs offer multiple choices for overwriting data. Special patterns of 1s and 0s, mathematical algorithms, random bits, and multiple overwrites can be used. With disk sizes reaching in excess of 2 terabytes, along with multiple overwrites, it might not be practical to use data wiping software, especially if you have many disks to wipe. Because data is stored magnetically on a hard drive, magnets can be used to erase them.

Degaussing

Degaussing disrupts or eliminates the magnetic field on a hard drive that allows for the storage of data. An electromagnet is a magnet that, when a current is applied, its magnetic field becomes very strong. A degaussing tool can cost $20,000 or more, so it is not a practical solution for most users. It takes about 10 seconds to degauss a hard drive, so it can save a lot of time and money if a large number of hard drives need to be securely erased.

There are also degaussing wands that can be used for smaller jobs, as shown in Figure 10-5. A degaussing wand uses powerful magnets instead of electromagnets and costs much less. To use a degaussing wand, a hard drive must be disassembled and the platters exposed to the wand for approximately 2 minutes.

Figure 10-5   Degaussing Wand

Hard Drive Destruction

Companies with sensitive data should always establish clear policies for hard drive disposal. It is important to be aware that formatting and reinstalling an operating system on a computer does not ensure that information cannot be recovered. Destroying the hard drive is the best option for companies with sensitive data. Drilling holes through a drive's platters is not the most effective method of hard drive destruction. Data can still be recovered using advanced data forensic software. To fully ensure that data cannot be recovered from a hard drive, carefully shatter the platters with a hammer and safely dispose of the pieces.

Solid State Drives

SSDs are comprised of flash memory instead of magnetic platters. Common techniques used for erasing data such as degaussing, and shattering are not effective. To fully ensure that data cannot be recovered from an SSD, perform a secure wipe or shred the drive into tiny pieces.

Other storage media, such as optical and floppy disks, must also be destroyed. Use a shredding machine that is designed to destroy this type of media.

Hard Drive Recycling

Hard drives that do not contain sensitive data should be reused in other computers. The drive can be reformatted, and a new operating system can be installed. Two types of formatting can be performed:

- **Standard format:** Also called *high-level formatting*, a boot sector is created and a file system is set up on the disk. A standard format can only be performed after a low-level format has been completed.

- *Low-level format*: The surface of the disk is marked with sector markers to indicate where data will be stored physically on the disk, and tracks are created. Low-level formatting is most often performed at the factory after the hard drive is built.

Security Procedures (10.2)

Protecting computers, networks, and data is the primary responsibility of a technician. This section discusses security procedures that protect equipment and data from security threats.

What Is a Security Policy? (10.2.1.1)

A *security policy* is a collection of rules, guidelines, and checklists. Network technicians and managers of an organization work together to develop the rules and guidelines for the security needs of computer equipment. A security policy includes the following elements:

- An acceptable computer usage statement for the organization.

- The people permitted to use the computer equipment.

- Devices that are permitted to be installed on a network, as well as the conditions of the installation. Modems and wireless access points are examples of hardware that could expose the network to attacks.

- Requirements necessary for data to remain confidential on a network.

- Process for employees to acquire access to equipment and data. This process may require the employee to sign an agreement regarding company rules. It also lists the consequences for failure to comply.

A security policy should describe how a company addresses security issues. Though local security policies may vary between organizations, there are questions all organizations should ask:

- What assets require protection?

- What are the possible threats?

- What should we do in the event of a security breach?

- What training will be in place to educate the end users?

Note

To be effective, a security policy must be enforced and followed by all employees.

Worksheet 10.2.1.2: Answer Security Policy Questions

In this activity, you answer security questions regarding the IT Essentials classroom. Refer to Worksheet 10.2.1.2 in *IT Essentials: PC Hardware and Software Lab Manual*, Fifth Edition.

Security Policy Requirements (10.2.1.3)

The value of physical equipment is often far less than the value of the data it contains. The loss of sensitive data to a company's competitors or to criminals can be costly. Such losses can result in a lack of confidence in the company and the dismissal of computer technicians in charge of computer security. To protect data, several methods of security protection can be implemented.

An organization should strive to achieve the best and most affordable security protection against data loss or damage to software and equipment. Network technicians and the organization's management must work together to develop a security policy that ensures that data and equipment are protected against all security threats. In developing a policy, management should calculate the cost of data loss versus the expense of security protection and determine which trade-offs are acceptable. A security policy includes a comprehensive statement about the level of security required and how this security will be achieved.

You may be involved in developing a security policy for a customer or organization. When creating a security policy, ask the following questions to determine the security factors:

- **Is the computer located at a home or a business?** Home computers are vulnerable to wireless intrusions. Business computers have a high threat of network intrusion because businesses are more attractive to hackers and because legitimate users might abuse access privileges.

- **Is there full-time Internet access?** The longer a computer is connected to the Internet, the greater the chance of attacks. A computer accessing the Internet must use a firewall and antivirus software.

- **Is the computer a laptop?** Physical security is an issue with laptop computers. There are measures to secure laptops, such as cable locks, biometrics, and tracking techniques.

When creating a security policy, these are some key areas to address:

- Process for handling network security incidents

- Process to audit existing network security

- General security framework for implementing network security

- Behaviors that are allowed

- Behaviors that are prohibited

- What to log and how to store the logs: Event Viewer, system log files, or security log files

- Network access to resources through account permissions

- Authentication technologies to access data: usernames, passwords, biometrics, and smart cards

The security policy should also provide detailed information about the following issues in case of an emergency:

- Steps to take after a breach in security

- Who to contact in an emergency

- Information to share with customers, vendors, and the media

- Secondary locations to use in an evacuation

- Steps to take after an emergency is over, including the priority of services to be restored

The scope of the policy and the consequences of noncompliance must be clearly described. Security policies should be reviewed regularly and updated as necessary. Keep a revision history to track all policy changes. Security is the responsibility of every person within the company. All employees, including non-computer users, must be trained to understand the security policy and notified of any security policy updates.

You should also define employee access to data in a security policy. The policy should protect highly sensitive data from public access, while ensuring that employees can still perform their job tasks. Data can be classified from public to top secret, with several different levels between them. Public information can be seen by anyone and has no security requirements. Public information cannot be used maliciously to hurt a company or an individual. Top secret information needs the most security because the data exposure can be extremely detrimental to a government, a company, or an individual.

Usernames and Passwords (10.2.1.4)

A username and password are two pieces of information that a user needs to log in to a computer. When an attacker knows one of these entries, the attacker needs only to crack or discover the other entry to gain access to the computer system. It is important to change the default username for accounts such as administrator or guest because these default usernames are widely known. Some home-networking equipment has a default username that cannot be changed. Whenever possible, change the default usernames of all users on computers and network equipment.

The system administrator usually defines a naming convention for usernames when creating network logins. A common example of a username is the first letter of the person's first name and then the entire last name. Keep the naming convention simple so that people do not have a hard time remembering it. Usernames, like passwords, are an important piece of information and should not be revealed.

Requiring Passwords

Password guidelines are an important component of a security policy. Any user who must log in to a computer or connect to a network resource should be required to have a password. Passwords help prevent theft of data and malicious acts. Passwords also help to ensure that logging of events is correct by ensuring that the user is the correct person.

Network logins provide a means of logging activity on the network and either preventing or allowing access to resources. If you are unable to log in to a computer, do not use another user's username and password, even if they are your coworker or your friend, because this can invalidate logging. Instead, inform the network administrator of any problems logging on to a computer or authenticating against secure network resources.

Using secure, encrypted login information for computers with network access should be a minimum requirement in any organization. Malicious software could monitor the network and record plaintext passwords. If passwords are encrypted, attackers must decode the encryption to learn the passwords.

Attackers can gain access to unprotected computer data. Password protection can prevent unauthorized access to content. All computers should be password protected. Three levels of password protection are recommended:

- **BIOS:** Prevents the operating system from booting and the BIOS settings from being changed without the appropriate password
- **Login:** Prevents unauthorized access to the local computer
- **Network:** Prevents access to network resources by unauthorized personnel

Password Requirements (10.2.1.5)

When you are assigning passwords, the level of password control should match the level of protection required. Passwords should be required to have a minimum length and include uppercase and lowercase letters combined with numbers and symbols. This is known as a strong password. It is common for a security policy to require users to change their passwords on a regular basis and monitor the number of password attempts before an account is temporarily locked out. These are some guidelines to creating strong passwords:

- **Length:** Use at least eight characters.
- **Complexity:** Include letters, numbers, symbols, and punctuation. Use a variety of keys on the keyboard, not just common letters and characters.
- **Variation:** Change passwords often. Set a reminder to change the passwords you have for email, banking, and credit card websites on the average of every three to four months.
- **Variety:** Use a different password for each site or computer that you use.

To create, remove, or modify a password in Windows 7 or Windows Vista, use the following path:

Start > Control Panel > User Accounts

To create, remove, or modify a password in Windows XP, use the following path:

Start > Control Panel > User Accounts > Change an account > click the account to change

To prevent unauthorized users from accessing local computers and network resources, lock your workstation, laptop, or server when you are not present.

Screensaver Required Password

It is important to make sure that computers are secure when users are away from the computer. A security policy should contain a rule about requiring a computer to lock when the screensaver starts. This will ensure that after a short time away from the computer, the screen saver will start and then the computer cannot be used until the user logs in.

To set the screen saver lock in Windows 7 and Windows Vista, use the following path:

Start > Control Panel > Personalization > Screen Saver

Choose a screen saver and a wait time, and then select the **On resume, display logon screen option.**

To set the screen saver lock in Windows XP, use the following path:

Start > Control Panel > Display > Screen Saver

Choose a screen saver and a wait time, and then select the **On resume, password** protect option.

File and Folder Permissions (10.2.1.6)

Permission levels are configured to limit individual or group user access to specific data. Both FAT32 and NTFS allow folder sharing and folder-level permissions for users with network access. Folder permissions are shown in Table 10-1. The additional security of file-level permissions is provided only with NTFS. File-level permissions are shown in Table 10-2.

Table 10-1   Folder Permissions

Permissions	Full Control	Modify	Read and Execute	List Folder Contents	Read	Write
Traverse Folder	Yes	Yes	Yes	Yes	No	No
List Folder	Yes	Yes	Yes	Yes	Yes	No
View Folder Attributes	Yes	Yes	Yes	Yes	Yes	No
View Extended Folder Attributes	Yes	Yes	Yes	Yes	Yes	No
Create Files Within the Folder	Yes	Yes	No	No	No	Yes
Create Folders	Yes	Yes	No	No	No	Yes
Write Folder Attributes	Yes	Yes	No	No	No	Yes
Write Extended Folder Attributes	Yes	No	No	No	No	Yes
Delete Subfolders and Files	Yes	No	No	No	No	No
Delete Folder	Yes	No	No	No	No	No
View Folder Permissions	Yes	Yes	Yes	Yes	Yes	Yes
Change Folder Permissions	Yes	No	No	No	No	No

Table 10-2   File Permissions

Permissions	Full Control	Modify	Read and Execute	Read	Write
Execute File	Yes	Yes	Yes	No	No
View Data	Yes	Yes	Yes	Yes	No
View File Attributes	Yes	Yes	Yes	Yes	No
View Extended Attributes	Yes	Yes	Yes	Yes	No
Write Data	Yes	Yes	No	No	Yes

Permissions	Full Control	Modify	Read and Execute	Read	Write
Append Data	Yes	Yes	No	No	Yes
Write File Attributes	Yes	Yes	No	No	Yes
Write Extended File Attributes	Yes	No	No	No	Yes
Delete Files	Yes	No	No	No	No
View File Permissions	Yes	Yes	Yes	Yes	Yes
Change File Permissions	Yes	No	No	No	No
Take Ownership	Yes	No	No	No	No
Synchronize	Yes	Yes	Yes	Yes	Yes

To configure file- or folder-level permissions, use the following path:

Right-click the file or folder and select **Properties > Security > Edit**

When configuring network share permissions for a computer that has NTFS, create a network share and assign shared permissions to users or groups. Only users and groups with both NTFS permissions and shared permissions can access a network share.

To configure folder sharing permissions in Windows 7, use the following path:

Right-click the folder > select **Share with**

There are four file sharing options to choose from:

- **Nobody:** The folder is not shared.

- **Homegroup (Read):** The folder is shared only with members of the Homegroup. Homegroup members can only read the contents of the folder.

- **Homegroup (Read/Write):** The folder is shared only with members of the Homegroup. Homegroup members can read the contents of the folder and create files and folders in the folder.

- **Specific People:** Opens the File Sharing dialog box. Choose the users and groups to share the contents of the folder, and choose the permission level of each.

To configure folder-sharing permissions in Windows Vista, use the following path:

Right-click a folder > select **Share**

To configure folder-sharing permissions in Windows XP, use the following path:

Right-click a folder > select **Sharing and Security**

All file systems keep track of resources, but only file systems with *journals*, which are special areas where file changes are recorded before changes are made, can log access by user, date, and time. The FAT32 file system lacks journaling and encryption capabilities. As a result, situations that require good security are usually deployed using NTFS. If increased security is needed, it is possible to run certain utilities, such as *CONVERT*, to upgrade a FAT32 file system to NTFS. The conversion process is not reversible. It is important to clearly define your goals before making the transition. A comparison of the two file systems is shown in Table 10-3.

Table 10-3   FAT32 and NTFS Comparison

	FAT32	NTFS
Security	Low security	File- and folder-level permissions, encryption.
Compatibility	Compatible with all versions of Windows	Compatible with all versions of Windows.
File size	Limit of 4 GB files/32 GB volumes	Limit of 1-terabyte files/256-terabyte volumes.
Files per volume	4.17 million	4.29 billion.
File size efficiency	Large clusters waste some space	Smaller clusters use more of the available space; built-in compression maximizes space.
Reliability	Does not track changes made to the file system	Includes journaling, which helps to rebuild the file system after a crash or power failure.

Principle of Least Privilege

Users should be limited to only the resources they need in a computer system or on a network. They should not be able to access all files on a server, for example, if they need to access only a single folder. It may be easier to provide users access to the entire drive, but it is more secure to limit access to only the folder that is needed to perform their job. This is known as the *principle of least privilege*. Limiting access to resources also prevents malicious programs from accessing those resources if the user's computer becomes infected.

Restricting User Permissions

File and network share permissions can be granted to individuals or through membership within a group. If an individual or a group is denied permissions to a network share, this denial overrides any other permissions given. For example, if you deny someone permission to a network share, the user cannot access that share, even if the user is the administrator or part of the administrator group. The local security policy must outline which resources and the type of access allowed for each user and group.

When the permissions of a folder are changed, you are given the option to apply the same permissions to all subfolders. This is known as *permission propagation*. Permission propagation is an easy way to apply permissions to many files and folders quickly. After parent folder permissions have been set, folders and files that are created inside the parent folder inherit the permissions of the parent folder.

Lab 10.2.1.7: Securing Accounts, Data, and the Computer in Windows 7

In this lab, you explore how to secure accounts, data, and the computer in Windows 7. Refer to Lab 10.2.1.7 in *IT Essentials: PC Hardware and Software Lab Manual*, Fifth Edition.

Lab 10.2.1.8: Securing Accounts, Data, and the Computer in Windows Vista

In this lab, you explore how to secure accounts, data, and the computer in Windows Vista. Refer to Lab 10.2.1.8 in *IT Essentials: PC Hardware and Software Lab Manual*, Fifth Edition.

Lab 10.2.1.9: Securing Accounts, Data, and the Computer in Windows XP

In this lab, you explore how to secure accounts, data, and the computer in Windows XP. Refer to Lab 10.2.1.9 in *IT Essentials: PC Hardware and Software Lab Manual*, Fifth Edition.

Software Firewalls (10.2.2.1)

A *software firewall* is a program that runs on a computer to allow or deny traffic between the computer and other computers to which it is connected. The software firewall applies a set of rules to data transmissions through inspection and filtering of data packets. Windows Firewall is an example of a software firewall. It is installed by default when the OS is installed.

Every communication using TCP/IP is associated with a port number. HTTP, for instance, uses port 80 by default. A software firewall, as shown in Figure 10-6, is capable of protecting a computer from intrusion through data ports. You can control the type of data sent to another computer by selecting which ports will be open and which will be blocked. You must create *exceptions* to allow certain traffic or applications to connect to the computer. Firewalls block incoming and outgoing network connections, unless exceptions are defined to open and close the ports required by a program.

Figure 10-6   Windows Software Firewall

How To

To disable ports with the Windows Firewall in Windows 7, follow these steps:

Step 1.   Select **Start > Control Panel > Windows Firewall > Advanced settings.**

Step 2.   In the left pane, choose to configure either Inbound Rules or Outbound Rules in the left pane and click **New Rule** in the right pane.

Step 3.   Select the **Port** radio button and click **Next.**

Step 4.   Choose **TCP** or **UDP.**

Step 5.   Choose **All local ports** or **Specific local ports** to define individual ports or a port range and click **Next.**

Step 6.   Choose **Block the connection** and click **Next.**

Step 7.   Choose when the rule applies and click **Next.**

Step 8.   Provide a name and optional description for the rule and click **Finish.**

How To

To disable ports with the Windows Firewall in Windows Vista, follow these steps:

Step 1.   Select **Start > Control Panel > Windows Firewall > Change Settings > Continue > Exceptions > Add port.**

Step 2.   Provide a name and port number or port range.

Step 3.   Choose either **TCP** or **UDP** and click **OK.**

To disable ports with the Windows Firewall in Windows XP, follow these steps:

Step 1. Select **Start > Control Panel > Windows Firewall > Exceptions > Add Port.**

Step 2. Provide a name and port number or port range.

Step 3. Choose either **TCP** or **UDP** and click **OK.**

Note

On a secure network, enable the internal OS firewall for additional security. Some applications might not operate properly if the firewall is not configured correctly.

Biometrics and Smart Cards (10.2.2.2)

Biometric security compares physical characteristics against stored profiles to authenticate people. A *profile* is a data file containing known characteristics of an individual. A fingerprint, face pattern, and *retina scan*, as shown in Figure 10-7, are all examples of biometric data.

Figure 10-7   Retina Scan

In theory, biometric security is more secure than security measures such as passwords or smart cards because passwords can be discovered and smart cards can be stolen. Common biometric devices available include fingerprint readers, retina scanners, and face and voice recognition devices. The user is granted access if their characteristics match saved settings and the correct login information is supplied.

Biometric devices, which measure physical information about a user, are ideal for highly secure areas when combined with a secondary security measure such as a password or pin. However, for most small organizations, this type of solution is too expensive.

Smart Card Security

A *smart card* is a small plastic card, about the size of a credit card, with a small chip embedded in it. The chip is an intelligent data carrier, capable of processing, storing, and safeguarding data. Smart cards store private information, such as bank account numbers, personal identification, medical records, and digital signatures. Smart cards provide authentication and encryption to keep data safe.

Security Key Fob

A *security key fob* is a small device that resembles the ornament on a key ring. It has a radio that communicates with a computer over a short range. The fob is small enough to attach to a key ring. The computer must detect the signal from the key fob before it accepts a username and password.

Data Backups (10.2.2.3)

A *data backup* stores a copy of the information on a computer to removable backup media that can be kept in a safe place. Backing up data is one of the most effective ways of protecting against data loss. Data can be lost or damaged in circumstances such as theft, equipment failure, or a disaster. If the computer hardware fails, the data can be restored from the backup to functional hardware.

Data backups should be performed on a regular basis and included in a security plan. The most current data backup is usually stored offsite to protect the backup media if anything happens to the main facility. Backup media is often reused to save on media costs. Always follow the organization's media rotation guidelines.

These are some considerations for data backups:

- **Frequency:** Backups can take a long time. Sometimes it is easier to make a full backup monthly or weekly and then do frequent partial backups of any data that has changed since the last full backup. However, having many partial backups increases the amount of time needed to restore the data.

- **Storage:** For extra security, backups should be transported to an approved offsite storage location on a daily, weekly, or monthly rotation, as required by the security policy.

- **Security:** Backups can be protected with passwords. The password is entered before the data on the backup media can be restored.

- **Validation:** Always validate backups to ensure the integrity of the data.

Data Encryption (10.2.2.4)

Encryption is often used to protect data. *Encryption* is where data is transformed using a complicated algorithm to make it unreadable. A special key must be used to return the unreadable information back into readable data. Software programs are used to encrypt files, folders, and even entire drives.

Encrypting File System (EFS) is a Windows feature that can encrypt data. EFS is directly linked to a specific user account. Only the user who encrypted the data will be able to access it after it has been encrypted using EFS.

To encrypt data using EFS, follow these steps:

Step 1. Select one or more files or folders.

Step 2. Right-click the selected data, and then click **Properties**.

Step 3. Click **Advanced**.

Step 4. Check the **Encrypt contents to secure data** check box.

Files and folders that have been encrypted with EFS are displayed in green, as shown in Figure 10-8.

Figure 10-8 Encrypting File System

In Windows 7 and Windows Vista Ultimate and Enterprise editions, a feature called *BitLocker* is included to encrypt the entire hard drive volume. BitLocker is also able to encrypt removable drives. To use BitLocker, at least two volumes must be present on a hard disk. A system volume is left unencrypted and must be at least 100 MB. This volume holds the files required by Windows to boot. Windows 7 creates this volume by default when it is installed.

When using BitLocker with Windows Vista, a special tool called *BitLocker Drive Preparation Tool* can be used to shrink the volume containing the operating system. Once the volume has been shrunk, a system file can be created to comply with the requirements of BitLocker.

After the system volume has been created, the *Trusted Platform Module (TPM)* must be initialized. The TPM is a specialized chip installed on the motherboard of a computer to be used for hardware and software authentication. The TPM stores information specific to the host system, such as encryption keys, digital certificates, and passwords. Applications that use encryption can make use of the TPM chip to secure things like user authentication information; software license protection;

and encrypted files, folders, and disks. Integrating hardware security, such as TPM with software security, results in a much safer computer system than using software security alone.

To initialize the TPM, follow these steps:

Step 1. Start the computer, and enter the BIOS configuration.

Step 2. Look for the **TPM** option within the BIOS configuration screens. Consult the manual for your motherboard to locate the correct screen.

Step 3. Choose **Enable** and then press **Enter.**

Step 4. Save the changes to the BIOS configuration.

Step 5. Reboot the computer.

To turn on BitLocker, follow these steps:

Step 1. Click **Start > Control Panel > Security > BitLocker Drive Encryption.**

Step 2. If the UAC message appears, click **Continue.**

Step 3. On the BitLocker Drive Encryption page, click **Turn On BitLocker** on the operating system volume.

Step 4. If TPM is not initialized, the Initialize TPM Security Hardware Wizard appears. Follow the instructions provided by the wizard to initialize the TPM. Restart your computer.

Step 5. Save your password using one of the options on the save recovery password page:

- **Save the password on a USB drive:** This option saves the password to a USB drive.

- **Save the password in a folder:** This option saves the password to a network drive or other location.

- **Print the password:** This option will print the password.

Step 6. After saving the recovery password, click **Next.**

Step 7. On the **Encrypt the selected disk volume** page, check the **Run BitLocker System Check** check box.

Step 8. Click **Continue.**

Step 9. Click **Restart Now.**

The Encryption in Progress status bar is displayed.

Malicious Software Protection Programs (10.2.3.1)

Certain types of attacks, such as those performed by spyware and phishing, collect data about the user that can be used by an attacker to gain confidential information.

You should run virus and spyware scanning programs to detect and remove unwanted software. Many browsers now come equipped with special tools and settings that prevent the operation of several forms of malicious software. It may take several different programs and multiple scans to completely remove all malicious software. Run only one malware protection program at a time.

- **Virus protection:** An *antivirus program* typically runs automatically in the background and monitors for problems. When a virus is detected, the user is warned and the program attempts to quarantine or delete the virus.

- **Spyware protection:** *Antispyware programs* scan for *keyloggers*, which capture your keystrokes, and other malware so that it can be removed from the computer.

- **Adware protection:** *Anti-adware programs* look for programs that display advertising on your computer.

- **Phishing protection:** *Antiphishing programs* block the IP addresses of known phishing websites and warn the user about suspicious websites.

Note

Malicious software can become embedded in the operating system. Special removal tools are available from security software development companies that clean the operating system.

Rogue Antivirus

When browsing the Internet, it is common to see advertisements for products and software. These advertisements can be a method for infecting a user's computer. Some of these ads display messages that indicate the user's computer is infected by a virus or other malware. The ad or pop-up may look like an actual Windows warning window stating that the computer is infected and must be cleaned, as shown in Figure 10-9. Clicking Remove, Clean, OK, or even Cancel or Exit may begin the download and installation of the malware. This type of attack is called *rogue antivirus*.

Figure 10-9   Rogue Antivirus

When faced with a warning window that is suspect, never click inside the warning window. Close the tab or the browser to see if the warning window goes away. If the tab or browser does not close, press **Alt+F4** to close the window or use the Task Manager to end the program. If the warning window does not go away, scan the computer using a known, good antivirus or adware protection program to ensure that the computer is not infected.

Remediating Infected Systems

When a malware protection program detects that a computer is infected, it removes or quarantines the threat. But the computer is most likely still at risk. The first step to remediating an infected computer is to remove the computer from the network to prevent other computers from becoming infected. Physically unplug all network cables from the computer and disable all wireless connections.

The next step is to follow any incident response policies that are in place. This may include notifying IT personnel, saving log files to removable media, or turning off the computer. For a home user, update the malicious software protection programs that are installed and perform full scans of all media installed in the computer. Many antivirus programs can be set to run on system start before loading Windows. This allows the program to access all areas of the disk without being affected by the operating system or any malware.

Viruses and worms can be difficult to remove from a computer. Software tools are required to remove viruses and repair the computer code that the virus has modified. These software tools are provided by operating system manufacturers and security software companies. Make sure that you download these tools from a legitimate site.

Boot the computer in Safe Mode to prevent most drivers from loading. Install additional malware protection programs and perform full scans to remove or quarantine additional malware. It may be necessary to contact a specialist to ensure that the computer has been completely cleaned. In some cases, the computer must be reformatted and restored from a backup, or the operating system may need to be reinstalled.

The system restore service may include infected files in a restore point. After the computer has been cleaned of any malware, the system restore files should be deleted. If system restore is used to restore the computer, restore points that contain infected files will not be listed and therefore; will not re-infect the computer.

To delete the current system restore files in Windows 7, follow these steps:

Step 1. Click the **Windows Start** button > right-click **Computer >** click **Properties > System Protection** tab.

Step 2. Select the drive that contains the restore points you want to delete.

Step 3. Click **Configure.**

Step 4. Click **Delete** next to Delete all restore points (this includes system settings and previous versions of files).

In Windows Vista and Windows XP, follow these steps:

Step 1. Create a restore point.

Step 2. Right-click the drive that contains the restore points you want to delete.

Step 3. Select **Properties > General** tab **> Disk Cleanup.**

Step 4. Windows will analyze the disk.

Step 5. In the Disk Cleanup for (C:) window, click the **More Options** tab **>** **Clean up.**

Step 6. Click **Delete** in the Disk Cleanup window to delete all but the most recent restore point.

Worksheet 10.2.3.2: Third-Party Antivirus Software

In this activity, you use the Internet, a newspaper, or a local store to gather information about third-party anti-virus software. Refer to Worksheet 10.2.3.2 in *IT Essentials: PC Hardware and Software Lab Manual*, Fifth Edition.

Signature File Updates (10.2.3.3)

Security strategies are constantly changing, as are the technologies used to secure equipment and data. New exploits are discovered daily. Attackers constantly look for new ways to infiltrate computers and networks. Software manufacturers must regularly create and dispense new patches to fix flaws and vulnerabilities in products. If a computer is left unprotected by a technician, an attacker can gain access. Unprotected computers on the Internet often become infected within a few minutes.

Threats to security from viruses and worms are always present. Because new viruses are always being developed, security software must be continually updated. This process can be performed automatically, but a technician should know how to manually update any type of protection software and all customer application programs.

Virus, spyware, and adware detection programs look for patterns in the programming code of the software in a computer. These patterns are determined by analyzing viruses that are intercepted on the Internet and on LANs. These code patterns are called *signatures*. The publishers of protection software compile the signatures into virus definition tables. To update signature files for antivirus and antispyware software, first check to see if the signature files are the most recent files. You can check the file status by navigating to the "About" option of the protection software or by launching the update tool for the protection software.

How To

To update signature file, follow these steps:

Step 1. Create a Windows restore point. If the file you load is corrupt, setting a restore point allows you to go back to the way things were.

Step 2. Open the antivirus or antispyware program. If the program is set to execute or obtain updates automatically, you may need to turn the automatic feature off to perform these steps manually.

Step 3. Click the **Update** button.

Step 4. After the program is updated, use it to scan the computer.

Step 5. When the scan is complete, check the report for viruses or other problems that could not be treated and delete them yourself.

Step 6. Set the antivirus or antispyware program to automatically update and run on a scheduled basis.

Always retrieve the signature files from the manufacturer's website to make sure the update is authentic and not corrupted by viruses. This can put great demand on the manufacturer's website, especially when new viruses are released. To avoid creating too much traffic at a single website, some manufacturers distribute their signature files for download to multiple download sites. These download sites are called *mirrors*.

Caution

When downloading signature files from a mirror, ensure that the mirror site is a legitimate site. Always link to the mirror site from the manufacturer's website.

Common Communication Encryption Types (10.2.4.1)

There are several different types of communication encryption used in computer and network security. The following paragraphs describe some of these types and how they encrypt data communication.

Hash Encoding

Hash encoding, or hashing, ensures that messages are not corrupted or tampered with during transmission. Hashing uses a mathematical function to create a numeric value that is unique to the data. If even one character is changed, the function output, called the *message digest*, will not be the same. However, the function is one way. Knowing the message digest does not allow an attacker to re-create the message, making it difficult for someone to intercept and change messages. Hash encoding is shown in Figure 10-10. The most popular hashing algorithms are *Secure Hash Algorithm (SHA)*, *message digest 5 (MD5)*, and *Data Encryption Standard (DES)*.

Figure 10-10 Hash Encoding

Symmetric Encryption

Symmetric encryption requires both sides of an encrypted conversation to use an encryption key to encode and decode the data. The sender and receiver must use identical keys. Symmetric encryption is shown in Figure 10-11. DES and *Triple Data Encryption Standard (3DES)* are examples of symmetric encryption.

Figure 10-11   Symmetric Encryption

Asymmetric Encryption

Asymmetric encryption requires two keys, a private key and a public key. The public key can be widely distributed, including emailing in clear text or posting on the web. The private key is kept by an individual and must not be disclosed to any other party. These keys can be used in two ways.

Public key encryption is used when a single organization needs to receive encrypted text from a number of sources. The public key can be widely distributed and used to encrypt the messages. The intended recipient is the only party to have the *private key*, which is used to decrypt the messages.

In the case of *digital signatures*, a private key is required for encrypting a message, and a public key is needed to decode the message. This approach allows the receiver to be confident about the source of the message because only a message encrypted using the originator's private key could be decrypted by the public key. Asymmetric encryption using digital signatures is shown in Figure 10-12. *RSA* is the most popular example of asymmetric encryption. RSA, is an algorithm for public key encryption. The acronym is actually the surname initials of Ron Rivest, Adi Shamir, and Leonard Adleman, the men who first described this algorithm for public key cryptography.

Figure 10-12   Asymmetric Encryption

Service Set Identifiers (10.2.4.2)

Because radio waves are used to transmit data in wireless networks, it is easy for attackers to monitor and collect data without physically connecting to a network. Attackers gain access to a network by being within range of an unprotected wireless network. A technician needs to configure access points and wireless NICs to an appropriate level of security.

When installing wireless services, apply wireless security techniques immediately to prevent unwanted access to the network. Wireless access points should be configured with basic security settings that are compatible with the existing network security.

The *service set identifier (SSID)* is the name of the wireless network. A wireless router or access point broadcasts the SSID by default so that wireless devices can detect the wireless network. Manually enter the SSID on wireless devices to connect to the wireless network when the SSID broadcast has been disabled on the wireless router or access point.

To disable SSID broadcasting, use the following path:

Wireless > Basic Wireless Settings > select **Disabled for SSID Broadcast > Save Settings > Continue**

Disabling the SSID broadcast provides very little security. If the SSID broadcast is disabled, each computer user who wants to connect to the wireless network must enter the SSID manually. When a computer is searching for a wireless network, it will broadcast the SSID. An advanced hacker can easily intercept this information and use it to impersonate your router and capture your credentials.

MAC Address Filtering (10.2.4.3)

MAC address filtering is a technique used to deploy device-level security on a wireless LAN. Because every wireless device has a unique MAC address, wireless routers and access points can prevent wireless devices from connecting to the network if the devices do not have authorized MAC addresses. To enforce MAC address filtering, enter the MAC address of each wireless device.

To set up a MAC address filter, follow these steps:

Step 1.   Select **Wireless > Wireless MAC Filter.**

Step 2.   Select **Enabled.**

Step 3.   Select **Prevent** or **Permit** for the access restriction type.

Step 4.   Click **Wireless Client List.**

Step 5.   Select the client.

Step 6.   Click **Save to MAC Address Filter List > Add > Save Settings > Continue.**

Repeat the steps for setting up a MAC address filter to add more wireless clients to the MAC Address Filter List.

The MAC address of a wireless NIC can be found by typing **ipconfig /all** at the command prompt. The MAC address is labeled Physical Address in the output. For devices other than computers, the MAC address is usually on the label of the device or within the manufacturer's instructions.

Filtering MAC addresses can be tedious if a lot of devices are connected to the network. Also, when using MAC address filtering, it is possible for an attacker to sniff a MAC address using wireless hacking tools. After the attacker has the MAC address, it can be used to impersonate the computer that has been approved through MAC address filtering. Use a strong encryption technology instead.

Wireless Security Modes (10.2.4.4)

Use a wireless encryption system to encode the information being sent to prevent unwanted capture and use of data. Both ends of every link must use the same encryption standard.

Most wireless access points support several different security modes. The most common ones are as follows:

- *Wired Equivalent Privacy (WEP):* The first-generation security standard for wireless. Attackers quickly discovered that WEP encryption was easy to break. The encryption keys used to encode the messages could be detected by monitoring programs. After the keys were obtained, messages could be easily decoded.

- *Wi-Fi Protected Access (WPA):* An improved version of WEP, WPA covers the entire 802.11i standard (a security layer for wireless systems). WPA uses much stronger encryption than WEP encryption.

- *Wi-Fi Protected Access 2 (WPA2):* An improved version of WPA. This protocol introduces higher levels of security than WPA. WPA2 supports robust encryption, providing government-grade security. WPA2 has two versions: Personal (password authentication) and Enterprise (server authentication).

Additions to WPA and WPA2

Other security implementations have been added to the WPA standard:

- *Temporal Key Integrity Protocol (TKIP):* This technology changes the encryption key on a per-packet basis and provides a method to check the integrity of messages.

- *Extensible Authentication Protocol (EAP):* Uses a centralized authentication server to increase security.

- *Protected Extensible Authentication Protocol (PEAP):* A protocol that does not use a certificate server.

- *Advanced Encryption Standard (AES):* A symmetric key encryption method added to WPA2 only.

To add wireless security, use the following path:

Wireless > Wireless Security > select a security mode **>** select an encryption type **>** type the pre-shared key **>** set **Key Renewal >** click **Save Settings > Continue**

Packet Tracer
☐ Activity

PT 10.2.4.5 - Wireless Security Techniques

In this Packet Tracer activity, you configure WPA2, MAC filtering, and single-port forwarding in the Linksys WRT300N. To access the activities found in this book, please refer to the instructions found in the Introduction.

Wireless Access (10.2.4.6)

Wireless communication is very easily monitored by unauthorized users. Making sure your wireless equipment and devices are protected is an important step in securing your network.

Wireless Antennae

The gain and signal pattern of the antenna connected to a wireless access point can influence where the signal can be received. Avoid transmitting signals outside of the network area by installing an antenna with a pattern that serves your network users.

Some wireless devices allow you to change the power level of the wireless radio. This can be beneficial in two ways:

- The size of the wireless network can be decreased to prevent coverage in unwanted areas. Use a laptop or mobile device to determine the coverage area. Decrease the radio power level until the coverage area is the desired size.

- Increase the power level in areas with many wireless networks to help keep interference from other networks to a minimum and help clients to stay connected.

Network Device Access

Many wireless devices built by a specific manufacturer have the same default username and password for accessing the wireless configuration. If left unchanged, unauthorized users can easily log in to the access point and modify the settings. When you first connect to the network device, change the default username and password. Some devices allow you to change both the username and the password, while others only allow you to change the password.

To change the default password, as shown in Figure 10-13, use the following path:

Administration > Management > type the new router password > reenter to confirm > click **Save Settings**

Figure 10-13 E2500 Management

Wi-Fi Protected Setup

For many people, setting up a wireless router and manually entering the configurations is difficult. In the past, a lot of people would simply plug in the device and use the default settings. These settings allowed devices to easily connect, but left a number of security holes, such as a lack of encryption, default SSID use, and default administration password use. *Wi-Fi Protected Setup (WPS)* was developed to help people set up a wireless network quickly, easily, and with security enabled.

With WPS, the most common way for a user to connect is the PIN method. With the PIN method, the wireless router has a factory-set PIN that is either printed on a sticker or shown on a display. When a wireless device tries to connect to the wireless router, the router asks for the PIN. After the user enters the PIN on the wireless device, they are connected to the network and security is enabled.

WPS has a major security flaw. Software has been developed that can intercept traffic and recover the WPS PIN and the pre-shared encryption key. As a security best practice, disable WPS on the wireless router if possible.

Firewalls (10.2.4.7)

A *hardware firewall* is a physical filtering component that inspects data packets from the network before they reach computers and other devices on a network. A hardware firewall is a freestanding unit that does not use the resources of the computers it is protecting, so there is no impact on processing performance. The firewall can be configured to block multiple individual ports, a range of ports, or even traffic specific to an application. The Linksys E2500 wireless router is also a hardware firewall.

A hardware firewall passes two different types of traffic into your network:

- Responses to traffic that originates from inside your network
- Traffic destined for a port that you have intentionally left open

There are several types of hardware firewall configurations:

- *Packet filter*: Packets cannot pass through the firewall, unless they match the established rule set configured in the firewall. Traffic can be filtered based on different attributes, such as source IP address, source port, or destination IP address or port. Traffic can also be filtered based on destination services or protocols such as WWW or FTP.

- *Stateful packet inspection (SPI)*: This is a firewall that keeps track of the state of network connections traveling through the firewall. Packets that are not part of a known connection are dropped.

- **Application layer:** All packets traveling to or from an application are intercepted. All unwanted outside traffic is prevented from reaching protected devices.

- *Proxy*: This is a firewall installed on a proxy server that inspects all traffic and allows or denies packets based on configured rules. A proxy server is a server that is a relay between a client and a destination server on the Internet.

Hardware and software firewalls protect data and equipment on a network from unauthorized access. A firewall should be used in addition to security software. Table 10-4 compares hardware and software firewalls.

Table 10-4   Hardware and Software Firewall Comparison

Hardware Firewall	Software Firewall
Dedicated hardware component.	Available as third-party software; cost varies.
Initial cost for hardware and software updates can be expensive.	Free version included with Windows operating system.
Multiple computers can be protected.	Multiple computers can be protected.
No impact on computer performance.	Uses the CPU; potential impact on computer performance.

To configure hardware firewall settings on the Linksys E2500, use the following path:

Security > Firewall > select **Enable for SPI Firewall Protection**

Then select other Internet filters and web filters required to secure the network:

Click **Save Settings > Continue**

> **Note**
>
> Even on a secure network, you should enable the internal operating system firewall for additional security. Some applications may not operate properly unless the firewall is configured correctly for them.

Demilitarized Zone

A *demilitarized zone (DMZ)* is a subnetwork that provides services to an untrusted network. An email, web, or FTP server is often placed into the DMZ so that the traffic using the server does not come inside the local network. This protects the internal network from attacks by this traffic but does not protect the servers in the DMZ in any way. It is common for a firewall or proxy to manage traffic to and from the DMZ.

On the Linksys E2500, you can create a DMZ for one device by forwarding all traffic ports from the Internet to a specific IP address or MAC address. A server, game machine, or web camera can be in the DMZ so that the device can be accessed by anyone. The device in the DMZ, however, is exposed to attacks from hackers on the Internet.

Worksheet 10.2.4.8: Research Firewalls

In this activity, you use the Internet, a newspaper, or a local store to gather information about hardware and software firewalls. Refer to Worksheet 10.2.4.8 in *IT Essentials: PC Hardware and Software Lab Manual*, Fifth Edition.

Port Forwarding and Port Triggering (10.2.4.9)

Hardware firewalls can be used to block ports to prevent unauthorized access in and out of a LAN. However, there are situations when specific ports must be opened so that certain programs and applications can communicate with devices on different networks. *Port forwarding* is a rule-based method of directing traffic between devices on separate networks. This method of exposing devices to the Internet is much safer than using a DMZ.

When traffic reaches the router, the router determines whether the traffic should be forwarded to a certain device based on the port number found with the traffic. Port numbers are associated with specific services, such as FTP, HTTP, HTTPS, and POP3. The rules determine which traffic is sent on to the LAN. For example, a router might be configured to forward port 80, which is associated with HTTP. When the router receives a packet with the destination port of 80, the router forwards the traffic to the server inside the network that serves web pages.

To add port forwarding, as shown in Figure 10-14, follow these steps:

Step 1. Click **Applications & Gaming > Single Port Forwarding**.

Step 2. Select or enter an application name. You might need to enter the external port number, Internet port number, and protocol type.

Step 3. Enter the IP address of the computer to receive the requests.

Step 4. Click **Enable > Save Settings > Continue**.

Figure 10-14   E2500 Single-Port Forwarding

Port triggering allows the router to temporarily forward data through inbound ports to a specific device. You can use port triggering to forward data to a computer only when a designated port range is used to make an outbound request. For example, a videogame might use ports 27000–27100 for connecting with other players. These are the trigger ports. A chat client might use port 56 for connecting the same players so that they can interact with each other. In this instance, if there is gaming traffic on an outbound port within the triggered port range, inbound chat traffic on port 56 is forwarded to the computer that is being used to play the video game and chat with friends. When the game is over and the triggered ports are no longer in use, port 56 is no longer allowed to send traffic of any type to this computer.

To add port triggering, follow these steps:

Step 1.   Select **Applications & Gaming > Port Range Triggering**.

Step 2.   Type the application name. Enter the starting and ending port numbers of the triggered port range and the starting and ending port numbers of the forwarded port range.

Step 3.   Click **Enable > Save Settings > Continue**.

Lab 10.2.4.10: Configure Wireless Security

In this lab, you configure and test the wireless settings on the Linksys E2500. Refer to Lab 10.2.4.10 in *IT Essentials: PC Hardware and Software Lab Manual*, Fifth Edition.

Physical Equipment Protection Methods (10.2.5.1)

Physical security is as important as data security. When a computer is taken, the data is also stolen. It is important to restrict access to premises using fences, door locks, and gates. Protect the network infrastructure, such as cabling, telecommunication equipment, and network devices, with the following:

- Secured telecommunications rooms, equipment cabinets, and cages
- Cable locks and security screws for hardware devices
- Wireless detection for unauthorized access points
- Hardware firewalls
- Network management system that detects changes in wiring and patch panels

Disabling AutoRun

Another method of hardware security is to disable the AutoRun feature of the operating system. *AutoRun* automatically follows the instructions in a special file called autorun.inf when it is found on new media. AutoPlay is different from AutoRun. The *AutoPlay* feature is a convenient way to automatically identify when new media, such as optical disks, external hard drives, or thumb drives, are inserted or connected to the computer. AutoPlay prompts the user to choose an action based on the content of the new media, such as run a program, play music, or explore the media.

On Windows, AutoRun is executed first, unless it is disabled. If AutoRun is not disabled, it follows the instructions in the autorun.inf file. On Windows Vista and Windows 7, AutoRun is not allowed to bypass AutoPlay. However, on Windows XP, AutoRun bypasses AutoPlay and might launch an application without prompting the user. This is a security risk because it can automatically run a malicious program and compromise the system, so it is recommended to disable AutoRun.

How To

To disable AutoRun in Windows XP, follow these steps:

Step 1.   Select **Start > Run**.

Step 2.   Type **regedit** and click **OK**.

Step 3.   Navigate to HKEY_LOCAL_MACHINE\SYSTEM\CurrentControlSet\ Services\Cdrom.

Step 4.   Double-click **AutoRun**. In the Value Data text box, type **0** and click **OK**, as shown in Figure 10-15.

Figure 10-15   Disabling AutoRun

Step 5.   Close the Registry Editor.

Step 6.   You might have to log out and then log back in for this change to take effect.

Two-Factor Authentication

Computer equipment and data can be secured using overlapping protection techniques to prevent unauthorized access to sensitive data. An example of overlapping protection is using a password and a smart card to protect an asset. This is known as *two-factor authentication*. When considering a security program, the cost of the implementation has to be balanced against the value of the data or the equipment to be protected.

Security Hardware (10.2.5.2)

Security hardware helps prevent security breaches and loss of data or equipment. Physical security access control measures include locks, video surveillance, and security guards. Card keys secure physical areas. If a *card key* is lost or stolen, only the missing card must be deactivated. The card key system is more expensive than security locks, but when a conventional key is lost, the lock must be replaced or rekeyed.

Network equipment should be mounted in secured areas. All cabling should be enclosed in conduits or routed inside walls to prevent unauthorized access or tampering. A *conduit* is a casing that protects the infrastructure media from damage and unauthorized access. Network ports that are not in use should be disabled.

Biometric devices, which measure physical information about a user, are ideal for highly secure areas. However, for most small organizations, this type of solution is expensive.

The security policy should identify hardware and equipment that can be used to prevent theft, vandalism, and data loss. Physical security involves four interrelated aspects: access, data, infrastructure, and the physical computer.

There are several methods of physically protecting computer equipment:

- Use cable locks with equipment.
- Keep telecommunication rooms locked.
- Fit equipment with security screws.
- Use security cages around equipment.
- Label and install sensors, such as Radio Frequency Identification (RFID) tags, on equipment.
- Install physical alarms triggered by motion-detection sensors.
- Use webcams with motion-detection and surveillance software.

For access to facilities, there are several means of protection:

- Card keys that store user data, including level of access
- Biometric sensors that identify physical characteristics of the user, such as fingerprints or retinas
- Posted security guard
- Sensors, such as RFID tags, to monitor equipment

Use locking cases, cable locks, and laptop docking station locks to protect computers from being moved. Use lockable hard drive carriers and secure storage and transport of backup media to protect data and media theft.

Protecting Data While in Use

For users who need to access sensitive network resources, a token can be used to provide two-factor authentication. A *token* can be hardware type, such as a pin card, shown in Figure 10-16, or a software type, such as a soft token program, as shown in Figure 10-17.

Figure 10-16   PIN Card

Figure 10-17   Soft Token Program

The token is assigned to a computer and creates a unique code at certain times. When users access a network resource, they enter a PIN and a number displayed by the token. The number displayed by the token is created from a calculation made with its internal clock and a random number encoded on the token at the factory. This number is authenticated against a database that knows the token's number and can calculate the same number.

The information on computer screens can be protected from prying eyes with a privacy screen. A *privacy screen* is a panel that is often made of plastic. It prevents light from projecting at low angles, so that only the user looking straight on can see what is on the screen. For example, on an airplane, a user can prevent the person sitting in the next seat from seeing what is on a laptop screen.

The Right Security Mix

Factors that determine the most effective security equipment to use to secure equipment and data include the following:

- How the equipment is used

- Where the computer equipment is located

- What type of user access to data is required

For instance, a computer in a busy public place, such as a library, requires additional protection from theft and vandalism. In a busy call center, a server may need to be secured in a locked equipment room. Where it is necessary to use a laptop computer in a public place, a security dongle ensures that the system locks if the user and laptop are separated.

Security Maintenance (10.3.1)

Implementing strong security policies and setting up protection from security threats is the beginning of protecting your network. All security procedures, software, and hardware must be maintained and updated regularly to ensure that data and equipment remain safe from security threats.

Operating System Service Packs and Security Patches (10.3.1.1)

Patches are code updates that manufacturers provide to prevent a newly discovered virus or worm from making a successful attack. From time to time, manufacturers combine patches and upgrades into a comprehensive update application called a *service pack*. Many devastating virus attacks could have been much less severe if more users had downloaded and installed the latest service pack.

Windows routinely checks the Windows Update website for high-priority updates that can help protect a computer from the latest security threats. These updates include security updates, critical updates, and service packs. Depending on the setting you choose, Windows automatically downloads and installs any high-priority updates that your computer needs or notifies you as these updates become available.

Updates must be installed, not just downloaded. If you use the Automatic setting, you can schedule the time and day. Otherwise, new updates are installed at 3 a.m. by default if the computer is on or in a low power state. If your computer is turned off during a scheduled update, updates are installed the next time you start your computer. You can also choose to have Windows notify you when a new update is available and then install the update yourself.

Because of constantly changing security threats, technicians should understand how to install patches and updates. They should also be able to recognize when new updates and patches are available. Some manufacturers release updates on the same day every month but also send out critical updates when necessary. Other manufacturers provide automatic update services that patch the software every time the computer is turned on or email notifications when a new patch or update is released.

To update the operating system with a service pack or security patch, follow these steps:

Step 1. Create a restore point prior to installing an update.

Step 2. Check for updates to ensure that you have the latest ones.

Step 3. Download updates using Automatic Updates or from the operating system manufacturer's website.

Step 4. Install the update.

Step 5. Reboot the computer if necessary.

Step 6. Ensure that the computer is operating properly.

Windows automatically downloads and installs updates to operating systems by default. However, the updates might conflict with an organization's security policy or other settings on a computer. The following Windows options allow you to control when software is updated:

- **Automatic:** Downloads and installs updates automatically without user intervention.

- **Only download updates:** Downloads the updates automatically, but the user is required to install them.

- **Notify me:** Notifies the user that updates are available and gives the option to download and install.

- **Turn off automatic updates:** Prevents any checking for updates.

To configure Windows Update, use the following path:

Start > All Programs > Windows Update > Change settings

If the user is on a dialup network, the Windows Update setting should be configured to notify the user of available updates or it should be turned off. The dialup user might want to control the update by selecting a time when the update does not interrupt other network activity or use the limited resources available.

In an enterprise environment, patch management policies detail downloading and testing updates offline before deployment to individual PCs in the network.

Worksheet 10.3.1.2: Operating System Updates in Windows

In this activity, you use the Internet to research operating system updates. Be prepared to discuss your research with the class. Refer to Worksheet 10.3.1.2 in *IT Essentials: PC Hardware and Software Lab Manual*, Fifth Edition.

Data Backups (10.3.1.3)

You can make a Windows backup manually or schedule how often the backup takes place automatically. To successfully back up and restore data in Windows, the appropriate user rights and permissions are required:

- All users can back up their own files and folders. They can also back up files for which they have the Read permission.

- All users can restore files and folders for which they have the Write permission.

- Members of the Administrators, Backup Operators, and Server Operators (if joined to a domain) can back up and restore all files, regardless of the assigned permissions. By default, members of these groups have the Backup Files and Directories and Restore Files and Directories user rights.

To start the Windows 7 Backup Files wizard for the first time, use the following path:

Start > All Programs > Maintenance > Backup and Restore > Set up backup

To change the backup settings in Windows 7 after the Backup Files wizard has been completed, use the following path:

Start > All Programs > Maintenance > Backup and Restore > Change settings > Change backup settings > Continue

To restore a backed up file in Windows 7, use the following path:

Start > All Programs > Maintenance > Backup and Restore > Restore my files

To start the Windows Vista Backup Files wizard, use the following path:

Start > All Programs > Maintenance > Backup and Restore Center > Back up files

To change the backup settings, use the following path:

Start > All Programs > Maintenance > Backup and Restore Center > Change settings > Change backup settings > Continue

To restore a backed up file in Windows Vista, use the following path:

Start > All Programs > Maintenance > Backup and Restore Center > Restore files

The Windows 7 or Windows Vista backup files have the extension .zip. Backup data is automatically compressed, and each file has a maximum compressed size of 200 MB. You can save a Windows 7 or Windows Vista backup file to a hard drive, any recordable media, or to another computer or server connected to your network. The backup can only be created from an NTFS partition. The target hard drive must be either NTFS or FAT formatted.

Note

You can manually exclude directories in the Windows 7 or Windows XP Backup or Restore Utility Wizard. This is not supported in the Windows Vista Backup Files Wizard.

To start the Windows XP Backup or Restore Utility Wizard, use the following path:

Start > All Programs > Accessories > System Tools > Backup

The Backup or Restore Wizard starts. To change the backup setting, use the following path:

Start > All Programs > Accessories > System Tools > Backup Advanced Mode > Tools > Options

To restore a backed-up file in Windows XP, in the Backup or Restore Wizard, use the following path:

Next > Restore files and settings > Next

Select the backed-up file, and then click **Next > Finish**.

The Windows Backup or Restore Utility Wizard and other backup applications commonly provide some of the backup types shown in Table 10-5.

The Windows XP Backup or Restore Utility Wizard files have the extension .bkf. You can save a .bkf file to a hard drive, a DVD, or to any other recordable media. The source location and target drive can be either NTFS or FAT.

You can perform backup operations for Windows XP at the command line or from a batch file using the **NTBACKUP** command. The default parameters for **NTBACKUP** are set in the Windows XP backup utility. The options that you want to override must be included in the command line. You cannot restore files from the command line using the **NTBACKUP** command.

On Windows 7 or Windows Vista, use the **WBADMIN** command. You cannot use backups made with the **NTBACKUP** command in Windows XP and restore them using the **WBADMIN** command in Windows 7 or Windows Vista. To restore backups from Windows XP to Windows 7 or Windows Vista, download a special version of the **NTBACKUP** command from Microsoft.

A combination of backup types allows the data to be backed up efficiently. Backup types are described in the Table 10-5. Backing up data can take time, so it is preferable to do backups when computer and network utilization requirements are low.

Table 10-5   Registry Backup Types

Type of Backup	Description
Full or normal	This backup type copies all selected files and marks each file as having been backed up.
Incremental	This backup type backs up only files that have been created or changed since the last full or incremental backup. Restoring files requires that you have the last full backup set and all incremental backup sets.
Differential	This backup type copies only files that have been created or changed since the last full backup. Restoring files requires that you have the last full and one differential backup.
Daily	This backup type copies all selected files that have been modified the day that the daily backup has been performed.
Copy	This backup type copies all selected files but does not mark them as having been backed up.

Lab 10.3.1.4: Data Backup and Recovery in Windows 7

In this lab, you back up data. You also perform a recovery of the data. Refer to Lab 10.3.1.4 in *IT Essentials: PC Hardware and Software Lab Manual*, Fifth Edition.

Lab 10.3.1.5: Data Backup and Recovery in Windows Vista

In this lab, you back up data. You also perform a recovery of the data. Refer to Lab 10.3.1.5 in *IT Essentials: PC Hardware and Software Lab Manual*, Fifth Edition.

Lab 10.3.1.6: Data Backup and Recovery in Windows XP

In this lab, you back up data. You also perform a recovery of the data. Refer to Lab 10.3.1.6 in *IT Essentials: PC Hardware and Software Lab Manual*, Fifth Edition.

Configuring Firewall Types (10.3.1.7)

A firewall selectively denies traffic to a computer or network segment. Firewalls generally work by opening and closing the ports used by various applications. By opening only the required ports on a firewall, you are implementing a restrictive security policy. Any packet not explicitly permitted is denied. In contrast, a permissive security policy permits access through all ports, except those explicitly denied. In the past, software and hardware were shipped with permissive settings. As users neglected to configure their equipment, the default permissive settings left many devices exposed to attackers. Most devices now ship with settings as restrictive as possible, while still allowing easy setup.

Configuring the Windows 7 or Windows Vista firewall can be completed in two ways:

- **Automatically:** The user is prompted to Keep Blocking, Unblock, or Ask Me Later for unsolicited requests. These requests might be from legitimate applications that have not been configured previously or from a virus or worm that has infected the system.

- **Manage Security Settings:** The user manually adds the program or ports that are required for the applications in use on the network.

To allow program access through the Windows Firewall in Windows 7, use the following path:

Start > Control Panel > Windows Firewall > Allow a program or feature through Windows Firewall > Allow another program

To allow program access through the Windows Firewall in Windows Vista, use the following path:

Start > Control Panel > Security Center > Windows Firewall > Change Settings > Continue > Exceptions > Add Program

To allow program access through the Windows Firewall in Windows XP, use the following path:

Start > Control Panel > Security Center > Windows Firewall > Exceptions > Add Program

To disable the Windows Firewall in Windows 7, use the following path:

Start > Control Panel > Windows Firewall > Turn Windows Firewall on or off > Turn off Windows Firewall (not recommended) > OK

To disable the Windows Firewall in Windows Vista, use the following path:

Start > Control Panel > Security Center > Windows Firewall > Turn Windows Firewall on or off > Continue > Off (not recommended) > OK

To disable the Windows Firewall in Windows XP, use the following path:

Start > Control Panel > Security Center > Windows Firewall

10.3.1.8 Lab: Configure a Windows 7 Firewall

In this lab, you explore the Windows 7 Firewall and configure some advanced settings. Refer to Lab 10.3.1.8 in *IT Essentials: PC Hardware and Software Lab Manual*, Fifth Edition.

10.3.1.9 Lab:- Configure a Windows Vista Firewall

In this lab, you explore the Windows Vista Firewall and configure some advanced settings. Refer to Lab 10.3.1.9 in *IT Essentials: PC Hardware and Software Lab Manual*, Fifth Edition.

10.3.1.10 Lab: Configure a Windows XP Firewall

In this lab, you explore the Windows XP Firewall and configure some advanced settings. Refer to Lab 10.3.1.10 in *IT Essentials: PC Hardware and Software Lab Manual*, Fifth Edition.

Maintaining Accounts (10.3.1.11)

Employees in an organization often require different levels of access to data. For example, a manager and an accountant might be the only employees in an organization with access to the payroll files.

Employees can be grouped by job requirements and given access to files according to group permissions. This process helps manage employee access to the network. Temporary accounts can be set up for employees who need short-term access. Close management of network access can help to limit areas of vulnerability that might allow a virus or malicious software to enter the network.

Terminating Employee Access

When an employee leaves an organization, access to data and hardware on the network should be terminated immediately. If the former employee has stored files in a personal space on a server, eliminate access by disabling the account. If the employee's replacement requires access to the applications and personal storage space, you can reenable the account and change the name to the name of the new employee.

Guest Accounts

Temporary employees and guests may need access to the network. For example, visitors might require access to email, the Internet, and a printer on the network.

These resources can be made available to a special account called Guest. When guests are present, they can be assigned to the Guest account. When no guests are present, the account can be disabled until the next guest arrives.

Some guest accounts require extensive access to resources, as in the case of a consultant or a financial auditor. This type of access should be granted only for the period of time required to complete the work.

To configure all the users and groups on a computer, type **lusrmgr.msc** in the Search box or in the Run Line utility, as shown in Figure 10-18.

Figure 10-18   lusrmgr.msc

Applying the Troubleshooting Process to Security (10.4.1)

Using the troubleshooting process to identify and correct security problems will help technicians maintain a consistent approach to managing and mitigating threats to data and equipment. Knowing some of the common problems and solutions that occur with security can help speed the troubleshooting process.

Identify the Problem (10.4.1.1)

The troubleshooting process is used to help resolve security issues. These problems range from simple, such as preventing someone from watching over your shoulder, to more complex, such as manually removing infected files from multiple networked computers. Use the troubleshooting steps as a guideline to help you diagnose and repair problems.

Computer technicians must be able to analyze a security threat and determine the appropriate method to protect assets and repair damage. The first step in the troubleshooting process is to identify the problem. Table 10-6 shows a list of open-ended and closed-ended questions to ask the customer.

Table 10-6   Step 1: Identify the Problem

Open-ended questions	When did the problem start?
	What problems are you experiencing?
	What websites have you visited recently?
	What security software is installed on your computer?
	Who else has used your computer recently?
Closed-ended questions	Is your security software up-to-date?
	Have you scanned your computer recently for viruses?
	Did you open any attachments from a suspicious email?
	Have you changed your password recently?
	Have you shared your password?

Establish a Theory of Probable Cause (10.4.1.2)

After you have talked to the customer, you can establish a theory of probable causes. Table 10-7 shows a list of some common probable causes for security problems.

Table 10-7   Step 2: Establish a Theory of Probably Cause

Common causes of security problems	Virus
	Trojan horse
	Worm
	Spyware
	Adware
	Grayware or malware
	Phishing scheme
	Password compromised
	Unprotected equipment rooms
	Unsecured work environment

Test the Theory to Determine Cause (10.4.1.3)

After you have developed some theories about what is wrong, test your theories to determine the cause of the problem. Table 10-8 shows a list of quick procedures that can determine the exact cause of the problem or even correct the problem. If a quick procedure corrects the problem, you can verify full system functionality. If a quick procedure does not correct the problem, you might need to research the problem further to establish the exact cause.

Table 10-8   Step 3: Test the Theory to Determine Cause

Common steps to determine cause	Disconnect from the network.
	Update antivirus and spyware signatures.
	Scan the computer with protection software.
	Check the computer for the latest OS patches and updates.
	Reboot the computer or network device.
	Log in as a different user to change your password.
	Secure equipment rooms.
	Secure the work environment.
	Enforce security policy.

Establish a Plan of Action to Resolve the Problem and Implement the Solution (10.4.1.4)

After you have determined the exact cause of the problem, establish a plan of action to resolve the problem and implement the solution. Table 10-9 shows some sources you can use to gather additional information to resolve an issue.

Table 10-9   Step 4: Establish a Plan of Action to Resolve the Problem and Implement the Solution

If no solution is achieved in the previous step, further research is needed to implement the solution.	Help desk repair logs
	Other technicians
	Manufacturer FAQs
	Technical websites
	Newsgroups
	Computer manuals
	Device manuals
	Online forums
	Internet search

Verify Full System Functionality and, If Applicable, Implement Preventive Measures (10.4.1.5)

After you have corrected the problem, verify full functionality and, if applicable, implement preventive measures. Table 10-10 shows a list of the steps to verify the solution.

Table 10-10 Step 5: Verify Full System Functionality and, If Applicable, Implement Preventive Measures

Verify full functionality.	Rescan that computer to ensure no viruses remain.
	Rescan the computer to ensure no spyware remains.
	Check the security software logs to ensure no problems remain.
	Check the computer for the latest OS patches and updates.
	Test network and Internet connectivity.
	Ensure all applications are working.
	Verify access to authorized resources such as shared printers and databases.
	Make sure entries are secured.
	Ensure security policy is enforced.

Document Findings, Actions, and Outcomes (10.4.1.6)

In the final step of the troubleshooting process, you must document your findings, actions, and outcomes. Table 10-11 shows a list of the tasks required to document the problem and the solution.

Table 10-11 Step 6: Document Findings, Actions, and Outcomes

Document your findings, actions, and outcomes.	Discuss the solution implemented with the customer.
	Have the customer verify the problem has been solved.
	Provide the customer with all paperwork.
	Document the steps taken to solve the problem in the work order and technician's journal.
	Document any components used in the repair.
	Document the time spent to solve the problem.

Identify Common Problems and Solutions (10.4.2.1)

Security problems can be attributed to hardware, software, or connectivity issues, or some combination of the three. You will resolve some types of security problems more often than others. Table 10-12 is a chart of common security problems and solutions.

Table 10-12   Common Problems and Solutions

Problem Symptom	Problem Causes	Possible Solutions
A wireless network is compromised even though 128-bit WEP encryption is in use.	A hacker issuing commonly available wireless hacking tools to crack the encryption.	Upgrade to WPA2 encryption. Add MAC address filtering for older clients that do not support WPA2.
A user is receiving hundreds or thousands of junk emails each day.	The network is not providing detection or protection for the email server from spammers.	Install antivirus or an email software program that removes spam from an email inbox.
An unknown printer repair person is observed looking under keyboards and on desktops.	Visitors are not being monitored properly, or user credentials have been stolen to enter the building.	Contact security or police. Advise users never to hide passwords near their work areas.
An unauthorized wireless access point is discovered on the network.	A user has added a wireless access point to increase the wireless range of the company network.	Disconnect and confiscate the unauthorized device. Enforce the security policy by taking action against the person responsible for the security breach.
Users with flash drives are infecting computers on the network with viruses.	The flash drive is infected with a virus and is not scanned by virus protection software when a network computer accesses it.	Set virus protection software to scan removable media when data is accessed.
A security alert is displayed.	The Windows Firewall is turned off. Virus definitions are out of date. Malware has been detected.	Turn on Windows Firewall. Update virus definitions. Scan the computer to remove any malware.
Windows Update fails.	The downloaded update is corrupted. The update requires a previous update that is not installed.	Download the update manually and install. Use System Restore to restore the computer to a time before the attempted update. Restore the computer from a backup.
System files have been renamed.	The computer has a virus.	Remove the virus using antivirus software Restore the computer from a backup.

Problem Symptom	Problem Causes	Possible Solutions
Your email contacts report spam coming from your address.	Your email has been hijacked.	Change your email password. Contact the email service support to reset the account.

Worksheet 10.4.2.2 is designed to reinforce your communication skills to verify information from the customer.

Worksheet 10.4.2.2: Gather Information from the Customer

In this worksheet, you gather data from the customer (a partner who has been assigned by your instructor) to begin the troubleshooting process, and then document the customer's problem in the work order. Refer to Worksheet 10.4.2.2 in *IT Essentials: PC Hardware and Software Lab Manual*, Fifth Edition.

Summary (10.5.1.1)

This chapter discussed computer security and why it is important to protect computer equipment, networks, and data. Threats, procedures, and preventive maintenance relating to data and physical security were described to help you keep computer equipment and data safe. Important concepts to remember from this chapter include the following:

- Security threats can come from inside or outside of an organization.

- Viruses and worms are common threats that attack data.

- Develop and maintain a security plan to protect both data and physical equipment from loss.

- Keep operating systems and applications up to date and secure with patches and service packs.

Summary of Exercises

Labs

The following labs cover material from this chapter. Refer to the labs in *IT Essentials: PC Hardware and Software Lab Manual*, Fifth Edition.

Lab 10.2.1.7: Securing Accounts, Data, and the Computer in Windows 7

Lab 10.2.1.8: Securing Accounts, Data, and the Computer in Windows Vista

Lab 10.2.1.9: Securing Accounts, Data, and the Computer in Windows XP

Lab 10.2.4.10: Configure Wireless Security

Lab 10.3.1.4: Data Backup and Recovery in Windows 7

Lab 10.3.1.5: Data Backup and Recovery in Windows Vista

Lab 10.3.1.6: Data Backup and Recovery in Windows XP

Lab 10.3.1.8: Configure a Windows 7 Firewall

Lab 10.3.1.9: Configure a Windows Vista Firewall

Lab 10.3.1.10: Configure a Windows XP Firewall

Worksheets

The following worksheets cover material from this chapter. Refer to the worksheets in *IT Essentials: PC Hardware and Software Lab Manual*, Fifth Edition.

Worksheet 10.1.1.7: Security Attacks

Worksheet 10.2.1.2: Answer Security Policy Questions

Worksheet 10.2.3.2: Third-Party Antivirus Software

Worksheet 10.2.4.8: Research Firewalls

Worksheet 10.3.1.2: Operating System Updates in Windows

Worksheet 10.4.2.2: Gather Information from the Customer

Check Your Understanding

You can find the answers to these questions in Appendix A, "Answers to 'Check Your Understanding' Questions."

1. What is an example of the implementation of physical security?

   A. Establishing personal firewalls on each computer

   B. Encrypting all sensitive data that is stored on the servers

   C. Requiring employees to use a card key when entering a secure area

   D. Ensuring that all operating system and antivirus software is up to date

2. A computer can successfully ping outside the local network but cannot access any World Wide Web services. What is the most probable cause of this problem?

   A. Windows Firewall is blocking port 80.

   B. Windows Firewall blocks port 23 by default.

   C. The computer network interface card is faulty.

   D. The BIOS or CMOS settings are blocking web access.

3. Which two methods would be acceptable to wipe data from a hard drive that has been used to store confidential information?

   A. Formatting

   B. Degaussing

   C. Drilling through the hard drive

   D. Data wiping

   E. Reinstalling the operating system

   F. Defragging

4. What is the purpose of a personal firewall on a computer?

   A. To protect the hardware against fire hazard

   B. To filter the traffic that is moving in and out of the PC

   C. To protect the computer from viruses and malware

   D. To increase the speed of the Internet connection

5. What must be done to ensure that the antivirus software on a computer is able to detect and eradicate the most recent viruses?

   A. Download the latest signature files on a regular basis.

   B. Schedule a scan once a week.

   C. Schedule antivirus updates using Windows Task Manager.

   D. Follow the firewall configuration guidelines on the antivirus manufacturer website.

6. Which statement is a characteristic of a differential backup?

   A. It copies all selected files and marks each as having been backed up.

   B. It copies all selected files that have been modified the day the daily backup has been performed.

   C. It copies all the files that have been changed since the last incremental backup.

   D. It copies all files which have been changed since the last full backup.

7. Which type of program causes banners and ads to appear on the desktop without any user intervention?

   A. Adware

   B. Spyware

   C. Stealth virus

   D. Trojan horse

8. In what type of attack does an attacker send a large number of requests to a server from several computers that are located at different geographical locations?

   A. DDoS

   B. DoS

   C. Email bomb

   D. Ping of death

9. Which action could be used to determine if a host is compromised and flooding traffic onto the network?

   A. Unseat and then reconnect the hard drive connectors on the host.

   B. Disconnect the host from the network.

   C. Check the host hard drive for errors and file system issues.

   D. Examine the Device Manager on the host for device conflicts.

10. When a support technician is troubleshooting a security issue on a system, which action should the technician take just before documenting the findings and closing the ticket?

   A. Boot the system in Safe Mode.

   B. Disconnect the system from the network.

   C. Ensure that all applications are working.

   D. Ask what the problem is that the customer is experiencing.

CHAPTER 11

The IT Professional

Objectives

Upon completion of this chapter, you will be able to answer the following questions:

- Why are good communication skills and professional behavior important?

- Does working with computer technology have ethical and legal aspects?

- What techniques can you use to keep the customer focused on the issue they need to have taken care of?

- What is the relationship between communication and troubleshooting?

- What are good stress and time management techniques?

- What is a call center environment, and what are the technician's responsibilities?

Key Terms

This chapter uses the following key terms. You can find the definitions in the Glossary.

Introduction (11.0.1)

Learning the technical knowledge required to work in the IT industry is just one aspect necessary to become a successful IT professional; however, it takes more than technical knowledge. An IT professional must be familiar with the legal and ethical issues that are inherent in this industry. Privacy and confidentiality concerns must also be taken into consideration during every customer encounter in the field, in the office, or over the phone in a call center. If you become a bench technician, although you might not interact with customers directly, you will have access to their private and confidential data. This chapter discusses some common legal and ethical issues.

Call center technicians work exclusively over the phone with customers. This chapter covers general call center procedures and the process of working with customers.

As an IT professional, you will troubleshoot and fix computers, and you will frequently communicate with customers and co-workers. In fact, troubleshooting is as much about communicating with the customer as it is about knowing how to fix a computer. In this chapter, you learn to use good communication skills as confidently as you use a screwdriver.

Communication Skills and the IT Professional (11.1)

This section addresses proper communication techniques for working with customers. It is necessary to explore these topics as a technician because it affects customer service. Developing a rapport and establishing a professional relationship with the customer will be beneficial to your information-gathering and problem-solving abilities.

Relationship Between Communication Skills and Troubleshooting (11.1.1.1)

Think of a time when you had to call a repair person to get something fixed. Did it feel like an emergency to you? Perhaps you had a bad experience with a repair person. Maybe that repair person did not seem to care about you or your problem. Are you likely to call that same person to fix a problem again?

Perhaps you had a good experience with a repair person. That person listened to you as you explained your problem and then asked you a few questions to get more information. Did you appreciate it when the repair person was sympathetic and responsive? Are you likely to call that person to fix a problem again?

A technician's good *communication skills* are an aid in the *troubleshooting* process. It takes time and experience to develop good communication skills and troubleshooting skills. As your hardware, software, and OS knowledge increases, your ability to quickly determine a problem and find a solution will improve. The same principle applies to developing communication skills. The more you practice good communication skills, the more effective you will become when working with customers. A knowledgeable technician who uses good communication skills will always be in demand in the job market.

To troubleshoot a computer, you need to learn the details of the problem from the customer. Most people who need a computer problem fixed are probably feeling some stress. If you establish a good rapport with the customer, they might relax a bit. A relaxed customer is more likely to be able to provide the information that you need to determine the source of the problem so it can be fixed.

Speaking directly with the customer is usually the first step in resolving the computer problem. As a technician, there are several communication and research tools available. All these resources can be used to help gather information for the troubleshooting process.

Relationship Between Communication Skills and Professional Behavior (11.1.1.2)

Whether you are talking with a customer on the phone or in person, it is important to communicate well and to represent yourself professionally. Your *professionalism* and good communication skills enhance your creditability with the customer.

If you are talking with a customer in person, that customer can see your body language. If you are talking with a customer over the phone, that customer can hear your sighs and sense that you might be sneering. Conversely, customers can also sense that you are smiling when you are speaking with them on the phone. Many call center technicians use a mirror at their desk to monitor their facial expressions.

Successful technicians control their own reactions and emotions from one customer call to the next. A good rule for all technicians to follow is that a new customer call means a fresh start. Never carry your frustration from one call to the next.

Worksheet 11.1.1.3: Technician Resources

In this worksheet, you use the Internet to find online resources for a specific computer component. Search online for resources that can help you troubleshoot the component. Be prepared to discuss the usefulness of the resources you found. Refer to the 11.1.1.3 worksheet in *IT Essentials: PC Hardware and Software Lab Manual, Fifth Edition*.

Working with a Customer (11.1.2)

Customers that seek support from a computer technician are generally doing so because they are experiencing problems with their systems. It is the responsibility of the technician to determine the problem while providing a positive customer experience with both professionalism and empathy. This section discusses how to identify customer types and relate to customers to provide quality support.

Using Communication Skills to Determine Customer Problems (11.1.2.1)

One of the first tasks of the technician is to determine the type of computer problem that the customer is experiencing.

Remember these three rules at the beginning of your conversation:

- **Know:** Call your customer by name.

- **Relate:** Use brief communication to create a one-to-one connection between you and your customer.

- **Understand:** Determine the customer's level of knowledge about the computer to know how to effectively communicate with the customer.

To accomplish this, practice active listening skills. Allow the customer to tell the whole story. During the time that the customer is explaining the problem, occasionally interject some small word or phrase, such as "I understand," "Yes," "I see," or "Okay." This behavior lets the customer know that you are there and that you are listening.

However, a technician should not interrupt the customer to ask a question or make a statement. This is rude, disrespectful, and creates tension. Many times in a conversation, you might find yourself thinking of what to say before the other person finishes talking. When you do this, you are not practicing active listening. Instead, try listening carefully when other people speak and let them finish their thoughts.

After you have listened to the customer explain the whole problem, clarify what the customer has said. This helps convince the customer that you have heard and understand the situation. A good practice for clarification is to paraphrase the customer's explanation by beginning with the words, "Let me see if I understand what you have told me." This is a very effective tool that demonstrates to the customer that you have listened and that you understand.

After you have assured the customer that you understand the problem, you will probably have to ask some follow-up questions. Make sure that these questions are pertinent. Do not ask questions that the customer has already answered while describing the problem unless it is for the sake of clarification. Doing this only irritates the customer and shows that you were not listening.

Follow-up questions should be targeted, closed-ended questions based on the information that you have already gathered. *Closed-ended questions* should focus on obtaining specific information. The customer should be able to answer a closed-ended question with a simple "yes" or "no" or with a factual response, such as "Windows XP Pro." Use all the information that you have gathered from the customer to complete a work order.

Displaying Professional Behavior with Customers (11.1.2.2)

When dealing with customers, it is necessary to be professional in all aspects of your role. You must handle customers with respect and prompt attention. When on a telephone, make sure that you know how to place a customer on hold, as well as how to transfer a customer without losing the call. The manner in which you conduct the call is important, and your job is to help the customer focus on and communicate the problem so that you (or another technician) can solve it.

Be positive when communicating with the customer. Tell the customer what you can do. Do not focus on what you cannot do. Be prepared to explain alternative ways that you can help them, such as emailing information, faxing step-by-step instructions, or using remote control software to solve the problem. Customers will quickly sense whether you are interested in helping them.

These are processes to follow before you put a customer on hold. First, let the customer finish speaking. Then explain that you have to put the customer on hold and ask the customer for permission to do so. When the customer agrees to be put on hold, thank the customer. Tell your customer that you will be away only a few minutes and explain what you will be doing during that time. Table 11-1 outlines the process to follow before you put a customer on hold.

Table 11-1   How to Put a Customer on Hold

Do	Do Not
Let the customer finish speaking.	Interrupt
Explain that you have to put the customer on hold and why.	Abruptly put the customer on hold
Ask the customer if it is alright to put them on hold.	Put the customer on hold without an explanation and the customer's consent
Once given consent, tell the customer that you will be away only a few minutes.	

This is the process for transferring a call. Follow the same process for a call transfer as you would when placing a customer on hold. Let the customer finish talking, and then explain that you have to transfer the call. When the customer agrees to be transferred, tell him the phone number that you are transferring him to. You should also tell the new technician your name, the name of the customer that you are transferring, and the related ticket number. Table 11-2 outlines the process for transferring a call.

Table 11-2   How to Transfer a Call

Do	Do Not
Let the customer finish speaking.	Interrupt
Explain that you will have to transfer the call and tell the customer to whom and why.	Abruptly transfer the call
Tell the customer the number you are transferring the call to.	Transfer without explanation and the customer's consent
Ask the customer if it is alright to transfer the call now.	Transfer without providing information to the new technician
Once given consent, make the transfer.	
Tell the new technician who you are, the ticket number, and the name of the customer.	

When dealing with customers, it is sometimes easier to explain what you should not do as a support technician. The following list describes things that you should not do when communicating with a customer:

- Do not minimize a customer's problems.
- Do not use jargon, abbreviations, acronyms, and slang.
- Do not use a negative attitude or tone of voice.
- Do not argue with customers or become defensive.
- Do not say culturally insensitive remarks.
- Do not be judgmental or insulting or call the customer names.
- Avoid distractions and do not interrupt when talking with customers.
- Do not take personal calls when talking with customers.
- Do not talk to co-workers about unrelated subjects when talking with the customer.
- Avoid unnecessary holds and abrupt holds.
- Do not transfer a call without explaining the purpose of the transfer and getting customer consent.
- Do not use negative remarks about other technicians to the customer.

Keeping the Customer Focused on the Problem (11.1.2.5)

Part of your job is to keep the customer focused during the phone call. When you focus the customer on the problem, it allows you to control the call. This makes the best use of your time and the customer's time on troubleshooting the problem. Do not take any comments personally, and do not retaliate with any comments or criticism. If you stay calm with the customer, finding a solution to the problem will remain the focal point of the call.

Just as there are many different computer problems, there are many different types of customers. There are multiple strategies for dealing with different types of difficult customers. The following tables represent different problem-customer types; these are not comprehensive. Often a customer can display a combination of traits, but these are intended to help the technician to recognize which traits their customer exhibits. Recognizing these traits can help manage the call accordingly.

Talkative Customers

During the call, a talkative customer discusses everything except the problem. The customer often uses the call as an opportunity to socialize. It can be difficult to get a talkative customer to focus on the problem. Table 11-3 outlines how to deal with talkative customers.

Table 11-3   Dealing with Talkative Customers

Do	Do Not
Allow the customer to talk for 1 minute.	Encourage non–problem-related conversation by asking social questions such as "How are you today?"
Gather as much information about the problem as possible.	
Politely step in to refocus the customer. This is the exception to the rule of never interrupting a customer.	
Ask as many closed-ended questions as you need once you have regained control of the call.	

Rude Customers

A rude customer complains during the call and often makes negative comments about the product, the service, and the technician. This type of customer is sometimes abusive and uncooperative and gets aggravated very easily. Table 11-4 outlines how to deal with rude customers.

Table 11-4   Dealing with Rude Customers

Do	Do Not
Listen carefully because you do not want to ask the customer to repeat any information.	Ask the customer to follow any obvious steps if there is any way you can determine the problem without the customer
Follow a step-by-step approach to determine and solve the problem.	
If the customer has a favorite technician, try to contact that technician to see if he or she can take the call. For example, tell the customer, "I can either help you right now or see if (the preferred technician) is available. He will be available in 2 hours. Is that acceptable?" If the customer wants to wait for the other technician, record this in the ticket.	Be rude to the customer
Apologize for the wait time and the inconvenience, even if there has been no wait time.	
Reiterate that you want to solve the customer's problem as quickly as possible.	

Angry Customers

An angry customer talks loudly and often tries to speak when the technician is talking. Angry customers are usually frustrated that they have a problem and upset that they have to call somebody to fix it. Table 11-5 outlines how to deal with angry customers.

Table 11-5   Dealing with Angry Customers

Do	Do Not
Let customers tell their problem without interrupting, even if they are angry. This allows customers to release some of their anger before you proceed.	Put this customer on hold or transfer the call (if at all possible).
Sympathize with the customer's problem.	Spend call time talking about what caused the problem. (Instead, you should redirect the conversation to solving the problem.)
Apologize for the wait time and inconvenience.	

Knowledgeable Customers

A knowledgeable customer wants to speak with a technician that is equally experienced in computers. This type of customer usually tries to control the call and does not want to speak with a level one technician.

Table 11-6 outlines how to deal with knowledgeable customers.

Table 11-6   Dealing with Knowledgeable Customers

Do	Do Not
If you are a level one technician, you might want to try to set up a call with a level two technician.	Follow a step-by-step process with this customer.
Give the customer the overall approach to what you are trying to verify.	Ask to check the obvious such as the power cord or the power switch. For example, you could suggest a reboot instead.

Inexperienced Customers

An inexperienced customer has difficulty describing the problem. These customers are usually not able to follow directions correctly and not able to communicate the errors that they encounter. Table 11-7 outlines how to deal with inexperienced customers.

Table 11-7   Dealing with Inexperienced Customers

Do	Do Not
Use a simple step-by-step process of instructions with this customer.	Use industry jargon
Speak in plain terms.	Be condescending to your customer

Using Proper Netiquette (11.1.2.6)

Have you read an online forum where two or three members have stopped discussing the issue and have begun to insult each other? These are called flame wars, and they occur in blogs and email threads. Have you ever wondered if they would actually say those things to each other in person? Perhaps you have received an email that had no greeting or was written entirely in capital letters. How did this make you feel while you were reading it?

As a technician, you should be professional in all communications with customers. For email and text communications, there is a set of personal and business etiquette rules called *Netiquette*. Here is a list the basic rules of Netiquette:

- Be pleasant and polite.

- Begin each email, even within a thread, with an appropriate greeting.

- Never send chain letters via email.

- Do not send or reply to flames.

- Use mixed case. UPPER CASE IS CONSIDERED SHOUTING.

- Check grammar and spelling before you post.

- Be ethical.

- Never mail or post anything you would not say to someone's face.

In addition to email and text Netiquette, some general rules apply to all your online interactions with customers and co-workers:

- Respect other people's time.

- Share expert knowledge.

- Respect other people's privacy.

- Be forgiving of other people's mistakes.

Employee Best Practices (11.1.3)

Effective time management is significant to a less stressful life. This section describes in detail various techniques for managing both.

Time and Stress Management Techniques (11.1.3.1)

As a technician, you are a very busy person. It is important for your own well-being to use proper time and *stress management* techniques.

Workstation Ergonomics

The ergonomics of your work area can help you do your job or make it more difficult. Because you spend a major portion of your day at your workstation, make sure that the desk layout works well. Have your headset and phone in a position that is both easy to reach and easy to use. Adjust your chair to a height that is comfortable. Adjust your computer screen to a comfortable angle so that you do not have to tilt your head up or down to see it. Make sure your keyboard and mouse are also in a position that is comfortable for you. You should not have to bend your wrist to type. If possible, try to minimize external distractions, such as noise.

Time Management

It is important to prioritize your activities. Make sure that you carefully follow the business policy of your company. The company policy might state that you must take "down" calls first, even though they might be harder to solve. A down call usually means that a server is not working and the entire office or company is waiting for the problem to be resolved to resume business.

If you have to call a customer back, make sure that you do it as close to the callback time as possible. Keep a list of callback customers and check them off one at a time as you complete these calls. Doing this ensures that you do not forget a customer.

When working with many customers, do not give favorite customers faster or better service. When reviewing the call boards, do not take only the easy customer calls. Do not take the call of another technician, unless you have permission to do so.

See Figure 11-1 for a sample customer call board.

Figure 11-1   Call Board

Stress Management

Take a moment to compose yourself between customer calls. Every call should be independent of other calls. Do not carry any frustrations from one call to the next.

You might have to do some physical activity to relieve stress. Occasionally, stand up and take a short walk. Do a few simple stretch movements or squeeze a tension ball. Take a break if you can, and try to relax. You will then be ready to answer the next customer call effectively. The following lists some ways to relax:

- Practice relaxed breathing: inhale-hold-exhale-repeat.

- Listen to soothing sounds.

- Massage your temples.

- Take a break; go for a quick walk, or climb a flight of stairs.

- Eat a small snack; protein is best.

- Plan your weekend.

- Avoid stimulants like coffee, carbonated drinks, and chocolate. They contain caffeine, and that can add to stress.

Observing Service Level Agreements (11.1.3.2)

When dealing with customers, it is important to adhere to that customer's *service level agreement (SLA)*. An SLA is a contract that defines expectations between an organization and the service vendor to provide an agreed-on level of support. As an employee of the service company, your job is to honor the SLA that you have with the customer.

An SLA is usually a legal agreement that contains the responsibilities and liabilities of all parties involved. The contents of an SLA usually include the following:

- Response time guarantees (often based on type of call and level of service agreement)
- Equipment and software that is supported
- Where service is provided
- Preventive maintenance
- Diagnostics
- Part availability (equivalent parts)
- Cost and penalties
- Time of service availability (for example, 24x7 or Monday to Friday, 8 a.m. to 5 p.m. EST)

Figure 11-2 shows an example of a service level agreement and some standard sections.

Figure 11-2   Service Level Agreement

Occasionally, there might be exceptions to the SLA. Some exceptions might include a customer's option to upgrade the level of service or to escalate a problem to management for review. Escalation to management should be reserved for special situations. For example, a long-standing customer or a customer from a large company might have a problem that falls outside the parameters stated in their SLA. In these cases, your management might choose to support the customer for customer-relation reasons.

Following Business Policies (11.1.3.3)

As a technician, you should be aware of all business policies related to customer calls. You would not want to make a promise to a customer that you cannot keep. Also have a good understanding of all rules governing employees.

Customer Call Rules

These are examples of rules a call center might use to handle customer calls:

- Maximum time on call (example: 15 minutes)

- Maximum call time in queue (example: 3 minutes)

- Number of calls per day (example: minimum of 30)

- Passing calls on to other technicians (example: only when absolutely necessary and not without that technician's permission)

- What you can and cannot promise to the customer (see that customer's SLA for details)

- When to follow the SLA and when to escalate to management

Call Center Employee Rules

There are also rules to cover general daily activities of employees:

- Arrive at your workstation on time and early enough to become prepared, usually about 15 to 20 minutes before the first call.

- Do not exceed the allowed number and length of breaks.

- Do not take a break or go to lunch if there is a call on the board.

- Do not take a break or go to lunch at the same time as other technicians (stagger breaks among technicians).

- Do not leave an ongoing call to take a break, go to lunch, or take some personal time.

- Make sure that another technician is available if you have to leave.

- Contact the customer if you are going to be late for an appointment.

- If no other technician is available, check with the customer to see if you can call back later.

- Do not show favoritism to certain customers.

- Do not take another technician's calls without permission.

- Do not talk negatively about the capabilities of another technician.

Customer Satisfaction

The following rules should be followed by all employees to ensure customer satisfaction:

- Set and meet a reasonable timeline for the call or appointment and communicate this to the customer.

- Communicate service expectations to the customer as early as possible.

- Communicate the repair status with the customer, including explanations for any delays.

- Offer different repair or replacement options to the customer, if applicable.

- Give the customer proper documentation on all services provided.

- Follow up with the customer at a later date to verify satisfaction.

Ethical and Legal Issues in the IT Industry (11.2)

As information technology professionals, it is important to recognize the responsibility and ethical obligations that come from having access to customers' personal and professional information.

Ethical Considerations in IT (11.2.1.1)

When you are working with customers and their equipment, there are some general ethical customs and legal rules that you should observe. These customs and rules often overlap.

You should always have respect for your customers, as well as for their property. Computers and monitors are property, but property also includes any information or data that might be accessible, for example:

- Emails

- Phone lists

- Records or data on the computer

- Hard copies of files, information, or data left on a desk

Before accessing computer accounts, including the administrator account, get the permission of the customer. From the troubleshooting process, you might have gathered some private information, such as usernames and passwords. If you document this type of private information, you must keep it confidential. Divulging customer information to anyone else is not only unethical, but might be illegal. Legal details of customer information are usually covered under the SLA.

Do not send unsolicited messages to a customer. Do not send unsolicited mass mailings or chain letters to customers. Never send forged or anonymous emails. All these activities are considered unethical and, in certain circumstances, might be considered illegal.

Legal Considerations in IT (11.2.1.2)

The laws in different countries and legal jurisdictions vary, but generally actions such as the following are considered to be illegal:

- It is not permissible to make any changes to system software or hardware configurations without customer permission.

- It is not permissible to access a customer's or co-worker's accounts, private files, or email messages without permission.

- It is not permissible to install, copy, or share digital content (including software, music, text, images, and video) in violation of copyright and software agreements or the applicable law. Copyright and trademark laws vary between states, countries, and regions.

- It is not permissible to use a customer's company IT resources for commercial purposes.

- It is not permissible to make a customer's IT resources available to unauthorized users.

- It is not permissible to knowingly use a customer's company resources for illegal activities. Criminal or illegal use typically includes obscenity, child pornography, threats, harassment, copyright infringement, trademark infringement, defamation, theft, identity theft, and unauthorized access.

- It is not permissible to share sensitive customer information. You are required to maintain confidentiality of this data.

This list is not exhaustive. All businesses and their employees must know and comply with all applicable laws of the jurisdiction in which they operate.

Legal Procedures Overview (11.2.2)

Many legal and ethical issues arise as companies use computers and computer networks in all aspects of business. All types of data are collected and stored about business processes as well as customers and employees. During criminal investigations, audits, and litigation that data may be required as part of a legal action. This section discusses different ways of handling data for legal purposes.

Computer Forensics (11.2.2.1)

Data from computer systems, networks, wireless communications, and storage devices may need to be collected and analyzed in the course of a criminal investigation. The collection and analysis of data for this purpose is called *computer forensics*. The process of computer forensics encompasses both IT and specific laws to ensure that any data collected is admissible as evidence in court.

Depending on the country, illegal computer or network usage may include the following:

- Identity theft

- Using a computer to sell counterfeit goods

- Using pirated software on a computer or network

- Using a computer or network to create unauthorized copies of copyrighted materials, such as movies, television programs, music, and video games

- Using a computer or network to sell unauthorized copies of copyrighted materials

- Pornography

This is not an exhaustive list.

Two basic types of data are collected when conducting computer forensics procedures: persistent data and volatile data:

- **Persistent data:** Persistent data is stored on a local drive, such as an internal or external hard drive, or an optical drive. When the computer is turned off, this data is preserved.

- **Volatile data:** RAM, cache, and registries contain volatile data. Data in transit between a storage medium and a CPU is also volatile data. It is important to know how to capture this data because it disappears as soon as the computer is turned off.

Cyber Law and First Response (11.2.2.2)

Cyber Law

There is no single law known as a cyber law. *Cyber law* is a term to describe the international, regional, country, and state laws that affect computer security professionals. IT professionals must be aware of cyber law so that they understand their responsibility and their liability as it relates to cyber crimes.

Cyber laws explain the circumstances under which data (evidence) can be collected from computers, data storage devices, networks, and wireless communications. They can also specify the manner in which this data can be collected. In the United States, cyber law has three primary elements:

- Wiretap Act

- Pen/Trap and Trace Statute

- Stored Electronic Communication Act

IT professionals should be aware of the cyber laws in their country, region, or state.

First Response

First response is the term used to describe the official procedures employed by those people who are qualified to collect evidence. System administrators, like law enforcement officers, are usually the first responders at potential crime scenes. Computer forensics experts are brought in when it is apparent that there has been illegal activity.

Routine administrative tasks can affect the forensic process. If the forensic process is improperly performed, evidence that has been collected might not be admissible in court.

As a field or a bench technician, you may be the person who discovers illegal computer or network activity. If this happens, do not turn off the computer. Volatile data about the current state of the computer can include programs that are running, network connections that are open, and users who are logged in to the network or to the computer. This data helps to determine a logical timeline of the security incident. It may also help to identify those responsible for the illegal activity. This data could be lost when the computer is powered off.

Be familiar with your company's policy regarding cyber crimes. Know who to call, what to do and, just as importantly, know what *not* to do.

Documentation and Chain of Custody (11.2.2.3)

Chain of custody is being able to validate how evidence is collected, protected, and kept track of so that its authenticity can be proven. This is crucial to using the evidence in legal actions. To ensure that the chain of custody is kept intact careful, detailed documenting must be kept.

Documentation

The documentation required by a system administrator and a computer forensics expert is extremely detailed. They must document not only what evidence was gathered, but how it was gathered and with which tools. Incident documentation should use consistent naming conventions for forensic tool output. Stamp logs with the time, date, and identity of the person performing the forensic collection. Document as much information about the security incident as possible. These best practices provide an audit trail for the information collection process.

Even if you are not a system administrator or computer forensics expert, it is a good habit to create detailed documentation of all the work that you do. If you discover illegal activity on a computer or network on which you are working, at a minimum, document the following:

- Initial reason for accessing the computer or network
- Time and date
- Peripherals that are connected to the computer
- All network connections
- Physical area where the computer is located
- Illegal material that you have found
- Illegal activity that you have witnessed (or you suspect has occurred)
- Which procedures you have executed on the computer or network

First responders want to know what you have done and what you have not done. Your documentation may become part of the evidence in the prosecution of a crime. If you make additions or changes to this documentation, it is critical that you inform all interested parties.

Chain of Custody

For evidence to be admitted, it must be authenticated. A system administrator may testify about the evidence that was collected. But he or she must also be able to prove how this evidence was collected, where it has been physically stored, and who has had access to it between the time of collection and its entry into the court proceedings. This is known as the chain of custody. To prove the chain of custody, first responders have documentation procedures in place that track the collected evidence. These procedures also prevent evidence tampering so that the integrity of the evidence can be ensured.

Incorporate computer forensics procedures into your approach to computer and network security to ensure the integrity of the data. These procedures help you capture necessary data in the event of a network breach. Ensuring the viability and integrity of the captured data helps you prosecute the intruder.

Call Center Technicians (11.3)

Call center technicians are required to have strong written and verbal communication skills in addition to their technical skills. This section describes the call center environment and the responsibilities of a call center technician.

Call Centers (11.3.1.1)

A call center environment is usually very professional and fast-paced. Customers call in to receive help for a specific computer-related problem. The typical workflow of a call center is that calls from customers are displayed on a callboard. *Level one technicians* answer these calls in the order that the calls arrive. If the level one technician cannot solve the problem, it is escalated to a *level two technician*. In all instances, the technician must supply the level of support that is outlined in the customer's SLA.

A call center might exist within a company and offer service to the employees of that company as well as to the customers of that company's products. Alternatively, a call center might be an independent business that sells computer support as a service to outside customers. In either case, a call center is a busy, fast-paced work environment, often operating 24 hours a day.

Call centers tend to have a large number of cubicles. Each cubicle has a chair, at least one computer, a phone, and a headset. The technicians working at these cubicles have varied levels of experience in computers, and some have specialties in certain types of computers, hardware, software, or operating systems.

All the computers in a call center have help desk software. The technicians use this software to manage many of their job functions.

Table 11-8 shows some of the features of help desk software.

Table 11-8 Features of Help Desk Software

Log and track incidents	The software may manage call queues, set call priorities, assign calls, and escalate calls.
Record contact information	The software may store, edit, and recall customer names, email addresses, phone numbers, location, websites, fax numbers, and the information in a database.
Research product information	The software may provide technicians with information regarding the products supported, including features, limitations, new versions, configuration constraints, known bugs, product availability, links to online help files, and other information.
Run diagnostic utilities	The software may have several diagnostic utilities including remote diagnostic software, in which the technician can take over a customer's computer while sitting at a desk in the call center.

Research a knowledge base	The software may contain a knowledge database that is pre-programmed with common problems and their solutions. This database may grow as technicians add their own records of problems and solutions.
Collect customer feedback	The software may collect customer feedback regarding satisfaction with the call center's products and services.

Each call center has business policies regarding call priority. Table 11-9 provides a sample chart of how calls can be named, defined, and prioritized.

Table 11-9   Call Prioritization

Name	Definition	Priority
Down	The company cannot operate any of its computer equipment.	1 (Most Urgent)
Hardware	One (or more) of the company's computers is not functioning correctly.	2 (Urgent)
Software	One (or more) of the company's computers is experiencing software or operating system errors.	2 (Urgent)
Network	One (or more) of the company's computers cannot access the network.	2 (Urgent)
Enhancement	There has been a request from the company for additional computer functionality.	3 (Important)

Level One Technician Responsibilities (11.3.1.2)

Call centers sometimes have different names for level one technicians. These technicians might be known as level one analysts, dispatchers, or incident screeners. Regardless of the title, the level one technician's responsibilities are fairly similar from one call center to the next.

The primary responsibility of a level one technician is to gather pertinent information from the customer. The technician has to accurately enter all information into the ticket or work order. These are examples of the type of information that the level one technician must obtain:

- Contact information
- The computer's manufacturer and model
- The computer's operating system
- Whether the computer uses AC or DC power

- Whether the computer is on a network and, if so, whether it is a wired or wireless connection

- If a specific application was being used when the problem occurred

- If any new drivers or updates have been installed recently and, if so, what they are

- Description of the problem

- Priority of the problem

Some problems are simple to resolve, and a level one technician can usually take care of these without escalating the work order to a level two technician.

Often a problem requires the expertise of a level two technician. In these instances, the level one technician must be able to translate a customer's problem description into a succinct sentence or two that is entered into the work order. This translation is important so that other technicians can quickly understand the situation without having to ask the customer the same questions again.

Level Two Technician Responsibilities (11.3.1.3)

As with level one technicians, call centers sometimes have different names for level two technicians. These technicians might be known as product specialists or technical-support personnel. The level two technician's responsibilities are generally the same from one call center to the next.

The level two technician is usually more knowledgeable than the level one technician about technology or has been working for the company for a longer period of time. When a problem cannot be resolved within a predetermined amount of time, the level one technician prepares an escalated work order. The level two technician receives the escalated work order with the description of the problem and then calls the customer back to ask any additional questions and resolve the problem.

Level two technicians can also use remote access software to connect to the customer's computer to update drivers and software, access the operating system, check the BIOS, and gather other diagnostic information to solve the problem.

Summary (11.4.1)

This chapter explored the relationship between communication skills and troubleshooting skills. These two skills need to be combined to make successful IT technicians. The chapter also discussed the legal aspects and ethics of dealing with computer technology and the property of the customer.

The following concepts from this chapter are important to remember:

- To be a successful technician, you must practice good communication skills with customers and co-workers. These skills are as important as technical expertise.

- You should always conduct yourself in a professional manner with your customers and co-workers. Professional behavior increases customer confidence and enhances your credibility. You should also learn to recognize the classic signs of a difficult customer and learn what to do and what not to do when you are on a call with this customer.

- There are techniques that you can use to keep a difficult customer focused on the problem during a call. Primarily, you must remain calm and ask pertinent questions in an appropriate fashion. These techniques keep you in control of the call.

- There is a right way and a wrong way to put a customer on hold or transfer a customer to another technician. Learn and use the right way every time. Doing either of these operations incorrectly can negatively affect your company's relationship with its customers.

- Netiquette is a list of rules to use whenever you communicate through email, text messaging, instant messaging, and blogs.

- You must understand and comply with your customer's SLA. If the problem falls outside the parameters of the SLA, find positive ways of telling the customer what you can do to help, rather than what you cannot do. In special circumstances, you might decide to escalate the work order to management.

- In addition to the SLA, you must follow the business policies of the company. These policies include how your company prioritizes calls, how and when to escalate a call to management, and when you are allowed to take breaks and lunch.

- A computer technician's job is stressful. You rarely meet a customer who is having a good day. You can alleviate some of the stress by setting up your workstation in the most ergonomically beneficial way possible. Practice time and stress management techniques every day.

- There are ethical and legal aspects of working in computer technology. You should be aware of your company's policies and practices. In addition, you might need to familiarize yourself with your local or country's trademark and copyright laws.

- Collecting and analyzing data from computer systems, networks, wireless communications, and storage devices is called computer forensics.

- Cyber laws explain the circumstances under which data (evidence) can be collected from computers, data storage devices, networks, and wireless communications. First response is the term used to describe the official procedures employed by those people who are qualified to collect evidence.

- Even if you are not a system administrator or computer forensics expert, it is a good habit to create detailed documentation of all the work that you do. Being able to prove how evidence was collected and where it has been between the time of collection and its entry into the court proceeding is known as the chain of custody.

- The call center is a fast-paced environment. Level one technicians and level two technicians each have specific responsibilities. These responsibilities might vary slightly from one call center to another.

Summary of Exercises

This is a summary of the worksheets associated with this chapter. Refer to the worksheets in the *IT Essentials: PC Hardware and Software Lab Manual*, Fifth Edition.

Worksheets

The following worksheets cover material from this chapter. Refer to the worksheets in the *IT Essentials: PC Hardware and Software Lab Manual*, Fifth Edition.

Worksheet 11.1.1.3: Technician Resources

Check Your Understanding

You can find the answers to these questions in Appendix A, "Answers to 'Check Your Understanding' Questions."

1. Which subject area describes collecting and analyzing data from computer systems, networks, and storage devices, as part of an investigation of alleged illegal activity?

    A. Cyber law

    B. Computer forensics

    C. Cryptography

    D. Disaster recovery

2. During computer forensics investigations, which type of data is lost when power is removed from the computer?

   A. Data that is stored on solid state drives

   B. Data that is stored in RAM

   C. Data that is stored on magnetic disk

   D. Data that is stored to an external drive

3. What is considered ethical behavior by a technician when communicating with a customer?

   A. A technician can send forged emails to customers.

   B. A technician can send mass emails to customers.

   C. A technician must only send solicited emails.

   D. It is normal to send chain emails to customers.

4. What does a technician need in order to make changes to software installed on the computer of a customer?

   A. The authorization of a more senior technician

   B. Customer authorization

   C. Verification that the software is legal

   D. Two witnesses

5. What is the definition of the term SLA?

   A. A contract that defines the expectations of the technician about supporting the customer

   B. A legal agreement that contains the responsibilities and liabilities of the service provider

   C. An acronym for stress level agreement

   D. The responsibilities a customer has with the technician to provide hardware and software support

6. What does it mean when a technician receives a "down" call?

   A. A call between a technician and a customer that was interrupted abruptly

   B. A call that is simpler to solve

   C. A call that has the maximum response time exceeded

   D. A call where a significant part of the IT infrastructure is down, affecting the ability of the company to do business

7. Which statement best describes a call center?

    A. It is a help desk used by customers to make an appointment to report their computer problems.

    B. It is a place to provide computer support to customers.

    C. It is a busy, fast-paced work environment that documents computer problems once they have been repaired by technicians.

    D. It is a help desk environment where the customers go with their computers to have them fixed.

8. What skill is essential for a level one technician to have?

    A. The ability to gather relevant information from the customer and pass it to the level two technician so it can be entered into the work order

    B. The ability to ask the customer relevant questions, and as soon as this information is included in the work order, escalate it to the level two technician

    C. The ability to translate a description of a customer problem into a few succinct sentences and enter it into the work order

    D. The ability to take the work order prepared by the level two technician and try to resolve the problem

9. Which two actions would be considered examples of poor communication skills when dealing with a customer? (Choose two.)

    A. Minimize customer problems.

    B. Make negative remarks about other technicians.

    C. Explain the purpose of transferring the call to another technician.

    D. Refuse personal calls while talking to a customer.

    E. Use a positive tone of voice.

10. Which task would require that a problem be escalated to a level two technician?

    A. Changing CMOS settings

    B. Cleaning a mouse

    C. Changing toner cartridges

    D. Checking loose external cables

CHAPTER 12

Advanced Troubleshooting

Objectives

Upon completion of this chapter, you should be able to answer the following questions:

- What is the six-step advanced troubleshooting process?

- How can I apply the troubleshooting process to computer components and peripherals?

- How can I apply the troubleshooting process to operating systems?

- How can I apply the troubleshooting process to networks?

- How can I apply the troubleshooting process to laptops?

- How can I apply the troubleshooting process to printers?

- How can I apply the troubleshooting process to security?

- What are some common problems and solutions for computer components and peripherals?

- What are some common problems and solutions for operating systems?

- What are some common problems and solutions for networks?

- What are some common problems and solutions for laptops?

- What are some common problems and solutions for printers?

- What are some common problems and solutions for security?

Key Terms

Blue Screen of Death (BSOD)   *page 643*

auto restart function   *page 643*

Introduction (12.0.1)

In your career as a technician, it is important that you develop advanced skills in troubleshooting techniques and diagnostic methods for computer components, operating systems, networks, laptops, printers, and security issues. Advanced troubleshooting can sometimes mean that the problem is unique or that the solution is difficult to perform. More often, advanced troubleshooting means that the probable cause is difficult to diagnose.

Advanced troubleshooting uses not only your advanced diagnostic skills when working with hardware and software, but also the interaction between technicians and customers or other technicians. The way in which you work with customers and other technicians can determine how quickly and comprehensively the problem gets diagnosed and solved. Take advantage of your resources, other technicians, and the online technician community to get answers to your diagnostic challenges. You might be able to help another technician with a problem.

Apply Troubleshooting Process to Computer Components and Peripherals (12.1.1)

This section describes how to apply the six-step troubleshooting processes to problems with computer components and peripherals and provides a chart of common problems and solutions that can be used by a technician troubleshooting these issues. Labs at the end of the section allow you to practice using the troubleshooting steps.

Six Steps for Advanced Troubleshooting Computer Components and Peripherals (12.1.1.1)

The troubleshooting process helps resolve problems with the computer or peripherals. These problems range from simple, such as updating a drive, to more complex problems, such as installing a CPU. Use the troubleshooting steps as a guideline to help you diagnose and repair problems.

The first step in the troubleshooting process is to identify the problem. Table 12-1 shows a list of open-ended and closed-ended questions to ask the customer.

Table 12-1 Step 1: Identify the Problem

Open-ended questions	What type of computer do you have?
	What is the brand and model of the computer?
	Can you describe what happens when the computer boots?
	How often does the computer fail to start?
	What is the first screen you see when you turn on the computer?
	What sound does the computer make as it starts?
Closed-ended questions	Has anyone done any repair work on the computer recently?
	Has anyone else used the computer?
	Is any media inserted in a floppy or optical drive?
	Does the computer have a USB drive attached?
	Can the computer be used to connect to a wireless network?
	Is the computer secured in a locked room at night?
	Do you have Windows installation media available?

After you have talked to the customer, you can establish a theory of probable cause. Table 12-2 shows a list of some common probable causes of computer or peripheral problems.

Table 12-2 Step 2: Establish a Theory of Probable Cause

Common causes of hardware problems	Computer power problems
	Loose external cable connection
	Loose data cable connection
	Loose adapter card
	Faulty RAM
	Incorrect device driver
	Dirty fans
	Incorrect jumper settings
	CMOS battery problem
	Incorrect firmware
	Failed parts

After you have developed some theories about what is wrong, test your theories to determine the cause of the problem. Table 12-3 shows a list of quick procedures that can determine the exact cause of the problem or even correct the problem. If a quick procedure corrects the problem, you can go to step 5 to verify full system functionality. If a quick procedure does not correct the problem, you might need to research the problem further to establish the exact cause.

Table 12-3   Step 3: Test the Theory to Determine Cause

Common steps to determine cause	Restart the computer.
	Disconnect and reconnect the external cables.
	Disconnect and reconnect the internal cables.
	Secure the adapter card.
	Roll back or reinstall the device driver.
	Replace the RAM.
	Clean the fans.
	Reset the jumpers.
	Secure or replace the CMOS battery.
	Update the firmware.
	Listen for beeps.
	Look for error codes or messages.

After you have determined the exact cause of the problem, establish a plan of action to resolve the problem and implement the solution. Table 12-4 shows some sources you can use to gather additional information to resolve an issue.

Table 12-4   Step 4: Establish a Plan of Action to Resolve the Problem and Implement the Solution

If no solution is achieved in the previous step, further research is needed to implement the solution.	Help desk repair logs
	Other technicians
	Manufacturer FAQs
	Technical websites
	Newsgroups
	Computer manuals
	Device manuals
	Online forums
	Internet search

After you have corrected the problem, verify full functionality and, if applicable, implement preventive measures. Table 12-5 shows a list of the steps to verify the solution.

Table 12-5   Step 5: Verify Full System Functionality and, If Applicable, Implement Preventive Measures

Verify solution and full system functionality	Reboot the computer.
	Restart external devices.
	Access all drives and shared resources.
	Print a document.
	Read and write to all storage devices.
	Validate the amount of RAM, the CPU, speed, and the date and time.
	Test network connectivity.
	Execute commonly used applications.

In the final step of the troubleshooting process, you must document your findings, actions, and outcomes. Table 12-6 shows a list of the tasks required to document the problem and the solution.

Table 12-6   Step 6: Document Findings, Actions, and Outcomes

Document findings	Discuss the solution implemented with the customer.
	Have the customer verify the problem has been solved.
	Provide the customer with all paperwork.
	Document the steps taken to solve the problem in the work order and the technician's journal.
	Document any components used in the repair.
	Document the time spent to resolve the problem.

Common Problems and Solutions for Components and Peripherals (12.1.1.2)

Computer problems can be attributed to hardware, software, networks, or some combination of the three. You will resolve some types of problems more often than others. Table 12-7 shows a chart of common problems and solutions.

Table 12-7   Common Problems and Solutions for Components and Peripherals

Identify the Problem	Probable Causes	Possible Solutions
An "OS not found" error message is displayed when the computer is started.	The hard drive has failed.	Replace the hard drive.
	The hard drive is not jumpered correctly.	Change the jumper settings on the hard drive.
	The boot order is not set correctly in BIOS.	Change the boot order in BIOS to boot the correct hard drive.
	The MBR is corrupted.	Boot the computer to the Recovery Console. At the command prompt, use the **bootrec /fixmbr** or **bootrec /fixboot** command in Windows 7 or Vista or the **fixmbr** command in Windows XP.
RAID cannot be found.	Cables connected to the hard drives are connected incorrectly.	Examine all the cable connections to all the drives in the array.
	The external RAID controller is not receiving power.	Check the power connection to the RAID controller.
	The RAID controller has failed.	Replace the RAID controller.
	The BIOS settings are incorrect.	Reconfigure the BIOS settings for the RAID controller.
RAID stops working.	The external RAID controller is not receiving power.	Check the power connection to the RAID controller.
	The RAID controller has failed.	Replace the RAID controller.
	The BIOS settings are incorrect.	Reconfigure the BIOS settings for the RAID controller.
A computer exhibits slow performance.	The computer does not have enough RAM.	Install additional RAM.
	The computer is running too many programs.	Close unneeded programs.
	The hard drive is full.	Run Disk Cleanup or replace the hard drive with a larger capacity hard drive.
The computer does not recognize a SCSI drive.	The SCSI drive has an incorrect SCSI ID.	Reconfigure the SCSI ID.
	The SCSI termination is not set correctly.	Ensure that the SCSI chain is terminated at the correct end points.
	The external SCSI drive was not powered on prior to booting the computer.	Turn on the drive before booting the computer.

Identify the Problem	Probable Causes	Possible Solutions
The computer does not recognize a removable external drive.	The OS does not have the correct drivers for the removable external drive. The USB port has too many attached devices to supply adequate power.	Download the correct drivers for the drive. Attach external power to the device or remove some of the USB devices.
After updating the CMOS firmware, the computer will not start.	The CMOS firmware update did not install correctly.	Restore the original firmware from the onboard backup if there is one available. Contact the motherboard manufacturer to obtain a new CMOS chip. If the motherboard has two CMOS chips, the second CMOS chip can be used.
The computer reboots without warning, locks up, or displays error messages or the BSOD.	The front-side bus is set too high. The CPU multiplier is set too high. The CPU voltage is set too high.	Reset to the factory default settings for the motherboard. Lower the front-side bus (FSB) settings. Lower the multiplier settings. Lower the CPU voltage settings.
After upgrading from a single-core CPU to a dual-core CPU, the computer runs slower and only shows one CPU graph in Task Manager.	The BIOS does not recognize the multicore CPU.	Update the CMOS firmware to support the multicore CPU.

Apply Troubleshooting Skills to Computer Components and Peripherals (12.1.1.3)

Now that you understand the troubleshooting process, it is time to apply your listening and diagnostic skills.

The first lab is designed to test your troubleshooting skills with computer and peripheral problems. You will troubleshoot and fix a computer that does not boot.

The second lab is designed to reinforce your communication and troubleshooting skills. In this lab, you perform the following steps:

Step 1.   Receive the work order.

Step 2.   Talk the customer through various steps to try and resolve the problem.

Step 3.   Document the problem and the resolution. The third, fourth, and fifth labs are designed to reinforce your skills with computer and peripheral problems. You will troubleshoot and repair a computer that has more than one problem.

Lab 12.1.1.4: Repair Boot Problem

In this lab, you troubleshoot and repair a computer that does not boot. Refer to Lab 12.1.1.4 in *IT Essentials: PC Hardware and Software Lab Manual*, Fifth Edition.

Lab 12.1.1.5: Remote Technician - Repair Boot Problem

In this lab, you gather data from the customer, and then instruct the customer on how to fix a computer that does not boot. Document the customer's problem in the work order. Refer to Lab 12.1.1.5 in *IT Essentials: PC Hardware and Software Lab Manual*, Fifth Edition.

Lab 12.1.1.6: Troubleshooting Hardware Problems in Windows 7

In this lab, the instructor introduces various hardware problems, and you diagnose the cause of these problems then fix them. Refer to Lab 12.1.1.6 in *IT Essentials: PC Hardware and Software Lab Manual*, Fifth Edition.

Lab 12.1.1.7: Troubleshooting Hardware Problems in Windows Vista

In this lab, the instructor introduces various hardware problems, and you will diagnose the cause of these problems then fix them. Refer to Lab 12.1.1.7 in *IT Essentials: PC Hardware and Software Lab Manual*, Fifth Edition.

Lab 12.1.1.8: Troubleshooting Hardware Problems in Windows XP

In this lab, the instructor introduces various hardware problems, and you diagnose the cause of these problems then fix them. Refer to Lab 12.1.1.8 in *IT Essentials: PC Hardware and Software Lab Manual*, Fifth Edition.

Operating Systems (12.2)

This section describes how to apply the six-step troubleshooting processes to problems with computer operating systems, and provides a chart of common problems and solutions that can be used by a technician troubleshooting these issues. Labs at the end of the section allow you to practice using the troubleshooting steps.

Six Steps for Advanced Troubleshooting Operating Systems (12.2.1.1)

The troubleshooting process helps resolve problems with the operating system. Use the troubleshooting steps as a guideline to help you diagnose and repair problems.

The first step in the troubleshooting process is to identify the problem. Table 12-8 shows a list of open-ended and closed-ended questions to ask the customer.

Table 12-8   Step 1: Identify the Problem

Open-ended questions	What operating system is installed on the computer?
	What programs have been installed recently?
	What updates or service packs have been installed?
	What error messages have you received?
	What were you doing when the problem was discovered?
Closed-ended questions	Does anyone else have this problem?
	Have you changed your password recently?
	Have you made any changes to your computer?
	Does anyone else have access to your computer?
	Has this problem happened before?

After you have talked to the customer, you can establish a theory of probable cause. Table 12-9 shows a list of some common probable causes for operating system problems.

Table 12-9   Step 2: Establish a Theory of Probable Cause

Common causes of operating system problems	Corrupted or missing system files
	Incorrect device driver
	Failed update or service pack installation
	Corrupted Registry
	Failing or faulty hard drive
	Incorrect password
	Virus infection
	Spyware

After you have developed some theories about what is wrong, test your theories to determine the cause of the problem. Table 12-10 shows a list of quick procedures that can determine the exact cause of the problem or even correct the problem. If a quick procedure corrects the problem, you can go to Step 5 to verify full system functionality. If a quick procedure does not correct the problem, you might need to research the problem further to establish the exact cause.

Table 12-10   Step 3: Test the Theory to Determine Cause

Common steps to determine cause	Reboot the computer.
	Examine the event logs.
	Run **sfc /scannow**.
	Roll back or reinstall the device driver.
	Uninstall recent updates or service packs.
	Run System Restore.
	Run **CHKDSK**.
	Log in as a different user.
	Boot to the last known good configuration.
	Run a virus scan.
	Run a spyware scan.

After you have determined the exact cause of the problem, establish a plan of action to resolve the problem and implement the solution. Table 12-11 shows some sources you can use to gather additional information to resolve an issue.

Table 12-11   Step 4: Establish a Plan of Action to Resolve the Problem and Implement the Solution

If no solution is achieved in the previous step, further research is needed to implement the solution.	Help desk repair logs
	Other technicians
	Manufacturer FAQs
	Technical websites
	Newsgroups
	Computer manual
	Device manual
	Online forums
	Internet search

After you have corrected the problem, verify full functionality and, if applicable, implement preventive measures. Table 12-12 shows a list of the steps to verify the solution.

Table 12-12   Step 5: Verify Full System Functionality and, If Applicable, Implement Preventive Measures

Verify solution and full system functionality.	Reboot the computer.
	Access all drives and shared resources.
	Check event logs to ensure there are no new warnings or errors.
	Check Device Manager to ensure there are no warnings or errors.
	Make sure applications run properly.
	Make sure the Internet can be accessed.
	Check Task Manager to ensure that there are no unidentified programs running.

In the final step of the troubleshooting process, you must document your findings, actions, and outcomes. Table 12-13 shows a list of the tasks required to document the problem and the solution.

Table 12-13   Step 6: Document Findings, Actions, and Outcomes

Document findings.	Discuss the solution implemented with the customer.
	Have the customer verify the problem has been solved.
	Provide the customer with all paperwork.
	Document the steps taken to solve the problem in the work order and the technician's journal.
	Document any components used in the repair.
	Document the time spent to resolve the problem.

Common Problems and Solutions for Operating Systems (12.2.1.2)

Operating system problems can be attributed to hardware, software, networks, or some combination of the three. You will resolve some types of OS problems more often than others. A stop error is a hardware or software malfunction that causes the system to lock up. An example of this type of error is known as the *Blue Screen of Death (BSOD)* and appears when the system is unable to recover from an error. The BSOD is usually caused by device driver errors.

The event log and other diagnostic utilities are available to research a stop error or BSOD error. To prevent these types of errors, verify that the hardware and software drivers are compatible. In addition, install the latest patches and updates for Windows. When the system locks up during startup, the computer can automatically reboot. The reboot is caused by the *auto restart function* in Windows and makes it difficult to see the error message.

The auto restart function can be disabled in the Advanced Startup Options menu. Table 12-14 shows common operating system problems and solutions.

Table 12-14   Common Problems and Solutions for Operating Systems

Identify the Problem	Probable Causes	Possible Solutions
The computer displays an "Invalid Boot Disk" error after the POST.	Media that does not have an operating system is in a drive. The boot order is not set correctly in the BIOS settings. The hard drive is not detected or the jumpers are not set correctly. The hard drive does not have an operating system installed. The MBR is corrupted. The computer has a boot sector virus. The hard drive is failing.	Remove all media from the drives. Change the boot order in the BIOS settings to start with the boot drive. Reconnect the hard drive cables or reset the hard drive jumpers. Install an operating system. Use the **bootrec /fixmbr** command from the System Recovery options of Windows 7 or Vista. Run **fdisk /mbr** from the CLI in Windows XP only. Run virus-removal software. Replace the hard drive.
The computer displays an "Inaccessible Boot Device" error after the POST.	A recently installed device driver is incompatible with the boot controller. BOOTMGR is corrupted in Windows 7 or Windows Vista. NTLDR is corrupted in Windows XP.	Use the last known good configuration to boot the computer. Boot the computer in Safe Mode and load a restore point from before the installation of new hardware. Restore the BOOTMGR file from Windows 7 or Windows Vista installation media. Restore the NTLDR from Windows XP installation media.
The computer displays a "BOOTMGR is missing" error after the POST in Windows 7 and Windows Vista.	BOOTMGR is missing or damaged. Boot configuration data is missing or damaged. The boot order is not set correctly in the BIOS settings. The MBR is corrupted. The hard drive is failing. The hard drive jumpers are not set correctly.	Restore BOOTMGR from installation media. Restore the Boot configuration data from installation media. Change the boot order in the BIOS settings to start with the boot drive. Use the **bootrec/fixmbr** command from the System Recovery options. Run **chkdsk /F /R** from the recovery console. Replace the hard drive. Reset the hard drive jumpers.

Identify the Problem	Probable Causes	Possible Solutions
The computer displays a "Missing NTLDR" error after the POST in Windows XP.	NTLDR is missing or damaged. Ntdetect.com is missing or damaged. Boot.ini is missing or damaged. The boot order is not set correctly in the BIOS settings. The MBR is corrupted. The hard drive is failing. The hard drive jumpers are not set correctly.	Restore NTLDR from installation media. Restore ntdetect.com from installation media. Restore boot.ini from installation media. Change the boot order in the BIOS settings to start with the boot drive. Run **fdisk /mbr** from the command prompt. Run **chkdsk /F /R** from the recovery console. Reset the hard drive jumpers.
A service failed to start when the computer booted.	The service is not enabled. The service is set to Manual. The failed service requires another service to be enabled.	Enable the service. Set the service to Automatic. Reenable or reinstall the required service.
A device did not start when the computer booted.	The external device is not powered on. The data cable or power cable is not connected to the device. The device has been disabled in the BIOS settings. The device has failed. The device has a conflict with a newly installed device. The driver is corrupted. The driver is still being installed.	Power on the external device. Secure the data cable and power cable to the device. Enable the device in the BIOS settings. Replace the device. Remove the newly installed device. Reinstall or roll back the driver. Allow the computer to finish booting.
A program listed in the Registry is not found.	One or more program files have been deleted. The uninstall program did not work correctly. The installation directory has been removed. The hard drive has become corrupted. The computer has a virus.	Reinstall the program. Reinstall the program and run the uninstall program again. Run **chkdsk /F /R** to fix the hard drive file entries. Scan for and remove the virus.

Identify the Problem	Probable Causes	Possible Solutions
The computer continually restarts without displaying the desktop.	The computer is set to restart when there is a failure. A startup file has become corrupted.	Press **F8** to open the Advanced Options Menu and choose **Disable, automatic restart on system failure.** Run **chkdsk /F /R** from the recovery console.
The computer displays a black or Blue Screen of Death (BSOD).	A driver is not compatible with the hardware. The RAM is failing. The power supply is failing. The CPU is failing. The motherboard is failing.	Research the STOP error and the name of the module that produced the error. Replace any failing devices with known good devices.
The computer locks up without any error messages.	The CPU or FSB settings are incorrect on the motherboard or in the BIOS settings. The computer is overheating. An update has corrupted the operating system. The RAM is failing. The hard drive is failing. The power supply is failing. The computer has a virus.	Check and reset the CPU and FSB settings. Check and replace any cooling devices as necessary. Uninstall the software update or perform a System Restore. Run **chkdsk /F /R** from the recovery console. Replace any failing devices with known good devices. Scan for and remove the virus.
An application does not install.	The downloaded application installer contains a virus and has been prevented from installing by virus protection software. The installation disk or file is corrupted. The installation application is not compatible with the operating system. There are too many programs running and not enough memory remaining to install the application. The hardware does not meet the minimum requirements. The security warning was ignored or canceled.	Obtain a new installation disk or delete the file, and download the installation file again. Run the installation application under compatibility mode. Close applications before installing a new program. Install hardware that meets the minimum installation requirements. Run the installation again and accept the security warning.

Identify the Problem	Probable Causes	Possible Solutions
A computer with Windows 7 installed does not run Aero.	The computer does not meet the minimum hardware requirements for running Aero.	Upgrade the processor, RAM, and video card to meet the minimum Microsoft requirements for Aero.
The search feature takes a long time to find results.	The index service is not running. The index service is not indexing in the correct locations.	Start the index services using services.msc. Change the settings of the index service in the Advanced Options panel.
The UAC no longer prompts the user for permission.	The UAC has been turned off.	Turn on the UAC in the User Account applet in the Control Panel.
No gadgets appear on the desktop.	The gadgets have never been installed or have been uninstalled. The XML necessary to render the gadget is broken, corrupted, or not installed.	Right-click the desktop > click **Gadgets** > right-click a gadget > click **Add**. Register the file msxml3.dll by entering **regsvr32 msxml3.dll > Enter** at the command prompt.
The computer is running slowly and has a delayed response.	A process is using most of the CPU resources. The hardware does not meet the requirements to run Aero.	Restart the process with services.msc. If the process is not needed, end the process with Task Manager. Restart the computer. Disable Aero.
The OS is missing.	Partition is not set as active. Missing startup files for Windows.	Set the active partition using the Disk Management utility. Run Windows Startup Repair.
When you run a program, a "Missing or corrupt DLL message" is displayed.	One or more programs using the DLL file was uninstalled and removed the DLL file that was needed by another program. The DLL file was not registered. The DLL file was corrupted during a bad installation.	Reinstall the program that has a missing or corrupt DLL file. Reinstall the application that uninstalled the DLL. Register the DLL file using the **Regsvr32** command. Run **sfc /scannow** in Safe Mode.

Identify the Problem	Probable Causes	Possible Solutions
RAID is not detected during installation.	Windows 7 does not include the proper drivers to recognize RAID. RAID settings in BIOS are incorrect.	Install the proper drivers. Change settings in BIOS to enable RAID.
A system file is corrupted.	Computer was shut down improperly.	Repair your computer from the Advanced Startup Options menu. Boot computer in Safe Mode and run **sfc /scannow**.
GUI is missing for all users, or GUI fails to load.	Missing startup files for Windows. Windows updates have corrupted the operating system.	Repair your computer from the Advanced Startup Options menu. Run Windows Startup Repair. Reinstall the OS.
The computer shuts down without warning.	A program is causing the Windows OS to shut down unexpectedly.	Boot to Safe Mode and manage startup applications using the msconfig command-line utility.
Computer boots to Safe Mode.	A program has been installed that causes the computer to boot in Safe Mode. The computer has been configured to boot in Safe Mode.	Use msconfig to adjust the startup settings for the program. Use msconfig to configure the computer to boot normally.
Computer boots only to VGA mode.	Corrupt video driver.	Reinstall the video driver.

Apply Troubleshooting Skills to Operating Systems (12.2.1.3)

Now that you understand the troubleshooting process, it is time to apply your listening and diagnostic skills.

The first lab is designed to reinforce your skills with the operating system. You will check restore points before and after using Windows Update.

The second lab is designed to reinforce your communication and troubleshooting skills. In this lab, you perform the following steps:

Step 1.   Receive the work order.

Step 2.   Talk the customer through various steps to try and resolve the problem.

Step 3.   Document the problem and the resolution.

The third, fourth, and fifth labs are designed to reinforce your skills with operating system problems. You will troubleshoot and repair a computer that has more than one problem.

Lab 12.2.1.4: Fix an Operating System Problem

In this lab, you troubleshoot and fix a computer that does not connect to the network. Refer to Lab 12.2.1.4 in *IT Essentials: PC Hardware and Software Lab Manual*, Fifth Edition.

Lab 12.2.1.5: Remote Technician - Fix an Operating System Problem

In this lab, you gather data from the customer and then instruct the customer on how to fix a computer that does not connect to the network. Document the customer's problem in the work order. Refer to Lab 12.2.1.5 in *IT Essentials: PC Hardware and Software Lab Manual*, Fifth Edition.

Lab 12.2.1.6: Troubleshooting Operating System Problems in Windows 7

In this lab, the instructor introduces various operating system problems. The student diagnoses the causes and solves the problems. Refer to Lab 12.2.1.6 in *IT Essentials: PC Hardware and Software Lab Manual*, Fifth Edition.

Lab 12.2.1.7: Troubleshooting Operating System Problems in Windows Vista

In this lab, the instructor introduces various operating system problems. The student diagnoses the causes and solves the problems. Refer to Lab 12.2.1.7 in *IT Essentials: PC Hardware and Software Lab Manual*, Fifth Edition.

Lab 12.2.1.8: Troubleshooting Operating Systems in Windows XP

In this lab, the instructor introduces various operating system problems. The student diagnoses the causes and solves the problems. Refer to Lab 12.2.1.8 in *IT Essentials: PC Hardware and Software Lab Manual*, Fifth Edition.

Apply Troubleshooting Process to Networks (12.3.1)

This section describes how to apply the six-step troubleshooting processes to problems with networks and provides a chart of common problems and solutions that can be used by a technician troubleshooting these issues. Labs at the end of the section allow you to practice using the troubleshooting steps

Six Steps for Advanced Troubleshooting Networks (12.3.1.1)

To begin troubleshooting a network problem, you should first try to locate the source of the problem. Check to see whether a group of users, or only one user, has the problem. If only one user has the problem, begin troubleshooting with that user's computer.

The first step in the troubleshooting process is to identify the problem. Table 12-15 shows a list of open-ended and closed-ended questions to ask the customer.

Table 12-15   Step 1: Identify the Problem

Open-ended questions	When did the problem start?
	Which network LEDs are lit?
	What problems are you experiencing?
	Is there anything else you can tell me about the problem?
	What other users are having problems?
	Can you describe your network configuration?
Closed-ended questions	Has any network equipment changed?
	Have any peripherals been added to your computer?
	Have any other computers been added to the network?
	Have you rebooted your computer?

After you have talked to the customer, you can establish a theory of probable cause. Table 12-16 shows a list of some common probable causes for network problems.

Table 12-16   Step 2: Establish a Theory of Probable Cause

Common causes of network problems	Incorrect IP information.
	Incorrect wireless configuration.
	Disabled network connection.
	Verify the wireless router configuration.
	Verify cabling and connections.
	Verify the network equipment settings.

After you have developed some theories about what is wrong, test your theories to determine the cause of the problem. Table 12-17 shows a list of quick procedures that can determine the exact cause of the problem or even correct the problem. If a quick procedure corrects the problem, you can go to Step 5 to verify full system functionality. If a quick procedure does not correct the problem, you might need to research the problem further to establish the exact cause.

Table 12-17   Step 3: Test the Theory to Determine Cause

Common steps to determine cause	Restart the network equipment.
	Renew the IP address.
	Reconnect all the network cables.
	Verify the wireless router configuration.
	Ping the local host.
	Ping the default gateway.
	Ping an external website.
	Verify the network equipment settings.

After you have determined the exact cause of the problem, establish a plan of action to resolve the problem and implement the solution. Table 12-18 shows some sources you can use to gather additional information to resolve an issue.

Table 12-18   Step 4: Establish a Plan of Action to Resolve the Problem and Implement the Solution

If no solution is achieved in the previous step, further research is needed to implement the solution.	Help desk repair logs
	Other technicians
	Manufacturer FAQs
	Technical websites
	Newsgroups
	Computer manuals
	Device manuals
	Online forums
	Internet search

After you have corrected the problem, verify full functionality and, if applicable, implement preventive measures. Table 12-19 shows a list of the steps to verify the solution.

Table 12-19   Step 5: Verify Full System Functionality and, If Applicable, Implement Preventive Measures

Verify solution and full system functionality.	Reboot all the network equipment.
	Reboot any computer that experienced network problems.
	Validate all LEDs on the network equipment.
	Use the **ipconfig /all** command to display IP addressing information for all network adapters.
	Use the **ping** command to check network connectivity to an external website.
	Use the **nslookup** command to query your DNS server.
	Use the **net view** command to show the available shared resources on a network.
	Print to a shared printer.

In the final step of the troubleshooting process, you must document your findings, actions, and outcomes. Table 12-20 shows a list of the tasks required to document the problem and the solution.

Table 12-20   Step 6: Document Findings, Actions, and Outcomes

Document findings.	Discuss the solution implemented with the customer.
	Have the customer verify the problem has been solved.
	Provide the customer with all paperwork.
	Document the steps taken to solve the problem in the work order and the technician's journal.
	Document any components used in the repair.
	Document the time spent to resolve the problem.

Common Problems and Solutions for Networks (12.3.1.2)

Network problems can be attributed to hardware, software, or a combination of the two. You will resolve some types of problems more often than others, while other problems may require more in-depth troubleshooting skills.

Network Connection Problems

These types of connection problems are often related to incorrect TCP/IP configurations, firewall settings, or devices that have stopped working, as shown in Table 12-21.

Table 12-21   Common Problems and Solutions for Network Connections

Identify the Problem	Probable Causes	Possible Solutions
A computer can connect to a network device by the IP address but not by the hostname.	Incorrect hostname. Incorrect DNS settings. DNS server is not operational.	Reenter the hostname. Reenter the IP address of the DNS server. Reboot the DNS server.
The computer does not obtain or renew the IP address.	The computer is using a static IP address. Loose network cable. Firewall is blocking DHCP.	Enable the computer to obtain an IP address automatically. Check the cable connections. Change the firewall settings to allow DHCP traffic.
An IP address conflict message displays when connecting a new computer to the network.	The same IP address is assigned to two different devices on the network.	Configure each device with a unique IP address.
A computer has network access but does not have Internet access.	The gateway IP address is incorrect. A router is configured incorrectly.	Reboot the router and reconfigure the router settings.
The computer automatically obtained the IP address 169.254.x.x but cannot connect to the network.	The DHCP server is not on. The computer cannot communicate with the DHCP server. Another computer has been assigned a static IP address that has been assigned from the DHCP pool.	Turn on the DCHP server. Run **ipconfig /release** and then **ipconfig /renew**. Reboot the computer. Remove the static IP address from the DHCP pool so the address is not assigned accidentally again, or change the static IP address on the computer to an IP address not included in the DHCP pool.
Users are experiencing slow transfer speeds on the wireless network.	Wireless security has not been implemented allowing unauthorized users access. There are too many users connected to the access point.	Implement a wireless security plan. Add another access point.
Users are experiencing intermittent connectivity on the wireless network.	User is too far away from access point. The wireless signal is experiencing interference from outside sources. There are too many users connected to the access point.	Ensure the access point is centrally located. Change the channels on the wireless network. Add another access point.

Email Failure

Not being able to send or receive email is often caused by incorrect email software settings, firewall settings, and hardware connectivity issues, as shown in Table 12-22.

Table 12-22   Common Problems and Solutions for Email Failures

Identify the Problem	Probable Causes	Possible Solutions
The computer cannot send or receive email.	The computer has incorrect email client settings.	Reconfigure the email client settings.
	The email server is down.	Reboot the email server or notify your email service provider.
	There is a loose or disconnected network cable.	Check the cable connections.
The computer can send email, but cannot receive email.	The inbox is full.	Archive or delete emails to create space.
The computer cannot receive a certain email attachment.	The email attachment is too large.	Ask the sender to split the attachment into smaller parts and resend them in individual emails.
	The email attachment contains a virus and has been blocked by virus protection.	Ask the sender to scan the attachment before sending it.
The computer cannot authenticate to the email server.	The email server settings are incorrect.	Enter the correct email server settings.

FTP and Secure Internet Connection Problems

File transfer problems between FTP clients and servers are often caused by incorrect IP address and port settings, or security policies. Secure Internet connection problems are often related to incorrect certificate settings and ports blocked by software or hardware, as shown in Table 12-23.

Table 12-23   Common Problems and Solutions for FTP and Secure Internet Connections

Identify the Problem	Probable Causes	Possible Solutions
The computer cannot access the FTP server.	Port forwarding is not enabled in the router.	Enable port forwarding on the router to forward port 21 to the IP address of the FTP server.
	The maximum number of users has been reached.	Increase the maximum number of simultaneous FTP users on the FTP server.

Identify the Problem	Probable Causes	Possible Solutions
The FTP client software cannot find the FTP server.	The FTP client has an incorrect IP address or port setting. The FTP server is not running.	Enter the correct IP address and port settings in the FTP client. Reboot the FTP server.
The FTP server disconnects the client after a short period of inactivity.	The FTP server does not allow connected clients to remain connected when no commands are being sent to the FTP server.	Increase the amount of time an FTP client is allowed to remain connected without performing any actions.
A computer cannot access a specific HTTPS site.	The browser certificate SSL setting is incorrect.	Clear the SSL state. Add the trusted root certificate. Select **Tools > Internet Options > Advanced** tab and ensure the SSL check box is enabled.

Problems Revealed by CLI Commands

Unexpected information reported from CLI commands is often caused by incorrect IP address settings, hardware connection issues, and firewall settings, as shown in Table 12-24.

Table 12-24   Common Problems and Solutions When Using Network Troubleshooting Tools

Identify the Problem	Probable Causes	Possible Solutions
Computer can ping an IP address but not a hostname.	The hostname is incorrect. The DNS settings of the computer are incorrect. The DNS server is not operational. NetBIOS over TCP/IP is not enabled.	Enter the correct hostname. Enter the correct DNS settings. Reboot the DNS server. Enable NetBIOS over TCP/IP.
A computer on one network cannot ping a computer on another network.	There is a bad connection or broken device between the two networks. ICMP echo request is disabled.	Use tracert to locate which link is down and fix the broken link. Ensure that the ICMP echo request is enabled.

Nslookup reports "Can't find server name for address 127.0.0.0: timed out."	The DNS IP address is not configured on the local computer. The DNS IP address is not correct.	Add the IP address of a valid DNS server to the TCP/IP properties of the LAN adapter. Correct the IP address to a valid DNS server to the TCP/IP properties of the LAN adapter.
A computer cannot connect to a shared network folder using the net use command.	The folder is not shared. The computer is not in the same workgroup.	Make sure the network folder is shared using the **net share** command. Set the computer to the same workgroup as the computer with the shared network folder.
When attempting to use the **ipconfig /release** or **ipconfig /renew** command, you receive the message:\ "No operation can be performed on the adapter while its media is disconnected."	The network cable is unplugged. The computer has been configured with a static IP address.	Reconnect the network cable. Change the TCP/IP properties of the LAN adapter to use DHCP.
The computer cannot telnet into a remote computer.	The Telnet service has stopped. The remote computer has not been configured to accept telnet connections.	Start the Telnet service on the remote computer. Configure the remote computer to accept Telnet connections.
The network icon in the notification area shows a yellow exclamation point. When attempting to use the **ipconfig /release** or **ipconfig /renew** command, you receive the message "The operation failed as no adapter is in the state permissible for this operation."	A static IP address has been assigned to the interface.	Change the configuration from a static IP address to **Obtain an IP address automatically**.

Apply Troubleshooting Skills to Networks (12.3.1.3)

Now that you understand the troubleshooting process, it is time to apply your listening and diagnostic skills.

The first lab is designed to reinforce your skills with networks. You will troubleshoot and fix a computer that does not connect to the network.

The second lab is designed to reinforce your communication and troubleshooting skills. In this lab, you perform the following steps:

Step 1.   Receive the work order.

Step 2.   Talk the customer through various steps to try and resolve the problem.

Step 3.   Document the problem and the resolution.

The third, fourth, and fifth labs are designed to test your troubleshooting skills with networking problems. You will troubleshoot and repair a router and computers that have more than one problem.

Lab 12.3.1.4: Fix a Network Problem

In this lab, you troubleshoot and fix a computer that does not connect to the network. Refer to Lab 12.3.1.4 in *IT Essentials: PC Hardware and Software Lab Manual*, Fifth Edition.

Lab 12.3.1.5: Remote Technician - Fix a Network Problem

In this lab, you gather data from the customer, and then instruct the customer on how to fix a computer that does not connect to the network. Document the customer's problem in the work order. Refer to Lab 12.3.1.5 in *IT Essentials: PC Hardware and Software Lab Manual*, Fifth Edition.

Lab 12.3.1.6: Troubleshooting Network Problems in Windows 7

In this lab, the instructor introduces various network problems. The student diagnoses the causes and solves the problems. Refer to Lab 12.3.1.6 in *IT Essentials: PC Hardware and Software Lab Manual*, Fifth Edition.

Lab 12.3.1.7: Troubleshooting Network Problems in Windows Vista

In this lab, the instructor introduces various network problems. The student diagnoses the causes and solves the problems. Refer to Lab 12.3.1.7 in *IT Essentials: PC Hardware and Software Lab Manual*, Fifth Edition.

Lab 12.3.1.8: Troubleshooting Network Problems in Windows XP

In this lab, the instructor introduces various network problems. The student diagnoses the causes and solves the problems. Refer to Lab 12.3.1.8 in *IT Essentials: PC Hardware and Software Lab Manual*, Fifth Edition.

Apply Troubleshooting Process to Laptops (12.4.1)

This section describes how to apply the six-step troubleshooting processes to problems with laptops and provides a chart of common problems and solutions that can be used by a technician troubleshooting these issues. Labs at the end of the section allow you to practice using the troubleshooting steps

Six Steps for Advanced Troubleshooting Laptops (12.4.1.1)

The troubleshooting process helps resolve problems with laptops. These problems range from the simple, such as updating a driver, to more complex problems, such as replacing an inverter. Use the troubleshooting steps as a guideline to help you diagnose and repair problems.

The first step in the troubleshooting process is to identify the problem. Table 12-25 shows a list of open-ended and closed-ended questions to ask the customer.

Table 12-25   Step 1: Identify the Problem

Open-ended questions	In what environment are you using the laptop?
	When did the problem start?
	What problems are you experiencing?
	What happens when the laptop boots?
	What can you see on your screen?
	Is there anything else you can tell me about the problem?
Closed-ended questions	Has anyone done any repair work on the laptop recently?
	Has anyone else used the laptop?
	Does the laptop connect to the Internet?
	Is there a wireless NIC in the laptop?
	Have you ever had any problems like this before?

After you have talked to the customer, you can establish a theory of probable cause. Table 12-26 shows a list of some common probable causes for laptop problem.

Table 12-26 Step 2: Establish a Theory of Probable Cause

Common causes of laptop problems	Laptop battery does not have a charge.
	Laptop battery will not charge.
	Loose cable connections.
	The inverter does not work.
	External keyboard does not work.
	Num Lock key is on.
	Loose RAM.
	A Fn key has disabled a capability.
	A button or slide switch has disabled the wireless connection.

After you have developed some theories about what is wrong, test your theories to determine the cause of the problem. Table 12-27 shows a list of quick procedures that can determine the exact cause of the problem or even correct the problem. If a quick procedure corrects the problem, you can go to Step 5 to verify full system functionality. If a quick procedure does not correct the problem, you might need to research the problem further to establish the exact cause.

Table 12-27 Step 3: Test the Theory to Determine Cause

Common steps to determine cause	Use AC power instead of the battery.
	Replace the AC adapter.
	Remove and reinsert the battery.
	Replace the battery.
	Check BIOS settings.
	Disconnect and reconnect cables one at a time.
	Replace the inverter.
	Check the Fn key settings.
	Verify the wireless connection button or slide switch is in the correct position.
	Disconnect and reconnect peripherals one at a time.
	Verify Num Lock key is off.
	Reinstall RAM.
	Reboot the laptop.

After you have determined the exact cause of the problem, establish a plan of action to resolve the problem and implement the solution. Table 12-28 shows some sources you can use to gather additional information to resolve an issue.

Table 12-28   Step 4: Establish a Plan of Action to Resolve the Problem and Implement the Solution

If no solution is achieved in the previous step, further research is needed to implement the solution.	Help desk repair logs
	Other technicians
	Manufacturer FAQs
	Technical websites
	Newsgroups
	Computer manual
	Device manual
	Online forums
	Internet search

After you have corrected the problem, verify full functionality and, if applicable, implement preventive measures. Table 12-29 shows a list of the steps to verify the solution.

Table 12-29   Step 5: Verify Full System Functionality and, If Applicable, Implement Preventive Measures

Verify solution and full system functionality.	Reboot the computer.
	Attach all peripherals.
	Operate laptop using only battery.
	Print a document from an application.
	Type sample document to test keyboard.
	Check Event Viewer for warnings or errors.

In the final step of the troubleshooting process, you must document your findings, actions, and outcomes. Table 12-30 shows a list of the tasks required to document the problem and the solution.

Table 12-30   Step 6: Document Findings, Actions, and Outcomes

Document findings.	Discuss the solution implemented with the customer.
	Have the customer verify the problem has been solved.
	Provide the customer with all paperwork.
	Document the steps taken to solve the problem in the work order and the technician's journal.
	Document any components used in the repair.
	Document the time spent to resolve the problem.

Common Problems and Solutions for Laptops (12.4.1.2)

Laptop problems can be attributed to hardware, software, networks, or some combination of the three. You will resolve some types of laptop problems more often than others.

If you need to replace laptop components, make sure that you have the correct replacement component and tools recommended by the manufacturer.

Table 12-31 is a chart of common laptop display problems and solutions. Before replacing laptop parts, make sure you understand the steps involved and the skills required for the installation.

Table 12-31   Common Problems and Solutions for Laptop Displays

Identify the Problem	Probable Causes	Possible Solutions
The laptop screen appears black or very dim. A buzzing noise may also be heard.	Laptop display screen inverter or backlight lamp failure.	Replace the display inverter. Replace the backlight lamp.
The laptop screen only displays vertical lines that can change colors.	Laptop display screen failure.	Replace the laptop display screen.
External laptop display connected to the laptop shows content, but the laptop screen is blank.	The laptop screen is not set to display output.	Press the Fn key with the appropriate multifunction key to display output on the laptop screen.
Laptop display screen and external monitor will not display images, while the laptop hard drive and fans are operating normally.	The laptop motherboard or the video card has failed.	Replace the laptop motherboard if it has onboard video. Replace the video card.
The laptop does not return from Standby or Hibernate mode.	The laptop has a conflict between the BIOS settings and the Windows power management settings.	Reconfigure the laptop BIOS settings and the Windows power management settings.

Table 12-32 is a chart of common storage device and RAM problems and solutions. Most replacement steps for storage devices and memory follow a generic installation process.

Table 12-32   Common Problems and Solutions for Laptop Storage Devices and RAM

Identify the Problem	Probable Causes	Possible Solutions
The laptop hard drive has data access errors and makes unusual noises.	The hard drive has failed.	Replace the hard drive.
The laptop will not boot or access a newly installed hard drive.	The hard drive is not connected properly. The BIOS does not recognize the new hard drive.	Reconnect the hard drive. Update the laptop BIOS.
The laptop accesses the hard drive excessively.	The virtual memory is set incorrectly. Additional RAM is needed. Free hard drive space is limited.	Change the virtual memory settings. Install additional RAM. Delete or remove unneeded files and applications.
The laptop makes a long beeping noise after installing new RAM.	The wrong type of RAM is installed. The RAM is installed incorrectly. A damaged RAM module is installed.	Install the correct type of RAM. Remove and reinstall the RAM. Replace the damaged RAM module.

Table 12-33 is a chart of common power and input device problems and solutions. Most replacement steps for a laptop battery follow a generic installation process.

Table 12-33   Common Problems and Solutions for Laptops Power and Input Devices

Identify the Problem	Probable Causes	Possible Solutions
The laptop LED power light is not on when the laptop is plugged into an AC outlet.	The AC power source is not working. The power cable is not securely connected to the laptop. The AC adapter is defective.	Plug the laptop into a known good power source. Unplug and securely connect the power cable to the laptop. Replace the AC adapter.
The laptop will not power on when only using the battery.	The battery is not connected correctly. The battery does not have a charge. The battery is defective.	Remove and reconnect the battery. Charge the battery. Replace the battery.
The laptop operation time while using the battery is very short.	The battery is old.	Replace the battery.

Identify the Problem	Probable Causes	Possible Solutions
Date and time are incorrect when the laptop is powered on.	The CMOS battery has failed. The CMOS battery is loose.	Replace the CMOS battery. Remove and reinstall the CMOS battery.
The laptop touchpad or pointer device is not responsive.	The touchpad or pointer device is disabled. The touchpad or pointer device is defective.	Enable the pointer device from the control panel. Replace the pointer device. Use a mouse as a new pointer device.
The laptop keyboard does not work, or individual keys do not work.	The keyboard has been damaged by liquid. The laptop keyboard has a loose connection. The keyboard is worn or old.	Clean the keyboard. Reconnect the laptop keyboard. Replace the laptop keyboard. Use an external keyboard.

Table 12-34 is a chart of common ventilation, CPU, sound, and expansion card problems and solutions. All PC expansion cards, including ExpressCards, are inserted and removed using similar steps.

Table 12-34   Common Problems and Solutions for Laptop Problems and Solutions

Identify the Problem	Probable Causes	Possible Solutions
The laptop shuts off randomly or is excessively hot.	The laptop has poor ventilation. The laptop has a faulty fan. The CPU heat sink is dirty or loose.	Clean all the vents. Replace any faulty fans. Clean and reseat the heat sink.
The laptop will not start up, and only the fans and LEDs are working.	The CPU has failed.	Replace the CPU.
The laptop's built-in speakers are not producing any sound.	The audio is disabled in BIOS. The sound is muted. The laptop built-in speakers are damaged.	Enable the audio in BIOS. Unmute the sound. Replace the speakers. Use external speakers.
Cannot insert a PC Card into the laptop.	The PC Card is not supported by the laptop. The plastic protector is installed in the card slot.	Replace the PC Card with an ExpressCard. Remove the plastic protector from the card slot. Purchase a PC Card to ExpressCard adapter.

Apply Troubleshooting Skills to Laptops (12.4.1.3)

Now that you understand the troubleshooting process, it is time to apply your listening and diagnostic skills.

The worksheets are about verifying work order information and investigating support websites and laptop repair companies.

The lab is designed to test your troubleshooting skills with laptop hardware and software problems. You will troubleshoot and repair a laptop that has more than one problem.

Lab 12.4.1.4: Fix a Laptop Problem

In this lab, you troubleshoot and fix a laptop that has a second monitor connected which does not display anything. Refer to Lab 12.4.1.4 in *IT Essentials: PC Hardware and Software Lab Manual*, Fifth Edition.

Lab 12.4.1.5: Remote Technician - Fix a Laptop Problem

In this lab, you gather data from the customer and then instruct the customer on how to fix a laptop that will not display anything on a secondary monitor. Document the customer's problem in the work order. Refer to Lab 12.4.1.5 in *IT Essentials: PC Hardware and Software Lab Manual*, Fifth Edition.

Lab 12.4.1.6: Troubleshooting Laptop Problems in Windows 7

In this lab, the instructor introduces various laptop problems. The student diagnoses the causes and solves the problems. Refer to Lab 12.4.1.6 in *IT Essentials: PC Hardware and Software Lab Manual*, Fifth Edition.

Lab 12.4.1.7: Troubleshooting Laptop Problems in Windows Vista

In this lab, the instructor introduces various laptop problems. The student diagnoses the causes and solves the problems. Refer to Lab 12.4.1.7 in *IT Essentials: PC Hardware and Software Lab Manual*, Fifth Edition.

Lab 12.4.1.8: Troubleshooting Laptop Problems in Windows XP

In this lab, the instructor introduces various laptop problems. The student diagnoses the causes and solves the problems. Refer to Lab 12.4.1.8 in *IT Essentials: PC Hardware and Software Lab Manual*, Fifth Edition.

Apply Troubleshooting Process to Printers (12.5.1)

This section describes how to apply the six-step troubleshooting processes to problems with printers and provides a chart of common problems and solutions that can be used by a technician troubleshooting these issues. Labs at the end of the section allow you to practice using the troubleshooting steps.

Six Steps for Advanced Troubleshooting Printers (12.5.1.1)

With printer problems, a technician must be able to determine if the problem exists with the device, cable connection, or the computer to which it is attached. Follow the steps outlined in this section to accurately identify, repair, and document the problem. In this chapter, you repair printers in both local and network configurations.

The first step in the troubleshooting process is to identify the problem. Table 12-35 shows a list of open-ended and closed-ended questions to ask the customer.

Table 12-35 Step 1: Identify the Problem

Open-ended questions	What type of printer do you have?
	What is the brand and model of your printer?
	What type of paper are you using?
	What problems are you experiencing with your printer?
	What software or hardware has been changed recently on your computer?
	What were you doing when the problem was identified?
	What error messages have you received?
Closed-ended questions	Is the printer under warranty?
	Can you print a test page?
	Is this a new printer?
	Is the printer powered on?
	Does the problem appear on every page?
	Has the paper been changed recently?
	Is the problem only with this printer?
	Does the problem occur when you use the other applications?
	Is your printer connected to the network wirelessly?

After you have talked to the customer, you can establish a theory of probable cause. Table 12-36 shows a list of some common probable causes for printer problems.

Table 12-36   Step 2: Establish a Theory of Probable Cause

Common causes of printer problems	Loose cable connections
	Paper jams
	Equipment power
	Low ink warning
	Out of paper
	Errors on equipment display
	Errors on computer screen
	Empty toner cartridge
	Print server not working
	Printer unable to establish a connection to the wireless network

After you have developed some theories about what is wrong, test your theories to determine the cause of the problem. Table 12-37 shows a list of quick procedures that can determine the exact cause of the problem or even correct the problem. If a quick procedure corrects the problem, you can go to Step 5 to verify full system functionality. If a quick procedure does not correct the problem, you might need to research the problem further to establish the exact cause.

Table 12-37   Step 3: Test the Theory to Determine Cause

Common steps to determine cause.	Restart the printer.
	Disconnect and reconnect the cables.
	Restart the computer.
	Check the printer for paper jams.
	Reseat the paper in the paper trays.
	Open and close the printer trays.
	Ensure the printer doors are closed.
	Clear the jobs in the printer queue.
	Restart the print spooler service.
	Reinstall the printer software.
	Remove the packing tape from the inkjet cartridge nozzles arm.
	Restart print server.
	Reconfigure the wireless settings of the printer.

After you have determined the exact cause of the problem, establish a plan of action to resolve the problem and implement the solution. Table 12-38 shows some sources you can use to gather additional information to resolve an issue.

Table 12-38 Step 4: Establish a Plan of Action to Resolve the Problem and Implement the Solution

If no solution is achieved in the previous step, further research is needed to implement the solution.	Help desk repair logs
	Other technicians
	Manufacturer FAQs
	Technical websites
	Newsgroups
	Computer manual
	Device manual
	Online forums
	Internet search

After you have corrected the problem, verify full functionality and, if applicable, implement preventive measures. Table 12-39 shows a list of the steps to verify the solution.

Table 12-39 Step 5: Verify Full System Functionality and, If Applicable, Implement Preventive Measures

Verify solution and full system functionality.	Reboot the computer.
	Reboot the printer.
	Print a test page from the printer control panel.
	Print a document from an application.
	Reprint the customer's problem document.

In the final step of the troubleshooting process, you must document your findings, actions, and outcomes. Table 12-40 shows a list of the tasks required to document the problem and the solution.

Table 12-40 Step 6: Document Findings, Actions, and Outcomes

Document findings.	Discuss the solution implemented with the customer.
	Have the customer verify the problem has been solved.
	Provide the customer with all paperwork.
	Document the steps taken to solve the problem in the work order and the technician's journal.
	Document any components used in the repair.
	Document the time spent to resolve the problem.

Common Problems and Solutions for Printers (12.5.1.2)

Printer problems can be attributed to hardware, software, networks, or some combination of the three. You will resolve some types of problems more often than others. Table 12-41 is a chart of common problems and solutions.

Table 12-41   Common Problems and Solutions for Printers

Identify the Problem	Probable Causes	Possible Solutions
Printer prints unknown characters.	The printer may be plugged into a UPS.	Plug the printer directly into the wall outlet.
	An incorrect print driver is installed.	Uninstall the incorrect print driver and install the correct driver.
	The printer cables are loose.	
	The printer has been set to Pause Printing.	Secure the printer cables.
	The printer has been set to Use Printer Offline.	Set the printer to **Use Printer Online**.
Paper jams when printing.	The wrong paper type is being used.	Replace the paper with the manufacturer's recommended paper type.
	Humidity causes the paper to stick together.	Insert new paper in the paper tray.
Printer will not print large or complex images.	The printer does not have enough memory.	Add more memory to the printer.
Laser printer prints vertical lines or streaks on every page.	The drum is damaged.	Replace the drum or replace the toner cartridge when it contains the drum.
		Remove and shake the toner cartridge.
The toner is not fusing to the paper	The fuser is defective.	Replace the fuser.
Paper is creased after printing.	The pickup rollers are obstructed, damaged, or dirty.	Clean or replace the pickup rollers.
Paper is not being fed into the printer.	The pickup rollers are obstructed, damaged, or dirty.	Clean or replace the pickup rollers.
Each time a network printer is restarted, users receive a "Document failed to print" message.	Printer's IP configuration set for DHCP.	Assign a static IP address to the printer.
	A device on the network has the same IP address as the network printer.	Assign a different static IP address to the printer.

Apply Troubleshooting Skills to Printers (12.5.1.3)

Now that you understand the troubleshooting process, it is time to apply your listening and diagnostic skills.

The first lab is designed to reinforce your printer troubleshooting skills.

The second lab is designed to reinforce your communication and troubleshooting skills with printers. In this lab, you perform the following steps:

Step 1.   Receive the work order.

Step 2.   Talk the customer through various steps to try and resolve the problem.

Step 3.   Document the problem and the resolution.

The third, fourth, and fifth labs are designed to reinforce your skills with printer problems. You will troubleshoot and repair multiple printing problems.

Lab 12.5.1.4: Fix a Printer Problem

In this lab, you troubleshoot and fix a printer that does not print documents for a user. Refer to Lab 12.5.1.4 in *IT Essentials: PC Hardware and Software Lab Manual*, Fifth Edition.

Lab 12.5.1.5: Remote Technician - Fix a Printer Problem

In this lab, you gather data from the customer and then instruct the customer on how to fix a printer that does not print documents for a user. Document the customer's problem in the work order. Refer to Lab 12.5.1.5 in *IT Essentials: PC Hardware and Software Lab Manual*, Fifth Edition.

Lab 12.5.1.6: Troubleshooting Printer Problems in Windows 7

In this lab, the instructor introduces various printer problems. The student diagnoses the causes and solves the problems. Refer to Lab 12.5.1.6 in *IT Essentials: PC Hardware and Software Lab Manual*, Fifth Edition.

Lab 12.5.1.7: Troubleshooting Printer Problems in Windows Vista

In this lab, the instructor introduces various printer problems. The student diagnoses the causes and solves the problems. Refer to Lab 12.5.1.7 in *IT Essentials: PC Hardware and Software Lab Manual*, Fifth Edition.

Lab 12.5.1.8: Troubleshooting Printer Problems in Windows XP

In this lab, the instructor introduces various printer problems. The student diagnoses the causes and solves the problems. Refer to Lab 12.5.1.8 in *IT Essentials: PC Hardware and Software Lab Manual*, Fifth Edition.

Apply Troubleshooting Process to Security (12.6.1)

This section describes how to apply the six-step troubleshooting processes to problems with security and provides a chart of common problems and solutions that can be used by a technician troubleshooting these issues. Labs at the end of the section allow you to practice using the troubleshooting steps

Six Steps for Advanced Troubleshooting Security (12.6.1.1)

Computer technicians must be able to analyze a security threat and determine the appropriate method to protect assets and repair damage. This process is called troubleshooting.

The first step in the troubleshooting process is to identify the problem. Table 12-42 shows a list of open-ended and closed-ended questions to ask the customer.

Table 12-42   Step 1: Identify the Problem

Open-ended questions	What problems are you experiencing?
	When did the problem start?
	How are you connected to the Internet?
	What type of firewall are you using?
	What security software is installed on your computer?
	What network resources can you access using wireless?
	What resource permissions do you have?
Closed-ended questions	Do you have a firewall?
	Has anyone else used your computer?
	Is your security software up-to-date?
	Have you scanned your computer recently for viruses?
	Have you ever had this problem before?
	Have you changed your password recently?
	Have you received any error messages on your computer?
	Have you shared your password?
	Do you have permissions for the resource?

After you have talked to the customer, you can establish a theory of probable cause. Table 12-43 shows a list of some common probable causes for security problems.

Table 12-43   Step 2: Establish a Theory of Probable Cause

Common causes of security problems	The user account is disabled.
	The user is using an incorrect username or password.
	The user does not have the correct folder or file permissions.
	The firewall configurations are incorrect.
	The user's computer has been infected by a virus.
	The wireless security configurations are incorrect on the client.
	The security configurations are incorrect on the wireless access point.

After you have developed some theories about what is wrong, test your theories to determine the cause of the problem. Table 12-44 shows a list of quick procedures that can determine the exact cause of the problem or even correct the problem. If a quick procedure corrects the problem, you can go to Step 5 to verify full system functionality. If a quick procedure does not correct the problem, you might need to research the problem further to establish the exact cause.

Table 12-44   Step 3: Test the Theory to Determine Cause

Common steps to determine cause	Verify the user's account settings.
	Reset the user's password.
	Verify the user's permissions for folders and files.
	Check firewall logs for errors.
	Verify the firewall settings.
	Scan and remove viruses from the computer.
	Verify the wireless security configuration of the client.
	Verify the security configuration on the wireless access point.

After you have determined the exact cause of the problem, establish a plan of action to resolve the problem and implement the solution. Table 12-45 shows some sources you can use to gather additional information to resolve an issue.

Table 12-45 Step 4: Establish a Plan of Action to Resolve the Problem and Implement the Solution

If no solution is achieved in the previous step, further research is needed to implement the solution.	Help desk repair logs
	Other technicians
	Manufacturer FAQs
	Technical websites
	Newsgroups
	Computer manual
	Device manual
	Online forums
	Internet search

After you have corrected the problem, verify full functionality and, if applicable, implement preventive measures. Table 12-46 shows a list of the steps to verify the solution.

Table 12-46 Step 5: Verify Full System Functionality and, If Applicable, Implement Preventive Measures

Verify solution and full system functionality.	Reboot the computer.
	Log in to the computer.
	Connect to the network using wireless.
	Verify file and folder access.
	Verify that no virus is found with a virus scan.

In the final step of the troubleshooting process, you must document your findings, actions, and outcomes. Table 12-47 shows a list of the tasks required to document the problem and the solution.

Table 12-47 Step 6: Document Findings, Actions, and Outcomes

Document findings.	Discuss the solution implemented with the customer.
	Have the customer verify the problem has been solved.
	Provide the customer with all paperwork.
	Document the steps taken to solve the problem in the work order and the technician's journal.
	Document any components used in the repair.
	Document the time spent to resolve the problem.

Common Problems and Solutions for Security (12.6.1.2)

Security problems can be attributed to hardware, software, networks, or some combination of the three. You will resolve some types of security problems more often than others.

Malware Settings

Malware protection problems are often related to incorrect software settings or configurations. As a result of these faulty settings, a computer may display one or more of the symptoms caused by malware and boot sector viruses, as shown in Table 12-48.

Table 12-48   Common Problems and Solutions for Malware

Identify the Problem	Probable Causes	Possible Solutions
Message "MBR has been changed or modified" appears at boot.	A boot sector virus has changed the master boot record.	Boot the computer with a bootable floppy or flash drive, and run antivirus software to remove the boot sector virus.
A Windows 7 or Windows Vista computer starts with the error message "Error Loading Operating System."	A virus has damaged the master boot record.	Boot the computer from the installation media. At the Install Windows screen, select **Repair your computer**. At the command prompt, type **bootrec.exe /fixmbr**.
A Windows 7 or Windows Vista computer starts with the error message "Caution: this hard disk may be infected by virus!"	A virus has damaged the boot sector.	Boot the computer from the installation media. At the Install Windows screen, select **Repair your computer**. At the command prompt, type **bootrec.exe /fixboot**.
A Windows XP computer will not boot.	A virus damaged the master boot record.	Boot the computer from the XP installation media. At the setup screen, select **R-Recovery Console**. At the command prompt, use the **fixmbr** command.
A Windows 7 computer will not boot.	A virus damaged Windows system files.	Boot the computer from Windows Preinstallation Environment (Windows PE) media. Access the Windows Startup Repair tool to recover corrupted system files.
Your contacts are receiving spam from your email account.	Your email account has been hijacked by a virus or spyware.	Run antivirus software and repair, delete, or quarantine the infected files. Run antispyware software and remove any spyware infections. After the computer is cleaned, change the email account password.

User Accounts and Permissions

Unauthorized access or blocked access is often caused by incorrect user account settings or incorrect permissions, as shown in Table 12-49.

Table 12-49   Common Problems and Solutions for User Permissions

Identify the Problem	Probable Causes	Possible Solutions
User can log in but receives an "access denied" message when trying to access some folders and files.	The user is not a member of the group that has access to the folders and files.	Add the user to the correct group. Add the correct user's permissions to the folders and files.
User can locate a file on the server but cannot download the file.	The user permissions are not correct.	Change the user's permissions on the file to read and execute.
User is gaining access to a subfolder that should be inaccessible.	The subfolder inherited permissions from the upper level folder.	Change the subfolder permission settings so it does not inherit the permissions from the parent folder. Set the proper permissions for the subfolder.
Users of a group cannot see one folder to which they are supposed to have access.	The folder permissions are set to deny.	Change the folder permissions to allow.
Encrypted files that are moved over the network to a new computer are no longer encrypted.	The new computer does not have an NTFS partition.	Convert the partition on the new computer to NTFS and reencrypt the files.

Computer Security

Computer security problems can be caused by incorrect security settings in the BIOS or on the hard drive, as shown in Table 12-50.

Table 12-50   Common Problems and Solutions for Computer Security Settings

Identify the Problem	Probable Causes	Possible Solutions
Computer runs slowly at the same time every day.	Antivirus software is set to scan the computer at the same time every day.	Configure the antivirus software to scan the computer when the computer is not in use.
User complains that the computer BIOS settings keep changing.	The BIOS password is not set, allowing others to change the BIOS settings.	Set a password to protect access to the BIOS settings.

Identify the Problem	Probable Causes	Possible Solutions
Trusted Platform Module (TPM) does not show up in Device Manager.	The TPM is disabled.	Enable the TPM in the BIOS.

Firewall and Proxy Settings

Blocked connections to networked resources and the Internet are often related to incorrect firewall and proxy rules and incorrect port settings, as shown in Table 12-51.

Table 12-51   Common Problems and Solutions for Firewall or Proxy Settings

Identify the Problem	Probable Causes	Possible Solutions
Computer cannot ping another computer on the network.	The Windows Firewall is blocking ping requests. A router is blocking ping requests.	Configure the Windows Firewall to allow ping requests. Configure the router to allow ping requests.
Laptop firewall exceptions are allowing unauthorized connections from rogue computers.	The Windows Firewall settings are incorrect. The Windows Firewall is disabled.	Set the Windows Firewall to **Do not allow exceptions when using a public network.** Enable the Windows Firewall.
Computer cannot telnet to another computer.	The Windows Firewall blocks port 23 by default. The router is blocking port 23.	Configure the Windows Firewall to open port 23. Configure the router to allow port 23.
Email program is properly configured but cannot connect to the email server.	The email server is down. The Windows Firewall is blocking the email software.	Verify that the email server is operational. Create a Windows Firewall exception for your email software.
Computer can ping outside the local network but has no Internet connectivity.	The Windows Firewall is blocking port 80. The router is blocking port 80.	Configure the Windows Firewall to open port 80. Configure the router to allow port 80.
Computer can ping the proxy server but has no Internet connectivity.	The browser proxy server settings are incorrect. The proxy server is offline.	Reenter the proxy server settings, including the IP address and port of the proxy server and any exceptions that should be defined. Reboot the proxy server.

Apply Troubleshooting Skills to Security (12.6.1.3)

Now that you understand the troubleshooting process, it is time to apply your listening and diagnostic skills.

The first lab is designed to test your troubleshooting skills with security problems. You will troubleshoot and repair a computer with a security problem that is preventing it from connecting to the wireless network.

The second lab is designed to reinforce your communication and troubleshooting skills. In this lab, you perform the following steps:

Step 1.   Receive the work order.

Step 2.   Talk the customer through various steps to try and resolve the problem.

Step 3.   Document the problem and the resolution.

The third, fourth, and fifth labs are designed to test your troubleshooting skills with security problems. You will troubleshoot and repair a network that has more than one security problem.

Lab 12.6.1.4: Fix a Security Problem

In this lab, you gather data from the customer, and then instruct the customer on how to correct a security issue that is preventing connection to the wireless network. Refer to Lab 12.6.1.4 in *IT Essentials: PC Hardware and Software Lab Manual*, Fifth Edition.

Lab 12.6.1.5: Remote Technician - Fix a Security Problem

In this lab, you gather data from the customer to begin the troubleshooting process. Document the customer's problem in the work order. Refer to Lab 12.6.1.5 in *IT Essentials: PC Hardware and Software Lab Manual*, Fifth Edition.

Lab 12.6.1.6: Troubleshooting Access Security in Windows 7

In this lab, the instructor introduces various access security problems. The student diagnoses the causes and solves the problems. Refer to Lab 12.6.1.6 in *IT Essentials: PC Hardware and Software Lab Manual*, Fifth Edition.

Lab 12.6.1.7: Troubleshooting Access Security in Windows Vista

In this lab, the instructor introduces various access security problems. The student diagnoses the causes and solves the problems. Refer to Lab 12.6.1.7 in *IT Essentials: PC Hardware and Software Lab Manual*, Fifth Edition.

Lab 12.6.1.8: Troubleshooting Access Security in Windows XP

In this lab, the instructor introduces various access security problems. The student diagnoses the causes and solves the problems. Refer to Lab 12.6.1.8 in *IT Essentials: PC Hardware and Software Lab Manual*, Fifth Edition.

Summary (12.7.1)

In this chapter, you were given multiple opportunities to hone your troubleshooting knowledge and skills.

This chapter covered advanced diagnostic questions to ask when gathering information about a computer hardware or software problem. It also presented more advanced versions of common problems and solutions for computer components and peripherals, operating systems, networks, laptops, printers, and security.

In labs you fixed a simple problem. You then talked someone else through that same fix, as a call center technician would. And finally, you had to troubleshoot more complex hardware and software problems in Windows 7, Windows Vista, and Windows XP.

Summary of Exercises

Labs

The following labs cover material from this chapter. Refer to the labs in *IT Essentials: PC Hardware and Software Lab Manual*, Fifth Edition.

Lab 12.1.1.4: Repair Boot Problem

Lab 12.1.1.5: Remote Technician - Repair Boot Problem

Lab 12.1.1.6: Troubleshooting Hardware Problems in Windows 7

Lab 12.1.1.7: Troubleshooting Hardware Problems in Windows Vista

Lab 12.1.1.8: Troubleshooting Hardware Problems in Windows XP

Lab 12.2.1.4: Fix an Operating System Problem

Lab 12.2.1.5: Remote Technician - Fix an Operating System Problem

Lab 12.2.1.6: Troubleshooting Operating System Problems in Windows 7

Lab 12.2.1.7: Troubleshooting Operating System Problems in Windows Vista

Lab 12.2.1.8: Troubleshooting Operating Systems in Windows XP

Lab 12.3.1.4: Lab - Fix a Network Problem

Lab 12.3.1.5: Remote Technician - Fix a Network Problem

Lab 12.3.1.6: Troubleshooting Network Problems in Windows 7

Lab 12.3.1.7: Troubleshooting Network Problems in Windows Vista

Check Your Understanding

You can find the answers to these questions in Appendix A, "Answers to 'Check Your Understanding' Questions."

1. A user is not able to open several files that are used frequently. A message appears indicating that the files are corrupted. What could cause this problem?

    A. The hard drive is beginning to fail.

    B. The amount of RAM is insufficient.

    C. The BIOS needs updating.

    D. The CPU needs upgrading.

2. A laptop is working very slowly. When inspecting the device, the technician sees that the hard drive LED activity indicator is lit for most of the time. A look at the properties of the hard drive shows that 196 GB are available. What would be the best possible solution to this problem?

    A. Reset the motherboard to the factory default settings.

    B. Add additional RAM.

    C. Replace the existing hard drive with a higher capacity one.

    D. Overclock the CPU.

    E. Reconfigure the BIOS settings.

3. When leaving a laptop for repair, a customer complains that searching for any file on the laptop is taking an excessive amount of time. The technician returns the laptop and explains that the index service has now been enabled for document folders. At what step of the troubleshooting process is this taking place?

    A. Identify the problem.

    B. Establish a theory of probable causes.

    C. Determine the exact cause.

    D. Implement a solution.

    E. Verify the solution and full system functionality.

    F. Document findings.

4. A network user is attempting to access email, but the email client is repetitively asking for a username and a password. Other users based in the same building are having no issues with the email service. What are the two most likely sources of the problem?

    A. The default gateway of the PC is set incorrectly.

    B. The username or the password entered are incorrect.

    C. There is a lack of connection with the DHCP server.

    D. The email server is not operational.

    E. The network cable is disconnected from the PC.

    F. The Caps Lock function is enabled.

5. A laptop keeps shutting down without warning while still connected to a power source. What could cause this problem?

    A. The laptop is overheating.

    B. The laptop battery is not seated properly.

    C. The BIOS needs to be updated.

    D. The power settings are incorrectly configured.

6. A user complains that a Windows XP laptop loads files very slowly. The technician notes that the laptop is accessing the hard drive excessively. What are two probable causes for this?

   A. The Power Options are not configured correctly.

   B. The laptop requires more RAM.

   C. The CPU is defective.

   D. The BIOS settings are wrong.

   E. The hard drive is fragmented.

7. A user reports that the date and time of a laptop is always incorrect every time the laptop is powered on. What is the problem?

   A. The LCD power inverter has failed.

   B. A driver is not configured properly.

   C. The CMOS battery requires replacement.

   D. A motherboard connector is failing or has a short.

8. A user complains that a laser printer outputs streaks and lines on every page. What could cause this problem?

   A. The drum is damaged.

   B. The toner level is low in the EP cartridge.

   C. The fuser has failed.

   D. The printer does not have enough memory.

9. A technician is attempting to fix a laser printer that jams when printing. Which two issues could cause this problem?

   A. There is dirt or debris in the printer.

   B. The fuser is failing.

   C. The drum is damaged.

   D. The wrong type of paper is being used.

   E. There is not enough toner in the EP cartridge.

10. A user needs to open some files that are being shared from a remote computer. However, the user receives an "access denied" message when trying to open some files and folders. What is a probable cause of this?

    A. The TPM must be enabled.

    B. The BIOS settings are not configured.

    C. A firewall is blocking access to those resources.

    D. The user is not a member of the group that has permission to access those resources.

Answers to "Check Your Understanding" Questions

Chapter 1

1. B. PC power supplies support 110V input, 220V input, or both. Dual-voltage power supplies normally have a selector that allows control of which voltage to use in the proper environment.

2. B. 1394—an IEEE serial bus interface standard also know as FireWire.

   1284—IEEE standard for faster throughput and bidirectional data flow is an enhanced parallel interface for PCs. It was used primarily for connecting printers and scanners, but USB is now used more often than parallel connections.

3. D. USB 1.0 maximum of 1.5 for low-speed devices and 12 Mb/s full-speed devices

   USB 2.0 maximum 480 Mb/s for high-speed devices

   USB 3.0 480 Gb/s for super-speed devices

4. D. A keyboard, video, mouse (KVM) switch is a hardware device that can be used to control more than one computer using a single keyboard, monitor, and mouse. KVM switches provide cost-efficient access to multiple servers using a single keyboard, monitor, and mouse.

   UPS is an uninterruptible power supply typically used to protect electrical equipment by providing emergency power when main power fails.

5. A. Do not open a power supply. Electronic capacitors located inside a power supply can hold a charge for extended periods of time, even after the main power has been disconnected.

6. C. Overclocking is a technique that is used to make a processor work at a faster speed than its original specification.

   Throttling is slowing down the CPU so it is not working hard unnecessarily.

   Multitasking is the CPU switches from one program to another so quickly that it gives the appearance of executing all of the programs.

   Hyperthreading is an Intel microprocessor technology that allows a single microprocessor to act like two separate processors to the operating system.

7. D. Redundant array of independent disks (RAID) provides a way to store data across multiple hard disks for redundancy and data protection.

8. C. Hot-swappable drives can be connected and disconnected to the computer without turning the computer off. Normally, to install a eSATA hard disk, you would shut down the computer, connect the drive, and turn the computer back on. A hot-swappable eSATA drive can be plugged into the computer at any time.

9. A. By surfing the Internet in a virtual environment, a virus would only affect the one virtual environment. A separate virtualized work environment would not be affected by the virus.

    Other functions of virtual computing include the following:

    To test software or software upgrades in an environment that does not hurt your current operating system environment

    To use other operating systems on one computer, such as Linux or Ubuntu

    To run old applications that are not compatible with modern operating systems

10. A, B, and E. The form factor pertains to the shape of the motherboard and case. In addition, the case must accommodate the shape of the power supply.

    The incorrect choices depend on the type of connectors and busses on the motherboard.

11. A. The power supply converts alternating current (AC) power coming from a wall outlet into direct current (DC) power, which is of lower voltage. DC power is required for all the components inside the computer.

Chapter 2

1. B. Touching the unpainted part of the computer case discharges any static built up on your body. The painted part of a computer case would not perform the same function. Both antistatic wrist straps and antistatic mats require constant contact to be effective.

2. B. The Material Safety Data Sheet contains this information. ESD is electrostatic discharge, OSHA is the Occupational Safety Health Administration, and UPS means uninterruptible power supply.

3. B and C. A and F refer to RMI and EMI. Static electricity will harm computer components whether or not the computer is plugged in. Keeping the air cool and dry will increase static electricity.

4. B. Always follow the emergency exit procedures, and never use an elevator during a fire or attempt to fight a fire that is out of control.

5. C. A surge protector helps protect against damage from power surges and spikes. A power strip is simply an extension cord with several outlets. A standby power supply provides a backup battery to supply power when voltages drop below normal. An uninterruptible power supply supplies a consistent level of electrical power to devices.

6. E. A firewall is designed to block unauthorized communication to and from a computer. Antivirus and anti-malware software help prevent infection from malicious software. Port scanners test network connections to determine which ports the PC is actively using. The security center in Windows keeps track of the security software and settings on the PC and provides warnings when protection software needs to be updated.

7. D. Glass cleaner and a soft cloth are used for cleaning mice. Never use ammonia or other harsh chemicals on an LCD screen. Rubbing alcohol can damage components; use isopropyl alcohol instead. Never use a cloth of any kind inside a computer case. Instead use canned air or a vacuum cleaner specially designed to clean inside computer cases.

8. A. System File Checker is used to find and replace corrupted system files in Windows. Chkdsk is used to scan file systems and the physical drive, fdisk creates and deletes partitions, and defrag optimizes space on a hard drive.

9. C. A spike exceeds 100 percent of the normal voltage on a line. A brownout is a reduced voltage level of AC power. A surge is a dramatic increase of voltage above normal. Sag is not used in your curriculum.

10. A. A multimeter also tests the integrity of circuits and the quality of electricity in computer components. A power supply tester is used only to test the power supply on a computer. A cable tester is used to verify the functionality of a cable, and the loopback plug, or adapter, is used to test computer ports.

Chapter 3

1. A. Incorrect answers are not mounting hardware.

2. D and E. EIDE is a standard electronic interface between a computer and its mass storage drives and attaches to the motherboard internally.

   Molex is a connector used to provide power to internal devices such as the motherboard, disk drives, and others.

   PATA is a standard electronic interface between a computer and its mass storage drives and attaches to the motherboard internally.

   PS/2 and USB are two common external cable connections.

3. C. Rubbing alcohol may contain a higher content of water than a higher percentage isopropyl alcohol.

   When reinstalling the heat sink, clean the base of the heat sink with isopropyl alcohol. This removes all traces of old thermal compound so the newly applied thermal compound works properly.

   Thermal compound helps to conduct heat away from the CPU.

4. A. Before you install a memory module, it is important to verify that there are no compatibility issues. A DDR3 RAM module will not fit in a DDR2 slot. Verification is best done by consulting the motherboard documentation or checking on the website of the manufacturer.

5. D. The Advanced Technology Extended (ATX) main power connector will have either 20 or 24 pins. The power supply may also have a 4-pin or 6-pin Auxiliary (AUX) power connector that connects to the motherboard. A 20-pin connector will work in a motherboard with a 24-pin socket.

    The incorrect answers are not real options for pin counts on the ATX motherboard.

6. C. Go to the motherboard manufacturer's site to get the correct software to update the BIOS program that is locationed on the BIOS chip.

7. A and B. LoJack is a two-part system for protecting computers. The first part, the Persistence Module, is installed in the BIOS by the manufacturer. The second part is the Application Agent and is installed by the user. The Persistence Module cannot be turned off once it is activated. If the computer is stolen, the owner can contact Absolute Software and perform the following functions: lock the computer remotely, display a message so that a lost computer can be returned to the owner, delete sensitive data on the computer, use geotechnology to locate the computer.

8. C. After the new motherboard is in place and cables are connected, you should install and secure all expansion cards. Finally, connect the keyboard, mouse, and monitor; then power on the computer to check for problems.

9. A. SCSI drives are configured in a chain, with each device having its own device ID. Floppy drives and SATA drives do not require any special configuration, simply that the correct cables be plugged in and in the correct orientation. Only PATA drives require that a master/slave setup be configured.

10. B. Increasing the CPU clock speed will make the computer run faster but will also generate more heat and cause overheating issues.

11. C. Molex connectors are used to connect the power supply to the internal disk drives to provide DC power.

    Berg and Mini Molex are terms used for connectors that connect the power supply to floppy disk drives and other components to provide DC power.

    20-pin ATX connector is a motherboard power connector.

12. B. The motherboard slots and the memory modules are keyed so that they will not install unless the notches on both components align.

Chapter 4

1. A. This is Step 2 in the troubleshooting process. The actions defined in B, C, D, and E occur in different steps of the troubleshooting process.

2. B. Holding the fan blades in place while blowing it with compressed air prevents damage from overspinning or spinning in the wrong direction. The CPU should not be removed when cleaning, you would not clean the hard drive heads, and you should never hold canned air upside down while spraying.

3. A. A failing power supply can cause a computer to not start or to reboot. A blinking curser and POST error code usually have other causes, and if the power cord will not attach properly, it is probably the wrong type of cord.

4. A and B. Incorrect drivers, overheating, and dirty read and write heads are not common problems associated with PATA drives.

5. B. Before beginning to troubleshoot a hard drive, you should always back up the user's data. Performing disk cleanup is part of preventive maintenance, contacting a data-recovery company is not part of the standard troubleshooting procedure, and replacing the hard disk is not indicated at this stage in the process.

6. D. This is part of Step 5 in the troubleshooting process: verifying full system functionality. The other answers are not part of this stage of troubleshooting.

7. C. Processor problems are often caused by BIOS compatibility issues. RAM and operating system issues would not produce this symptom, and installing the wrong CPU type would cause other symptoms.

8. A. Extending the life of computer components reduces cost and downtime. The other answers do not apply to preventive maintenance.

9. C. Visually inspecting the fan is the best way to determine whether it is spinning properly. Spinning the blades with a finger or with canned air can cause damage to the fan, and listening for the sound of a fan spinning can be confusing, as there is more than one fan in the computer.

10. C. If the computer is functioning normally, it is likely the cable from the motherboard to the LED light has come loose. The data cable and power supply would cause noticeable problems if they were malfunctioning, and the BIOS may need to be updated, but it would not cause the problem with the LED light.

Chapter 5

1. D. Sysprep is used in conjunction with imaging software to deploy the same Windows operating system on multiple computers that may have different hardware.

Third-party tools can be used to create a disk image.

Device Manger and Windows Update can be used to install or update device drivers for hardware.

2. A. A Windows XP computer upgraded to Vista may not have the memory and processing resources to both perform adequately and run Aero.

3. A. Thread is a small piece of a program in execution.

Multiprocessing is related to a system with more than one processor.

Multiuser is related to a system that supports more than one user at the same time.

Multitask is a system that can perform more than one task at the same time.

4. A and C. The correct answers produce no errors, but the following list shows the errors that would be produced from the incorrect answers:

When NTLDR is missing or damaged, the computer displays one of these messages (after the POST):

- "Missing NTLDR"
- "Inaccessible Boot Device"

When MBR is corrupted, the computer displays one of these messages (after the POST):

- "Invalid Boot Disk"
- "BOOTMGR Is missing"
- "Missing NTLDR"

When the boot order is not set correctly in BIOS, the computer displays one of these messages (after the POST):

- "Missing NTLDR"
- "Invalid Boot Disk"
- "BOOTMGR Is missing"

5. A. Virtual PC is a Type 2 (hosted) hypervisor because it is hosted by an operating system and does not run directly on the hardware.

Windows XP Mode is a program available for Windows 7 Professional, Enterprise, and Ultimate. Windows XP Mode uses virtualization technology to allow users to run Windows XP programs in Windows 7.

OpenGL and DirectX are application programming interfaces (APIs).

6. A. Possible causes for the error shown are as follows:

   - Media that does not have an operating system is in a drive.
   - The boot order is not set correctly in the BIOS.
   - The hard drive is not detected or the jumpers are not set correctly.
   - The hard drive does not have an operating system installed.
   - The MBR is corrupted.
   - The computer has a boot sector virus.
   - The hard drive is failing.

7. D. The at command is used from a Windows command prompt to schedule commands and programs to run at a specific date and time. Any command followed by /? will list the options associated with a particular command.

8. C. Restore points are used to roll the system and Registry settings back to a specific date and time.

   The Automatic Updates utility ensures that the OS and applications are constantly being updated for security purposes and added functionality

   NTBackup is the built-in backup application introduced in Windows NT in all subsequent versions up to and including Windows 2000, Windows XP, and Windows Server 2003. A different version is used in Windows Vista and Windows 7.

   Scanreg is a Windows Registry checker tool.

   With driver rollback, a driver can be rolled back to a previous version.

9. D. Closed-ended questions tend to have a yes/no response.

   Open-ended questions leave more room for the customer to explain in more detail. Technicians should use open-ended questions to help identify the problem.

10. B and C. During the troubleshooting process, if a quick procedure does not correct the problem, further research should be conducted to identify the exact cause of the problem.

11. B. The **attrib** command shows the file attributes that are associated with each file. The possible attributes are as follows:

    - **r:** The file is read-only.
    - **a:** The file will be archived the next time that the disk is backed up.
    - **s:** The file is marked as a system file, and a warning is given if an attempt is made to delete or modify the file.
    - **h:** The file is hidden in the directory display.

12. C. A hard drive is divided into specific areas called partitions. Each partition is a logical storage unit that can be formatted to store information, such as data files and applications. A primary partition is usually the first partition on a drive, and any remaining space can be used to create an extended partition. Up to four primary partitions can be created per physical disk.

13. A. Hard drives are divided into specific areas called partitions. Only one primary partition can be marked as active at any time. The active partition is the partition where the operating system files are stored and is used to boot the computer.

14. B. The Performance tab is commonly used to check current computer performance. Two key areas that are shown are memory and CPU usage.

Chapter 6

1. A. Hubs regenerate the signal. All devices connected to the hub share the same bandwidth (unlike a switch, which gives each device dedicated bandwidth). Routers segment networks and modems modulate and demodulate between digital and analog signals.

2. C. Category 5e meets the requirements and is the most common cable type. Category 3 is for phones. Category 6 and 7 support speeds up to 10 Gb/s, but these are not the most common.

3. A. Host is a general term for any device on a network that can send and receive data. The other terms could all be referred to as "hosts," if they are capable of sending and receiving information on the network.

4. B. The IEEE standards describe current Ethernet features. The IEEE standard for Ethernet is 802.3. EIA/TIA is the Telecommunications Industry Association and Electronic Industries Alliance. ANSI is the American National Standards Institute, and CCITT is older name for ITU-T, the International Telecommunications Unions Telecommunication Standardization Sector.

5. B. The closer to the central office the connection is located, the higher the possible DSL speed. Distance from the service provider facility does not affect the other technologies.

6. B. A full-mesh network requires a link between every site that can be calculated with the formula $n * (n - 1) / 2 =$ total links, where n is the number of sites, so $4 * (4 - 1) / 2 = 6$.

7. C. A physical topology defines the way in which computers and other network devices are connected to a network. The addressing scheme and type of network may be included, but do not define how network devices connect to the LAN, and a physical topology does not show the order in which devices access the network.

8. A and E. In troubleshooting, once data is gathered from the user, the technician must identify the problem. According to the troubleshooting process, A and E are the next steps to help a technician determine the problem when connectivity is lost. None of the other answers would help a technician identify the problem at this stage in the process.

9. C. A LAN is smaller or more contained than a WAN, which can span several cities. A MAN is usually contained in one city. A PAN is a very small network of devices that are located in close proximity to one another, usually within range of a single person.

10. C. HTTP is associated with the application layer. IP and ICMP are associated with the Internet layer. TCP is associated with the transport layer.

11. A. An 802.11a NIC operates within the 5-Ghz band and cannot operate in a 2.4-GHz wireless network. Wireless cards that are 802.11b, 802.11g, and 802.11n can work in a mixed environment. Wireless cards that are 802.11a can only work in a mixed environment with 802.11n.

12. C. The manufacturer website is always the best place to find the most up-to-date drivers. The other answers are not the best location for finding new drivers.

13. D. When a PC does not have a static IP address or cannot pick one up from a DHCP server, Windows automatically assigns the PC an IP address using APIPA (Automatic Private IP Addressing), which uses the range of addresses from 169.254.0.0 to 169.254.255.255. None of the other answers would cause the computer to assume this address.

Chapter 7

1. A. Laptops have space restrictions. Therefore, they use small outline dual in-line memory modules (SODIMM).

   SRAM is not used for desktops or laptops as a RAM module, but as L1 cache inside the CPU.

   SIMMs were replaced by DIMMs on desktops as RAM modules.

2. B. Laptop CPUs are designed to generate less heat and therefore require smaller cooling mechanisms than their desktop counterparts.

   Because of the compact nature of a laptop, internal components are not usually interchangeable with desktop computers.

   CPU throttling is used to modify the clock speed as needed to reduce power consumption and heat resulting in a slight decrease in CPU performance on laptops.

Laptops need components that require less power consumption because a main feature of laptop is portability and that means using battery power rather AC power like a desktop.

3. C. A Bluetooth Class 2 has a maximum distance of 10 meters.

A Bluetooth Class 1 network has a maximum distance of 100 meters.

A Bluetooth Class 3 network has a maximum distance of 1 meter.

4. C. Some laptops contain a PC Card or ExpressCard slots.

AGP, ISA, and EISA are not laptop slots.

USB is a port.

PCI is an internal slot, not external.

5. A. Being proactive in keeping the laptop clean is to anticipate possible accidents such as fluid spills or food drops over the equipment.

The incorrect options are scheduled tasks to clean the computer after it gets dirty.

6. B. Use compressed air or a nonelectrostatic vacuum to clean out the dust from the vents.

Incorrect answers do not pertain to cleaning vents.

Clean the keyboard, touchpad, and LCD with a damp cloth and mild detergent and only use cleaning solutions that are specifically designed for that type of component.

Clean the optical drive with a cleaning disc.

7. A. A closed-ended question is one that is used to determine the exact cause of a problem. It focuses on a specific aspect of the problem and is used to establish a theory of probable cause.

B and C are open-ended questions.

D does not relate to a possible laptop battery failure.

8. D. Some common problems related to the keyboard are usually caused by having the Num Lock key on.

The incorrect options are not related to the keyboard.

9. C. S4: The CPU and RAM are off. The contents of RAM have been saved to a temporary file on the hard disk.

S0: The computer is on and the CPU is running.

S1: The CPU and RAM are stilling receiving power, but unused devices are powered down.

S2: The CPU is off, but RAM is refreshed.

S3: The CPU is off, and the RAM is set to a slow refresh rate.

S5: The computer is off.

10. D. Laptops with integrated cellular WAN capabilities require no software installation and no additional antenna or accessories.

    With any integrated device, ensure that the device is enabled in the BIOS settings.

Chapter 8

1. A. A Quick Response (QR) code is a type of bar code that is designed to be scanned by the camera of a mobile device. It is a different pattern than a standard bar code, and it has nothing to do with device camera calibration or visual assistance for users.

2. A and B. Devices can use a GPS radio receiver or information from Wi-Fi and cellular networks to calculate their position. Many devices use both. The user profile is not used to find position, nor does a device use images from the camera or the relative position to other devices.

3. C. Because mobile device apps are run in an isolated location, or sandbox, it is harder for malicious programs to infect the device. The carrier may prevent access to some features and programs based on the service contract, but this is not a security feature. The passcode and remote lock are used to protect the physical device.

4. B and E. Rooting and jailbreaking both refer to unlocking the bootloader of the device. Patching, remote wipe, and sandboxing are all terms that refer to operating system features.

5. C. The technician has already identified the problem, in Step 1 of the troubleshooting process. The next step is to establish a theory of probable cause and test the theory, Steps 2 and 3. The other answers are later steps in the troubleshooting process.

6. A. The technician has identified the problem, which is the first step in the troubleshooting process. The other answers are later steps in the process.

7. B. The ability to add a docking station is considered a feature because it enhances the functionality of the device. Having to upgrade memory or repair parts would not be considered a feature, and most mobile hardware is not upgradeable.

8. C. The General Packet Radio Service was an extension of the 2G standard and is considered a 2.5G standard. GSM and CDMA are part of the 2G standard, and LTE is considered a 4G standard.

9. A. Pairing is considered the correct term for establishing a connection between two Bluetooth devices. The other terms are incorrect in this context.

10. B. Most airlines do not allow the use of wireless devices during takeoff and landing. Airplane mode turns off any service that can transmit data, but allows the user to continue to use the device for other work. It does not adjust the volume, allow the device to roam, or lock the device.

Chapter 9

1. B. The more complex the structure of the printout, the more time it takes to print.

   Photo-quality picture, high-quality text, and draft text are less complex than a digital color photograph.

2. D. The greater the number of dots per inch, the better the resolution of the picture and therefore the quality of printing

3. B. Enabling print sharing allows a computer to share the printer over the network.

   Print drivers do not provide the ability to share printers.

   Installing a USB hub allows a number of peripheral connections to the same computer.

4. C. Hardware print servers permit several users to connect to a single printer without the need for a computer to share the printer.

   USB hubs, LAN switches, and docking stations are incapable of sharing printers.

5. C. The inability of a printer to print a test page usually indicates a driver problem.

   Paper jams and the lack of power are printer hardware problems.

   LED does affect the printer operation.

   A print queue problem is usually indicated when a printer experiences a problem with one particular document or application.

6. A. If the printer is connected to the wrong computer port, the print jobs will appear on the print queue but documents will not be printed by the printer.

7. B and E. The computer sharing the printer uses its own resources to manage all the print jobs coming to the printer.

More than one computer can send print jobs to the shared printer at the same time.

Not requiring the other computers to be cabled directly to the printer is an advantage of printer sharing.

To share a printer, computers do not need to be running the same operating system.

The computer directly connected to the printer does needs to be powered on, even if not in use.

8. A. Before performing maintenance on a printer, or any computer or peripheral, always disconnect the power source to prevent exposure to dangerous electrical voltages.

9. A and B. Using components not recommended by the manufacturer may result in poor print quality and void the manufacturer warranty.

The price and availability of nonrecommended parts may be advantageous, and the cleaning requirements may vary.

10. D. Inkjet print heads cannot usually be effectively cleaned by physical means. The vendor-supplied printer software utility is recommended.

Chapter 10

1. C. Employees should be required to use a key card when entering a secure area. Encrypting data, keeping software up to date, and the use of personal firewalls are all security precautions but will not restrict physical access to secure areas.

2. A. The World Wide Web (HTTP) protocol uses port 80; port 23 is used by Telnet. Successful pings to other devices indicate that the network interface card is working correctly. BIOS and CMOS settings control system hardware functions, not network applications such as the World Wide Web.

3. B and D. Degaussing disrupts or eliminates the magnetic field on a hard drive. Data wiping uses software specifically designed to overwrite data multiple times. Formatting a hard drive does not erase the data, and data can still be recovered after drilling through the plates of a hard drive. Reinstalling the operating system and defragging do not erase data on a hard drive.

4. B. The purpose of a firewall is to filter the traffic that is moving in and out of the PC. A computer firewall cannot deny all illegal traffic from a computer or increase the speed of any connection. It is also not able to protect hardware against fire hazards.

5. A. Having an antivirus program on a computer does not protect a PC from virus attacks unless the signature updates are done regularly to detect newer and emerging threats. A scan will not be able to detect new threats without updated signatures. Windows Task Manager does not perform this function. The firewall configuration is not used to update antivirus software.

6. D. Answer D describes a differential backup. A full backup copies and marks all selected files, a daily backup copies all files modified the day it is performed, and an incremental backup backs up any files changed since the previous incremental or full backup.

7. A. The primary difference between adware and spyware is that adware is designed to display advertisements on the target system and spyware is designed to collect information about user activity on the target system. Both C and D are types of viruses.

8. A. A distributed denial-of-service (DDoS) attack uses many infected computers, called zombies, to launch a coordinated attack against a target, with the primary goal of denying access to the target from legitimate hosts. Both C and D are denial-of-service (DoS) attacks, which generally come from one source.

9. B. If a network is experiencing an extremely high volume of traffic, disconnecting a host from the network may confirm that the host is compromised and is flooding traffic onto the network. The other issues are hardware issues and not usually security related.

10. C. The last step before documenting findings is to verify full system functionality, which means all the applications are working. Asking what problem the user is experiencing is part of the first step: identifying the problem. Disconnecting from the network and rebooting in Safe Mode are both examples of the third step: determining an exact cause.

Chapter 11

1. B. The field of computer forensics involves collecting and analyzing data from computer systems, networks, wireless communications, and storage devices.

   Cyber law is a term to describe the international, regional, country, and state laws that affect computer security professionals.

   Cryptography is the practice and study of techniques for secure communication.

2. B. Volatile data that is contained in cache, RAM, and CPU registers is lost when power is removed from the computer.

   Incorrect answers are all nonvolatile storage media.

3. C. Unsolicited, chain, and forged emails are unethical, and maybe illegal, and must not be sent by a technician to a customer.

4. B. To make any changes to a computer, a technician needs authorization from the customer.

   The presence of either another technician or other witnesses does not entitle the technician to either install or modify software, even if it is legal.

5. B. A service level agreement (SLA) defines the level of service that a technician or service provider is obligated to provide to a customer. It outlines responsibilities and liabilities such as when and where service is to be provided, response time guarantees, and the penalties that are applied if the agreement is broken.

6. D. A "down" call usually means that a server is not working and the entire office or company is waiting for the problem to be resolved to resume business.

7. B. A call center might exist within a company and offer service to the employees of that company as well as to the customers of that company. Alternatively, a call center might be an independent business that sells computer support as a service to outside customers. In either case, a call center is a busy, fast-paced work environment, often operating 24 hours a day.

8. C. The level one technician must be able to translate the description of a customer problem into a succinct sentence or two that is entered into the work order.

9. A and B. Dealing with customers is a very sensitive task. It is very important to show highly professional behavior during the call and to avoid making the customer upset, anxious, or angry. There are certain things a technician should not do, such as arguing with customers, using jargon, and taking personal calls while talking to a customer.

10. A. Straightforward tasks such as cleaning the mouse, changing printer toner, and checking cables can be managed by a level one technician. More complex tasks such as changing CMOS settings and running diagnostic software would usually be escalated to a level two technician.

Chapter 12

1. A. Files becoming corrupted is a symptom of a failing hard disk drive. An outdated BIOS, a lack of RAM, or an underpowered CPU could not cause files to become corrupted.

2. B. The symptoms that are described point toward a shortage of RAM in the laptop and not a lack of space available on the hard drive. When the RAM is full, the computer is using the hard disk drive (HDD) as a temporary storage device. Overclocking the CPU, reconfiguring the BIOS settings, or resetting the motherboard to the factory default settings would not fix this issue.

3. F. Discussing with a customer the solution that is implemented is one of the tasks completed at the end of the troubleshooting process and is part of documenting the findings. The other answers are different steps of the troubleshooting process.

4. B and F. Because the user is prompted for a username and a password, the email server is operational. This means that the network cable is connected and that the DHCP server is working correctly. It is highly unlikely in this situation that the gateway is wrongly configured. The username and password are case sensitive, and if the Caps Lock has been turned on inadvertently, the username and password would not be recognized.

5. A. Overheating can cause the laptop to shut down as a safety precaution. If the laptop is connected to a power source, an unseated battery would not cause the shutdown. BIOS updates and incorrectly configured power settings are very unlikely to cause this problem, although when searching for the cause of the overheating, make sure you research the manufacturer's website for critical notices that may involve BIOS updates.

6. B and E. The pagefile or virtual memory on a system is used for long-term storage of RAM data and for overflow when RAM becomes full. Having too little RAM will cause high rates of paging writes and degradation of system performance. A highly fragmented drive will also cause the system to slow down as the data has to be accessed from several different areas of the drive. Misconfigured power options, incorrect BIOS settings, and a defective CPU are unlikely to cause these symptoms.

7. C. When a CMOS battery is old it loses the ability to hold a charge. This would cause the system clock on the laptop to gain or lose time. Misconfigured drivers would not have this effect. A failure in the LCD power inverter results in a dim screen and a motherboard connector failure or short would cause different symptoms than the loss of date and time.

8. A. A damaged drum results in lines and streaks on the printed page. Lower toner results in faded or incomplete printed output. A faulty fuser causes the toner to not be embedded (melted) into the paper. Insufficient memory results in high-detail, complex print jobs failing or printing incomplete output.

9. A and D. Dirt and debris in a printer or loading the wrong paper can cause a printer to jam. A damaged drum results in lines and streaks on the printed page. The fuser failing will mean that toner is not melted onto the page. Not enough toner causes a faded or incomplete image.

10. D. An "access denied" message occurs when a user lacks the privileges that are required to access a resource. An improperly configured BIOS setting would not block access to files. A firewall has nothing to do with file system access, and TPM is used for secure access to a system.

Glossary

This Glossary defines many of the terms and abbreviations related to PC hardware and operating systems. It includes the key terms used throughout the book. As with any growing technical field, some terms evolve and take on several meanings. Where necessary, multiple definitions and abbreviation expansions are presented.

10BASE-T A 10-Mb/s baseband Ethernet specification that uses two pairs of Category 3, 4, or 5 twisted-pair cabling. One pair of wires is used to receive data, and the other pair is used to transmit data. 10BASE-T, which is part of the IEEE 802.3 specification, has a distance limit of approximately 328 feet (100 m) per segment.

2.5G extensions Transitional cell phone standards between 2G and 3G. Some common extensions: General Packet Radio, CDMA2000, and Enhanced Date Rates for GSM Evolution.

AC power connector A socket that is used to connect the AC power adapter to a computer or docking station.

Accelerated Graphics Port (AGP) A high-speed, 32-bit bus technology designed to support the acceleration of 3D computer graphics.

accelerometer A sensor in a mobile device that detects the orientation of the device. An example of this technology at work is the auto rotate screen mode.

active partition The operating system uses the active partition to boot the computer.

ActiveX control An applet or small program created by Microsoft to control interactivity on web pages that has to be downloaded to gain access to the full functionality.

ActiveX filtering Allows web browsing without running ActiveX controls.

adapter card An expansion card that increases the number of controllers and ports available on a computer.

address bus The address portion of the collection of wires known as the bus, the address bus carries the memory addresses of the locations where data is read or written by the CPU.

Advanced Configuration and Power Interface (ACPI) An interface that allows the operating system to control power management. Replaces Advanced Power Management (APM).

Advanced Encryption Standard (AES) A symmetric key encryption method added to WPA2 only.

Advanced Power Management (APM) An interface that allows the BIOS to control the settings for power management. This has been replaced by the Advanced Configuration and Power Interface (ACPI).

Advanced Technology Attachment (ATA) An early drive controller interface that connects computers and hard-disk drives. *See also* IDE.

Advanced Technology Attachment (ATA-2) An updated version of the IDE drive controller interface. *See* EIDE.

adware A software program that displays advertising on a computer, usually distributed with downloaded software.

airplane mode A setting on a mobile device that turns off all cellular, Wi-Fi, and Bluetooth radios. Airplane mode is useful when traveling on an airplane or when located where accessing data is prohibited or expensive.

alert badge Apple iOS uses badges displayed as a small icons above an application to show that the application needs attending such as a new text message or an application is ready for update.

all-in-one A multifunctional device designed to provide services such as printing, fax, scanning, and copier functions.

alternating current (AC) Current that changes direction at a uniformly repetitious rate. This type of electricity typically is provided by a utility company and is accessed by wall sockets.

American National Standards Institute (ANSI) A private, nonprofit organization that administers and coordinates the U.S. voluntary standardization and conformity assessment system. ANSI identifies industrial and public requirements for national consensus standards. It also coordinates and manages their development, resolves national standards problems, and ensures effective participation in international standardization.

analog telephone adapter (ATA) A telephone system that uses audio signals on copper wire.

anti-adware program A program that is installed on a system to detect programs that display advertising on a computer.

antiphishing program A program installed on a computer that blocks the IP addresses of known phishing websites and warn the user about suspicious websites.

antispyware program Protects against software that sends information about web surfing habits to an attacker.

antistatic bags Packaging material that protects components from electrostatic discharge (ESD).

antistatic mat A surface that provides a safe environment for computer components by dissipating ESD.

antistatic wrist strap A device worn on the wrist to dissipate electrostatic discharge (ESD) between a person and electronic equipment.

antivirus program A program that is installed on a system to prevent computer viruses from infecting the computer.

Apple OS X A proprietary operating system used by Apple computers.

application (app) Programs that are executed on mobile devices. Mobile devices come with a number of different apps preinstalled to provide basic functionality.

application programming interface (API) A set of guidelines to ensure a new application is compatible with an OS.

architectural model A common frame of reference for explaining Internet communications and developing communication protocols. It separates the functions of protocols into manageable layers. Each layer performs a specific function in the process of communicating over a network.

aspect ratio The horizontal to vertical measurement of the viewing area of a monitor.

asymmetric DSL (ADSL) Currently the most common DSL implementation. Speeds vary from 384 Kb/s to more than 6 Mb/s downstream. The upstream speed is usually lower.

asymmetric encryption A method of encrypting data on a network. Uses a private key to write messages and a public key to decode the messages. Only the private key needs to be kept secret. Public keys can be distributed openly.

audio and video editing workstation This type of workstation is used during many stages of development when creating audio and video material.

auto restart function When the system locks up during startup, the computer can automatically reboot. The reboot is caused by the auto restart function in Windows.

automatic rotation A feature on a mobile device which enables the display screen to change from portrait to landscape when the device detects that it has been turned on its side.

auto-negotiate Ethernet NICs will auto-negotiate the fastest speed that is common between the NIC and the other device. For instance, if you have a 10/100-Mb/s NIC and a hub that is only 10 Mb/s, the NIC operates at 10 Mb/s. If you have a 10/100/1000-Mb/s NIC and a switch that is only operating at 100 Mb/s, the NIC operates at 100 Mb/s.

AutoPlay Identifies new media when inserted and prompts the user to choose an action based on the contents of the media.

AutoRun A feature of the operating system, AutoRun automatically follows the instructions in a special file called autorun.inf when it is found on new media. This can be a security risk and should be disabled.

backlight Supplies the main source of light to the screen of the laptop display. Without it the image on the screen would not be visible. The backlight shines through the screen and illuminates the display. Two common types of backlights are cold cathode fluorescent lamp (CCFL) and LED.

backoff algorithm Calculates random times in which the end station tries transmitting again. This random time is typically in 1 or 2 milliseconds (ms). This sequence occurs every time there is a collision on the network and can reduce Ethernet transmission by up to 40 percent.

backup app An application used for data and system backups. Mobile devices provide a means to centrally store information through the use of backup client software that stores data remotely on the cloud.

Backup utility Allows users to access backup settings and create schedules for backups.

bandwidth The amount of data that can be transmitted within a fixed amount of time.

base station A device that attaches a laptop to AC power and to desktop peripherals.

basic disk Contains primary and extended partitions, in addition to logical drives.

basic input/output system (BIOS)   A program stored in a ROM chip in the computer that provides the basic code to control the computer's hardware and to perform diagnostics on it. The BIOS prepares the computer to load the operating system.

battery   Allows the laptop to function when it is disconnected from an external power source.

battery latch   A tool used to insert, remove, and secure the laptop battery.

battery status indicator LED   A light that indicates the condition of the laptop battery.

beep codes   An audible reporting system for errors that are found by the BIOS during the POST, represented by a series of beeps.

bench technician   Bench technicians do not usually work directly with customers and are often hired to perform computer warranty service.

Berg power connector   A keyed connector that supplies power to a floppy drive.

biometric security   Compares physical characteristics against stored profiles to authenticate people.

BitLocker   A Windows feature that encrypts an entire hard-drive volume.

BitLocker Drive Preparation Tool   Shrinks the volume containing the operating system.

blackout   A complete loss of AC power.

Blue Screen of Death (BSOD)   A stop error that causes the system to lock up because of a hardware or software malfunction. The BSOD appears when the system is unable to recover from an error.

Bluetooth   A wireless industry standard that uses an unlicensed radio frequency for short-range communication, enabling portable devices to communicate over short distances.

Bluetooth pairing   When two Bluetooth devices establish a connection to share resources. For the devices to pair, the Bluetooth radios are turned on, and one device begins searching for other devices. Other devices must be set to discoverable mode, also called visible, so that they can be detected.

BNC connector   Uses a push, twist, and lock connector.

bootloader   Code that is run before the OS starts. It provides instructions for the hardware to start the OS; they are locked to prevent modification and access to sensitive areas of the file system.

botnets   Computers that have been commandeered by hackers and unwillingly launch attacks against networks and servers. Also called zombies.

bridge   Segments network traffic by filtering and forwarding packets based on MAC addresses.

broadband   Multiple signals using multiple frequencies over one cable.

broadcast topology   A host broadcasts a message to all hosts on the same network segment. There is no order that hosts must follow to transmit data. Messages are sent on a first in, first out (FIFO) basis.

brownout   A temporary drop in AC power.

built-in LCD   Similar to a desktop LCD monitor, except that you can adjust the resolution, brightness, and contrast settings using software or button controls. You cannot adjust the laptop monitor for height and distance because it is integrated into the lid of the case.

bus topology   A network in which each computer connects on a common cable.

cable   Connects one computer to the next.

cable tester   A device that checks for wiring shorts or faults, such as wires connected to the wrong pin.

cache   A data storage area that provides high-speed access for the system.

cache memory   A separate RAM memory used to optimize performance by storing frequently accessed data.

call center employee rules   Rules that cover general daily activities of employees.

cancellation   Effect produced by the twisted-wire pairs that limits signal degradation caused by electromagnetic interference.

card key   Secures physical areas. Card keys can be easily activated and deactivated.

carrier sense multiple access collision detect (CSMA/CD)   An access control method that allows any end station to send a message at any time, assuming it first listened and heard no other end station transmitting. If two end stations send at the same time and the collision is detected, a jam signal is sent and every host stops sending. Each end station must wait a number of milliseconds before it can transmit again. That wait time can be randomly assigned or based on the MAC address, depending on the specific protocols.

cathode ray tube (CRT)   An older display technology that uses electron beams to light up colored phosphor dots on the screen. The combination of light and dark areas on the screen creates the image.

CAx workstation   A workstation used to design products and control the manufacturing process.

CDMA2000   A mobile technology standard used to send voice, data, and signaling data.

cellular data network   A wide-area network that has the technology for the use of a cell phone or laptop for voice and data communications.

cellular technology   Enables the transfer of voice, video, and data. With a cellular WAN adapter installed, a user can access the Internet over the cellular network.

cellular WAN   A wide-area network that has the technology for the use of a cell phone or laptop for voice and data communications.

central processing unit (CPU)   Interprets and processes software instructions and data. Located on the motherboard, the CPU is a chip contained on a single integrated circuit called the microprocessor. Most calculations take place in the CPU.

charging   Step two in the laser printing process. The previous latent image on the drum is removed and the drum is conditioned for the new latent image.

chipset   Chips on a motherboard that enable the CPU to communicate and interact with the computer's other components.

chkdsk   A command used to check the integrity of files and folders on a hard drive by scanning the disk surface for physical errors.

cleaning   Step seven in the laser printing process. The toner remaining on the drum is removed using a blade or an AC charge.

cleaning tools   Cleaning tools such as a soft cloth used to clean without scratching or leaving debris; compressed air, which can be used to blow away dust and debris from components; cable ties to cables neatly inside and outside of a computer; and parts organizers for screws, jumpers, and other small parts to prevent them from getting mixed together or lost.

clock speed   The speed at which data travels through the bus. This is measured in megahertz (MHz) or gigahertz (GHz).

closed source   The source code is not released to the public.

closed-ended questions   Questions that generally require a yes or no answer. These questions are intended to get the most relevant information in the shortest time.

cluster   Also called a file allocation unit. Smallest unit of space used for storing data and made up of one or more sectors.

coaxial cable   Copper-cored cable surrounded by a heavy shielding. Used to connect computers in a network.

code division multiple access (CDMA)   Protocols used in second-generation (2G) and third-generation (3G) wireless communications that uses multiplexing to optimize the use of available bandwidth.

collision   When a device wants to gain access to the network, it checks to see if the network is free. If the network is not free, the device waits a random amount of time before retrying. If the network is free and two devices access the line at exactly the same time, their signals collide. When the collision is detected, they both back off and wait a random amount of time before trying to transmit again.

command-line interface (CLI)   An interface, such as a DOS prompt, that requires commands to be entered manually on the command line.

communication skills   A skill set that allows a technician to communicate information so that it is understood by the customer.

complementary metal-oxide semiconductor (CMOS)   A type of semiconductor, or low-power memory firmware, that stores basic configuration information.

Complex Instruction Set Computer (CISC)   This CPU architecture uses a broad set of instructions, which requires fewer steps per operation.

CompTIA A+ certification   This certification signifies that a candidate is a qualified PC hardware and software technician.

computer case   The enclosure that contains and protects the computer components.

Computer Management   A management console utility that allows a user to manage many aspects of a computer.

conditioning roller   A roller in a laser printer that receives a charge of approximately −600V DC uniformly across the surface of the drum..

conduit   A casing that protects the infrastructure media from damage and unauthorized access.

content source   Applications are used on mobile devices the same way that programs are used on PCs. Instead of being installed from an optical disk, apps are downloaded from an online database either directly provided by the device vendor or a third party.

contrast ratio   The measurement of difference in intensity of light between the brightest point (white) and the darkest point (black).

Control Panel applets   A collection of programs and utilities that can be used to configure the operating system.

Convert   A utility that can be used to upgrade a FAT32 file system to NTFS.

copy backup   Copies all selected files. It does not mark files as archived.

counterfeit components   A component that is represented as new or produced by the original manufacturer but is used or has been altered to look like a brand name or new component.

CPU throttling   Manually setting the CPU to run slower, usually to conserve power or reduce heat.

crimper   Used to attach connectors to wires.

critical battery level   Low battery warning with an alarm that is set to warn the user to connect the portable device to a power source very soon or risk a shutdown and potentially the loss of data. The default for critical battery level is 5 percent. You can also set the type of notification and the action to take, such as whether to sleep, hibernate, or shut down the laptop when the battery capacity reaches the specified level.

crossover cable   Uses both wiring schemes, T568A on one end of the cable and T568B on the other end of the same cable.

cross-platform   The exchange of data between two or more devices running different operating systems, while maintaining consistent data on those devices.

crosstalk   Interfering energy, such as electromagnetic interference (EMI), that is transferred from one circuit to another.

current   The movement of electrons.

customer call rules   Rules a call center might use to handle customer calls.

customer-replaceable unit (CRU)   A component that customers may install at their location.

cylinder   A stack of tracks lined up one on top of another to form a cylinder shape.

daily backup   Only backs up the files that are modified on the day of the backup. Does not modify the archive bit.

data backup   Information on a computer stored on removable backup media that can be kept in a safe place or cloud storage. If the computer hardware fails, the data backup can be restored so that processing can continue.

data bus   The data portion of the collection of wires known as the bus. The data bus carries data between the computer components.

data cable   The cable that connects drives to the drive controller located on an adapter card or on the motherboard.

Data Encryption Standard (DES)   A popular type of hash encoding algorithm.

data synchronization   The exchange of data between two or more devices while maintaining consistent data on those devices.

data threats   Events or attacks that remove, corrupt, deny access to authorized users, allow access to unauthorized users, or steal information.

data wiping   Also known as secure erase, is a procedure performed to permanently delete data from a hard drive.

DC jack   Receives power from a laptop's AC/DC power converter and supplies the power to the system board.

de-encapsulation   Reverse process of encapsulation.

default gateway   A node or router on a network that provides access to another network or the Internet.

Defrag   Disk Defragmenter gathers fragmented data that is spread over the clusters in the hard drive and puts them in one place on the drive, increasing speed and efficiency.

defragmentation   Consolidates files for faster access, and disk error checking, which scans the hard drive for file structure errors.

degaussing   Disrupts or eliminates the magnetic field on a hard drive that allows for the storage of data.

demilitarized zone (DMZ)   A subnetwork that provides services to an untrusted network.

denial of service (DoS)   A form of attack that prevents users from accessing normal services, such as email or a web server, because the system is busy responding to an abnormally large number of requests. DoS works by sending an abundance of requests for a resource. This causes the system to overload and stop operating.

developing   Step four in the laser printing process. The toner is applied to the latent image on the drum.

device driver   A program that allows the operating system to access and communicate with a hardware component.

Device Manager   An application that displays a list of all the hardware that is installed on the system.

diagnostic tools   Used to test and diagnose equipment; examples are loopback adapter and toner probe.

dialup networking (DUN)   Using the public telephone system or network to communicate.

differential backup   Backs up all files and folders created or modified since either the last normal or last incremental backup. Does not mark the files as archived.

Digital Light Processing (DLP)   A technology used in projectors that uses a spinning color wheel and an array of mirrors to project an image.

digital multimeter   A device that can take many types of measurements. It tests the integrity of circuits and the quality of electricity in computer components.

digital signatures   Used for authentication with asymmetric encryption, a private key is required for encrypting a message and a public key is needed to decode the message.

digital subscriber line (DSL)   A public network technology that delivers high bandwidth over conventional copper wiring at limited distances. Always-on technology that allows users to connect to the Internet.

Digital Visual Interface (DVI) port   A digital video port that allows backward compatibility to analog video signals. It can transmit very large amounts of data and is often used for applications that require a large monitor resolution.

direct current (DC)   Current flowing in one direction, as used in a battery.

DirectX   Collection of APIs related to multimedia tasks for Microsoft Windows.

disk cleanup   Disk-management software that is used to clear space on a hard drive by searching for files that can be safely deleted, such as temporary Internet files.

disk cloning   Copying the contents of an entire hard drive to another hard drive, thereby decreasing the time it takes to install drivers, applications, updates, and so forth on the second drive.

Disk Management   A system utility used to manage hard drives and partitions, such as initializing disks, creating partitions, and formatting partitions.

display cables   These cables transfer video signals from the computer to display devices.

distributed DoS (DDoS)   A denial of service attack launched from multiple infected PCs called zombies or botnets. The intent is to obstruct or overwhelm access to the targeted server.

DNS poisoning   Changing the DNS records on a system to point to false servers where the data is recorded.

docking station   A device that attaches a laptop to AC power and desktop peripherals.

docking station connector   The port through which a laptop connects to a docking station. Details regarding the shape and design of docking station connectors vary widely among manufacturers.

domain   A logical group of computers and electronic devices with a common set of rules and procedures administered as a unit.

domain controller   A specialized server that manages all security-related aspects of users and network resources, centralizing security and administration.

Domain Name System (DNS)   A system that provides a way to map friendly hostnames, or URLs, to IP addresses.

dot pitch   The distance between pixels on the screen.

dots per inch (dpi)   A measurement of print quality on a dot-matrix printer. The higher the dpi, the higher the print's quality.

Double Data Rate (DDR)   RAM that reads on the rising and on the falling side of the clock cycle, thereby doubling the access speed. Normal SDRAM is read once per clock cycle.

Double Data Rate 2 (DDR2)   DDR RAM with a modified bus speed that allows RAM to be read four times every clock cycle.

Double Data Rate 3 (DDR3)   DDR RAM that expands memory bandwidth by doubling the clock rate of DDR2.

double touch   Mobile devices can detect when two or more points of contact are made on the screen. For example, for zoom items such as photographs, maps, and text, touch the screen twice quickly to zoom in, and touch the screen twice quickly again to zoom out.

downloading   The receiving of data from the server to the end user.

dual in-line memory module (DIMM)   A circuit board that holds SDRAM, DDR SDRAM, DDR2 SDRAM, and DDR3 SDRAM chips.

dual in-line package (DIP)   An individual memory chip with dual rows of pins used to attach it to the motherboard.

dual-core CPU   Two cores inside a single CPU. Both cores can process information at the same time.

DxDiag   Tool used to test video and sound cards as well as the functionality of DirectX.

Dynamic Host Configuration Protocol (DHCP)   A software utility that automatically assigns IP addresses to client devices in a large network.

dynamic link library (DLL)   Consists of program code that can be used by different programs to perform common functions.

dynamic RAM (DRAM)   RAM that stores information in capacitors that must be periodically refreshed with pulses of electricity in order to maintain the data stored on the chip.

electromagnetic interference (EMI)   Is the intrusion of outside electromagnetic signals in a transmission media, such as copper cabling. In a network environment, EMI distorts the signals so that the receiving devices have difficulty interpreting them.

electronically erasable programmable read-only memory (EEPROM)   Also called flash ROM, an EEPROM chip can be erased and rewritten without having to remove the chip from the computer.

electrostatic discharge (ESD)   The discharge of static electricity from one conductor to another conductor of a different potential.

email protocol   Interactions between email servers and clients are governed by email protocols and different protocols provide different email services.

encapsulation   Source data has header control information from successive layers added to it before transmission across a network.

Encrypting File System (EFS)   A windows feature that can encrypt data. EFS is directly linked to a specific user account.

encryption   A security feature that applies coding to a file so that only authorized users can view the file.

Enhanced Data Rates for GSM Evolution (EDGE)   A protocol that achieves near broadband data transfers over existing GSM technology. It is found in 3G and 4G phones.

Enhanced Integrated Drive Electronics (EIDE)   An enhanced version of the standard IDE interface that connects hard disks, CD-ROM drives, and tape drives to a PC. *See also* ATA-2.

erasable programmable read-only memory. (EPROM)   Information is written to an EPROM chip after it is manufactured and the chip can be erased with exposure to UV light by using special equipment.

error-correcting code (ECC)   Technology that can detect multiple bit errors in memory and correct single bit errors in memory.

Ethernet   A baseband LAN specification invented by Xerox Corporation and developed jointly by Xerox, Intel, and Digital Equipment Corporation. Ethernet networks use CSMA/CD and run on a variety of cable types at 10 Mb/s or more. Ethernet is similar to the IEEE 802.3 series of standards.

Ethernet port   An RJ-45 socket that is used to connect a computer to a cabled LAN.

EUCIP (European Certification of Informatics Professionals)   IT Administrator program that offers a recognized certification of competence in IT. The certification covers the standards prescribed by the Council of European Professional Informatics Societies (CEPIS).

Event Viewer   Application that monitors system events, application events, and security events.

Evolution-Data Optimized (EV-DO)   A data protocol that provides fast download rates and is found on many 3G phones.

exceptions   Exceptions allow certain traffic or applications to connect to a computer through the firewall.

expansion slots   Slots on the motherboard where a PC adapter card can be inserted to add capabilities to the computer.

exposing   Step three in the laser printing process. To write the image, the photosensitive drum is exposed with the laser beam.

extended data out (EDO)   RAM memory that overlaps consecutive data accesses, speeding up the access time to retrieve data from memory.

extended partition   The second partition on a hard drive. This partition can be separated into logical drives.

extended-star (hierarchical) topology   A star topology that is expanded to include additional networking devices.

Extensible Authentication Protocol (EAP)   Uses a centralized authentication server to increase security.

external diskette drive connector   A port that connects older laptops to floppy disk drives.

external hard drive enclosure   Often used when diagnosing and repairing computers. The customer hard drive is placed into the external enclosure for inspection, diagnosis, and repair using a known-working computer.

External Serial ATA (eSATA)   Provides a hot-swappable external interface for SATA drives.

external threats   Users outside of an organization who do not have authorized access to the network or resources.

factory recovery partition   A partition that contains an image of the bootable partition created when the computer was built.

fast page mode (FPM)   An older type of DRAM that supports paging. Paging enables faster access to data.

field-replaceable unit (FRU)   A component that should be replaced rather than repaired, by the user or a trained service technician, rather than sending the entire device back to the manufacturer.

field technician   A field technician works in a variety of locations, including private homes, businesses, and schools.

field-serviceable parts   Components that can be repaired or refurbished on the job site without having to replace the part.

File Allocation Table, 32-bit (FAT32)   A table that the operating system uses to store information about the location of the files stored on a disk. Used by Windows XP and earlier OS versions.

FireWire (i.LINK or IEEE 1394)   A high-speed hot-swappable interface that connects peripheral devices to a computer flash drive.

first generation (1G)   Mobile devices that primarily used analog standard in which voice and noise signals were hard to distinguish.

flash card   A data storage device that uses flash memory to store information. Flash cards are small, portable, and require no power to maintain data.

flash card reader   Device that reads flash cards. Most modern laptops feature a flash card reader for Secure Digital (SD) and Secure Digital High Capacity (SDHC) flash cards.

flash drive   Also known as a thumb drive, is a removable storage device that connects to a USB port. An external flash drive uses the same type of nonvolatile memory chips as a solid state drive (SSD).

flash memory chips   A rewritable memory chip that retains data after the power is turned off.

flat-head screwdriver   Used to tighten or loosen slotted screws.

floppy drive   An older type of storage drive that uses magnetically coated floppy disks to read and write data.

form factor   The physical size and shape of computer components.

fourth generation (4G) Standards that provide ultra-broadband Internet access. Higher data rates allow users to download files much faster, perform video conferencing, or watch high-definition television.

frame   When data is sent over a computer network, it is broken up into small chunks called packets. Address information is added to the beginning and end of the packets before they are transmitted. The packet, with the address information added, is called a frame.

Freedom of Mobile Multimedia Access (FOMA)   A third-generation standard (3G) that enables mobile devices to go beyond voice and data communications.

frequency   Used to measure processing or clock speed. Usually measured in megahertz (MHz) or gigahertz (GHz).

front-side bus (FSB)   The front-side bus is the path between the CPU and the Northbridge. It is used to connect various components, such as the chipset and expansion cards.

F series connector   A coaxial RF connector commonly used for cable modems.

full backup   *See* normal backup.

full-duplex transmission   Data transmission that can go two ways at the same time. An Internet connection using DSL service is an example.

function key (Fn key)   A modifier key usually found on laptop computers. It is used in combination with other keys to perform specific functions.

fusing   Step six in the laser printing process. The toner is permanently fused to the paper.

General Packet Radio Service (GPRS)   Found mainly in 2G and 3G cell phones, a method of sending data to and from portable devices.

geocaching   A mapping app that shows the location of geocaches (hidden containers) around the world. Users find them and often sign a logbook to show that they found it.

geotagging   Embeds location information into a digital object, like a photograph or a video, to record where it was taken.

gestures   Using the multitouch function on a mobile device touchscreen to perform certain function such as slide, double touch, long touch, and scroll.

Global Positioning System (GPS)   A navigation system that determines the time and location on Earth using messages from satellites in space and a receiver on Earth.

Global System for Mobile (GSM)   A worldwide cellular network.

graphical user interface (GUI)   An interface that allows the user to navigate through the operating system using icons and menus.

grayware   Similar to adware, grayware may be malicious and is sometimes installed with the user's consent. For example, a free software program may require the installation of a toolbar that displays advertising.

half-duplex transmission   Data transmission that can go two ways, but not at the same time. A two-way radio is an example.

hand tools   Tools that are powered or controlled by a person. They are normally small and have dedicated functions. Examples include a screwdriver, pliers, and a drill.

hard disk drive (HDD)   A device that stores and retrieves data from magnetic-coated platters that rotate at high speeds. The HDD is the primary storage medium on a computer.

hard drive access panel   The panel that allows access to a hard drive in a laptop.

hardware   Physical electronic components that make up a computer system.

hardware compatibility list (HCL)   A utility that verifies that existing hardware is compatible with an operating system.

hardware firewall   A freestanding hardware device that inspects data packets from the network before they reach computers and other network devices.

hash encoding   Also called hashing, an encryption method that uses a mathematical function to create a numeric value that is unique to data.

headphone connector   Also called a headphone jack. Allows audio output for headphones.

heat sink/fan   A device that dissipates heat from electronic components, usually the CPU into the surrounding air.

hex driver   Used to tighten or loosen nuts in the same way that a screwdriver tightens or loosens screws (sometimes called a nut driver).

hexadecimal   A base-16 number system where values are defined as a range of the numbers from 0 to 9 and the letters *a* to *f*.

hibernate   A power level in which the computer is essentially off. RAM is copied to the hard drive so the computer does not need send power to RAM. It is very efficient but takes longer to recover from hibernate than from standby.

hierarchical addressing   Organized groupings within a collection. In networking, IP addressing is considered hierarchical because the addresses are grouped by network portion of the address and a host portion of the address.

High-Definition Multimedia Interface (HDMI)   Carries digital video and digital audio signals. Digital signals provide high-quality video and high resolutions.

high-efficiency particulate air (HEPA) filtration   A specialized vacuum filter that catches microscopic particles.

high-level formatting   A boot sector is created and a file system is set up on the disk. Also called standard formatting.

home screen   Multiple screens organized for easy access to icons and widgets. These screens can be customized to user preference.

Home Theater Personal Computer   A specialized PC system used to control high-quality video and audio systems.

HomeGroup   Allows computers on the same home network to automatically share files and printers.

host   A computer system on a network. Similar to the term node, except that host usually implies a computer system. Node generally applies to any networked system, including access servers and routers.

hub   Extends the range of a network by receiving data on one port and then regenerating the data and sending it out to all other ports.

hyperthreading   When multiple pieces of code (threads) are executed simultaneously in the CPU.

hypertransport   Used to enhance CPU performance, a high-speed, low-latency connection between the CPU and the Northbridge chip.

hypervisor   The software that creates and manages a virtual machine on a host.

iCloud   Provides email and the ability to store content on remote servers for Apple mobile device users.

IEEE 802.11   An IEEE the standard that specifies connectivity for wireless networks. IEEE 802.11, or Wi-Fi, refers to a collective group of wireless standards

IEEE 802.3   An IEEE LAN standard that specifies that a network implement the carrier sense multiple access with collision detection (CSMA/CD) access control method.

image-based installation   Uses Sysprep and a disk-imaging program, such as ImageX, that copies an image of the OS directly to the hard drive with no user intervention.

impact printer   A printer that uses print heads that strike an inked ribbon. These printers include dot matrix and daisy wheel.

incremental backup   Backs up all files and folders created or modified since either the last normal or last incremental backup. It marks the files as archived by clearing the archive bit.

industry standard architecture (ISA)   8- or 16-bit expansion slot. This is older technology and seldom used.

information technology (IT)   The design, development, implementation, support, and management of computer hardware, software, and network systems to organize and communicate information electronically.

infrared port   A line-of-sight wireless transceiver that is used for data transmission.

infrared (IR) wireless technology   Electro-magnetic waves whose frequency range is above that of microwaves but below that of the visible spectrum. LAN systems based on this technology represent an emerging technology.

inkjet printer   A type of printer that uses liquid-ink-filled cartridges that spray ink to form an image.

InPrivate browsing   InPrivate browsing prevents the web browser from storing personal information about you or your browsing habits.

input devices   An input device enters data or instructions into a computer. Typical input devices are keyboards and mice.

input/output (I/O) ports   Connects peripheral devices, such as displays, printers, scanners, portable drives, and audio devices. They also connect the computer to network resources, such as modems or external network drives.

Institute of Electrical and Electronics Engineers (IEEE)   An organization that oversees the development of communication and network standards.

Integrated Digital Enhanced Network (iDEN)   A first-generation cellular network designated by Motorola for specialized mobile radio service.

Integrated Drive Electronics (IDE)   An early drive controller interface that connects computers and hard disk drives interlaced. *See also* ATA.

Integrated Services Digital Network (ISDN)   A communication protocol, offered by telephone companies, that permits telephone networks to carry data, voice, and other source traffic.

internal threats   Users and employees who have access to data, equipment, and the network.

International Organization for Standardization (ISO)   An international organization that sets standards for networking. ISO developed the OSI reference model, a popular networking reference model.

Internet appliance   Also called a Net appliance, a smart appliance, or an information appliance.

Internet Control Message Protocol (ICMP) Used for network testing and troubleshooting, ICMP enables diagnostic and error messages. The ping utility uses ICMP echo messages to determine whether a remote device can be reached.

Internet Message Access Protocol (IMAP) Used by local email clients to synchronize and retrieve email from a server and leave email on the server.

Internet service provider (ISP)   A company that provides Internet and email services to consumers and businesses.

inverter   Converts DC power to the higher voltage AC power that is required by the backlight.

iOS Home button   Apple iOS navigation button that allows a user to perform a variety of functions such as, wake the device, start Siri, open Search, and more.

IP address   The Layer 3 logical address that has been assigned to a networked computer or device.

IP address classes   IPv4 addresses are divided into five classes: Class A, Class B, Class C, Class D, Class E. Only Class A, B, and C addresses can be assigned to hosts.

IP phone   A device that connects to an IP network using an RJ-45 Ethernet connector or a wireless connection.

IP phone software   This application connects by using a microphone, speakers, and a sound card to emulate the IP phone functionality.

ipconfig   A command-line utility used to verify that a NIC has a valid IP address.

IPv4   Fourth version of development of Internet Protocol (IP) consists of a series of 32 binary bits (1s and 0s).

IPv6   Latest revision of the Internet Protocol (IP), it is a three-part hierarchy consisting of 128 bits. It is intended to replace IPv4.

IT industry certifications   Industry-standard certifications for IT professionals obtained through standardized testing.

iTunes   Apple's media player and media library that can be used to download and install content and applications to Apple devices.

jailbreaking   A hack that involves unlocking the bootloader and giving iPhone users access to the underlying operating system of iOS and opens the phone to customization that is not normally available to the user.

Java APIs   Collection of APIs related to the development of Java programming.

journals   Special areas where file changes are recorded before changes are made.

keyboard port   A PS/2 socket used to connect older keyboards to the computer.

keyed connectors   Connectors that are designed to be inserted in one direction only.

keyloggers   Malicious programs installed on a computer to capture the user's keystrokes.

KVM switch   A hardware device that can be used to control more than one computer while using a single keyboard, monitor, and mouse.

LAN architecture   Describes both the physical and logical topologies used in a network.

laptop   A small form factor computer designed to be mobile. Operates much the same as a desktop computer. Laptop hardware is proprietary and usually is more expensive than desktop hardware.

laptop latch   A lever used to open the laptop lid.

laser printer   A high-quality, fast printer that uses a laser beam to create an image.

latency   The amount of time it takes data to travel from source to destination.

LC connector   A snap-in connector that latches with a simple push-pull motion.

LCD cutoff switch   A small pin on the laptop cover contacts a switch when the case is closed and helps conserve power by extinguishing the backlight and turning off the LCD when the laptop is closed.

LCD monitor   An output device that passes polarized light through liquid crystals using cold cathode fluorescent lamp (CCFL) backlighting to produce images on the screen.

light-emitting diode (LED)   This display is an LCD display that uses LED backlighting to light the display.

liquid crystal display (LCD)   Commonly used in flat panel monitors, laptops, and some projectors, it consists of two polarizing filters with a liquid crystal solution between them.

LED monitors   An output device that uses light emitting diodes replacing the cold cathode fluorescent lamps (CCFL) for the backlighting while using an LCD screen.

level-one technician   The primary responsibility of a level-one technician is to gather pertinent information from the customer. Level one technicians may also resolve simple customer problems.

level-two technician   Usually more knowledgeable than level-one technicians, level-two technicians resolve problems that have been escalated from level-one technicians.

like devices   Devices that are directly connected and use the same pins for transmit and receive.

line-in connector   Allows audio input from pre-amplified sources like iPods.

line of sight   A characteristic of certain transmission systems such as laser, microwave, and infrared systems in which no obstructions in a direct path between transmitter and receiver can exist.

line-of-sight wireless Internet   Is an always-on service that uses radio signals for transmitting Internet access. Radio signals are sent from a tower to the receiver that the customer connects to a computer or network device. A clear path between the transmission tower and customer is required. The tower may connect to other towers or directly to an Internet backbone connection.

link lights   LEDs located next to the Ethernet port on the NIC that indicate activity on the link.

link-local IP address   An IP address the Windows OS automatically assigns if your computer cannot communicate with the DHCP server to obtain TCP/IP configurations.

Linux   A popular open source version of UNIX that offers a much more user-friendly GUI than previous versions of UNIX offered.

lithium-ion (Li-Ion) battery   It is a lightweight battery for the power that has no memory effect so the battery can be recharged before completing discharging. Li-Ion batteries can easily overheat, so should be kept cool, and can degrade quickly, so they have a short lifespan of 2 to 3 years.

lithium-polymer (Li-Poly or LiPo)   A battery that can charge quickly and hold the charge for long period. A LiPo battery has no memory effect, so the battery can be recharged before completing discharging it.

local-area network (LAN)   A communication network that covers a small geographic area and is under the control of a single administrator.

logical drive   A logical drive is a section of an extended partition.

logical topology   The method (ring or bus) by which different computers and other equipment in a network communicate with one another. Contrasts with physical topology.

Long Term Evolution (LTE)   A 4G wireless broadband technology that supports mixed data, voice, video, and messaging traffic.

long touch   A gesture used on Android mobile devices when a user presses on an application icon for a few seconds that allows the application to be moved to the desktop, and long touches on the desktop clock allow you to remove it.

loopback adapter   Also called a loopback plug, tests the basic functionality of computer ports. The adapter is specific to the port that you want to test.

low battery warning   An alarm warning the user to connect the portable device to a power source.

low-level formatting   The surface of the disk is marked with sector markers to indicate where data will be stored physically on the disk.

MAC address filtering   A technique used to deploy device-level security on a wireless LAN.

main distribution facility (MDF)   A building's primary communications room. Also, the central point of a star networking topology, where patch panels, hubs, and routers are located.

malware   A term taken from the phrase malicious software. Malware is designed to infiltrate or damage a computer system without the user's knowledge.

man-in-the-middle attack   An attacker intercepts communications between computers to steal or manipulate information transmitting through the network.

material safety data sheet (MSDS)   A fact sheet that summarizes information about material identification, including hazardous ingredients that can affect personal health, fire hazards, and first-aid requirements.

mean time between failures (MTBF)   The average length of time that the device will work without failing. This information can be found in the manual or on the manufacturer's website.

Media Access Control (MAC)   The lower of the two sublayers of the data link layer defined by the Institute of Electrical and Electronics Engineers (IEEE). The MAC sublayer handles access to shared media, such as whether token passing or contention will be used. Also, the rules for coordinating the use of the medium on a LAN.

media reader   A device that reads and writes to different types of media cards.

memory modules Special circuit boards with memory chips soldered on to them.

mesh topology A method of connecting users that provides alternative paths for data. If one path is severed or unusable, the data can take an alternative path to its destination.

message digest The function output of hash encoding.

message digest 5 (MD5) A popular type of hash encoding algorithm.

Messaging Application Programming Interface (MAPI) A proprietary messaging MAPI is used by Microsoft Office Outlook to connect to Exchange servers, to provide email, calendar, and contact management.

metropolitan-area network (MAN) A network that spans across a large campus or a city. The network consists of various buildings interconnected through wireless or fiber-optic backbones.

microphone jack A socket used to connect a microphone used for audio input.

Microsoft Exchange A mail server, contact manager, and calendaring software created by Microsoft.

Microsoft System Preparation (Sysprep) Is a tool to install and configure the same OS on multiple computers. *See* disk cloning.

Microsoft Windows The family of Microsoft operating systems that includes Windows XP, Windows Vista, and Windows 7. It also includes operating systems for network servers and for portable devices. Legacy Windows OSs include Windows 3.1, NT, 95, 98, Me, and 2000.

Mini-PCI Commonly used by older laptops. Mini-PCI cards have 124 pins and are capable of 802.11a, 802.11b, and 802.11g wireless LAN connection standards.

Mini-PCIe Most common type of wireless card in laptops. Mini-PCIe cards have 54 pins and support all wireless LAN standards.

mirrors Antivirus signature download sites used by manufacturers to avoid heavy traffic at a single website.

Mobile WiMAX A wireless standard that provides ultra-broadband Internet access. Even though Mobile WiMAX and LTE fall short of the data rate to be compliant with 4G (128 Mb/s and 100 Mb/s, respectively), they are still considered 4G standards because they offer so much improvement over the performance of 3G.

modem A device that converts digital computer signals into a format that is sent and received over an analog telephone line.

modem port An RJ-11 jack that connects a computer to a standard telephone line. The modem port can be used to connect the computer to the Internet to send and receive fax documents and to answer incoming calls.

modulation/demodulation The process of converting analog signals to digital and back again.

Molex power connector A four-wire computer power connector used to connect many devices, such as optical drives and hard drives.

monitor resolution Refers to the level of image detail that can be reproduced.

motherboard   The main printed circuit board. Connects all the computer's components, such as the CPU, BIOS, memory, mass storage interfaces, serial and parallel ports, expansion slots, and controllers required for standard peripheral devices.

Motocast USB   A free service used to synchronize data and content when using a Motorola with the Android OS.

mouse port   A PS/2 socket that is used to attach an external mouse.

Msconfig   A Windows utility designed to aid in troubleshooting the operating system. Allows the user to edit start-up applications and access the BOOT.INI, SYSTEM.INI, and WIN.INI files.

Msinfo32   The filename of System Information utility. It provides very detailed information about the hardware, OS, and key applications.

Multimedia Messaging Service (MMS)   The protocol used in picture or video text messaging.

multimode   Optical fiber that has a thicker core than single-mode. It is easier to make, can use simpler light sources (such as LEDs), and works well over short distances. This type of fiber allows light waves to be dispersed into many paths as they travel through the fiber.

multiple-input multiple-output (MIMO)   Wireless technology that uses additional antennas to increase the potential throughput.

multiprocessing   To enable programs to share two or more CPUs.

multipurpose devices   Network devices that perform more than one function. It is more convenient to purchase and configure one device that serves all your needs than to purchase a separate device for each function.

Multipurpose Internet Mail Extensions (MIME)   A standard that extends the email format to include text in ASCII standard format, as well as other formats, such as pictures and word processor documents. Normally used in conjunction with SMTP.

multitasking   Capable of operating multiple applications at the same time.

multitasking bar   Features the iOS home button performs. Double-press the Home button to open the multitasking bar. The multitasking bar shows the most recent apps that have been used.

multithreading   To divide a program into smaller parts that can be loaded as needed by the operating system. Multithreading allows individual programs to be multitasked.

multi-touch   Mobile devices have the ability to recognize when two or more points of contact are made on the screen.

multiuser   Two or more users running programs and sharing peripheral devices, such as a printer, at the same time.

native resolution   The best quality resolution setting for an LCD monitor.

navigation   A mapping app that provides turn-by-turn directions to a place, address, or coordinates.

navigation icons   Android OS uses navigation icons on the home screen to perform functions such as returning to the home screen, accessing recently opened apps, context screen menu, and a back button.

net commands   Commands used to manage network computers, servers, and resources like drives and printers.

netiquette   Being polite in email, text, forums, and all Internet-based interactions.

Network Address Translation (NAT)   The process used to convert private addresses to Internet-routable addresses. With NAT, a private (local) source IP address is translated to a public (global) IP address. The process is reversed for incoming packets.

network discovery   A network setting that affects whether your computer can find other computers and devices on the network and whether other computers on the network can see your computer. There are three network discovery states: on, off, and custom.

network installation   To install Windows 7 by network installation, all setup files are copied to a network server.

network interface card (NIC)   A computer interface with the LAN. This card typically is inserted into an expansion slot in a computer and connects to the network medium.

network LED   A light that shows the status of the network connection. The green link light indicates network connectivity. The other LED indicates traffic.

network location profile   Computers running Windows 7 and Windows Vista can detect different types of network locations called profiles, based on these profiles the firewall and security setting are made.

network operating system (NOS)   An operating system designed specifically to provide additional network features.

network-attached storage (NAS)   A device consisting of one or more hard drives, an Ethernet connection, and an embedded operating system rather than a full-featured network operating system. The NAS device connects to the network, allowing users on the network to access and share files, stream media, and back up data to a central location. NAS devices that support multiple hard drives can provide RAID-level data protection.

networking media   Material (either cable or air) by which signals are sent from one network device to another.

networks   Systems that are formed by links.

New Technology File System (NTFS)   A type of file system that provides improved fault tolerance over traditional file systems, and also provides file-level security.

nickel-cadmium "Ni-Cad" (NiCd) battery   First type of battery commonly used in laptop computers. It is heavy and has a short charge life; memory effect can be a problem so the battery must be completely discharged before it can be recharged to prevent the problem.

nickel-metal hydride (NiMH) battery   Older type of laptop battery, not expensive, moderate capacity, and memory effect can be a problem so the battery must be completely discharged before it can be recharged to prevent problems.

noise   Interference, such as EMI or RFI, that causes unclean power and may cause errors in a computer system.

noninterlaced   Noninterlaced monitors create the image by scanning the screen, one line at a time from top to bottom. Most CRT monitors today are noninterlaced.

nonparity   A type of memory that does not check for errors in memory.

nonvolatile memory   Type of memory that does not need power to retain data.

normal backup   Also called a full backup. All selected files on the disk are archived to the backup medium. Files are marked as having been archived by clearing the archive bit.

Northbridge   Although the functions may vary depending on the manufacturer, the Northbridge usually controls access to the RAM, video card, and the speeds at which the CPU can communicate with them.

notification center   Displays all of the alerts from apps in one location on an iOS device.

Nslookup   A command that returns the IP address of a given hostname. This command can also do the reverse and find the hostname for a specified IP address.

NT Loader (NTLDR)   A boot file that loads Windows-based operating systems.

Occupational Safety and Health Administration (OSHA)   A government agency in the Department of Labor to maintain a safe and healthy work environment.

Ohm's law   A basic equation that states that voltage is equal to current multiplied by resistance: $V = IR$.

OLED   An organic LED display uses a layer of organic material that responds to electrical stimulus to emit light.

Open Graphics Library (OpenGL)   Cross-platform standard specification for multimedia graphics.

open source   The developer's programming code, known as source code, is published when it is released. The public can change, copy, or redistribute the code without paying royalty fees to the software developer.

Open Systems Interconnect (OSI)   A reference model to standardize the way devices communicate on a network. This model was a major step toward ensuring interoperability between network devices. The OSI model divides network communications into seven distinct layers.

open-ended questions   Questions that allow customers to explain the details of a problem in their own words.

operating system (OS)   Software program that performs general system tasks, such as controlling RAM, prioritizing the processing, controlling input and output devices, and managing files.

optical drive   A disk drive that uses a laser to read and/or write CDs and DVDs.

optical fiber   Is a glass or plastic medium that transmits information using light. Fiber-optic cable has one or more optical fibers enclosed in a sheath or jacket

organic LED (OLED) monitor   An output device that requires a small amount of power for the amount of light produced and requires no backlight; they are lightweight

output devices   Presents information to the user from a computer. Typical output devices are monitors and printers.

overclocking   A technique used to make a processor work at a faster speed than its original specification.

packet   A logical grouping of information that includes a header that contains control information and usually user data. The term packet is most often used to refer to network layer units of data.

packet filter   A network filter that uses IP addresses, protocols, or ports to allow or deny packets through.

Page Description Language (PDL)   Code that describes the contents of a document in a language that the printer can understand.

pages per minute (ppm)   The measure of a printer's speed.

Parallel ATA (PATA)   The parallel version of the ATA drive controller interface. PATA uses a 40-pin/80-conductor cable. PATA hard drives are older technology.

Parallel ATA (PATA) power connector   Provides power to a drive from the power supply.

parallel data transfer (IEEE1284)   Faster than serial data transfer. Parallel data transfer moves multiple bits of information in a single cycle.

parallel port   A standard Type A DB-25 female connector, usually used to connect a printer or scanner.

Parity   Parity memory contains eight bits for data and one bit for error checking. The error-checking bit is called a parity bit.

part retriever   Used to retrieve parts from locations that are too small for your hand to fit.

passcode lock   Locks a device and puts it in a power-saving state. The lock can also be delayed to engage after a specified amount of time passes after the device goes into the power-saving state.

patches   Code updates that manufacturers provide to prevent a newly discovered virus or worm from making a successful attack.

PC Card   An expansion card used in laptops to conform to PCMCIA standards.

PC Card/ExpressCard slot   Two legacy laptop expansion slots that allowed early laptops to install wireless NICs, external hard drives, and other devices that typically connect through USB ports today.

PC combo expansion slot   Receives expansion cards like PCMCIA and PC Card/ExpressCard.

PC virtualization   Occurs when a host machine uses its system resources to host a virtual machine, sometimes called a guest.

PCI Express (PCIe)   PCIe is a serial bus expansion slot. It is replacing AGP as an expansion slot for video adapters and can be used for other types of adapters.

PCI Express Micro   Commonly found in newer and smaller laptops, such as Ultrabooks, because they are half the size of Mini-PCIe cards. PCI Express Micro cards have 54 pins and support all wireless LAN standards.

PCI Extended (PCI-X)   A 32-bit bus with higher bandwidth than the PCI bus.

peer-to-peer network   Each network device runs both client and server portions of an application. Also describes communication between implementations of the same OSI reference model layer in two different network devices.

Performance Monitor   A tool that shows the real-time levels of CPU and RAM usage.

Peripheral Component Interconnect (PCI) slot   A 32-bit or 64-bit expansion slot. PCI is the standard slot currently used in most computers.

permission levels   Configured to limit individual or group user access to specific data.

permission propagation   A way to apply permissions to many files and folders quickly. When the permissions of a folder are changed, you are given the option to apply the same permissions to all sub-folders.

personal-area network (PAN)   A network that connects devices, such as mice, keyboards, printers, smartphone, and tablets within the range of an individual person. All of these devices are dedicated to a single host and are most often connected with Bluetooth technology.

Personal Computer Memory Card International Association (PCMCIA)   An industry trade association that defines laptop expansion card standards.

Personal Digital Cellular (PDC)   A second-generation technology used in digital cellular telephone communication in Japan.

personal reference tools   Include troubleshooting guides, manufacturer manuals, quick reference guides, and repair journals.

Phillips-head screwdriver   A tool used to tighten or loosen crosshead screws.

phishing   A type of spam intended to persuade the recipient to provide the sender with information that will enable the sender to access the recipient's personal information.

physical threats   Events or attacks that steal, damage, or destroy equipment, such as servers, switches, and wiring.

piezoelectric printer   An electrically charged plate changes the nozzle's size and shape. This change in size causes the nozzle to act like a pump. The pumping action forces ink out through the nozzle and onto the paper.

pinch   Zoom out from objects, such as photographs, maps, and text. Touch the screen with two fingers and pinch them together to zoom out from the object.

ping   A simple but highly useful command-line utility that is included in most implementations of TCP/IP. Ping can be used with either the hostname or the IP address to test IP connectivity. Determines whether a specific IP address is accessible by sending an ICMP echo request to a destination computer or other network device. The receiving device then sends back an ICMP echo reply message.

pinout   A description of the purpose of each pin in a multi-pin hardware connection interface.

pixel   An abbreviation for picture element. Pixels are the tiny dots that comprise a screen. Each pixel consists of red, green, and blue.

plain old telephone service (POTS)   The regular phone system, which typically uses analog signals to transmit voice and data. Sometimes called the public switched telephone network (PSTN).

plasma   A type of flat-panel monitor that uses tiny cells of ionized gas that light up when stimulated by electricity.

plasma displays   Rarely found in laptops because they consume a large amount of power made up of tiny fluorescent lights to create the image.

plenum cable   A cable that is safe for installation between a dropped ceiling and the structural ceiling of a building where air circulation takes place. Plenum-rated cables are made from a special plastic that retards fire and produces less smoke than other cable types.

plug-and-play (PnP)   Technology that allows a computer to automatically configure the devices that connect to it.

Power over Ethernet (PoE) switch   A device which transfers small amounts of DC current over Ethernet cable, along with data, to power PoE devices.

pop-up   An online advertisement that suddenly appears, blocking what you intended to see on the web page.

pop-up blocker   A tool that is built into a web browser or operates as a standalone program. It enables a user to limit or block most of the pop-ups that occur while browsing the Web.

port   Is a numeric identifier used to keep track of specific conversations. Every message that a host sends contains both a source and destination port.

port forwarding   A rule-based method of directing traffic between devices on separate networks.

port replicator   A fixed-base unit in which a laptop is inserted and can connect to peripheral devices.

port triggering   Allows a router to temporarily forward data through inbound ports to a specific device.

Post Office Protocol Version 3 (POP3)   An application layer protocol used to allow clients to communicate with email servers.

PostScript (PS)   Adobe Systems developed PostScript to allow fonts and text types to share the same characteristics on the screen as on paper.

power fluctuation   Unsteady voltages.

power protection device   Used to protect the data and computer equipment.

power supply   Converts AC (alternating current) into the lower voltages of DC (direct current), which powers all the computer's components. Power supplies are rated in watts.

power supply tester   A device that checks whether the computer power supply is working properly. A simple power supply tester might just have indicator lights; more advanced versions show the amount of voltage and amperage.

power surge   Dramatic increase in voltage above the normal flow of electrical current. A power surge lasts for a few nanoseconds, or one-billionth of a second.

power-on self-test (POST)   A diagnostic test of memory and hardware when the system is powered up.

Preboot Execution Environment (PXE) installation   Uses a PXE boot program and a client's network card to access the setup files from the network server.

preventive maintenance   A detailed program that determines maintenance timing, the type of maintenance performed, and the specifics of how the maintenance plan is carried out.

primary corona wire   A voltage device that erases the charge on the printing drum. Also called the grid or conditioning roller.

primary partition   The first partition on a hard drive. A primary partition usually contains the operating system and cannot be subdivided into smaller sections.

Principle of Least Privilege   A security measure that limits user access to only the folder that is needed to do their jobs.

print server   The device that interfaces between a computer and a printer.

Printer Command Language (PCL)   Hewlett-Packard developed PCL for communication with early inkjet printers. PCL is now an industry standard for nearly all printer types.

printer driver   Software that must be installed on a PC so that the printer can communicate and coordinate the printing process.

privacy screen   A plastic panel that attaches to a computer screen and keeps light from projecting at low angles, so that only the user looking straight at the screen can see the contents.

private key   Used to decrypt messages sent using asymmetric encryption.

processing   Step one in the laser printing process. Data is converted into a printable form. The printer converts data from common languages, such as Adobe PostScript (PS) or HP Printer Command Language (PCL), to a bitmap image stored in the printer's memory.

professionalism   Acting in a manner that reflects well on the company and yourself.

profile   A data file containing known characteristics of an individual.

programmable read-only memory (PROM) Information is written to a PROM chip after it is manufactured, and the chip cannot be erased or re-written.

Protected Extensible Authentication Protocol (PEAP)   A protocol that does not use a certificate server.

protocol   A formal description of a set of rules and conventions that govern how devices on a network exchange information.

protocol data unit (PDU)   A unit of data that is specified in a protocol of a layer of the OSI reference model. For example, the PDU for Layer 1 is bits or the data stream, Layer 2 is framing, Layer 3 is the packet, and Layer 4 is the segment.

proximity sensor   Turns off the touchscreen when the phone is up to your ear and turns it on when you pull the device away from your ear on some smartphones. This prevents icons or numbers from being activated by contact with your face or ear, and also saves power.

proxy firewall   A firewall installed on a proxy server that inspects all traffic and allows or denies packets based on configured rules.

PS/2 port   A 6-pin mini DIN female connector that connects a keyboard or a mouse to a computer.

public key encryption   Used when a single organization needs to receive encrypted text from a number of sources. The public key can be widely distributed.

public switched telephone network (PSTN)   A general term that refers to the variety of telephone networks and services in place worldwide. Sometimes called plain old telephone service (POTS).

punch-down tool   Used to terminate wire into termination blocks.

push and pull   When a user runs the Google Play app or the Apple App Store app from a mobile device, apps and content that are downloaded are pulled from a server to the device. With Android devices, a user can browse Google Play using any desktop or laptop computer and purchase content. The content is pushed to the Android device from the server. iOS users are able to purchase content from iTunes on a desktop or laptop computer that is then pushed to an iOS device.

quality of service (QoS)   Also called 802.1q. QoS, is a variety of techniques that control the flow of network traffic, improve transmission speeds, and improve real-time communications traffic.

Quick Response (QR) code   A type of bar code that is designed to be scanned by the camera of a mobile device. It is similar to a bar code but can contain much more information.

radio frequency (RF)   A generic term that refers to frequencies that correspond to radio transmissions. Cable TV and broadband networks use RF technology.

radio frequency interference (RFI)   Radio frequencies that create noise that interferes with information being transmitted across unshielded copper cabling.

RAM access panel   The panel that grants easy access to RAM on a laptop.

Rambus DRAM (RDRAM)   A memory chip that was developed to communicate at a very high rate of speed.

Rambus in-line memory module (RIMM)   A circuit board that holds RDRAM chips.

random-access memory (RAM)   The temporary storage for data and programs that are being accessed by the CPU. RAM is volatile memory, which means that the contents will be erased when the power is turned off.

read-only memory (ROM)   Memory that permanently stores prerecorded configuration settings and data on a chip that can only be read. This type of memory retains its contents when power is not being supplied to the chip.

Reduced Instruction Set Computer (RISC)   A CPU architecture that uses a small set of instructions and executes them very rapidly.

redundant array of independent disks (RAID)   Provides a way to store data across multiple hard disks for redundancy.

reflective   An infrared network in which the signal is sent to an optical transceiver and is redirected to the receiving device.

refresh rate   The refresh rate is how often per second the image on a monitor is rebuilt. A higher refresh rate produces a better image.

Regedit   A Windows application that allows users to edit the registry.

registers   Storage areas used by the CPU when performing calculations.

Registration, Evaluation, Authorization and Restriction of Chemicals (REACH)   In the European Union, the regulation Registration, Evaluation, Authorization and restriction of Chemicals (REACH) came into effect on June 1, 2007, replacing various directives and regulations with a single system.

Registry   A systemwide database used by the Windows operating system to store information and settings for hardware, software, users, and preferences on a system.

remote assistance   Allows technicians to assist customers with problems from a remote location.

remote backup   When a device copies its data to a website using a backup app.

Remote Desktop   A utility that can be used to remotely control one networked computer from another networked computer via a graphical interface

remote installation   Downloads the installation across the network. The installation can be requested by the user or forced on to a computer by an administrator.

remote lock   Allows a user to lock a mobile device with a passcode.

remote technician   A remote technician might work at a help desk answering calls or emails from customers.

remote wipe   Deletes all data from the device and returns it to a factory state. To restore data to the device, Android users must set up the device using a Gmail account, and iOS users must synchronize their devices to iTunes.

replay attack   Data transmissions are intercepted and recorded by an attacker. These transmissions are then replayed to the destination computer, which believes they are sent by the original source. An attacker then gains entry to a system or a network.

resistive touchscreen   An input device that consists of transparent layers of material capable of conducting electricity, and it allows users to physically interact with what is shown on the screen and type on a virtual keyboard.

restore point   A system restore point is a set system date and time. A user can "roll back" to this restore point when troubleshooting problems with the operating system.

retina scan   A biometric security device that scans the retina of the eye to authenticate a user.

ring topology   A network topology that consists of a series of repeaters connected to one another by unidirectional transmission links to form a single closed loop. Each station on the network connects to the network at a repeater. Although logically they are a ring, ring topologies are most often organized in a closed-loop star.

RJ-11 modem port   Serial port that connects to allow communication on analog phone networks.

rogue antivirus   Adware that may look like a genuine Windows virus warning. Clicking on the warning will cause malicious software to download and install on the computer.

rooting   A hack that involves unlocking the bootloader and giving Android users access to the root directory and the OS which opens the phone to customization that is not normally available to the user.

rootkit   A malicious program that gains full access to a computer system.

router   Network layer device that forwards packets from one network to another based on network layer information.

RSA   The most popular type of asymmetric encryption. The acronym is the surname initials of Ron Rivest, Adi Shamir, and Leonard Adleman, the men who first described this algorithm for public key cryptography.

sandbox   A location of the OS that keeps code isolated from other resources or code.

SATA data cable   The cable that connects the motherboard and the SATA drive. Most commonly they have 7 pins. Some cables can also provide power to the drive as well as data.

satellite   The use of orbiting satellites to relay data between multiple Earth-based stations. Satellite communications offer high bandwidth and broadcast capability at a cost that is unrelated to the distance between Earth stations. Because of the satellite's altitude, satellite communications can be subject to long propagation delays.

SC connector   A snap-in connector that latches with a simple push-pull motion.

ScanDisk   A Windows utility used to examine all files on a drive.

scatter   An infrared network in which the signal is bounced off ceilings and walls.

Scheduled Tasks utility Enables users to schedule events such as backups or updates.

screen brightness   The glow of the display on a laptop screen. Levels can be adjusted to make the screen more readable in varying degrees of light.

scroll   When items are too large for the display screen viewing area, touch and hold the screen, moving your finger in the direction you want to move the item so that an area you want to examine comes into view.

second generation (2G)   Mobile devices that made the change from using analog standard to digital standards which provided better call quality.

sector   A hard drive area that contains a fixed number of bytes, generally at least 512.

Secure Hash Algorithm (SHA)   A popular type of hash encoding algorithm.

Secure Sockets Layer (SSL)   Developed to transmit files securely across the Internet.

security key fob   A small radio system that communicates with the computer over a short range. The computer must sense the signal from the key fob before it accepts the user login name and password.

security keyhole   A hard point in the case that is used to attach a security cable.

security policy   A document that outlines procedures regarding physical security, and the protection of data, research and development, and customer information.

segment   A portion of a computer network in which every device communicates using the physical layer of the OSI reference model. Hubs and repeaters extend and become part of a network segment, whereas switches and routers define and separate network segments.

Serial ATA (SATA)   SATA hard drives use 7-pin, 4-conductor cables. SATA is replacing IDE and EIDE as the standard interface for hard drives and SSDs serial port.

serial ATA (SATA) power connector   Provides power to a drive from the power supply.

serial data transfer   The movement of single bits of information in a single cycle.

serial ports   Connects a computer to a peripheral device such as a mouse or trackball.

service level agreement (SLA)   A contract that defines expectations between an organization and the service vendor to provide an agreed-upon level of support.

service pack   System patches and upgrades that are combined into a comprehensive update application.

service set identifier (SSID)   The broadcast name of a wireless network.

Shadow Copy   A feature of Windows Operating System that automatically creates backup copies of files and data on a hard drive.

shielded twisted-pair (STP)   A two-pair wiring medium used primarily with Token Ring networks. STP cabling has a layer of shielded insulation to reduce electromagnetic interference (EMI). Compare with UTP.

Short Message Service (SMS)   The protocol used in text messaging.

sideloading   Another way to install apps on mobile devices. Apps can be downloaded from different sources on the Internet and transferred to a mobile device through Wi-Fi, Bluetooth, data cable, or other methods. It is not recommended because many sources for apps cannot be trusted it is recommended to only install apps from trusted sources and developers.

signatures   The list of known virus code patterns to which antivirus software compares files to determine if the file is infected with a virus.

Simple Mail Transfer Protocol (SMTP)   An email protocol servers use to send ASCII text messages. When augmented by the MIME protocol, SMTP can carry email with pictures and documents. Email clients sometimes use SMTP to retrieve messages from an email server. However, because of the limited capability to queue messages at the receiving end, other protocols such as POP or IMAP are typically used to receive email.

simplex   The capability for data transmission in only one direction between a sending station and a receiving station.

single in-line memory module (SIMM)   A small circuit board that holds several memory chips. It must be installed in pairs.

single-core CPU   One core inside a single CPU that handles all the processing.

single-mode   A fiber cable that has a very thin core. Uses a high-energy laser as a light source. Can transmit signals over longer distances than multimode fiber-optic cable.

Siri   Special software that understands advanced voice controls.

site survey   Physically inspecting a building to help determine a basic network topology.

slide/swipe   The user slides an icon, such as a lock or an arrow, to unlock the device. This option is the least secure.

Small Computer System Interface (SCSI)   A parallel interface that connects SCSI devices to a computer.

small outline DIMM (SODIMM)   A SODIMM is a smaller version of DIMM that is ideal for use in laptops printers and in other devices where conserving space is necessary. SODIMM has 72-pin and 100-pin configurations for support of 32-bit transfers and 144-pin, 200-pin, and 204-pin configurations for support of 64-bit transfers.

smart card   A credit-card-sized device that includes a processor and memory. Used to store information and authenticate network users.

SmartScreen Filter   Detects phishing websites, analyzes websites for suspicious items, and checks websites against a list of websites and files that are known to be malicious.

social engineering   An attacker tries to gain access to equipment or a network by tricking people into providing the necessary access information.

software   The operating system and programs used by a computer.

software firewall   A program that runs on a computer to allow or deny traffic between the computer and other computers to which it is connected.

solid state drives (SSD)   A solid state drive has no moving parts and uses semiconductors to store data. Nonvolatile flash memory chips manage all storage on an SSD.

Southbridge   Usually allows the CPU to communicate with the hard drive, sound card, USB ports, and other I/O ports.

spam   Also known as junk mail, is unsolicited email.

spike   Sudden increase in voltage that lasts for a short period and exceeds 100 percent of the normal voltage on a line. Spikes can be caused by lightning strikes, but can also occur when the electrical system comes back on after a blackout.

spoofing   A computer pretends to be a trusted computer to gain access to resources. The computer uses a forged IP or MAC address to impersonate a computer that is trusted on the network.

Spotlight   Apple iOS search feature.

spread   Zoom in on objects, such as photographs, maps, and text. Touch the screen with two fingers and spread them apart to zoom in on the object.

spyware   Malware that monitors activity on the computer. The spyware then sends this information to the organization responsible for launching the spyware.

ST connector   A bayonet mount connector that is spring loaded.

standby   A power level that leaves data in RAM and reduces power or turns off peripheral devices. Recovering from Standby is quicker than recovering from Hibernate but consumes more power.

standby power supply (SPS)   Battery backup that is enabled when voltage levels fall below normal.

standoff   A barrier/screw used to physically separate parts (in particular, the system board) from the case.

star topology   A LAN topology in which endpoints on a network are connected to a common central switch by point-to-point links. A ring topology that is organized as a star and implements a unidirectional closed-loop star instead of point-to-point links.

stateful packet inspection   A firewall that keeps track of the state of network connections traveling through the firewall. Packets that are not part of a known connection are dropped.

static IP addressing   An IP address is manually assigned to each node on the same network. The IP address must be unique for each node.

static RAM (SRAM)   A type of RAM that retains its contents for as long as power is supplied, and is usually used as cache memory. SRAM does not require constant refreshing, like dynamic RAM (DRAM).

stereo headphone jack   A small round plug that uses cylindrical bands as contacts. Two audio signal wires (right and left) transmit analog audio signal.

straight-through cable   Is the most common cable type. It maps a wire to the same pins on both ends of the cable. In other words, if T568A

is on one end of the cable, T568A is also on the other. If T568B is on one end of the cable, T568B is on the other. This means that the order of connections (the pinout) for each color is the exact same on both ends.

stress management   Techniques or activities used to reduce stress.

stylus   A writing utensil. Typically used as an input method for the touch-sensitive screens of PDAs and graphics tablets.

subnet mask   The second group of numbers used when configuring an IP address on a device. End devices use the subnet mask to determine the network portion of an IP address.

subnetting   A logical division of a network. It provides the means to divide a network, and the subnet mask specifies how it is subdivided.

Subscriber Identity Module (SIM) card   This small card contains information used to authenticate a device to mobile telephone and data services. SIM cards can also hold user data such as contacts and text messages.

surge suppressor   A device that ensures that the voltage going to another device stays below a certain level.

S-Video   A display cable that carries analog video signals.

S-Video connector   A 4-pin mini-DIN connector that is used to output video signals to a compatible device. S-Video separates the brightness and color portions of a video signal.

switch   A Layer 2 network device also known as a multiport bridge.

switching table A table that contains a list of all MAC addresses on the network and a list of which switch port can be used to reach a device with a given MAC address. The switching table records MAC addresses by inspecting the source MAC address of every incoming frame, as well as the port on which the frame arrives. The switch then creates a switching table that maps MAC addresses to outgoing ports.

symmetric encryption Requires both sides of an encrypted conversation to use an encryption key to encode and decode data. The sender and receiver must use identical keys.

SYN flood attack Randomly opens TCP ports at the source of the attack and ties up the network equipment or computer with a large amount of false SYN requests.

synchronous DRAM (SDRAM) DRAM that operates in synchronization with the memory bus.

System Center Configuration Manager A Microsoft systems management feature pack that can be used to simplify an OS deployment.

System File Checker (SFC) Enables you to check all the protected system files, such as krnl386.exe, and replace them with known good versions if they have become corrupted or deleted.

System Information tool Used to collect and display information about local and remote computers.

System Utility Allows all users to view basic system information, access tools, and configure advanced settings. Found in the Control Panel.

T568A/T568B Two standards for connecting Category 3, Category 5, and Category 6 wire to connectors. Both are appropriate for high-speed data.

tablet A portable PC that can be folded back on the keyboard or, more commonly, has no moving parts and is read and handled like a piece of paper. They often use touchscreen technology in place of a mouse and keyboard.

Task Manager Displays active applications and identifies those that are not responding so that they can be shut down.

TCP/IP model A model used by those working with networks to provide a common ground for communicating about devices, processes, protocols, and services. It is an architectural model used as a common frame of reference for explaining Internet communications and developing communication protocols. It separates the functions of protocols into manageable layers. Each layer performs a specific function in the process of communicating over a network.

Telecommunications Industry Association (TIA) An organization that develops standards that relate to telecommunications technologies. Together, the TIA and the Electronic Industries Association (EIA) have formalized standards, such as EIA/TIA-232, for the electrical characteristics of data transmission.

Temporal Key Integrity Protocol (TKIP) Changes the encryption key on a per-packet basis and provides a method to check the integrity of messages.

tethering A mobile device can connect to another mobile device or computer to share a network connection.

theory of probable cause   The second step in the six-step troubleshooting process, the technician will create a list of the most common reasons why an error might occur.

thermal compound   A substance that increases thermal conductivity between the surface of two of more objects. Used between the CPU and heat sink/fan assembly.

thermal printer   A printer that marks special thermal paper by applying heat to areas of the paper that are to be darkened to represent characters.

thicknet   Coaxial cable that was used in older networks and operated at 10 Mb/s with a maximum length of 500 meters. Also called 10BASE5.

thinnet   Coaxial cable that was used in older networks and operated at 10 Mb/s with a maximum length of 185 meters. Also called 10BASE2.

third generation (3G)   Standards that enable mobile devices to go beyond simple voice and data communications. It is now common for mobile devices to send and receive text, photos, audio, and video. 3G even provides enough bandwidth for videoconferencing. 3G mobile devices are also able to access the Internet to browse, play games, listen to music, and watch video.

Time Division Synchronous Code Division Multiple Access (TD-SCDMA)   A 3G mobile telecommunications standard, being developed initially for People's Republic of China triangulation.

time management   The act of organizing time efficiently in order to increase productivity.

token   A way to provide two-factor authentication. It can be a hardware or software type.

token-passing topology   Controls network access by passing an electronic token sequentially to each host. If a host wants to transmit data, the host adds the data and a destination address to the token, which is a specially formatted frame. The token then travels to another host with the destination address. The destination host takes the data out of the frame. If a host has no data to send, the token is passed to another host.

toner probe   A two-part tool in which the toner part is connected to a cable at one end using specific adapters, such as an RJ-45, coaxial, or metal clips and generates a tone that travels the length of the cable. The probe part traces the cable.

Torx screwdriver   A tool used to tighten or loosen screws that have a star-shaped depression on the top, a feature that is mainly found on laptop screws.

total cost of ownership (TCO)   The overall cost of owning a printer that includes many factors, such as initial purchase price, cost of supplies, and maintenance costs.

touchscreen   An interactive LCD or CRT monitor that detects when something is pressed on it.

touchpad   An input device considered to be a field-replaceable unit.

Tracert   A Windows utility that traces the route that a packet takes from source computer to destination host.

track   A complete circle around a hard-drive platter made up of groups of 512-byte sectors.

transferring   Step five in the laser printing process. The toner attached to the latent image is transferred to the paper.

Transmission Control Protocol Internet Protocol (TCP/IP)   Defines the rules computers must follow to communicate with each other over the Internet.

Triple Data Encryption Standard (3DES)   A type of symmetric encryption.

Trojan horse   A program that appears harmless but actually contains malicious software.

troubleshooting   A systematic approach to locating the cause of a fault in a computer system or network.

Trusted Platform Module (TPM)   A specialized chip installed on the motherboard of a computer to be used for hardware and software authentication.

TV tuners and cable cards   A TV tuner converts analog and digital television signals into audio and video signals the computer can use and store. Cable cards can be used to receive television signals from a cable company.

twisted pair   A pair of insulated wires wrapped together in a regular spiral pattern to control the effects of electrical noise.

two-factor authentication   The practice of using two different methods of authentication, such as a password and a smartcard.

unattended installation   A custom installation of an operating system with minimal user intervention. Windows performs unattended installations by using an answer file called unattend.txt.

uninterruptible power supply (UPS)   A device that maintains a continuous supply of electric power to connected equipment by supplying power from a separate source when utility power is unavailable.

Universal Mobile Telecommunications System (UMTS)   A 3G mobile technology that will deliver broadband of voice and data, UMTS will deliver audio and video to wireless devices anywhere in the world through fixed, wireless, and satellite systems.

Universal Serial Bus (USB) port   An external, hot-swappable, bidirectional connection for USB cables connecting to peripheral devices.

unlike devices   Two devices directly connected and using different pins for transmit and receive.

unshielded twisted-pair (UTP)   A four-pair wire medium used in a variety of networks. UTP is rated in categories, with higher categories providing the best performance and highest bandwidth. The most popular categories are Category 3, Category 5, Category 5e, Category 6, and Category 6A.

Upgrade Advisor   Microsoft tool to advise customers on what hardware is compatible with an OS. It is used to determine whether an OS upgrade will be successful.

uploading   The sending of data from the end user to the server.

USB ports   Standard interfaces that connect peripheral devices to a computer. A single USB port can support up to 127 separate devices with the use of multiple USB hubs.

User Account Control   The User Account Control monitors programs on a computer and warns users when an action might present a threat to the system. Users can adjust the level of monitoring by using the User Account Control settings.

User State Migration Tool   This downloadable tool migrates all user files and settings to a new operating system.

ventilation   A series of vents that allow hot air to be expelled from the interior of the device.

video accelerator card   An integrated circuit board that contains a processor and memory to increase the speed of video graphics. Video accelerator cards are primarily used for 3D and gaming applications.

video adapter card   An integrated circuit board that stores digital data in VRAM and converts it to analog data. The interface between a computer and a display monitor.

Video Graphics Array (VGA)   Supplies analog video to an analog monitor. The connector is a 15-pin D-subtype connector.

video port   Connects a monitor cable to a computer. There are several video ports and connector types.

Virtual Desktop Infrastructure (VDI)   Allows users to log in to a server to access their own virtual computers. Input from the mouse and keyboard is sent to the server to manipulate the virtual computer.

virtual private network (VPN)   An encryption system that protects data as it travels, or tunnels, over the Internet or another unsecured public network.

virtualization   Simultaneously running two or more operating systems on one computer.

virus   In computer terms, a malicious piece of software or code sent by attackers that can copy itself and infect a computer without the user's knowledge or permission.

virus protection software   Software designed to detect, disable, and remove viruses, worms, and Trojans before they infect a computer.

voice control   An iPhone 3G and iOS 3.0 feature that allows users to control the device by speaking into its microphone and to have the phone speak information to the user.

Voice over IP (VoIP)   A method to transmit telephone calls over the Internet using packet-switched technology.

volatile memory   With volatile memory, the contents are erased when the computer is powered off. RAM is an example of volatile memory.

Wake on LAN (WoL)   Settings are used to wake up a networked computer from a very low power mode state. Very low power mode means that the computer is turned off but is still connected to a power source. To support WoL, the computer must have an ATX-compatible power supply and a WoL-compatible NIC.

web tools   Tools that are used to make web pages more powerful and versatile. These can be used by attackers to make computers more vulnerable to attacks.

well-known ports   Port numbers reserved by ICANN to be assigned to each type of application, service, or protocol such as port 80 which is assigned to HTTP. Clients use well-known ports for each service so that the client requests can be identified by using a specific destination port.

wide-area network (WAN)   A data communications network that serves users across a broad geographic area and often uses transmission devices provided by common carriers.

widgets   A small program that runs to launch larger programs.

Wi-Fi   Brand originally licensed by the Wi-Fi Alliance to define the embedded technology of a wireless network (based on the IEEE 802.11 specifications).

Wi-Fi networks   Any type of computer network that is not connected by cables of any kind.

Wi-Fi Protected Access (WPA)   A security standard for Wi-Fi wireless technology. Provides better encryption and authentication than the earlier WEP system.

Wi-Fi Protected Access 2 (WPA2)   Wireless encryption that uses 128-bit AES block ciphering to encrypt data. WPA2 can be enabled in two versions: Personal (password authentication) and Enterprise (server authentication). It is not backward compatible with WEP.

Wi-Fi Protected Setup (WPS)   Commonly uses a PIN method to allow users to set up a wireless network quickly, easily, and with security enabled.

Wi-Fi Sync   A wireless sync between an iPad or iPhone and PC allowing a user to keep files in sync without having to connect their devices to a PC via the sync /charge cable.

Windows 7 Action Center   Checks the status of essential security settings. The Action Center continuously checks to make sure that the software firewall and antivirus programs are running. It also ensures that automatic updates download and install automatically.

Windows 7 Firewall   Runs continuously to protect against unauthorized communications to and from your computer.

Windows application programming interface (API)   Also known as WinAPI. Allows applications from older versions of Windows to operate on newer versions.

Windows Automatic Updates   The Automatic Updates utility scans the system for needed updates, and then, depending on the user settings, downloads and installs the updates or recommends the updates be installed. This ensures the OS and applications are constantly updated for security purposes and added functionality.

Windows Boot Manager (BOOTMGR)   Controls several installation steps during the startup process, depending on the system configuration.

Windows Easy Transfer   Migrates personal files and settings from an old computer to a new one.

Windows Preinstallation Environment (PE)   A basic operating system created to prepare a computer for Windows installation and help users troubleshoot operating system failures.

Windows Recovery Environment (WinRE)
A recovery platform based on the Windows Preinstallation Environment, which helps users troubleshoot operating system failures.

Windows Virtual PC   The virtualization platform for Windows 7.

Windows XP Mode   Windows XP Mode uses virtualization technology to allow users to run XP programs in Windows 7. XP Mode is a fully functional version of Windows XP available for Windows 7 Professional, Enterprise, and Ultimate.

wire stripper   A tool used to remove the insulation from wire so that it can be twisted to other wires or crimped to connectors to make a cable.

Wired Equivalent Privacy (WEP)   A first-generation security standard for wireless technology.

wireless access point (WAP)   A device that connects wireless devices to form a wireless network. An access point usually connects to a wired network, and it can relay data between wired and wireless devices. Connectivity distances can range from several feet or meters to several miles or kilometers.

wireless adapters   A device to add wireless connectivity to a laptop. Adapters can be built-in to the laptop or attached to the laptop through a laptop expansion port. Three major types of wireless adapters used in laptops are Mini-PCI, PCI Express Micro, and Mini-PCIe.

wireless LAN (WLAN)   A network that uses radio signals instead of cables to connect computers to access points and wireless routers.

wireless locator   Software utility that allows a user to see SSID broadcasts, encryptions, channels, and locations of wireless networks in the immediate area.

workgroup   A collection of workstations and servers on a LAN that are designed to communicate and exchange data with one another.

workstation ergonomics   Efficient arrangement of equipment and supplies to increase productivity and reduce the risk of injury.

Worldwide Interoperability for Microwave Access (WiMAX)   An IP-based wireless 4G broadband technology that offers high-speed mobile Internet access for mobile devices. WiMAX is a standard called IEEE 802.16e.

worm   A program that copies itself and spreads exponentially, consuming bandwidth and filling hard drives.

zero insertion force (ZIF)   A chip socket that permits the insertion and removal of a chip without using tools or force. This is common for delicate chips such as a CPU.

zombies   Computers that have been commandeered by hackers and unwillingly launch attacks against networks and servers. Also called botnets.

Index

Symbols

A

I

M

N

S

Try Safari Books Online FREE for 15 days

Get online access to Thousands of Books and Videos

Safari™ Books Online

FREE 15-DAY TRIAL + 15% OFF*
informit.com/safaritrial

> ### Feed your brain
> Gain unlimited access to thousands of books and videos about technology, digital media and professional development from O'Reilly Media, Addison-Wesley, Microsoft Press, Cisco Press, McGraw Hill, Wiley, WROX, Prentice Hall, Que, Sams, Apress, Adobe Press and other top publishers.

> ### See it, believe it
> Watch hundreds of expert-led instructional videos on today's hottest topics.

WAIT, THERE'S MORE!

> ### Gain a competitive edge
> Be first to learn about the newest technologies and subjects with Rough Cuts pre-published manuscripts and new technology overviews in Short Cuts.

> ### Accelerate your project
> Copy and paste code, create smart searches that let you know when new books about your favorite topics are available, and customize your library with favorites, highlights, tags, notes, mash-ups and more.

* Available to new subscribers only. Discount applies to the Safari Library and is valid for first 12 consecutive monthly billing cycles. Safari Library is not available in all countries.

Leabharlanna Poibli Chathair Bhaile Átha Cliath
Dublin City Public Libraries